Frontiers of World Socialism Studies

Yellow Book of World Socialism

Frontiers of World Socialism Studies
Yellow Book of World Socialism
Year 2013

edited by Li Shenming

Volume II

CANUT INTERNATIONAL PUBLISHERS
Istanbul - Berlin - London - Santiago

This edition is an authorized translation from the Chinese language edition, published in cooperation with **Social Sciences Academic Press**, Beijing, China.

Published with financial support of the Innovation Program of the Chinese Academy of Social Sciences

Frontiers of World Socialism Studies
Yellow Book of World Socialism - Year 2013 - Volume II
Edited by Li Shenming
Chinese Title: 世界社会主义跟踪报告 (2012-2013), (ISBN: 978-7-5097-4482-6)
Copyright © SSAP China, 2013

Canut International Publishers
Canut Intl. Turkey, Teraziler Cad. No.29. Sancaktepe, Istanbul, Turkey
Canut Intl. Germany, Heerstr. 266, D-47053, Duisburg, Germany
Canut Intl. United Kingdom, 12a Guernsay Road, London E11 4BJ, England
Copyright © Canut International Publishers, 2017

All rights reserved. No part of this book may be used or reproduced in any manner whatsoever without the written permission of the publishers.

ISBN: 978-605-9914-36-9
Printed in UK
Lightning Source Ltd. UK
Chapterhouse, Pitfield Kiln Farm
MK11 3LW
United Kingdom
www.canutbooks.com

About the Editor of the Book

Li Shenming, born in 1949, native of Wenxian city of Henan Province. For long years he served in the PLA and PLA Medical Research Institute, led major central publications and newspapers of the PLA, later worked as the secretary of Central Military Commission in 1998 he was assigned as the vice president of the Chinese Academy of Social Sciences and was elected as the director of World Socialism Research Center attached to CASS. His major research areas include world socialism, global economic and political crises, international strategies of major world powers, and Mao Zedong Thought. He has authored and co-authored and edited abundant books and articles, including *Globalization and Party Building* (1991), *Globalization and Chinese Strategy* (2007), *Trend of History, The Reasons Behind The Collapse of the CPSU and the Soviet Union, History's Reflection: Memorial for the 20th Anniversary of the Disintegration of Soviet Union* (2013), *Return to Truth* (History of Mao Zedong Thought and Truth of Facts Related To Mao Zedong, co-edited by Lie Jie, (2015) published by Social Sciences Press, Beijing. His two major articles in recent years include: "At the End of Hegemonism and Power Politics Is the Revival of Socialism" and "The New Features of the Present Capital Empire: Financial, Scientific and Technological, Cultural and Military Hegemonies."

Contents

Acknowledgements for the Second Volume — i
Acknowledgement by the Chinese Publisher — iii
List of Scholars of the WSRC attached to CASS — vii

PART THREE
Studies on the Theories of Socialism Theoretical Consciousness and Having Confidence in the System

Y. 28
Democratic Politics Has A Distinct Political Nature
—Reading Notes On Democracy
Wang Weiguang — *1*

Y. 29
Several Issues of Deepening the Concept of
Socialism with Chinese Characteristics
Zhu Jiamu — *17*

Y. 30
Following the Basic Line of the Party Unswervingly throughout one Hundred Years: A Review on Deng Xiaoping's Speeches in the Southern Tour
Zhu Jiamu — *33*

Y. 31
On Essential Distinction between Socialist State-owned Economy and Capitalist State-owned Economy
Yu Bin — *51*

Y. 32
Building the Chinese Discourse System,
Based on the Practice of Reform and Opening up
Cao Suhong — *61*

Y. 33

A Popular Theoretical Reader That Clarifies the Causes of
the Demise of Soviet Union: Be Vigilant Against Danger:
World Socialism Book Series Well Received after Release

Yi Yuan   *77*

Y. 34

What Do People Live For?
—An Abstract from the Keynote Speech at the Opening Ceremony for
Grade 2012 Freshmen of Graduate School, CASS on September 7, 2012

Li Shenming   *91*

Y. 35

There Are No Universal Values as Supra-ideology:
Why is there a Lack of Consensus on the Core Socialist Values?

Hou Huiqin   *105*

Y. 36

Grasp the Hypocritical Nature of
"Universal Values" and Refine Socialist Core Values

Li Zongfang   *119*

Y. 37

An In-depth Investigation among Worker Groups of Beijing:
Experience and Reflection

Lu Gang   *131*

PART FOUR
Developments and Struggles of Communist and Workers' Parties around the World

Y. 38

The Major Changes and Transformations in the Contemporary World Socialist Movement

Nie Yunlin   137

Y. 39

The Communist Party of the Russian Federation and Russia: Their Future

Ouyang Xiangying   153

Y. 40

The Successful Practice of Chavez's Socialist Exploration

Zhu Jidong   167

Y. 41

The New Struggle of the Communist Party of Greece under Circumstances of the European Debt Crisis

Yu Haiqing   179

Y. 42

The Active Position of the Communist Party of Greece in the Debt Crisis

Tong Jin   191

Y. 43

The Views of the Swedish Communist Parties Regarding the Capitalist Economic Crisis

Li Kaixuan   201

Y. 44

Vulnerable Countries Help Themselves: The Bolivarian Alliance — The Present Situation and Prospects of the Bolivarian Alliance for the Peoples of Our America (ALBA)

Chen Airu   213

Y. 45

Why Marxism is on the rise again

Stuart Jeffries translated by Song Lidan 227

Y. 46

The Communist Party of India (Maoist) as the Major Component Part of Communist Movement in India

Wang Jing 233

Y. 47

Review of the New Program of the Communist Party of Belarus

Kang Yanru 247

Y. 48

New Exploration of the Socialist Development Path of the South African Communist Party in the New Period

Nie Yunlin & Cheng Guangde 259

Y. 49

Post-War History of the Japanese Communist Party's Movement as Narrated in the Autobiography Book by Mrs. Tetsuzo Fuwa

Zheng Ping 273

Y. 50

On the Nature of the Current International Meetings of Communist and Workers' Parties

Nie Yunlin 283

Y. 51

An Analysis of the "International Meetings of the Communist and Workers' Parties" from 1999 to 2011

Wang Ximan & Wang Zifeng 295

Y. 52

The Brussels Meetings: The Analysis of the 21st Meeting of the International Communist Seminar

Wang Ximan 311

Y. 53
For Equality, Democracy, Peace and Socialism
—On the 26th Congress of the Communist Party of Israel
Wang Ximan & Wang Zifeng 323

Y. 54
The 17th and 18th Meetings of the Sao Paulo Forum and the Development and Consolidation of the Latin American Left Forces
Xu Shicheng 337

Y. 55
Review of the Eleventh Congress of the Communist Party of Turkey: Forging Socialist Alternative against Reactionary Power and Push Forward Socialism
Yu Weihai 349

PART FIVE

Lessons Drawn from the Collapse of the Soviet Union

Y. 56
Ideological Realm and the Role of Intelligentsia during the Reverse Evolution of the Soviet Union
Zhou Xincheng 367

Y. 57
Twenty Years Since the Fall of the USSR: Whose Fault? And What to Do?
Yuri Prokofyev 379

Y. 58
A Round Table Discussion: The Disintegration of the Soviet Union and the International Financial Crisis
— The Yin-Yang Imbalance
Li Shenming, hosts guests from the Austrian Academy of Sciences led by Helmut Denk
Wang Xiaoju 387

Y. 59
Soviet Scholars' Debates on the 20th Congress of the CPSU and "the Sixties Generation"
Ma Xiaoming 397

Y. 60
The Social Situation in the Former U.S.S.R. Territories, 20 Years after Its Disintegration
Xu Hua 409

Y. 61
The Russian Scholars Are Beginning to Explore the Contemporary Value of the "Soviet Civilization"
Li Ruiqin 421

Y. 62
A Proposal to Translate and Publish the Revised Editions of Stalin's Collected Works, Volumes 14-18
Ouyang Xiangying 433

Y. 63
The Analysis of Social Structure and Classes of Russia by the Russian Communists
Liu Shuchun 443

Y. 64
The Collapse of the Soviet Union and East Europe: Reflection and Criticism by the Communist Party of Australia
Yang Chengguo 457

Y. 65
Scientifically Revealing the Reasons Behind the Collapse of the Soviet Union
Gao Yong 469

Y. 66
Unveiling the Truth and Thought-provoking "8/19" Event
— The Archives of the Beijing Television (BTV)
The documentary film "The Disintegration of the Soviet Union
Li Yan 481

Y. 67
The Party Committees of Various Regions and Departments Have Organized A Campaign of Group Watching of the TV Documentary: "20 Years' Reflections on the Soviet Union's and CPSU's Perishment: The Russians Narrating"
A News Report by China Fangzheng Press   487

Y. 68
A Review of A Spectacular Event : The Educational TV Film "20 Years' Reflections on the Soviet Union's Collapse and the CPSU's Perishment: The Russians Are Narrating"
Liu Ruisheng & Li Yan   495

Acknowledgements for the Second Volume

The second volume of Yellow Book includes three parts: Part III includes articles probing into the theories of socialism; part IV includes articles debating on the struggles of world's communist and workers' parties; part V includes articles debating on the lessons drawn from the disintegration of the Soviet Union and demise of the CPSU.

The Yellow Book, a yearly catalogue book of world socialism studies of 2 volumes has been a valuable book created by the World Socialism Research Center attached to China Academy of Social Sciences and published by Social Sciences Academic Press in Beijing for years. This regular publication is one of best in China among its kind in this sphere. It is the first time such a meticulous work has been translated into English and made available for the global readers. With the publishing this catalogue of academic articles, I have intended to reflect the current trends and mature level of Marxism and socialism studies in China, especially the researches on the history of the world socialism, history of the socialist camp and the Soviet Union.

Due to several other reasons and especially due to language barriers, little is known about Chinese academic studies of Marxism and socialism.

Most of the academic journals in China are published in Chinese, which means that much of the current research achievements are not readily available to non-Chinese readers, those who are interested can only read an abstract of the work in English, from the national data base, cnki.net. But it is no secret that China's scholars in this sphere are very keen to communicate with their colleagues throughout the world, some have already started to write and publish in foreign languages, yet being rare.

Throughout my editing work, I have experienced that the studies on the theoretical system of Marxism, and scientific socialism in China enjoys an unprecedented vitality and academic diversity plurality in this country, especially their works on the newly added characteristics of capitalism and inevitable crises of capitalism, focusing on the new developments of the capitalist monopoly which is the core of hegemonism. Also in my deep conversations and interviews, I have personally experienced that Chinese academy has never given up the truth and methodology of Marxism in revealing the essence of current realities and trends of capitalism, monopoly capitalism and imperialism, which is misinterpreted by some, outside this country. Besides this sphere of academy has nurtured an abundant number of masters which lead an army of middle age and young theoreticians, which means that China is still following the desire mentioned by Mao Zedong and Deng Xiaoping.

Marxism is gaining anew brightness and attraction, besides development of the world socialist movement shows clear signs of recovery and reunion, the current facts have proven that "barbarism" and wars can only be a temporary trend, and the prospects of socialist development trend is bright and its victory is inevitable as Wang Weiguang has solidly analyzed. In the second volume, you will read vivid discussions by renowned socialism researchers Li Shenming, Hou Huiqin, Zhu Jiamu, Zhou Xincheng, Zhu Jidong, Zheng Ping and Nie Yunlin and many others from the younger generation, like Wang Ximan, Yu Weihai, Wang Jing. In this respect the readers will find valuable informative articles, related to communist, socialist and progressive movements in Russia, Japan, India, Greece, Venezuela, South Africa, Latin America and Caribbean Region, Belarus, Turkey, USA, Australia, Sweden, Israel.

Prof. Nie Yunlin and Wang Ximan has especially focused on the International cooperation and meetings of the communist and workers' parties, their scope of cooperation, their cooperation mode and mechanisms which has blazed a trail in the studies of international cooperation and its improvement. I hope this book will increase the exchange of debates and theories among Marxism and socialism scholars of the world.

I am thankful that Canut Publishing International has assigned me this task of editing and proofreading of this valuable book with rich content and writing this with acknowledgment for it. I am thankful to scholars of the World Socialism Research Center and Social Sciences Academic Press in Beijing who have very cooperatively helped me in accomplishing this task and especially the latter who enabled the co-realization of this book.

Daivya Jindal
June, 2017
Bombay, India

Acknowledgement by the Chinese Publisher

The Yellow Book of World Socialism is a collection of authoritative, cutting-edge and representative research achievements made by the World Socialism Research Center. During the past year, the economic crisis in the Western capitalist have continued deepening, also the sovereign debt crisis which spread especially to European countries and to others has been persistent, besides the uncertainties and risks in the world economy rose sharply. In spite of deepening crises and uncertainties throughout the world, the theory and practice of building socialism with Chinese Characteristics has made world-acclaimed achievements. With the current crisis the theories of Marxism has been popular again and revisited by people with foresight, the issue of direction and fate of human development has become a new reflection and study subject, globally.

The yellow book consists of 5 parts: part I, on the general theories of Marxism and socialism, which may also be read as an introduction; part II, includes articles on the Crisis of the Capitalist System; Part III includes articles probing into the theories of socialism; part IV includes articles debating on the struggles of world's communist and workers' parties fighting against exploitation and oppression; part V includes articles debating on the lessons drawn from the disintegration of the Soviet Union and demise of its historical party, the CPSU.

In the Part III of the book the first article by the president of China Academy of Social Sciences, Prof. Wang Weiguang has discussed the distinct features of socialist democracy as compared with bourgeois democracy. Li Shenming has discussed, with the guests from Austrian Academy of Sciences, the dialectic of the Soviet Upheaval and global financial crisis. Zhu Jiamu, has analyzed an important period of the Reform of Opening, the spirit of Southern Talks of Deng Xiaoping.

In the Part IV of the Yellow Book readers can find recent important research articles regarding communist, socialist parties, and their latest achievements. This part also includes 2 articles, related "International Meetings of the Communist and Workers' Parties" and the annual Brussels Communist Seminars, hosted by the Labor Party of Belgium.

We hope that readers from all walks of life can benefit and broaden their views on the issues of socialism, the current world socialism and other crucial issues of the contemporary world. The book includes two valuable articles written by foreign scholars Stuart Jeffries and Yuri Prokofyev, to whom we owe special thanks.

We would particularly thank to the executive leaders and staff of the WSRC, who have cooperated with us during the realization process of the book, and we are grateful to Mr. Huang Changzhuo who has revised the English parts.

Social Sciences Academic Press, Beijing

List of Consultants and Scholars Contributing to World Socialism Research Center attached to Chinese Academy of Social Sciences as of 2013

Consultants

Chen Kuiyuan, Former Vice Chairman of the CPPCC and Chinese Academy of Social Sciences

Wang Jiarui, Vice Chairman of the CPPCC National Committee, the Minister of Foreign Relations attached to CPC Central Committee

Dai Bingguo, Former State Councilor

Wang Weiguang, Dean of the Chinese Academy of Social Sciences, Party Secretary

Liu Huaqiu, Former Director of the Foreign Affairs Leading Group Office of the CPC Central Committee

Li Anan, Former General Secretary of the Central Advisory Commission

Zhang Panjing, Former Minister of the Organization Department of the CPC Central Committee, the president of the National Party Building Research Association

Zheng Keyang, Former Deputy Director of the Central Policy Research Office, vice chairman of the Party Building Research Association

Yu Hongjun, Vice Minister of the International Department attached to CPC Central Committee

Wei Jianhua, Former Director of the Compilation and Translation Bureau attached to CPC Central Committee

Director of the World Socialism Research Center

Li Shenming

Executive Directors of the World Socialism Research Center

Xia Weidong, Wu Enyuan, Cheng Enfu, Hou Huiqin, Deng Chundong Wang Xuedong, Yan Shuhan, Li Hongqi, Zhang Shuhua, Jiang Hui, Fan Jianxin, Wang Liqiang, Wang Tingzhi, Wang Yicheng, Wang Lei, Wang Zhenya, Wang Xuejian, Wang Wen, Chung Yeung, Ma Yan, Feng Gang, Feng Jinhua, Tian Yongxiang, Anqi Ren, Huayu Wu, Liu Shulin, Liu Shuchun, Liu Tong, Liu Ruisheng, Lu Weizhou, Ren Zhijun, Sun Haiquan, Xu Xingya, Xu Zhengfan, Zhu Bingyuan, Zhu Jidong, Zhuang Qiansheng, Chen Xueming, Chen Zhanan, Chen Zhihua, Chen Yue, He Bingmeng, He Qianqiang, He Junchen, Li Bingyan, Li Chongfu, Li Hanlin, Li Jianping, Li Qiqing, Li Xinggeng, Li Xiangjun, Li Jun (ambassador), She Zhiyuan, Song Xiaoping, Li Xiangjun, She Zhiyuan, Song Xiaoping, Wu Bo, Wu Shangmin, Wu Xiongcheng,

Zhang Guozuo, Zhang Guanzi, Zhang Shunhong, Zhang Haibin, Zhang Zaixing, Zhang Shulin, Zhang Wenmu, Yang Haijiao, Fang Guangshun, Fang Ning, Meng Jie, Lin Gang, Luo Wendong, Luo Hong, Wu Zhaoling, Zhou Zhaoguang, Zhou Hong, Zhou Qi, Zhou Xincheng, Zhao Jianying, Hu Lemin, Hu Zhenliang, Hu Zhenliang, Jiang Shanyian, Shihe An, Rao Ninghua, Jin Baoping, Gao Yongzhong, Gao Qiufu, Gao Xiang, Guo Yuzhou (ambassador), Guo Jiezhong, Guo Jianning, Qin Xuan, Sang Yucheng, Tang Kunxiong, Xu Chongwen, Xu Shicheng, Cui Yaozhong, Huang Haotao, Huang Jinhui, Huang Xiaoyong, Huang Rongsheng, Huang Ping, Mei Rongzheng, Huang Rongsheng, Huang Hong, Mei Rongzheng, Cao Yaxiong, Cheng Wei, Dong Jingquan, Dong Xiaoyang, Dong Zhengping, Jiang Lifeng, Wen Bo, Xie Shouguang, Jinhui Ming.

Visiting Scholars of World Socialism Research Center

Ding Bing, Ding Yuanhong, Ding Xiaoqin, Ding Shujie, Yu Zuyao, Yu Haiqing, You Suzhen, Wei Jianlin, Ma Xiaoquan, Ma Zhongcheng, Ma Xiaoming, Ma Weixian, Wang Jing, Wang Shaoxian, Wang Zhongbao, Wang Wene, Wang Zhengquan, Wang Lincong, Wang Jiafei, Wang Jingli, Wang Zhenhua, Wang Xiaoquan, Wang Xiaoju, Wang Haiyun, Wang Ximan, Mao Xianglin, Kong Tianping, Lu Gang, Ye Weiping, Shen Yajie, Tian Chunsheng, Qiu Jin, Feng Yumin, Feng Shaolei, Feng Yanli, Qu Wei, Qu Yanming, Zhu Andong, Quan Lin, Yuan Liu, Liu Junmei, Liu Zhiming, Liu Guoping, Liu Chunyuan, Liu Haixia, Qi Fengtian, Jiang Shixue, Xu Hua, Xu Xin, Xu Yuanrong, Sun Li, Sun Hongbo, Ji Jun, Su Zhenxing, Du Han, Du Xiaolin, Li Qian, Li Weil, Man Liyan, Li Changjiu, Li Fenglin, Li Weiheng, Li Zhengle, Li Minqi, Li Yazhou, Li Kaixuan, Li Zongfang,

Li Yanyan, Li Runhai, Li Ruiqin, Li Fuchuan, Yang Shuang, Yang Bin, Yang Shengguo, Yang Chengguo, Yang Huichun, Yang Jianmin, Yang Chengxun, Yang Zugong, Yang Hongxi, Xiao Feng, Xiao Lian, Xiao Bin, Xiao Guozhong, Wu Qian, Wu Jian, Wu Guoping Wu Jinping, He Xin, Tong Yuhua, Yu Li, Yu Bin, Yu Wenli, Yu Jincheng, Yu Weihai, Wang Tingyou, Shen Qiang, Shen Xiaoquan, Shen Zongwu, Song Lidan, Song Mengrong, Zhang Li, Zhang Jie, Zhang Ji, Zhang Zhongyun, Zhang Wendai, Zhang Yuliang, Zhang Ximing, Zhang Xinghui, Zhang Shouhua, Zhang Xiaodong, Zhang Tiezhu, Zhang Haipeng, Zhang Xinning, Lu Shucheng, Chen Yue, Chen Renjiang, Chen Chengxin, Chen Airu, Chen Shuoying, Fan Lei, Lin Xinhai, Ouyang Xiangying, Shang Wei, Luo Yunli, Jin Ying, Jin Liqun, Zhou Miao, Zhou Zhiwei, Zhou Suiming, Pang Dapeng, Pang Zhongying, Zheng Ping, Zhao Shi, Zhao Yao, Zhao Minghao, Zhao Changqing, Hu Junqing, Zhong Yaping, Duan Lijuan, Duan Qizeng, Hou Aijun, Yu Su, Jiang Li, Jiang Lin, Jiang Weiping, He Shuangrong, Geng Lihua, Yuan Qun, Nie Yunlin, Xia Dongmin, Gu Yumin, Chai Shangjin, Xu YunFeng, Xu Zhongwei, Xu Xiaofeng, Xu Haiyan, Luan Wenlian, Gao Yong, Gao Hong, Gao Gexiu, Gao Yixin, Gao Zengjie, Guo Yuanzeng, Guo Jianping, Tang Xiuzhe, Tang Yanlin, Huang Dengxue, Cao Changsheng, Cao Suhong, Chang Weiguo, Cui Xuedong, Kang Yanru, Yan Zhimin, Yan Hongju, Liang Xiao, Ge Xinsheng, Jinghui Zhichun, Cheng Chunhua, Fu Ning, Fu Junsheng, Shu Chang, Tong Jin, Xie Xiaoguang, Pei Yuanying, Liao Jian, Tan Suo, Tan Yangfang, Xue Xinguuo, Xue Fuqi, Wei Yongwang, Wei Nanzhi.

PART THREE

Studies on the Theories of Socialism Theoretical Consciousness and Having Confidence in the System

Y. 28

Democratic Politics Has A Distinct Political Nature
—Reading Notes On Democracy

Wang Weiguang[1]

Abstract: Democracy is an important and a sensitive concept with theoretical and practical implications. This article approaches the issue of democracy from historical and practical perspectives in terms of three aspects: democratic politics has a distinct political nature; democracy is always unique and historically determined, and formed itself in a developing process; and finally people's democracy is the fundamental requirement of socialist democracy.

Key words: democracy; political nature; process; people's democracy

---

1 Prof. Wang Weiguang, President of the CASS, Secretary of the leading Party members' group of CASS.

I. Unique political features of democratic politics

Democracy is an important and a sensitive concept with theoretical and practical implications. It is an issue that has been in the political realm of socialism in China and that of the international society for a long time. Generally speaking, democracy has three connotations.

First, in terms of a state system, namely, democratic politics, democracy is a policy having distinct class nature, political nature and ideological nature. Socialist democracy and capitalist democracy are two political systems, which belong to superstructure, and which fundamentally contradict each other. Socialist democratic policy basically serves the socialist economic base, while capitalist democratic policy serves the capitalist economic base. For instance, the fundamental political system of China, as a socialist country, is to exercise people's democratic dictatorship, namely democracy for the people and dictatorship over the reactionaries. The basic democratic political system of China rises upon four pillars: the National People's Congress system, the system of multi-party cooperation and political consultation under the leadership of the CPC, the system of ethnic and regional autonomy and citizens' grass root autonomy system. Our above elucidation discusses democracy from the aspect of the connotation of the state system.

Second, in terms of specific organizational form, procedures democracy has its own distinct organizational forms distinct operating systems, institutions, mechanisms, operational procedures, and principles.

Organizational form of a state serves certain state system, certain politics and certain class and it belongs to or determined by what it serves, and acquires the nature of what it serves. It takes a form according to the ruling class it serves and acquires its nature. Generally speaking, the organizational form of democratic politics, itself alone has no specific political nature, class nature or ideological nature. For example, whether it is a western parliamentary system or a people's congress system in a socialist county, president or chairmanship of the state—this organ—does not specify the nature of a state. If we take the renowned principle, "the minority is subordinate to the majority" as another example; this principle itself, as one general rule of democracy, does not imply a specific political nature, or class nature or an ideological nature.

Third, democracy also refers to democratic values, such as democratic value pursuit, democratic value judgment, democratic way of thinking, including democratic theories, opinions and understanding, and includes the pursuit of democratic style, like maintaining close ties with the masses and being open to different opinions. In this sense, democracy has an obvious ideological and class natures. That is to say, any democratic theory is inevitably imbued with belongs the democratic value of a certain class, the bourgeoisie or the working class.

Fourth, the aforesaid different aspects of democracy are interconnected, and supplement each other and assimilate the best aspects of each other. For instance, it is inevitable that the principle of democratic centralism accords with socialist democracy. To implement democratic centralism, socialist democratic politics must adhere to democratic values and also the leaders and cadres must develop an excellent democratic style and should stick to democratic ideas. For example the public servants should refuse to use the advantages of being in the ruling positions and laws should restrict all privileges in the socialist society. However, every aspect is different from the other, consequently we must not confuse their different connotations. Some specific organizational forms, institutions, mechanisms, operating principles, procedures. In another word, rules of democratic politics can either be applied to the socialist democratic system or the capitalist democratic system.

Democratic politics as the system of the state is unique, historically determined and changeable. Such an exclusive, supra-class, supra-historical, permanent and universal democratic politics or a democratic state system, do not exist. In the development of the human societies, the primitive society was the one without classes. In its later period, men created more mature democratic discussion process, in accordance with the organizational forms and mechanisms. That is because the public ownership in the primitive society determined that for the people, democratic system should be the democratic politics of its commune, possessing a set of procedures and rules.

In the slave society, which had been the first class society and where the system enjoyed a distinct class nature, the minority ruled over the majority—the slave owners had absolute power to dominate and exploit their slaves. Thus the democratic politics was impossible in the slave society. However, in the Greek city states, which also implemented slavery system, some sort of the democratic politics of the state was implemented. Yet, the democratic practices in the slave society were only enjoyed and shared among the slave owners and thus belonged to the minority who ruled over the majority. In the feudal society, a monarchic dictatorial system which fundamentally opposed to democratic politics was implemented. In the feudal society of China which lasted for thousands of years, an absolute monarchical system which was fundamentally distinct from democratic politics was established. And in the period when China was a semi-colonial and semi-feudal society, a dark despotic dictatorial system had been implemented.

As a new class that ascended within the feudal society, the bourgeoisie represented the development of the new productive forces. To establish the capitalist relations of production and to liberate and develop productive forces that was obstructed by feudal relations of production, the bourgeoisie firstly needed to abolish the despotism implemented by the feudal landlord class and set up a bourgeois democratic system which could fit and serve the development requirements of private ownership and market economy.

In that way, the interests of the bourgeoisie was secured within the basic political system and with the bourgeois democratic revolution where democratic system replaced despotism. To put it in a different way, in accordance with the development of capitalist market economy, bourgeoisie had created a democratic political system which was in accordance with the needs of progress in the history of humanity. Hence, bourgeois democracy has been progressive and revolutionary in the rising stage of capitalism.

However, bourgeois democracy has a dual nature: on the one hand, bourgeois democracy was progressive and revolutionary compared to feudal political system. Yet its progressive character was temporary, historical and limited. On the other hand, compared with the political system of the working class, we can say it is deceptive and reactionary.

After all, bourgeois democracy is the hegemony of the minority who rules over the majority and it seeks to protect the economic interest of the bourgeoisie. Thus, although bourgeois democracy in the rising stage of capitalism was progressive and revolutionary, it is also limited, temporary, reactionary, hypocritical and deceptive. For the proletariat and working class, capitalism uses democracy to camouflage its class nature of dominance and oppression over the majority. After the success of bourgeois revolution and establishment of capitalist system, bourgeois democracy has lost its progressive and revolutionary nature.

The modern era has witnessed the competition between the socialist and the capitalist forces, which has been a new phenomenon in the history, in terms of historical progress, prospect and final destination to reach. When the bourgeois revolution won the victory, the hypocritical and reactionary nature of bourgeois democracy has become evident. Right from the moment when the capitalist system was established as an economic system, the working class also emerged as the class opposing the bourgeoisie. Socialist factors that negate and substitute the capitalist system arose in the womb of the capitalist society itself. After since socialism has defeated the power of capitalism, won victory and emerged as a new social system, it has been besieged and exterminated by the capitalist economic, political, ideological and military forces.

The bourgeoisie during its revolutionary period, when it strived to overthrow the feudal forces, carried the ideological and political weapons of democracy: like human rights, freedom, equality, solidarity and its weapons were indeed stronger than those of the feudal despotism and has been used to fight against feudal autocracy in that period. However, with the closure of the revolutionary period of the bourgeoisie, the bourgeoisie started ideological attacks on socialist countries with the very same weapons and tried to westernize and dissolve them, besides fortifying its economic basis with bourgeoisie democracy and protecting itself with those weapons. In the socialist system, the democracy which serves the vast masses of the people is the democratic system based on the socialist public ownership. Since socialism is a new phenomenon and socialist democracy, which is a new-type democracy, has to be perfected gradually. We can obviously see that it still has many defects and shortcomings. Therefore, it is understandable that there is a life-and-death struggle between socialist and bourgeois democracies in the contemporary era.

II. Democracy is unique and historically determined and always establishes itself within a process

It has been five years since the global financial crisis broke out in 2008. It was caused by the American subprime mortgage crisis, and in the end it led to the European sovereign debt crisis. Politics is the concentrated expression of economy. Consequently, the economic crisis in 2008 has led to the lasting "Occupy Wall Street" movement and later "Occupy London" movement in the developed Western capitalist countries and gave rise to a succession of strikes, demonstrations and parades. The economic crisis turned into social crisis and then to an ideological crisis, triggering ideological disputes. Many of those living in the West, be it politicians, theorists, or civilians, began to criticize and oppose the Western capitalist system from different standpoints and cast doubts on the Western bourgeois democratic system. Zbigniew Brzezinski, former National Security Advisor of the United States and famous expert on international affairs, once said, "the question today is whether democracies can thrive with financial systems that are out of control, that are capable of generating selfishly beneficial consequences only for the few, without any effective framework that gives us a larger, more ambitious sense of purpose. That is the real problem."[2] With these words he criticized the Western democracy, saying "Western Democracy is the Real Problem" has been a heavy blow to those who advocate the "universal value" of Western democracy.

2　See article by Can Kao, Xiao Xi, "Western Democracy is the Real Problem", quoted from Zbigniew Brzezinski's keynote address on April 3, 2012. in the Columbia Law School Faculty House.

Democracy is unique and historically determined, establishing itself within a specific and special process. It does not transcend history, time, space or national conditions; nor is it abstract, permanent, static or universal. Democracy is unique to the societies, and historical conditions within it emerges and develops. It is a special, unique and objective social existence, such as socialist democratic politics with distinctive Chinese characteristics, American bourgeois democratic political system, British bourgeois democratic political system, and so on. These are by no means abstract and universal systems that can survive without specific historical and social conditions. Democracy is a historical concept. Democracy is a product emerging under certain historical conditions and it evolves with the historical developments, the transitions of history and the accumulation of practices. Hence, it presents itself in a historical process. There is no such thing as permanent, fixed, unchangeable and thus there is no absolute democratic system. Democracy, be it in democratic politics as part of the political system, democratic thoughts of ideology, or specific forms, procedures and rules of democratic political system, is the product of certain historical periods, special national conditions and certain unique conditions. It is a historical product which is gradually generated and perfected and develops along with a certain nation, party, class and groups of people.

Different democratic politics, democratic thoughts, democratic forms, procedures and rules share certain common intrinsic natures with other democracies. That is to say, democracies have similarities and general and universal characteristics. Still, in reality these characteristics do not lead specific democracies to transcend history, time, or space or to be abstract or be "universal". Those are the dialectic relationships between the individuality and similarity, particularity and generality, exceptionality and universality of democracy, which can be summarized as democratic particularity and democratic generality. Particularity of democratic refers to particular, unique and historically formed democracies in the real history, such as the inner-party democracy of the Chinese Communist Party, special multi-party system of China led by the CPC, and the multi-party democracies of the Western bourgeois societies. Universality of democracy refers to the common characteristics of democracy that dwells within its particularities. Universality of democracy is embedded in its particularity and it is the common characteristics that demonstrates itself through comparisons we make among different specific democracies. That is to say, universality of democracy is the general expression of specific democracies. In terms of epistemology, democratic particularity and democratic generality represent the relationships between "individuality" and "similarity", "particularity" and "generality", "exceptionality" and "universality". In the history of Chinese philosophy, the discussion over "name" and "substance" is one important example that demonstrates the relationship between particularity and generality, in the Chinese sense "name" refers to generality and "substance" refers to particularity. For instance, table is the "name" used for a category of objects, while the specific tables that people can see and touch, such as long table, round table, wood table, stone table, large table and small table, all refers to "substance". "Name" is the abstraction of the common nature of "substance" and exists inside it, "name" cannot exist without "substance" and where there is "substance", there is a "name".

"Individuality", "particularity" and "specificity" refer to individual, particular and specific things that objectively exist. "Similarity", "generality" and "universality" refer to the general characteristics and universal rules that is shared by individual, particular and specific things. "Similarity", "generality" and "universality" exist within all the "individual", "particular" and "specific" concepts. Universality cannot stand alone, that is because all specific, individual and particular things share a general nature and universal rules when compared to each other. Individuality and similarity, particularity and generality, specificity and universality are dialectically merged into each other in the individual, particular and specific things. Similarity, generality and universality cannot exist without individual, particular and specific things. Hence, democratic politics, democratic thoughts and democratic rules all exist within a specific country, class, political party, people and individual. That is to say, democracy is a soul and cannot survive without a lively flesh.

The similarity, generality and universality of democracy should not be negated due to its specificity, particularity and individuality. We should object the idea that democracy is universal and will transcends history and class and that it can be detached from democratic particularity. Nevertheless, we are not against the opinion that every specific democracy shares certain similarity, generality and universality.

Lenin had argued that absolutization of a fragment of human cognition ultimately leads to idealism. The relationships between individuality and similarity, particularity and generality, exceptionality and universality, which are a node of human cognition, reflect the cognition process and rules of the human cognition. Generally speaking, human cognition starts with the understanding of individual, specific and particular things, goes through repetitive practices and understandings. Then a circular process emerges where sensible cognition turns into rational cognition and then again turns back into sensible cognition. Through this process, human cognition grasps the similarity, generality and universality of individual, specific, particular things by abstracting them. Hence, people first learn about individual, specific and particular things and then gradually abstract the similarity, generality and universality embedded inside the specific things by comparison. For instance, people summarize the general characteristics of different kinds of peaches covering flat peach, wild peach, juicy peach, etc., and of different shapes of peaches and then categorize them as "peach" and thus the concept of "peach" comes into being. Besides, specific peaches share common genetic natures. Almost everyone has ever eaten specific, fresh peaches in different shapes, but none of them has tasted its concept, namely its generality. The abstract generality of a peach does not equal to its specificity which allows it to be eaten. Epistemologically, overstating people's abstract understanding of the peach will lead to idealistic conclusions.

Take human beings as another example. Almost everyone has ever seen specific individuals like Zhang San, Li Si, etc. they are not abstract individuals that are neither male nor female, neither foreigner nor Chinese. "Human being" is just a general concept abstracted from specific individuals and is embodied inside each of them. During the Warring States Period of China, Gongsun Longzi raised the famous paradox: "a white horse is not a horse". A "white horse" is an individual, particular and specific horse, while "horse" is a general concept that covers all the common characteristics of specific horses. Since universal is embedded within particularity, the general concept of horse's species characteristics naturally exists within each specific horse. If universality is detached from particularity, then the general concept of horse would be detached from specific horses. Overstating the general concept of horse will lead to a mistaken judgment.

So is that with democracy. What is democracy? It embraces the specific democratic systems of different parties, different classes, different countries and different historical periods. But also it refers to the general characteristics—democratic generalities—abstracted from the corresponding democratic thoughts and rules. Democratic similarity, democratic generality and democratic universality only exist within specific, individual and particular democracies. Take the democratic politics as an example. It is unrealistic to apply the democratic system of a certain historical period to all historical periods, or to apply the democratic system of a country to all the countries, regardless of their specific historical conditions, historical periods, geographical conditions and ignore their stages of development. No democratic system is applicable to all the people, parties, classes, countries and historical periods. As the phrase goes, "tangerine grow into tangerine in the south, but becomes trifoliate orange in the north." Without a specific soil, environment, climate conditions and process, a tangerine will into a trifoliate orange. American democracy which mainly features a two-party system has been gradually formed since the national liberation and the War of Independence due to the national conditions of the America, the developmental requirements of American capitalism, the requirements of the American bourgeoisie and the subjectivity of the American people who have adjusted themselves to it. It is distinct from British democracy, let alone from socialist democracy. In the British democracy, the democratic politics is based on the constitutional monarchy which is the result of the specific historical development that is the bourgeoisie has compromised did not make a complete bourgeois revolution. Although British democratic system and American democratic system are both bourgeois democracies, they differ from each other in some aspects due to different historical conditions. Yet, they still share similarities as two bourgeois democratic systems. Therefore, it is unrealistic to assume any democracy under certain conditions as something absolute, permanent and applicable to all. It is inevitable that democracy arises from and exists in specific historical conditions. But the limitations and requirements of those historical conditions also make it necessary to perfect democracy in new historical periods with arduous efforts.

To abstract the universal democratic principles from a unique, specific democracy and fit them into everything is nothing but a joke, from which the pretext to interfere other countries and democracies is produced. Some Western politicians and theorists claim that American "democracy" and Western "democracy" represents the "universal values". Thus they bully others with their democracies. For the American politicians, American democracy is the best system in the world imbued with universal values and it should be the right model for others. They publicize it all around the world, try to impose it on those countries that they are unsatisfied with based on their own standards and bully those that are different from them in terms of understanding of democracy. Double standards are applied against those Americans don't like and they are labeled as "despotic", "dictatorship" and even as "evil" states and that they should be transformed and eliminated. For instance, they tries hard to intervene and manipulate the general elections in Russia and became furious when Putin was elected. They also interfere to other countries' domestic affairs, impose arbitrary sanctions and blackmail on them. We have also seen their military attacks and invasions which were camouflaged as promoting "universal democracy".

The financial crisis has indeed awakened a lot of Westerners about the hypocrisy of Western democracy. Some people allegorically call Western democracy as "democracy of the money" and consider "money is the mother's milk for democracy", which sharply reveals the nature of Western democracy. According to a report by Agencia EFE on January 27, 2012, some of the well-known scholars who attended to the World Social Forum have argued that the "European democracy has been blackmailed by the greedy financial markets and moreover the markets do not have any base line to stop threatening human rights and political rights of the European people."

The Portuguese sociologist A. de Santos once said that neither European democracies nor their constitutions are qualified because their control is now subordinated to Goldman Sachs. The current crisis gives people a "basis to believe that capitalism is anti-democratic." The Famous French economist Paul Jorion commented to a reporter from the Tribune of France in December 2011 that, "the election won't change anything... Politicians have no turning back in the face of a gradually declining system. Regardless of the camp they are fighting for, they can do nothing but only pretend to be in charge under these circumstances. The people who have been considered as a hope in solving this problem stands just in the center of the problem itself"[3].

So far, those who are concerned about this reality have raised this critical question: "What are the drawbacks and deficiencies of the Western democracy?" Isn't it the "universal, perfect and eternal democracy" that is advocated? Is the democracy that brings fortune to the minority instead of happiness to the majority what the people need? Consequently, it becomes evident that the specific Western democracies which advocate the so-called "universal values" is an historical product that will inevitably exit the stage of the history when the conditions are ripe.

III. People's democracy is the essential requirement of the socialist democracy

Socialist democracy is the broadest democracy for the people, which is in essence completely different from bourgeois democracy. The bourgeoisie has created bourgeois democracy that is distinct from despotism and superior to other previous forms of class states. Its main features are as follows: firstly, it has ended the rule of feudal despotism and promoted a distinct anti-despotic character. Secondly, it was adapted to the needs of the capitalist market economy and aimed a catalyzer role to promote capitalist economic and social development. Thirdly, compared to other social forms such as the slave society and feudal society, it has endowed certain political rights—freedom, equality and human rights—to all sectors of the society such as recognizing each citizen's voting right to vote and right to be elected, but only within the scope and limits allowed by the bourgeoisie interests. Fourthly, it has formed democratic politics in line with bourgeois democratic ideology and bourgeois democratic theories and consequently created a set of democratic forms, mechanisms, procedures and rules advanced than any other former democratic politics in human history. Thus bourgeoisie democracy has provided prerequisites and patterns for a more advanced, reasonable and more sophisticated socialist democratic thoughts,

---

3 Quoted from "Western Democracy is Indeed a Problem", Can Kao and Xiao Xi, April 3, 2012/10 in the Journal of Political Reference

theories, forms, procedures and principles. These four points are strengths of the bourgeois democracy.

However, hitherto existing democracies, humans have encountered in any historical period and democracies of any exploiting classes have their historical and exploitative class limitations. Their narrow interests play the decisive role in these limitations. The exploiting classes of any historical age were the minority classes. So, undoubtedly that the democracies it created would inevitably serve and obey the interests of the minority and this democracy is minority class democracy, and this is an obvious ironclad fact.

Even though the bourgeois democracy is more advanced than its precedents, it still abides by this iron law. To put it correctly, bourgeois democracy is still a minority and one that the exploiting class as a minority uses it to maintain its class interests, and this is the class nature of the bourgeois democracy.

Of course, while serving the overall and long-term interests of the capitalist minority, the bourgeois democracy has taken into consideration the interest and the demands of the other classes and the strata in the society. In this sense, compared to the former exploiting classes, bourgeoisie grants more rights and a broader democracy to other classes. While implementing democracy, the bourgeoisie has never forgotten and forsake dictatorship. Democracy and dictatorship are the two sides of the same coin, they are twin brothers. Where there is democracy, there is dictatorship. Hence, the dictatorship must be fortified when the democracy is expanded and strengthened. In order to protect bourgeois democracy, capitalist states need to establish and maintain gigantic state apparatuses of dictatorship, on the basis of which the democracy has been implemented.

Bourgeois democracy during the revolutionary period of bourgeoisie possessed a highly revolutionary and progressive nature. In order to unite the working class, the peasantry, the petty bourgeoisie and other strata, the bourgeoisie had to claim their democracy being universal and "democracy for all the people". That is also true that in the early period of the establishment of the bourgeois state, bourgeoisie promised more equal rights, freedom and democracy to the other classes.

Bourgeois democracy although being revolutionary was at the same time hypocritical and deceptive. Bourgeois democracy although claims to be democracy for all the people, but if we examine its essence and ultimate goal, it is a democracy serving the minority exploiting class.

Bourgeois democracy, under its cloak of democracy, and with the slogan of universal democracy for all, and with a broad range of formally defined rights, in fact has a strong dualistic characteristic. Engels wrote in one of his late works: "classical outlook of bourgeoisie, is the juristic world outlook" and this world outlook worships formality.

Of course, bourgeois democracy is not totally deceptive or an illusion because it indeed satisfies some basic requirements of other classes and grant more democratic rights compared to former exploiting classes.

However, along with the decline of capitalism, the progressiveness of the bourgeois democracy becomes reduced, while its deceptive, formal, decorous, character will increase more and more, and it will become more and more reactionary.

Three are mainly three differences between the socialist democracy and the bourgeois democracy. Firstly, the socialist democracy is the true democracy for the majority, democracy for the oppressed and the exploited. Secondly, in the socialist democracy, dictatorship and democracy are dialectically implemented at the same time, which was called as the dictatorship of the proletariat by the classical authors of the scientific socialism. This also applies for the people's democratic dictatorship practiced in China, which is a specific form the proletarian dictatorship. Thirdly, while the socialist democracy openly claims to be democracy for the overwhelming majority of the people, but it does not conceal that it is the people's dictatorship on the minority. That is different from the attitude of the bourgeois democracy which claims to be universal and embracing "all the citizens."

During the Revolution of 1911, Sun Yat-sen led China's old type of democratic revolution adopted the democratic theories to fight against the feudal despotism in the rising period of the bourgeoisie, tried to establish a bourgeois democratic republic and lead China into the path of independence, liberation and prosperity.

The democratic revolution led by Sun Yat-sen was progressive, because the democratic theories was used by him as the weapons to awaken people and armed them with lofty ideals to join the revolution. However, in that period China was in the status of a semi-colonial and semi-feudal country and the world had entered the era of imperialism and the colonies were divided among big powers, consequently China was not allowed to enter into an independent path of bourgeois democracy. Nor could China's weak national bourgeoisie lead bourgeois democratic revolution to victory as the Western bourgeoisie had done in its revolutionary period. Hence, Sun Yat-sen's old type democratic revolution was strangled by the siege of domestic and international reactionary powers.

Although Chiang Kai-shek called himself as the successor of Sun Yat-sen, his dictatorial rule only put China further into civil war and darkness and brought no changes in the miserable life of the masses.

Chinese Communists, armed with Marxism, inherited and developed the democratic ideals and thoughts of Sun Yat-sen and put forward the programme of the new democracy that were in the line with China's national conditions to start the new democratic revolution.

The new democratic revolution is a new-type of a bourgeois democratic revolution led by the Communist Party of China, therefore it was radically different from the former old type of democratic revolution.

First of all, it is led by the working class and its party rather than bourgeoisie and its party. Secondly, it is based on the alliance between the working class and the peasantry, and also embraces patriotic factions of bourgeoisie and other classes in a most extensive democratic revolutionary united front. Lastly, new democratic revolution, after its victory, without any interruption transits to socialist revolution so as to establish the socialist system.

The new democratic revolution, led by the CPC aimed to establish a new democratic economy, a new democratic politics and a new democratic cultural system, among these the new democratic politics means a brand new type of democracy. The new democracy is different from the old-type of bourgeois democracy, being the most extensive democracy led by the Communist Party of China based on the alliance of working class and the peasantry. Later the new democracy has evolved towards the establishment of the socialist democratic politics with Chinese characteristics.

The path of democracy building led by the CPC is in accordance with China's national conditions and the most advanced ideology of democracy in the history of China. The thoughts of new democracy by the Communist Party of China inherits and develops the former democratic thoughts of Sun Yat-sen, as well. And today's socialist democracy of China has inherited and developed the democracy of the new democracy.

The new democracy theory is created by the CPC based on the conditions of China, and designed to meet the requirements of China's society, it includes two organic components: the most extensive democracy for the people and most effective dictatorship over a handful of reactionaries. Hence, the essential characteristics of the new democracy is people's democratic dictatorship. Comrade Mao Zedong in his famous "On New Democracy" has elaborated on the institutions, systems, procedures and rules of the new democratic politics, which is his innovative contribution to the Marxist views on democracy and important part of Mao Zedong Thought. The new democracy and the socialist democracy which the CPC further deepens are inseparable. The new democratic democracy has been the prerequisite of and the preparation for the socialist democracy while the socialist democracy is the continuance and the development of the democratic new democracy.

The further establishment of the socialist system in China provides the fundamental guarantee for the establishment of the socialist democracy. Comrade Mao Zedong has led the Chinese communists through an arduous exploration for the establishment of the socialist democratic politics and claimed that socialist democracy should: first of all, adhere to the guidance of CPC, the political party of the working class and adhere to the socialist path guided by Marxism; secondly, socialist democratic politics should be conducive to the consolidation of the public ownership of the means of production and the system people's democratic dictatorship; thirdly, socialist democratic politics should practice democratic centralism and realize the unity between the extensive democracy and centralized guidance; fourthly, socialist democratic politics should establish and carry out a set of democratic practices, such as the democratic system suited to the rule of law, democratic forms, rules and procedures that are in accordance with Chinese conditions; fifthly, promote socialist democracy through implementing intra-party democracy of the ruling party.

Through the practices of building socialist democratic politics, the Party has successfully established the following institutions such as the system of the People's Congress, the system of regional national autonomy, the system of multi-party cooperation and political consultation under the leadership of the CPC, and regulations for the grass-roots democracy and so on. These theoretical and practical explorations on the theories and the practices have created a new situation for China's socialist democratic system, and laid the theoretical and practical foundation for the building of socialist democratic politics with Chinese characteristics.

Although the socialist democracy is supposed to be a more extensive and advanced than the bourgeois democracy, and since there wasn't any ready made available model for our inspiration our Party has gone through a process of cognition, practice, re-cognition/examination and re-practice when pursuing to establish the socialist democracy in our country. Currently, the democratic politics of China still needs further development and perfection.

In the meantime, due to the deep-rooted influence of the remnants of the old feudalism, we have encountered with great detours in our path to achieve socialist democracy in China, such as the "Great Cultural Revolution" period in which the people's democracy and the legal system were greatly damaged.

Since the Third Plenary Session of the 11th Central Committee of the CPC in 1978, China has entered the new period of Reform and Opening-up when the Party resumed the ideological line of seeking truth from facts, and established the correct line of "One Central task and Two Basic Points" and began to form the theoretical system of socialism with Chinese characteristics, so as to lead the correct path of socialism with Chinese characteristics. In line with the reform process and establishment of the socialist market economy, the Party leads the people to the building of socialist democratic politics with Chinese characteristics.

Socialist democratic politics with Chinese characteristics should critically inherit all the excellent achievements of democracy experienced in the history of humanity, including the positive results of the bourgeois democracy, simultaneously discarding the dross of the bourgeois democracy and inheriting the fine tradition of new democracy, it should also summarize the experiences and lessons from the democratic politics of former socialist countries in the international communist movement and those of the socialist democratic political construction practice led by the CPC since the founding of New China, so as to create the socialist democracy with Chinese characteristics.

First of all, socialist democracy with Chinese characteristics is a democracy with socialist characteristics (nature), and also suits to the transition period till China will passage to the higher stage of socialism and communism; it is the democracy of China corresponding to the primary stage of socialism. Socialist democracy with Chinese characteristics also conforms to its economic foundation in which public ownership plays a dominant role and other diverse forms of ownership also develops side by side with it; besides conforms to distribution according to labor contribution being the dominant mode and a variety of modes of distribution coexisting besides the former. It is the most extensive type of people's democracy led by the working class, with workers, peasants and intellectuals being the main basis, including all the patriotic strata. It is a democracy, formed during the specific history of China which upholds "the system of multi-party cooperation and political consultation under the leadership of the CPC", and includes this system as the basic feature. It is a democracy which applies democracy for the majority and dictatorship over the few. Since China in the current situation has evolved from a semi-feudal and semi-colonial society, it is particularly crucial to eliminate the influence of feudal residuals and carry forward people's democracy;

On the other side since China is under the influence of the mature bourgeois democracies of the West, it has to guard against the invasion of the Western democracy as well as learn from them. Consequently, socialist democracy with Chinese characteristics is in a historical process of gradual establishment, gradual improvement and maturation.

As Lenin asserted, "proletarian democracy is a million times more democratic than any bourgeois democracy" (quoted from "The Proletarian Revolution and the Renegade Kautsky", Lenin, V.I.) Currently we should strive for the goal of building socialist democratic politics which can accomplish the people's democracy for the broadest possible of the citizens. The essence and the form of socialist democracy with Chinese characteristics are consistent. In order to fulfill the goals of people's democracy for the broadest, the democratic systems, institutions, forms, procedures, rules and mechanisms in accordance with Chinese conditions should be established. As Comrade Mao Zedong depicts in his work "The Situation in the Summer of 1957," "[o]ur aim is to create a political situation in which we have both centralism and democracy, both discipline and freedom, both unity of will and personal ease of mind and liveliness" Since the foundation of the New China, the Party has led the people to create a set of democratic politics in accordance with the conditions of China, but we are still far away from the goal we strive to arrive, therefore concerted efforts are necessary. To realize socialist democracy with Chinese characteristics, neither should we copy the practice of Western democratic politics blindly; nor should we ignore the circumstances of the current stage and attempt to go beyond the times. We should bear in mind that the realization of socialist democracy is a lengthy and a gradual process which requires down-to-earth efforts. We should not deny our achievements or underestimate ourselves just because our democracy does not sound enough. We should never consider the bourgeois democracy as the civilization of the millennium and accept total democratic Westernization. Certainly we should continue to promote and perfect our socialist democracy with Chinese characteristics. I would like to note that the bourgeois democracy has been improved and evolved throughout several hundred years, however socialist democracy with Chinese characteristics has just emerged and being established; we know that novel phenomena are not perfect in the beginning, but their future is always bright and radiant.

Y. 29

Several Issues of Deepening the Concept of Socialism with Chinese Characteristics

Zhu Jiamu[1]

This is a keynote speech of the author at the 12th Annual Academic Conference on National History on October 10, 2012, which was published in the journal of World Socialism Research Trends (Issue 92, October 30, 2012), an in-house periodical of the World Socialism Research Center attached to Chinese Academy of Social Sciences.

Abstract: The issue of "what socialism is" has acquired a relatively clear explanation through the practice of the reform and opening up over 30 years. Now, however, it is more important to clarify what is socialism with Chinese characteristics (SCC). Those two problems are closely related, but completely different. Understanding the former is cannot lead to the understanding of the latter, automatically. The report delivered by the CPC Central Committee to the 17th National Party Congress had offered a classic definition related to the path of SCC. This paper argues that, in order to deepen our understanding of the SCC, it is necessary to deeply analyze the three unities embodied in the path of SCC according to this definition, namely, the unity of the CPC's maximum program with basic program, the unity of the principles of scientific socialism with China's reality and the characteristics of the times, as well as the unity of the two historical periods before and after the reform and opening up.

Key words: socialism with Chinese characteristics; basic program; three unities

---

1 Zhu Mujia, Vice President of Chinese Academy of Social Sciences.

2012 witnessed the 30th anniversary of the appeal of "establishing socialism with Chinese characteristics" offered by Deng Xiaoping in the 12th National Party Congress of the CPC. In the early stage of reform and opening up, Deng Xiaoping pointed out that "we haven't fully clarified" what socialism was "in the past".[2] To some extent, Deng Xiaoping Theory, Reform and Opening up and the path of SCC were step by step established, clarified and improved during constant exploration on the question of "what socialism is and how to establish it". At present, even the ordinary people know that socialism as a concept cannot be equaled to class struggle, poverty, eating from the same big pot or sluggish development. Then, what is socialism? According to Deng Xiaoping, "the essence of socialism is to liberate and develop productive forces, eliminate exploitation, do away with polarization and ultimately achieve common prosperity."The definition grants us more accurate and profound understanding of socialism. Although we still need to improve our understanding of the definition, currently we should focus on another question: what socialism with Chinese characteristics is, or what kind of SCC should be established, and how to establish the SCC? Although the two questions are directly linked to each other, they are not exactly one and same question. That is to say, understanding what socialism is does not clarify what the SCC is. In the report of the 17th National Party Congress of the CPC, a classic explanation related to the path of SCC was given: "taking the path of socialism with Chinese characteristics means we will, under the leadership of the CPC and in light of China's basic conditions, take economic development as the central task, adhere to the Four Cardinal Principles and persevere in reform and opening up, release and develop the productive forces, consolidate and improve the socialist system, develop the socialist market economy, socialist democracy, an advanced socialist culture and a harmonious socialist society, and make China a prosperous, strong, democratic, culturally advanced and harmonious modern socialist country."

According to this definition, the path of SCC is a new path guided by the basic theories, programs, line and experiences of the Party in the primary stage of socialism, it is related to socialism before the Reform and Opening Up yet different from it. Therefore, in order to deepen our understanding of it, it is necessary to deeply analyze three unities embodied in this path according to this definition, namely, the unity of the CPC's maximum program with basic program, the unity of the principles of scientific socialism with China's reality and the characteristics of the times, as well as the unity of the two historical periods before and after the reform and opening up.

2　Xiaoping Deng. Selected Works of Deng Xiaoping. Volume 3, p. 234, People's Publishing House, 1993.

I. Socialism with Chinese characteristics is the unity of the CPC's maximum program with the basic program

In conformity with the Communist Manifesto, the ultimate goal of its struggle as well as the maximum program of the CPC is to eliminate private ownership and realize communism. However, "Everybody knows that the Communist Party has an immediate and a future programme, a minimum and a maximum programme, with regard to the social system it advocates,"[3] so it is impossible to skip the minimum program or the basic program and realize communism. Based on the basic program for the primary stage of socialism, the Party put forward that it is the goal and task of the Chinese people, at the present and for a relatively long time in the future, is to establish the SCC. In order to deepen our understanding of the SCC, we must clarify the relationship between the maximum program and the basic program of the Party.

It is specified in the basic program of the Party that we must establish a socialist market economy, socialist democratic politics, socialist advanced culture and socialist harmonious society. To sum up, we must establish a prosperous, strong, democratic, culturally advanced and harmonious modern socialist society. In terms of its content, the program is basically in line with the path of SCC. It is based on the reality that China is and will be in the primary stage of socialism for a relatively long time in the future and takes into consideration our lofty goal of communism, laying an essential foundation for the higher stage of socialism or the primary stage of communism.

In retrospect, the success of the new democratic revolution led by the Party was to a great extent due to the correct understanding and handling of the relationship between the minimum program and maximum program. At that time, on the one hand, the Party required all the members to fight for the minimum program of the democratic revolution, because of the belief that "those who look down upon the bourgeois democratic revolution and take it lightly, without loyalty, passion or readiness to sacrifice their blood and life, and empty-talk about socialism and communism"[4] are more or less traitors of socialism and communism rather than conscious and loyal communist. On the other hand, the Party should educate the cadres and members with communist ideological system and require that all the members bear two goals—struggling for new democratic revolution and struggling for future socialism and communism—when they join the Party, "regardless of the ignorance, hostility, slander and ridicule from the enemies of

---
3 Zedong, Mao. Selected Works of Mao Zedong, Volume 2, p. 421, People's Publishing House, 1991.
4 Zedong, Mao. Selected Works of Mao Zedong, Volume 3, p. 421, People's Publishing House, 1991.

communism."⁵ For one thing, if the publicity of communist thoughts is not strengthened and study of Marxism and Leninism is not taken strictly, "Chinese revolution will not be led to the socialist stage, nor can the current democratic revolution be led to success."⁶ For another, the whole Party should be reminded from time to time that, "the publicity of communist ideological system and social system should be differentiated from the action program of new democracy; communist theories and methods for observing problems, studying knowledge, handling affairs and training cadres should be differentiated from the guideline of new democracy, which is national culture."⁷ The Party dialectically unites the maximum program with minimum program, without overlooking the latter when struggling for the former or forgets the former in the implementation of the latter, so it only took it 28 years to lead the people to overthrow the "three mountains" that oppressed the Chinese people.

Today, the Party should correctly understand and balance the relationship between maximum program and basic program, while leading the people to establish the SCC. There are stringent differences as well as close connection between the basic program in the primary stage of socialism and the maximum program of the Party. Struggle for the maximum program cannot be achieved without the fulfillment of the basic program of establishing the SCC; yet without the maximum program, the establishment of the SCC will be the product of direction or orientation and soul. It is like a person heading south. It can slow his pace, march on the spot or even take a few steps backward, but it cannot walk towards the north which will never lead it to the final destination even if it is fully prepared. Therefore, whether the maximum program and final goal of the Party are borne in mind will decide whether the Party can lead the people to complete the tasks of basic program and whether the Party will lead the path of SCC towards the great ideal of communism. As General Secretary Hu Jintao said, "the realization of communism is a lengthy historical process, which requires that China is and will be in the primary stage of socialism for a long time and that we should continuously struggle to realize the basic program of the Party at current stage in a down-to-earth manner…and march towards the ultimate goal of the Party unswervingly. If we focus on the present and forget the lofty ideal, we will lose our direction; if we just make empty-talk about the lofty ideal without working, we will be divorced from reality."⁸

---

5   Zedong, Mao. Selected Works of Mao Zedong. Volume 3, p. 422, People's Publishing House, 1991.
6   Zedong, Mao. Selected Works of Mao Zedong. Volume 2, p. 422, People's Publishing House, 1991.
7   Zedong, Mao. Selected Works of Mao Zedong. Volume 2, p 422, People's Publishing House, 1991.
8   Selected Documents Since 16th National Party Congress of the CPC, Volume 1. Central Party Literature Press, 2005.

The Party has gone all the way through several tests including the long-term governance, market economy and reform and opening up. Emphasizing that Party members should bear the maximum program and the lofty ideal in mind does not mean that they should implement the communist policies immediately, it is to remind everyone that the Party sticks to governance and implements market economy and reform and opening up in order to enhance social productive forces, realize an affluent life for the people and pave the way for the realization of communism, rather than allow the party members and cadres to build up fortunes by means of their positions and powers. Although the realization of communism will be a lengthy path, it is by no means an unforeseeable future or illusion; nor is it an utopia. That is the reason why Party members have to make the oath of "…fight for communism throughout my life, be ready at all times to sacrifice my all life, to the struggle for communism."Communism refers to the ideal system of human society, it is an ideological system as well as a movement. "In China, the publicity of communist thoughts and practices for the ultimate realization of communism have already started at the moment when the Chinese Communist Party was founded and when it started the new democratic revolution…communist thoughts and practices have long existed in our real life."[9]

We can be closer to communism if the will of the Party members was supported by the communist ideals, we possessed in the Jinggang Mountains period, Yan'an period and Xibaipo period. It was pointed out by Comrade Jiang Zemin that, "we are now fighting to realize the maximum program of realizing communism. A qualified Party should not forget this lofty goal or ignore the struggle for the realization of the basic program of the primary stage of socialism."[10]

As the General Secretary Hu Jintao said, "Martyrs in the revolution defy steadfastly all brute forces in the test of life and death, because they are loyal through thick and thin and were absolutely determined about the ideal of communism" and "the reason why currently some Party members hesitate when faced with difficulties or contradictions, and abandon themselves to despair and become corrupted in the face of temptations is that they do not have enough faith in the ideal of communism and the path of SCC."[11] These passages demonstrate that it is achievable and is a must that members should bear in mind the maximum program and have faith in the ideal of communism, in the period when the Party is fighting for the current basic program.

---

9 Selected Documents Since 12th National Party Congress of the CPC, Volume 1. Central Party Literature Press, 1986.
10 Selected Documents Since 15th National Party Congress of the CPC, Volume 1. People's Publishing House, 2000.
11 Selected Documents Since 16th National Party Congress of the CPC, Volume 2. Central Party Literature Press, 2006.

There are objective criteria for judging whether a Party member bears in mind the maximum program and has faith in the ideal of communism when struggling for the basic program. For the ordinary Party members, the criteria are whether they serve the people faithfully, whether they are the first to bear hardships and the last to enjoy comforts, whether they work hard and are honest in performing their official duties, whether they study Marxism hard and whether they throw themselves into the breach in times of emergency, when they are implementing all the guidelines and policies of the Party and the state. As to the party cadres and leaders, apart from the aforementioned, the criteria also include whether they carry out the basic theories, path and program of the Party in a comprehensive, complete and accurate manner, whether they adhere to Four Cardinal Principles when promoting the reform of economic, political and cultural systems and whether they pay attention to spiritual civilization and self-building of the Party while they are leading the establishment of material civilization. Only when they meet the aforesaid criteria, we can fully confirm that they bear the maximum program in mind and have faith in the ideal of communism.

Therefore, it can be concluded that the SCC does not transcend the stages of social development, nor is it perpetual. Rather, it is socialism that calls for long-term adherence and requires that we keep abreast of time based on objective conditions and "march towards the ultimate goal of the Party."

II. Socialism is the unity of the principles of scientific socialism with China's reality and the characteristics of the times

Scientific socialism is a theory established by Marx and Engels who critically inherited the utopian socialism based on theories of historical materialism and surplus value, with seeking the truth from facts as its most important theoretical quality. Practice has proved that a good combination of the principles and practice of scientific socialism will result in a successful socialist movement, or else, it will be the other way round. The fundamental reason why the new democratic revolution was successful lies in the Mao Zedong Thought, which is the result of the combination between principles of scientific socialism and the reality of Chinese revolution. The same reason gave rise to the successful socialist revolution at the early stage of New China. Other cases like the "Great Leap Forward", "Organization of People's Communes throughout the Country" and "Great Cultural Revolution" which have induced heavy losses to the Party and the people were caused by the "Left" mistakes of the Party that blindly and dogmatically understood and applied some principles of scientific socialism and which separated theory from reality.

As a political theory, social practice and social system, socialism with Chinese characteristics belongs to the scope of scientific socialism, which determines that it should follow the principles of it. For instance, in terms of economic system, we should implement the public ownership of the means of production instead of privatization; in terms of politics, put into practice the dictatorship of the proletariat and leadership of the Communist Party instead of "a state of the whole people" and a multi-party system of the Western type; in terms of ideology, stick to the guidance of Marxism instead of pluralism of guiding thoughts, etc. Without following these principles, it will be anything but scientific socialism. Yet, in the meantime we must combine the principles of scientific socialism with the national conditions of China and consciously accept that we will be in the primary stage of socialism for a long time, and be clear that peace and development are the two main themes of the times. To deepen our understanding of the SCC, firstly we must understand the relationships among the three..

First of all, looking from the aspect of economy, based on the low level of productive forces in China, the SCC encourages, supports and guides the development of non-public sector of the economy, creates a new situation in which all economic sectors compete on an equal footing and reinforce each other, gives a better play to the basic role of market forces in the allocation of resources, pushes forward the establishment of a modern property right system and a modern enterprise system, improves the distribution system in order to allow the factors of production such as labor, capital, technology and managerial expertise to have fair shares according to their respective contributions; sticks to the basic economic system where public ownership and distribution according to labor are dominant, adheres to carry out macroeconomic regulations on market economy by means such as the state plans, effectively combines giving play to the strengths of socialist system and allocating market resources; prohibits the use of market principle of exchange of equal values in the political field, especially within the Party.

At the early stage of reform and opening up, in order to eliminate the long-standing "equalitarian" practices and the tendency of "dining from the same big pot", the Party launched the policy of "allowing some people and some regions to be rich earlier than others", which played an important role in releasing people's initiative and speeding up economic development. However, such a policy also brought some negative effects during its implementation, such as income gap between different regions, income gap between different groups of people and different industries, unfair distribution of income, money-driven mindset and various corruption and hideous phenomenon that followed. As a result, strong dissatisfaction among the masses has become the underlying cause of social instability and mass disturbances, and which triggered the attacks from both right and "left" thoughts and rising criticisms from the capitalist countries. To tackle the question and improve the situation, the Party put forward the guideline of "taking the path of common prosperity" and "gradually reversing the trend of growing gap in income distribution" and made some adjustments related to distribution policies. For instance, the principle of "giving priority to efficiency and stressing fairness" which was proposed before was changed into the policy of "highlighting both efficiency and equity, with putting equity in a prominent position". It was correct and necessary that the stress should be put on social construction to protect and improve people's livelihood and promote social equity and justice on the basis of economic development; a proper balance should be achieved between efficiency and equity in both the primary distribution and the secondary distribution, with particular emphasis given to equity in the secondary distribution; the share of people's personal incomes in the distribution of national income should be gradually increased, and that of labor remuneration in primary distribution raised. Besides according to this policy, vigorous efforts were made to raise the income of low-income groups, and poverty-alleviation aid and the minimum wage, etc. were gradually increased. Preliminary results have been achieved, such as the decrease in the income gap between the urban and rural areas and increases in the poverty-alleviation aid and the minimum wage. To be exact, there appears phenomenon of labor shortages and rise of labor costs in some regions.

It should also be noted that it is no mean feat to balance efficiency and equity, let alone dissolving the big gap between the wealthy and the poor. For example, it is said that "the gap between the wealthy and the poor in China is not big enough. Only by enlarging the gap, can society make progress and is harmonious society possible," and that "without the gap, it is none other than eating from the same big pot." There are even opinions that the growing gap is caused by the government's economic management and "state-owned monopoly", which gave rise to slogans like "priority should be placed on the people's wealth", "state-owned enterprises withdraw and private-owned enterprises enter", "private economy should be the main body", etc. Socialist society with Chinese characteristics is not classless, because both concepts of "nation" and "the people" are of class nature. Hence, elaboration should be given on "the people are poor", "the people are rich", "the nation is wealthy" and "the nation is poor". At present, there are still 130 million people whose daily living expense is less than 1 dollar. However, China is currently the second largest luxury goods market in the world and soon will be the largest. The state-owned and state-holding enterprises take up less than 30% of the industrial enterprises in both production and asset values; state revenues amounts to only 30% of the national income. The average tax bearing of the 24 industrialized countries is %45.3

and that of the 29 developing countries is %35.5, both higher than that of China. Therefore, we cannot make such a generalization like "the people are poor" or "the state is wealthy".

As Marx had pointed out in Critique of the Gotha Program, "Any distribution whatever of the means of consumption is only a consequence of the distribution of the conditions of production themselves. The latter distribution, however, is a feature of the mode of production itself."[12] After reform and opening up, Deng Xiaoping has repeated that the two cardinal principles of socialism are "public ownership as the main body and common prosperity".[13]

Some economists have given elaboration on this basic tenet of Marxism in light of current situation and pointed out that "when it comes to the cause of growing income gap, normally people will think of growing urban-rural gap, aggravating regional development imbalance, trade monopoly, corruption, uneven supply of public goods, redistribution control lag, etc. Those are indeed corresponding causes but not the major ones. According to Marxist views, ownership system decides distribution system; property relation decides distribution relation. Difference in possession is the major factor of difference in income distribution."[14] Hence, while advancing ownership reform, the Party has always highlighted that ownership is the main body and state-owned economy is dominant. It is stated in the Decisions on Several Significant Problems of Reform and Development of State-owned Enterprises of the Fourth Plenary Session of the Fifteenth Central Committee of the CPC that "public sector of the economy including state-owned economy is the economic foundation of socialist system in China, state-owned economy is the basic force with which the country guides, promotes, regulates and controls economic and social development and it is the important guarantee for the realization of the fundamental interests of the masses and common prosperity."It is required in the report of the 17th Central Committee of the CPC that "we stick to and improve the basic economic system in which public ownership is dominant and different economic sectors develop side by side" and "perfecting modern enterprise institution, optimizing layout and structure of state economy, and enhancing the vigor, control power, and influence of state economy" Facts have proven that only by upholding the basic economic system in which public ownership is dominant can we avoid polarization and guarantee the implementation of socialism with Chinese characteristics. Otherwise,

---

12　Selected Works of Marx and Engels by Karl Marx, Friedrich Engels. Volume 3, p. 82, People's Publishing House. 1996
13　Xiaoping Deng. Selected Works of Deng Xiaoping. Volume 3. People's Publishing House, 1993.
14　Guoguang, Deng. Deepen Understanding of the Status and Role of the Public Sector of Economy. People's Daily. June 21, 2011.

polarization will get serious, which will undermine social cohesion as well as well social consumption power, diminishing domestic market and reducing the motive force of economic development.

Secondly, in the light of politics, based on the conditions of centralized leadership, excessive concentration of power and overlooking the building of democracy and the legal system, SCC always puts political restructuring on the important position of reform and development, unswervingly advances it and has made great progress. Yet in the meantime, socialist political development path with Chinese characteristics should always adhere to the people's democratic dictatorship of the country, uphold the leadership of Communist Party, stick to the basic political system and then adhere to the socialist direction of political restructuring.

Some people say that it doesn't matter whether reform takes a socialist path or capitalist one, referencing Deng Xiaoping's opinions that we should ignore whether it is socialist or capitalist and that contention should be discouraged. In effect, throughout the Selected Works of Deng Xiaoping, Deng Xiaoping never mentioned about those opinions; rather, Deng Xiaoping kept reminding us that "it is of paramount importance to adhere to socialist path during reform and opening up."[15]

In his speeches during the Southern Tour, he stressed that "we must uphold Four Cardinal Principles during reform and opening up"[16] and that "If we do not uphold them in our effort to correct ultra-Left thinking, we shall end up ``correcting'' Marxism-Leninism and socialism."[17] In this sense, when Deng Xiaoping said that "The crux of the matter is whether the road to take should be capitalist or socialist," he meant that we must clarify what capitalism and socialism are and find out the criteria for correct judgment of socialism. Besides, Deng Xiaoping never said he discouraged contention over reform direction. Instead, after the political turmoil in 1989, he said, "the 'reform' advocated by certain people should be renamed liberalization, that is, going capitalist. The essence of their 'reform' is to go capitalist. The reform we are carrying out is different from theirs. There will be more debate on this subject."[18]

---

15 Xiaoping Deng. Selected Works of Deng Xiaoping. Volume 3. People's Publishing House, 1993.
16 Xiaoping Deng. Selected Works of Deng Xiaoping. Volume 3. People's Publishing House, 1993.
17 Xiaoping Deng. Selected Works of Deng Xiaoping. Volume 3. People's Publishing House, 1993.
18 Xiaoping Deng. Selected Works of Deng Xiaoping. Volume 3. People's Publishing House, 1993.

Comrade Jiang Zemin and General Secretary Hu Jintao have the same proposition over whether we should adhere to the correct direction of reform and are consistent about it throughout. In the meeting to commemorate the 70thfounding anniversary of the CPC, Comrade Jiang Zemin said, "Our reform is the self-perfection and development of socialist system"; "without reform, our socialist system will not continue to be vigorous, while without adherence to the socialist direction in reform, the achievements of the Party and the people over the past 70 years will be gone. We must fundamentally distinguish two views of reform and opening up, namely reform and opening up with adherence to Four Cardinal Principles and that with bourgeois liberalization—going capitalist."[19]

In the meeting to commemorate the 30thanniversary of the Third Plenary Session of the 11th Central Committee of the CPC, General Secretary Hu Jintao said that "we must stick to the combination of Four Cardinal Principles with reform and opening up, firmly grasp economic construction, the center, and always maintain the correct direction of reform and opening up" and that "the Four Cardinal Principles are the foundation underlying all our efforts to build the country and the political corner stone of the survival and development of the Party and the country; reform and opening up is the path to a powerful nation and the energy source of the development and progress of the Party and the country...without the Four Cardinal Principles and reform and opening up, economic construction will lose its way and motivation."[20] Their demonstration shows that the Party has always insisted that we must stick to the right direction of reform—socialism, namely the Four Cardinal Principles. Negation on a direction for reform is groundless.

Some people criticize that our political restructuring stagnates and retrogresses. To judge whether a political restructuring is stagnant, we must determine what the goal of reform is in the first place. If the goal is Western political system and we use it as the criterion for failure and success of the reform, our political restructuring is not only "stagnant", but never starts. However, if the goal is self-perfection and development of socialist political system and we use it as the criterion, then our restructuring is by no means stagnant or retrogressive but significantly successful.

It should be noted that it is still a long way to go in establishing democracy and legal system, which calls for further reform and serious implementation of reformed system and laws. However, the goal of reform falls on the self-perfection of socialist system, with the principle of upholding the organic unity among leadership of CPC, the people as the masters of the country

---

19 Selected Significant Works Since 13th National Party Congress of the CPC. Volume 3. People's Publishing House, 1993.
20 Selected Significant Works Since 17th National Party Congress of the CPC. Volume 2. Central Party Literature Press, 2009.

and rule of law, and with a prerequisite that is conducive to political stability, solidarity among the people, economic development and improvement of livelihood. We have never and will not copy the system where multi-parties take turns to be in power and three powers are separated, because it is not in line with Chinese conditions. If we copy it mechanically, we will not be able to bring real democracy to the people or dissolve corruption; instead, we will induce political turmoil, result in social chaos, national secession and civil war, render our people refugees and put us back in the time when the country was divided by foreign powers, with all our achievements ended in smoke.

The "constitutional" reform advocated by some people in essence calls for the implementation of capitalist regime covering multiparty system, parliamentary system and civilian control of the military. In this sense, it is no longer about political restructuring but fundamentally changing the political system of SCC. In the capitalist country, different parties representing different interest groups and taking turns to be in power does not influence the state nature—dictatorship of bourgeoisie, so the military can and must be nationalized, or else the multi-party system cannot be materialized. As to the people's democratic dictatorship based on worker-peasant alliance led by the working class, CPC represents the interest of the working class as well as the common interest of the majority. Under market economy, though there are conflicts between different interests among the people, there isn't and is not allowed to be fundamental conflict of interests. Therefore, interest groups and their representing parties which are opposite to the people's interest are not allowed to exist. In this case, military must and absolutely can be led by CPC. Such a leadership does not hinder the operation of political system or influence the military's nature as national defense forces; rather, it is conducive to the implementation of socialist political system with Chinese characteristics and it is the indispensible condition to the adherence of people's democratic dictatorship and the guarantee of solidarity of the Party and the people.

Therefore, it can be concluded that SCC does not copy the principles of scientific socialism dogmatically and mechanically, or go against the basic principles of scientific socialism; instead, it is the socialism that sticks to the system in which public ownership and distribution according to labor are the main body, with coexistence of many different kinds of economic sectors and forms of distribution; puts the market under the macro-control of the country while basing resource allocation on the market and; takes the path of common prosperity and prevents polarization while opposing to equalitarianism and eating from the same big pot; always uphold the organic unity among leadership of CPC, the people as the masters of the country and rule of law while deepening political restructuring; grasps the construction of both material and spiritual civilizations.

III. Unity of the two historical periods before and after the reform and opening up

SCC is initiated after reform and opening up, based on the condition that China has been establishing socialism for more than 20 years before reform and opening up. To deepen our understanding of SCC, we must deepen our understanding of the two historical periods before and after the reform and opening up. It is easy to see that in real life, those who are doubtful about or against reform and opening up tend to negate the history after it with the history before it; those who are doubtful about or negate the Four Cardinal Principles tend to negate the history before reform and opening up with the history after it; those who regard SCC as the "return of new democracy", "democratic socialism", "social democracy" or "restoration of capitalism" tend to separate the two historical periods and consider them antagonistic to each other. Once the two periods are separated and considered antagonistic, people will oppose to or distort SCC. Hence, how to understand the two historical periods before and after reform and opening up and their relation is closely related to our understanding of SCC.

Looking back on history, it becomes clear that if reform and opening up was not implemented in 1978 or was abandoned after 1978, the history of New China would not have been possible and the Party and the state must have been gone, which has been proved by the history of some former socialist countries. However, if New China was not founded in 1949, did not choose socialist path, did not carry out large-scale industrialization and basic construction of farmland, did not establish independent and integrated industrial system and national economic system and did not cultivate a large number of talents in the field of economy, science and technology, culture and education, reform and opening up would not have been started. If it was started, but took the path of capitalism rather than socialism, the Party and the state would also have been gone, which is also proved by the history of former socialist countries.

To correctly judge the history before reform and opening up, we must draw a clear distinction between the mainstream and sub streams of that period. Changes in economic development and people's life before reform and opening up are far less prominent than those after it, but it by no means shows that achievements in the period are not great or important. It is the same case with building houses. It is not easy to see whether the foundation is firm enough when it is being laid, but it can be proved when the houses are quickly erected. Besides, to correctly judge the history before reform and opening up, we must understand the significance of that history to reform and opening up. When the first generation of leaders of the New China led people to establish socialism, they carried out arduous exploration on the rules of establishment and formed many correct guidelines. For instance, politically, we must strictly differentiate and correctly handle two kinds of conflicts, mobilize all positive factors and turn all negative factors into positive ones, because ideological and political work is the lifeline of economic work and all other work; economically, we must be independent and self-reliant, make overall plans and appropriate arrangements, take all factors into consideration, increase production and practice economy and build the country with diligence and thrift, with agriculture as the base and industry as the leading factor; culturally, we must allow all flowers to bloom together and a hundred schools of thought to contend with each other, make the past serve the present and foreign things serve China, etc. Though those correct guidelines were not implemented before the reform and opening up, they have been seriously carried out and given full play to after it and will play an important role in the establishment of SCC.

Despite the huge differences between the two periods in both policy and practical work, they have not been separated or stood antagonistic because they are both stages of development of Chinese socialist society. The previous period is the basis of the later one, while the later one is the reform, renewal and development of the previous one; both periods have worked together to give rise to SCC. General Secretary Hu Jintao pointed out in his demonstration on the historical course of reform and opening up in the report of the 17th Central Committee of the CPC, "the great cause of reform and opening up was conducted on a foundation laid by the Party's first generation of central collective leadership with Comrade Mao Zedong at its core, which founded Mao Zedong Thought, led the whole Party and the people of all ethnic groups in establishing the People's Republic and scoring great achievements in our socialist revolution and. construction, and gained invaluable experience in its painstaking exploration for laws governing socialist construction"; "reform and opening up and socialist modernization inherit and develop the great cause of establishing socialism in China after the founding of New China"[21], which guides us to correctly understand the dialectic relationship between two historical periods before and after reform and opening up.

Correct understanding of the relation between two historical periods decides the correct understanding of the connotation of SCC, the evaluation on the contribution of the Party, state leaders, cadres and the masses at the early stage of New China and the safety of regime and survival of the country. "If we want to destroy a country, we must eliminate its history."[22] At

---

21 Selected Significant Works Since 17th National Party Congress of the CPC. Volume 2. Central Party Literature Press, 2009.
22 Zizhen, Gong. "On Ancient History II", Complete Works of Gong Zizhen. Shanghai People's Publishing House, 1975.

present, hostile forces at home and abroad enjoy making an issue of history, especially contemporary history, in order to oppose the leadership of CPC and socialist system. On the one hand, they distort and slander the Chinese history of revolution and the history of New China, attack and smear the Party and national leaders; on the other hand, they try to reverse the verdicts on some overthrown representatives of the reactionary class and whitewash the squires and traitors and sing the praises of them. To protect the honor and interests of People's Republic of China, we must attach great importance to the ideological confrontations in the fields of historical research and publicity. We do not allow slanders on history of New China and words opposing two historical periods to run rampant.

Negating a person's history is equivalent to negating the person himself; likewise, negating the history of one's own is equivalent to negating oneself. For instance, Mikhail Gorbachev initiated a movement that negated the history covering Stalin, Lenin, the October Revolution and the Soviet Union and then that of Marx, Engels and international Communist Movement, which resulted in serious confusion and crises of confidence and faith among the masses and led to the collapse of the Soviet Union. To learn a lesson from it, the Communist Party of China does not negate the historical period before reform and opening up simply because the faults and distortions of it but righteously takes the 60 years of history of New China as a glorious whole and publicizes it. With such a correct attitude, it fundamentally protects the history after reform and opening up, which is conducive to the people's ideal and faith of establishing SCC as well as the consolidation and development of the cause of SCC.

Therefore, SCC does not completely affirm the history before reform and opening up or completely negate it. Instead, on the one hand, it admits and corrects the mistakes of that period and learns lessons from it; on the other hand, it affirms the nature and mainstream of the history, establishes itself on the basis of its great achievements and precious experience and unites the two historical periods.

From General Secretary Hu Jintao's talk on July 23, we can conclude that the theme of the upcoming 18th Central Committee of the CPC is the same as those in the previous ones, namely, upholding the great banner of SCC, unswervingly marching on the path of SCC and struggling for the comprehensive establishment of a well-off society. To respond to the appeal of the Party, we must continuously deepen our understanding of SCC and clarify what is SCC so as to realize the great rejuvenation of the Chinese nation on the path of SCC.

Y. 30

Following the Basic Line of the Party Unswervingly throughout one Hundred Years: A Review on Deng Xiaoping's Speeches in the Southern Tour

Zhu Jiamu[1]

Abstract: The core idea of Deng Xiaoping's Speeches in the Southern Tour is "unswervingly adhering to the basic line of the Party throughout one hundred years". The speeches made a comprehensive dialectical analysis on a series of important relations involving the Party's and the nation's development, among which the following eight relations are most important: the relation between do not be afraid of too many elements of capitalism and must adhere to the socialist path, the relation between setting up more "three-capital"[2] enterprises and building bigger and stronger large and medium-sized state-owned enterprises, the relation between planned economy is not equivalent to socialism and market economy is not equivalent to capitalism, the relation between allowing a part of people get rich first and common prosperity, the relation between concentrating on economic construction and attaching equal importance to material and spiritual civilization without any letup, the relation between avoiding quarrels and opposing bourgeois liberalism, the relation between following Party's basic line and training successors, the relation between the protracted and tortuous nature of the socialist path and the general trend of history along which socialism will replace capitalism. Today, these analyses still bear an important enlightening role and guiding significance.

Key words: Southern Speeches; basic line; eight relations

---
1 Zhu Jiamu, Vice President of Chinese Academy of Social Sciences.
2 "Three capital" (sanzr') enterprises stands for the three different forms of foreign capital: Sino-joint ventures, contractual joint ventures and exclusively foreign-funded ventures in China.

20 years ago, at an important historical moment of severe ordeal of domestic and international political disputes, Deng Xiaoping, at an age of 88 years, travelled for an inspection to South China and delivered important speeches (hereinafter referred to as Speeches). In the Speeches, he comprehensively summarized the lessons and experiences from the 14 years' of reform and opening up, fully expounded on the lines, principles and policies instituted since the Third Plenary Session of the 11th Central Committee of the CPC, profoundly answered many important cognitive issues that had troubled the people and constrained their thinking for a long time and systematically put forward important thoughts that are of real and long-term guiding significance to build an entire socialist modernization, making great contributions to pushing forward China's reform and opening up as well as the building of socialist modernization into a new stage. Upholding the basic line of the Party at the primary stage of socialism with Chinese characteristics, and being a manifesto of the innovation of the theory of socialism with Chinese characteristics, the Southern Speeches is a very important historical literature of Marxism in the history of People's Republic of China, especial the history of reform and opening up, and a masterpiece of Deng Xiaoping Theory. Its foresighted and truthful features have been fully confirmed by the rapid economic growth and the constant enhancement of the overall national strength of China in the past 20 years, as well as by the profound changes in international situation and economic crises of the capitalist countries. As a saying goes, "If a man keeps cherishing his old knowledge, so as continually to be acquiring *new*, he may be a teacher of others." Reviewing the speeches on the occasion of their 20th anniversary, re-reading them several times together with 20 years of practice and re-grasping their spiritual essence and profound connotation are not only the best commemoration of them, but will also help us correctly understand and solve various complex problems at present so as to advance the cause of socialism with Chinese characteristics.

It is declared at the outset of the Speeches that "in adhering to the line, principles and policies instituted since the Third Plenary Session of the Eleventh Central Committee of the CPC, the key lies in adhering to 'one central task and two basic points'"; "failing to adhere to socialism, carry out reform and opening up, develop the economy and improve people's livelihood can only lead up to a blind alley. The basic line of the Party governs one hundred years and must not be shaken."[3] This shows clearly that unswerving adherence to the basic line of "one central task and two basic points" for one hundred years is the core idea of the Speeches. When we

---

3   Selected Works of Deng Xiaoping. Volume III. People's Publishing House, 1993, p. 370-371; available at: https://dengxiaopingworks.wordpress.com/2013/03/18/excerpts-from-talks-given-in-wuchang-shenzhen-zhuhai-and-shanghai, accessed on February 20, 2015.

review the Speeches, we should firmly grasp their core idea, profoundly comprehend and continue to implement the basic line of "one central task and two basic points" and fully understand and correctly interpret the truth of "failing to adhere to socialism, carry out reform and opening up, develop the economy and improve people's livelihood can only lead up to a blind alley" so as to earnestly accomplish to unswervingly adhere to the basic line of the Party throughout one hundred years.

Although the Speeches are quite short in size with only 8,000 characters altogether, their content is very rich. They revolve around the core idea of "following the basic line unswervingly throughout one hundred years" and make a comprehensive dialectical analysis on a series of important relations involving the development of the Party and nation, among which the following eight relations are most important: the relation between do not be afraid of too many elements of capitalism and must adhere to the socialist path, the relation between setting up more "three-capital"[4] enterprises and building bigger and stronger large and medium-sized state-owned enterprises, the relation between planned economy is not equivalent to socialism and market economy is not equivalent to capitalism, the relation between allowing a part of people get rich first and common prosperity, the relation between concentrating on economic construction and attaching equal importance to material and spiritual civilization without any letup, the relation between avoiding quarrels and opposing bourgeois liberalism, the relation between following Party's basic line and training successors, the relation between the protracted and tortuous nature of the socialist path and the general trend of history along which socialism will replace capitalism. The analysis of those relations runs through the spirit of emancipating the minds and seeking truth from facts and embodies the standpoint, viewpoint and method of Marxism, which still bear an important enlightening role and guiding significance for us today. Reviewing the Speeches, we must take those analyses as our focus of study and earnestly accomplish a good grasp of them.

I. On the relation between do not be afraid of too many elements of capitalism and must adhere to the socialist path

Reform and opening up and adherence to the Four Cardinal Principles are the two indispensible integral parts in Party's basic line. The unity decides whether the country will end in success or failure, because the former is the way to make China powerful and the vitality source of the Party's and the country's development and progress, while the latter is the foundation to the building of China and the political cornerstone of the Party's and the

---

4 "Three capital" (sanzr') enterprises stands for the three different forms of foreign capital: Sino-joint ventures, cooperative joint ventures and exclusively foreign-funded ventures in China.

country's survival and development. However, since reform and opening up, there have always been some people who tend to, consciously or unconsciously, consider these two basic points in separation and even in opposition, talk only about one of them, ignoring or denying the other. What often serves them as basis of argument is the so-called wording "whether it is called 'social' or 'capital'" proposed by Deng Xiaoping in the Speeches. In fact, as long as we take a careful look at the original text of the Speeches, we will find out what Deng Xiaoping actually talked about: "The reason some people hesitate to carry out the reform and the open up policy and dare not break new ground is, in essence, that they're afraid it would mean introducing too many elements of capitalism and, indeed, taking the capitalist path. The crux of the matter is whether it [the path] is called 'capital' or 'social'."[5] Here, he not only said "whether it [the path] is called 'social' or 'capital'", but, on the contrary, he said right after these words, "special economic zones are 'social', not 'capital'. In the case of Shenzhen, the publicly owned sector is the mainstay of the economy."[6] Hence, the so-called "whether it is called 'social' or 'capital'" is completely a misinterpretation of the Speeches. Since reform and opening up, Deng Xiaoping has reminded us again and again that we must adhere to the socialist path, socialist orientation and socialist principles and never engage in capitalism. He pointed out: "we are engaged in four modernizations, which are four modernizations of socialism, none other modernizations"[7]; "in the course of reform it is very important for us to maintain our socialist orientation"[8]; "the mainland will maintain the socialist system and not turn off onto the wrong road, the road to capitalism"[9]; "that public ownership has the mainstay, common prosperity, this is the fundamental principle of socialism we must adhere to."[10] In the Speeches, he also emphasized that "in the course of reform and opening up, we must always adhere to the Four Cardinal Principles"[11], and added that "If we do not uphold these Four Cardinal Principles in our effort to correct ultra-Left thinking, we shall end up "correcting" Marxism-Leninism and socialism."[12] This shows that the so-called

---

5 Selected Works of Deng Xiaoping. Volume III. People's Publishing House, 1993, p. 372, available at: https://dengxiaopingworks.wordpress.com/2013/03/18/excerpts-from-talks-given-in-wuchang-shenzhen-zhuhai-and-shanghai; accessed on February 20, 2015.
6 Ibid.
7 Ibid., p. 110, available at: https://dengxiaopingworks.wordpress.com/2013/03/18/reform-is-the-only-way-for-china-to-developed-its-productive-forces; accessed on February 20, 2015.
8 Ibid., p. 138, available at: https://dengxiaopingworks.wordpress.com/2013/03/18/reform-is-the-only-way-for-china-to-developed-its-productive-forces; accessed on February 20, 2015.
9 Ibid., p. 123, available at: https://dengxiaopingworks.wordpress.com/2013/03/18/bourgeois-liberalization-means-taking-the-capitalist-road; accessed on February 20, 2015.
10 Ibid., p. 111.
11 Ibid., p. 379.
12 Ibid., p. 137, available at: https://dengxiaopingworks.wordpress.com/2013/03/18/reform-is-the-only-way-for-china-to-developed-its-productive-forces; accessed on February 20, 2015.

"the crux of the matter is whether it is called 'social' or 'capital'" said by Deng Xiaoping is not "whether it is called 'social' or 'capital'", but rather, to clarify what capitalism and socialism are, we have to find out the correct judgment on the criteria of socialism. In his opinion, the major criteria to make a judgment on socialism are whether public ownership is the mainstay and whether there is polarization in the society; as long as public ownership has the mainstay and the path of common prosperity is taken, it is socialism. Therefore, his saying "do not be afraid of too many elements of capitalism and, indeed, taking the capitalist path" has a premise, that is, adhering to socialist orientation and principles. Furthermore, even under such a premise, we must make sure that what we do is conducive to developing socialist productive forces, to enhancing comprehensive national strength and to improving people's livelihood in order to make bold attempts and take bold steps, unlike "not being afraid" without premise and "being bold" without conditions as interpreted by some people.

II. On the relation between setting up more "three-capital" enterprises and building bigger and stronger large and medium-sized state-owned enterprises

In the Speeches, when it comes to not being afraid of too many elements of capitalism, it is stressed that "have more 'three-capital' enterprises. There is no reason to be afraid of them."[13] Why should we not be afraid? As Deng Xiaoping explained, "as long as we keep level-headed, there is no cause for alarm. We have our advantages: we have the large and medium-sized state-owned enterprises and the rural enterprises. More important, political power is in our hands."[14] Moreover, he took Shenzhen as an example and pointed out that "in the case of Shenzhen, the publicly owned sector is the mainstay of the economy, while the foreign-invested sector accounts for only a quarter."[15] Therefore, he pointed out that "subject to the constraints of China's overall political and economic conditions, 'three-capital' enterprises are useful supplements to the socialist economy, and in the final analysis they are good for socialism."[16] From these remarks, it can be easily seen that the reason why Deng Xiaoping thought that the "three-capital" enterprises are useful supplements to the socialist economy instead of the development of capitalism lies in the restriction on the "three-capital" enterprises by the socialist power of China as well as that by the public ownership, especially the economic restriction on the "three-capital" enterprises by

---

13 Ibid., p. 372-373, available at: https://dengxiaopingworks.wordpress.com/2013/03/18/excerpts-from-talks-given-in-wuchang-shenzhen-zhuhai-and-shanghai; accessed on February 20, 2015.
14 Ibid.
15 Ibid.
16 Ibid.

China's large and medium-sized state-owned enterprises. China's large and medium-sized state-owned enterprises are different from capitalist state-owned enterprises. According to Article 7 of the Constitution, "the state economy is the sector of socialist economy under ownership by the whole people; it is the leading force in the national economy." With such a state-owned economy, the bloodline of the national economy can be controlled in the hands of the socialist state power, people's democratic dictatorship has a solid economic base, socialist market economy has a powerful main strength, the country is endowed with a fundamental strength to participate in international competition, the negative influence of the mercenary profit-seeking of "three-capital" enterprises will be limited within a controllable scope and they will be beneficial to China to increase tax revenue, arrange employment, expand overseas markets, absorb international advanced technologies and managerial experience and other useful effects will be fully brought into play. Based on this analysis of Deng Xiaoping, the Central Committee of the CPC later put forward that "public ownership is the foundation of China's socialist economic system, while the non-public sector of the economy is an important part of China's socialist market economy"[17]; "we must further deepen our understanding of the meaning of the basic economic system in which public ownership is the mainstay and diverse types of ownership develop side by side, and continuously improve this system in the practice"[18]; "we must unswervingly consolidate and develop the public-owned economy, unswervingly encourage, support and guide the development of the non-public-owned economy"; "deepen the reform to introduce the enterprise system and shareholding system in state-owned enterprises, perfect the modern corporate structure and optimize the composition and structure of the state-owned economy to enhance its dynamism, dominance and influence."[19] These elaborations further deepened our understanding of the relationship between the public-owned economy including large and medium-sized state-owned enterprises and the non-public-owned economy including the "three-capital" enterprises, provided an important theoretical support for the rapid development of national economy in recent 20 years and also laid a solid theoretical foundation for the co-development of diverse sectors of economy, including the future state-owned economy, collective economy, private-owned economy, individual economy as well as foreign-funded enterprises.

---

17 Jiang Zemin on Socialism with Chinese Characteristics (Excerpts). Central Party Literature Press, 2002, p. 685.
18 Selected Significant Works Since 17h National Party Congress of the CPC. Volume 2. Central Party Literature Press, 2009, p.52.
19 National Party Congress of the CPC. Volume 2. Central Party Literature Press, 2009, p. 52.

III. On the relation between socialism has also market and capitalism has also planning

As to the relationship between plan and market, these two constitute an important pair of category in economics, especially in Marxist economics. In the past, over a long time, people tended to link them with the ownership system, thinking that the market economy can only be established based on the capitalist private ownership system, while the socialist public ownership system can only implement planned economy. As early as the 1950s, CPC had made a breakthrough in this understanding and proposed the conception of "Three Mains and Three Supplements", which failed to be implemented for various reasons. After reform and opening up, CPC gradually cast off the past traditional concept and successively put forward an economic operation system taking planned economy as mainstay and market regulation as supplement, having a planned commodity economy and combining planned commodity and market regulation, etc. However, these formulations could not fundamentally get rid of the thought constraint that considers that planned economy and market economy belong to the category of basic economic system. That means, people could not develop new understanding on the relation between planned economy and market economy, until Deng Xiaoping's clear statements in the Speeches in his Southern Tour: "The proportion of planning to market forces is not the essential difference between socialism and capitalism. A planned economy is not equivalent to socialism, because there is planning under capitalism too; a market economy is not capitalism, because there are markets under socialism too. Planning and market forces are both means of controlling economic activity."[20] This enabled the people to make a new major breakthrough in the understanding of the relation of planning and market. Based on this judgment, the 14th National Congress of the CPC took socialist market economic system as the goal of reform of the economic system. In this economic system, the market is allowed to play a fundamental role in resource allocation, full play is given to market's advantage of quite sensitively reacting to all sorts of economic signals, the prompt coordination between production and demand is promoted, while it is also emphasized that the display of this function have to be realized under the premise of the macro-control of the state that restricts the weaknesses and negative influences of the market and leads the market to healthy development with economic policies, economic laws and regulations, planning guidance and necessary pubic administration. Hence, we can see that this kind of economic system does not exclude planning, but takes both market and planning as economic means. Comrade Jiang Zemin pointed out in his report to the 14th

---

20 Selected Works of Deng Xiaoping. Volume III. People's Publishing House, 1993, p. 373; available at: https://dengxiaopingworks.wordpress.com/2013/03/18/excerpts-from-talks-given-in-wuchang-shenzhen-zhuhai-and-shanghai, accessed on February 20, 2015.

National Congress of the CPC that "during the process of establishing the socialist market economy, the extent to which planning is combined with market regulation and the form the combination takes may vary at different times, in different places and in different sectors of the economy."[21] He also said that "the state plan is an important means of macro-control. To establish the socialist market economy system, we must reform the past model of planned economy, but it does not mean that we should discard planning. Western countries that implement market economy also highlight the role of planning. We are a socialist country, it is more necessary and more likely to correctly apply the necessary means of planning."[22] General Secretary Hu Jintao also said, "We will give play to the guiding role of national development programs, plans and industrial policies in macroeconomic regulation."[23] Those remarks have fully demonstrated the essence of the Southern Speeches about the dialectical relation between planning and market regulation and have an important guiding significance in improving our understanding and handling of the relations. In recent years, with the deepening of the economic crisis of capitalism, many people and progressive figures in Western countries begin to reflect upon capitalism and some politicians and economists begin to throw doubt on neo-liberalism, stress the role of state and advocate reinforcing the supervision on the market and financial sector. It also proved that, from the reverse side, it is in line with the economic rules of commodity economy and the best way to handle the relations between planning and market regulation that socialist market economy allows market forces, under the macroeconomic control of the state, serve as the basic means of regulating the allocation of resources and use state plan as an important means of macroeconomic regulation. If the success of reform and opening up has any secret that is different from other transition economies, this is that it does not copy the Western laissez-faire market economic model, which is probably an important secret.

VI. On the relation between allowing a part of people get rich first and the goal of common prosperity

To tackle the long-standing problem of equalitarianism, Deng Xiaoping put forward an important policy at the Third Plenary Session of the 11th Central Committee of CPC that a part of the Chinese people and a part of the regions of the country should be allowed to have a higher income and better livelihood first. 30 years of reform and opening up witnessed the full play of people's enthusiasm and creativity and the flow of fountains of

---

21　Zemin, Jiang. Selected Works. Vol. I, People's Publishing House, 2006, p. 228; available at: http://www.bjreview.com.cn/document/txt/2011-03/29/content_363504_3.htm.
22　Zemin, Jiang. On Socialist Market Economy. Central Party Literature Press, 2006, p.31
23　Selected Significant Works Since 17h National Party Congress of the CPC. Volume 2. Central Party Literature Press, 2009, p. 21.

fortune, which were the direct result of the policy. However, when Deng Xiaoping proposed this major policy, he made clear that encouraging a part of the people to get rich first is to "make the entire national economy develop forward continuously in a wave pattern and enable people of all nationalities get rich quite quickly."[24] In his Southern Speeches, he also mentioned: "the concept of common prosperity is formulated as follows: some regions have the conditions to develop first, some regions develop slowly; those that develop first can help promote the development of those that lag behind, until all achieve common prosperity. If the rich keep getting richer and the poor poorer, polarization will emerge."[25] He also specified how to make it possible, namely, "the regions that become prosperous first to support the poor ones by paying more taxes or turning in more profits to the state" and highlighted that the problem should be solved by the end of 20th century "when our people achieve a fairly comfortable level."[26] Moreover, he further raised common prosperity to the height of essential features of socialism, pointing out that "the essence of socialism is to liberate and develop productive forces, eliminate exploitation, do away with polarization and ultimately achieve common prosperity", and saying that "taking the path of socialism is to gradually achieve common prosperity."[27] After his Southern Speeches, he associated common prosperity with distribution and repeatedly emphasized its importance, saying that "after China develops to a certain degree, distribution must be considered... There will always be certain disparity between different regions, but they should be neither too large nor too small. If only a few get rich, it will fall into capitalism... Our policy should neither be to encourage lazybones nor to cause to fight in 'civil war'"[28]; "how to realize prosperity among 1.2 billion people and how to distribute the wealth after prosperity are big problems... when we said that polarization has to be prevented, in fact, it has of course appeared"; "in the past we talked about development first. But now we can see problems are not less than those before the development."[29] In recent 20 years, differences between urban and rural areas, regional differences and income differences have been growing, which fully prove that those views of Deng Xiaoping are full of foresight and completely correct. In order to solve this problem, the Party Central Committee with Comrade Hu Jintao as the General Secretary put forward the historical task of establishing a

---

24 Xiaoping, Deng. Selected Works of Deng Xiaoping. Volume II. People's Publishing House, 1994, p.152.
25 Xiaoping, Deng. Selected Works of Deng Xiaoping. Volume III. People's Publishing House, 1994, p. 373-374.
26 Ibid., p. 374.
27 Ibid., p. 373.
28 Xiaoping, Deng. Chronicle of Deng Xiaoping from 1975 to 1997. Central Party Literature Press, 2004, p. 1356-7.
29 Ibid., p. 1364.

socialist harmonious society; requiring to handle the relationship between efficiency and equity well in both primary distribution and redistribution, with a particular emphasis on equity in redistribution; deciding that the share of citizen income in the distribution of national income should be gradually increased, and that of work remuneration in primary distribution raised, with vigorous efforts to raise the income of low-income groups, gradually enhancing poverty-alleviation aid and the minimum wage, etc. All those are to fulfill the goal of common prosperity and reverse the trend of a growing gap in income distribution.

V. On the relation between concentrating on economic construction and attaching equal importance to material and spiritual civilization without any letup

Since the Third Plenary Session of the 11th CPC Central Committee which established the general policy of shifting the Party's work focus to economic construction and implementing reform and opening up, Comrade Deng Xiaoping repeatedly reminded the whole Party to "attaching equal importance to material and spiritual civilization without any letup". As early as 1980, he pointed out that "to establish a socialist country, we must have a high degree of material civilization as well as a high degree of spiritual civilization."[30] Later he also proposed that we must "attach equal importance" to economic development as well as legal system, on reform and opening up and fight against all sorts of crime, arrest corruption and oppose bourgeois liberalism, in a tough manner. Why must we "attach equal importance" to economic development as well as legal system, on reform and opening up and" on them "in a tough manner"? According to him, "without the central task of economic development, there is the risk of losing our material base"[31]; "but if our ethos deteriorates, it will be pointless to achieve economic success. It will, on the other hand deteriorate, which will in turn affect the deterioration of the whole economy."[32] However, in the practical work, it is always easier to be tough in material civilization than in spiritual civilization. Regarding this, he made several criticisms. In 1985, in the Party Congress, he said, "we have proposed to build a socialist spiritual civilization very early, for which the central and local governments as well as the military have done a lot of work and a lot of advanced figures have appeared with positive influence. However, the effect is far from ideal nationwide, mainly because the whole Party fails to pay enough attention on it."[33]

---

30 Xiaoping, Deng. Selected Works of Deng Xiaoping. Volume II. People's Publishing House, 1994, p. 367.
31 Ibid., p. 250.
32 Ibid., p. 154.
33 Ibid., p. 143.

After the political turmoil in 1989, when Deng Xiaoping met the cadres of Beijing Martial Law Department, he repeated that "in retrospect, we can now see the distinct drawback—imbalanced emphasis on material civilization and spiritual civilization."[34] In the Southern Speeches, he spent most of the time stressing the policy of "attaching equal importance". He said, "Since China opened its doors to the outside world, some decadent things have come in along with the others, and decadent social phenomena such as drug abuse, prostitution and economic crimes have emerged in some areas. Special attention must be paid to these evils, and resolute measures must be taken to stamp them out and prevent them from spreading. After the founding of New China, it took only three years to wipe these things out. Who in this world has ever been able to eliminate the abuse of opium and heroin? Neither the Kuomintang nor the capitalist countries. But facts have proved that the Communist Party was able to do it."; "as long as our productive forces are developed and a certain economic growth rate is maintained, we will adhere to attaching equal importance and we shall be able to build a socialist society with advanced spiritual standards."[35] Hence, the spirit of the Southern Speeches include: we must grasp opportunities, development should proceed as fast as possible, development is the absolute principle, we should be bolder than before in conducting reform and opening up, once we are sure that something should be done, we should dare to experiment and break a new path, we must place equal emphasis on material and spiritual civilization and we must oppose corruption, bourgeois liberalism and decadent social phenomena. The idea that development is only understood as economic development or that material civilization is the absolute principle overlooking or even scarifying spiritual civilization goes against the spirit of Southern Speeches, nor do they belong to Deng Xiaoping Theory.

VI. On the relation between avoiding quarrels and opposing bourgeois liberalism

Avoiding quarrels is an important opinion of Deng Xiaoping in Southern Speeches. But, what is "avoiding quarrels"? Some people say that it means avoiding quarrels on ideological issues and avoiding quarrels on whether we take socialist path or capitalist path. Is that true? Only when we refer back to the original text, it becomes can become clear. In the Southern Speeches, Deng Xiaoping raised the opinion of avoiding quarrels after he talked about whether things like securities and stock markets are good or bad, dangerous or not, whether they are unique to capitalism and whether they can be applied by socialism and he proposed that we should allow ourselves to look at them and must be resolute to have a try. As he said,

---
34 Ibid., p. 306.
35 Ibid., p. 379.

"Avoiding quarrel is an invention of mine"[36]; "in the very beginning opinions were divided about the reform and opening up. That was normal"; "In carrying out the line, principles and policies adopted since the Third Plenary Session of the 11th Central Committee, we did not resort to coercion or mass movements. People were allowed to follow the line on a voluntary basis, doing as much or as little as they wished. In this way, others gradually followed suit"; "no quarrel is to win time for action. Once disputes begin, they complicate matters and waste a lot of time. As a result, nothing is accomplished. Don't argue; try bold experiments and blaze new trails. That's the way it was with rural reform, and that's the way it should be with urban reform."[37] From what he said, we can see that Deng Xiaoping proposed the policy of avoiding quarrels in terms of some concrete measures of reform and opening up in order to gain time so that things can be done without missing the best timing by indulging into debates. Was this policy not right? The policy was completely right, because it is in line with human law of cognition, in line with the Marxist viewpoint of "practice comes first" and conforms to our work experiences. However, we can one discover in these words that we should avoid quarrel in terms of ideological issues and on whether to take the socialist path or capitalist one. Completely impossible to find, not even the shadow. On the contrary, there are a lot of arguments for the view that we must adhere to the Four Cardinal Principles and oppose bourgeois liberalism and peaceful evolution in reform and opening up in the Southern Speeches. For instance, he said, "we must always adhere to the Four Cardinal Principles in the process of reform and opening up", "at the Sixth Plenary Session of the 12th Central Committee I said that the struggle against bourgeois liberalism must be conducted for another twenty years. Now it seems it will take longer. The rampant spread of bourgeois liberalism may have grave consequences. It has taken the special economic zones more than ten years to reach the present stage. They can collapse overnight"[38]; "The imperialists are pushing for peaceful evolution towards capitalism in China, placing their hopes on the generations that will come after us."[39] What is bourgeois liberalism? According to Deng Xiaoping's explanation, bourgeois liberalism is "the worship of democracy and freedom of the capitalist countries in the West and denial of socialism,"[40] "to make the current policies of China to take the capitalist path."[41] What is peaceful evolution? As Deng Xiaoping also explained, it is "a world war without smoke"[42] as termed by the Western politicians and "the so-called world

---

36 Ibid., p. 374.
37 Ibid., p. 374-5.
38 Ibid., p. 379.
39 Ibid., p. 380.
40 Ibid., p. 123.
41 Ibid., p. 181.
42 Ibid., p. 325-6.

war without smoke wants the peaceful evolution of socialist countries."[43] Hence, bourgeois liberalism and imperialist peaceful evolution are both attempts at a pincer attack on socialist China from inside and outside, pushing China to the capitalist path. Deng Xiaoping repeatedly emphasized that "we cannot give way [to bourgeois liberalism]. The struggle against it is embedded in the process of four modernizations and will be persisted throughout this and next centuries."[44] He also said, "To realize four modernizations, we must implement the policy of reform and opening up instead of bourgeois liberalism. The idea of liberalism has been sown in the society and the Party since a couple of years ago. Once it develops, it will disturb our cause.[45] He severely criticized those who turn a deaf ear to wrong ideas and pointed out that it was even worse that "few people step forward to wage serious ideological struggles" with wrong opinions and thoughts and even some open opinions against leadership of the Party and against socialism "on newspapers or in the inner-Party life"[46]. It is obvious that he did not mean that we should avoid quarrels on ideological issues or the direction of reform and opening up; instead, he proposed that we must firmly fight with those issues, with the direct use of the word "quarrel". After the turmoil in 1989, he said, "the so-called 'reform' advocated by certain people should be renamed liberalization, namely, going to capitalism. The essence of their 'reform' is going to capitalism. The reform we are carrying out is different from theirs. The debate must be continued on this issue."[47] Of course, the debate here is different from the mass criticism in the "Cultural Revolution" because it requires us to convince others with facts and through reasoning. It is by no means "no quarrel", "no crossfire" or hanging a "war-free license". As Comrade Jiang Zemin said, "it is detrimental and threatens the stability and unity of the country and society that we are indifferent to erroneous ideological and political opinions and allow them to confuse people's thoughts and mess up our ideology without criticism or fight."[48] Also, as Comrade Hu Jintao said, "we must not let erroneous thoughts and comments drift or allow corruptive and downfallen thoughts and culture to be uncurbed."[49] Thus, it is a misinterpretation of Deng Xiaoping theory and goes against the consistent spirit of the Party Central Committee to say that the policy of "no

---

43 Ibid., p. 344.
44 Ibid., p. 204.
45 Ibid., p. 124.
46 Xiaoping, Deng. Selected Works of Deng Xiaoping. Volume II. People's Publishing House, 1993, p. 365.
47 Xiaoping, Deng. Selected Works of Deng Xiaoping. Volume III. People's Publishing House, 1993, p. 297.
48 Zemin, Jiang. Jiang Zemin on Socialism with Chinese Characteristics (Excerpts). Central Party Literature Press, 2002, p. 412-3.
49 Selected Significant Works Since 16th National Party Congress of the CPC. Volume 2. Central Party Literature Press, 2008, p. 686.

quarrel" for specific measures of reform and opening up in the Southern Speeches is one about ideological issues.

VII. On the relation between following Party's basic line and training successors

"A correct political line must be guaranteed by a correct organizational line"[50] is an important experience of the CPC as well as a basic viewpoint of party building. Deng Xiaoping reiterated the view in Southern Speeches and clearly pointed out that "in some sense, whether we can manage our domestic affairs well, whether we can keep to the socialist road and adhere to reform and opening up, whether we can develop the economy more rapidly and whether we can maintain long-term peace and stability will all be determined by people"; "if any problem arises in China, it will arise from inside the Communist Party."[51] Thus, "in the final analysis, we must manage Party affairs in such a way as to prevent trouble."[52] Such a judgment is based on the Communist Party's system of democratic centralism as well as the lessons learned from the collapse of the former Soviet Union and tremendous changes in Eastern Europe and from two general secretaries after reform and opening up who "stumbled over the question of opposing bourgeois liberalism"[53] Why did the Soviet Union, a big socialist country with a history of more than 70 years, collapse and its Communist Party, a working-class Party with a history of more than 80 years and more than 10 million members, break down overnight? There are a lot of reasons accounting for them. Yet it is undeniable that the most critical reason lies in the Central Committee of the Communist Party of the Soviet Union, especially in the major leaders. According to *Critique of the Gotha Program* and the experience of the socialist movement, socialism is a transitional social formation from capitalism to communism. Therefore, in such a society, there is always one force driving forward to communism and another pushing back to capitalism. If the former is stronger, the socialist system becomes stable; if the latter is stronger, socialist system might be overthrown. In the contest between those two forces, the Communist Party as the ruling party, especially its Central Committee, plays the decisive role. Shortly after the turmoil of 1989, Deng Xiaoping said, "that Communist Party with a sound political bureau, especially a sound Standing Committee of the Political Bureau, is the key to issues about China. China will maintain stable as long as this part remains sound"[54]; "if problems arise from

---

50　Xiaoping, Deng. Selected Works of Deng Xiaoping. Volume III. People's Publishing House, 1993, p. 380.
51　Ibid., p. 380.
52　Ibid., p. 381.
53　Ibid., p. 380.
54　Ibid., p. 365.

inside the Central Committee, the result might be the other way round. That is the most crucial problem." Based on this understanding, he proposed in the Southern Speeches that "we must pay attention to training people, selecting and promoting to positions of leadership persons who have both ability and political integrity, in accordance with the principle that they should be revolutionary, young, well educated and professionally competent." and that "we must educate the army, persons working in the organs of dictatorship, the Communist Party members and the people, including the youth."[55] He warned us that "this is of vital importance to ensure that the Party's basic line is followed for a hundred years and to maintain long-term peace and stability"[56]; "whether the line for China's development that was laid down at the Third Plenary Session of the 11th Central Committee will continue to be followed depends on the efforts of everyone, and especially on the education of future generations."[57] Those remarks grasped the fundamental reason for the invincibility of the proletarian party and the socialist country. They are of critical significance to the Party to stand the tests of a long-term rule, market economy and reform and opening up as well as the country's adherence to the socialist path. There are a lot of reasons accounting to the fact that the Party can still lead the people to calmly tackle various international emergencies related to sovereignty and safety and overcome various risks in political and economic fields one after another after the old generation of revolutionists like Deng Xiaoping passed away. However, the key reason lies in that the leadership of the Party Central Committee is in the hand of Marxists, which together with a good education on the members, the people and the youth, will enable the Party to lead the people to advance the cause of socialism with Chinese characteristics, no matter what storms we will face.

VIII. On the relation between the protracted and tortuous nature of the socialist path and the general trend of history along which socialism will replace capitalism

There is a distinct feature of Southern Speeches. That is, it remains clear about the protracted and tortuous nature in pursuing the socialist road and yet confident about its final success; it stresses that it is the inevitable for the socialist countries to meet setbacks and that socialism will replace capitalism through zigzags, as it is a fundamental rule for human society to develop from low level to high level. As Deng Xiaoping said, "We have been building socialism for only a few decades and are still in the primary stage. It will take a very long historical period to consolidate and develop the

---

55 Ibid., p. 380.
56 Ibid., p. 380.
57 Ibid., p. 380.

socialist system, and it will require persistent struggle by many generations, a dozen or even several dozen. We can never rest on our oars."[58] Why will it take so long? Apart from special reasons like large population, weak base, low economic starting point and relative shortage of resources and that "we have been building socialism for only a few decades and are still in the primary stage", he also mentioned a general reason—"a new, rising class that has just taken power is, generally speaking, weaker than the opposing classes."[59] Here he refers to opposing classes both at home and abroad. When Lenin was analyzing the reasons why the proletariat was weaker than the bourgeoisie a long time after the former overthrew the latter, he said that "it is because the bourgeoisie has broad international relations"[60] and "because of the power of international capital" and "its firm international relations."[61] Deng Xiaoping also said that after we appeased the turmoil of 1989, the G7-Summit in Paris "decided to impose sanctions on China and they applied both economic and political means, such as preventing senior officials from interacting with China" and "after the founding of China, we were isolated, blocked and sanctioned for several decades."[62] Based on this fact and unlike those who believe in "the rapid success of socialism", Deng Xiaoping believed that the establishment of socialism was "a lengthy process" and "require persistent struggle by many generations, a dozen or even several dozen"[63]; "the road has many twists and turns" and "temporary restorations are usual and can hardly be avoided".[64] On the other hand, his ideas differed from those who believe in the "remoteness of communism". First of all, he believed that since the power of the opposing classes was stronger in a certain period, "the socialist system must be defended by the dictatorship of the proletariat"[65]. He pointed out that "Marx once said the theory of class struggle was not his discovery. His real discovery was the theory of the dictatorship of the proletariat"[66] and that "it is right to consolidate the people's power by employing the force of the people's democratic dictatorship. There is nothing wrong in that."[67] In the meantime, he insisted that we should not show weakness in the face of the sanction and threat from Western countries. As he said, "the more you fear and show your weakness, the more they will push their luck. Showing

---

58 Ibid., p. 381.
59 Ibid., p. 379-80.
60 Ibid., p. 379.
61 Selected Works of Lenin, Vol. IV, People's Publishing House, 1995, p. 179.
62 Ibid., p. 135.
63 Xiaoping, Deng. Selected Works of Deng Xiaoping. Volume III. People's Publishing House, 1993, p. 329.
64 Ibid., p. 379-80.
65 Ibid., p. 383.
66 Ibid., p. 379.
67 Ibid., p. 379.

weakness will not make others treat you better but look down on you."[68] Besides, he believed that "some countries have suffered major setbacks, and socialism appears to have been weakened. But the people have been tempered by the setbacks and have drawn lessons from them, and that will make socialism develop in a healthier direction."[69] Furthermore, he held that "feudal society replaced slave society, capitalism supplanted feudalism, and, after a long time, socialism will necessarily supersede capitalism. This is an irreversible general trend of historical development."[70] At the end of the Speeches, he confidently pointed out that "Marxism cannot be defeated", "because Marxism is the irrefutable truth"[71]; "I am convinced that more and more people will come to believe in Marxism, because it is a science"; "don't think that Marxism has disappeared, that it's not useful anymore and that it has been defeated. Nothing of the sort!"[72] Those words remind people that after the disintegration of Soviet Union, some Western bourgeois scholars were hysterical and asserted that "history ends" and that "capitalism finally succeeds." However, we are going through times when socialist China's economy rose from the seventh to the second place in the globe while financial crises broke out, spread and deteriorated in the capitalist world; more and more people cast doubt on capitalist system while the works of Marx and Engels were reprinted and became bestsellers in the capitalist countries. All those are the best proof for the aforesaid predictions of Deng Xiaoping.

Since the publication of Southern Speeches, the international situation has gone through broad and profound changes and China has undergone broad and profound transformations. In the past 20 years, the third generation of the central collective leadership with Comrade Jiang Zemin at its core and the Party Central Committee with Comrade Hu Jintao as the General Secretary, hold high the great banner of socialism with Chinese characteristics, keep abreast of the times and make continuous innovation in face of new practice; the second generation of the central collective leadership with Comrade Deng Xiaoping at its core first explored and answered important theoretical and practical questions like what is socialism and how to build socialism and then continued to explore and answer what kind of Party we will establish, how to materialize it, what kind of development we will achieve, how to realize the development and put forward the important theory of "Three Represents" and "Scientific Outlook on Development", further enriching the basic theories, basic line, basic program and basic experience of the Party. Moreover, since the 17th CPC National Congress,

---

68 Ibid., p. 379.
69 Ibid., p. 320.
70 Ibid., p. 383.
71 Ibid., p. 382-3.
72 Ibid., p. 382.

the Party Central Committee inherited the spirits of the Southern Speeches and realized many new developments. For instance, it put forward that the fundamental requirement of adhering to development being the absolute principle is sticking to scientific development; the important content of adhering to development being the absolute principle is cultural prosperity and development; we must pay more attention to the idea of people first, to comprehensive coordination of sustainable development and to making overall plans and taking all factors into consideration; we must seek improvement in stability and maintain steady and fast economic development; a large part of the focus of expanding domestic demand must be shifted to protecting and improving people's livelihood, etc. At the 20th anniversary of Southern Speeches, while reviewing it, we should profoundly comprehend and seriously implement a series of new guidelines, new policies and new decisions by the Party Central Committee based on the new reality, which is also the best commemoration of Deng Xiaoping's Southern Speeches.

Y. 31

On Essential Distinction between Socialist State-owned Economy and Capitalist State-owned Economy

Yu Bin[1]

Abstract: The media of western developed countries affix the label of liberal capitalism to the oligarchic capitalism. At the same time, they affix the label of state capitalism for the economies of the emerging countries which support their own private enterprises, just like the developed countries. Thus they fabricate the illusionary dispute between liberal capitalism and state capitalism. They sometimes threaten the emerging countries with interference and war so as to coach and force them resume to the neo-liberal path so that they can transfer the economic crisis to these countries and maintain the old international economic order. They also affix the label of state capitalism to China. However, there is an essential distinction between socialist state-owned economy and capitalist state-owned economy. China should hold high the banner of socialism with Chinese characteristics, rename the state-owned enterprises as the enterprises owned by the whole people, and strengthen the economic alliance with the other BRICS countries which are also suppressed by developed capitalist countries. By south-south cooperation and marketing alliances, BRICS alliance will pave the way for the establishment of a new international economic order.

Key words: state capitalism; oligarchic capitalism; socialist state-owned enterprises; enterprises owned by the whole people

---
[1] Yu Bin, researcher at the Institute of World Socialism attached to CASS, also researcher at the Academy of Marxism.

In January, 21st, 2012, the famous British magazine published a special issue on "state capitalism" including multiple articles written by Western scholars.

These articles violently criticizing "state capitalism" have on the one hand, lamented over the decline of neo-liberalism and demonstrated the uneasy sentiments of the international monopoly capitalist groups in the face of vigorously rising emerging economies, on the other hand.[2]

I. Capitalism with the mistaken label

As we will deal below, we have noticed many confused claims in these articles, published in the above issue of the Economist.

Firstly, in some articles, Boris Yeltsin's privatization of state companies or Yeltsin's "anti-state-capitalism" acts Russia has been equaled to the infrastructure support of governments in other countries and to the so-called "state capitalism" support of these countries to the flagship companies of these countries. Secondly, some of articles affirm the positive role of "state capitalism" in the history of developed countries, but these articles suggest that emerging economies should not copy this "old way" followed by the developed countries. Thirdly, some articles hold two ideas, firstly, in the "state capitalist" countries which "play West's original game" (namely, learning from the "old way" of the West) this state capitalism will cause the "self-elimination" of the ruling class in these countries. Second idea, they claim that the "state capitalist" countries which "play West's original game" will certainly enhance their political status, in the world stage. Fourthly, although some of the articles have frequently mentioned the judgment that "state-owned enterprises are frustrated with low efficiency", they admit that it is difficult to figure out the accurate productivity and efficiency rates of state-owned sector and compare them with private sector's productivity and efficiency. Fifthly, some articles have confused China's private enterprises with state-owned enterprises of China, such as the Geely (the reknown auto manufacturer) which is a private enterprise in China. Sixthly, some articles have evaluated state-owned enterprises in China as "state capitalist" enterprises.

Those articles obviously have ulterior motives, when labeling the practice of emerging countries' supporting their private enterprises as "state capitalism".

In fact, in developed countries of the Europe and the US America, private enterprises enjoy huge government support, openly or covertly, which is a common practice especially in the crisis periods.

---

2 Internal Reference Bulletin, February, 15, 2012.

For instance, during the US financial crisis in 2008, tycoon companies of the automobile industry and some big banks received huge sum of relief funds from the US government. But when the Chinese private enterprise like Geely Holding Group who purchased part of Volvo Automobile Motor's shares from the United States company by capital borrowed from international finance institutions, such case was used as evidence of "state capitalism". This demonstrates that British magazine's opposition to "state capitalism" is essentially targeting the state owned enterprises of emerging countries.

As the state-owned enterprises are the embodiments of the "state capitalism" in emerging capitalist the countries; thus the British magazine has admitted that there are still many state-owned or stately–steered companies in the rich developed countries, currently. Therefore, we can say that the dispute between "laissez-faire capitalism" and "state capitalism" is a pseudo-proposition or a pseudo classification. The truth is that the developed capitalist countries at the core of the world system are dissatisfied with the emergence of peripheral countries and try to "persuade" them to continue the neo-liberal path so that they can transfer the burden of economic crisis to these countries and maintain the old international economic order.

II. Why emerging countries copy the developed countries

The Economist admits that the history of state capitalism is as long as that of capitalism and every big emerging power has relied on the government support to push the growth of or protect their key but feeble industries.

For example, even U.K. the Mecca of free trade in history has established a gigantic state-owned enterprise—the East India Company. For emerging countries, "state capitalism" has successfully created some excellent national state-owned enterprises that are competent enough to adapt to global competition. Those companies from emerging countries that are included in the ranking of Fortune 500, two thirds of them are state-owned enterprises and we can say that others in the list have also received certain support from their countries.

Successful state owned enterprises of emerging countries can help formulate international trade measures and policies for their governments so that they don't have to follow others' rules.

In fact, some of the emerging countries have not only copied the state capitalist economic path of the developed countries, but in some periods they have also followed their oligarchic capitalist path. When, these countries have adopted the neo-liberal policies advocated by the Anglo-American countries since the 1980s, they have allowed the magnate enterprises of the developed countries to thoroughly defeat many of their smaller enterprises which were not yet organized and strong enough. This meant allowing the foreign magnate enterprises, plundering of their own resources, which have monopolistic advantages.

Nowadays, learning from their bitter experience, they find it inevitable to reject the path of oligarchic capitalism. Drawing lessons from the "lost decade", some of the Latin American countries have also decided to take a socialist path. Developing countries including those in the Latin American gradually learn to choose their own path instead of following the orders and manipulations originating from the developed countries of Europe and the USA.

Many emerging countries fail to understand that the developed countries have both state capitalism and oligarchic capitalism, why shouldn't they imitate that As the British magazine admits, they are just "playing our old game". Once the emerging countries begin to learn from the earlier developed ones, the latter are afraid that their monopolistic power and position will be weakened, consequently to defend their privileged interests severely criticize the "followers".

III. The British magazine "criticizes" emerging countries' mode of copying

The British magazine criticizes emerging countries' mode of copying is especially directed at the so-called "copying of state capitalism".

It questions, the following: how can states manage their own companies? How can states avoid heavy losses, due to badly management and use of subsidies by the "saved" companies? How can they continue to be innovative when innovation needs freedom of free and private entrepreneurship?

According to the invited authors of the British magazine, when these governments support some companies, others will suffer losses and when the large state-owned enterprises are unfairly given capital funds and talents that can "surely" play much better effects when used by private enterprises, thus a big damage will be caused regarding the overall competitiveness of these countries.

After all, state-owned enterprises have a lower efficiency in using capital funds and slower growth rate compared to private enterprises. If some enterprises openly or secretly enjoy government support, it will be even very difficult to guarantee fair trade in the market.

Governments that follow state capitalism can be often capricious and do not quite care for fairness; after all, these government supported companies are only responsible towards the government instead of private shareholders, because the state not only owns the majority of the shares, but controls the economic and financial administration and also controls the legal system.

Governments can be good in providing seeds for innovation, but they are bad in turning them into bread. State-owned enterprises do worse than publicly owned[3] enterprises in cost controlling, because they pursue commercial goals and profit as well as social goals. However, the British magazine also confesses that state-owned enterprises usually enjoy more freedom in management and have trained generations of perfect professional managers. It is self-contradictory that the British magazine casts these doubts, when the Bank of England is also a state-owned company.

In effect, "within colossal trusts, free competition turns into monopoly and the unplanned production of capitalist society will surrender to the planned production of socialist society… no nation will tolerate production led by trusts or the stark exploitation on the whole society by a small group (a huge stratum of rentiers, capitalists) live by clipping coupons. In all cases, whether there are trusts or not, the state, the official representative of the capitalist society, is compelled to assume the leadership of these means of production and communication."[4]

Analysis of the aforesaid ambiguities and confusions in the British magazine, Economist:

(1) The British magazine admits that remunerations and wages offered by state-owned enterprises are higher than those of the private ones, they offer shorter working hours, better and stable jobs.

If there are no state-owned enterprises, talented professionals prefer working in the foreign enterprises at home and abroad rather than private enterprises that offer poor conditions. Hence, state-owned enterprises are able to attract talents domestically and from abroad. So, will they damage the overall competitiveness of their own countries, and how ? When government supports some companies, others, will indeed suffer damage and mainly foreign companies, will suffer damage.

(2) Marx pointed out long ago that "the profit earned by a capitalist that controls a larger sum of capital is larger than that earned by a small capitalist who seemingly makes handsome profit… The accumulation of capital increases and the competition between capitalists decreases, when capital and landed property are united in the same hand..."[5] Therefore, state-owned enterprises' low efficiency in using capital funds and their slow growth rate are just common phenomenon of big capital.

---
3 The shares of publicly owned enterprises, are held by individuals or private capitalist groups.
4 Marx & Engels Selected Works. Volume I. People's Publishing House, 1995, p. 239.
5 "Capital". Volume 3, People's Publishing House, 2004, p. 250.

(3) There is no fair trade in the current old international economic order. Many enterprises in developed countries constantly receive open or secret support from the government. State capitalism is able to bring certain fairness to the old order.

(4) The governance and the legal systems in the Western countries are in line with the excess profit pursuit of magnate capitalist trusts, for whom the government is just an agent. "State capitalist" government, does not care about the minority shareholders, as is the case within private enterprises, are there majority shareholders that care about minority shareholders, within private enterprises?

(5) History of both developed and emerging countries demonstrates that state-owned enterprises are also good enough in turning seeds into bread.

(6) The strength of state-owned enterprises lies in their pursuit of social goals. In effect, large enterprises do better than small and medium-size enterprises in the treatment of workers. Nowadays, people are more and more demand that private enterprises should assume more social responsibilities rather than just focusing on commercial goals.

VI. International competition with the mistaken label

There are both state-owned and oligarchic enterprises in developed countries and emerging developing countries but the difference lies in the proportion between the two. The Federal Reserve, in the United States' (the central bank) is private while the central banks of most countries including that of the U.K., Bank of England, are state-owned.

Therefore, labels like "old capitalism" and "emerging capitalism" are more suitable do define the difference between the Western developed countries and the countries like Russia, Brazil and South Africa, rather than labeling them as "liberal capitalism" and "state capitalism".

So, why does the British magazine affix those wrong labels on them? When financial crisis broke out in the United States in 2008, developed countries suffered from economic crisis while emerging countries did not live such crises directly. People in the developed countries raised doubts about the financial oligarchs ruling their lives and the Occupy Wall Street movement erupted in the United States.

On the one hand, developed countries feel their traditional monopolistic privileged status has weakened; on the other hand, they have to find scapegoats for the economic crisis and the ongoing recession in their economies.. In the meantime, they feel it necessary to shift their burden of crisis over the emerging countries and eliminate possible obstacles which can occur during this burden shifting. Thus, developed countries shirk their problems to the emerging countries, criticize that they use state's power in order to build an unfair competition power, consequently they accuse the latter by destroying the free market system, and require that the latter group privatizes their state-owned enterprises so that they can continue their plunder.

Consequently, Western developed countries threaten the emerging countries with war, so the British magazine believes that if a war would erupt in the 21st century, it will be between different versions of capitalism rather than between capitalism and socialism.

Such a belief again proves that capitalism is the source and root of contemporary war threat. The fight between emerging capitalist countries and old ones competing for global markets might indeed lead to a war and they have already launched a local war in Libya and others, recently. However, although old capitalist countries possess powerful military forces, the outcomes of the war will not necessarily be favorable for them. Therefore, it is best option for them to use both their political and economic powers in coordination, rather than just employing hard power, i.e militarism against the latter group.

V. Market competition means exchanging market for market

Among all the emerging countries, the most remarkable ones are the BRICS group. Originally, the BRICS was BRIC, and only included Brazil, Russia, India and China. Later, with South Africa joining it, it has become BRICS. Those large size developing countries enjoy large domestic markets which they enhance and independently form an independent pole in the international market.

Yet, small countries like Singapore, Korea and Chile fail to do the same due to their small domestic market, limited or single type of resources. Italy, Greece and Ireland has gained some advantages only by joining the European Union. At the early years of its development, Japan had proposed "leaving Asia and approaching towards Europe", which meant that Japan alone could not form a pole. With the failure of this attempt, Japan has become dependent on the United States ever since.

China had once proposed exchanging market for technology. However, what can you do with technology, alone?

Yet in market economy, production is for none other than markets. Hence, if China had exchanged market for technology, it would have used the market to occupy more markets and even contend for more markets.

But, where is the market? First comes the domestic market and secondly the international market. However, it is not so easy to enter the markets of others. Developed countries have protective custom tariffs, which is the most important means of state intervention to prohibit foreign enterprises from entering their domestic markets.

Today, developed countries still use all sorts of other means of state intervention other than tariff barriers or use regional intervention means like EU regulations to protect their markets and also defend their foreign markets with various international laws and treaties. When fighting for control over colonies so as to obtain exclusive rights in the markets of colonies, developed countries started two world wars by using all their powers. Apparently, market competition cannot do without state power.

China would not be able to propose "exchanging market for technology" if it could not limit others entering its market, by its own state power.

For emerging countries, with the strengthening of their economic power and production capacity, it becomes necessary for them to enter foreign markets so as to push their economic development, and this target needs two integrated policies: the opening up of their domestic markets but besides, use their state power in the market competition, which means exchanging markets for markets.

In the other way round, if foreign markets are not opened for their domestic enterprises, there is no reason to allow foreign enterprises to enter our domestic markets. That is to say, if other countries do not open their market for free trade with China, it should not open our markets for free trade to them, either. This is also the principle of establishing equal free trade zones. Of course, this principle roughly applies to "equal" market treaties, like the Korea-US, Free Trade Agreement signed in June 2007, due to the inequality between the owners of the two markets, the U.S.' restrictions against North Korea are far more restrictive than South Korea's restrictions against on the United States.

Since the developed countries have capacity to protect their own markets and can control world markets, weaker emerging developing countries can only develop their economy with the permission of major big capitalist countries. For example, South Korea's economy was developed in a time when United States and Soviet Union fiercely competed for hegemony and also when United States confronted North Korea and China. As another case, Singapore provoked United States with the big red slogan of "Against Capitalism" during Singapore strikes, with this provocation U.S. began to help Singapore and thus Singapore acquired textile export quotas from the U.S., and the textile sector in Singapore has developed rapidly, reaching high production capacity.[6]

---

6   See, Yan Chongtao, "The secret of success in Singapore: a chief civil servants memories and ideas" Lee Kuan Yew, GCMG, CH, SPMJ (born Harry Lee Kuan Yew, 16 September 1923-23 March 2015), informally known by his initials LKY, was the first Prime Minister of Singapore, governing for three decades. Lee is recognized as the nation's founding father. Singapore Thomson Press Study Publishing Group, 2007, p. 243.

On the other side, when we evaluate especially the bigger developing countries, if they are good at protecting and using domestic market and good in cooperating with other developing countries, they might be able to win more equal terms of trade internationally and enjoy fairer conditions of competition in the international markets.

Besides, apart from a large domestic market, those developing countries are also required to be equipped with large and competitive enterprises that can be ranked among the top Fortune Global 500, we think this is the reason why those countries support their state-owned and oligarchic enterprises.

Y. 32

Building the Chinese Discourse System, Based on the Practice of Reform and Opening up:
An Overview of the Workshop on "Building the Chinese System and Theoretical Research and Discourse"

Cao Suhong[1]

This article is co-edited by Wang Liqiang, Chen Airu and Liu Ruisheng, Written by Cao Suhong, World Socialism Research Center of the Chinese Academy of Social Sciences.

Abstract: On June 21, 2012, the Workshop on Building the Chinese System of Theoretical Research and Discourse was held in Beijing under the sponsorship of the World Socialism Research Center, of the CASS. The workshop focused on the topic of "interpreting the Chinese path and China's practice in terms of the Chinese system of theoretical research and discourse". The participants have argued that given the remarkable progress made in the reform and opening-up, we should be confident enough of making theoretical achievements in studying China's achievements and its socialist system. And that a scientific attitude should be adopted in building the academic discourse of philosophy and social sciences with Chinese characteristics, Chinese style and Chinese spirit.

In response to the multifarious manifestations of discourse power in the fields of politics, economy, culture, history and education, the participants have further suggested that the Chinese academy should set up, and improve a discourse system which safeguards the fundamental interests of China and the Chinese people, so that it can become the general consensus of the Chinese people; that we should adopt a critical attitude when studying foreign cultures and foreign research achievements, so that we can distinguish the essence from the dross; that we should make a thorough and systematic review of the terms and concepts that have been introduced into Chinese academic disciplines over the years, besides a Chinese discourse dissemination strategy should be developed thereof.

Key words: building the Chinese system of theoretical research and discourse; suggestions and advice

---
[1] Cao Suhong, Guest Researcher of World Socialism Research Center of Chinese Academy of Social Sciences; Director of the Editing Division and Associate Editor of World Socialism Research Trends.

On June 21, 2012, the Workshop on Building the Chinese System of Theoretical Research and Discourse was held in Beijing under the sponsorship of the World Socialism Research Center of the Chinese Academy of Social Sciences. Executive Vice President, Wang Weiguang extended welcome to the participants of the workshop.

Li Shenming, Vice President of Chinese Academy of Social Sciences and Secretary of World Socialism Research Center attended the workshop and delivered a speech. Leaders and comrades from Party History Research Center, Chinese Soft Power and Culture Research Center, Xinhua News Agency, Hongqi Wengao Magazine, Party School of the CPC Central Committee, Peking University, Renmin University of China, Beihang University, some research institutes of CASS, Chinese Social Sciences Today, Xinhuanet, Chinese Social Sciences Net, Academy of Marxism of CASS, etc. together with experts and scholars gathered in the room and had heated discussion on the topic of "interpreting the Chinese path and practice in terms of the Chinese system of theoretical research and discourse."

Among the participants were Sha Jiansun, Ru Xin, Liu Haifan, Wei Xinghua, Zhou Xincheng, Fang Keli, Zhang Guozuo, He Juncheng, He Bingmeng, Cheng Enfu, Hou Huiqin, Fan Jianxin, Yang Shengming, Zhang Jiong, Cai Fang, Wang Zhenzhong, Li Lin, Wang Yicheng, Yu Pei, Huang Ping, Wu Shangmin, Zhang Wenmu, Zhu Jidong, Li Ling, Pei Xiaoge, Dong Xiaoyang, Yu Bin, Xin Xiangyang, Wang Liqiang, Wang Tingyou, etc. They actively participated making comments, engaged in the discussions, proposed practical measures and solutions.

I. Study and grasp the spirit of Li Changchun's speech: "Building the Chinese System of Theoretical Research and Discourse"

As a socialist country, China must establish a discourse system that safeguards the fundamental interests of China and the Chinese people

As Li Shenming has pointed out, on June 2nd, 2012, Comrade Li Changchun, on behalf of the Party Central Committee with Comrade Hu Jintao at the core, clearly proposed in his "Speech at the Working Conference for Research and Establishment of Marxist Theory" that "how to use China's theoretical study and discourse system to decipher China's practice and China's path, continuously summarize scientifically and blaze a trail to propose new concepts, new categories and new expressions that can link theory with practice. We should build the academic discourse of philosophy and social sciences with Chinese characteristics, Chinese style and Chinese spirit by learning from the achievement of human civilization is an important and urgent task of the times for the theorists and academics."

Li Shenming added: "It is indeed an important proposition with profound significance."

Wang Tingyou, Associate Prof. from the School of Marxism Studies of Renmin University of China has argued that the Chinese discourse system that we aim to establish should be built on the premise and basis of adherence to Marxism. We should not only regard Marxism as a belief, but also a science and truth, because the basic tenets, world outlook and methodology of Marxism reflect the objective law of the development of human society. We should always stick to Marxism in establishing socialism with Chinese characteristics and when promoting and following China's own path. To make this aim possible, we must develop and conduct in-depth investigation so as to establish Chinese discourse system based on the requirements of the development of science and technology.

Prof. Hou Huiqin, also secretary of the Party committee of the Academy of Marxism attached to CASS, has pointed out that: "guiding thoughts are the theoretical basis of the foundation of a party and a country and the basic methodology and world outlook that philosophy and social sciences must follow. We must unify our theories and guiding thoughts and unswervingly stick to the guidance of Marxism, this cannot be shaken. However, there various different opinions on the subject (discipline) system, for instance, my colleagues as philosophy researchers are inclined to talk about Chinese philosophy, Western philosophy and Marxist philosophy and our research schools and achievements are encouraged to be diverse. Also, there are different views on the establishment of Chinese discourse system, for example the relations between the natural formation of and consciously building of the discourse system, relations between discourse and thought, relations between theory and practice, relations among discourse power, between soft power and hard power, relations between Marxism as the guiding thought and Marxism as a disciplinary system, etc., which all call for further study".

Wang Yicheng, Former Director of Institute of Politics of CASS, held that "to establish a discourse system, we must adhere to the internal consistency of discourse within the system, so as to express consistent inner thoughts, if we fail to maintain consistency when applying discourse, but follow fashion instead, this may seem fresh and captivate or attract some people, but to speak the truth it will often cause internal confusion and internal contradictions among the concepts of the theory, consequently this will prevent theory from playing the role of providing guidance to the people. Our theory should be consistent with practice and our words should conform our actions, otherwise we will not be able to convince people whatever language we adopt.

"With the remarkable progress made in reform and opening-up, we should be confident of socialism" and strive to make theoretical achievements in studying the Chinese miracle and the socialist system

In the above article by Prof. Liu Haifan, the former Vice president of Party School of the CPC Central Committee, claimed: "although there are 30 Nobel Economics Prize winners in the West, economy of the West since the financial crisis in 1997, and the international financial and economic crisis in 2008, is brought to its knees. Though there are no Nobel laureate of economics in China, it has made tremendous achievements in economic reform and economic construction, a great leap in its economic aggregate, has become which the second largest economy next to US."

Prof. Zhou Xincheng, former Dean of the Graduate School of Renmin University of China, commented: "although Western scholars have made countless mathematical models to explain economic phenomena, only few of them could give pre-warning for the approaching subprime crisis in the US that has influenced the world. On the contrary, under the guidance of Marxist theories, experts of the World Socialism Research Center successfully predicted this financial crisis and raised their relevant opinions in many international and national conferences. Facts prove that we are equipped with a solid foundation for establishing Chinese system of theoretical research and discourse.

Researcher, Zhang Jiong, former Director of the Institute of Literature of CASS, has pointed out: "theoretical discourse power is different from political discourse power and economic discourse power and theoretical discourse power cannot be measured by the latter two. In the political field, as a permanent member state of United Nations Security Council, China has a greater political discourse power than any non-permanent member states. In the economic field, since China is the second largest economy, it now enjoys a much greater economic discourse power than in the past. It is the truthfulness of China's discourse power that enables it to be acknowledged and supported by the world. If we review the history of New China, China's international discourse power is not decided by the ranking of its economy, but its convincing thoughts, theories and views, which are the key."

Researcher Wang Liqiang, Deputy Director, Academic Secretariat Bureau of Scientific Research Management of the CASS, has also argued that discourse alone cannot bring hegemony. He added: "the US relies on its military superiority and financial hegemony, to boost its discourse power and its discourse control and manipulation, and in turn US' discourse power consolidates its hegemonic status. At present, although China lags behind United States in economically, it does not mean that China is not able to establish an influential global discourse system. We can confidently publicize the strengths of socialism with Chinese characteristics. Thanks to the practice of reform and opening up by the Chinese people, we have developed a path different from that of the capitalist countries, which is the fundamental basis for our theorists to build the Chinese discourse system. As long as we stand on the side of the truth, we will eventually win the discourse power."

So as to build the academic discourse of philosophy and social sciences with Chinese characteristics, with Chinese style and Chinese spirit, in a scientific manner, first of all, we must adhere to the guidance of Marxism.

Liu Haifan has pointed out: "China's rich historical practices of socialist revolution and construction have laid a solid foundation for the contemporary Chinese Marxism to establish China's theoretical discourse by inheriting its former achievements. I think this inheritance is the primary source why China's contemporary theoretical discourse can and will inevitably go global and be accepted. Currently, people all over the world are talking about Chinese miracle, we should confidently affirm that this achievement is made under the guidance of Marxism, namely the three—Chinese, modern and popular—versions of Marxism and that it is the socialist system that has led us to Chinese miracle."

Researcher Zhang Wenmu from Research Center of the Beihang University of Aeronautics & Astronautics has points out: "the discourse power comes from cultural self-consciousness and cultural confidence. Cultural self-consciousness in China means faith in and consciousness of the "two inevitables", namely inevitable extinction of capitalism and inevitable victory of socialism.

Cultural confidence starts with confidence in Marxism-Leninism. It is Leninism that has made Marxism a practical reality. The core of Leninism is the dictatorship of the proletariat, which orients us to communism, the former is the means and the latter is our goal. The two cannot be separated or partitioned. As Comrade Deng Xiaoping clearly stated, "It is completely righteous to consolidate people's political power by using the power of people's democratic dictatorship." This can be our model for high cultural self-consciousness and cultural confidence. Since Leninism is the direct source of Mao Zedong Thought, indifference to Leninism is equivalent to indifference to Mao Zedong and indifference to the core part of CPC's ideological foundation, which will mean there is a lack of cultural self-consciousness and cultural confidence."

Researcher Xin Xiangyang from the Academy of Marxism attached to CASS held that: "currently, some people use Western discourse system to substitute Marxist discourse system and use Western discourse system to explain China's development, but they not only fail to explain the nature of its problems, but also cause various confusions. For example, they prefer the term "citizen" and "civilian" instead of the term "people", they praise "tolerance" but do not like the term "criticism", they talk about "volunteering" instead of talking about "communist selfless dedication", praise "universal values" but do not speak about "proletarian internationalism", they like to talk about "top" leadership, but do not speak about "grass roots", etc., This is detrimental to the guiding position of Marxism. If we opt to analyze the development and achievements of China with the terms such as "citizen", "civilian", "universal values" and "tolerance" it will only mean that we are adopting Western neo-liberalism, Western market economy, civil society and social welfare policy mentality of the West. Firstly, practical problems of China must be studied based on Marxist terminology and Marxist discourse system. Without Marxism, various practical questions of China's practices and questions of its development cannot be correctly answered. Secondly, we must be in close contact with contemporary practices and enhance, promote innovation by summing up our new practices.

Researcher He Bingmeng, former Secretary General of the Academic Divisions of CASS has argued: "if, the Chinese academy wants to have a deserved place in the world academy, just following suit will take us nowhere. If China wants to embrace the world, it need to have a discourse power, should bring to the fore its own things. Firstly, we should insist on innovation while adhering to the guidance of Marxism, secondly, we should emphasize the importance of basic research, especially basic theoretical research; thirdly, we should focus on the researches of comprehensive, important strategic problems, only in this way can China will have a discourse power on certain issues and besides it will also have a discourse power on major, macroscopic theoretical issues.

Deputy Director of Party History Research Center, Sha Jiansun pointed out that China's discourse power or discourse system should be expression of the achievements of socialist path with Chinese characteristics. This discourse system hold high the basic theories, basic experience, basic political system and economic system of socialism with Chinese characteristics unswervingly. People's democratic dictatorship is China's state system, its basic political system mainly includes the system of people's congress, system of regional ethnic autonomy, system, the system of multi-party cooperation and political consultation under the Leadership of the CPC and community level grass-root self-governance. Under such a political system, Chinese people rally around the CPC, to build socialism with Chinese characteristics with concerted efforts and have made remarkable achievements. We cannot sacrifice the stable and benign political situation of China to copy the multiparty system and constitutional government system of the West. China enjoys a basic economic system where public ownership plays a dominant role and diverse forms of ownership develops side by side and distribution according to work is dominant and where multiple different modes of distribution coexist. Currently, some people hold that if state-owned enterprises are not privatized, they are bound to be inefficient. This is quite erroneous concept since the key problem of state-owned enterprises lie in management.

Dogmatism of fetishizing Western thoughts and theories must be opposed

Sha Jiansun has mentioned the following: "Comrade Li Changchun has pointed out that dogmatism of fetishing Western thoughts and theories must be opposed and that we should resist the invasion of decadent Western ideology, culture and values, which is an important prerequisite of developing Chinese philosophy and social sciences. I think, this is an important point with strong pertinence. The mainstream ideology of the developed capitalist countries reflects their state-capitalism economy and politics. In essence, that mainstream ideology serves to protect the political rule of the bourgeoisie and consolidate the economic system of capitalism, that means socialist countries should not copy them. Deng Xiaoping was an active advocate of opening to the outside world, but he also opposed "the wholesale westernization theory" namely blindly worshipping Western dogmatism. Deng Xiaoping, also said that some comrades fetishized all kinds of Western philosophical, economic, social political and literature and art trends without analysis, differentiation and criticism and that phenomena of allowing decadent Western bourgeois culture corrupting the youth should never be tolerated. Such a warning by Deng Xiaoping is still of practical significance."

As Zhou Xincheng pointed out: "language does not have class nature, but thoughts that the language system expresses, do have class nature. Thus, what the language should reflect is of great significance. At present, economics professors in some universities tend to use the terminology of Western economics, one form of its expression is total mathematicization, in this mathematicization, economic relations between people are fully described and demonstrated with mathematical models.

Consequently, some facts which can be explained by simple propositions or even by common sense are explained with a load of mathematical formulas, which is in fact an example of fetishizing the West. I do not mean that we should be completely against mathematical models. Under certain conditions, mathematical models can be used as a means for quantitative analysis on economic phenomena are conducive to the analysis of economic phenomena. Mathematical models, can play a favorable role only when they are based on scientific qualitative analysis. Without Marxism, mathematical models alone cannot explain any problems. Generally speaking, the more macroscopic a problem is, the less reliable it is to use mathematical models, since there are too many factors influencing the outcome and since it is difficult to determine the influence of each factor. Fundamentally speaking, it is difficult to grasp the essence of productive relations with mathematical models. Hence, to build the Marxist discourse system of Chinese economics, a scientific attitude should be adopted towards mathematical models, mathematical model should be placed in an appropriate position so that people won't be caught in fetishizing the mathematics of Western economics.

The director of the China Soft Power Cultural Research Center, Zhang Guozuo stated: the West had monopolized the global discourse power in international exchanges, later this monopoly was weakened by the successes of the Soviet Union and the birth and development of New China. However, with the transformation of the Soviet Union and the CPSU, the Western discourse system led by the US was further enhanced. Consequently, this Western discourse system has successfully "coached and governed the vast majority of developing countries and non-western countries to do things what is completely favorable to Western countries, and follow the practices of the Western countries themselves", as said by Joseph Nye—a US scholar, and a representative strategist advocating neo-liberalism. This soft power consolidates the unreasonable international political, economic and cultural world order established by Western countries with hard power consisting of military force and capital.

The former Vice president of Party School of the CPC Central Committee, Li Haifan stated: we cannot export revolution, but we can confidently publicize our successful experiences. For instance, due to the financial and economic crisis in the West, its politics and ideology suffers a serious impact and even the Davos Forum has brought fore a topic discussing the alternatives of capitalism.

Evaluating the above speeches, we can have a say and make some comments. Participants generally emphasize that an independent discourse system with Chinese characteristics should be established as a means in the international exchanges so as to effectively defend China's economic, political and cultural rights and so as to contribute to the establishment of a fair and reasonable new international order.

II. Specific manifestations of discourse power in the fields of politics, economy, culture, history and education

Political field

Researcher Ru Xin, former Vice President of the CASS has pointed out: after China entered the modern era in the 19th century, we have introduced a large amount of Western thoughts academics, as a result of which many people tend to adopt Western thinking about an issue. For example, there are different understandings of the term "democracy", but currently when people talk about democracy, naturally many people are inclined to put some Western concepts into it. For example, when some people are talking about "party politics" they define it vying of groups with each other to seize power, which completely distorts its own principle. Therefore, some terms must be accurately grasped and must be reinterpreted based on the practical experience of Chinese socialism in order to create an independent discourse system. To make it possible, two measures should be taken. Firstly, we should rigorously review and make correct interpretations of foreign terms and concepts; secondly, terms and concept unique to China must be created. China has acquired a lot of new experience from practices since reform and opening up, which gave rise to many new theories that can no longer be expressed with old terms. Indeed, the establishment of such a system calls for arduous academic efforts.

Researcher Li Lin, director of Institute of Law Studies attached to CASS has pointed out that: "the major problems of the law field are as follows. Firstly, academic discourse of law studies is seriously divorced from China's conditions and social realities, thus it fails to meet the requirements of China's economic and social development , besides it fails to meet the requirements of establishing of democracy and rule of law on legal theories or cannot lead the scientific development of China's rule of law; nor can this academic discourse be incorporated into China's excellent law culture, due to its lack of historical and cultural background.

Secondly, in our academy Western legal concepts and legal discourse are copied based on temporary needs without comprehensive or in-depth study, analysis or criticism and even its terms are borrowed. Therefore, Legal discourse system with socialist nature and Chinese characteristics must be established."

Zhang Wenmu has pointed out: "it is worth paying attention to the concept of "civil society" that is being used by some people. According to the Western discourse system, the concept "civil" is inseparable from the concept of "state", because state defends civil rights of the citizens while the civilians pledge loyalty to the state, this is a two side relationship and neither can be neglected. This is the original idea as well as valuable side of the term "civil". However, the so-called "civil society" term used by some people separate the "civil" from the "state", emphasizing the state's responsibility of protecting the civilians without highlighting the civilians' obligation to pledge loyalty to the state. In fact, this mistaken interpretation encourages civilians to confront the state. On this basis, the nature of "constitutional road" propagated by these people advocates confrontation between the civilians and the state.

The bourgeoisie took the same position in the period when it fought against feudalism period, but it became the ruling class, it highlighted the consistency between the civilians and the state. Since China has long become a socialist country based on worker-peasant alliance, with this fundamental change, the "constitutional government" system is already completely outdated. Currently, when people bring fore the concept "civil society ", they deliberately conceal the content in which "civil" pledges loyalty to the state, besides they keep the separation between the two only. If this is not intentional, at least it ignores the facts.

I think with some political motives, they only emphasize demanding civil rights, but do not require civilians to be loyal towards state. We should not be misled by their mistaken conceptualization, instead we should always consider the historical context behind the term, "civil". Instead, we should not highlight the state's responsibility of defending civil rights, but also emphasize the obligation and loyalty of citizens towards the state.

Researcher Yu Bin, from the Academy of Marxism attached to CASS, held that discourse power is our right to live. Without discourse power, political power will be deprived from legitimacy, thus people and state will not have the right to live. Yu Bin has also mentioned that a vice president of Peking University once said in an alumni gathering in North America that people at Peking University speak another dialect or language compared to other parts of China. There are now many foreign professors at the Peking University who all communicate in foreign languages. But people of Guangdong province speak Cantonese while people of Shanghai speak the Shanghai dialect. Although language is different from discourse, the loss of discourse power is equivalent to the loss of right to language. Once the people lose their discourse power, the state and nation will fall apart. Hence, discourse power is not a trivial matter.

Wang Liqiang has commented: "we should carefully consider and think over whether China's government departments at all levels should aim to "serve the people" or realize "rule of law". Some scholars have examined and studied the management attitudes of various local governments, especially examined those grass-root management units political power and they have discovered one central issue. When grass-root management units were asked, what they considered when implementing the tasks given to them by their superiors: "mostly they replied, our supreme consideration is "satisfaction of the ordinary people".

However, since the rule of law is a high priority in foreign countries, their judgment criteria is based on the strict implementation of laws and enforce the authority of law system, rather than seeking satisfaction of the people. Consequently, in the West, an official that abides by laws and strictly enforces the law is a good official. I think the principle of "serving the people" itself contains the connotations of the "rule of law", accordingly, we must adhere to the discourse system of "serving the people".

According to Prof. Yu Bin: "it is extremely necessary to attach great attention to Marxist discourse power. It is the very scientific nature of the Marxist discourse power that it can lead a relatively backward nation to have a place in the world and effect the future direction of the world. Hence, China's discourse power is in fact the discourse power of Marxism. Some people argue that Marx also belongs to the "West", but term "West" is not a territorial or geographical concept, but an ideological one. Marxism is not a part of Western mainstream discourse, because they believe that Marxism belongs to China. In the past, we said and insisted "only socialism can save China". Yet in recent years, China's discourse system has encountered some imbalance. Some people think that since we are the second largest economy in the world, socialist discourse power is not necessary, they think that in this way we can be closer to the West. Instead, I think the discourse "only socialism can save China" is still necessary, not only because it saved China in 1949, but can save China in 2012."

Economic field

Researcher Yang Shengming, former Secretary of the Party Committee of Institute of Finance and Trade Economics, attached to CASS held that: "ideological confusion is the source of language and discourse confusion. For instance, after the founding of New China, our economics discipline used the Marxist terminology developed based on Marx's Kapital. But, currently Marxism is absent in the textbooks or in academic papers. Western economics hasn't gone beyond the macroeconomics theory. In fact, when we are talking about the effects of the current virtual economy, we can see that Marx has long ago predicted that the potential economic crisis that might be triggered by the virtual capital. The reason why there is ideological confusion lies in education.

Researcher Cheng Enfu, the president of Academy of Marxism attached to CASS has pointed out: "a serious crisis has occurred in the Western ideology. However, many people in the Chinese economic circles clearly complain that Western discourse power dominates our education and research fields. It is expressly regulated in many of our universities that anyone who wants to be the dean of School of Economics should be equipped with a Western university degree, which is a serious problem. We should exceed Western economics in both economic methodology and economic theories while learning and absorbing from it. In this way, we will be its counterpart and compete against it, for a stronger discourse power. The same approach should be applied regarding sociology and political science.

Cai Fang, director of the Institute of Population and Labor Economics, attached to CASS said: "Comrade Li Changchun has emphasized that discourse power is of stark pertinence in the economics circle. After all, the carrier of discourse power is theoretical power, and theoretical power is expressed through concepts and categories and thinking and actions. It will be dangerous, if Western discourse power governs our thinking and actions. Friedman, founder of economic liberalism and Nobel Prize winner, once said, "Inflation is always and everywhere a monetary phenomenon", which is of profound meaning, which indicates that price rises and production level has no relationship or prices of agricultural products and commercial farmers have no relationship, in the final analysis price rises phenomena are all related with the currency phenomenon, namely, issuance of excess currency. But, this is inconsistent with our understanding of China's conditions. Especially after 1990s, there occurred a trend of thought in China that inflation was the only target of macroeconomic policy, and suggested to base the macroeconomic policies on currency volume and currency expansion. In the past, we placed employment growth in the first place, second priority was the economic growth and currency stability. Currently, there is no direct target of "employment" in the macroeconomic policy."

Wang Zhenzhong, former vice director of Institute of Economics, attached to CASS, has pointed out that discourse system of economic reforms should not be vague, especially general reform direction discourse system should be clear. Since 2005, Comrade Liu Guoguang determinedly criticizes the vague discourse which avoids talking about "socialism" and only talks about adhering to the economic reform direction of "market economy" and he has pointed out that such vague discourse poses a great harm to the reform of economic system and establishment of the discourse system of economics. Currently, some people think that state-owned economy does not work because it is of low efficiency, which is an erroneous idea. Recently two articles were published in the newspapers, I think they are jus for academic research. The articles have argued that we should not have public sector of the economy as the main pillar, but it should be the dominant sector. Concepts of "main pillar" and "dominant" is substantially different from each other.

According to Prof. Wei Xinghua from Renmin University of China: "it is a common phenomenon in China's economics that Western economics discourse power enjoys superiority over Marxist economics discourse power. This phenomenon not only happens at universities, but in academic forums, at home and abroad. But, who are the media more concerned about? It seems to be a trend that media is more indifferent to our economists that stick to Marxism. Recently, during his research visit to the School of Economics of Renmin University of China, Comrade Xi Jinping pointed out that with Marxism as guidance, our Party must attach great importance to the study of classic Marxist theories. Mao Zedong Thought and theoretical system of socialism with Chinese characteristics are the two great achievements of localization of Marxism in China. Marxism is a truth that can stand the test of time and practice. In recent two years, many people, especially Westerners, have gone through profound introspection and some Western scholars re-inspect Marx's Capital, pay attention to it and develop a panoramic view of its truthfulness and value. Therefore, we must strengthen studies on Capital in order to guide our practice of construction and reform and further develop the socialist system with Chinese characteristics. China's economics discipline is open to take in all excellent achievements of Western human civilization, but also it is selective based on Marxist stance, view and methodology. Especially in terms of teaching, we must hold fast to it and be confident with a clear-cut stand. Those words by Comrade Xi Jinping are quite inspiring and support for us.

According to Huang Ping, Director of Institute of American Studies of CASS, there is no ground for the argument that only those who hold the economic power can have discourse power. For instance, during the rectification movement in Yan'an, the guiding role of Mao Zedong Thought was determined and became very influential despite our weak economic power and technology in our revolutionary base areas. Nevertheless, why was the social influence of Mao Zedong Thought so great? According to materialistic dialectics, not always the "wealthy and propertied" can exert ideological influence. At that time, CPC has expanded its social influence and seized political power after winning the support of from workers, peasants, cadres, intellectuals and the masses. In another case, when China put forward the Five Principles of Peaceful Coexistence, when it was under the siege and blockade of the West. How much goods and materials did China possess in those days ? However, those five principles were widely acknowledged and well received at that time and are still being acknowledged as norms of the for international relations, currently.

Philosophy, history, culture, education and the international issues

According to Prof. Fang Keli, the former Dean of Graduate School of the CASS, "history of Chinese Philosophy is a discipline that demonstrates independent problem awareness, seeks unique discourse system and rich Chinese characteristics and reflects the universal laws of philosophical thinking.

However, we should see that during the past hundred years, it has been gradually "Westernized". Hu Shi has attempted to combine it with pragmatism, Feng Youlan has combined it with neo-realism, and Mu Zongsan has combined it with Kantian theory while dogmatic Marxists have turned it into footnotes (un-important status) and saw it as the exception (margin) of history of Western philosophy. Consequently, several years ago, some people prompted the debate on "the legitimacy crisis of the Chinese philosophy.

To overcome such a "crisis", Chinese philosophy should absorb all the achievement of human civilization, on the basis being self-reliant, and sovereign, it should also return to its own development of problem awareness and cherish the discourse system formed in the past centuries till today. For instance, heaven and man, principle and vital force, mind and matter, body and function, being and nothingness, duality and unity, opposition and recovery, subject and object, knowing and doing, learning and thinking, group and individual, righteousness and profit, etc. are all unique discourse (and category) system of Chinese philosophy. The basic philosophical problem raised by Engels (materialism versus idealism) is of universal significance but has special manifestations in the Chinese philosophy, similar to the struggle between materialism and idealism, we have the struggle between heaven and humanity (man). "Exploring the profundities of Yin and Yang" is the dialectics with Chinese characteristics; "affiliation with ethics and seeking good to acquire knowledge" is epistemology with Chinese characteristics; "grasping and understanding the evolution from ancient to modern" is Chinese philosophy of history; "cultivation of the ideal personality" is Chinese philosophy of life. Chinese philosophical problem awareness shares something in common with those problem awareness of many national philosophies of the world, but it has also its unique manifestation. We should not be marginal footnotes of the Western philosophy, but should return to our own problem awareness and discourse system, since the so-called "universal values" does not belong to the mainstream in Western discourse system."

Former Director of Institute of World History of CASS Yu Pei has argued that: "there are three issues in the study of Chinese history. Firstly, it negates the history of 1917, which argues that it is political preaching rather than being scientific. Secondly, it holds that scientific history study started to develop in 1980s when theories and methods of Western historiography were adopted to reform Chinese historical studies. Thirdly, although we have entered the 21th century, we still do not have systematic or comprehensive planning for the theoretical and methodology for the Chinese history studies.

Those problems mirror a realistic practical problem—if we do not have a complete Marxist theoretical system for Chinese historiography, we would not be able to establish a Chinese discourse system. We are passing through a very critical struggle period, I am not exaggerating, to have a complete Marxist theoretical system for Chinese historiography, is the key to the future of Chinese history and the way out."

Zhang Jiong has explained that: "for over one hundred years, Chinese Marxists have been striving constantly to establish the Marxist theoretical system and discourse of literature and art with Chinese characteristics. Mao Zedong's Speech in the Forum on Literature and Art in Yan'an and other relevant works have laid a particular cornerstone for the establishment of Marxist theoretical system and basic discourse of literature and art with Chinese characteristics. We must better sort out and take in the cream of traditional Chinese literary theories and transform them based on Marxist historical materialism and dialectical materialism. Also, we must critically take in the scientific part of contemporary Western literary theories, including Western Marxism's literary theories and various thoughts of modernism and postmodernism, in this process we should absorb the rational content from them and leave aside the dross. Moreover, we must start from summarizing the experience and lessons of both China's social practices, and literary and art practices of China, especially practice of socialist literary and art, and enhance a proper theoretical understanding. If we can make sound achievements in the aforesaid aspects, we will be able to acquire due discourse power status in the field of literary and art theory—in the world stage.

Discourse on the international issues

Li Shenming, has argued: "as a socialist country, China should not pursue a hegemonic discourse but must establish a discourse system to protect China's and Chinese people's fundamental interests. We should hold an objective and clear attitude towards the certain buzz words (terminology) in the international relations. I will discuss the eleven aspects as an example:

Firstly, "international society" does not simply refer to powerful Western countries, but also includes developing countries, too.

Secondly, "terrorism" does not include people's resistance against oppression, exploitation and repression with military means.

Thirdly, "acting in the framework of international rules and conventions" should exclude those international treaties that infringe the fundamental interests of China.

Fourthly, as to "blending into economic globalization" which is the basis and what is behind political globalization, legal globalization and cultural globalization, China should actively engage with it but not blend into it.

Fifthly, "national interests above all" is true within a socialist country, but in international relations, we should acknowledge that the United Nations Charter and the Five Principles of Peaceful Coexistence are above all. In international relations, "national interests above all" means following hegemonism and following power politics.

Sixthly, "global governance" should not deprive any sovereign state of its sovereignty or its territorial integrity. Seventhly, "being a responsible power" means that any nation should not require other countries to sacrifice their interests or their people's interests to meet its assuming requirements regardless of the United Nations Charter and the Five Principles of Peaceful Coexistence.

Eighthly, "solidarity during the international financial crisis" was raised by Unites States Secretary of State Hilary Clinton. Fundamentally speaking, the current international financial crisis belongs to capitalist system. In the fight against this crisis, the superiority of socialist system with Chinese characteristics has been fully demonstrated. There is no ground or advantage for us to save capitalism.

Ninthly, "there are no permanent friends, nor permanent foes ." Countries, be it small or large, powerful or weak, we should promote friendship as long as they abide by the United Nations Charter and the Five Principles of Peaceful Coexistence. We must reject Western countries attempting to alienate friendship among the vast majority of developing countries with such a view.

Tenthly, the expression "countries in transition or transformation" should be prevented from being used by Western countries to turn socialist countries into capitalist ones through "peaceful evolution" through reforming their economic and political systems.

Eleventhly, "there is no war between (western) democratic countries". Firstly, according to this view, socialist countries are classified as "autocratic" and "dictatorial" countries. Secondly, it advocates excuses for interference in and invasion of other countries. Thirdly, the two world wars were in effect initiated by imperialist countries, and so on.

Y. 33

A Popular Theoretical Reader That Clarifies the Causes of the Demise of Soviet Union: Be Vigilant Against Danger: World Socialism Book Series Well Received after Release

Yi Yuan

Abstract: This meeting review narrates the meeting arranged for the release of the book series titled as Be Vigilant against Danger: World Socialism co-sponsored by the World Socialism Research Center and the Social Sciences Academic Press of the Chinese Academy of Social Sciences. The 10-part book series received favorable comments from the participants: it presents abroad view of the magnificent and tortuous history of world socialist movements in the 20th century ; it follows a distinct theme and reviews the history when different schools of thought clashed and mingled with each other; it provides an incisive analysis of the history when pioneers blazed the trail and made it through socialist movements; and it warns against the erroneous trends of thought that have potential harm to Chinese socialism, demonstrating the Marxists' firm conviction in building socialism with Chinese characteristics.

Key words: publication of World Socialism Series; press release; overview

October 10, 2012 witnessed the book release meeting of the "Be Vigilant against Danger: World Socialism Series co-sponsored by the World Socialism Research Center and the Social Sciences Academic Press attached to the Chinese Academy of Social Sciences. The book series was thought as a commemorative event for the successful convening of the 18th National Congress of the CPC.

Over 100 leaders, comrades, experts and scholars from ministries and commissions covering Organization Department of the CPC Central Committee, Publicity Department of the CPC, International Department of the CPC Central Committee, Policy Research Office, Central Compilation and Translation Bureau, Party School of the CPC Central Committee, Xinhua News Agency, National Defense University PLA China, Chinese Academy of Social Sciences, etc., universities including Peking University, Tsinghua University, Renmin University of China, Wuhan University, etc., and media like Xinhua News Agency, People's Daily, Guangming Daily, Red Flag Manuscript, etc. participated in the meeting or submitted written statement. Among them were, Li Li'an, Wang Weiguang, Zhao Keming, Li Shenming, Li Jie, Huang Haotao, Jiang Wei, Jiang Shuxian, Yu Yuan, He Bingmeng, Liang Zhu, Liu Shulin, Cheng Enfu, Hou Huiqin, Tian Xinming, Wu Xiongcheng, Xu Chongwen, Xie Shouguang, Jiang Lifeng, Chen Zhan'an, Gu Yuanyang, Guo Fenglian, Wang Hong, Deng Chundong, Fan Jianxin, Li Xiangjun, Li Ling, and other leaders were present at the meeting.

In tune with modern life tempo, each part of the series were limited around 40,000 to 50,000 words so that readers can finish reading it, at one go after work or during a trip. The series are also suitable for cadres of the party and government at all levels, university students and readers who are interested in or passionate about theory and practice of world socialism.

They can also be evaluated as theoretical books popularizing scientific socialism, or rigorous academic works by experts and scholars from inside and outside World Socialism Research Center, based on their long-term research and painstaking efforts, as well as an effective attempt of popularization of Marxism.

The series includes ten parts: Be Concerned about the People and the Party—Mao Zedong's Exploration on the Party's Evergreen Ideas and (by Li Shenming), October Revolution of Russia (by Chen Zhihua), Cuba: Feasible Local Socialism (by Mao Xianglin), Contemporary Socialist Ideological Trends and Practices in Latin America (by Xu Shicheng), Socialist Thought Trends in the West, (by Jiang Hui & Yu Haiqing), On Neoliberalism (by He Bingmeng & Li Qian), On Democratic Socialism (by Zhou Xincheng), On Historical Nihilism (Liang Zhu), On Universal

Values (by Wang Tingyou); Gorbachev and "Humanistic and Democratic Socialism" (by Wang Zhengquan). Since publication, it has been well-received among leaders and comrades of Party Central Committee and Central Military Commission and readers from all walks of life.

In the premiere of the series, Wang Weiguang, Executive Vice President of Chinese Academy of Social Sciences, pointed out that since reform and opening up, China had undergone rapid development in all aspects and thoughts among people have become more diversified, which may present a great challenge to mainstream ideology, if nor handled well.

At such a critical juncture, experts and scholars that are indulged in mainstream thoughts fail to properly explain the problems that have occurred in world socialist movement to ordinary people, were not able answer the question why the Soviet Union has disintegrated, etc.

On the other side other scholars, due to being too focused on summarizing experiences, studying the current theories and facts of the world socialist movement, have neglected the more popularization of socialist values, theories and common basis of socialism theory. Therefore, for the first time, "implementing innovation projects related to philosophy and social sciences and promoting prosperity and development of philosophy and social sciences" was included into the 12thFive-year Plan.

Sponsored by Innovative Academic Publishing Project of the Chinese Academy of Social Sciences, the book series is another achievement in exerting the frontline spirit of Marxism following Be Vigilant against Danger: Historical Lessons from the Collapse of Soviet Union Communist Party, a series of political commentary and interpretation films by World Socialism Research Center.

Theoretical achievements have to be tested by practices, they should be tested by the majority of people—the masses. How to popularize the profound, but boring and dull looking theories among the ordinary people?

The question seems simple, but is actually difficult to answer. As an important achievement of the "innovation project" mentioned above, the books series have been innovative in form, as "pocket books", and thus have been reader-friendly. Though the series aims to introduce basic common sense and basic common characteristics of scientific socialism to the ordinary people, it still enjoys the rigor and depth of academic and theoretical content. Moreover, it is a series of excellent books that are conducive to the promotion of socialist ideology and thoughts and will play a significant role in the realization of socialist spiritual (intellectual) progress.

I would like to summarize the statements made by the meeting participants as follows.

I. It offers a broad view on the magnificent and tortuous history of world socialist movements of the 20th century

The participants have praised : "with high self-consciousness of theory and firm conviction to socialism, scholars of the World Socialism Research Center have unveiled the mystery over the socialist movement cast by Western capitalism and demonstrated the vitality of socialism in the contemporary world with the series."

Former Secretary of the Advisory Commission, Li Li'an has pointed out: "the world socialist movement is recovering and this is great. The "series" sheds light on the history, the current situation and development of world socialism from different facets and angles, including latest research achievements regarding the October Revolution, Cuba's socialist practice, contemporary socialist trends of thoughts and current practices in Latin America, socialist trends of thought in the West. It also includes the ideas refuting the erroneous trends of thought, in China such as the historical nihilism, democratic socialism, neoliberalism and the doctrine of universal values. Although "the series" starts with expounding on specific points yet does not lose the holistic panoramic picture, uses rigorous logic and strong argumentation and boasts macroscopic perspective as well as microscopic analysis.

Li Jie, Vice President of CASS has stated: "all sorts of feelings crowd in when we look back into the world socialist movements since the October Revolution of Russia. Before the October Revolution, socialism was a thought and theory and had undergone a lengthy development from fantasy to science, which we should mainly attribute to Marx and Engels. After the October Revolution, socialism evolved into practices with country as the space of development , later embraced more and more countries, it conquered the powerful fascist Germany, Italy and Japan, resisted the cold war initiated by the Western camp led by the United States and developed into splendid socialist camp between 1950s and 1960s. At one time, the east wind tended to prevail over the west wind. However, it was inevitable that the world socialist movement, as a brand new practice, have faced setbacks on its path ahead. Few people had anticipated incidents like the collapse of the Soviet Union and the tremendous changes in the Eastern Europe. But we must be good in drawing lessons from those incidents and transform them into our treasure for pushing forward the development of socialism with Chinese characteristics. There are mainly three lessons that we must bear in mind. Firstly, to establish socialism, we must promote the policy of reform and opening up, instill vitality and power into the development of socialism. Secondly, we must adhere to socialist path and hold a scientific and correct view regarding our history and its important representative figures so as to guarantee the correct direction for our reform and opening up. Thirdly, we must attach great importance to the selection of successors, stick to collective succession and collective leadership principles."

Jiang Wei, Deputy Secretary of the Central Political and Legal Affairs Commission of CPC, asserted: since the end of 1980s, world socialist movement arrived at its low tide, whereas some socialist countries including former Soviet Union degenerated, which has pleased the politicians and theorists in the capitalist countries but filled the scholars in the socialist countries with worry, shook their faith in Marxism and eroded their confidence in the future of socialism. However, world socialist practices we observe in the last recent years, especially the great practice of socialism with Chinese characteristics have eloquently proven to the world the truth of Marxism cannot be defeated and socialism has a promising future. Yet the crisis that broke out in 2008 and hasn't come to an end up to now, which demonstrates to all that capitalism is on the decline. Against such historical background, it becomes the responsibility of the theoretical workers of Marxism to abide by the rules of historical development, help people to hold firm to the ideal of communism and raise people's confidence in socialism. In current China, theories of scientific socialism advocated by Marxism not only need to be localized but also popularized in China. As the builders of socialism with Chinese characteristics, the masses will not have a firm political stand without a clear grasp of theories, and they will be deprived of the enthusiasm to make further achievements without confidence in the system. Based on the new developments of human civilization and with faith in Marxism and confidence in socialism, the authors of "the series" wrote their works from the perspective of exploring the future prospects of socialism. We should pay our highest tribute to the editors and authors of the series."

Zhang Quanjing, former director of the Organization Department of the CPC Central Committee, commented that: some books and articles related to theory are often dull and they tend to patronize and baffle readers. Marxist theories are lively and vivid, this also applies to theories and practices of scientific socialism. "The series" was an attempt to change this situation, as the authors were trying to bring readers into a lively and vivid world of theories with a rich content and fluent language. For instance, in October Revolution of Russia, Chen Zhihua has described the roar of the guns from the cruiser Aurora, readers can immediately find themselves embraced by the atmosphere of the October Revolution. In the Contemporary Socialist Ideological Trends and Practices of Latin America, with rigorous logic, Xu Shicheng has shed light on the Cuban socialism, Chilean socialism and Allende, "Socialism of the 21st century" advocated by Venezuela and Chavez, "socialism of the 21st century" of Ecuador and Rafael Correa1, "communitarian socialism" of Bolivia and Eva Morales and "syndicalism" of Brazil and Workers' Party."

Each book of the series contained about 40,000 to 50,000 words, as short as pamphlets, so that readers could finish them within a short time. We should not look down on pamphlets, because the Communist Manifesto itself was a pamphlet. Besides, Lenin wrote many pamphlets and Chairman Mao's On the Protracted War was also published as a pamphlet. To publish pamphlets was very important for the publicity, spread and education of the Party's thoughts and theories and a good tradition of the Party. The series was not only a theoretical reader popularizing common ideas of scientific socialism, but also an academic work that included the long-term research results of experts and scholars. Although the books were short regarding the number of words, they were correctly pinpointed, carefully structured and hit the nail on the head with thorough analysis.

Director of Publicity Department of BAIC Group Wang Hong commented the following: "the series is reader-friendly, adheres to and embodies the basic tenets of Marxism, I think such characteristics meet the requirement of popularization of socialism theories, and demonstrates the materialization of socialist core value system. For instance, the articles on universal values and democratic socialism tell us that there are indeed trends of thought that negate Marxism-Leninism and the path of socialism with Chinese characteristics. If we don't discriminate such mistaken trends , our faith in Marxism-Leninism and our confidence in taking the path of socialism with Chinese characteristics will be shaken. It is by reading those articles that people can realize the danger of various trends of thoughts fighting against Marxism and thus enhance their political awareness and discerning power.

---

1 Correa said: communitarian socialism is characterized by "well-being, making the wealth communal, drawing on our heritage…" The process "will not be easy, it could take decades, even centuries, but it is clear that the social movements cannot achieve true power without implanting a socialist and communitarian horizon."

Liang Zhu's book, "On Historical Nihilism", has given vivid description and incisive analysis on the issue. Out of personal interest, I have focused reading Li Shenming's "Be Concerned about the People and the Party—Mao Zedong's Exploration on the Party's Evergreen Ideas" which was both convincing and thought provoking owing to its content with rich historical data and including the author's own experiences.

II. The series have chosen distinct themes and has reviewed the history world socialism in which different schools of thoughts clashed and intertwined with each other.

Participants have pointed out that the world socialist movement has gone through twists and turns and its thought and theories are not unitary, but instead includes diversity.

During the development of the world socialist movement, different schools of thought have had clashes among them from time to time, this has never ended. There were also clashes or conflicts between different understandings within the same school (internal confrontations), such as the clash between different understandings regarding the basic tenets of Marxism and also confrontation between Marxism and dogmatism.

Also, there has been external struggles by Marxism against the different schools of thought, such as liberalism, neo-liberalism, and historical nihilism, and against rumors attacking Marxism. Besides, fighting against the use of "faint" academic discourse which aims to weaken and offset the influence of Marxism.

Moreover, there is the specific trend of democratic socialism thought, which we can say that it is both combined product of external and internal aspects. We should carry out a careful struggle against this trend of thought.

Wang Xuedong, Deputy Director of Central Compilation and Translation Bureau, commented: "the ten-part series have discussed some important contemporary theoretical and practical issues of the world socialist movement, such as Mao Zedong's exploration on the Party's evergreen ideas, such as neo-liberalism, historical nihilism, socialism in the Western world, etc.

A lot of people still have vague understanding of those major theoretical and practical issues, which call on us social sciences research workers to give scientific answers, we should raise ourselves to leading position regarding theoretical issues, adhere to the principle of offering correct theoretical guidance and guide the public opinion accordingly.

Li Shenming in his book "Be Concerned about the People and the Party—Mao Zedong's Exploration on the Party's Evergreen Ideas" has based himself on the important document of the Party "Resolutions on Several Historical Problems for the Party since the Founding of China" and ideas put forward in the Sixth Plenary Session of the 11th CPC Central Committee and also based himself on the speeches by Deng Xiaoping with the same spirit. In this book, Li Shenming has also expounded on the sources, development context and practice of Mao Zedong's ideas about keeping the Party and political power evergreen, which can help us make truthful and appropriate evaluation on Mao Zedong's exploration of socialism building and Mao Zedong's mistakes in his late years and in this way this work is conductive to develop our current work, especially it can enable us to grasp Mao Zedong's strategic thinking about keeping the Party and state (government) evergreen, thus they should never degenerate. Thus the book confidently answers to a series of other similar major issues, can inspire the readers and endow them with strong beliefs and confidence."

Li Jie has pointed out that: democratic socialism trend, has given the largest negative impact and it is the most deceptive trend in the world socialist movement, for this reason it is a daunting and lengthy task, even currently to make a clear distinction between scientific socialism and democratic socialism.

In effect, at the beginning of reform and opening up in the 1980s, Comrade Deng Xiaoping, put forward the Four Cardinal Principles, namely, the principle of upholding the socialist path, the principle of upholding the people's democratic dictatorship, the principle of upholding the leadership of the Communist Party of China (CPC), and the principle of upholding Marxism-Leninism and Mao Zedong Thought, in order to draw a clear line between socialism with Chinese characteristics and other erroneous thoughts like democratic socialism.

Practices have proven that as long as we uphold and develop the spirit of Four Cardinal Principles, they will continue to be the inexhaustible source and impetus for advancing reform and opening up and the path of socialism with Chinese characteristics.

Dazhai Village party secretary from the Xiyang Guo Fenglian has commented: "I have just finished reading the book "Be Concerned about the People and the Party" in one breath and was deeply touched, because this book gave me insights regarding multiple historical facts. Thus we can see that Mao Zedong and the older generation of revolutionaries, had nurtured lofty ideals, no matter what evaluation is made regarding them and Mao Zedong by others, especially those working in our Tachai production brigade, will evaluate them as great leaders.

I have myself lived the practice of the 1950s, I know very well that every word, every line and every page and chapter of the history of the Republic of China were written by excellent Chinese people with blood, sweat, ideal, faith, labor, courage and wisdom. Thus, this history is imbued with the ambition and spirit of our nation. Time is elapsing and there are new generations. What had happened and what was happening have and will become history, but the patriotic spirit of Chairman Mao and the older generation will last forever and the heroes and people with lofty ideals who have made selfless contributions to the nation and these people will never be forgotten by our people or the history. Hence, I have bought more than a hundred copies of the book and gave them to cadres, youth and students around me in Tachai (Dazhai). Party members, cadres and the managers and leaders of the county affiliated business enterprises in my region have received great inspiration and enlightenment from this book.

Song Liying, a 83-year-old retiree, has arranged some younger people to read her each chapter of the said book and recalled a series of theoretical and ideological systems proposed by Mao Zedong on strengthening the Party building. She said, "Without the Communist Party, New China would not have been possible, and without Chairman Mao, the happy life of today would not have been possible. As a senior Party member, I believe we must remain honest, serve the people whole-heartedly, think for the people, work for the people and take the problems of the majority of the masses as priority. We can be pleased only when the masses are happy. As long as everyone leads a good life, we will also lead a good life."

III. The "series" provides an incisive analysis of the history, within which great pioneers have blazed new trails and propelled the world socialist movement

Lenin, Mao Zedong and Stalin

Scholar Li Jie held that: "Lenin had not only developed Marxism into Leninism, but announced the arrival of the new epoch of imperialism and proletarian revolution. He also led the great October Revolution, created the new era of building socialist countries, properly put forward the New Economic Policy in the Soviet Union and raised the slogan of uniting with all the oppressed nations, and he established a model that can be followed by the economically and culturally backward countries when they are taking a socialist path. Mao Zedong creatively solved the issue of carrying out new democratic revolution in a semi-colonial and semi-feudal Eastern country, opened the path of localization of Marxism in China and established the Mao Zedong Thought which still guides us. Later, Mao Zedong creatively put into practice the idea of implementing policy of redemption on the national bourgeoisie which was the idea raised by classical Marxist authors, successfully led the socialist transformation. Later, based on the past achievements Mao Zedong started the socialist modernization task and made great achievements, providing precious experience through arduous and hard exploration on the law of building socialism in line with China's conditions. Despite his general error of Cultural Revolution in his late years, Mao Zedong's contributions to China's revolution and socialist construction will shine all the way throughout history.

Li Jie has also commented that in the history of world socialist movement, Stalin was a controversial figure who had made grave mistakes, as the following: Stalin's way of thinking was absolutist, simple and metaphysical, he seriously magnified the struggle of different ideas in the Party, and employed a simple and crude approach when dealing with social contradictions in the socialist society and state. In the political life of the party and society, Stalin promoted personal worship and promoted personal arbitrary decision making, all of which induced extremely severe consequences to the construction of socialism in the Soviet Union and also to world socialist movement. However, we cannot no deny that he had also made great contributions and achievements in speeding up the industrialization of the SU, made excellent contributions to the Soviet Union's Great Patriotic War against Nazi Germany and the world anti-Fascist war and provided help and support to China's revolution and construction. I think on this controversial issue of historical evaluation of a representative historical figure, we must carry out a comprehensive, objective, realistic and truthful research and judgment, since Stalin has exerted a significant influence on the world socialist movement. While learning lessons from his mistakes, we should also truthfully acknowledge his contributions and achievements and never repeat his errors.

IV. We should be vigilant and resolutely resist all the erroneous trend of thoughts that can have potential harm to Chinese socialism, demonstrate a firm Marxist conviction in building socialism with Chinese characteristics

Zhao Keming, former political commissar of the National Defense University of the PLA, has commented: "several books in "the series"—on democratic socialism, on neo-liberalism, on "humanistic and democratic socialism" of Gorbachev, on historical nihilism—which elaborate on their basic connotations and which reveal their erroneous and reactionary nature have been very well written. I think, in the current situation, when we are faced with complex social thought trends, "the series" play an important role by lifting the veil of these social thought trends in the eye of cadres and masses and convincing them that only the leadership of the Party and the path of socialism with Chinese characteristics can help China develop." Zhao Keming, especially commented on Li Shenming's work, "Be Concerned about the People and the Party": this book, while brilliantly demonstrates Comrade Mao Zedong's strategic thoughts on keeping the Party and political power (state) evergreen, the book also correctly differentiates Mao Zedong's this thought system, from his grave mistake of expanding class struggle, especially during the Cultural Revolution. Since the reform and opening up, comrades Deng Xiaoping, Jiang Zeming, Hu Jintao and many other leaders and cadres of the Central Committee have been emphasizing the idea of keeping the Party and the state (regime) evergreen in the face of struggles at home and abroad, they have repeatedly stressed the issue of preventing the party and the state from degeneration. Considering the tragic lessons of the Soviet Union and the past problems we have lived in our Party, their above emphasis is not "baseless", their warnings not only included ringing "alarm bells" but they have also put forward a series of specific thoughts on this issue and also led the establishment of systems and institutions to prevent such degeneration."

Jiang Wei has commented the following: authors of "the series" are all experts and scholars in their specific fields. They have by focusing a specific aspect of a big topic, have put the essence of their long term research achievements into this well-founded series with historical proofs and well-founded arguments.

"The series" offer clear and thorough comments and analysis on several trends of thought that have exerted influence on China in recent years, such as the, democratic socialism, doctrine of universal values, neo-liberalism, historical nihilism, etc. so as to silence the noise they have generated. Thus, "the series" has been strong weapon and theoretical source, against their mistaken interference to our socialist practice.

The authors, have organically combined historical analysis with realistic analysis, phenomenal analysis with essence analysis, theoretical analysis with practical analysis in those quite short articles, the authors not only specify the cause and effect of those mistaken trends of thoughts, but have analyzed their nature, especially their ideological connotations, which endow the readers with a clear view of their ideological harm and thus can prevent their mistaken interference to their practices.

Guo Fenglian said, "I was born under the red flag in October 1946 and grew up happily, singing "The East is Red" and walking on yellow soil. I am supported and nurtured with the Mao Zedong thought for 67 years. I love the Party, motherland, the people and especially my hometown. Back in the 1950s when I was a kid, my Granny always taught me to pinch and scrape without wasting anything with quotations from Mao Zedong that waste is the biggest crime. As a result, with the annual grain ration, Granny and I have managed to survive and still had some left. Our coarse clothes were full of patches, but we have never complained. In the 1960s, I led 23 young girls to take up the task of building Tachai. We worked from dawn to night time, carrying soil and stones for 365 days in succession without complaining. Even though we were not paid, no one was lazy, instead, everyone rushed to laboring and undertook dirty and dangerous labor tasks, which won us the name "Iron Girls". Our model was Chen Yonggui, the Secretary of the Tachai Party branch. As he said, party and government cadres should always be first to step fore and be best in work tasks. Cadres should act like locomotives that lead the train to run faster. So the Party members and cadres should take the lead so that the masses will have more enthusiasm for work. Chen Yonggui, did what he said. In those days, cadres, always bore the people's needs in mind, solved people's difficulties in a timely manner and were better than others in work tasks, therefore everyone called them as the good cadres of Tachai. With those veteran revolutionaries playing leading roles, the fine traditions of Tachai were maintained and passed down to later generations.

In order to build a better today and a bright tomorrow, under the correct guidance of the Party Central Committee, Tachai's party organization led the movements of emancipation the mind, made bold innovations supported the reform and opening and scientific development, thus Tachai changed the mode of economic construction. As a result, great changes have taken place, the economic structure has been adjusted, economic incomes has increased, people have become wealthier, collective family businesses grew rapidly, quality of life and living environment was improved, cultural undertakings have prospered, electricity network strengthened, modern electrical appliances were greatly introduced and people's bank accounts prospered, bringing people more satisfaction.

With the development of times, Tachai people's living standards were constantly improved. However, we must bear in mind that whatever has changed, the soul of our nation, namely, hard work, plain living and self-reliance should never change; nor should the communist styles of "love for the country and love of the collective". This is the treasure heritage of Tachai. We must hold it tight and do well in reform and opening up, be pioneers in building model villages and in the movement of establishing the new socialist countryside.

Deng Chundong, Party Secretary of the Academy of Marxism attached to the CASS, commented the following: in modern China, with the development of socialist market economy and formation of different interest groups, different groups of people develop different thoughts and ideas under the influence of different social thoughts of trends and under the influence of various cultures, all these differences are demonstrated as the differences in world outlook, values, ideas, etc. It is not at all surprising that the differences are great.

But the Communist Party members should be clear in the following: in the face of diverse thoughts and ideas, considering the influence of multiple world outlooks at home and abroad and people's increasing freedom of choice, we must systematically and confidently publicize mainstream outlook and mainstream values and guide and educate people in grasping and practicing core socialist values. This is necessary and urgent because some paradoxical, vulgar and even erroneous ideas have spread in the society due to the influence of diverse world outlooks, irresponsible publicity of individualism we can observe in the media and also some local governments' and units' mistake of "relaxed approach regarding ideological education", which was also warned by Deng Xiaoping. We know that this problem has not been effectively resolved for a long time, Consequently, social life of people are faced with all sorts of paradoxes, low-level vulgar ideas or even fallacies, and harmful ideas have spread wantonly. The failure to address this "relaxation" problem has resulted in skepticism and doubts regarding Marxist scientific theory, has caused distortion attempts and slandering of the Party's glorious history, the emergence of money worship and money first mentality, and other unhealthy beliefs.

Therefore, it is more necessary to carry out systematic and comprehensive publicity of Marxist ideology, the system of socialist core values and relevant correct theories and ideas, which means that Marxist theory workers should realize the necessity and urgency and bravely undertake such a historical task. The "series" is an attempt to elaborate on the basic principles of Marxism, Marxist outlook, and Marxist values, and also elaborate on basic tenets of socialism, which will play a positive role in promoting correct values in the society, help the people, especially the youth, to distinguish between the right and wrong theories, thoughts and ideas, thus strengthen the system of core socialist values. The book publishing community and theoretical circles should work together to realize such an orientation of literature.

Y. 34

What Do People Live For?
—An Abstract from the Keynote Speech at the Opening Ceremony for Grade 2012 Freshmen of Graduate School, CASS on September 7, 2012

Li Shenming[1]

Abstract: "What Do People Live For? This is an important question. Our life can be in the right direction only when we are absolutely clear on this question. At present, an aspiring young people should set up a correct world outlook and also a correct life outlook. He should believe in Marxism, socialism and communism and must serve the people whole heartedly. Only in this way, we can recognize the responsibility, accept the challenge and grow into a useful timber.

Key words: person; young people; conviction

---

1 Li Shenming, Deputy Secretary of Party Committee, Vice President, Researcher, Director of World Socialism Research Center attached to CASS.

Today, I would like to share with you my feelings and meaning of "What Do People Live For? Currently people are talking about "top-level design", but the "top-level" meant by some people is in fact the level below four and five, or even two or three. I suggest that everyone should think about the question "What Do People Live For?" so as to be a qualified and be an excellent postgraduate, because as far as I am concerned, this question can be the top-level question in our life. Once you figure it out, there is nothing that can prevent you from being a qualified and excellent postgraduate of the People's Republic of China and grow into a useful timber of the Party, the state and the nation.

What Do People Live For? This question deserves a lifetime exploration. To clarify this question is to find out what belief people should have.

Currently, there are three major religions that are universally accepted. The Christians believe in God and believe that people are born with original sin and they can only been saved by God. The Islamists believe in Allah and believe that if they do good and righteous deeds in this life, they will go to heaven in the next life. The Mahayana Buddhists believe that Theravada Buddhism is for self-cultivation and the Mahayana Buddhism to deliver all living creatures from torment. According to the Article 36 of the Constitution of the PRC, "Citizens of the People's Republic of China enjoy freedom of religious belief." We do not oppose that some students have their freedom of religious belief, but Communist Party members must abide by the Party constitution and believe in Marxism. Cuban leader Castro holds that there are only two faithful followers in the world: one is an adherents of religion, the other a genuine Communists.

A true communist believes in Marxism, socialism and communism. Comrade Deng Xiaoping once said that Marxism, socialism and communism in nature are synonyms. Then the ultimate nature and goal of this belief is to ultimately fulfill the free and comprehensive development of everyone as expected by Marx and Engels. How to materialize this ultimate nature and goal? Every true communist has to serve the people whole-heartedly. Chairman Mao Zedong once encouraged the whole Party, "We must keep going. We must work incessantly and we will touch God eventually. The God is none other than the people of China."[2]

Therefore, we can say the belief of true communists is the people who are the "God" in the communists' heart. Within classes and in class society, the people are always the majority of the society and thus the interests, will, volition and power of the majority are the real impetus for the creation of history and ultimately determine where the history is developing. Such is the true meaning of historical materialism. Trusting the people, relying on

---

2 Selected Works of Mao Zedong. Volume III. People's Publishing House, 1991.

the people and believing the people (namely, for the people) mean that we must believe in the people so that such a belief becomes glorious and noble and is the social reality and historical truth instead of social and historical illusion.

In essence, the basic economic, political and cultural systems which are based on the private sector of economy serve very few people, which thus requires that the ordinary people, namely, the majority should have such values and ideas as self-salvation, doing the good in this life and self-cultivation and serving the social system where the minority oppress and exploit the majority so as to achieve the lasting political stability and sustainable development of the society. Therefore, the basic economic, political and cultural systems which are based on the private sector of economy are not in line with the values and ideas they promote. However, the basic economic, political and cultural systems of socialist countries are for the people, which demand that Party members and government staff should implement the purpose of serving the people whole-heartedly. That is to say, the basic economic, political and cultural systems of socialist countries are in line with the values and ideas they promote. Undeniably, there are some Party members and government officials whose acts belie their words and who even pervert justice for a bribe, but these individual cases by no means imply that the basic economic, political and cultural systems of China are not in line with the values and ideas they promote, because those incidents are caused by people who break away from, deviate from or betray the purpose of the Party and the government.

The goal "serve the people wholeheartedly" pursued by communists shares similarity with the doctrines of Christianity, Islam and Buddhism. Several years ago, I read online an article called "In Memory of Norman Bethune, an article that completely Changes my American Colleague' Opinion on Mao Zedong", which was the dialogue between a Chinese entrepreneur who started a business in the United States and his colleague. As a pious Christian, the colleague could not understand and even detested what Chinese communists did in China.

The Chinese entrepreneur told his colleague that, "before I came to the United States, I thought it was a paradise of freedom. But as I landed here, I found that it is an extremely religious country. The American people believe that America is the blessed land and they are the blessed ones, which make them proud and passionate about their nation, especially the walking missionaries who wear simple clothes and eat simple food. Their sincere, simple and determined eyes always remind me of the communists in the old Chinese movies. Or TV series. There used to be a group of Chinese communists who similarly were fully devoted, selfless and willing to bear whatever hardships they faced or sacrificed themselves for their beliefs.

The only difference was that the missionaries were guided by God while the communists by communist beliefs, and Mao Zedong, to be exact."

Through two-month difficult conversation, the colleague finally said, "I think I am a little bit touched, if everything was true."Later, after he read the English version of Mao Zedong's In Memory of Norman Bethune, recommended by the Chinese entrepreneur, he said, "I was shocked. If you didn't tell me that it was written by Mao Zedong, if I could delete words related to communism and ideology, I would think I was listening to God when someone read it to me. What Mao Zedong said is exactly the same as what I heard in the church." Also, he said to the Chinese, "Thank you so much for showing me a different Mao Zedong. I think I am beginning to respect him. I am more grateful that my heart is more open and I feel the door of the world is open to me. Communism and Mao Zedong are no longer obstacles to my understanding of China. Now I understand China better. I am glad that I can embrace all these." If anyone is interested in the dialogue, you can search for it on the Internet.

According to Marxist philosophy, the universe is boundless and time infinite. Each and every one of us came into being as a result of the intersection of space and time. To some extent, it is inevitable that human beings are born into the Earth. However, it is also contingence. As a part of the leading living creatures, it is fortunate that we can live for around a hundred years on the Earth and we should be proud of it and cherish it. Bearing that in mind, we can all be optimists and live a happy life but cannot go too far.

Therefore, it is extremely important for us to decide and make our life more meaningful and valuable, which requires us to clarify what is human being, namely, where are realistic human beings come from, what kind of a state we are in, where we are going and how we should live, what we should do and what we will leave behind after the (may be) one hundred years on Earth.

First of all, humans are "species-being" that are different from other natural living creatures. As a special form of product of material movement when nature evolves to certain historical period, humans are the only "species-being" that gets rid of sheer animal state because of labor activity. Therefore, humans are the leader of existing living creatures which can perceive the world and actively transform it. Humans do not differ from other animals just for satisfying physiological needs like eating and sleeping, but for higher spiritual needs. Hence, we should be proud of laboring for it makes us the only "species-being". Yet, the extension of laboring is expanding with the development of times. The current Constitution of China includes love of labor into the social morality that it proposes. Only by being proud of laboring, can each individual and the whole human race make progress and realize free and comprehensive individual development. It is a fundamental and basic truth that anyone who loves laboring should not be money-driven. Those who are driven by money will lose the correct direction of struggle, violate discipline and even break the bottom line of law. As long as we are alive, we should never make it our bottom line not to violate discipline and break law but should have higher spiritual pursuit, which calls for a correct ideal and faith. What is a correct ideal and faith?

For communists, it is what is laid down in the current Party Constitution, "Members of the Communist Party of China must serve the people wholeheartedly, dedicate their whole lives to the realization of communism, and be ready to make any personal sacrifices", living and struggling for the interests of the people. This is what makes a communist a "noble-minded and pure" man, a man of moral integrity and above vulgar interests, a man who is of value to the people". Such a man will always be remembered by the people and recorded in the history.

Secondly, human society is the aggregation of each individual formed by all social members. Humans are concrete and realistic rather than abstract and imaginary. Concrete and realistic humans always exist in certain space and time and in practical individual living process and activities of different times. Therefore, each individual should have specific and reasonable needs and interests which are satisfied by possible individual labor and social help. However, human society enjoys common interests for human survival and development, such as a sound ecological environment. Yet, what we can see now are some individuals, groups and even countries are desperately plundering resources and polluting the environment for huge fortune or extravagant life, which is typically gaining benefit by harming other countries, other people and others' posterity. A country or nation consists of certain society which is formed by "numerous" individuals, both each individual and the whole nation should nurture collectivist and internationalist spirits. Proposing the positive but failing to oppose the negative will lead to utopism since in this way positive cannot be sustained and promoted.

Thirdly, humans include both those who exist in the "present tense" and those who exist in the "past tense" and "future tense". On the one hand, we contemporary people cannot regard ourselves as concrete and real people while our ancestors as abstract and imaginary people; or else, we will be trapped in historical nihilism. Human civilization is the product of history and heritage passed down through generations. Without the bloody struggle and arduous undertaking of people in the "past", we could not have had the material basis for our happy life and further development. Hence, while we are building socialism with Chinese characteristics, we must cherish our revolutionary tradition and "bear our ancestors in mind". In a sense, we should place the people in the "past" first. That is, we must respect history and cherish the material and spiritual fortunes that our ancestors created and accumulated for us; we must not "sell the field of our father without feeling heartbreak' but inherit and carry forward the sound tradition and revolutionary spirit of our ancestors. On the other hand, we contemporary people cannot regard ourselves as concrete and real people and our posterity as abstract and imaginary people; or else, we will weaken the idea of sustainable development and prevent our posterity from developing. Thus, we should not only continue to work hard based on the material and spiritual fortunes of our ancestors and create and accumulate more material and cultural wealth for our posterity, but protect the environment, cherish resources and highlight the historical inheritance.

Fourthly, in a class society or a society where classes exist, when we talk about "serving the people", "the people" refer to the majority of the masses, rather than everyone, let alone the minority. In a class society or a society where classes exist, individuals belong to certain class or hierarchy caste. In order to thoroughly free those individuals and help them become freely and comprehensively developed individuals, we must "overthrow all the relations, in which man is a debased, enslaved, forsaken, despicable being"[3].

Fundamentally speaking, in a class society or a society where classes exist, we cannot place all the people and their fundamental interests first, or the proletariat will never be able to break away from being exploited and oppressed, not to mention freeing the human race. In a class society or a society where classes exist, the fundamental interests of the majority, namely, the majority of the masses, are in full accord, while those of the minority stay in the opposite. Serving the fundamental interests of the minority is inevitably at the sacrifice of the fundamental interests of the majority. When the Great Harmony is realized, there will exist the concepts like communism, communist party and the working people, because then the social governance bodies of the state will serve all the people.

Our motto of serving the majority of the masses and defending their fundamental interests—in a class society or a society where classes exist—will change as the following: serve all the people and their fundamental interest in the future classless society. Without doubt, we must have a sober and firm understanding of this change since building the advanced socialism needs the hard work of numerous generations and we must avoid the errors like the "Great Leap Forward" of the 1950s. Jiang Zemin and Hu Jintao repeatedly emphasized, "putting people first" is equivalent to putting the fundamental interests of the majority of the masses first. We should bear this important point in mind.

---

3 Selected Works of Marx and Engels. Volume I. People's Publishing House, 1995, p. 234.

In order to clarify our life-long purpose, we should look at how the revolutionary martyrs and our predecessors lived their live and made it vigorous as immortal.

Some people regard living as a faith with the philosophy of "better live like a coward than a dead hero" and became renegades and traitors. Comrade Cai Hesen, member of the fifth and sixth Standing Committee of the Political Bureau, was betrayed in June 1931 by traitor Gu Shunzhang who had been responsible for security work of the Central Committee, consequently Cai Hesen had suffered from cruel torture in the jail. In the end, Comrade Cai Hesen was nailed to the wall by the enemy with thick spikes and his chest was completely mashed by a bayonet. Though, aged 36, he was staunch and unyielding.

Some people make it a creed to eat and drink well. However, Comrade Yang Jingyu, one of the leaders of the Anti-Japanese Amalgamated Army of the Northeast, led his army to prevent hundreds of thousands of Japanese from entering China in the nine-year armed combat against Japanese invaders, creating amazing achievement and forcibly assisted the people in the War of Resistance against Japan. Later, he was betrayed by traitor Ding Shoulong and was killed by Japanese invaders. The invaders did not understand how Yang Jingyu managed to persist in the war for more than a year without any food, so they dissected his body, only to find there was "no rice in his stomach" but just weeds, bark and torn cotton fiber. He died at the age of 35.

Some people live for money. However, it is not the case with Peng Pai who was a communist who believed in saving the country and people and transforming the society as his mission. He was one of the leaders of early peasant movement and founder of Hailufeng peasant movement and revolutionary base area. Although he was born into a rich family, he burnt in public all the proprietorship certificates his family possessed and announced that "from now on people farm their own lands to support their own needs and do not have to submit grain for rent." After that he devoted himself to revolution and became a martyr of revolution due to the betrayal by traitor Bai Xin on August 24, 1929 at the age of 33.

Some people live for money. However, it is not the case with Peng Pai[4] who was a communist who believed in saving the country and people and transforming the society as his mission. He was one of the leaders of early peasant movement and founder of Hai-feng peasant movement in 1923 and revolutionary base area. Although he was born into a rich family, he burnt in public all the proprietorship certificates his family possessed and

---

4 Peng Pai, in in 1925 of the CPC's committee for the districts of Hai-feng and Lu-feng. In 1927 hebecame a member of the Central Committee of the CPC.

announced that "from now on people farm their own lands to support their own needs and do not have to submit grain for rent." After that he devoted himself to revolution and became a martyr of revolution due to the betrayal by traitor Bai Xin on August 24, 1929 at the age of 33.

As a saying goes, "No man was ever immune from death, so let me but leave a loyal heart shining in the pages of history." Cai Hesen, Yang Jingyu and Peng Pai will never be forgotten by the Party and New China. At the 60th anniversary of the founding of New China, comrades Cai Hesen, Yang Jingyu and Peng Pai are included into the 100 hero models that have made significant contribution to the founding of New China, while those traitors will forever labeled as shame in history.

Some people take bribes, manipulate power for personal ends and even fall into renegades and traitors so as to "enjoy life", naively believing that those ill achievements and sins will be gone and unknown with their decease and passing of time. It is true that some historical details will be forgotten and even distorted with the elapsing of time and changes in human affairs. However, they hardly realized that based on historical materialism, we don't need many trivial historical details for a broad outline and social practice is the sole criterion for testing truth. The influence of what one has done on history can never escape the inspection of history and the more important a person is and the more significant an event is, the more people and history will discriminate him/her and it and make records.

In the final analysis, "What Do People Live For" is all about belief and world outlook. A correct ideal is a shining sun. We, communists should not have only one kind of belief which passes to to the revolutionary period, and be brave enough to make sacrifice, while hold another belief during the ruling and socialism building epochs, honestly make good money.

To answer the question of "What Do People Live For" is the key of to have a firm and correct world outlook. With a correct world outlook, we will have correct outlook on life, death, power, status and hardship and happiness.

To have a correct world outlook, we must stay away from the doctrine that "every man for himself, and the Devil take the hindmost." Is man's nature at birth good or evil? This question has been under debate for several thousand years and will not stop in the days to come. Those who believe that man's nature at birth is good hold that since man's nature is good or inclined to goodness, we must establish a sound system which includes people's democratic dictatorship. As long as everyone's conscience is awakened, with good nature and kind will, people can build an ideal society. However, those who believe that man's nature at birth is evil, hold that since people are born to focus on self-interest, they will harm others for personal gains. Therefore, a strict system should be designed for prevention. Yet, now that people are born to focus on self-interest, some people think, spokesmen of certain class and group also focus on self-interest and thus they will formulate policies and regulations that are beneficial to their own interests and force others to implement them when exercising their powers.

According to these ideologists, the social system where people exploit and oppress people is reasonable and will live forever. Such reasoning in essence aims to introduce the law of jungle into human society and solidify it. According to the theoretical assumption of Adam Smith, humans are rational economic men, namely, men are born to be selfish and focus on self-interest. Whether man's nature is good or evil is a question belongs to the category of morality. As Chairman Mao pointed out in 1943, "morality is a reflection of what people require in their economic life and other social lives and…. different classes have different views of morality. This is our view of good and evil."

Mao Zedong, also mentioned: "the special characteristic, feature or trait of humanity is its social nature—men are social animals. Natural traits, animal traits, and features are not humanity's distinguishing characteristics.

There is no doubt or question that men are animals, not plants or minerals. The question we are faced is, what kind of animals men are. And this is a question that until Marx, nobody could correctly answer for tens of thousands of years, not even Ludwig Feuerbach, of the capitalist class. That is humans have only one basic characteristic—their social nature. We should not say that they have two basic characteristics—one being their animal nature, and the other being their social character. Such a statement is not good because it falls into dualism, which actually is idealism."

Mao Zedong also stated: "ever since the day when men separated themselves from monkeys, everything, including their physique, their intelligence and their instinct, has become social"…"men's facial features, the entire body, intelligence and capabilities are all inherited. People often call these things innate so as to differ them from social influences received after birth, but everything a person has inherited is social and is the result of hundreds of thousands of social production. We will lapse into idealism, if we are not clear about this point.[5]

It shows us that whether man's nature is good or evil reflects the requirements of economic life and social life at that time. So far, archaeological discoveries have proven that human history spans at least 2 million years and some physiological features are the result of genetic inheritance

---

5 Mao Zedong Wenji. Volume III. People's Publishing House, 1999, pp. 81-85, it is reproduced from Mao's handwritten manuscript.

through those years, which will continue to be passed down, but they are reflection of realistic society and historical society. Throughout history, there is no abstract but concrete humanity and sociality; in a class society or a society where classes exist, humanity and sociality tend to have class nature. Ideas and opinions of thinkers preceding Marx are generally based on whether man's nature is good or evil and the differences between humanity and other animals. Negating those two thinking bases, Marxist philosophy put forward that human nature in terms of reality is the sum total of all social relations and proposes that human nature should be inspected against certain social background, thus pointing out the correct thinking path.

Some people are good, some are evil and some are both good and evil. However, those manifestations are not human nature or instinct, but the reflection or embodiment of certain social relations. Therefore, we should neither propose that man's nature is good nor advocate that man's nature is evil. In the primitive communist society, people essentially helped each other, which was decided by the sum total of the then relations of production. People's selfishness arose along with the disintegration of primitive communist society and the birth of slave society, the first society with private ownership in human history. Such selfishness enjoys certain progressiveness for a long time in human society. However, with the development and progress of history, its limitation and decadence became more and more apparent. Since selfishness was developed later in human history, it will not be permanent, either.

With the comprehensive progress of human society and the final establishment of public ownership, people's selfishness will eventually be eliminated from history. This is negation of negation on a higher level. So far, modern biology fails to provide acceptably sufficient evidence to prove that men are innately selfish, unchangeable as our skin color which is genetic. Observing the animals, we can easily find that not all the animals are selfish in any circumstances and situations; a lot of animals are strongly communal and altruistic. For instance, when ants in the forest meet fire, they all gather into a ball and roll over the fire area and those on the surface of the ball will sacrifice. Even animals small as ants can do this, let alone men, the head of all living creatures. As far as I am concerned, there are three groups of people. The first group of people is the extremely selfish. "They think of themselves before others at every turn" and harm others and even betray the fundamental interests of the country and the nation for personal benefit.

The second group of people always harbors public spirit and thinks about the destiny of the country, the people and the nation. Yet, with a little selfishness, they may place individual interest first when it conflicts with the public interests. Some ordinary people may belong to the second group. The last group of people are those that boast communist personalities, including especially the qualified communists and those who do not join the

Party but enjoy excellent communist personalities.

The last group of people also have their personal consideration and interests, but when public interests conflict with personal ones, the former always comes first. In this sense, they are selfless and always put everything personal in the second place. They may even sacrifice their personal interest and life for the destiny of the country and the nation.

Can we say those martyrs are born selfish when they dedicated their lives to the Party and the people? We propose that both public and personal interests should be taken into consideration and that when the fundamental interests of the country and the nation conflict with personal ones, we should take national interests as the priority. The opinion that man's nature is selfish is in essence the product of the idea of private ownership as well as the fundamental theoretical basis for protecting private ownership. By no means should we agree with the opinion that man's nature is selfish. If it is established, it would not be possible for us to explain the great maternal love; nor are we able to understand the struggle and sacrifice our martyrs have made for the ideal and our present happy life. Also, such an opinion cannot be used to explain capitalism or prove that it will last forever. After all, the working class that takes up an overwhelming majority will not stand the ruthless and cruel exploitation for too long. They will eventually understand that to gain completely personal freedom, the whole human race should be freed at the first place. If the opinion that man's nature is selfish is carried through, socialism which represents fairness and justice will be the inevitable outcome of the development of human society. We should not overlook the opinion for it is corrupting part of our cadres and the people and sent some of the people and even senior Party cadres into prison where they receive extreme penalty. To some extent, the opinion gives them out. It is known to all that under traditional economic system, while collective and national interests are being emphasized, personal interests are seriously ignored. However, we should not make the same mistakes of extreme individualism, hedonism and money worship in the West, while establishing socialist market economy.

A correct world outlook requires that we must establish firm and correct ideal and faith. It is widely acknowledged that world history will never "develop smoothly" and "sometimes may make a big leap backward."[6]

Yet we must firmly believe that however winding the road of history is, it will inevitably lead to communism. As Deng Xiaoping once said, "In the past, however weak our Party was, it always maintained powerful fighting capacity in the face of various difficulties. That was because we had Marxism and communist faith", which is "our true strength."[7]

---

6 Selected Works of Vladimir Lenin. Volume II. People's Publishing House, 1995, p 139.
7 Selected Works of Deng Xiaoping. Volume III. People's Publishing House, 1993, p. 423.

When world socialist movement is at its low tide, it is even more necessary for us to hold firm to our belief in Marxism. Such a belief will thus become more precious for it can identify, trail and hone a person. A correct and firm belief is the "true gold" which does not fear fire. Having such a belief will make a world of difference. Without such a belief, cadres and leaders at all levels will probably bite others as well as get bitten themselves. In recent years, when being published according to Party disciplines and state laws for their mistakes, many cadres and leaders reflected over tears that they should have work hard and should not have lost their belief in Marxism and communism. Those are indeed the fundamental reasons.

After the collapse of the former Soviet Union and tremendous changes in the Eastern Europe, some people have completely lost their belief in Marxism, for they believed that "the nation is in peril" and that Marxism would also collapse in China sooner or later. Some people are fishing for personal gains, because they believe that if they don't, others will do it, anyway. Once their belief has collapsed, the doors of the jail will be open for them.

A correct world outlook also requires that we must practice what we preach. If we recite Marxist expressions, but rather act for our own selfish interests, it will not be "ossification" or "dogmatism" but essentially separation, deviation and even betrayal of Marxism. To the masses, it is the most disgusting that a person fails to do what he says. That is one of the fundamental reasons for the collapse of Soviet Communist Party. Hence, we must carefully implement correct ideal and belief and the Party's purpose of serving the people whole-heartedly in our study, work and life.

The Kingdom of Bhutan, a country among the Himalayas put forward the concept Gross National Happiness (GNH) in the 1970s. The concept began to catch the attention of many scholars and countries that juxtapose and compare it with GDP. On July 8, 2012, Arthur Brooks, President of American Enterprise Institute pointed out in his article that "The Occupy Wall Street protesters may have looked like a miserable mess. In truth, they were probably happier than the moderates making fun of them from the offices above. And none, it seems, are happier than the Tea Partiers, many of whom cling to guns and faith with great tenacity."[8]

Undoubtedly, different people in the world have different beliefs and happiness index. Nevertheless, dear fellows, with firm and correct world outlook, we will have a correct direction, a great ambition and a broad vision and mind, and we will be brave in emancipating our minds and shoulder

---

8 Brooks, Arthur. "Why Are Conservatives Happier Than Liberals?" New York Times. July 8, 2012. http://www.nytimes.com/2012/07/08/opinion/sunday/conservatives-are-happier-and-extremists-are-happiest-of-all.html.

historical undertakings and activate our passion to transform our society and create a better world and take up various difficulties and challenges for the future and fate of our country and nation; thus we will write great chapters for our life with genuine overwhelming masculinity rather than being confined to our personal life and concentrated on constructing our small life and family; we will be imbued with self-respect, self-love, confidence, self-improvement, self-reliance, work and think harder in a down-to-earth manner, firm and indomitable, tenacious, creative, rather than playing fast and loose, shrink back from difficulties, confused, drift along; we will have social justice and conscience, instead of being an on-looker or simple criticizer of negative social phenomena; we will have a more optimistic and active attitude towards life, perfectly combine idealism, realism and heroism, willing to listen to and accept others' opinions, continuously adjusting and improving our practices, instead of quarreling with Providence, indulging in self-pity, pessimistic and idle about; we will strengthen our mutual cooperation and collective consciousness, help each other with learning, communicate with each other, debate with each other, incessantly release new thirst for knowledge, and interact with ordinary working people and peasants, be aware of the pulse of the times, listen to the people's demands, rather than shutting ourselves in a greenhouse, as dumb as an oyster, ignorant or narcissistic; we will be able to stand all kinds of tests and storms and make ourselves useful to the Party, the country and the nation until we become the pillar of society.

As is known to all, on July 23, 2012, General Secretary Hu Jintao delivered an important speech in which he made it clear that we are in the period of unprecedented chances as well as challenges; the external risks are also unprecedented. Dear fellows, we have to understand the meaning and weight of this speech and recognize the responsibilities upon our shoulders and should never live up the expectations of the Party, the country and the people, from us.

Y. 35

There Are No Universal Values as Supra-ideology: Why is there a Lack of Consensus on the Core Socialist Values?

Hou Huiqin[1]

Abstract: "Universal values" of men are not abstract value consensuses, but core values that represent concrete social institutions and a concrete national ethos.

Therefore, the so-called "universal values" vary across diverse social formations. When theorizing and refining the core values of socialism, priority should be given to the essential properties of socialism and the objective law of historical development rather than targeting maximum inclusiveness. We suggest that the core values of socialism should be built upon the primary principles of the supremacy of the people, the priority of labor, and common prosperity. Values like freedom, democracy, justice, and human rights have to be premised on these primary principles and be different from the capitalist core values, thus become component part of the system of core socialist values.

Key words: core socialist values; objective truth; universal values; class nature; inclusiveness

---
1 Hou Huiqin, Deputy Director of World Socialism Research Center, attached to CASS, and researcher in the Academy of Marxism.

It is a significant strategy for the strengthening and reinforcing the socialist mainstream ideology and the "spirit of national rejuvenation" to strengthen the establishment of core socialist values system. During our practices in the recent years, appeals are running high for "theorizing and refining the socialist value system and concisely putting forward the socialist core values that are easy to publicize" while on the other hand "it requires us to continue exploration through practices to refine core socialist values that can be widely acknowledged."[2]

What lies behind such a contradiction is very thought-provoking. To sum up, there are three focal points of the contradiction. Firstly, in terms of content, how values reflect the organic unity of socialist characteristics and humanity; secondly, in terms of main body, how values embody the internal consistency between regulating the country and regulating the citizens; thirdly, in terms of basis, how values mirror the historical unity between reality and ideality.

I. Lack of consensus on core socialist values primarily demonstrates the inconsistency regarding some major and even basic theories

Values are the summary of a certain thought and theoretical system, consequently we can say that world outlook and view of history determine people's values. The key to understand the lack of consensus on socialist core values is not whether the theorization conveys contemporary people's consensus on values and the inheritance of excellent tradition of our values but the key is what socialist core values are. That is to say, there are fundamental disagreements on the fundamental question whether and how core socialist values integrate humanity and nationality through "socialist nature".

One major tendency is to take maximum inclusiveness, namely, "universality" as the highest principle for the theorization of values, which not only, intentionally or unintentionally, blurs the boundary between socialism and capitalism, but opens a gap or loophole for the West to influence our values. According to this mistaken view, socialism and patriotism are just "special values" while the supra-class "human values" are the essence of values. It is not difficult to perceive that behind such an obsession on abstract supra-class and supra-ideology "universal values" are the doubt on the truthfulness and vitality of Marxism and the submission to currently popular or currently strong values and strong dominant discourse system. The key question is whether the basic tenets of Marxism, that in a class

---

2 Changchun, Li, "Elaboration on "Decisions on Several Questions about Deepening Cultural System to Promote Development and Prosperity of Socialist Culture" by the CPC Central Committee". People's Daily. October 27, 2011.

society, supra-class human values can only exist in abstract forms and they inevitably yield to the ruling class, that among the actually existing conflicts of various values, only appeals and orientations from the advanced class more or less represent the interests of the majority and will eventually be admitted or recorded by history, that only the appeal for "elimination of classes" by the modern proletariat truly represents the future of man and that the negation of the "class nature" of working class with "humanity" as the essence is, in fact the appeal of the bourgeois class.

The inclination to take "universal values" as the highest principle in the theorization and refinement of core socialist values is undoubtedly the negation on the aforementioned basic tenets of Marxism.

According to the source of epistemology, the above mentioned inclination is an inevitable misjudgment due to boiling truthfulness down to value and also negating objective truth with the truth of value. Value is one of the multiple characteristics of truth rather than the fundamental one or the only one. The fundamental characteristic of truth is objective universality that cannot be changed based on people's subjective will and subjective cognition. Akin to the unceasing attempts to replace "dialectical materialism and historical materialism" with "practical materialism" in recent years, there is also an unceasing attempt to replace "objective truth" with "truth of value" and the crux behind all these attempts, is their world outlook and view of history that negate materialism.

Founders of Marxism has repeatedly pointed out that the existence of the world is not because of its "unity" or "thinking" but its "objective reality", namely "materiality". Similarly, the fundamental characteristic of truth, the correct reflection and grasp of the objective world, is none other than "objective universality". Today, at a time when international capitalism is still in a powerful position and promotes hegemonism, neocolonialism, etc., talking about "mankind's interests are superior than class interests of the proletariat" and that "universal values are superior than socialist values" is not only daydreaming, but a hostile intention to help a tyrant to victimize his subjects.

From the standpoint of countering ideological infiltration, it is the new tendency of the West's strategy of "Westernizing" and "dividing' China to break through core values so as to overthrow Marxism and subvert the mainstream ideology of socialism. The overflow of abstract "universal values" (based on the abstract theory of human nature) is premised on the "deconstruction" of Marxist theory of "class struggle". Hence, we are currently faced a daunting challenge: is Marxist theory of class struggle a basic tenet of Marxism? Should we hold on to it and develop it? How should we understand this basic tenet of Marxism?

For this point, Lenin particularly pointed out that "we should call ourselves Communists as Marx and Engels did. We should affirm that we are Marxists, based on The Communist Manifesto."[3]

Then, what basis the Manifesto offers us to determine this basic tenet of Marxism? As, Engels stated in the preface of the German version in 1883, "The basic thought running through the Manifesto — that economic production, and the structure of society of every historical epoch necessarily arising there from, constitute the foundation for the political and intellectual history of that epoch; that consequently (ever since the dissolution of the primeval communal ownership of land) all history has been a history of class struggles, of struggles between exploited and exploiting, between dominated and dominating classes at various stages of social evolution; that this struggle, however, has now reached a stage where the exploited and oppressed class (the proletariat) can no longer emancipate itself from the class which exploits and oppresses it (the bourgeoisie), without at the same time forever freeing the whole of society from exploitation, oppression, class struggles—this basic thought belongs solely and exclusively to Marx." Also, Marx and Engels always emphasized that "the application of those tenets, as laid out in the Manifesto, can be changed based on the then historical conditions in any place at any time in the future."[4]

This summary of the basic thoughts above clearly demonstrates the essence of the materialist conception of history, namely, the mode of economic production as historical basis, class struggle as historical cardinal line, and dictatorship of the proletariat as the historical direction, thus completing the objective historical laws of the development of human society since the disintegration of primitive society. Our task is to creatively apply it to the historical conditions of contemporary China.

Based on the current situations, apart from the seemingly small disagreement over the basic theory of mode of economic production as the basis, there are open disagreements over the other above two basic principles or theories. Since socialist countries have made the mistake of magnifying class struggle, the status of class struggle as the historical cardinal line should inevitably be the first to be negated. It has become a fashion that some people argue that class struggle is no longer the principal contradiction in China and tend to generalize that class struggle has never been the principal contradiction in the development of human society and then by deviating from this cardinal line, they go and "rewrite history". Hence, we should make a scientific elaboration on the class struggle theory of Marxism.

---

3 Complete Works of Vladimir Lenin. Volume XXIX. People's Publishing House, 1985, p. 192.
4 Selected Works of Marx and Engels. Volume I. People's Publishing House, 1995, p. 238.

Today, the class struggle theory of Marxism can be elaborated in three aspects.

In terms of narration of history, it is the basic method and fundamental discourse for us to analyze the recorded written history

If we can say materialist conception of history has opened the course of and has initiated the course of scientific study of history, the theory of class struggle is the beacon light of this course. As Lenin pointed out, "the striving of some of its member's conflict with the strivings of others, that social life is full of contradictions, and that history reveals a struggle between nations and societies, as well as within nations and societies, and, besides, an alternation of periods of revolution and reaction, peace and war, stagnation and rapid progress or decline. Marxism has provided the guidance—i.e., the theory of the class struggle—for the discovery of the laws governing this seeming maze and chaos."[5]

Since the written history of all hitherto existing society is all about the history of class struggles so far history is all about class societies, the narration of history must be based on social-economic formations, with class struggle being its cardinal line, which cannot be fundamentally negated with the excuse of some parochial and contingent cases.

Marxist theory of class struggle should be applied differently inside and outside contemporary Chinese society

If we evaluate the situation of contemporary mainland China, class struggle is no longer the principal contradiction, but class struggle will exist for a long time, although limited within certain spheres. If ill managed, it may intensify again. Considering the overall structure of the contemporary world, what decides the direction of history is not the so-called "clash of civilizations" or "common global issues", but the struggle between socialist path and capitalist path, between socialist system and capitalist system. Such a struggle decides the fate of the contemporary people and their way out and this contradiction remains the principal contradiction of the contemporary world. We can almost be certain that Western capitalism will be caught in economic and social crises for a long time, reflecting the increasing parasitic and moribund nature of contemporary capitalism and the accumulation of risks and invasiveness. Marxist judgment on the nature of imperialism is still our sharp weapon to observe the changes in the contemporary world.

We must stick to and enrich the theoretical system of socialism with Chinese characteristics when applying it into China

As the second historical leap of localization of Marxism in China, theoretical system of socialism with Chinese characteristics applies the basic

---

5 Selected Works of Lenin. Volume II. People's Publishing House, 1995, p. 423.

tenets of Marxism and creatively answers a series of major questions, such as how to free China, a large developing country with a population of more than one billion, from poverty, how to speed up it its modernization, and how to strengthen and develop socialism. It is a correct theory that guides the Party and the people to march along the path of socialism with Chinese characteristics and to continuously consolidate, to reform and to improve the basic system of socialism with Chinese characteristics. The actual application of Marxist theory of class struggle is shown in the following aspects:

Firstly, based on the fact that exploiting class no longer exists in China, the theoretical system of socialism with Chinese characteristics does nothing but strengthen the leading position and class consciousness of the working class while the wording like "exploiting class", "exploitation" and "oppression" are avoided.

Secondly, based on the fact that class struggle is no longer the principal contradiction of China, while making concrete analysis of the concrete contradictions, focusing on resolving contradictions among the people and being careful not to raise theses contradictions among the people to the level of "class struggle" are being emphasized, I think, the Marxist method of class analysis must not be abandoned in the analysis of major social contradictions, such as when combating against corruption and the building of a clean government.

Thirdly, based on the general situation of adhering to and advancing socialism with Chinese characteristics, with firm grasp of the political direction of socialist modernization, we must unswervingly prevent polarization, strive for common prosperity, continuously practice the nature of socialism and present the superiority of socialist system while promoting reform and opening up, continue to allow some people to get rich first, but we should not ignore the critics like the following : "there is a big gap between the wealthy and the poor" and "there are unfair distribution phenomenon like 'polarization' and 'class polarization'".

To sum up, when theorizing the socialist core values—with Marxism as the guidance—the following should be our cardinal principles: a) take fundamental values of socialism as the key attribute, b) full inheritance of the excellent Chinese cultural traditions, c) continue to absorb the world's moral and cultural resources on the basis of refining integration.

II. Lack of consensus on core values also shows major disagreement over the social functions and modes of influence of core values

At first glance, we all acknowledge that the function of core values lies in building consensus and raising public spirits. However, with a closer look, we will find that the behavioral agent of the regulation could either be the country or the citizens and the narration differs when emphasis is placed differently. The reason why we lack consensus on the theorization of core values is that many theorizations are based on individual citizens instead of the country, which makes it difficult to agree on whether "patriotism" and "integrity" should be included among the core socialist values.

In effect, core values can be theorized as "institutional spirit", the soul based on which a state institution and a state operation mode are established, expanded and sustained. Thus they are also the ideology of a country and the core of state's "soft power". Core values have three major functions.

Core values have three major functions:

Firstly, core values lay a moral foundation for the state institutions, form the basis for its legitimacy and thus determine the national image. Hence, arguments over the core values is first of all, an argument over the commanding heights the two: who will hold the commanding heights in history and morality. While exposing the class nature and historical limitations of freedom, democracy and human rights of the West, Marxism successfully seizes the moral commanding height of contemporary human civilization.

Core values provide basic thinking for the establishment of corresponding state institutions and determine the basic direction for their reform and adjustment. Core values seem to be abstract universal discourse that has nothing to do with concrete institutional construction. In fact, this is not the case. As the expression of ideas of a certain social-economic formation, core values adopt universal discourse, but they have obvious interest orientation. Therefore, argument over core values is fundamentally one over power struggle regarding institutional construction.

Thirdly, core values determine the leading values of the relevant society and the mainstream will of the people under certain historical conditions. The ruling class transforms their ideas into ruling ideas through the influence and effect of core values. When people see the core values that belong to a certain class and certain social form as "universal values", the ideas of the ruling class become widely, generally accepted ruling ideas of the society. Such a hidden value consensus become people's daily life criteria, based on which they cultivate their lifestyle, and determine people's internal scale for good and evil, right and wrong, and beauty and ugliness, and influence the mainstream will of the people, greatly. Hence, the argument over core values is one over dominant power of ideas. Without core values, we will not able to guide different social trends of thoughts in the society.

It can be easily concluded that, obviously core values regulate citizens' behaviors by forming social cohesion and consensus. But the formation of this consensus, after all, comes from identification with the state, in the final analysis it comes from the state system and citizens' identification with the spirit of the state. Therefore, proper successful core values, do not directly pose requirements regarding the civilians, but receive identification form the civilians by shaping the spirit of the state and emphasize the spirit of the system, state to obtain identification, in this way individual civilians can regulate their own behaviors consciously.

There are other two points that we should pay attention to: Firstly, which one is the primary and which one is the secondary, and the issue of relations between the two: state and civil society. The spirit of the state determines the spirit of citizenship, a kind of state, gives you a kind of citizens. The formation of the spirit of state precedes the spirit of citizenship. Only after successful internalizing the spirit of the state, can the citizens of a civil society become "citizens". This is what Hegel called "state is the internal purpose of civil society."

Secondly, second question is which one is conscious will and which one is the passive will (obedience). Only when a state represents and organically represents the integral interests of an individual, so that the citizens feel that there is an internal unity between the interests of the state and their individual interests, under these conditions the state's will can become the will of the individual citizens.

In turn, there are two ways in which civilians obtain identification with the state: First way, the conscious identification is based on the recognition of sameness between interests and goals. And the second way is the passive obedience which is the result of great pressure from political and economic thoughts.

It is beyond doubt that socialist core values should reflect the following ideological characteristics that: state's interests and purpose are consistent with the interests and purpose of the citizens. Thus the spirit of the state can be with conscious will is turned into citizens' inner moral principles.

Based on the above explanations and based on the above requirements, I can say that: the theorization or refinement of core socialist values should reflect the fundamental properties of our socialist system in China: a) the nature of the state: the people's democratic dictatorship led by the working class and based on the worker-peasant alliance.

Consequently, we can reach the following:

a) "priority of labor" and "honor of labor" that reflect labor's and laboring people's lofty status in the national life;

b) "supremacy of people" and "serve the people" that reflect the people being the masters of the state (country);

c) "common prosperity", "fairness and justice" and "harmonious development" that reflect the superiority of socialist system, etc. these are certainly, all the essence of national spirit of China.

Only by regulating national behaviors and manifesting our national spirit in this way, can China have a sound international image and an increasingly strong international influence be established and widely recognized by the people so as to form sound social mood and moral spirit. Only on this basis, can the core socialist values of China, be established as the core of China's soft power, in the world arena.

Therefore, I can argue for another view, when theorizing socialist core values: we should construct and demonstrate the national "institutional spirit" as the keynote task, while at the same time regulate the operation of the state power and institutional construction, in this way we must continue to regulate civilians' social behaviors and promote sound social spirit and atmosphere and formation of morality.

III. Lack of consensus on core values, demonstrates that there are major disagreements over the ways in forming and nurturing core values

What is our basis in the theorization of core values? Core values as the fruit of spiritual civilization are believed to originate from life and play a guiding and normative role in reality. But there is disagreement over whether their basis is "the current time" or "the future". The two opinions evidently stand opposite to each other.

The former view emphasizes that core values are rooted in current life, which requires that refinement of core values should be made starting from the actual needs of the current stage and possibility of current reality. The latter view highlights that core values, especially the core socialist values, that can play a guiding role in establishing healthy life style and new social fashion, which means that refinement of the core socialist values should start from aiming to change the world and transcend beyond the current status.

If we look from a deeper level, this disagreement of views also involves the question of the role of consciousness in the formation of core values.

The former view in fact, believes that core values are formed spontaneously, thus core values and lifestyle are naturally formed in the society, which is a lengthy historical process.

The latter view holds that socialist core values can only be established consciously and they rely on the advanced social forces in the society, spiritual crystallization of advanced theories, thoughts (ideology) thus they can play a significant guiding role in real life.

To have a correct judgment on these two different opinions, we must further observe the properties of core values.

In the final analysis, core values are moral and spiritual forces whose formation and development are subordinate to the law of spiritual development. Looking from the standpoint of Marxism, the laws of spiritual development are in the final analysis determined by the basic contradictions of the society, and in a class society, the law of spiritual development always fits the consumption needs of the people, and in the final analysis, serves the rule needs of the ruling class.

Therefore, we can say culture arises spontaneously in daily life. However, such spontaneity is always dominated by the ruling class which has the dominant social power in the society, and this means that it is the dominance of the consciousness of the ruling class. Therefore, spontaneity is equivalent to the domination of the ruling class.

More importantly, the bourgeoisie uses its dominance in the commodity production process, in such a way that the spontaneity in the commodity production and cultural manipulation by the bourgeoisie is closely integrated, thus we can say that spontaneous bourgeois ideology and cultural hegemony are synonymous. Consequently, the worship of spontaneity, becomes an important means for the bourgeoisie to carry out its ideological rule.

The reason why I emphasize cultural consciousness is that—the relation with the past and current time—if we fail to break the ideological cage of the bourgeoisie, from the past revolution, we must strip away all superstition of the past, in the current time, we will be unable to resist the cultural infiltration of the West, and the Western strategy to push us towards capitalism, with peaceful evolution.

For, advanced cultural consciousness, most fundamental factor is the working class party and its advanced theories leading the cultural and spiritual construction. Lenin wrote: This shows that all worship of the spontaneity of the working class movement, all belittling of the role of "the conscious element", of the role of Social-Democracy (communist movement), means, quite independently of whether he who belittles that role desires it or not, a strengthening of the influence of bourgeois ideology upon the workers.6

Consciousness should be instilled into the entire process of socialist cultural construction, of course including the refinement of core values.

To peel one more layer off it, socialism is a new thing whose value and life are not "accumulated" on existing things but shown by constantly expanding its future development. Therefore, the fundamental characteristics of scientific socialist world outlook is not to "interpret the world" but "change the world", it teaches not to yield to the reality but change the existing state.

As Marx pointed out: "The social revolution of the nineteenth century cannot take its poetry from the past but only from the future. It cannot begin with itself before it has stripped away all superstition about the past."[7]

On the contrary, although Western capitalism is still in a strong position and by the virtue of its strong position in economic and social development, it has an advantageous for its cultural expansion, but also as Marx has long ago predicted, the strength of Western capitalism is in "the past and current status quo" not in "reality (Wirklichkeit) and future."

As to its cultural hegemony, Western capitalism—due to its nature—fails to occupy the commanding height of cultural development or fails to guide the trend and future of cultural development, it can only rely on some formal cultural branches such as entertainment, commodity and spontaneity, etc, and its "innovation" is restricted to form, rather than true content.

It is only Marxism that reveals the human needs and law of human development, at the same time unveils the laws of social and historical development, it is only Marxism that stands on the historical height of contemporary human's cultural development, thus only Marxism can truly grasp the inherent requirements and objective trends of cultural development.

"Facing the world and facing the future" are the inexhaustible motive force, for the development of socialist advanced culture, at the same time the irresistible power of socialist core values.

In the final analysis, the essence of the disagreement over whether socialist core values should focus starting from the future and nurturing consciousness is in fact the disagreement over the Marxist truth: the law of history that capitalism will eventually and necessarily be replaced by communism, which the proponents of "one side" does not admit.

---

6 Lenin, Selected Works, Volume II. People's Publishing House, 1995, p. 235.
7 Marx and Engels. Selected Works, Volume I. People's Publishing House, 1995.

Since the collapse of the Soviet Union and great changes in Eastern Europe in the early 1990s, there has been an almost prevalent mindset in the West: whether or not you like capitalism, people must accept it.

According to this view: no matter how many ideological trends are competing and struggling with each other, when challenging the reality, they will never be able to exceed the system of liberal democracy. That is to say, you can criticize liberal democracy but you will be never be able to replace it.

You cannot transcend beyond capitalism, this is the mood in the ideological sphere of the West and which even the left-wing scholars—in this certain epoch of time—cannot get rid of.

When the Western style liberal democracy, and its advertisement of freedom, democracy, human rights democracy, they altogether propagated, human society has reached an insurmountable "historical end", fundamentally they have altogether canceled the future history, because they have regarded capitalism as the absolute combination of ideal and reality.

Hence, the disagreement over whether we should start from ideal and the future on the one side, or we should start from reality and from the current struggle on the other side, is in fact the disagreement over two different development blueprints in China and the disagreement over two kinds of paths for China's social development.

The view that emphasizes that the theorization and refinement of the core socialist values should "respect" the existing reality, is probably quite obsessed with British and American capitalism and lacks confidence in communism. Therefore, currently the following questions stand sharply before us: isn't the path leading to communism, revealed by Marxism the only road to history?, namely, proceed forward under the leadership of the working class and its party, to eliminate private ownership and classes, and achieve that the people masters their own destinies and achieve that they can realize free, comprehensive and all-sided development. In the middle of 21st century, we aim to reach a higher status, wherein modernization and the great rejuvenation of the Chinese nation will be achieved, here arises another question: whether this achievement will be a solid foundation for communism or whether this achievement will become a bourgeoisie "Enlightenment value" founded on contemporary capitalist society?

These are the theoretical focus points, when we discuss on the core values of contemporary China, but also the question "where China should go" under new circumstances. The cultivation and promotion of core socialist values should vigorously promote China to successfully marching unswervingly along the path of socialism with Chinese characteristics.

We can obviously conclude that the refinement of the core socialist values is not only the "spirit" of socialism with Chinese characteristics, offering the basis for the communist morality, such as the communist "Leifeng spirit" and the basis for essence of socialism, such as the "achieving common prosperity" in current stage of development in China, but at the same time, the refinement of the core socialist values also differentiates socialist modernization from capitalist modernization, so that it can organically combine socialism with Chinese characteristics with the long-term goal of communism, thus the refinement of the core socialist values, is a strategy that will carry us towards our grand cause.

Because of this, a consensus cannot be easily achieved on such an important issue. We should take the theorization of the core socialist values as the starting point, when carrying out an in-depth education on the lofty ideal of communism and the common cause of socialism with Chinese characteristics. Thus we can expect that, we will be able to reach a genuine consensus on the refinement of the core socialist values, when we can make great headways in cultivating communist ideals and beliefs.

Y. 36

Grasp the Hypocritical Nature of "Universal Values" and Refine Socialist Core Values

Li Zongfang[1]

Abstract: From both historical and realistic aspects, this paper generalizes and criticizes the so-called "universal values", demonstrates its bourgeois attributes, exposes the real purpose of advertising "universal values" by US-led Western countries, and reveals the truth that socialism will eventually replace capitalism. The article discusses the significance of criticizing "universal values", and ideas to strengthen core socialist values. As viewed from China's international environment, and the debate on the issue of values is not only a purely academic dispute, but a struggle for the power of discourse in the field of ideology among different classes and different types of countries. Therefore, we must deeply understand the significance of adhering to core socialist values, since it is a discourse power struggle in the sphere of value system.

Key words: critiques, "universal values", core socialist values

---
1 Li Zongfang, Guest Researcher in the World Socialism Research Center attached to CASS, Doctoral Student in the branch of Marxism Study in the Graduate School of CASS.

Recent years has witnessed a wide repercussion aroused by the dispute on "universal values". Those who are dissatisfied with the existing system of China, attempt to make an issue of the topic and promote bourgeois liberalization, have hyped the slogan of "universal values". The article aims to offer people a clear view of the hypocritical nature of "universal values" by analyzing the concept and shedding light on the history of capitalism and capitalism in real life, so as to contribute to the refinement of core socialist values and firmly strengthen the faith in socialism with Chinese characteristics.

I. Analysis on several different versions of "universal values"

The "democracy, freedom, equality, fraternity and human rights" as the pursuits of humankind's "universal values"

Owing to the Western countries' all-out efforts in advertising, the concept of "democracy" has become a panacea in contemporary society. In effect, "democracy" is but a form of power relationship, namely, power belongs to "all the people" or "the majority", different from the power controlled by "one person" (as in monarchy) and "a few people" (as in aristocracy, oligarchy or elite system).

Throughout history, the progressiveness of "democracy" as the political demand of the bourgeoisie is widely acknowledged. However, there are several obstacles to the attempt of equaling the progressiveness of the specific historical period to the universally applicable "universal values". Based on the theoretical analysis of pure political science, so far there is no definite answer to whether the "democracy" is excellent among other forms of power relationships.

In the Chinese context, there is not a clear definition of "freedom" as a Western bourgeois value. According to the Qin Hui's explanation in Idyll and Symphony: Rethinking Guanzhong Mode and Pre-modern Society Mode, "freedom" in the Western context is opposite to "dependence on the (feudal lord)" which includes two meanings: divorce from restriction of feudal lord and secondly loss of protection from feudal lord (second aspect referred by Rousseau as "men are forced to freedom").

In the Chinese context, freedom is laissez-faire (that is, the first meaning) there is no second meaning in Chinese context. Hence, talking about "freedom" in a sweeping manner will result in confusion of concepts and the discussion will lose its meaning. "Freedom" is meaningful only when it is discussed in relation with subjects, or else the discussion will be an empty talk.

Currently, some Chinese advocate the bourgeois "freedom" without seeing the danger that is accompanied by such "freedom". They are confused by the Western subversive forces and tend to believe that once China implements the liberal capitalist economy, separation of three powers in the political system and the so-called freedom of speech, all the problems will be readily solved. However, even in their birthplace, those so-called "universal values" do not enjoy peace and prosperity and problems caused by erroneous economic policies can be found everywhere.

The recent economic crisis in the West—to a great extent—is caused by over exaggeration liberalism in the economic sphere and greed of magnate financial capitalists.

The view that common interests of all the mankind kind generates the "universal" value consciousness

The above view, advocates that due to commonality of interests, of all the mankind, the solution to problems can be resolved by relying ourselves on the criteria of "universal values". We can clearly see that, the advocates of "universal values" have never put problems faced by the whole mankind kind as the top-priority but have sacrificed weak countries for their particular gains.

On the United Nations Climate Change Conference in Copenhagen held in 2009, Western countries overlooked the demands and interests of smaller countries, which has induced strong criticism. Some people have compared the increasing serious environmental problem faced by the humankind to "a sinking ship where sea water floods the passenger cabin for the small countries and the Western countries sitting on the deck of the ship and do not feel concerned for others. "

In fact, with the rise of sea level, some small island countries in the Pacific ocean, face the danger of being flooded in the next few years. However, the major industrialized countries like the U.S. still keep their habits of high consumption, high energy consumption and high pollution, constantly emitting greenhouse and carbon dioxide gases, and they continue to be the prime culprit of environmental and climate problems.[2]

This fully demonstrates that the so-called "universal values" are not shared by the whole humankind or serve the all humankind, instead, this only demonstrates that the "universal values" is an advertising tool with which some countries use for their particular interests.

Traditional Confucianism and Confucian ethics proposed as the common pursuit of whole humankind This proposition advocates that the value

---

2 International Division of China Energy News. Copenhagen on the Journey. China Environment and Science Publishing House, 2010.

norms of traditional Confucianism and Confucian ethics have "universality". This erroneous understanding is mainly caused by the popularity of "Sinology" and "Neo-Confucianism" around the world. Thus some people desire to advertise "universal values" together with traditional Chinese moral and ethical norms, in an epoch when national sentiments are high across the country.

However, mechanically fitting Western "universal values" into traditional Chinese morals and ethics will bring reverse effect. For instance, it is an obvious mistake to literally translate "Ren, Yi, Li, Zhi and Xin" in the Confucianism into "fraternity, integrity, civility, reason and integrity" found in the Western bourgeois values, because Confucianism fundamentally serve the rule of feudal emperors and thus has distinct class nature.

"Ren" in Confucianism refers to "benevolent love", whereas, "Yi" refers to "serve the country with supreme loyalty" and "Li" refers to "rites throughout all states" and all these values are closely related with the feudal rule , which is different from the anti-feudal slogans of "freedom, equality and fraternity" proposed by the bourgeoisie.

Besides, "Zhi" in Confucianism is quite different from the "reason" in West behind which lies the tradition of scientism in the Western context and also "Xin" in Confucianism does not fit and completely different from the Western concept of "integrity" behind which hides the modern spirit of contract in the Western context.

Therefore, no matter how contemporary people re-interpret Confucianism or other traditional values, they cannot become fellows of Western bourgeois values, let alone undertaking the heavy task of being the "universal values" for the whole humankind. 4. Among the advocates of "universal values" the most deceptive approach is that which regards the universal law revealed by Marxism as "universal values" and argues that Marxism is a "universal value".

The main reason why this opinion can attract popularity is that the majority, including those who are ideologically identify themselves with Marxism and socialism, lack scientific understanding of Marxism.

They believe it would be a good thing to raise Marxism to the height of "universal values" that guide the whole humankind in its struggles, without realizing that it is but a trap set by the Western capitalist forces that are making use of them.

If the opinion that, Marxism is a "universal value" is accepted, then the very concept of "universal values" itself, will be justified, and openly enter the room. And, when this mistaken opinion, wins two wings , it will easily kick away Marxism and serve for the bourgeois liberalism. By then, it will be only more difficult to negate and reject: Marxism is a "universal value".

In fact, that is an erroneous understanding to equal Marxism with "universal values" which represents bourgeois interests, because Marxism is a scientific truth that surpasses the so-called "value debate" or "controversy on morals".

In fact, Marxism—in a theoretical sense—is a universal truth and—in a practical sense—the ideological guide of proletarian struggle, it is the organic unity of the both aspects.

How will Marxism which leads proletariat's revolutionary struggle become a "universal value" and be accepted by the bourgeoisie, although it aims to put an end to capitalist system?

Marx had never regarded his doctrine as the only truth that is applicable to all classes, but clearly stated that they are the theoretical weapon of the proletariat to fight against the bourgeoisie.

On April 8, 2011, U.S. Department of State submitted to the Congress the Country Reports on Human Rights Practices of 2010, which was the 35th annual report on human rights. In the section about China, the Report has distorted a lot of facts and made irresponsible remarks on human rights in China.[3]

In this US report which covers more than 190 countries, also criticized the human rights situation in many of these countries. In order to restore the facts and reveal the hideous purpose of the US based report, the State Council Information Office of China struck back with Report on the U.S. Human Rights Record for 2010, which exposed the human rights problems of the US to the world.[4]

In this China based report, the human rights problems were classified in six categories. Firstly, there are serious violent crimes and crime rate stays at a very high level in the US. About one fifth of the population fall victim to crimes every year and this ratio (%20) ranks the first in the world. In 2009, US citizens above the age of 12 became targets of 4.3 million violent crimes, 15.6 million property related crimes and 133,000 personal theft crimes, with a crime rate of 17.1 every thousand persons.

In the US use of guns run rampant due to slack control. About 90 million people out of the total population of 300 million possess 200 million guns, leading to a high ratio of shooting and murder crimes. Statistics have reveled that there occur approximately 12,000 shooting cases every year.

---

3 Country Report on Human Rights Practices of 2010, China (including Tibet, Hong Kong and Macau).
4 State Council Information Office of China. Report on the U.S. Human Rights Record of 2010. Xinhua News Agency. April 10, 2010.

Secondly, civil and political rights are seriously deprived in the US. Under, the pretext of anti-terrorism, citizens' privacy is infringed as a usual practice. And the police forces quite frequently use torture and use it to get a statement from a suspect.

The number of prisoners in the US tops the world, with one out of every one hundred adults serving a prison sentence. There are unjust and misjudged cases are quite frequent.

In the past 20 years, charges on 266 suspects were acquitted after DNA identification, including 17 sentences of death penalty. Politics is highly related with money,(money politics) funds raised during election constantly reach new heights and political bribery is a usual occurrence. Besides, strict control of Internet communication infringes citizens' freedom of speech.

Thirdly, due to deterioration of the US economy, people's living standards have fallen to a worrisome degree. Unemployment rate stays at a high level, with 9.8%, that is, 15 million people, were registered as unemployed in November 2010. Poverty-stricken population has increased to a record high of 14.3%, the highest since 1994, amounts to 44 million people at the end of 2009.

The number of people suffering from hunger is increasing. 2009 witnessed 14.7% of the families facing food shortage, a 30% increase compared to 2006. There is also a surge in the number of the homeless people. In the financial year 2008 to 2009, the number of homeless families increased by 7%, adding up to 170,129.

The number of people without medical insurance has increased progressively every year. In 2009, the figure has increased from 46.3 million in 2008 to 50.7 million and amounts to 16.7% of the population, which presents an increase for nine consecutive years.

Fourthly, racial problems are prominent. Ethnic minorities do not enjoy equal political status as the white Americans and ethnic minorities are discriminated both employment and assess to occupation.

The black Americans are unfairly treated or discriminated in promotion, welfare, position, etc. Ethnic minorities suffer from high unemployment rate and their poverty rate remains at a high level. They are also apparently unequal in education opportunities. The health situation of black Americans is worrisome. Racial discrimination is obvious in law enforcement and before judiciary. Crimes caused by racial hatred happen frequently. And the rights of immigrants living in the USA, are not properly protected.

Fifthly, human rights situation of women and children are particularly serious. There is a wide spread of sex discrimination. Women often fall victim to sexual assault, mobbing and violence and the occurrence rate of domestic violence is increasing each year. There is no sufficient protection for women's health rights and interests. Children live in poverty and suffer from severe violence. Their physical and psychological health is not well protected.

Sixthly, the US' record in the field of international human rights is quite bad. The Iraq War and War in Afghanistan, initiated and launched by the U.S., has led to a large number of civilian casualties. From March 2003 to the end of 2009, during the Iraq War 285,000 people were injured and killed, at least 109,000 people were dead, 63% of which were civilians. In 2009, during the War in Afghanistan, 535 civilians were injured and killed, with 113 of them shot to death, a 43% increase compared to 2008. Many scandals of maltreating and abusing the prisoners were revealed during the war against terrorism. USA, severely infringes Cuban people's rights to survive and develop. The US refused to ratify some important international human rights conventions or rejects to fulfill its international obligations.

II. Expose the bourgeois attribute of "universal values" and recognize the objective historical truth that socialism will inevitably replace capitalism.

Socialism will inevitably prevail over capitalism, due the basic contradiction of capitalism, between capitalist private ownership and socialization of production. Driven by interests, dispersive and fragmented production units tend to centralize resources in a few fields, which not only results in unfair social distribution, but makes the rich become richer and the poor become poorer, but significantly waste the social resources, due to irrational duplicate investments.

However, owing to its systematic and scientific planning, socialist production can promote the optimal allocation of resources among various departments of the national economy and effectively leads the production activities, enabling the healthy development of the economy on the whole.

Scientific planning, can also minimize the concentration of wealth in the society,so that Gini coefficient remains at a reasonable level.

As to the problems brought by capitalism, Engels once pointed out: "industry can lead to national affluence, but it also results in rapid growth of poverty-stricken proletariat who strive to keep body and soul together. The proletariat will never be eliminated, because they will never obtain property."

The private ownership of means of production in capitalism directly leads to the class antagonism between owners of the means of production and the proletariat. The latter includes the working class in the cities where they sell their labor and the capitalists exploit their surplus value as well as the peasants in the rural areas, where they are exploited by the central government, local bureaucrats, landlords, squires and tyrants. The two groups, together with the "social conscience"—the intellectual class, surround the evil capitalist system in the mid-1900s and gradually developed into a mainstream socialist movement across the globe. This movement, with the founding of the Soviet Union and the PRC as the representatives, have thoroughly changed the world and the international political pattern.

Western countries could not tolerate the existence of the Soviet Union. The bourgeoisie knew very well that before capitalism is eventually replaced by capitalism, capitalism would not raise the white flag, but struggle to the end and counterattack against the newborn proletarian country. Hence, they first gave secret support to the reactionary white forces, the remnants of the old Russia, attempting to stop the establishment and development of the Soviet Union with the tool of the civil war.

Later, they have provoked Finland to brazenly invade the Soviet Union; in the end, they lifted all the disguise and stepped onto the front stage and launched the military intervention against the Soviet Union. However, the Soviet people bravely beat off the crazy attacks by the imperialist countries one after another until this conspiracy went bankrupt.

In the mid-1920s, Western countries had no other option but recognize the Soviet Union. Moreover, when economic crisis broke out, European and American countries admired the rapid economic development of the S.U. and went to S.U. to learn from it. They were overwhelmed when they observed there prospering socialism in the Soviet Union, its well organized economy and sound social security system. That was the reason why in the 1930s, there were a lot of people in Western countries who have immigrated to the Soviet Union. By then, the increasingly apparent superiority of socialism has caused sleepless nights for the bourgeoisie.

At that time, the international communist movement was developing strongly up and the birth of the P.R. China and the establishment of communist party led governments in many countries of the Eastern Europe, North Korea, Cuba, Vietnam, etc. which has instilled vitality into the international communist cause. Such surging of the world socialist movement has imposed strong impact on bourgeois governments of the West.

In the United States, a common fear of communism began to spread inside the political parties, which gave rise to the notorious McCarthyism. In the countries like Greece and Turkey, the influence of the forces led by the communist party has increased, while in the countries like the U.K., France and Spain, the communist party, social democratic party and various left wing forces have vigorously carried parliamentary struggles against the right wing forces.

Before World War II, colonies of the U.K., France, Germany and Japan in Asia, Africa and Latin America launched a wave of national independence against colonialism. As a counter movement against the national independence movement, the Korean War and Vietnam War were launched by the U.S and its allies, all ended in failure. The 1960s saw the most acute social conflicts and most severe crisis in the West. In the U.S., people have cast great doubt on the legitimacy of the administration by reflecting on why their country was involved in the Vietnam War. Economic depression and distortion of social morality influenced as well as shaped the values of the whole generation, which was one of the main reasons why President Johnson put forward the "Great Society" programs. In France and other countries in Western Europe, student movements where students wore Che Guevara -red badges, waved quotations from Mao Zedong and appealed for a society with genuine equality, freedom and democracy were unprecedentedly high and intense. Thus, capitalism around the world was trapped bogged in an unprecedented crisis. The US citizens had predicted that communist regimes would spring up in every state and would form a domino effect. If they did not prevent it, capitalist regime would collapse and that capitalism was faced with the threat of elimination across the world. Therefore, after the war, The US citizens built defense corps to prevent communist forces from further spreading.

Since the early 1990s, the collapse of the former Soviet Union and tremendous changes in the Eastern Europe have seriously frustrated the world communist movement and there was a sharp decrease in the numbers, territory, population, economic aggregate, etc. of socialist countries. This temporary low tide once aroused ecstasy among the ideologues of the Western capitalist forces, since they believed that they won the battle against communism and socialism and they have loudly that it was "the end of history". However, historical necessity cannot be changed by the will of a person, a country or a class.

As we have entered the 21st century, rapid economic development of the socialist countries like China and various political and economic crises occurring in the capitalist countries present sufficient ground for the belief that international communist movement, which was once in its low tide will flourish again.[5]

---

5 Yue, Xiao & Liqun Zhu.Concise History of International Relations from 1945 to 2002. World Knowledge Publishing House, 2011.

III. Advocate the core socialist values and resolutely reject the "universal values"

Now that we can prove in terms of scientific principles that "universal values" have never existed both in history or reality, both in capitalist or socialist countries, why do some people still insist on such a delusive concept? Simply to say, those hostile forces at home and abroad aim to change the direction of China's socialist development.

The US hegemonism through cultural infiltration has launched a series of color revolutions, such as the Rose Revolution in Georgia, Orange Revolution in Ukraine, and Yellow Revolution in Kyrgyzstan and recently started the reactionary wave of so-called "liberalization and democratization" in the countries like Egypt, Libya, Syria and Yemen.[6]

During those plots and attempts, they US has always kept an eye on China and vainly attempted to implement the same "peaceful evolution" strategy against the largest socialist country in the world, which can be detected in their full support for the Taiwan, Tibetan and Xinjiang independence separatist forces.

In China, a group bourgeois liberals who were confused by the Western countries seized every opportunity to advocate the concepts like "political parties take turns in government" and "the right to private property" and made use of "universal values" to delude the public (for instance, the Charter 2008 signed by 303 activists was based on the doctrine of "universal values").

They aim has been to prepare the public opinion basis, and lay theoretical preparation for diverting the development path of China. Therefore, we must reinforce our confidence, make a sober judgment and respond calmly against the threats.

We must oppose the confusion of "universal values" with the core values of scientific socialism; we must systematically and comprehensively reveal the hypocritical and abstract nature of "universal values" based on the truth that socialism will inevitably replace capitalism, marching unswervingly along the path of socialism with Chinese characteristics.

We must adhere to and develop Marxism consciously in the practice of building socialism with Chinese characteristics, develop Marxism in practice, practice it during development.

Only in this way can we draw a clear line between the core values that we propose and the Western advocate of "universal values". Clarifying the hypocritical nature of "universal values" is conducive to the refinement of

---

6   Da, Chen.Color Revolutions: Choices made by Central Asia. Lanzhou University Press, 2007.

socialist core values. To establish the socialist core values, we must grasp the three principles, namely, its essence, its close relation to the masses and its loftiness.

Firstly, we must understand the socialist core values as the inevitable path of mankind's historical development, instead of taking them as short-term and utilitarian ideological tools.

Secondly, socialist core values adapt to times and consider the real demands of the people, and be established based on China's excellent culture and traditions.

Thirdly, we should highlight the lofty nature of core socialist values and recognize that communism as an advanced theory, represents the long-term interest and future development direction of the society and men.

If we consider the issue, from China's international environment, the debate on the issue of values is not only a purely academic debate, but a struggle of discourse power in the field of ideology among different classes and different types of countries.

Therefore, we must deeply understand the significance of adhering to socialist core values in this struggle of discourse power. We must incorporate core socialist values into the national education, into the construction of spiritual civilization and the party building undertaking, implement them throughout the reform and opening up and socialist modernization and reflect them in the creation, production and spread of spiritual and cultural products. We should guide social trends of thought with socialist core values, in order to form unified guiding ideology, in order to promote common ideals and beliefs, strong spiritual strength and basic morality and ethics throughout the party and the society.

Y. 37

An In-depth Investigation among Worker Groups of Beijing: Experience and Reflection

Lu Gang[1]

Abstract: Marxists hold that the proletariat is the basic driving force of social transformation. For the hundreds of millions of workers, the poor and difficult factory work and life experience and hard living environment compel them to launch strikes again and again as an instinctive resistance to these conditions. Since the "May workers movements and strikes" in 2010, existing labor conflicts hidden in the industrial field have revealed themselves and have become an important factor of social conflict and unrest. Since the May 4th movement in 1919. Chinese proletariat obviously appeared on the stage of history show their will and power to change the Chinese society. The history of international communist movement indicates that labor movement is not born to be the fellow traveler of socialist cause and its vanguard party. For the Communist Party of China, just from the beginning the power of labor movement has been an important driving force to change the society, but it can also deliver unpredictable risks under certain circumstances, consequently how to win and lead this force for the cause of socialism with Chinese Characteristics is an important historical issue. The campaign of "observing and studying our national conditions" initiated by the CASS leadership for the CASS Graduate School students gave an opportunity for Marxists to go among the worker groups and make further investigations. .

Key words: building socialism with Chinese characteristics; labor movement; Communist Party of China; investigating national conditions

---
[1] Lu Gang. Guest Researcher at World Socialism Research Center attached to Chinese Academy of Social Sciences; Doctoral Student of Marxism Study at the Graduate School of CASS.

During the last year, the Chinese Academy of Social Sciences has initiated the campaign of "Concentrate on the Grass roots, Alter the Style of Work, Change the Style of Writing" which included going into the masses and making investigations among them to better learn the real conditions of the people and country, which has achieved significant fruits. As a grade 2011 doctoral student studying Marxism at the Graduate School of CASS, I came up with the idea of making investigations among the worker groups. Also, being one of the leaders of the Society of Seeking the Truth at the Graduate School, a student organization which focuses on the study of Marxism, I do not only read the classics of Marxism-Leninism, but actively participate in social practices. Consequently, I chose to be a day laborer in the Beijing Economic and Technological Development Area-Yizhuangi for one day, with the intention to explore the practicability of organizing students for day labor and permanent work during the school holidays so that we could develop in-depth understanding of the working class and acquire first-hand materials useful for our investigation. In the history of socialism, carrying out investigations by directly observing the workers' factory life have produced a large number of literature with academic value such as The Condition of the Working Class in England by Engels and The Condition of the Working Class in Russia by L. I. Ostrover and others.

In order to get a day work in a factory, laborers need to apply submit to a professional employment agent company and have to gather in front of the company door at 6 a.m. Hence, I went to Yizhuang the day before and stayed in a simple and low-budget hotel for 20 yuan a night, and early in the morning through an agent I got a job in a printing factory and worked for a day.

The day's labor made me exposed to the harsh living conditions of the workers – their long working hours, intensive work, poor environment and low income.

I worked from 8am to 8pm, with less than two hours for lunch and supper. There was no overtime wage for day laborers but only several yuan per hour for overtime for the permanent workers. Working in the factory, I realized that workers eat to work and in order to better cooperate with the machines. My job during the day was sorting out the semi-finished products that came out of the folding machine. The work was simple but it was extremely intensive. The daily workload of a folding machine is 48,000 revolves, each revolve with one semi-finished product. That is to say, I sorted out 48,000 semi-finished products a day. Worse still, I had to work standing on my feet, without a slim chance to sit down. As a result, I could not feel my legs in the afternoon. The working environment was like the salt on the wound. The workshop was full with folding machines and overwhelming noise came along when they were on. Despite the warning of "Wear Ear

Protectors" on the wall, most of the workers did not wear protectors and just only a few wore earplugs. You cannot imagine how harmful it is to work under those conditions for a long time.

Then, what is their payment? Through chats with the workers during the meal time, I learned that the monthly salary of a common permanent male worker is 3,000 yuan, with 12 hours a day, meager overtime wage and less than 2 days off per each month. It was worse with day laborers. Their daily wage is 120 yuan, 50 yuan of which is commission fee for the employment agent. Hence, they are actually paid 70 yuan for a day. To me, I had only 50 yuan left because I had to spend 20 yuan on the accommodation for the night before. Many people worked as day laborers in Yizhuang during weekends, but not all of them stay in a hotel like me. Some young people chose to save 10 yuan by staying overnight in a net bar at a cost of 10 yuan.

I met a 22-year-old girl coming from a village in Hebei, who worked in an electronics factory for a monthly salary of 2,000 yuan. After paying 300 yuan for house rent, plus other daily expenses, she almost had no money left. In order to pay her brother's tuition fee, she had to work as day laborer for two days for 140 yuan, but most girl students like us cannot cover the cost of a dress with this money. However, it was a good sum for her family. Moreover, day laborers do not sign official labor contracts with the employers, so if any accidents happen, they have to bear the consequences on their own. In spite that the agents got 50 yuan fee, they take no responsibility for the day laborers.

The day's labor made me exposed to the workers' discontent and even anger towards social injustice.

The workers I met complained to each other about low wages and bad treatment, they seemed somewhat hopeless for themselves and their families, and worked by counting the day. They also complained that the boss of the factory was ruthless and the foreman worker was mean to the workers and even sometimes beat and scolded them. Stories about workers who got injured in the factory but was not compensated was openly talked among them, which intensified their unrest about future and anger against the boss. They are clear that they are in the lowest rung of the social ladder and that most of the people associate them with the rascal yellow-hair hooligans, shameless prostitutes and high crime rate, but they feel they can do nothing about it.

The aforementioned girl envied that I am a student and she proudly told me that she is going to send her brother to university. She said, "Well-educated people like you tend to look down on us poor people, but my brother won't." Those words made me—a so-called well-educated person—ashamed.

In his book Korean Workers, Hagen Koo, a Korean American scholar, described a similar story where a factory female worker who sponsored her brother for education wrote to her mother, "I would also like Siki to receive good education and wear the square academic cap and school badge, on his school uniform. But recently I began to think: maybe college education does not grant the prospect of being a wholesome person. During my eight years away from home. I have seen many cases where the educated look down on the poor and bullied others with the college education they have received." Hagen Koo commented that the story shows that "the girl has seen clearly the ideological fallacy in the mainstream education ideology and felt the social injustice."[2]

The day's labor has improved my understanding on of some the tenets of Marxism in practice

Marx mentioned in Capital that under the conditions of massive industrial production, worker, technology, knowledge and labor will be unceasingly separated.[3]

The only chance for workers to have a rest during the work hours is when the machines break down. Once they break down, the foreman will arrange a repairmen, which allows the worker a short break. Short as it is, it is precious for the extremely tired workers. Hence, they often hope that the machines break down and even wish to learn some tricks to make them break down. Such mentality enables me to better understand the Luddite Movement where workers have destroyed the machines in England in the 19th century.

Of course, the introduction of the machines, a modern means of production, represents the progress of human productive forces. However, based on my experience in the factory, I have realized that the more advanced a folding machine can operate more than 48,000 revolves and the chance of it breaking down is slimmer. While it represents the glorious achievement of humans' master of science and technology, it brings longer work hours and more intensive work for the ordinary workers in the printing factory.

The experience has led me to deeper thinking: how Marxists deal with their relations with giant worker groups in modern China.

---

2 Hagen Koo.Korean Workers. Translated by Guangyan Liang & Jing Zhang. Social Sciences Academic Press, 2004.
3 Marx mentioned in Section V "The Strife Between Workman and Machine" of Chapter XIII "Machinery and Modern Industry" of Capital that "the character of independence and estrangement which the capitalist mode of production as a whole gives to the instruments of labor and to the product, as against the workman, is developed—by means of machinery—into a thorough antagonism." (Marx, Karl. Capital. People's Publishing House, 1975)

It is noteworthy that recent years has witnessed the increase of workers' movements to safeguard their legal rights, which generally occurred in eastern coastal areas. In May 2010, thirteen people in Foxconn Shenzhen leapt to their deaths, which has triggered the "May Strike Movement". With the strikes started by the workers in Honda Nanhai and 70,000 others in Dalian Development Area, conflict between labor and capital came on to the front stage of public opinions. Some scholars termed the year 2010 as the "labor-capital relationship year".[4] Workers' ability to organize, their sense of discipline and struggle tactics they used in the movement were amazing. Since 2010, workers movement to safeguard legal rights began to arouse public attention. Hostility between capital and labor was no longer covert in industrial field, and became one major part of social unrest in the society. By then, Chinese industrial workers' collective movement to safeguard their legal rights has become a force to be reckoned with.

What makes it worse is that liberals at home and abroad and the underground Christian church affected by pro-Western anti-China forces have tried to influence the worker groups through workers' rights protection network, which has become an important threat to national security. As Lenin said, worker groups on the whole possess poor education, so their movement could not give rise to the consciousness of scientific socialism, automatically. Therefore, the development of worker movement harbors unpredictable risks to the building of socialism with Chinese characteristics. During the great upheavals and adverse changes in Eastern Europe, in Poland where the "Solidarity Union" that united most of the Polish workers by the support of the Catholic church enabled the union leader Wałęsa to realize peaceful evolution, and we should be on alert against such risks.

As Engels mentioned in the preface of The Condition of the Working Class in England, "the conditions of the working class are the real basis and starting point of all social movements, because they are the acutest and most barefaced expression of all social disasters...in order to offer a solid foundation for socialist theories and opinion that socialist theories have the rights to exist and in order to clean up all fantasies and fabrication that are for or against socialist theories, it is necessary to study the conditions of the proletariat."[5] Therefore, to guarantee both national security and the future of our socialist cause, we should be in close contact with workers movement. How to instill the consciousness of scientific socialism into workers movement and correctly guide the working class forces is an important historical issue that needs long-term attention all through our path of building

---

4 Guanghuai, Zheng & Jiangang, Zhu. ed. New Working Class: Relation, Organization and Collective Actions. China Social Sciences Publishing House, 2011.
5 Marx, Karl & Engels Friedrich. The Complete Works of Mark and Engels. Volume II. People's Publishing House, 1957.

socialism with Chinese characteristics. For researchers of Marxism, it is an urgent task to delve deeper into the current conditions of Chinese working class and provide prompt and necessary theoretical support for decision making by the government. For a long time, worker groups have been an object of study and analysis in sociology studies but their historical role has always been ignored by researchers. The Party Committee's campaign of "Concentrate on the Grass roots, Alter the Style of Work, Change the Style of Writing" and "investigate and study our national conditions" practiced by the Graduate School of CASS, provides an important opportunity for Marxists to delve deeper into the worker groups.

As a major in the program of "Basic Tenets of Marxism", I believe that in terms of practice, Marxism requires us to use this opportunity to learn more about the real conditions of the working class, observe and study their conditions, demands and confusion. In this way, not only we the intellectuals will have a clearer understanding of the reality but also the workers will better understand both their status and role in the social production process and in historical progress. As Lenin said, (we should) instill Marxist ideology into the workers movement, jointly promote social progress with them and actively rather than passively promote the historical change. In terms of theoretical study, Marxism requires us to analyze the conditions of the Chinese working class, reveal the source of problems about payment conditions, living standards, religion and ethics, and how to develop class awareness, etc. of the working class and at the same time analyze and criticize various non-socialist schools by means of historical materialist views and methods.

Further research, analysis and criticism of these problems above will not only provide a larger space for innovation of the Chinese Marxism, but more importantly, we will be able to grasp the ways to correctly guide the working class forces and ways to raise the socialist consciousness of the working class, and we win this force that may transform China's society under the banner of socialism with Chinese characteristics, and ensure the long-term, stable and healthy development of China.

PART FOUR

Developments and Struggles of Communist and Workers' Parties around the World

Y. 38

The Major Changes and Transformations in the Contemporary World Socialist Movement

Nie Yunlin[1]

This paper is the initial research result of Major Project in the field Philosophy and Social Sciences Researches, and "Research Project on the Theories and Practices of the Communist Parties in Contemporary Capitalist Countries".

Abstract: The contemporary world socialist movement has changed significantly and new adjustments have been accomplished. The mode of world socialist movement has changed from one having a single center, all across the world, single leadership, one single revolution path, and a single and unitary socialist construction mode. The new mode includes, different communist parties following their own independent revolution paths suited to their national conditions and constructing socialism that suits to distinctive features of their countries. The transformation of the contemporary world socialist movement is mainly characterized by the following aspects: it has transformed from being a movement outside the capitalist system, to the one inside the capitalist system; it has abandoned the way of proletarian revolution to overthrow capitalism, and embraced the way of peaceful, democratic and revolutionary transformation of capitalism; world socialist movement has developed from one in which an advanced social class fights for the interests of the majority into a one, wherein majority of the people rise up and fight for the interests of the majority, i.e, themselves.

Key words: contemporary world socialist movement; major changes; changes and transformations

---
1 Nie Yunlin, Professor of Central China Normal University, Institute of Research on Marxism Abroad.

I. Nine significant contemporary changes in the world socialist movement

Contemporary changes related to the goals of the socialist movement

World socialist movement aims to realize socialism and communism, but socialist movements in different times have different interpretations of this goal, which leads to different judgments and results. During the Second International, workers' parties in Europe also specified the goal of socialism in their programs, but they failed to elaborate on their thinking and theories for the fulfillment of this goal, could not define the targeted transformations in economic and political structure and also could not define different stages of social development, especially the stages of development in the socialist revolution and socialist construction path after winning power.

During the Third International, communist parties of each country have elaborated on how to achieve the goal of socialism, defined different stages of social development, especially the path to socialist revolution, which were relatively more clear than the Second International, but these elaborations were quite monotonous, and generally followed the Soviet model.

The collapse of the former Soviet Union, tremendous changes that occurred in the socialist Eastern Europe and the success of socialism with Chinese characteristics have demonstrated that there will be no unitary pattern for the establishment of socialism and each country will construct socialism suited to its national characteristics and suited to characteristics, spirit of the times.

Therefore, communist parties of different countries have began to pay special attention to their own national conditions and characteristics and have set the goal of establishing socialism suited to their national characteristics. Apart from their emphasis on unique characteristics in establishing the socialist society, they also propose common characteristics of this society: Firstly, they all propose to establish mixed economic system with public ownership being in the dominant status. Secondly, they propose to organically combine planned economy with market economy. Thirdly, they propose to protect ecological environment and realize harmonious development between man and nature. Fourthly, they call for the organic combination between parliamentary democracy and participatory democracy or direct democracy. Fifthly, they propose a multi-party system. Sixthly, they propose to implement the policy of building the most broad alliance. Seventhly, they propose the spirit of science and oppose sectarianism, advocate ensuring freedom of thought and beliefs, etc.

New interpretations regarding the contemporary capitalist society

After the collapse of the former Soviet Union and tremendous changes in the Eastern Europe, most of the communist parties in the capitalist countries got rid of the misleading idea of "General Total Crisis of Capitalism" and developed a more realistic and dialectical understanding of contemporary capitalism.

Different national development and national socio-historical characteristics impact the communist parties of different countries to reach different interpretations of capitalism. For instance, about the stages of world capitalist development, some still hold that contemporary capitalism is monopoly capitalism stage, some believe that it has developed from monopoly capitalism into state monopoly capitalism, some think that it has developed from monopoly capitalism into financial monopoly capitalism, some consider that it has developed from monopoly capitalism into international monopoly capitalism, etc. Nevertheless, there are some basic common understandings.

Firstly, significantly different from laissez-faire capitalism and monopoly capitalism, contemporary capitalism enjoys strong abilities of self-regulation, self-renewal and self-development. Secondly, those abilities do not and cannot or will not eliminate the basic contradictions of capitalist society because their fundamental solution is socialism replacing capitalism. Thirdly, during the current development of capitalism, the new social factors are growing and increasing within its womb, paving the way for the future realization of socialism. Four, opposing the capitalist globalization calls for a struggle of anew globalization that can be beneficial to the humankind, etc.

Strategies of contemporary world socialist movement

The strategies designed by socialist movements are not immutable, instead they change continuously according to the objective environment of struggle and the historical mission of the party, because Marxism requires to combine firmness in strategic goals with flexibility in tactics.

At the beginning of the 20th century when laissez-faire capitalism entered the stage of imperialism and war and revolution featured the then epoch, Lenin formulated the strategy of violent revolution for the Russian proletarian revolution, and regarded the peaceful development of the revolution as a "rare" exceptional case.

After the victory of the World War II, tremendous changes took place in international situation, which triggered fierce debates over the strategy of revolutionary struggle and constituted one of the reasons for the split of international communist movement in the 1960s. After the collapse of the former Soviet Union and tremendous changes in the Eastern Europe, based on the new developments and changes in the economic and political life at home and abroad, communist parties in most of the capitalist countries proposed to realize socialism through a peaceful and democratic path, discarding violent revolution and the dictatorship of the proletariat. However, in those countries with relatively less-developed economy and culture, communist parties were divided into two groups, one proposing the path of parliamentary struggles and the second path of using rural areas to encircle the cities and using armed struggle to seize power.

Thoughts on the arrangement of class forces in the contemporary socialist movement

Correct thoughts on the arrangement of class forces for developing the socialist strategy is one of the key issues for the success of any socialist party or movement. There were somewhat mistaken ideas regarding determining attitudes towards the middle classes and strata by the Third International parties. This was mainly demonstrated by "left" theories and policies adopted towards the intellectuals, well earning workers, the wealthy peasants and the majority of middle and petty bourgeoisie, which have caused losses in the socialist movement.

After the end of cold war era, since great changes have occurred in the social class structure of the capitalist society, under the effect of the third scientific and technological revolution and revolutionary development of productive forces, communist parties of different countries have drawn lessons from the collapse of the former Soviet Union and tremendous changes in the Eastern Europe, gave up the previous sectarian strategies, proposed to implement the policies of broad alliances and began to target winning of the broad middle class as well as some other class forces against the monopoly capital class.

All these new adjustments have greatly expanded the social basis of the socialist movement. If we generally look at the target of arrangement of class forces in today's socialist movement led by communist parties in different countries, the working class, among whom the number of mental workers or intellectual working class is increasing, and this group has become the leading force of socialist movement; secondly the majority of the workers, peasants and the intellectuals are the reliable backbone or main forces; thirdly middle and petty bourgeoisie are class forces regarded as forces, we should apply a dual policy: both struggle against and unite with. And generally monopoly capital is taken as the target of socialist revolution.

The development stages of revolution towards socialism

In general Marxist communists tended to believe that those countries with backward economic and cultural conditions should go through two stages of in the revolutionary process, first a people's democratic revolution and secondly socialist revolution. While they believed that developed capitalist countries may directly transit to socialism after the victory of revolution. The collapse of the former Soviet Union and tremendous changes in the Eastern Europe have triggered new understanding among the leaders of the socialist movement of the developed capitalist countries, currently most of them think that the establishment of a socialist society would probably be a long-term, complex, and arduous process. Consequently the communist parties of many developed countries were prudent in formulating specific program for transiting to socialism and have begun to adopt a two-step strategy. First step would be the establishment of a democratic coalition government, which will carry out the democratic transformation of the national economy and politics by targeting or isolating the monopoly capitalist class. As the second step, socialist transformation should be carried out related to national economy and political system and socialist society will be established. Communist Party of the United States believed that "socialist revolution in the U.S. would be divided into two stages, democratic revolution against monopoly capitalism and socialist revolution."[2]

Communist Party of Japan has stated in their program that the first step of the revolution in Japan will be a "democratic revolution" against the US imperialism and the rule of Japanese monopoly capital and pointed out that "the revolution will uninterruptedly develop from one fighting for sovereignty and democracy into one for socialism."[3]

Marxist politic party leading the socialist movement

In different historical periods, socialist movement of Marxist workers underwent different historical development forms. Since the birth of Marxist workers' parties, their development can be roughly divided into three stages, for every stage there are three according historical forms. The first stage lasted from mid-19th century to the beginning of the 20th century, there is a party with mass character. The second stage is from mid-20th century to 1970s, there is the vanguard party. The third stage started from 1970s up to now, the contemporary party has a new (modern) mass character.

---

2 Shujie, Ding. Socialist Theories and Practices of Communist Party of U.S. China Social Sciences Publishing House, 2006.
3 Tianlu, Cao. "Japanese Socialism" Theories and Practices of the Communist Party of Japan, China Social Sciences Publishing House, 2004.

At the end of the 20th century and the beginning of the 21st century, communist parties in most of the capitalist countries put forward the policy of modernization of their party organization and tried to establish a party of a (new) mass character. They began to think that such a new organization would be more suitable to the demand of times at home and abroad.

Currently, there is no fixed pattern regarding "the party building structure" of communist parties in capitalist countries. However, in terms of relevant theories and practices, they do not only inherit the traditions of vanguard party pattern—theory, organization principle and political tradition—but they develop and boast new features, such as: mass character, openness, more democracy, transparency, independence and so on.

Marxism has always been the theoretical basis that guided the world socialist movement.

Marxism has always been the theoretical basis that guides the world socialist movement. However, since Marxist theory constantly develops and people's understanding of Marxism deepens, people's understanding and attitude to Marxism in different periods are not completely the same. In contemporary world socialist movement, but some parties mention that only Marxism is their theoretical basis, most parties believe that both Marxism and Leninism are their theoretical bases and some communist parties in the developing countries hold that Marxism, Leninism and Mao Zedong Thought are their theoretical basis.

There is also a significant transformation in attitude towards Marxism, change from dogmatic approach to creative application of Marxism and a change from adherence to traditional socialism theory to exploration of modern socialist theory. The ups and downs and the collapse of the former Soviet Union, and CPSU and tremendous changes in East Europe have exposed clearly the harm of dogmatism to the communist parties of all countries, and at the same time they have seen how dogmatism has corrupted the CPSU and how the approach of "authority of theory" has damaged the party. All gave the lesson that to creatively apply Marxism is a must to create favorable conditions.

At present, it has been the mainstream approach in the world socialist movement to combine Marxism with specific practice of a country. Communist parties of all countries explore their own path of socialist development and form their own theories and strategies. The Communist Party of Japan put forward the "Japanese Socialism", Communist Party of Greece put forward "anti-imperialist and anti-monopoly socialism", Communist Party of India "people's democratic revolution theory", Communist Party of Brazil "new socialism with Brazilian characteristics", Communist Party of Russian Federation put forward the "Russian socialism", etc. Although communist parties in some countries have not yet given localized names to their theories, they also try to follow the basic guiding principle of combining Marxism with local/national realities.

World socialist movement began to adopt a new form of solidarity and cooperation in its internal relations

The first half of the 20th century had embraced united international organizations of the communist movement including the Third International and the Communist Information Exchange Bureau (COMINFORM) established by nine countries of Russia and Europe. But in the 1950s and 60s, although there was no such organizations as above, but some worldwide unity and cooperation occurred through international conferences. (Moscow, Bucharest meetings etc.)

After the mid-1960s, due to sharp split there was neither a tangible international organization nor a intangible unity or cooperation, because the past unity and cooperation mode, could no longer respond to the needs of socialist movements in different countries, instead the old mode had become an important obstacle to them.

After the collapse of the former Soviet Union and tremendous changes in the East Europe, the international ties of the world socialist movement encountered a serious damage. However, in nearly 20 years of development since 1991, there arose new forms of international solidarity and cooperation in the world socialist movement.

Firstly, developing bilateral relationships between parties became a main form of international connection, which includes experience exchanges and mutual support. In this new period, the relationship between communist parties features: independence, equality, mutual respect and mutual non-interference in each other's internal affairs. In this way, unhealthy practices that have occurred in the past can be avoided, especially the situation of one certain big party being in the center of the cooperation has been avoided.

Secondly, the annual International Meeting of Communist and Workers' Parties is an important form for communist parties to strengthen contacts, exchange thoughts, ideas and exchange work experiences and promote development of world socialist movement. It has been held 11 times in different continents in turn and in South Africa in 2012 and in Istanbul Turkey, in 2015. Besides, International Communist Seminar (ICS) held annually in Brussels is a similar form. It has been held for 18 times, participated by about 150 parties and organizations from five continents. Last, the meetings under the title of Socialist Scholars Conference is a supplementary form of theoretical exchanges in the world socialist movement.

Relationship between the socialist movement and other social movements

After the collapse of the former Soviet Union and tremendous changes in the East Europe, people have gained a more profound understanding on the nature and development of socialism and a more profound understanding on the diverse (plural) development path from capitalism to socialism. And gradually eliminated the influence of the mistaken idea that "socialist struggle has a privileged superior status" and adopted a more tolerant attitude towards other progressive social movements criticizing and fighting against capitalism. With this new understanding, communist parties generally support those social movements which help to the freedom (release) and development of productive forces, social movements favorable to eliminate polarization and aiming to realize fairness and justice, communist parties also respect their exploration for a different path towards socialism. Many communist parties show an attitude of willingness to learn from the experiences of these social movements. What is particularly important is, the relationship between communist parties and socialist parties has turned from hostility into a relationship of co-existence and mutual tolerance and mutual accommodation. The relations between communist and socialist parties in major countries have become normalized.

The improvement of the relations between these two different parties has promoted the convening of the international conference by the left-wing parties, among which Sao Paulo Forum in 1990 was the most influential one and this Forum has become an important annual gathering for left-wing parties of the globe. World Social Forum has many sub-branches or sub-problem areas it deals with.[4]

Meanwhile, the improvement the relations between these two different parties have also promoted the establishment of regional coalition of left-wing parties. In May 2004, 15 left-wing parties from Europe met in Rome and founded the Party of the European Left, which developed the unity and cooperation of Europe's left movement.

---

4 The World Social Forum on Migrations (WSFM) was born as a key feature of the World Social Forum, and was first held in Porto Alegre in 2005. This year, São Paulo in Brazil will be hosting the forum from 7 to 10 July 2016 under the slogan "Migrants: building alternatives to disorder and the global capital crisis". Hosted by members of civil society, non-governmental institutions, academics and activists, the Social Forum of Migration aims to create an environment enabling reflection on migration and democratic debate that is opposed to neoliberalism and capitalism. The Forum is plural, non-confessional, non-government, organized in a decentralized and horizontal form, bringing together social movements from all countries and strengthening their ties. This year's six themes are: 1. Systemic crisis of the capitalist model and its consequences for migrations, 2. Resistance and alternatives for migrants, 3. Migrations, gender and body, 4. Human rights, habitat, decent work, political participation and social movements, 5. Migration, rights of Mother Earth, climate and the North-South dispute, 6. Right to the city, social inclusion and migrants as citizens.

II. New transformation achieved by the contemporary world socialist movement

The world socialist movement has not encountered a general change, instead a comprehensive and profound changes have occurred in world socialist movement. Owing to the deepening of the goal of socialist movement, many transformations have occurred as follows: transformations in the strategies of revolutionary struggle and path, new understanding related to the status and function of parliamentary struggle, new developments in the organization form of communist parties; expanding of the social class and strata basis of the movement; formation of a new understanding on the relationships between two different social systems (socialism and capitalism), etc.

All these new approaches mean a new transformation in world socialist movement. World socialist movement has also transformed from one led by a strong international center (in the past) and from one which advertised "a single correct revolution path" and "unitary socialist construction path"; consequently world socialist movement has embraced a new pattern, with independent parties seeking for their "own revolution path" suited to national characteristics, and "a native socialist construction path" in line with national conditions.

Ricardo Alarcón, President of the National Assembly of People's Power from 1993 to 2013, in Cuba sums up this learning well:

"What characterizes Latin America at the present moment is the fact that a number of countries, each in its own way, are constructing their own versions of socialism. For a long while now, one of the fundamental errors of socialist and revolutionary movements has been the belief that a socialist model exists. In reality, we should not be talking about socialism, but rather about socialisms in the plural. There is no socialism that is similar to another. As Mariátegui said, socialism is a 'heroic creation'".

The main features of transformation we can observe in the contemporary world socialist movement are as follows. It has changed from a movement outside the capitalist system into one within the system; it has transformed from one aiming to overthrow capitalism through a proletarian revolution into a one which aims to implement a revolutionary transformation of capitalism with peaceful and democratic means; world socialist movement has developed from one in which an advanced social class fights for the interests of the majority into a one, wherein majority of the people rise up and fight for the interests of the majority, i.e, themselves. We think the above significant changes and transformations in world socialist movement have profound social roots.

The factors behind the changes

Revolutions in high technology and revolutionary developments in the productive forces are the material prerequisites and basis for the changes and transformations in the world socialist movement

Revolutions in the high technology and revolutionary developments in the productive forces which can be dated back to World War II, and these two have induced profound changes in the structure and operation of capitalist economy and its political systems including political operation, social class structure in the capitalist society, new stratification in the working class, new developments in the social contradictions of the capitalist society, etc., which are the profound social roots of the significant changes and transformations in world socialist movement. All of which are highlighted and demonstrated by vigorous development of economic globalization, vigorous development of science and informatization technology, political democratization, social welfare, middle classes, etc.

The above new trends in the capitalist development, have effected all social classes and their parties (including those of the bourgeoisie and working class) and these parties were faced by a crisis of institutional inadequacy and "ill-adaptation" which meant, all these parties were forced to adjust themselves to new changes in the society, they were forced to change their theories and strategies.

Bourgeois parties

The bourgeois parties have undergone through the stage of "powerful parties" (between the late 17th century and late 18th century), secondly the "mass parties" stage (between the late 18th century and beginning of 20th century) and thirdly the "catch-all parties"[5] stage since the mid-20th century.

The appearance of "catch-all parties" was closely related to new developments in the capitalist economy and politics since the 1960s. Firstly, with the development of economy and society, the former strong divisions and distinctions between social classes have weakened compared to early industrialization period, thus highly distinctive collective identities of social groups became pale and obscure.

---

5 Kristina Weissenbach wrote: "Catch-all parties is the result of increasing erosion of traditional social boundaries in Western Europe in the late 1950s and 1960s implied a weakening of formerly highly distinctive collective identities, making it less easy to identify separate sectors of the electorate and to assume shared long-term interests. Secondly, economic growth and the increased importance of the welfare state facilitated the elaboration of programmes which were no longer necessarily devisive or partisan, but which were formulated to serve the "interests of all", or at least nearly all." See. http://www.kas.de/wf/doc/kas_21710-1522-1-30.pdf?110126062034.

Secondly, owing to continuous economic development and establishment of welfare state policies, many parties tend to formulate programs for the majority of voters and even for the vast majority of voters.

Thirdly, with the vigorous development of mass media, party leaders can directly appeal to the majority of the voters, without needing to rely on a tightly organized electoral/social groups organized in their parties. Under these new circumstances, all kinds of parties have transformed into "catch-all parties" consequently the main features of these new parties are as follows: political ideologies of the parties have weakened, besides differences and opposition between political parties began to fade. Also, the status and role of the upper-level leadership groups in these parties continue to strengthened, while the role of party members are declining. Thus the new parties, intentionally or unintentionally, reduce their reliance on certain social class or certain social group, and began to attract supporters from all walks of the society. Besides these transformed parties do their best to strengthen their ties with numerous diversified interest groups.

Living in the environment of contemporary capitalism, communist parties in the capitalist countries were forced to formulate and adopt new development goals/patterns, new strategy and tactics suited to new economic and political conditions. Consequently, the communist parties needed to reform themselves so that their theoretical concepts, organizational structures, operational mechanisms and means and ways of struggle are in line with new developments that have occurred in the capitalist society.

The change in theme(s) of the times—after the first half of the 20th century—has been an important external environment which has promoted changes and transformation in the world socialist movement.

In the first half of the 20th century, as the internal contradictions of the capitalist imperialism intensified, consequently war and revolution became the 2 themes of the times. Therefore the communist parties of most countries needed to carry out illegal struggles, and Third International was forced to formulate the strategy of armed seizure of power.

However, after the World War II, especially after 1960s and 70s, thanks to the new developments in the economic and political spheres and due to the absence of global-level war and big revolutions, peace and development became the 2 new themes of the times. Consequently, peace and development has become the heartfelt inspiration for the people of all countries.

Under such circumstances, only by understanding the people's mind and spirit, and correctly analyzing the public opinions, can the Marxist working class parties, adjust their theories and strategies and can follow a revolutionary path containing peaceful and democratic policies, and only in this way can they win people's support and achieve new successes.

New changes in capitalism is the objective basis for the changes and transformations in the world socialist movement

Capitalist countries have achieved a new round of development by properly adjusting and renewing—to a certain degree—their economic, political, cultural and social systems—in order to adapt to the revolutionary changes of high technology and development of productive forces. As a result, tremendous changes have taken place in the external living environment of the communist parties in the capitalist countries.

Firstly, political and economic strength of capitalist forces have relatively enhanced and the capitalist law system and capitalist institutions were reformed to gain an inclusive and flexible nature.

Secondly, there were profound changes in social class structure of the society. The pyramid form of social class structure turned into an olive shaped one, with a remarkable increase in the number of middle class, decrease in blue-collar workers and expansion of the proportion of white-collar stratum in the working class.

Thirdly, the majority of the working people's living standards have seen a new increase, their welfare protection was greatly improved, they were offered multiple ways to participate in the decisions related to politics and economic sphere.

Fourthly, with improvements in their economic and political conditions, the broad masses of people have lost their anxiety to change the current status quo, instead they became enthusiastic about improving or reforming the flaws of the existing system.

Fifthly, communist parties have won or given legal status one after another, and they encountered a change from being parties outside the system to parties within the system.

All these above have, to a certain degree, eased the basic contradictions of the capitalist society, especially the basic contradiction between labor and capital. This new situation was greatly different from the sharp class contradictions before the World War II and even greatly different from the early postwar period. Therefore, communist parties of all countries needed to transform themselves and innovate their theories and strategies in order to adapt to new changes in their external environment, and objective conditions.

Grave asymmetry of power between opposing class forces constitutes the internal requirement for the changes and transformation in the world socialist movement

During the 1950s and 60s, although we cannot say that "the East wind"[6] had gained the upper hand against "the West wind", the socialist camp led by the S.U.-led socialist countries was indeed an important force to counter the U.S.-led imperialist camp, which was beneficial to the development of socialist movements in the capitalist countries. The great upheaval in the former Soviet Union and tremendous changes in the East Europe led to a grave asymmetry of power between opposing class forces and causing a change in the balance of forces inside the capitalist countries, thus the situation developed in a direction favorable to big monopoly capital class. This struck a serious blow to the forces fighting for peace, democracy and socialism in the capitalist countries, sped up the marginalization of communist parties in the political life of European and American continent countries. When power relations between class forces at home and abroad change unfavorably in terms of socialist movement the communist parties of capitalist countries need to reform their theories and strategies, change position from attack to defense and opt for accumulating strength to use it in a better future situation.

Marxist theory still remains to be the theoretical basis for the changes and transformations in the world socialist movement

Marx and Engels formulated different revolution strategies for the proletariat in different periods and suggested that firmness in terms of principles should be combined with the flexibility in designing strategies. We think this approach has been the basis in the formulation of revolutionary paths including peaceful and democratic strategies by the communist parties of capitalist countries. At the same time, communist parties of capitalist countries have shifted their strategy to gradually transform capitalism, due to their consideration of Marx and Engels' theory which points to "the new social factors developing in the womb of the old society"[7].

---

6 "The East wind" and "the West wind" refers to the forces of socialism and capitalism.
7 Marx and Engels, Collected Works, Volume II. People's Publishing House, 1965, p. 625.

III. Conclusive remarks on the changes and transformations in the contemporary world socialist movement

The changes and transformations in the world socialist movement is the product of adaptation to economic, political and social developments by the communist parties and product of their efforts to reform themselves accordingly.

If we look into the history of bourgeois parties, it can be clearly seen that, none of the old parties that have survived 100-plus years were able to develop and progress forward without multiple changes and transformations. Therefore, reforms and transformations implemented by the communist parties as the leaders of the world socialist movement conform to the law of development of political parties, in general, and also in line with development law of the socialist movement.

These changes and transformations are the result of struggles of the working class and the vast majority of the working masses over several centuries, and also result of social progress.

Until 1975, the communist parties of the old capitalist countries such as Spain, Portugal and Greece have still struggled as underground parties.

In the 1990s, we have also observed that some states, as the former Soviet and Eastern European regions, have forced communist parties to an illegal status. However, through tenacious struggles of the masses, by the end of the first decade of the 21st century, communist parties of all developed countries and most of the developing countries have won legal status. Thus, they won the conditions wherein they can adopt a new struggle mode different than in the past and the conditions to launch a new struggle mode by undertaking smaller cost and sacrifice in their cause to achieve the victory of socialism. This deserves our appreciation. On February 15, 1845, Engels made it clear in an assembly in Elberfeld that "gentlemen, if these conclusions are correct, if the social revolution and practical communism are the necessary result of our existing conditions—then we will have to concern ourselves above all with the measures by which we can avoid a violent and bloody overthrow of the social conditions. And there is only one means, namely, the peaceful introduction or at least preparation of communism."[8]

In 1847, in the Principles of Communism, Engels answered the question "Will the peaceful abolition of private property be possible? It would be desirable if this could happen, and the communists would certainly be the last to oppose it. Communists know only too well that all conspiracies are not only useless, but even harmful."[9]

---

8 Selected Works of Marx and Engels. Volume II, People's Publishing House, 1995, p. 292.
9 https://www.marxists.org/archive/marx/works/1847/11/prin-com.htm.

In the struggle to realize socialism, communist parties should have the right to independently formulate their theories and strategies, and we should respect this fundamental right

When talking about "European communism", Deng Xiaoping pointed out that "only independence is the true demonstration of Marxism." ... "we should be blamed to some extent. We didn't well understand the special environment of parties in Eastern European countries."[10]

He also said: "what has happened tells us that it won't work for a party to make comments on the right or wrong of foreign brother parties according to the already existing formula or some stereotype programme"; "We must respect all other countries and people and let them explore their own road thus address and solve their own problems. No Party should act like a patriarchal party and issue orders to others. We object to being ordered about and we, for our part, will never issue orders to others. This should be regarded as an important principle." "Since situations, people's consciousness, national class relations and balance of class forces vary in different countries, how will it be feasible for them to apply a fixed formula? Even if your formula is a combination of Marxism and national reality, it is still difficult to avoid mistakes.[11]

Therefore, "we must respect parties and the people of all countries in handling their own affairs and allow them to find their own paths, "also mistakes should be summarized by themselves independently" so that they can make new explorations"[12].

The path in which mankind will achieve socialism will be tough, tortuous and lengthy—with twists and turns—in this struggle path practice is the only criterion for testing truth. It is only the history which will judge the right and wrong of the current contemporary world socialist movement.

Deng Xiaoping once pointed out that: "domestic principles (policies) and routes of political parties of different countries, the right or wrong of others' practices. These should be judged by their own parties and their own people, After all, their people understand their national situations the best.", "we couldn't blame them for exploring new roads, in line with their reality", Party-to-party relations should be "new, healthy and friendly". Secondly each party should handle its internal affairs in an independent and self-determined way, not subject to the decision, interests or wishes of others. No party should give orders to others".[13]

---

10 Selected Works of Deng Xiaoping. Volume III. People's Publishing House, 1993, p. 189.
11 Selected Works of Deng Xiaoping. English Version, Volume II. People's Publishing House, 1994, p. 239.
12 Selected Works of Deng Xiaoping. English Version, Volume II. People's Publishing House, 1994, p. 238.
13 Selected Works of Deng Xiaoping. English Version, Volume II. People's Publishing House, 1994, p. 237.

Y. 39

The Communist Party of the Russian Federation and Russia: Their Future

Ouyang Xiangying[1]

Abstract: In 2011, the Communist Party of Russian Federation won nearly 20% of the votes at the sixth State Duma elections and entered the new State Duma as the largest opposition party. The rise of its votes is caused by a number of internal and external reasons. The reflection of the people on the current system in Russia and changes in the image and practice of the Communist Party of Russian Federation in the new era and new situation of the Russia has been the main reasons behind this success. Historically looking—in this latest State Duma elections of 2011—the influence of the Communist Party of Russian Federation did not yet return to the highest level it had achieved in the past years. How to overcome the continuous inner splits and struggles in the party and strengthen the inner unity is the major problem before the Communist Party of Russian Federation. Currently, we can say the report delivered by Zyuganov, in the 2nd Session (stage) of the 14thCongress of this party is the programmatic document guiding its struggle. The said document proposes new foreign policies in three fields and seven new economic policies as well as five social priorities, and analyzes five threats brought by capitalism to Russia: enormous inequalities in the society, demographic catastrophe, Economic collapse, planted on the raw needle, spiritual and moral degradation,, decline of Russia's national defense capacity and loss of its key allies and friendly countries; the party has committed itself to face these five major problems.

Key words: Communist Party of the Russian Federation; Duma elections; regime and state; program; international communist movement

---
1 Ouyang Xiangying, Associate Researcher in the Institute of World Economics and Politics, attached to CASS

On December 25, 1991, Gorbachev announced his resignation, putting an end to the Soviet Union that was founded 69 years ago. On December 24, 2011, the campaign activities of "strive for a clean election" were held in Moscow, St. Petersburg, Chelyabinsk, Tomsk, Astrakhan, etc. where tens of thousands of people have participated in the demonstrations, pointing the arrow towards Putin. Is Russia, 20 years after the disintegration of the Soviet Union, whether Russia is preparing for a radical political change, and whether the Communist Party of Russian Federation stand out, and play a relevant role are important issues to study.

I. The number of voters supporting the Communist Party of Russian Federation is increasing

At the sixth State Duma election, the Communist Party of Russian Federation won nearly 19.19 % of the votes, corresponding to 92 seats in the Federal Assembly, entered the new State Duma as the largest opposition party and was deemed the biggest winner in the elections by the media. Zyuganov, the leader of the Party, was not satisfactory, since he believed that 12 % to 15 % of their votes were stolen and that the CPRF votes should be as many as those of the rival party, the ruling party namely the United Russia.

Just before the election, a report released by Russian Public Opinion Research Center showed that nearly 30% of the public favored the Communist Party of Russian Federation, among which 26% firmly supported and favored Communist Party of Russian Federation and its leader and 48% of the respondents held a neutral position.

On the other side, the election results have proved that the support rate of Communist Party of Russian Federation has indeed increased. Such an increase was caused by three main reasons:

Firstly, the social and economic situation after the world economic crisis has affected the system. Before 2007, Russia under Putin's leadership had achieved a fast economic development, including abundant oil and natural gas export revenues brought by the rise in energy prices, Russia also saw substantial increases in wages and pension payments, this has raised patriotism and optimism among all social classes. The alleged grave corruptions, polarization between the rich and the poor, descending of Russia's scientific and technological level, etc. criticized by the opposition parties like Communist Party of Russian Federation were regarded as critiques by the losers and not supported by the public.

But currently, the global capitalist economic crisis has exposed the structural and institutional contradictions in the Russian economy, the gap between society and the government has widened and the existing regime in

Russia "although it is has long been believed to be effective, is unfair." The intellectuals and the working class make reflections and criticize privatization, people begin to miss the stable life they had during the socialist period and more and more appeal for social fairness and justice, and even the middle class is worrisome that their future is not secure enough, and demands a more proactive policy. The current crisis has reinforced the social class basis of the Communist Party of Russian Federation, which has been an important reason for the increase of support rate.

Secondly, the ruling party, the United Russia was caught in a trust crisis in the public and labeled as "the party of cheaters and thiefs", thus creating an opportunity for the main opposition party to ascend to power. The presidential-prime ministerial "castling" between Putin and Medvedev has made "democratic public and figures" feel themselves fooled, which means the images of the two leaders are quite damaged.

Manipulation in the elections has further evoked the anger of the liberals and the anarchists and their critique against Putin has increased, doubting the political ethic of the system. More importantly, as a ruling party, United Russia is accused to be responsible for the problems like economic downturn, increase of the unemployment rate, decrease in life expectancy of citizens, failures in satellite launching, sinking of oil drilling platform, increase of terrorism, and capital flight.

Against such a background, those populist parties in the left of the political spectrum -who have always supported United Russia shifted their support to the CPRF and some prominent intellectuals due to absence of a right-wing liberal party that could enter the Duma, have supported the CPRF as a protest tendency.

The great achievements of the Soviet era lay a solid political foundation for the direct inheritor party, the CPRF, the public compares it with the "tarnished scandalous" ruling party, all this explains why CPRF's support rate has increased.

Thirdly, the third main reason is related with the changes in the CPRF itself. Through several ups and downs, the CPRF has finally recovered the core values of freedom of labor, democracy, justice and socialism and revered new and modern theories based on social values. It spared no efforts to strengthen the role and function of the state in economic and social life, defended the easing of people's burden and their access to better social welfare. CPRF has not only maintained its socialist orientation as a communist Party, but also to some extent adapted itself to modern party politics and absorbed some new theories in this regard, corrected some of its drawbacks and malpractices, which all means that CPRF has gradually clarified its ideological stand and recovered its deep roots in the society.

Also, the Party has intensified its ideological and theoretical research activities, to solve the new realistic issues basing itself on the new situation and strives hard to innovate Marxist-Leninist theories. CPRF, has reinforced the establishment of regional "people's militia" (in Nizhny Novgorod) and Communist Youth League and consolidated its leading political team made up by celebrities, scientists and authorities, trying to win support from people of different ages and from different social groups. Zyuganov said: Forum of the People's Militia in Nizhny Novgorod accelerated mobilization of our supporters to actively participate in the election work and protest against the manipulations.

CPRF attaches great importance to learning from China, bur also increases communication with European countries. These measures have enabled the CPRF to better cope with the challenges of times. With the goal of overthrowing the current social system, rebuilding Soviet regime and eventually establish the new socialism suited to 21st century, besides CPRF has achieved to isolate the Westernization idea propagated by the liberals with raising the slogans "Love our country" and "Make our Country Stronger" and won extensive support from the voters.

II. Can the CPRF wrest political power nationwide?

With the recent Duma elections, the "one party dominant position" of the United Russia Party has changed, compelling it to carry out benign interactions and exchanges based on interests with other parties, this new political pattern in Russia better serves the practical interests of the Communist Party of Russian Federation.

However, since the ultimate goal of the Communist Party is to wrest the political power nationwide, can this goal be fulfilled in the near future? As far as I am concerned, in the long-term, this goal is not entirely impossible, but in the short run or even in the next 20 years, it is quite unlikely.

The CPRF has designed a secure policy of conquering the nation-wide political power in two steps. Firstly, it should target to establish alliances, achieve vertical and horizontal expansion and strive to be the biggest political party in Russia, so that it can hold the discourse power in the State Duma.

As the secondly, it should speed up training of influential younger successors for the future of Party, thus strive to win in the presidential elections.

In retrospect, in the 1995 and 1999 State Duma elections, the Communist Party of Russian Federation won the majority of the seats in the State Duma, by winning 22.3% and 24.2% of the total votes respectively, and became the strongest party in State Duma. It is clear that, currently the CPRF is far away from the zenith it has achieved in 1999, which is related to the current situation in Russia, especially with the strength of Putin and increasing suppression upon the CPRF, besides due several internal splits in the Party.

How to prevent constant internal splits and struggles in the Party and achieve to unite all that can be united is an important puzzle facing the CPRF. Worse still, Seleznev's "the Party of Russia's Rebirth", Sergei Glazyev's Motherland Bloc and Tikhonov's All-Russian Communist Party of the Future have—which are all in the left camp of the spectrum—significantly undermined the strength of the CPRF. Besides, Mironov's "A Just Russia", a center-left-wing nationalist party with social democratic ideology, has gained 64 seats in the Duma by winning the 13.25% of the total votes, thus gradually expanded its influence.

In light of these developments, CPRF leader Zyuganov declared his hope "to win the support of A Just Russia and Liberal Democratic Party of Russia" but "A Just Russia's", leader Mironov said: "we will not enter into official alliance agreements with those parties in Duma, but depending on the situation, we will ally with other parties to progress on certain partial issues." It shows that Mironov does not fully reject alliance, but the CPRF needs to look for common interest points to achieve such an alliance. Surely, political interests is the most difficult to split. If we evaluate optimistically, we can say that if CPRF could establish an alliance with "A Just Russia" and other left-wing parties, it can not only obtain larger discourse power in State Duma, but can achieve strong impetus for its future development.

According to the latest public opinion polls for the next elections, Putin is expected to be the winner of Russia's 2012 Presidential elections, with a support rate of 42%. Other powerful candidates, Zyuganov, 11%, Zhirinovsky, 9% and Minorov, %5, still lag far behind Putin. The reasons why Zyuganov lags far behind Putin are that, on the one hand, after the collapse of Soviet Union, and restoration of the capitalist system in Russia, the communist ideology was strongly suppressed and demonized, on the other hand, CPRF has many internal problems such as the differences in political opinions, constant internal splits, Zyuganov's relative lack of personal charisma, aging of the party members, etc.

Although Zjuganov's support rate lags far behind Putin, we should also see that the CPRF has made a series of achievements under his leadership. For instance, in the last spring and autumn of 2009, during the regional and city level council elections CPRF has been very successful, it has held ideological activities including commemoration for the 140th birthday of Lenin, launched a strong campaign to overcome the severe financial crisis of the party and led protests against the increased tax on second-hand imported cars, criticizing mainly local authorities in the Far East region, area, and retain its position as the second largest party in the regional (provincial) oblast parliaments.

In the recent elections of 2011, CPRF has won the majority votes in the provinces of Novosibirsk, Omsk, Vladivostok, Voronezh, Ryazan and Orenburg and there was a remarkable increase of votes in Kostroma, Nizhny Novgorod, Irkutsk, Moscow, Kaliningrad, Pskov, Smolensk, Magadan, Murmansk, Altay, Krasnoyarsk, Primorsky Krai, Perm and other areas, which demonstrates that CPRF's primary-level, grass-root organizations have done a good job in the major cities of Russia, and its influence has grown greatly.

After the collapse of the former Soviet Union and tremendous changes in the East European socialist countries, currently the left-wing parties which were formerly communist parties have entered a new epoch wherein they are ascending to power in the countries like Moldova, Hungary, Republic of Lithuania, Poland, Czech Republic, Romania, Albania, Serbia, Macedonia, etc. Considering this fact we can predict that if there are proper conditions, the CPRF can embrace new opportunities and prospects. Although currently the Party of the European Left is in its low tide, the upheavals in international and domestic political and economic situations tend to bring more opportunities than challenges, in general. If the CPRF can achieve to seize the opportunities, it will probably win the same glory of the (former) Communist Party of the Soviet Union.

III. The report of the 2nd Session of the 14thCongress of the Communist Party of Russian Federation is the programmatic document for guiding struggle

At the 2nd Session (stage) of the 14thCongress of the Communist Party of Russian Federation on December 18, 2011, Zyuganov, on behalf of the Central Committee, made a long report "Russia on the Threshold of Great Revolution, which will be the programmatic document for guiding struggle of the Communist Party for a certain time in the future.

Divided into eight parts, the report of the Central Committee made judgments on global economic situation and international situation, criticized Russia's current situation, proposed the economic and social policies of the Communist Party of Russian Federation, criticized the government's manipulations in the elections and called on the people to strive for the establishment of Soviet regime.

The report pointed out that the world has been turning to left, and that capitalism in Russia cannot not solve five major threats, namely, enormous inequalities in the society, demographic catastrophe, Economic collapse, planted on the raw needle, spiritual and moral degradation,, decline of Russia's national defense capacity and loss of its key allies and friendly countries.

The CPRF report has proposed the "Three + Seven + Five" policies to deal with these five major threats: namely, new foreign policies in three fields, seven new economic policies, as well as five social priorities.

New foreign policies in three fields include:

(1) To redefine priorities in the grand foreign policy: establish fair relations in the global stage, , reinforce the function and the role of United Nations in the global affairs and restrict the influence of NATO; increase the number of long-term partners from allied countries.

(2) To speed up re-integration of the nation (new great Soviet Union), advance the re-establishment of the Soviet Union and build a new national brotherhood alliance in the new great Soviet Union.

(3) To strengthen the national defense, promote the revival of armed forces and military complex of Russia.

Seven new economic policies include:

Economy growth of the economy instead of the well.

1. We will carry out the nationalization of the raw materials and other industries.

During the years of privatization and "reform" destroyed more than two thirds of the country's industrial potential. It's time to rectify the situation. Nationalization would allow the state to concentrate in the hands of large financial resources, direct them to the recovery of the economy and other challenges.

In the mining industry in Russia now working 9850 companies. Only 416 of them–the public. As a result, profit oligarchs in more than 400 times greater than what it gets our whole country from the exploitation of natural resources. Is it any wonder that the poor in Russia is not diminished, but the infrastructure is falling apart before our eyes.

In addition to the primary industries affected by the nationalization of the steel industry, aircraft construction, machinery, electricity and other basic industries. Country will get rid of the destructive rule of the "wild" market. Will restore the state regulation of economic life, its core planning, industrial and agricultural policy.

2. We will hold the new industrialization of the country, implementing the principle: "Modernization without stopping."

New industrialization would be based on the latest achievements of scientific and technological progress. Science returns in all sectors of the economy and, above all in electronics, machine tools, instrumentation, mechanical engineering, aircraft industry, automotive, shipbuilding, chemical industry. The output of these sectors will again be produced in Russia, rather than be acquired abroad. There will be industrial parks with a single ecosystem and "zero emissions". Earn the Unified Energy System of the country. Electricity tariffs, prices for coal, oil and lubricants will be reduced and will be strictly regulated. Will be established a system of rewards people for buying environmentally friendly vehicles and household appliances, and other innovative products.

3. Agriculture–the subject of our special care.

Communist Party guarantees the revival of the Russian village on the basis of a number of priorities.

New Land, Forest and Water Codes consolidate state ownership of land and forests, water areas. The land will be transferred free of charge for agricultural purposes. Land speculation will cease.

State support of agriculture will be provided at the level of advanced countries. The provision for its development will be from 10 to 15% of the expenditure part of the federal budget. Price discrepancies would be resolved.

The Government will ensure the restoration of large collective farms. It will hold a technical re-equipment of agriculture, and will finance the development program of agricultural machinery.

The village will receive a new life. Rural residents will be provided with housing, cultural institutions, schools, hospitals and clinics, kindergartens. Food security is restored. Russia will not join WTO on disadvantageous terms.

4. Government of national trust pass to the new financial policy.

The basis of the Russian banking system amount to the state by banks, including Vneshtorgbank, Sberbank, Construction Bank, Selkhozbank. They will provide a rational use of financial resources of the country and the effective circulation of money. State Savings Bank will provide free services to citizens at subsidized public utilities and other services.

Will be curtailed speculative banking system, stifling the economy excessively high interest rates for credit. Commercial banks will continue to provide services that promote economic and social development.

5. The Government will revise the taxation system.

Will be introduced progressive income tax on individuals, with the liberation of the poor from paying it. Significant benefits will be those of production that produce high-tech, competitive products, committing resources to research and development activities. Taxes for the real sector of the economy will decline.

6. The People's Government will ensure effective interaction with the sphere of Russian science production.

Government of public confidence will do anything to increase the intellectual potential of the nation. Will be done away with the shameful situation in which the proportion of high-tech products in exports has reached 40% U.S., Germany and Japan, exceeded 30%, and Russia fell 0.5%. During the first three years we will increase funding for domestic science at least twice. Our government will maintain and ensure the development of science cities created by the Soviet regime. Scientific centers of Russia will receive state support and will support its revival.

Decent wages will raise the status of scientists. Promising young researchers will be guaranteed housing and other support and encouragement. Postgraduate and doctoral scholarships will rise an average of 4 times.

Russian science will participate in the development of all major government decisions. Will be improved value analysis, forecasting and planning activities of government. The National Security Strategy will now be aligned with the strategy of scientific and educational priorities. Key decisions of the president and the government will not be taken without the approval of the Supreme Council of Mining.

7. Our government is implementing a comprehensive program "The Conquest of Space."

Communist Party will return to the Soviet experience of all forms of transport, and enriched it with modern world achievements. Regulation of tariffs for transportation costs will reduce the businesses and give citizens the freedom of movement.

We will return to the state railways. New highways will connect the country, will provide travel from Vladivostok to Moscow for two days.

Destroyed infrastructure fleet will be restored. Aeronautic get sufficient investment. Consolidation of the airline will be the prospect of monopolizing the industry by the state. This will create a modern regional aircraft.

Five social priorities are:

The third direction of our politics–a change of social priorities. "Social Jungle," will give way to public justice. Russia will become a country without a "backwoods".

1. Would have received a new social legislation.

The current government and the "United Russia" drastically worsened it in just a few years. Being introduced paid education and health care, limited public access to culture.

Communist Party is ready for two years to refocus the Russian legislation to the needs of citizens. The state will expand the network of social institutions, protection of motherhood and childhood, and ensures a dignified old age, to take care of people with disabilities. Unemployment will be eradicated as a sign of capitalist savagery. Working people rebuild their warranty on decent wages and working conditions, rest and recovery, to increase educational and cultural level.

2. Children and young people receive support from the state.

Fundamentals of our youth policy will be: free access to quality education, provision of professional work, providing free housing for young families and strengthen family values. The State will actively support gifted children and youth, young inventors, scientists, authors of promising projects. Country will have developed a network of clubs, sports clubs, art studios, tourist centers.

Child benefits will be paid based on actual expenses for the child. We finish with a deficit of childcare facilities. The Company will forget about the "juvenile technologies" destruction of the family. For families with many children will act developed a system of privileges. Significantly expand the organization's programs of child health holidays.

Will be given full cooperation to the activities of children and youth associations.

3. Our motto: "Quality education–for everyone!"

Communist Party will return to the people the greatest achievement of Soviet power–universal free education. Universities and schools will not be closed. Will begin the revival of vocational education. Work of the teacher and the teacher will be adequately paid, and prestige–to strengthen.

Public spending on education reached 10% of GDP. Education policy will allow for the program "From the desk to the sky" and other ambitious projects. Pupils will be provided with hot meals. Increase student scholarships, expand the number of their recipients.

4. Will strengthen the nation's health.

Quality health care, including the most complex operations will all be free. Private clinics can exist only as an addition to a full public health care system. We will restore the health service to major industries. Program will earn the organization of emergency medical care in rural areas.

The average salary in health care will be higher than the national average. Doctors qualifications will be included in the category of the most highly paid people.

The full service will be restored maternal and child health, antenatal care, delivery care. Lump sum benefit to the newborn will be from 40 to 50 thousand rubles. Monthly child allowance will be equal to its actual cost of living.

The state will provide comprehensive prevention of disease, the availability of spa treatments and a large-scale promotion of healthy lifestyles.

Strengthen the nation's health will contribute to the program "Cities of Russia." A special place in it will take the project "Green City"with the new rules of land use, landscaping of streets, houses grouped around small squares.

5. New cultural growth–a condition Russia's revival.

The people's government will provide favorable conditions for the revival of Russian culture and all the peoples of Russia. We firmly defend our history from the encroachments of those who distort and denigrate her, casts doubt on the exploits of previous generations. Cinema and television once again become a source of education basic moral values, patriotism and civic responsibility.

The most important criterion for evaluating the activities of government will be the country's cultural flowering. As soon as possible, we pass the law "On Culture". The budget for this area will double within three years. Will be enhanced preservation of historical monuments.Earn large-scale program for the protection of language and the traditions of Russian and all the peoples of Russia, promoting the outstanding works of Soviet culture.

Creative unions will have ample opportunities for development. This will create a National Public Council for Culture to develop the principles and ways of spiritual development.

Without a new cultural policy of the Communist Party does not see any possible solution and the national question. Therefore, it is our party really has developed a Russian theme, overriding any of its vulgarization nationalism. This question refers to four-fifths of Russia's population, and hence, again, the majority. Togo majority that is required to recognize their special role–the role of unifier of our multinational homeland. To address the question is Russian, in particular, you should:

- A responsible public policies aimed at creating an atmosphere of friendship between the peoples of our country;

- Active resistance to attempts at spiritual aggression against the national cultural traditions of Russia;

- Punishment under the law for any manifestations of extremism as a form of Russophobia incite ethnic hatred;

- Adequate presence of indigenous culture in the information environment of the country;

- To achieve real equality for all peoples of Russia in the field of public administration, business and resource rent receipt;

- The protection of our compatriots abroad, use all the features of state and social impact of the ruling regimes, which violated their civil, cultural, and socio-economic rights.

The party leader Zyuganov has emphasized that the conceptions brought forward by the CPRF was no Utopia, "they are real plans, and the implementation of these plans will be ensured by laws approved in the State Duma, plus the implementation in different fields will be supervised and followed under the guidance of committee of experts." The report has once again reiterated that nationalization is the cornerstone of the all measures, because privatization and the so-called "reform" destroyed more than two thirds of the country's industrial potential. It's time to rectify the situation.. If the CPRF ascends to power, it would nationalize the key sectors: nationalization would allow the state to concentrate in the hands of large financial resources, direct them to the recovery of the economy and other challenges.

In the mining industry in Russia now working 9850 companies. Only 416 of them–the public. As a result, profit oligarchs in more than 400 times greater than what it gets our whole country from the exploitation of natural resources. Is it any wonder that the poor in Russia is not diminished, but the infrastructure is falling apart before our eyes.

In addition to the primary industries affected by the nationalization of the steel industry, aircraft construction, machinery, electricity and other basic industries. Country will get rid of the destructive rule of the "wild" market. Will restore the state regulation of economic life, its core planning, industrial and agricultural policy.

Besides, the CPRF promises to follow a policy of national reconciliation when nationalizing the oligarchic ownership: "Our opponents are particularly fond of the myth that the Communist victory would provoke a civil war in Russia. Now this lie comes to an end. And we affirm that only a policy of the Communist Party could become the policy of national reconciliation." CPRF's ultimate goal is a peaceful and stable development of Russia and return of people's wealth back to people.

In this meeting, Zyuganov was again unanimously elected as the candidate for the next presidential elections. Amid multiple problems, this unanimous support has given Zyuganov the opportunity to recover the internal strength and unity of the party and maintain continuity and stability in organization. At present, the CPRF is still the party that enjoys the most rigorous organization, which has the most mature program and enjoys a relatively stable support and social basis in Russia. Only when the CPRF seriously summarizes the lessons learned, overcomes the negative influence of internal splits and factional struggles, adjusts its strategies based on the new situations, effectively represents the interests of the people, it will play its due role in Russia's political stage and usher in the spring of socialist movement.

Y. 40

The Successful Practice of Chavez's Socialist Exploration

Zhu Jidong[1]

Abstract: Although there are some controversial issues in his concept of Socialism of the 21st Century which Chavez has advocated, it is certain that he has made a major contribution to the world socialist movement after the drastic changes and collapse of the Soviet Union and Eastern European socialist countries. Chavez has resolutely criticized the Western free market economy. He raised the Venezuelan people's political status, improved their living standards, and elevated their happiness indices and hopes. By his reforms and achievements Venezuelan people gained an increasingly firm belief in socialism, thus with Venezuela's participation a powerful force was added to the Latin American socialism forces camp. After these developments we can say that Venezuela became the vanguard of the socialist forces in the Southern hemisphere. The successful exploration and practice of Chavez and his concept of Socialism of the 21st Century has not only strengthened the power of the world socialist forces and expanded the influence of Marxism in the world, but also contributed to the innovation and development of Marxism.

Key words: Chavez, Venezuela, Socialism of the 21st Century.

---

[1] Zhu Jidong, Executive Director of World Socialism Research Center of Chinese Academy of Social Sciences; Doctoral Student of Marxism Study of Graduate School; Associate Senior Editor of Xinhua News Agency.

On October 10, 2012, the National Electoral authority of Venezuela officially announced that Chavez had won and elected as the new president of Venezuela for the next 7 years till 2019. This was his fourth election victory. Despite some controversies, Chavez, is honored as the Red Star of Latin America", "the Second Castro", "Hope and Savior of the Poor", "Anti-American Banner Bearer", etc., and has initiated the concept of the 21stCentury Socialism which became a new highlight in the world socialist movement, which is at the low ebb, after the collapse of the Soviet Union and the drastic changes in Eastern Europe. Then, how did Chavez embark on the exploration of a socialist path? What kind of socialism is his Socialism of the 21st Century? What was achieved in his exploration, and what are its influences and significance?

I. Chavez is actively exploring socialism as the national leader of Venezuela

Chavez's later determined fight for socialism is closely related to his life experiences. Born into an ordinary family of teacher parents in the West of Venezuela on July 28th, 1954, Chavez was born the second of seven children and led a difficult life, because his three-generation family living in the same house relied on his parents' meager income for living. Since he was a child, he has been in the streets, peddling snacks made by his grandmother for some extra income for the family. Those experiences allowed him to gain experience on the lives of the poor people and led him to work for the well-being of them after he came to power.

Chavez initiated and led the "Revolutionary Bolivarian Movement" in order to win the presidential election

Chavez initiated and organized the "Revolutionary Bolivarian Movement-200" in 1982 and later he was sentenced to imprisonment for organizing a military coup in 1992, after his attempt had failed. In 1994, after he was released from prison, he devoted himself to political activities to publicize political ideas of eliminating corruption and advocated social fairness. He tirelessly visited poverty-stricken areas around the country where he disseminated his revolutionary ideas to the low-income groups.

With his efforts, Revolutionary Bolivarian Movement-200 evolved into a political party and was renamed Movement for the Fifth Republic in 1997 July.

His party advocated to lead Venezuela onto a path different from traditional socialism and also neo-liberal capitalism which was popular in those days. At the parliamentary elections of November 1998, the Movement for the Fifth Republic (party) obtained 49 out of the 189 seats in the National Assembly and become the second largest party of the country.

A month later, as the candidate recommended by the alliance of left-wing parties, Chavez easily defeated his rivals in the presidential elections and was elected as president with 56.6% of the votes, highest rate in the last 40 years.

After his inauguration on the February 2nd, 1999, he changed the country's name as Bolivarian Republic of Venezuela. Promoted by him, civil rights and democratic transformations were started and a new Constitution was passed by a people's referendum. The new Constitution highlighted "material guarantees for people's comprehensive development" and stipulated protecting "everyone's right to freely develop her/his individuality". The people were given more democratic rights. The new Constitution was highly supported by the people and provided the legal basis for Chavez's further revolution.

Chavez took a clear position against the laissez-faire market economy of the West

After he took office, Chavez took a clear position against the laissez-faire market economy of the West, followed a national economic policy of nationalization and also nationalized some important key enterprises and carried out "Anti-US foreign policy", which was supported by the lower classes and the Anti-western groups. But these policies also offended the vested interests of certain domestic forces as well as the U.S.

In April 2002, opposition parties attempted coup with the support of the U.S., but miraculously 48 hours later Chavez was able to return back to his office. The thrilling unsuccessful coup taught Chavez that he should design more effective policies benefiting the poor people in order to further increase his strength and enhance mass base of the government. Therefore, after the constitutional amendment, he was to be re-elected as president and in the elections of July 2000, he made openly declared "not to follow the capitalist path" and yearned for socialism. And after 2005, he repeatedly announced his ideas to replace "capitalism" with "new socialism" and openly advocated the "21st Century Socialism."

The "21st Century Socialism" proposed by Chavez was based on Simon Bolivar's thoughts and took in many theories including Christian doctrines, national hero General Samora's ideas of defending national sovereignty and Marx's scientific socialism and some other theories. But the core of the "21st Century Socialism" advocates social fairness, equity, justice, democracy, freedom, and so on. On August 15, 2004, with the firm belief that people would support him, Chavez agreed to accept a "recall referendum" and won 58.25% of the votes. From then on, Chavez, more strongly advocated the "21st Century Socialism" and was even more well-received and loved by the people.

Chavez stayed close with the people and became the most popular president.

In order to have close relations and contacts with the people, Chavez even used his presidential office as an important bridge to interact with the ordinary people. The Miraflores Palace, in the west of Caracas—his presidential office—is a spectacular office is loosely guarded and surrounded by slums resided by poor people. It was the place where Chavez's supporters gathered to interact with him. On April 13, 2002, the third day after the unsuccessful coup attempt, hundreds of thousands of supporters gathered outside the Palace asking the coup leaders for their beloved president, with deafening slogan "I am also Chavez". Among countries in Latin America and even the whole world, Venezuela's office of the president is the one that is surrounded by the largest number of poverty-stricken people.

Ever since he put forward the "Socialism of the 21st Century", Chavez has become people's spiritual power and national leader and his repeated successes in many elections has delivered great happiness for the majority of the Venezuelans.

II. How did Chavez fill the hearts of Venezuelans with confidence in socialism?

2006 that the Socialism of the 21st Century, he wanted to build was different from that in the 20th century, the Socialism of the 21st Century, would aimed to ensure "the free development of each as the condition for the free development of all the people"—a statement in Marx's Communist Manifest. In fact, Chavez thought "changing the political status of the laborers as the biggest happiness brought to the people should be mission of the Socialism of the 21st Century, which granted Chavez wholehearted support of the people.

Chavez gave the people the feeling of being masters of their own affairs for the first time.

Chavez's primary important measure to raise people's political status was protecting their political rights through a democratic legislation, therefore he always emphasized and promoted the participation by the people, granting the people the feeling of being the masters of their own affairs and freedom for the first time.

After being elected, Chavez started the political reforms and made up his mind to make important amendments to the 1962 Constitution; he strongly proposed democratic participation in state and political affairs and elimination of corruption, encouraged all social classes the society to take part in national decision making, on the other side adhered to the policy of "using all means to guarantee people's say on the fate of the country" besides he actively promoted the peaceful and democratic revolutionary way to establish socialism.

Propelled by him, since April 25, 1999, Chavez's government had initiated several referendums, he supported the Constituent Assembly decision-making system, supported free elections for the Assembly and recall general elections with new Constitution, so that voters could fully exercise their rights to vote and decide the affairs of the country.

The new constitution passed in the referendum of December 1999 stipulated that: "apart from the three powers of legislation, executive and judicial power, constitution endows civil rights and political rights—to propose, use their rights to supervise state institutions and use their rights to organize and jointly nominate candidates for the Supreme Court, National Election Committee and Ethics Council of the Republic". With the new constitution the House of Representatives and Senate were combined into a single organ called the National Congress, made up by 167 members to be elected for a term of 5 years. Moreover, indigenous people of Venezuela (the Indians) were included in the Constitution as legal subjects for the first time and they were endowed with political, economic, social and cultural rights.

Chavez implemented participatory democracy, so that the people can practice their rights as the masters of the country

Chavez emphasized that Socialism of the 21st Century was in essence people's democracy, participatory democracy and democracy of the people, and they should play the leading role. For Chavez, another important way to raise people's political status was implementing grass roots democracy organs and other grass roots organizations such as community councils, in order to realize the principle of participatory democracy, people being the masters of the country. For the participation by the people, Chavez promoted the establishment of Communal councils and the parliament passed a bill for that.

The law promulgated in 2006, said: "Communal councils are a group of elected persons from a self-defined residential neighbourhood of about 150 to 400 families in urban areas, or closer to 20 families in rural areas, and potentially 10 in indigenous communities. The principal decision making body of a communal council is the citizens' assembly. The formal functioning committee is composed of the following five units:

- Citizens' Assembly
- Executive Body
- Financial Management Unit
- Unit of Social Oversight (Anti-corruption)
- Community Coordination Collective

All council persons are people within the community elected by the citizens' assembly for a period of 2 years. No person can occupy positions in more than one unit at time."

And communal councils were officially established in April 2006, which marked that Venezuela entered a brand-new and important stage of establishing a "new political system" and local power organs as the basis of the "new political system" By 2008, 500 community councils were established in the urban districts and 50,000 throughout the country, and a large proportion was organized in these councils. Chavez called them as the "embryo and a space of the new socialist country" and "basic organizations of the new state". It is particularly noteworthy that It is also enshrined in the constitution that the Venezuelan National Assembly is obliged to consult with these community organizations,. therefore since after 2006, according to the law of communes, the community parliament should have an elected spokesperson for each community council that forms that commune. Another three elected spokespeople for the socio-productive organizations, and one spokesperson to represent the Bank of the Commune. The term of each spokesperson is three years, after which they are eligible for re-election.

Besides, two "little brothers", were established as the Workers' Councils and the Peasants' Councils, as the basic grass-root organizations of the people which supplemented each other. The activities of the Communal Council were financially sponsored by the government.

Chavez emphasized ideological work and held high the banner of socialism

In the world socialist camp, Chavez, who has studied and praises the Selected Works of Mao Zedong, seems to inspire him, he not only quoted sayings from Mao from time to time but also grasped the essence of Mao Zedong thought better than many Chinese and tried to apply it.

In order to turn his idea of Socialism of the 21st Century into reality, Chavez, has attached great importance to ideological work, often reads the works of Marx and Lenin and tries to creatively apply the ideas written in the works of Marx, Engels, Lenin, Mao Zedong, so on. Not only did he himself tries hard to learn Marxism, he also called on the whole nation to study the works of Marx and Lenin. With Chavez's determined positioning both the more and more Venezuelans and people around the world began to understand the significance of Mao Zedong thought and China, his studies on the Mao Zedong Thought not only provided strong spiritual impetus for Venzuala's exploration of socialism but helped him to win great support from socialist countries and enabled Venezuala's close cooperation with the socialist countries.

Since he came into power, Chavez has held high the banner of "Socialism of the 21st Century" so that socialism can enjoy more and more popularity in Venezuela. On January 30, 2005, in his speech in the fifth World Social Forum, Chavez said, "I am increasingly confident that we need less and capitalism, and more and more socialism." It was the first time that Chavez had clearly showed his faith on socialism and opposition to capitalism.

On February 25, in the same year, he stated in the opening ceremony of Fourth Social Debt Summit that: Venezuela's "revolution should be of socialist nature, otherwise it will not be a revolution" and "this socialism should be the socialism of the 21st century". It was the first time that he had publicly used his concept of "Socialism of the 21st Century". Later, he repeatedly expressed: "I am a 21st century socialist".

III. Significant improvements in the life of Venezuelan people has strengthened their hope and faith in socialism

Chavez who has continuously praised and studied Mao Zedong and China is quite aware that, in order to get the people's support for socialism, not only raising their political status will be enough, especially constant improvement of people's well being would be the key factor.

Therefore, during the period he has been in power for more than a decade, he has committed himself to improve people's well- being. He took ordinary people's concrete interests into account in the formulation of national policies and tried to do everything with people's interests as the starting point of all his policies, which has made Socialism of the 21st Century take deeper roots among the people. He has implemented a series of policies beneficial for the masses, which constitutes the main reason for his election victories.

Chavez has vigorously promoted nationalization as the basic government policy

Considering himself to be the gravedigger of "neo-liberalism", Chavez has vigorously promoted nationalization as the basic government policy. He first nationalized those enterprises that are the economic lifeblood of the country as petroleum and other key industries and regarded this policy as an important measure to realize socialism.

On December 15, 2006, Chavez pointed out in his speech: "in the Communist Manifesto when Marx and Engels discussed the scientific socialism, they emphasized the extreme importance of economic transformation. If we want to establish true socialism, our economy should be socialized. We have to create a new production mode, which is our concern. Yet we are still exploring this path. In the end, the essence of socialism is to eliminate private ownership of means of production and replace it with collective management so as to meet the needs of people, needs of the society and the environment."

On January 10, 2007 when Chavez held the new cabinet meeting, after the cabinet was sworn in , he said in his speech: our government should speed up the reforms, nationalize enterprises in main industries like communications and electric power that had been privatized by the former governments, expand the government's shares in the oil industry and we should restrict the independence of the national central bank. To speed up the nationalization of the industries like energy, electric power and telecommunication aims to make the people the major beneficiary in the economy and will also be good to consolidate the foundation of their political power. These measures by Chavez enabled "Socialism of the 21st Century" .to have a solid economic foundation.

Chavez repeatedly expressed: "those that is feasible to be nationalized will be nationalized and it must be done". After nationalizing the assets of oil companies worth of billions of dollars, he turned his attention towards the service companies with smaller scale. On February 28, 2009, rice processing factories all over the country refused to produce rice at the price regulated by the government, so Chavez ordered Venezuelan army to take over those all these factories, temporarily. In August, he announced that the government would take over two large national coffee enterprises whose production amounted 80% of the whole domestic production and coffee market and would carry the nationalization through to the end. The nationalization policies by Chavez not only helped Venezuela to control the country's economic lifeline, but also enabled him to carry out his gigantic social development plans and foreign aid to needy countries, which all paved the way for improving people's well-being and winning international status.

Chavez actively carried out a land reform and vigorously developed economy

Due to the underdeveloped status of Venezuela's agriculture, 70% of the food need of Venezuela was being imported. Chavez believed that unreasonable land ownership was an important reason for the long-term awful situation of country's agriculture so he decided to start the land reform.

And in November 2001, with a special legislative power endowed by the constitution, he led the formulation and promulgation of 92 laws and regulations, among which Land Law was the most influential. According to the Land Law, land owners should truthfully declare their amount of land property within a specified time and the government would have the right to to recover those lands or purchase them at a low price and then redistributes it to the needy farmers, those lands over 5,000 hectares and those lands which are not tilled nonproductive land. It meant that the "private property" of big land owners will be no longer protected by the state and landless peasants will benefit from the new law. On March 25, 2007, Chavez announced the confiscation of 2 million hectares of non-tilled land from big land owners and declared that as one part of the socialist reforms, the government would try to realize the goal of "land to the tiller" through land reform. In 2011, the Chavez government also launched a massive "Venezuelan Housing Plan" sponsored the government which included the building of 3 million houses all around the country between 2011 and 2017 and sell them to medium income families at a low price or give them to low income families that need to move and re-settle.

Chavez actively promoted collective ownership such as cooperatives and those enterprises which would produce public goods as a part of "people's economy", in order to enable people become the masters of social and economic organizations and the new Constitution stipulates the following: developing cooperatives is a special mission of the new Constitution a key measure to solve the issues of livelihood for the people. With these efforts, cooperatives have developed rapidly.

By August 2007, the number of registered cooperatives have amounted 215,000, with more than 3 million members. The production value they created amounted to 14% of national GDP and they employed % 18 of the economically active population of the country. Inside the cooperatives, leaders and members are equal, profits generated are distributed among workers, workers can elect the managers and the supervisors of the cooperatives and environmental issues are managed by workers' representatives.

Chavez seems to deeply realize that vigorous development of the economy is the prerequisite and basis of successful implementation and consolidation of his Socialism of the 21st Century project. He called on to all economic sectors to undertake concerted efforts in vitalizing economy so as to realize rapid economic development. Between 2000-2005, the annual economic growth rate of Venezuela has been 10% and between 2000-2006, the annual growth in the minimum wage of workers have increased %20 to %30, which demonstrates that the majority of the people have benefited from economic growth and development.

Chavez has established a life-long social security system which covers all the citizens, without any discrimination

In the sphere of social development, Chavez has emphasized social justice, equity and mutual help, solidarity and actively established a lifelong new social security system, which covers all the citizens, without any discrimination.

First of all, drawing lessons from the anti-government strikes that was supported by the chain stores that sold imported foodstuffs, Chavez government started the project of "Mission Mercal" which aimed to establish a chain store network of 140,000 stores covering the whole country to control the supply system within 3 years, between 2005-2007. The stores were especially established in the poverty-stricken neighborhoods.

Today, "Mission Mercal" has become the biggest chain store and the second largest enterprise of Venezuela, where people can make shopping and buy basic consumption products with subsidized prices, besides each and every citizen can sell their products to Mercal stores.

Secondly, Chavez called for the "cultivation" of socialism through education of the people, which should be truly democratic and which respects the values of the nation. The government initiated a nationwide Bolivarian literacy Campaign called as Mission Robinson with which free public education was greatly improved.

Mission Robinson established full-day Bolivarian schools, where two free daily meals were offered. In the framework of Mission Robinson tens of thousands of military and administrative personnel were sent to rural areas to promote education. On July 1, 2003, Chavez has announced the Robinson mission, and the nation-wide illiteracy campaign was officially started. With this campaign, illiteracy was greatly eliminated illiteracy and hundreds of thousands of people were elevated to the level of primary school education.

In October 2005, UNESCO has praised Venezuela as a country without illiteracy. Later, "Mission Ribas" and "Mission Sucre" allowed hundreds of thousands of adults and teenagers to attend the middle school and college courses, which greatly enhanced the cultural qualities of the people. Besides, Chavez spent a large portion of the oil export revenues for the health care programs which especially served the poor people. He started a nation-wide public health network of health clinics, called as the "Go Deep Into the Slums" project to provide free basic medical care and health services to poor people.

In these clinics, people could see a doctor for free, get drugs for free, and can enjoy 12-hour medical services, 24-hour emergency treatment, call a doctor for house visits, and so on. Thus all citizens are provided with free medical services financed by the state. Moreover, with the help of tens of hundreds of Cuban doctors, the above system of cooperative basic level medical has spread to all over the country. In addition, Chavez has repeatedly initiated minimum wage increases, thus enabling Venezuelan workers get highest minimum wages among Latin American countries.

Since Chavez came to power, the number of poverty-stricken people of the country has decreased by half. In 2009, the United Nations included Venezuela among those countries with high level of development.

In many countries, social stability can be undermined by the continuous increases in prices. However, Chavez's iron solid policies increases the trust and confidence of the people which facilitates government's ability to stabilize prices. The Venezuelan government formed a research group to examine the inflation and it found out that that inflation was caused by the speculators' manipulations of the prices and consequently the prices of more than 100 basic foodstuff ranging from sugar, milk to beef had rampantly increased.

Therefore, on July 14, 2010 Chavez announced the establishment of a new governmental department to regulate the commodity prices and deal with speculators so that the increasing inflation could be controlled. On the same day, Chavez issued a new decree to control the prices and approved the establishment of the prices regulation department. He said, in a cabinet meeting that was live broadcasted on the national television: the new "government decree on checking the costs and price of goods will prevent speculators from "plundering" the Venezuelan people or opportunistically making excess profits".

The new price regulation department would try to guarantee that the traders would not set the prices too excessively and ensure "fair price and costs" and "it will end the market speculations."

The practice has showed that these measures were effective, they did not only ensure a stable life for the Venezuelan people, but gave them a sense of security for their future life. Currently, all the Venezuelan people can enjoy free public medical care, free education and cheap water, electricity and natural gas. Although inflation is high, in the recent years, many low-income families living poorer neighborhoods can purchase their foodstuff needs, with subsidized lower prices, and by law the government is obliged to supply them foodstuffs at subsidized lower prices. As a result, a large number of ordinary people has become firm supporters as well as voters for Chavez and his "Socialism of the 21st Century".

For many years, Chavez has been holding high the banner of "Socialism of the 21st Century", not only for raising the political status of the Venezuelan people and improving their living standards, and elevating their happiness, so as to gain their increasing support in building socialism, but also to foster the socialist forces in Latin America, consequently Venezuela has become a vanguard of the socialist forces in the Southern Hemisphere.

Moreover, Chavez led Venezuelan people in resolutely supporting Cuban people in their socialist revolution and socialist construction and he continuously strengthened cooperation with China and other socialist countries, which significantly expanded the joint socialist forces of socialism in Latin American and in the world.

Although, some countries' exploration of socialism may not tally with the traditional definition of socialism and socialism building, we can comfortably say that there can be no fixed model for socialism and socialism building, And such new explorations do not only enhance the vitality and enrichment of the world socialism, but also expands the influence of Marxism in the world, innovates and develops Marxism. We should observe them with optimistic expectations and support them for future victories.

Y. 41

The New Struggle of the Communist Party of Greece under Circumstances of the European Debt Crisis

Yu Haiqing[1]

Abstract: The Communist Party of Greece is leading various struggles against capitalism since the eruption of European debt crisis. Recently, the party has formed some new viewpoints on such problems as debt crisis and criticized some false arguments on the mass struggles.

Key words: Communist Party of Greece; the European Debt Crisis; mass struggles

---

1 Yu Haiqing, Guest Researcher of World Socialism Research Center, attached to CASS, and Associate Researcher in the Academy of Marxism.

Since the eruption of the European sovereign debt crisis in the end of 2009, Greece, the eye of storm in the crisis, became the main battlefield of European radical left's anti-capitalist struggle. In the crisis that has lasted for two years, the Communist Party of Greece has been standing in the forefront of the battle, leading the Greek people to achieve a wave after wave of resistance to the climax.

Since June 2011, as the crisis deepened and Greece's economic situation deteriorated, the Communist Party of Greece (KKE) started a new round of struggle climax. During the struggles, the Communist Party of Greece contemplated on the capitalist crisis and the Greece's debt problem and raised some new viewpoints and opinions. At the same time, the Party criticized some false opinions and thoughts on the masses' protest movement and underlined communists' basic standpoint and attitude under the crisis.

I. Latest progress in the anti-capitalist struggle of the Communist Party of Greece

In the anti-capitalist struggle during the crisis, the Communist Party of Greece pointed the arrow towards the government's austerity measures to counter the crisis, targeting the Greek government, the EU, NATO and major economic monopoly capitalist groups and organizations by means of protests and strikes.

From the latter half of 2011 up to now, the strikes and demonstrations led and supported by the Communist Party of Greece include:

On June 15, the General Confederation of Workers of Greece led by the Communist Party of Greece took part in the 24-hour general strike where tens of thousands of people staged a demonstration against the government's austerity measures to cope with the debt crisis in the center of Athens.

On June 16, the Communist Party of Greece organized demonstration in Athens and 55 other cities.

On June 28, the left-wing labor confederation of Greece (PAME) participated in and organized a 48-hour general strike, pressing the government when the parliament was voting on the new austerity plan.

On September 29, the Communist Party of Greece organized tens of thousands people for demonstration against the government's new tax scheme in the center of Athens.

On October 5, the left-wing labor confederation of Greece (PAME) took part in and organized a 24-hour general strike held by employees from both state-run and private sectors against the government's new austerity measures. Participants included employees working in the local municipal government offices, taxing offices, public hospitals, schools, airports, etc.

From October 19 to 20, the left-wing labor confederation of Greece (PAME) took part in and organized a 48-hour general strike protesting the government's continuation of financial austerity policies and against such measures as increasing tax levy and reducing welfare. Strikers called for the resignation of the Papandreou government to assume responsibility, carrying the banner "Government Should Step Down".

At the beginning of 2012, the Communist Party of Greece played a more active role in leading strikes and protests.

On January 17, February 7, February 10 and February 11, the labor confederation of Greece (PAME) launched strikes against the government's new financial austerity policies.

In addition to leading and organizing strikes against the government's austerity measures, the Communist Party of Greece also actively supported workers in various strikes to protect their rights, which brought great spiritual support to the workers' struggles of the steel industry that had lasted for 100 days.

The "Occupy" Movement that began in the US and swept the capitalist world could also be seen in the struggles of the Communist Party of Greece. As early as June 3, 2011, the Communist Party of Greece led several hundred protestors to block the entrance of the office building of Ministry of Finance of Greece, where Greek government negotiated with the EU authorities and IMF on the issues of financial aid, and occupied the building. Protestors hung a gigantic poster outside the building, calling on all the people to stage a general strike. In the strike on February 10, 2012, strikers and protestors occupied the Ministry of Labor.

Moreover, the Communist Party of Greece also carried out fierce struggles against all sorts of anti-communist activities. For instance, the Communist Party of Greece actively criticized and fought against the Georgia's anti-communist Freedom Charter[2], anti-communist measures by Slovakian government the anti-communist speech from Martin Schulz, the new social-democrat speaker of the European Parliament.

The Party spoke highly of the historical achievements of the Soviet Union and other socialist countries and emphasized that those socialist countries tackled huge difficulties and completed huge tasks that capitalism could only achieve in a period of few centuries, and solved the unemployment problem. Socialism, protected laborers' social and economic rights and achieved historical breakthroughs in medical treatment, education, culture and physical education.

---

2 On the 31th of May 2011, the Parliament of Georgia adopted the so-called „Freedom Charter", which prohibits the Communist ideology and the use of Soviet symbols in the public areas. After the change of governing power the new Parliament of Georgia extended the list of symbols that are prohibited by law and there were specified sanctions for violation of the law.

Although various mistakes and deviations happened during the establishment of socialism and although these deviations has led to a counter-revolutionary restoration occurred, the achievements of socialist countries should be fully acknowledged. The Communist Party of Greece appealed to the working class and the people to study the experiences of building socialism and the history of communist movement and fight against the reactionary forces' attacking communism and fascism in the same breath and equation of communism and fascism and called on to fight back vigorously against anti-communist measures.

II. Basic viewpoints of the Party on the capitalist economic crisis and debt crisis

With the worsening of European debt crisis, the Communist Party of Greece has deepened its understanding of the economic crisis and debt problems. The Party, with sharp eyes saw through the phenomenal appearance and grasped the essence of developments and raised viewpoints and opinions which are distinct from the mainstream of public opinions. Its basic viewpoints include the following:

The aim of the bourgeoisie launching unprecedented offensive on people's income and rights cannot solve public debt problem, but rather to strengthen European monopoly groups' competitiveness in the international capitalist market.

July 2012 memorandum of understanding between Greece and the Troika (the International Monetary Fund, European Central Bank, and the European Commission) failed miserably The Memoranda of Understanding in the Greek Debt Crisis was promoted among EU members, in accordance with this Memoranda all EU states renewed their economic reform plan and implemented stabilization plans which contained anti-people commitments targeting the majority of the wage earners.

The propaganda by the capitalist states blurs the real cause of the debt problem. Workers should not be made responsible to pay the public debt

There are five causes behind the Greek debt problem.

Firstly, Social Democratic Party's (PASOK) fiscal policy served the interests of Greek monopoly capitalist groups. Its main features included: legal measures to radically reduce taxes for big capitalists, which created conditions for wider tax evasion, thus PASOK used public wealth to support capitalist groups, namely, the state borrowed from other countries to meet higher profit demand of the capitalist groups.

Secondly, the military spending has been huge, which increased to 4% of the GDP in 2009.

Thirdly, during the integration of the Greek economy into the EU and into the European Monetary Union, its industrial production departments were faced with the shrinkage of production, due to huge pressure of competition from the other EU countries.

The radical increase in imports also influenced an increasing trade deficit with the EU countries, besides the increasing trade deficit had also a corresponding impact of increasing public debts.

Fourthly, the terms of borrowing have deteriorated, including interest rates, maturity of debts, repayment conditions, consequently Greece's loan interest payments increased from 9 billion Euros per year increased to 15 billion Euros in 2011, compared to beginning of the 21st century.

Fifthly, after the eruption of the capitalist economic crisis, due to decrease in economic activities, tax income reduction has occurred, coupled with the increased financial support to the banks and to other monopoly groups by the government, the public budget deficit and foreign debt stock has increased radically.

Fueled by the general EU strategy, the anti-people political line followed by the Greek bourgeois regime has increased the debt burden of the country.

Since the outburst of the debt crisis, the GDP growth of Greece has plummeted while public debt has increased. At the end of the third quarter of 2011, the proportion of the public debt of the state to GDP figure has increased to 160%, compared to 127.1% in the 2009.

This fact has showed that any change in the bourgeois regime (another capitalist party getting the helm of the government) cannot not and will not create a people-oriented solution which can release the burden over people.

Even bourgeois economists have admitted that reduction of debts with a memoranda treaty with the EU and austerity measures would only lead to piling up of debts again, that means that will not overcome the vicious cycle of economic recession.

What the central imperialist powers worry is not the scale of Greek's debt stock, rather they are afraid from a chain effect, impacting Spain, Italy and others in EU, which they think will endanger Euro's status as international reserve money and negatively affect the future of the Euro zone.

Although the working class is bankrupt, the EU and big financial magnates are still discussing how to strengthen their control over Greek economy which is on the verge of bankruptcy.

They have contradictions among them about how to share the losses and how to distribute the necessary capital depreciation among themselves, but they vigorously join forces to implement and maintain offensive anti-people policies.

Although different major EU countries have different plans, it seems that those who hold government debt bonds in their hands (especially major EU banks and institutional investors who hold them) accept delays (re-scheduling) of repayments by the Greek government, but Greece should be ready to pay the cost of interest for delayed payments. Thus, they think that they could avoid the full loss of their money brought by Greece's immediate bankruptcy.

For example, the debt restructuring plan proposed by the Bank of France and the consortium led by it, included a delay of the 50% of the current debts, to be repaid in 30 years, but the interest rate proposed was raised to 8% (crisis period premium rate) compared to 5.5% (the interest rate of stable period).

In order to secure a cheaper labor force, the dominant capitalist class has speeded up restructuring and privatization of the economy and sell public property to monopoly groups at cheapest prices, the dominant capitalist class will continues to upgrade its offensive against the people even if Greek government achieves relief of its debts.

Any short time achievement by the government regarding relief of its debts, will only lead to new tax reductions and further support for the big Greek capitalists by the Greek state, such a relief will not cause any improvements regarding the demands of the people.

That means, Greece will face another debt build up, that is a new round of increase of its debts.

The state revenues are only sufficient enough to pay the salaries and monthly pension payments of the people but cannot repay the debtors. In 2009 and 2010, the total budget revenues of the Greek state was 48.5 billion Euros and 51.1 billion Euros respectively, while subsidies for the social security payments, salaries and monthly pension payments were 42.3 billion Euros and 37.9 billion Euros respectively. However, the interest sums to be paid in 2009 and 2010, were 12.3 billion Euros and 13.2 billion Euros respectively.

Currently, while the government is emphasizing the danger of the state going bankrupt, it is still gives plenty of financial support to the Greek banks, expands Greece's military spending and cuts the tax rate on undistributed profits. During the crisis, the bailout financial support given by the Greek state to the banks has amounted to 108 billion Euros.

According to the Greek Communist Party, should not dream any propeople solution, because all the measures were formulated by the capitalist parties remain under the framework of Euro Pact and Europe 2020 Strategy, which aims push down the labor costs and labor wages, across the EU and all the measures concentrate on strengthening the competitive ability of monopoly capitalist groups in the international market.

III. On the several questions that should be underlined regarding the current struggles in Greece

The Communist Party of Greece has criticized some problems that occurred during the mass struggles, and developed some strategic ideas regarding the policies the Party should follow during the capitalist crisis and it has clarified Party's attitude towards parliamentary struggles.

These problems discussed by the Communist Party of Greece are, generally also the problems of the other communist parties and the working class movements and the social movements in the developed countries, the problems they need to face, think and solve.

The problems and limitations of the "movements of the squares"[3]

In June 2011, three months before the outburst of Occupy Wall Street movement, "indignados" (Indignant Citizens Movement) in Greece had already occupied the Syntagma Square outside the Parliament House in capital Athens. Several thousands of people have positively echoed the calls from the Facebook and occupied the Syntagma Square, thus began a spontaneous protest movement in this Square. The "movement" lasted for several weeks and reached many other cities and towns of Greece. The Communist Party of Greece analyzed this kind of spontaneous mass movement and criticized such slogans shouted by the crowd during these demonstrations such as "the left-wing should leave the Square", "Political parties should leave the Square", "Labor Unions should leave the Square", etc. The Party newspaper wrote: "such slogans, cast doubt on the democratic character of the "square movements", cast doubts on its goals, and cast doubts on their practical significance.

---

3 Movements of the squares: among the common features of these "movements of the squares" is that they have drawn large numbers of youth into political life – often with a sweeping sense of rejecting previous politics (both existing governments and the oppositional parties). There is a sense that everything "before" is corrupt, complicit and exhausted, and everything "after" must now make a break.

The square movements" oppose to organized and class-oriented labor union movement and advocated that the labor unions should leave the squares. However, labor union movement itself is not homogeneous: there are different kinds of labor unions—-such as the yellow ones that are led by the government and that collude with the employers, but the left-wing labor confederation of Greece (PAME) that organizes strikes and mass assemblies, is completely different from them. It is obvious that, the former ones insidiously support the austerity measures."

The party newspaper added: "that slogan demanding "political parties should leave the Square" shouted also represents a conservative view. A political party is an organizations that express the interests of a certain class and a stratum via its ideology and political line, consequently and different parties serve the interests of different classes.

The slogan "political parties should leave the Square" shouted by the crowd, equals the Communist Party that represents the interests of working class with the bourgeois parties and thus conceals the real enemy of the people, namely "the slogan" conceals the big capitalist monopoly groups that are in power."

The "movements of the squares" define themselves as a "non-political alliance", with the slogan of "real democracy", which has won the sympathy of the bourgeois media. But facts prove their claims about themselves is quite hypocritical. Under the vague theme of protest against the austerity measures, the "movements" have united the people but aimed and demanded to exclude labor unions, political parties and the left-wing parties and groups from the movement, as such this practice itself cast doubts on its democratic characteristics.

Preventing laborers to express themselves in the movement, and trying to censure their political and ideological opinions not only goes against democracy, but also restrains democracy from developing. Also, there is something problematic with the goals of the movement.

Although the "movement" allegedly, struggles against austerity measures and opposes the "EU memoranda on Greek debts" but it fails to point its finger at the Greek government, the EU and those political forces that obviously favor and support these above policies. All in all, the "movement" opposes organized allied struggles, by preventing different social groups from participating in the common movement of people.

According to the views of the Communist Party of Greece, it is impossible that the "movements of the squares" can liberate workers from problems, old and new, because this movement hasn't originated or rooted in the anti-capitalist class movement in the factories and work-places, it lacks the very solid basis, for a sustainable development.

The Communist Party of Greece highlights the significance of struggles in the factories in the struggle, since it believes that the real sphere of class struggles is the factory space. Only in this space, can the workers carry unremitting struggles—every moment of every day—against big capitalists, and can achieve the ultimate victory.

When the Western left-wing political trends generally speaking highly of "the occupy" or "square" movements, above analysis and thoughts by the Communist Party of Greece provides us a new perspective for our in-depth understanding of these movements.

The left should "unite with the Greek people"

The Communist Party of Greece has stressed that the working class should not be misled by the slogans like "We are all Greeks" shouted in the strikes and demonstrations of the left forces in some Western European countries.

Whom should the left ally with in Greece? There are two main forces in Greece. There are Greek capitalists who try to get new loans from the EU and IMF so as to increase their profits, on the one side, and the Greek working class and the ordinary people that shoulder the burden of the capitalist crisis. Whom should the left ally with in Greece?

According to the views of the Communist Party of Greece: the above slogan does not give a clear answer to this question. There are two main reasons for this situation. On the one hand, certain left forces, mainly the democratic socialists, opportunists in the Party of the European Left and "the Green Party", tend to use such vague slogans to whitewash the Maastricht Treaty Criteria, and try to disguise their support EU treaties, disguise the reactionary character of the EU, the Communist Party of Greece vigorously underlines: "democratization" can never be achieved, by the big capital led EU.

On the other hand, some people have harbored ulterior motives by placing Greek debt problem in the competition among imperialist forces within and outside the EU. Doubtlessly, the working class of Greece should like to unite with workers in Europe and the whole world, but this unity should aim to coordinate struggles and strikes against capitalism, support class-oriented labor union movements and prevent capitalism from exploiting and oppressing workers. The statement released by Central Committee of the Communist Party of Greece stated that there was no need for the workers in Europe to "become Greeks". Instead, they should join the struggle to acquire modern rights for the working class and hardworking people, overthrow the dictatorship of big capitalist class in all countries, aim to realize the socialization of monopoly capitalist property system and quit the imperialist EU and NATO. Thus the slogan for the moment should be the "Workers of all countries, unite for common struggles."

"National" sovereignty or people's sovereignty

In the face of EU's second round of aid scheme to solve the Greek debt crisis, there emerged an opinion in the leaders of mass protestors in Greece—they think, if the EU's memorandum conditions for the aid is accepted, the "national government will be executing orders of the foreign governments" which will mean "we" the Greek nation will lose its national sovereignty". The Communist Party of Greece opposed this kind of deceptive opinion as it disguised the root cause of the crisis, namely, the inherent contradiction of capitalism, between labor and capital. Such opinion can easily be exploited by the bourgeois politicians. At the same time, it cannot scientifically reveal the true situation under the current world imperialism framework: the interdependence in the current imperialist alliances, "state sovereignty" of all allies are already nullified in the EU mechanism.

"The reason why the ruling bourgeoisie of each country has joined the imperialist alliance is not that they have betrayed the nation or state that represent their interests. The reason they have joined the imperialist alliance, is to serve their narrow class interests, reinforce their class status and cope with the working class with various suppression mechanisms and tools controlled by the common alliance organization. They have transferred their sovereignty to various inter-state agencies in order to better compete against other major monopoly capitalist forces as the U.S., Japan, Russia, etc.

The Communist Party of Greece thinks: the abolition of this kind of dependence and interdependence can only be realized by the working class-people's[4] regime through fundamental socialization of means of production, central planning and workers' control over economy, instead of those ideas or slogans which humanizes the "imperialist alliance", such as praising the EU institutions as implementing "democratic" operation.

Myths created about the crisis and solutions

The Communist Party of Greece has criticized various "solutions" against the crisis and pointed out that the general direction of "EU Memoranda" and the "painless" exit plan from the crisis as advertised by the so-called mid-term plan (known in Greece as Mesoprothesmo) raised by the EU and its member states in 2010 and 2012, both do not contradict with the demands of the monopoly capitalist class forces.

The political groups such as the Coalition of the Radical Left and anti-capitalist left front have proposed to quit the Euro zone and cancellation the debt, as a solution that will benefit the people. Yet in fact, these proposals

---

[4] Working class-people is an original terminology developed by the KKE (The Communist Party of Greece).

are based on some mistaken ideas, they think that huge amount of public debt and Greece being part of the Eurozone are the main causes why the government enforces various reactionary measures.

For countries outside the Euro zone, such as the Sweden, the U.K. and Germany—the leader of Eurozone—which do not suffer from grave debt problem, offensive against the workers' rights can be mainly attributed to the general capitalist development path.

The above opportunist tendencies in current the socialist forces are misleading the people by the slogans like, "overthrow the occupation of Greece by IMF", or "overthrow the occupation by the European Central Bank and European Commission" which disguise the important role played by ruling classes of Greece, in attacking people's rights and income and also disguised the intertwined relationship between Greek capitalists and international capitalist class. The opportunist tendencies put forward various crisis exit planes, but in essence all these proposals aim to develop a version of crisis management solution within the framework of capitalist system, which can temporarily recover the capitalist profit rates.

The Communist Party of Greece argues that the current crisis is the crisis of capitalism rather than a simple debt crisis. Even if certain measures can recover the development of capitalism, people's prosperity and well-being will not be possible. So long as there occurs a fundamental change in terms of economic and political power and so long as monopoly capitalist class dominates the EU countries, there will never be a people-oriented solution.

To solve the crisis, the working class should not retrogress to the past economic forms or go back to capitalist economic protectionism, i.e. back to the national level; instead, the working class should strive for working class-people power and head towards socialism.

At the current stage, a class-oriented labor movement should be developed. The working class must carry out struggle against the economic rule of monopoly capitalism, struggle against capitalist countries and imperialist alliances and the working class should not be trapped by the impasse and dilemma of capitalist power. Different left forces should be coordinated to struggle against the bourgeois forms of management, demand that big capitalists should undertake the social security costs and put forward a political line that opposes abandonment of labor and social security rights. The basic direction of the struggle should be to overthrow capitalism. The only way to resolve the crisis is to mobilize people's power and "break away from EU and cancel multi-lateral debts agreements."

The correct understanding on the parliamentary struggle

Under the contemporary capitalist condition that the big capitalist groups are holding the ruling position, it is an important question for the current international communist movement to deeply think over, contemplate how the greatly marginalized and weakened communist party should understand its tasks and missions, especially how to correctly consider the parliamentary struggles, electoral tactics, participation in and even establishment of coalition governments. This issue is closely linked with the direction of future development.

Should the communist parties be indulged in parliamentary struggle, be content with the increase in its votes and be content with participating the government, or should it stick to the path of promoting people's movements and commit itself in establishing people's regime?

Regarding these questions, the Communist Party of Greece holds an unyielding opposition line which opposes the opportunistic parliamentarianism line.

On January 5, 2012, in the face of insistent questioning by journalists, Papariga, General Secretary of the Communist Party of Greece explicitly expressed the basic standpoint of the Party, regarding parliamentary struggle in the morning show of Greece's ANT 1 TV. She answered: at the current stage of Greece, our Party will not seek to participate in the formation of a government, because participating in the government will not be able stop the consequences of the crisis or be able to solve people's problems. As long as the monopoly power exists, it is impossible to establish any progressive government in Greece."

"If a so-called SYRIZA led radical left government, or a central right or a central left government is formed, soon after they will immediately embark on a path to arrange more memoranda and foreign loans to consolidate the alliance of Greece's big enterprises and employers. Under the current conditions, it is impossible for Greece to form a people-oriented government. As long as the current political status quo cannot be changed, there will be no correct or favorable solution to the crisis.

Under the current debt crisis, the Party's task should be organizing and mobilizing all people in anti-capitalist struggle rather than seeking to form government that would operate within the framework of capitalist system."

The Communist Party of Greece, does not rule out the possibility of a radical overthrow of the existing system, but it also emphasizes that the revolutionary struggle can not achieve victory overnight, so people need to achieve progressive incremental small victories, bit by bit. Papariga, stated: it is impossible, to determine the exact time schedule for the revolutionary change of the current political regime because, everything will depend on the will of the overwhelming majority of the people."

Y. 42

The Active Position of the Communist Party of Greece in the Debt Crisis

Tong Jin[1]

Abstract: The debt crisis, a chronic problem of Greece, has caused a chaotic situation in this country, and to date, no reasonable and effective solution is visible. Currently, public demonstrations and strikes occur frequently.

The Greek Communist Party, as the most influential left-wing party in Greece, actively call and organize protests against the government, urging it to take measures as to alleviate the domestic contradictions, in favor the interests of the working class. The Communist Party of Greece not only focuses on the participation and organization of practical struggles, but also actively carries out ideological persuasion and propaganda work, which exposes the essence of capitalist society and its fundamental contradiction, in order to safeguard the interests of the working class. At the same time, the Greek Communist Party tries to use all the opportunities and favorable conditions within the parliament, thus pays attention to carrying out struggles in the Parliament, to defend people. The Party does not miss any opportunity to express its own position, regarding the crisis and its solution, in order to educate and create a more favorable condition for the working class.

Key words: Communist Party of Greece; debt; crisis

---

[1] Tong Jin, Special Researcher of World Socialism Research Center attached to CASS; Doctoral Student of Marxism Study of Graduate School.

The Communist Party of Greece can be rated as an influential one among the communist parties of Europe in adhering to the basic tenets of Marxism-Leninism. After the collapse of the former Soviet Union and tremendous changes in the Eastern Europe, communist parties of the Western Europe have generally adjusted their theories and policies. Among them, some, which are represented by the Communist Party of France, the Communist Re-foundation Party of Italy and the Communist Party of Spain, adopted an innovative policy that "completely transcends the traditional" guiding ideological line. While others including the Communist Party of Greece and the Communist Party of Portugal took a gradual adjustment strategy that stuck to the tenets and sought a gradual and stable new exploration. The Communist Party of Greece firmly defends the Marxism-Leninism as always. In recent years, in the face of the most serious debt crisis and economic crisis of the country, this Party has directly and profoundly exposed to the drawbacks of capitalism and has thoroughly revealed various contradictions and problems of international financial monopoly capitalism.

I. History of the Communist Party of Greece

Formerly known as Socialist Workers' Party of Greece, the Communist Party of Greece was renamed, in 1924 under the influence of the October Revolution. During World War II, the Party actively carried out anti-fascist struggle and was widely supported by the people in the post-War era. In terms of performance in the parliamentary elections of Greece, the Party won as much as 24.4% of the votes in 1958 and 10.9% in 1981. Although its votes decreased in the elections of the 1990s and in the 21st century, it managed to be the third largest party in the parliament, except for 1993 when it became the fourth biggest. In a time when world socialist movement is in a low tide, it has not been so easy for the Communist Party of Greece to win such achievements.

The global economic crisis that broke out in 2008 has again proved that there are drawbacks and contradictions of capitalism that cannot be overcome and that periodic economic crises will always perplex the development of capitalism. In the global economic crisis, Greece's debt crisis continues to intensify, bringing serious impacts and triggering outstanding contradictions in Greece. In order to overcome the crisis break, the parliament passed a new round of financial austerity measures with 2/3 of the votes in favor, on February 13, 2012.

To acquire the second round of aid from the EU and IMF and so on, the Greek government promised to cut its expenditures by 3.2 billion Euros, downsize 15,000 civil servants and lower the minimum wage of workers in the private sector by 22% in 2012.

By 2015, altogether 150,000 civil servants are planned to be laid off. As the debt crisis heated up, the Communist Party of Greece that represents the interests of the workers actively criticized the austerity countermeasures, cast doubt on the government's measures in the crisis and called for the working class and other people to unite so as protect their interests from being exploited.

The Communist Party of Greece has showed an increasingly outstanding performance in the debt crisis and the policies it adopted became more active. On the one hand, it attached great importance to its leading role in the actions and tactics of the workers 'demonstrations, parades and strikes. On the other hand, it laid stress on counterattacking the misleading and opportunistic trends in the field of ideology which the bourgeois government used to deceive the working class. Thus the Party raised its ideological and political level to better convince the working class so that it, together with the ordinary people, acquired a better picture regarding the nature of the debt crisis, its causes and future trend, thus the Party have put forward more clear solutions, against the crisis.

At the same time, the Communist Party of Greece actively carried out parliamentary struggles, where it expressed its viewpoints, called on the deputies of other parties to be careful in their votes and pointed out that it was unwise to borrow new loans at the expense of the ordinary people, and held that such new loans would bring huge losses, which could never be remedied.

II. Active participation in and organization of mass actions

In October 2011, leaders of the EU decided to offer a second round of bail out aid to Greece, totaling 130 billion Euros, would be collectively funded by the EU, the IMF and the European Central Bank, but forcing the conditions that Greece should further deepen its economic reform and further implement financial austerity policies. In the last ten days of the March 2012 when a debt of 14.5 billion Euros was about to due, in order to repay the debt in time and avoid breach and bankruptcy, the Greek government passed new austerity policies in the parliament. In fact, since Greece got the first aid in May 2010, its economy was already caught in grave recession. Data has showed that unemployment rate of Greece in November 2011 had already reached 20.9%, among which 48%were the young people.[2]

Economic depression and rising unemployment rate has caused great resentment and discontent among the Greek people towards the financial austerity policies. Hence, large-scale strikes and demonstrations have frequently occurred in Greece, such as the protests against the measures like downsizing civil servants and reducing pension.

2　Lejun, Wu, "Greece's Pain over New Austerity Plan". People's Daily. February 14, 2012.

Since after, the government took its own way to implement the financial austerity policies at the cost of people's interests and chose the option to protect the interests of the financial monopoly groups, the Communist Party of Greece and the General Confederation of Workers of Greece and Greece's left-wing labor confederation PAME led by the KKE or GCP have intensified the struggles and participated in and organized more and more strikes and demonstrations.

The two-day general strike starting from February 10, 2012 was initiated and organized by the Greece's left-wing labor confederation PAME. The strike broke out in Athens and also in dozens of other cities at the same time, attended by the working class, poverty-stricken people and women, showing the significant improvement in the Confederation's support during the debt crisis.

The Communist Party of Greece also took an active part in this strike leading team. On February 11th, hundreds of members from the Communist Party of Greece held high red flags and shouted protest slogans against the strict austerity policies adopted by the financial monopoly groups leading the EU. During this strike, the Communist Party of Greece, called on the working class, poverty-stricken people and young people to join strongly in the protests and raise the following demand: "End the EU's monopolistic dictatorship, overthrow the current government, quit the EU and cancel the debts unilaterally."[3]

Aleka Papariga, the General Secretary of the Communist Party of Greece, also took part in protests and strikes that took place in Athens and told the media: "even if the people succumb to the government and sacrifice their interests to repay the debts in this way, the bankruptcy is inevitable. The only solution is the separation of Greece from the EU and the unilateral cancellation of the debts. Otherwise, the working class will have to face a grave disaster." She added: communist movement has the task of both enabling the extensive union of the working class, and also should carry out struggles in the ideological field.[4]

The Communist Party of Greece has realized that the political party should lead and play a significant role in protecting the legal interests and rights of the working class and ordinary people. In the final statement of the 13thInternational Meeting of Communist and Workers' Parties in Athens which was held in December 9 to 11, 2011, communist and workers' parties from different countries have advocated that, with continuous intensifying of the contradictions of capitalism, the power and the unity of the communist and workers' parties needed to be strengthened so that they

---

3 http://inter.kke.gr/News/news2012/2012-02-11-48ori-2mera.
4 http://inter.kke.gr/News/news2012/2012-02-10-48ori2.

would be able to play a historical role in this critical moment of intensifying contradictions.

Only by strengthening the power of the communist parties, can the fighting capacity of the workers increase and ordinary people can defend their rights, effectively, thus the socialist movement can better use the opportunity of increasing contradictions of capitalism and imperialism. The statement said: all forces should be united to overthrow the bourgeois governments' control on economy and politics and fight for the realization of the fundamental interests of the majority of the people. Without the leadership of the communist parties, workers' parties or vanguard parties of the working class, the working class and ordinary people are bound to get confused about the current complicated situation, they will be unable to clearly understand the political situation and will possibly be mislead and perverted by the pro-imperialist government that represents the monopoly plutocrats.[5]

III. Active ideological persuasion and publicity work

There occurred fierce confrontations between the government that represents the bourgeois financial monopoly groups and the Communist Party of Greece that represents the interests of the working class and ordinary people. Those confrontations include protests as well as serious ideological struggles.

Based on the current situation, the Communist Party of Greece had been devoting more publicity efforts on winning over the people, which include critical ideological and political attacks targeting the ruling bourgeois government, extensive critique regarding the bourgeois government's discourse system that deceives the working class, here KKE uses scientific analyses. Both in the communist parties, and in the working class to increase the combat capacity, ideological work and ideological propaganda play an important role: Besides, ideological work and ideological propaganda is key to maintain and strengthen the belief in scientific socialism: without ideological work and ideological propaganda, it is impossible to defeat anti-socialist thoughts, disclose various bourgeois trends of thought, oppose to those opportunist trends and mistaken theories that divide and weaken the working class struggle and unswervingly fight against the forces that defame the working class struggles. In a word, communist movement not only needs extensive unity with the working class, but need to carry out ideological struggles.[6]

---

5 http://www.solidnet.org/13-international-meeting/2289-13-imcwp-final-statement-en.
6 http://www.solidnet.org/13-international-meeting/2289-13-imcwp-final-statement-en.

Grasping the true nature of the crisis

The Communist Party of Greece believes that the crisis is one about the capitalist system itself, instead of any partial problem about economic operation as alleged by the bourgeoisie and opportunist trends in the working class movement. Capitalist crisis is also an opportunity and excuse for the bourgeoisie to promote those economic policies that benefit themselves and undermine the interests of the working class. In fact, such policies have been continuously implemented and the strict austerity policies, greatly infringe economic and legal interests of the working class.

The Communist Party of Greece holds that the bourgeois government and the financial monopoly groups behind the Greek governments deceive the working class with a series of falsifying discourses, such as "protecting national sovereignty" and "Greeks should unite to tackle the difficulties together", in order to disguise the obvious fact that the capitalist crisis is caused by the insurmountable contradictions of capitalist system and to disguise the fundamental antagonistic contradiction between the bourgeoisie and the working class. Therefore, the Communist Party of Greece believes that, currently it is urgent to further awaken the class consciousness of the working class and help them to understand that the pro-government ideologues and parties paralyze people's thinking by exploiting the concept of "unity spirit". This "unity" is a concept distinct from the people's unity raised by the Communist Party of Greece.

The Communist Party of Greece thinks that the reason why the bourgeois government conceals the cause of the crisis is to maintain the solutions within the framework capitalist rule. That is to say, the government wants to solve the crisis by maintaining the stability of the current order, and the current economic mechanism where the capitalists freely exploit the surplus value of the working class. However, but the two aspects of the capitalist solution are contradictory, because under the capitalist framework, the periodic capitalist economic crises cannot be avoided, and the debt crisis as a result of it cannot be eliminated. To eliminate the periodic capitalist economic crises, the current capitalist system must be abandoned and thorough reform of this system is a must.

Analysis on the victims of the crisis

The Communist Party of Greece believes that with this crisis, the bourgeoisie aims to achieve two purposes:. Firstly, they can reduce wages of the laborers, and further lower the wages of the working class and reduce social welfare of the people. Secondly, they aim to widely, press down and squeeze small and medium-sized enterprises so as to strengthen the dominance of financial monopoly groups.[7]

---

7 http://inter.kke.gr/News/news2012/2012-02-16-metra/.

The bourgeois government propagates that the re-scheduling of the loans will restore the national economy, in fact they are actually damaging the interests of the working class and want the working class to pay the burden of the debt crisis, which is caused by the narrow interests of the bourgeoisie, in the final analysis the working class will sacrifice more, but will benefit less. Moreover, the repayment of serious indebtedness the Greek government has swallowed today, will last for 150 years. Even if, the people will obey that their wages and welfare are reduced and even they obey to work voluntarily for one, two or three years, the threat of bankruptcy still cannot be avoided.[8]

In fact, in accordance with the interest requirements of the EU, European Central Bank and IMF, if the Greek government wants to obtain the bailout aid of 130 billion Euros, it must legislate the following curettage-like reform measures in the parliament: the reduction of government expenditures by 1.5% of the GDP and cutting the ordinary people's monthly minimum wage (currently 750 Euros) by at least 20%. Obviously, these new measures will dramatically affect the people's life.[9]

The party follows a wise policy to divide the enemy front

The Communist Party of Greece realizes that party's strong ties with the working class can be the best weapon to solve the crisis, as a part of this policy the working class should be protected from being utilized or manipulated by the bourgeois government. During the strikes and demonstrations, the Communist Party of Greece paid great attention to directly appeal to the working class, poverty-stricken people, women and the youth, who are the main allies and subjects that the Party wants to unite, against the government.

At the same time, the Communist Party of Greece propagates that not only the Greece's working class should unite alone, but those in the Europe and the world should be united for an extensive and comprehensive unity, against capitalism and imperialism. Such a unity should be realized through struggles, strikes and other radical ways. As to the debt crisis, the Communist Party of Greece believes the working class should point the main attack at the Greek government, demand to overthrow the current government that represents the financial monopoly groups, quit the EU and unilaterally cancel debts, and if conditions permit, establish a new government that truly represents the interests of the working class.[10]

---

8   http: //inte.kke.gr/News/news2012/2012-02-13-info.
9   Ye, Cai. Greece Caught in Dilemma: Reform or Bankruptcy. Guangming Daily. February 10, 2012.
10 http: //inter.kke.gr/News/news2012/2012-02-13-info.

The Communist Party of Greece is strongly aware of the power of united working class. Even if there is a street blockade made by the armed police forces or any other measures to disrupt a demonstration of the working class, as long as the working class unites with each other in an organized manner and firmly struggles to realize its goal, no such force can stop it from marching forward. The Party has clearly pointed: "while the GCP (KKE) actively works as brother in arms with the working class, the working class should also firmly support the Communist Party. In the face of common enemy, only our mutual support, will generate a stronger power that is necessary."

The party demonstrates a pioneering internationalist vision

In its development process, the Party continuously summarizes its own experiences and values high to learn from others, in the world communist movement. In the 13thInternational Meeting of Communist and Workers' Parties, Aleka Papariga specified in her speech: "the reason why our Party was able to put forward active policies, countermeasures and tactics, since the very beginning of the crisis, is we have always adhered to our ideology, and devoted ourselves to unremitting struggle. To sum up, there has been two interconnected reasons, both of which are, in fact sourced out of the Greek soil, yet have affected the development of the Communist Party of Greece significantly and deeply: firstly, the Party had always adhered to socialism, defended the great contribution made by the Soviet Union and fought against all sorts of reactionary thoughts; secondly, we have paid attention to study of the EU, focused our efforts to analyze the contradictions and cruel competition among its members—- the imperialist system of the EU complex."[11]

While coping with the debt crisis, the Communist Party of Greece also actively called on the working classes of Greece, Europe and the world to unite with each other, to jointly deal with the crisis as comrade in arms, so as to defend their interests and hold high their banner again: "Proletarians in the world unite!" It can be seen that no matter in the past or currently when the debt crisis is worsening, the Communist Party of Greece has always been in the forefront of the struggle against the bourgeois governments and has maintained an internationalist vision when it examines and predicts the future development trends in Greece, the EU and the world.

11　http://inter.kke.gr/News/news2011/2011-12-13-kke-omilia. Speech by Aleka Papariga, General Secretary of the Communist Party of Greece in the 13th International Meeting of Communist and Workers' Parties.

IV. Active Parliamentary Struggle

The Communist Party of Greece lays emphasis on developing the struggles both inside and outside the parliament. It uses every opportunity to express its stance and views in the parliament and favored progressive steps, suited to the development trend of the society. For long years, the Party has always maintained stable seats in the parliament

In 2012, when the parliament was deliberating on whether it would pass the new round of bailout austerity scheme and loan re-scheduling agreement, the Communist Party of Greece explicitly expressed its critical attitude. The Party believed that the representatives serving in the parliament were not sovereign enough to vote according to their own will: whether the strict austerity policies that are destructive to the life of the ordinary people, especially the working class, would be passed. They didn't feel the true responsibility, to bear the consequences of their votes. And those who voted for the approval of the bill, knew that they will never be forgiven, in the face of history. Although, the said bill was approved with 199 affirmative votes and 74 negative votes, this did not mean that the efforts by the Party to defend the interests of the working class were fruitless, and the GCP never gave up.[12]

Currently, the Communist Party of Greece is one of the most influential communist parties in Europe. When observing its performance, especially its position and active response to the complex international financial and economic crisis and to Greece's debt crisis, all these demonstrate that the Party is in a process of gradual maturity.

The Communist Party of Greece encounters healthy growth through practices, and its struggles help it to further develop, and all this process continues to reinforce its power. Its increasing support in Greece is the best proof of its influence. It can be seen that the Communist Party of Greece, which pursues relatively "radical" policies is gradually attracting the laboring people from all walks of life, and gaining more approval and support from the people. We think these positive achievements of the Party, are inseparable from its adherence to traditional socialist values, this is also why, it is still one of the few communist parties, which is not effected with democratic socialist ideological characteristics or democratic socialist, at the political stage of Europe. Currently, when the world socialist movement is generally developing in a low tide, and in the European region where the capitalist forces are relatively strong, the Communist Party of Greece, constantly adheres to the traditional mission of socialism, seeks development and successfully realizes its transformation towards perfection.

---

12   http://inter.kke.gr/News/news2012/2012-02-13-info.

Y. 43

The Views of the Swedish Communist Parties Regarding the Capitalist Economic Crisis

Li Kaixuan[1]

Abstract: The Swedish communist parties which have split for various reasons in the history have had a greater impact in the history of Sweden. Since the collapse of the Soviet Union, the Swedish communist parties and groups have been greatly affected and the communist movement in this country has fallen into a low ebb. However, Swedish the two communist parties have continually participated in and supported the domestic workers' movements and international conferences in order to exert their influence and publicize their own thoughts. According to the contemporary Swedish communist parties—Sweden, the model country of welfare state in the capitalist world, has started to cut its welfare expenditures since the outbreak of the global economic crisis. In this unfavorable situation, the Swedish Social Democratic Party not only failed to make forward-looking decisions and take active measures, but also fell into a confusion regarding its stand and role in the society, thus suffered a defeat in the Swedish election of 2010. The Swedish communists have also criticized the relationships between Sweden and the European Union, and between Sweden and NATO, etc.

Key words: Swedish Communist Parties; economic crisis; Swedish Social Democratic Workers' Party; democratic Socialism, The Left Party(V)

---

1 Li Kaixuan, Specially invited researcher in World Socialism Research Center, attached to CASS, and research assistant at the Marxism Research Institute.

There are two communist parties in Sweden. One of them is currently named Communist Party (KP) since 2005, the predecessor of which is the Communist Fraction of the Marxist-Leninists, (KFML (r) the revolutionary). It was founded in 1970, and in 1977, it further changed its name to Communist Party Marxist-Leninists (the KPML (r) revolutionary).

In 1980, the KPML party split, and the Swedish Communist Workers' Party (SKP/WPK) came into being. In 1982, the party split again, during the process of which, the pro-Albania faction quitted and formed another communist party.

The two latter pro-Albanian and the (SKP/WPK) were both practically dissolved in 1993. In January 2005, the Communist Party Marxist-Leninists (the KPML (r) revolutionary) changed its name to Communist Party and the organ of the party has been The Proletarian Weekly.

This Party has been one of the first communist parties participating in the International Communist Seminar held in Brussels since 1992. The other communist party is named Swedish Communist Party (SKP).

In 1970, the pro-Soviet "left wing" communists quit the party and established the Communist Workers Party. But, the Communist Workers Party was declared bankrupt by the Swedish state in 1995, the first case in the history of parties in Sweden. However, the core members of the Party soon reorganized the party, namely the Swedish Communist Party, under the leadership of Rolf Hagel[2] and published the party journal Policy to propagate the Party's thoughts and propositions. The SKP (Sveriges Kommunistiska Parti) has participated in the International Meeting of Communist and Workers Parties since its first meeting in 1999. The Party took part in the parliamentary general elections of Sweden in the years of 2006 and 2010, and has won 438 votes and 375 votes respectively, both around 0.01%.[3]

The son of a worker, Hagel is an electrician in the ship-building industry by trade. In 1950, he joined the Communist Youth League of Sweden (later renamed the Democratic Youth League) and in 1951 he became a member of the Communist Party of Sweden (renamed the Left Party-Communists in 1967). From 1950 to 1960 he worked in a division of the metal workers' trade union at a shipyard in Göteborg; he was a member of the division's administrative board from 1953 to 1960. He was deputychairman of the Democratic Youth League from 1960 to 1962 and chairman from 1962 to 1964.

2　Rolf Hagel, Born Oct. 6, 1934, in Göteborg. Figure in the Swedish working-class movement.
3　Detailed information for the history and current condition of the two communist parties the readers may refer to http://www.kommunisterna.org/en/about, http://skp.se/tmp_index.htm.

From 1965 to 1976, Hagel worked in the Göteborg division of the electricians' trade union, serving onthe division's administrative board from 1971 to 1975. He was a member of the Administrative Committee of the Communist Party from 1959 to March 1977 and chairman of the Göteborg districtorganization of the party from 1966 to March 1977. After the Left Party-Communists split in March 1977, Hagel was elected chairman of the Administrative Committee of the Workers' Communist Party of Sweden. From 1966 to 1976 he was a deputy to the Göteborg municipality. Hagel was first time elected to the Parliament (Riksdag) in 1976.

I. Propositions of the Swedish Communist Party[4] (SKP)

Its opinions regarding the capitalist economic crisis

The SKP believes that the periodical attack of the capitalist crisis has caused the current financial crisis, which has led to massive unemployment and low life quality. However, it is affluence rather than poverty that has caused the capitalist crisis – many commodities have no market, simply because the workers who produce these products cannot afford them.

The capitalist mode of production, due to anarchic pattern of production and government regulation, results in imbalances and mutual destructive competition of different economic sectors. In the name of structural changes, the current capitalist production destroys the whole production department, and damages capital as well as the generations of the skilled professional force. The capitalist crisis shatters the myth of "humane capitalism" and demonstrates the true character—the mercilessness and inhuman character—of the current society. The investment in livelihood of people, welfare and education keeps decreasing in Sweden because of the crisis. On the contrary, most of the social wealth has been used for financial speculations, bank bailouts, or escaped to other countries. In the capitalist society, the so called free competition is nothing but a myth. The capitalism disrupts free competition by creating stronger and greedier monopoly organizations, which seize more surplus profits, through the policies of divide and control, in the markets. The whole capitalist society supports the exploitation of workers by the big enterprises to facilitate the handful of few capitalists who pursue higher profits. The whole strength of the developed countries

---

[4] In the 37th congress of the party, Sörensen was elected as the chairman party.Its party newspaper is the Riktpunkt (montly). SKP participates in elections as "Kommunisterna" (the Communists). It contest elections to the national parliament (1998: 1,868 votes, 1994: 2,038), and elections to some regional and municipal councils; Municipal election results are (1998 results) Pajala 2,23% (109 votes, 1 seat), Gällivare 1,97% (245 votes, 1 seat), Värnamo 2,45% (470 votes, 1 seat), Piteå 0,48% (127 votes, 0 seats), Västerås 0,33% (243 votes, 0 seats), Järfälla 0,14% (53 votes, 0 seats), Malmö 0,05% (74 votes, 0 seats) and Stockholm 0,04% (200 votes, 0 seats).

have been devoted to serving the minority, even though this small group of people no longer shoulder the responsibility of national development.

A struggle goal of the SKP – withdrawal from the EU

Sweden is too small for the Swedish capitalists and they need to expand overseas. After becoming a member of the EU in 1994, Sweden witnesses a radical increase of its enterprises' overseas activities, but this caused that the Swedish people's right of independent decision-making has been castrated before the interests and market dictatorship of the EU. In the new competition area of EU and the world, the big enterprises of Sweden totally neglect the rights, development and welfare of the Swedish workers. Thus the Swedish Communist Party believes that withdrawal from the EU remains a necessary aspect of the struggle of the Swedish working class.

After joining the EU, Sweden has encountered numerous problems – societal democracy (democracy in social life) and labor union organizations are damaged, welfare is reduced, unemployment is serious, women's working rights are restricted, and profits take precedence over environmental protection. In addition, Sweden became a part of an aggressive military agreement. The fight against the EU is a class issue. The EU consolidates the status of and adds strength to the Sweden's bourgeoisie and facilitates the implementation of their anti-people policy. Their target of attack are not only women, but the whole working class.

Secondly, the fight against the EU is a democracy issue. Because the Sweden became a member state of a higher authority, i.e. the EU, the Swedish people's right of self-determination, for example, their demand to unite with other peoples of the world, who oppose against the EU's expansion or non-democratic foreign policies, is restricted. Thus the SKP aims, withdrawal from the EU and play a leading role in this struggle, for both two reasons: for class struggle and for democracy.

The SKP's internationalist stance

The capitalist world is both united and divided. According to the law of jungle, powerful capitalist countries have been struggling for the domination of the world. After the World War II, the US has become the strongest leader of the capitalist world, but in recent years, its status has been challenged with the rise the EU and Japan, which jealously eye and aim taking the control of the world markets.

Although Sweden is not so powerful, it is still one of the imperialist countries of the world. It still participates in the various imperialist organizations and alliances among the capitalist countries and exploits the third world countries through capital export, exploit them via unfair trade and loans. The SKP is against the further enslaving of the third world people in any form and opposes the strengthening of any capitalist country's power contend for world hegemony. It supports people of all countries' and nations' struggles for freedom. The SKP expresses their internationalism stance with concrete action since the global financial crisis. In July 2009, the SKP and the Socialist Party of Latvia have published a joint statement, denouncing all attempts to divide Swedish workers and workers coming from other Baltic States to work in Sweden. The statement demands that the salary of workers, regardless of their nationality, should conform to the Swedish Collective Salary Agreement, and wage cuts should be avoided. In December 2009, when the ant-communist Czech government authorities tried to ban the activities of the Communist Party of Bohemia and Moravia, the SKP protested the Czech government immediately, believing that the real intention of Czech government was to prevent the Communist Party from influencing the state and defend the interests of the workers. The SKP has strongly supported the Communist Party of Bohemia and Moravia in defending its legitimate right of political struggle and participated in the protest activities in front of the Czech embassy in Sweden.

II. Propositions of the Communist Party[5] (KP)

After the outbreak of the financial crisis in 2008, the SKP expressed its propositions and stance on the following aspects such as the root of financial crisis, social welfare of Sweden, the crisis of the Swedish Social Democratic Party and the relationship between Sweden and the NATO, etc.

Root of the financial crisis

On the 10th session of the International Meeting of Communist and Workers' Party held in 2008, the KP pointed out that the fundamental cause of the global 2008 financial crisis was the basic contradiction of capitalism. Since the mid-19th century, the contradiction between the socialization of production and the private ownership of means of production has never changed or stopped, and therefore, economic crises have kept erupting, time and again. The controllers of capitalist system obtain most of the social surplus by exploiting the working class, and then this social surplus is partly consumed and partly put into reproduction, also some part is used for financial speculations together with the fictitious capital generated in the financial services sector.

With the rapid development of speculation, and increase of financial activities and financial derivatives the purchasing power of the public has greatly declined.

---

5   Its central party news organ is Proletaren (Proletarians).

Secondly, credit operations have become a major tool for the capitalists to solve the problem of economic stagflation. When the capitalist world suffered from stagflation in the 1970s, the bank loans have become the best means to fill up the gap between production and people's purchasing power. Loans, to name them, from the borrower's side, is debt. The capitalists' strong desire for capital accumulation requires that the working class should earn less salary while spend more to buy commodities. And the only solution for this capitalist demand is to push the blue-and-white collar wage earning classes to the abyss of debt. Therefore, both the developed capitalist countries and neo-colonies of the third-world are trapped in the debt of ocean. Besides, the real economy is shrinking. In 1980s, the capitalists shifted their capital to the financial sector for capital accumulation, because the real economy didn't bring has lucrative profits and there was over-capacity in the real economy. By the end of the 1980s, the financial sector contributed to the 55% of the GDP, in the OECD member states, while the contribution of the real economy sectors, accounted about 45-50%.

Thirdly, the economy and the ideology of the capitalist society contradicts each other. When the real economy is severely damaged and debts keeps rising, the ideologues of capitalism still insist that the self-regulating and self-adjustment power of the capitalist market can ensure economic prosperity. Despite these, ideologues, in reality the disasters caused by capitalism cannot be solved within the framework of capitalism. Many people have already witnessed the incapability of the market, they have witnessed the collapse of real economy and the explosion of the speculative bubbles. The real economy cannot be saved unless the capitalists are ready return the surplus value exploitation to the working class. Yet historical experience prove that the capitalists will never do so.

Aggravation of the global economic crisis

In November 2009, the KP has pointed the following in the 11th gathering of the International Meeting of Communist and Workers' Parties: one of the features of fascist state is to strengthen and generalize state monopoly capital, this is implemented, in the form of joint committees, which steal the decision right of from people, and these committees give important decisions and design the strategic plans. In fact what they do is, to use funds of the public, to support and bailout the banks, bankrupt enterprises, insurance companies and other financial institutions, this is the truth behind so called large-scale bailouts. The US has spent 23 trillion dollars to save the markets, the Sweden government has also spent half of its GDP, for the same purpose, without any loan length, or without any maturity date. The target of the Sweden's bailout operations have been the two major Swedish banks, which have controlled the economy of neighboring Baltic States and Sweden since the mid-1990s, while some markets in the region have long been suffering from speculative bubbles.

However, the Swedish government does not undertake, any such commitments when it comes to people's economic interests, such as the people's endowment insurances, unemployment compensation moneys, sickness allowance or health care costs. In the capitalist society, the creditor who provides any financial aid to any bank or enterprise for any salvage should demand some part of the ownership, as compensation. However, in the recent crisis, the governments of most countries who provided financial aid to private enterprises and private banks have not demanded to get the shares (ownership) of these enterprises and banks. The private enterprises and private banks were saved, and the governments closely cooperated and colluded with the financial monopoly capital groups.

The KP believes that unlike what is advocated by the European media, the bailout of the financial institutions does not indicate the end of financial crisis. Actually, the economic world has divided into two parts – one part is finance, and the other part is commodity production and non-financial service sector. For example, on the Newspapers of Sweden, the headline on this page is "President of the Swedish Riksbank Suggests Remaining Cautious and Optimistic", while the other page reports the dismissal of 400 workers by the Swedish Agricultural Company Union. The term so-called, "jobless recovery" accurately describes the phenomenon that the creation of new employment opportunities, and decreasing the jobless rate falls behind the economic recovery. The financial derivative products, which best represent speculative financial operations and fictitious capital, has increased geometrically, far ahead of other industries. At present, the nominal value of financial derivative products markets accessed via big banks of the West is 1,500 trillion dollars, while the GDP of the whole world is 50 trillion dollars, accounting for 3.3% of the financial derivative products markets; on the other hand the real estate value of the whole world is 20 trillion dollars, accounting for the 1.3% of the financial derivative products markets.[6]

Therefore, the biggest secret is that, the major capitalist banks do not present the value of the derivative products, or incomes from derivative operations in their balance sheet. If they dare to do so, they will immediately be declared bankrupt, in fact the western bank system has already gone bankrupt.

The real economy is still depressed, the unemployment rate is high, poverty spreads all across the world, and famine victims of the world has exceeded 1 billion for the first time. The Baltic Dry Bulk Freight Index (BDI) is a reliable measurement index to measure the volume of industrial activities.

---

6 The continuing crisis and the advance of the new Fascism, Statement of the Communist Party of Sweden (SKP) at the International Meeting of Communist and Workers' Parties in New Delhi, 20-22 November 2009, http:// solidnet.org /Sweden-communist-party-of-sweden/232 – 11 imcwp-intervention-by-cp-of-sweden.

As a measurable indicator, this index above is immune to speculation, and thus it can provide an accurate reflection of the worldwide industrial activity. And unlike other economic data, it is updated every day. From January to December in 2008, the BDI has dropped by 94%. Until, December 2009, it has only recovered 30% compared to January 2008. The data suggests that economy is not recovering, rather the crisis is aggravating.

Stand of the Communist Party on the crisis of the Swedish Social Democratic Workers' Party

In 2010 elections, the Swedish Social Democratic Workers' Party and the Red-Green Alliance formed by the Green Party and the Left Party were defeated by the Swedish Centre-Right Coalition in the general elections.[7]

In the article "Crisis of the Social Democratic Workers' Party", the KP analyzes the reasons of Social Democratic Workers' Party's crisis and proposes suggestions on how this Party can overcome its crisis and lead better future development path.[8]

The KP believes that in Sweden, no party is so close to the lives of the common people and the trade union movement than the Swedish Social Democratic Workers' Party (SAP). The internal crisis of the Social Democratic Workers' Party does not only concern involve this party itself, but also affects the public.

The Party's failure in the 2010 election has completely revealed its crisis, but the hidden crisis for this Party was rooted much earlier, when they had decided to give up the socialism goal in its program

In traditional sense, the SAP should have recognized the essence of the capitalist crisis and its exploitation and damages over the working people. They have made some concessions to the workers, established a powerful public sector of economy which has been the strongest in the capitalist world, it has set up "people's houses"[9] for the workers, and adopted Keynesianism in economy, all of which have been proved to be effective till the end of the 1970s. Then under the fierce ideological attack started by the neoliberal right wing, the SAP retrogressed in its thoughts and policies. The first manifestation of this retrogression was the closing of daily newspaper. Consequently, the daily initiative in the ideological debate has passed to

---

[7] The Swedish Social Democratic Workers' Party (SAP) was established in 1889, and in 1917, a faction was separated from the SAP and formed the current Swedish Left Wing Party (VP). The SAP has the theoretical foundation of Bernstein revisionism and calls its ideology as democratic socialism. The Party has 100 thousand members. From 1940 to 1988, the support rate of the Party has maintained at 40% to 55% in the consecutive elections. In recent years, the SAP has started to pay attention to the issues of feminism and sexual equality.

[8] Swedish Communist Party: The crisis of the social democracy, http://solidnet.org/sweden-communist-party-of-sweden/1109-cp-of-sweden-the-crisis-of-the-social-democracy.

[9] Economic housing for workers.

the right-wing bourgeoisie forces, and the people who carried retrogressive thoughts were allowed to be employed in the labor union organizations.

The original modern social democracy has told the middle class that the ownership of means of production determines the people's social status in the society. In Sweden there are the bourgeoisie and working class, the latter has gained some power due to the increase of the public service sector of the economy. If a workers' party has a sense of responsibility, it should approach to the middle class and arouse their consciousness, because like the working class, the improvement of the living conditions of the middle class also relies on the struggle of the labor union organizations.

The KP believes that the Swedish Social Democratic Labor Party wants to re-shape itself as a bourgeoisie liberal Party, but it is impossible for the SAP to transform itself into such a bourgeoisie liberal party, because this seat has already been occupied by the right-wing parties. The KP argues: the SAP should realize that due to the severe impact generated by current capitalist overproduction crisis which gives a serious blow to the working class, the space for an affluent capitalism—social welfare state—does not exist."

Consequently, the SAP should strongly fight against the privatization of schools education, privatization of health care and welfare, and resist against the slacking off of social welfare functions of the state.

If the SAP wants to have any future in the political stage, it must support the struggle of the workers' unions and thus try to weaken the capitalist exploitation of the workers and should also support and participate the struggles outside the parliament.

All in all, the SAP should realize that fairness and righteousness in a society cannot be only achieved through distribution sphere, for fairness and righteousness, the reforms in the distribution sphere should also be accompanied by changing the ownership of the means of production. And a healthy production should be measured by its satisfaction of the social demand, its measure should not be the satisfaction of profit pursuit of individuals and capitalist groups.

Stand of the Communist Party[10] on the collapse of the Soviet Union, economic crisis and Swedish welfare system

On the 13th gathering of the International Meeting of Communist and Workers' Parties held in December 2011, the SKP first pointed out the influences of the collapse of the Soviet Union and the drastic changes in the Eastern European countries on Sweden. Among those countries with higher

---

10 Andreas Sörensen is the current party chairman, and its party newspaper is the Riktpunkt (montly). SKP participates in elections as „Kommunisterna" (the Communists).

social welfare, policies, Sweden has created the biggest public service sector and became famous for its practice of the so called "welfare state of the Sweden model."

The working class of Sweden, following the example of the Soviet Union, has made certain progress in the fields of economics, society, politics and culture, but since the fall of the SU in 1991, their achievements have been targeted by the capitalists of Sweden.

20 years after the collapse of the Soviet Union, the social welfare policies of Sweden has been severely damaged. Between, 1991-2011, 350 thousand jobs were lost in Sweden, among which the jobs regarding the public service departments were 175 thousand. But, there were already some problems regarding the development of the welfare system in Sweden, due the opportunism of the leaders of the Swedish Social Democratic Workers' Party, and secondly due to its class collaboration with state capitalism.

To cite a simple fact, Swedish Krone has appreciated circa hundreds of times between 1970 and 1997. The SAP, which has been the ruling party in this period, has been credited for Sweden's welfare state and enjoyed good reputation.

In the EU, although the social democrat Swedish Minister of Finance Borg was praised as "the best minister of finance", he has responsible for the jobless of the youth, 25% of the youth between 16 and 24 years old had become jobless, plus this "excellent" minister has spent 15 trillion Krona, for the "first aid emergency room" to help the banks. And, that was why Sweden could only spend 20 billion to 25 billion Krona in helping the crisis-affected working class.

At present, most of the Sweden's tax revenues are being used for the privately-owned health care, educational and welfare enterprises that operate for more and more profits, and their social obligation towards the laborers are no more priority for them, the workers are forced to pay the major part of their health expenses from their own individual family budgets. These enterprises, operate independently solely responsible for their profits or losses. These enterprises are outsourced by the Swedish laissez-faire capitalism for health services, besides the collective wage bargaining system of Sweden is greatly undermined.

Sweden and the EU

The SKP believes that since Sweden has joined the EU, labor unions of Sweden gradually became passive and voiced their opinions less frequently, and they were prevented from voicing critical attitudes towards the EU, instead they had accommodate to the demands of the EU bodies.

Obviously, for the majority of the Swedish people, the EU is not a democratic or a peaceful organization, the people's belief—when it joined the EU in 1994—that "joining the EU would provide higher quality life for the working people and would enhance fairness and righteousness" when it joined the EU in 1994 has been proved wrong.

The SKP points out that, currently 80% of the Swedish laws are determined by Brussels. In face of the current sovereign debt crisis in the Eurozone, the SKP pleasantly notes that Swedish people's "no to EU" vote, in 1994 has been a wise decision.

Sweden and the NATO

Neutrality and non-aligned status of Sweden has merely become a scrap of paper. The SKP points out that Sweden actually has a very close relationship with the NATO during the recent decades. Despite people's support and demand for the non-alignment status, the Swedish government has sent the Swedish "Gripen fighter jets" to participate in the military action targeting Libya which was led by the NATO. Such a policy has aroused more critical voices among the public, consequently the government still continued to collude "secretly" with the NATO. As early as 2002, Sweden has sent 500 troops to Afghanistan war, and this fighting force was under the command of the NATO army. In addition, if you enter the NATO's official website, and click "Sweden" under the column of "partners" all the truth regarding the "partnership for peace" between Sweden and the NATO would be glass clear revealed. Obviously, the "partnership for peace" has become a tool to coordinate, prepare and train the Swedish army for the NATO strategy, which means participating in the future "crisis management" operations of it.

The reason behind the large-scale and evil massacre in Libya was the "crisis management"[11] strategy of the NATO, as the police force of the world. Obviously, the NATO apparently aims to make Finland and Sweden its northern wing fortress, to contain Russia and these two countries are thought to be a necessary supplement for the so called "missile defense systems" established by the US in several European countries. The SKP strongly opposes, to such a political development as a dangerous and undesirable possibility.

---

11 Crisis management is one of NATO's fundamental security tasks. It can involve military and non-military measures to address threats.

Stand of the Communist Party against the "indiscriminate" use of the term socialism to stigmatize communism

According to the propaganda of the Western media, all social democratic parties are socialist. Following this logic, the Papandreou government of Greece and the social democrat (PSOE) government in Spain are socialist governments. But the problem is, these parties, as a matter of fact, do not have such features conforming with the trend of political movement they represent, of course such propaganda of the Western media, cause confusions in the minds of the young people, who still lack a mature class consciousness.

The SKP points out that, with such a confusion in the eyes of these young people, socialism becomes capitalism and capitalism becomes socialism, and that the final stage of capitalism already includes socialism.

The SKP has strongly criticized the "Living History Forum" of the Swedish government, which claims to focus on calling attention to crimes against humanity under communist regimes, and concentrates on those crimes against humanity that were committed during the communist regimes in the Soviet Union, China and Cambodia during the period between the Russian revolution and the fall of the wall (1917-1989) has done researches on "the crimes of communism against people".

The SKP points out these so called "researches" funded and published by this Forum, have been criticized by many renown historians in 2008, since they have no scientific or historical significance, but only serve as an ideological tool. An increasing number of people in Sweden also believe that such a "History Forum" should be closed.[12]

---

12 For more information please refer to the Swedish Communist Party, 13. IMCWP, Contribution of CP of Sweden, http://solidnet.org/sweden-communist-party-of-sweden/2335-13-imcwp-contribution-of-cp-of-sweden-en.

Y. 44

Vulnerable Countries Help Themselves: The Bolivarian Alliance — The Present Situation and Prospects of the Bolivarian Alliance for the Peoples of Our America (ALBA)

Chen Airu[1]

Abstract: The Bolivarian Alliance for the Americas has appeared as an integration platform in Latin America and the Caribbean region, targeting and opposing the FTAA led by the US. At the same time, it is also a strategic political coalition. The Alliance plays an important role in promoting the collective security of its member states and other Latin American and Caribbean countries, and aims to help them to cope with the challenges of the economic crisis. And in a global context, the Alliance also represents to some extent the interests of the vast number of developing countries in coping with the strong tide of economic globalization, it also opposes power politics and hegemonism pursued by a handful of big powers, and pursues global justice and equality.

Key words: Latin America; Bolivarian Alliance; justice

---

1 Chen Airu, specially invited researcher in World Socialism Research Center, attached to CASS, doctoral student in the Marxism Research Institute.

The Bolivarian Alliance for the Americas has appeared as an integration platform in Latin America and the Caribbean region, targeting and opposing the FTAA led by the US. Since its establishment in 2004, and especially after the global economic crisis of the 2008, aims to help them to cope with the challenges of the economic crisis and also plays an important role in promoting the collective security of its member states and other Latin American and Caribbean countries. And in a global context, the Alliance also represents to some extent the interests of the vast number of developing countries in coping with the strong tide of economic globalization, it also opposes power politics and hegemonism pursued by a handful of big powers, and pursues global justice and equality.

At present, the international financial crisis, instead of coming to an end, still exerts a deep influence across the world. The crisis has dealt a heavy blow to the world economy, thus people can feel and observe the insurmountable problems and contradictions of the capitalist development, and directs people's attention to Marxism again, globally. Against such a background, some developing countries seek to explore new alternative development modes based on their respective national or regional conditions. Some member states of the ALBA are such as Cuba, develops socialism – Cuba is now implementing the "Guidelines of the Economic and Social Policy of the Party and the Revolution " set in the 6th Congress of the Cuba Communist Party which aims "to update" its socialist economic mode without changing its socialist path, on the other hand, Venezuela and Ecuador have put forward and practice "the 21st century socialism" Bolivia, has put forward and carries out the Communitarian Socialism.

In addition, the ALBA tries to find new ways of economic and trade integration and establishing new regional trade mechanisms among its members. The Alliance also pursues poverty relief and fight against social exclusion, on the basis of true political, economic and social integration. Since its establishment, the Alliance has made steady progress, the number of its members have increased and various cooperation mechanisms have been established gradually. It plays a significant role in the balance of forces, across the world, in defending the interests of developing countries, the influence of big countries, its practice and orientation represents the shaping of a new world order.

I. The Current Situation of the Bolivarian Alliance for the Americas

In December 2001, Venezuela's president Chavez, has proposed to establish "the Bolivarian Alternative for the Americas" (which was later changed into Bolivarian Alliance for the Americas), in the 3rd Summit meeting of the organization. Chavez, announced: "countries of Latin America and the Caribbean should unite", he added: "Without the integration of the countries and people of Latin America and the Caribbean, there would be no independence for our Venezuela."

In December 2004, Chavez visited Cuba, issued the joined statement and signed the implementation agreement of the future ALBA with the Cuban State Council President Castro. On 24th June 2009, the Sixth Summit of the Bolivarian Alternative for the Americas was held in Maracay, the capital of Paraguay, and changed the name of the association into "Bolivarian Alliance for the Americas".

The principles of the Alliance include: fairness, mutual assistance, equality, cooperation, economic complementarity and the cooperation between the participating countries and non competition between countries and productions, Cooperation and solidarity that are translated into special plans for the least developed countries in the region, respect for sovereignty, these principles are imbued by Simon Bolivar's ideas[2] who once fought to integrate the continent and who put forward the idea of "united continental-wide country. Under his aspiration the current leaders have hailed strengthening of political, economic and social cooperation in the region, and the strength of each country should be given full play to, the urgent social problems of the region should be solved, poverty and social inequality should be eliminated, people of all countries should benefit from the cooperation, sustainable development should be promoted, people to people communications and solidarity among the peoples of Latin American countries should be promoted. Members generally agree that an alternative to the U.S.-backed Free Trade Agreement of the Americas should be established

The goals purpose of the Alliance: Defense of the Latin-American and Caribbean culture and of the identity of the peoples of the region, with particular respect for and promotion of the autochthonous and indigenous cultures.

Creation of the Television of the South (TELESUR) as an alternative instrument to the service of the dissemination of our realities.

Promotion of Latin American capital investments within Latin America and the Caribbean, with the aim to reduce the dependence of the countries of the region on the foreign investors. To that effect, a Latin-American Investment Fund, a Bank of Development of the South, and the Latin-American Mutual Guarantee Company would be created, among others.

---

2 Simón Bolívar (-1830) was a Venezuelan military leader who had the revolutions against the Spanish empire. In 1825, the „Republic of Bolivia" was created in honor of the inspirational leader, hailed by many as El Libertador (The Liberator).

Creation of the Social Emergency Fund, proposed by the President Hugo Chávez in the Summit of the South American Countries, recently celebrated in Ayacucho.

Inclusive development of the communications and the transport between the Latin-American and Caribbean countries, which includes joint plans of roads, railroads, maritime routes and airlines, telecommunications and so on.

Actions to enable the sustainability of the development by means of procedure, and which protect the environment, stimulate a rational use of the resources and prevent the proliferation of wasteful patterns of consumption that are foreign to the realities of our peoples.

Defense of the Latin-American and Caribbean culture and of the identity of the peoples of the region, with particular respect for and promotion of the autochthonous and indigenous cultures. Creation of the Television of the South (TELESUR) as an alternative instrument to the service of the dissemination of our realities.

Measures for intellectual property norms, while protecting the heritage of the Latin-American and Caribbean countries against the voracity of the transnational companies, which must not become an obstacle to the necessary cooperation in all areas between our countries.

Coordination of the positions in the multilateral spheres and in the processes of negotiation of all kinds with countries and blocks of other regions, including the fight for the democratization and transparency in the international organizations, particularly in the United Nations and its agencies.

Eliminate inequality, unbalanced economic development and unfairness in trade. Reject the policies of structural adjustment proposed by the IMF and the World Bank which might damage the social and political foundation of Latin American and the Caribbean countries.

There are eight member countries in the Alliance (as of December, 2014): Venezuela, Cuba, Antigua and Barbuda, Bolivia, Dominica, Ecuador, Nicaragua, Saint Lucia, and Saint Vincent and the Grenadines. Honduras joined as a member state in 2008, but withdrew in 2010 following a coup d'état against President Manuel Zelaya the previous year.

Alba has With a population of 75 million, the member countries cover an area of 2.5 million square kilometer. On December 14, 2014, three days after its 10th anniversary, the Bolivarian Alliance for the Peoples of Our America (ALBA) welcomed two new member countries: Grenada and St. Kitts and Nevis.

Both new ALBA members are Commonwealth realms, with Queen Elizabeth II as their formal head of state. Countries awaiting full incorporation into ALBA include Haiti, currently an observer country, and Suriname, which holds "guest member" status. Haiti, an observer since 2007, was confirmed as a permanent observer during the summit and has also expressed interest in becoming a full member. Iran and Syria are observers.[3]

The institutional framework of the Alliance is as follows:

The Presidential Council is the most powerful council in the alliance, made up of heads of state from each country. The Council is responsible for the highest levels of decision-making for the alliance.

The Political Council comprises foreign ministers from each member country, and is tasked with advising the Presidential Council on strategic policy issues.

The Economic Council consists of ministers appointed by member countries within the fields of economy, finance, trade, and development. Members coordinate strategy, policy, and projects related to an "economic area of shared development" within ALBA. Working groups play an important role, and cover areas such as energy, food safety, technology, commerce, and infrastructure.

The Social Council incorporates ministers that manage social areas in their home countries, and seeks to provide oversight for work related to education, health, employment, and culture.

The Social Movements Council is the "principle mechanism that facilitates integration and direct social participation" in ALBA. This Council is responsible for articulating the social movements of member and non-member countries.

Social Council

Formed by ministers in charge of the social affairs of the member countries, Social Council serves for coordinating and controlling strategies, policies, actions and schemes in the key social fields for the purpose of promoting people's basic social rights. The principle of the Council is to implement, promote and maintain equal opportunity between the two sexes and to advance the endeavors in the fields of health, education, science and technology, employment, housing, culture and sports in the member countries during the procedure of integration.

---

3 The website of the Alliance is http://www.alianzabolivariana. org.

(2) Economic Council

Formed by ministers in the economic fields (industry, finance, commerce, planning and development), the Economic Council makes and coordinates the strategies, policies and plans in the fields of complementary production, agricultural food products, industry, energy, commerce, finance and technology for the purpose of establishing joined development economic zone. This Council has ten working teams dealing with ten different fields.

(3) Political Council

Formed by foreign ministers, the Political Council provides suggestions for the Presidential Council in terms of strategic concepts and international policies to facilitate it in policy making. At the same time, the Council coordinates the works of other councils and offers strategic guide to ensure the normal operation of the Alliance. Under the Political Council there are Political Committee, Standing Coordination Committee and Executive Secretariat to assist the implementation of the orders.

(4) Social Movement Council

The Social Movement Council is a new institution to facilitate integration and direct public participation in the Alliance so as to safeguard social justice and protect national sovereignty, the task of which is to coordinate the social movements of the member countries as well as the social movements of the non-member countries conforming to the principles of the Alliance.

II. Previous Summits of the Bolivarian Alliance for the Americas and Their Contents

Since its founding, the ALBA has held 11 summits to negotiate and solve the problems faced by the Alliance. Here is a short introduction:

The first Summit was held in Havana, Cuba on14th December2004. President Chavez of Bolivarian Republic of Venezuela and Cuban State Council President Castro signed the joined statement and the implementation agreement for the establishment of the Bolivarian Alliance for the Americas.

The Second Summit was held on 28th April, 2005 in Havana Cuba. The Communication and Information Department of Bolivarian Republic of Venezuela signed a memorandum of understanding with the Technology and Industry Department of Saint Vincent and the Grenadines for the purpose of consolidating bilateral ties based on mutual benefit and deepening cooperation in the field of information. The Summit decided to establish Caribbean Petroleum Company to coordinate energy policies and plans so that the sovereignty over energy resources could be enhanced and that the people could directly benefit from the resource revenues. The Summit also decided to promote the integration of Caribbean countries. At the same time, the establishment of the common Fund of ALBA was decided, which would support social and economic projects. The Fund would raise money through financial and non-financial means, and different parties could come to an agreement in terms of using oil revenues and different parties could come to an agreement in terms of direct trade savings.

The Third Summit was held on 29th April, 2006 in Havana, Cuba. President Eva Morales from Bolivia signed the agreement and joined the Alliance. At the suggestion of President Morales, the bloc added the Peoples' Trade Treaty (TCP) upon Bolivia's incorporation

The Fourth Summit was held on 11th January 2007 in capital Managua, of Nicaragua. Nicaragua joined the Alliance, the then President of which was Ortega.

Between the Fourth Summit and the Fifth Summit, 16 agreements have been signed between Cuba and Venezuela (24th January 2007), 2 agreements have been signed between Venezuela and Dominica (16th February 2007). The agreements covered many important fields, such as marine transport, railway transportation, insurance, energy, metallurgy, tourism, agriculture, telecommunication and human resources training.

The Fifth Summit was held on 29th April, 2007 in Tintorero city of Lara Province of Venezuela. Representatives from Venezuela, Bolivia, Nicaragua and Cuba signed the Political Statement of the Fifth Summit of the ALBA; they also signed the Energy Treaty of the ALBA. Under the framework of the treaty, Venezuela also signed several energy agreements with Nicaragua, Bolivia and Haiti government. Venezuela, Cuba and Haiti also signed the Framework Agreement of ALBA-Haiti Cooperation.

The Sixth Summit was held during 24-26th January 2008 in Caracas, Venezuela. This time Caribbean island nation Dominica joined the Alliance, the then Premier was Roosevelt Skerrit. This Summit also established the ALBA Social Movement Council and the ALBA Bank started its operations.

The Seventh Summit was held on 24th June 2009 in Maracay, Venezuela. Ecuador, Saint Vincent and the Grenadines, Antigua and Barbuda joined the Alliance. This Summit published the Statement of the ALBA Political Council regarding Honduras, denounced the coup d'état in this country, demanded that the legal and constitutional President Zelaya should return to the country safely without preconditions and resume his power granted by the Constitution. The Alliance also stated that they would not recognize the illegal government which was formed through election manipulations.

The Eighth Summit was held during December 13-14th, 2009 in Havana Cuba. The Summit published the ALBA declaration regarding the climate change for the purpose of reiterating their stance with regard to Fifteenth General Assembly for climate change held in Copenhagen.

The Ninth Summit was held on 19th April, 2010 in Caracas, Venezuela. This Summit passed Caracas Bi-centenary Manifesto to commemorate the bi-centenary anniversary of Venezuela War of Independence against Spain. With this Manifesto, the member countries confirmed their commitments, namely their common aim of consolidating people's sovereignty and national idependence and struggle for socialism: the 21st Century Ayacucho. This part of the manifest reads as follows: Reviving the people's victory of Ayacucho, which The Liberator described as the "Summit of the American Glory", in every sphere of social life, ALBA will orient each one of its actions to contribute to seal the definite end of colonial domination, consolidating independence and sovereignty. But the 21st Century Ayacucho will be the victory of Socialism, the only guarantee of legitimate independence and sovereignty with justice for the people.

ALBA has set the goal to advance, jointly and simultaneously, toward political, economic and social unity, toward the fullest integration and unity, with a view to guaranteeing the "greatest possible measure of happiness, the highest degree of social security and the highest measure of political stability" for the people, in accordance with the mandate of The Liberator, by turning transition to Socialism into a rewarding experience for Humankind.

In this sense, amidst the Bicentennial Era, we, Heads of State and Government of the member countries of the Bolivarian Alliance for the Peoples of our America, have decided to adopt a number of decisions to accelerate the consolidation process of our independence.

The Tenth Summit was held on 25th June 2010 in Otavalo, Ecuador. This Summit signed the Otavalo Statement. The leaders of the member countries proposed the principles and made their commitments together with the appointed leaders of the local Indians and Africans. It means that the Alliance has made a big step forward in building a just and fair new world. The commitments and confirmations made on the Summit included: the commitment of the ALBA member states in their struggle against the exploitation of human beings.

Likewise, it also validates the concept of multinational state, instituted in the constituent processes of Ecuador and Bolivia, while it also reaffirms it as an expression of unity within diversity.

The commitment of the nations making up the bloc of boosting the Peoples' Trade Treaties and the construction of an alternative model of economic sovereignty, are also some of the aspects included in the document.

It also considers the ALBA's Bank—with the new currency Sucre[4]—and ALBA Fund as instruments of a new financial architecture.

The summit also published an universal declaration with regard to the rights of the Mother Earth within the framework of the UN and vowed to respect the Mother Earth.

The Summit also published the ALBA released a statement on June 28 reaffirming its commitment to the Honduran people's struggle for a return to democracy one year after the coup that overthrew president Manuel Zelaya,

The Eleventh Summit was held during 4- 5th February, 2012 in Caracas, Venezuela. In the Summit, Haiti joined the ALBA as a permanent observer country. In addition, Suriname and Saint Lucia joined the Alliance as "special guest member" countries. The Summit signed the ALBA agreement on establishing economic platform. The economic platform included banks and multilateral foundation to facilitate the use of common regional currency.

The heads of state also discussed the possibility of increasing the commercial use of the sucre, the bloc's virtual currency. The sucre is currently used for direct trading between the ALBA countries, allowing them to circumvent the U.S dollar and minimise the foreign-exchange risk.

According to Ricardo Menendez, Venezuelan Vice-minister of Production and Economy, 431 financial transactions using the sucre were carried out between ALBA countries last year, amounting to over US$216 million worth of trade. However, Ecuadorean president, Rafael Correa, called for the use of the currency to be increased.

"Those free trade agreements, free markets, [with]...zero indemnity, annihilating the weak, that's suicide for our countries...We should encourage fair trade; unite our reserves and financial capacity in the Bank of the Alba and avoid using foreign currencies," he urged.

Daniel Ortega, the Sandinista president of Nicaragua, also expressed his desire to boost the use of the bloc's currency. In statements, Ortega said that he hoped to begin using the sucre within the next few weeks, subject to approval from Nicaragua's national assembly.

At present, the ALBA has become an unprecedented regional alliance and cooperation mechanism and is gradually moving towards economic integration. In face of the international-scale financial crisis, the ALBA persists in safeguarding the development of the Alliance through the strengthening of regional economies and cooperation so as to make the Alliance more attractive for the countries in the region.

---

4 Sucre, is a virtual regional currency proposed for commercial exchanges between members of the regional trade bloc, ALBA.

III. Practical Activities and Future Development Prospects of the ALBA

The Alliance organizes implementation of projects through People's Trade Treaty, Work Plan and via the framework of Grannational Enterprise5 These established institutions promote the potential and capacity utilization of the member countries in a practical, cooperative and fair method to meet their people's basic social demands, so as to achieve sustainable development. People's Trade Treaty is a framework advocating international integration and promoting trade and the exchange of commodities and services in a larger scale based on complementariness principle, mutual benefit and cooperation to improve people's lives. Different from the US-led Free Trade Agreement which favors minimize public sector and favors privatization, People's Trade Treaty recognizes the significant role played by the state in social economic development and in economic regulation.

Implementation of the Grannationals ALBA projects

Grannationals ALBA projects can covers all aspects of the national life of the Alliance member countries, including culture and women issues. Grannationals ALBA projects is an innovative approach of People Trade Treaty, which gives full play to the strength and experiences of each country, reduces information asymmetry, optimizes allocation of resources, enhances mutual aid, promotes structural-development projects, and

---

5   The concept of Grannational is enshrined in the conceptual substratum of ALBA. It is an essentially political concept, but it encompasses all the aspects of the life of our nations. It has several components:

Historical and Geopolitical Basis: focused on the Bolivarian vision of the union of the Latin-American and Caribbean republics for the shaping of the great nation. The grannational concept can be assimilated to the mega-state concept, within the meaning of the joint definition of shared guidelines for political action between the states that share the same view on the exercise on national and regional sovereignty, where each develops its own political identity, without creating supranational structures.

Socio-Economic Basis: Based on the fact that the strategy for the development of the economies of our countries in order to meet the social needs of the great majorities cannot only be restricted to the local sphere. It is a matter of overcoming the national barriers to strengthen the local capacities by merging them in a whole in order to be able to face the challenges of the global reality.

Ideological Basis: It is determined by the conceptual affinity between us who comprise ALBA, regarding the critical conception of the neoliberal globalization and the need to break the world trade patterns based on the free market fiction.

Grannational Project: Program of action intended to comply with the principles and objectives of ALBA, validated by the member countries and its implementation involves two or more countries, for the benefit of the social majorities.

Grannational Enterprise: Enterprises from the productively integrated ALBA countries, whose productions will be fundamentally destined for the INTRA-ALBA, market to shape up a fair trade area, and its operation will be carried out efficiently.

aims to benefit majority of the people. Contrary to transnational corporations, the products and services produced by the companies supported by Grannationals ALBA projects aim at satisfying the needs of the people rather than promoting the profits of capitalists or capital accumulation. The common properties in the operation of the Grannationals ALBA projects all aim to achieve complementariness, joint development, mutual benefits, sustainability, comprehensiveness and reciprocity so as to promote the process of integration under the framework of ALBA.

Member States are free to decide on the mechanisms and projects that they are willing to accede, and non-member States that accept the principles of the ALBA may also join these projects. The above-mentioned Grannationals ALBA projects is part of a numerous of projects in the ALBA. The member countries take advantage of their respective resources and strength and conduct activities with an eye on the present and future benefits of their society and people.

The ALBA Bank and the Uniform Regional Settlement System (Sucre)

The emergence of the uniform settlement (payment) system has been established in the new regional context of financial and trade relations among member states. The headquarter of the ALBA Bank was set in Caracas in 2009 with an initial working capital of 1 Billion dollars. The major functions of the ALBA Bank include projects financing; promoting, establishing and managing grants to promote the development of economy, society and environment; it also provides technological support, pre-investment feasibility studies, supports research and development, technology transfer and technology introduction or absorption; promoting the implementation of equitable trade regarding goods and services.

The regional uniform settlement (payment) system is established in order to develop the economic space of the ALBA. In order to promote the Sucre-based trade among member countries, each member country must provide 1% of its international reserves for the ALBA as an initial fund. Venezuela has provide more than 0.3 billion dollars. The birth of Sucre symbolizes that the countries of Latin America and the Caribbean have made a significant step forward towards trade integration. With the decreasing use of dollars in the region, regional currency integration in Latin America has witnessed an important development. At present, 431 Sucre-based transactions have been completed with a total worth of 0.27 billion dollars (as of 2011), which marks a big breakthrough in the system. In addition, Sucre can also promote the use of local currency as payment for import goods so that the country is able to achieve effective compensation in its balance of trade, and Sucre can also be used as credit financing to increase the production of high-value-added products for export.

CELAC

The Community of Latin American and Caribbean States (CELAC) is the most precious work of ALBA alliance. It's the mechanism to forge unity in diversity, through political concentration. This Community has had to endure the pushback of the defenders of the failed Pan-Americanism.

The declaration of the 14th summit says: "our commitment with the Proclaim of Latin America and the Caribbean as a Peace Zone guides our international policy. It's coherent with our strict compliance with the principles of the UN Charter and with International Right, and it reaffirms our respect to self-determination, to national sovereignty and to equality between States. It expresses the will to settle differences peacefully, through dialogue and negotiation, and recognizes the inalienable right of States to choose their political, economic, social and cultural system.

The small economies of the Caribbean, who have suffered genocides against their native populations, slavery, and plundering through colonial and neocolonial systems, nowadays are facing the effects of climate change, natural disasters and global crises, which make them the most vulnerable ones in our family. The Caribbean, decidedly supported by the generous initiative of Petrocaribe, deserves our utmost solidarity and all of our attention."

Great unity of the people in the region

ALBA declaration of 2004 says: Bolivarian Alliance for the Peoples of Our America takes concrete actions which materialize in the field of the Missions and Social Programs that contribute decisively to the universality of the fundamental rights to Education and Health among our peoples.

Based on the huge achievements realized through Mission Miracle and Missions in the field of health, education, care for people with disabilities, among others, the ALBA considers granting universality to the Social Missions in all our countries.

In terms of national unity, several projects which represent, solidarity and humanitarianism, developed with principle of social inclusion are as follows:

The Literacy and Post-literacy program: This program has allowed the eradication of illiteracy in 4 ALBA-TCP countries, which have been declared "illiteracy-Free Territories" by UNESCO. Venezuela (2005), Bolivia (2008), Nicaragua (2009) and Ecuador (2009).

Based on the "Yes I Can" Educational Method, developed by Cuba, more than 3.500.000 persons nowadays can read and write. The program also guarantees the continuation of studies and the inclusion of the citizens in the formal education system of our countries.

Miracle Mission Foundation: It is a humanitarian project, that is focused on the care and free intervention in patients with ophthalmic conditions in the Latin American and the Caribbean countries, mainly for the low-income persons.

Mission Miracle has not only attended to patients from the ALBA-TCP countries , but it has also been extended to 21 countries around the world, restoring visual capability in more than 1.880.000 persons with vision impairment, who did not have access to specialized health services.

Aid Program for the Disabled: In the member countries of the ALBA, there are 800.000 disabled people without receiving any special care. The Program develops a Psychosocial and Clinical Genetics Study for Persons with Disabilities, which allows for the identification of the population of this sector who, for years, had been deprived of any human and social right, by ensuring their integration, without discrimination, in the socio-productive, political and cultural area as well as the promotion of their individual potentials.

More than 3.000.000 persons who did not have access to medical care, have been identified with disability in six of the countries of ALBA-TCP: Cuba, Venezuela, Ecuador, Bolivia, Nicaragua and Saint Vincent and the Grenadines. Study will be carried out soon in Dominica, and Antigua and Barbuda.

The assistance offered to this sector of the population is provided through Jose Gregorio Hernández Mission in Venezuela, Manuela Espejo in Ecuador, "Todos con Vos" program in Nicaragua and Moto Méndez Mission in Bolivia.

The program also includes the strengthening of the installed capacities in order to produce prostheses and orthoses for the persons with disabilities, counted in the study in the ALBA-TCP countries.

Latin American School of Medicine: The Latin-American School of Medicine (LASM) seeks to train community doctors with solid scientific, technical, ethical and humanistic background, deeply committed to social purposes, and they shall act as a force for social and political change, by integrating themselves into their own community.

The LASM, with its headquarters in Cuba and Venezuela, has enabled more and more students to be trained in health sciences, project which will solve in the medium term, the problems of access to health care with which our peoples are confronted. There are more than 2.000 young students from different parts of Latin America, the Caribbean and Africa.

ALBA Culture Fund: The creation of a ALBA Culture Fund for the promotion of creation, production and distribution of goods and cultural services of our peoples, gave birth to the Grannational ALBA Cultural Project.

ALBA Cultural is intended to contribute to the unity of the creators, artists and intellectuals, institutions and social movements of Our America, opposed to the pseudo-cultural trends, fostered and promoted by the so called entertainment industry.

Its actions have been framed in the strategic lines: Production, Distribution and Promotion of cultural goods and services.

Articulation and development of networks with social movements and cultural entities. Training of human resource for culture. Legitimating of the Latin-American and Caribbean cultural values. Socio-cultural impact development among our peoples. In addition, the creation of the network of Houses of ALBA Cultural stands out, with the aim of enriching social and cultural life and favoring the expression and development of ideas and, as well as, the most representative artistic and literary creation of our peoples.

2008 to present, TV Station of ALBA, TV Station of the South, TV Channel of the South have been set up. These TV stations facilitate the integration of the people living in the member states, strengthen their national identity of and promote the transformation of politics, economics and culture of these countries.

To sum up, the ALBA, intends both to protect the national and regional sovereignty, promotes members' respective social and political features, designs wide range of activities based on the common policies of member states, and leads ALBA countries to become a "great community of nations". The ALBA has initiated a completely innovative course, incorporates and implements some projects with regard to social economic development and culture which were neglected in the past during the integration efforts in Latin America.

The practices of the ALBA, offer us enlightment in the following two aspects. Firstly, when the current world is faced with new situations and new problems, and as the developing countries are exploring a path of development that is in line with their own development interests and needs, the basic tenets of Marxism still has strong vitality and can offer a strong inspiration.

Secondly, in the face of unequal and unfair economic and political world order dominated by the West, the developing countries, when seeking an alternative development mode, to the current neo-liberalism and capitalist development mode, should enhance their political and economic relations so as to reinforce their position in North-South dialogue, thus can promote the establishment of an equitable and just new international economic and political order.

Y. 45

Why Marxism is on the rise again

Stuart Jeffries translated by Song Lidan[1]

Abstract: With the deepening of the capitalist crisis, the sales of classical works of Marxism and the interest in Marx and Marxist thought are on the rise again in the West. An article "Why Marxism is on the Rise Again" in The Guardian on 4 July 2012 analyses this phenomenon tentatively. The author points out that the rich make the mass pay for its crisis and the rest of us have to struggle to live in the dilemma caused by the crisis and this confirms that the analysis of the crisis by Marxism is a truth. The theory of the "end of the world" has to end in front of the crisis and the so called "middle class" illusion is disillusioned in the crisis. The author, who is influenced by the mainstream thought of the West, has to admit that capitalism could solve the crisis within the system itself. He assumes that "the proletarians have nothing to lose but their chains. They have a world to win." This article provides a sketch of perspectives from different classes on Marxism and would be useful for us to observe Why Marxism is on the rise again in the West.

Key words: Marxism; capitalism; crisis

---

[1] Song Lidan, visiting researcher of CASS World Socialism Research and associate researcher of CASS Institute of Marxism Studies.

Capitalism is in crisis across the globe – but what on earth is the alternative? Well, what about the musings of a certain 19th-century German philosopher? Yes, Karl Marx is going mainstream – and goodness knows where it will end.

Class conflict once seemed so straightforward. Marx and Engels wrote in the second best-selling book of all time, The Communist Manifesto: "What the bourgeoisie therefore produces, above all, are its own grave-diggers. Its fall and the victory of the proletariat are equally inevitable." (The best-selling book of all time, incidentally, is the Bible – it only feels like it's 50 Shades of Grey.)

Today, 164 years after Marx and Engels wrote about grave-diggers, the truth is almost the exact opposite. The proletariat, far from burying capitalism, are keeping it on life support. Overworked, underpaid workers ostensibly liberated by the largest socialist revolution in history (China's) are driven to the brink of suicide to keep those in the west playing with their iPads. Chinese money bankrolls an otherwise bankrupt America.

The irony is scarcely wasted on leading Marxist thinkers. "The domination of capitalism globally depends today on the existence of a Chinese Communist party that gives de-localised capitalist enterprises cheap labour to lower prices and deprive workers of the rights of self-organisation," says Jacques Rancière, the French Marxist thinker and Professor of Philosophy at the University of Paris VIII. "Happily, it is possible to hope for a world less absurd and more just than today's."

That hope, perhaps, explains another improbable truth of our economically catastrophic times – the revival in interest in Marx and Marxist thought. Sales of Das Kapital, Marx's masterpiece of political economy, have soared ever since 2008, as have those of The Communist Manifesto and the Grundrisse (or, to give it its English title, Outlines of the Critique of Political Economy). Their sales rose as British workers bailed out the banks to keep the degraded system going and the snouts of the rich firmly in their troughs while the rest of us struggle in debt, job insecurity or worse. There's even a Chinese theatre director called He Nian who capitalised on Das Kapital's renaissance to create an all-singing, all-dancing musical.

And in perhaps the most lovely reversal of the luxuriantly bearded revolutionary theorist's fortunes, Karl Marx was recently chosen from a list of 10 contenders to appear on a new issue of MasterCard by customers of German bank Sparkasse in Chemnitz. In communist East Germany from 1953 to 1990, Chemnitz was known as Karl-Marx-Stadt.

Clearly, more than two decades after the fall of the Berlin Wall, the former East Germany hasn't airbrushed its Marxist past. In 2008, Reuters reports, a survey of east Germans found 52% believed the free-market economy was "unsuitable" and 43% said they wanted socialism back. Karl Marx may be dead and buried in Highgate cemetery, but he's alive and well among credit-hungry Germans. Would Marx have appreciated the irony of his image being deployed on a card to get Germans deeper in debt? You'd think. Later this week in London, several thousand people will attend Marxism 2012, a five-day festival organised by the Socialist Workers' Party. It's an annual event, but what strikes organiser Joseph Choonara is how, in recent years, many more of its attendees are young. "The revival of interest in Marxism, especially for young people comes because it provides tools for analysing capitalism, and especially capitalist crises such as the one we're in now," Choonara says.

There has been a glut of books trumpeting Marxism's relevance. English literature professor Terry Eagleton last year published a book called Why Marx Was Right. French Maoist philosopher Alain Badiou published a little red book called The Communist Hypothesis with a red star on the cover (very Mao, very now) in which he rallied the faithful to usher in the third era of the communist idea (the previous two having gone from the establishment of the French Republic in 1792 to the massacre of the Paris communards in 1871, and from 1917 to the collapse of Mao's Cultural Revolution in 1976). Isn't this all a delusion?

Aren't Marx's venerable ideas as useful to us as the hand loom would be to shoring up Apple's reputation for innovation? Isn't the dream of socialist revolution and communist society an irrelevance in 2012? After all, I suggest to Rancière, the bourgeoisie has failed to produce its own gravediggers.

Rancière refuses to be downbeat: "The bourgeoisie has learned to make the exploited pay for its crisis and to use them to disarm its adversaries. But we must not reverse the idea of historical necessity and conclude that the current situation is eternal. The gravediggers are still here, in the form of workers in precarious conditions like the over-exploited workers of factories in the far east. And today's popular movements – Greece or elsewhere – also indicate that there's a new will not to let our governments and our bankers inflict their crisis on the people."

That, at least, is the perspective of a seventy something Marxist professor. What about younger people of a Marxist temper?

I ask Jaswinder Blackwell-Pal, a 22 year-old English and drama student at Goldsmiths College, London, who has just finished her BA course in English and Drama, why she considers Marxist thought still relevant. "The point is that younger people weren't around when Thatcher was in power or when Marxism was associated with the Soviet Union," she says. "We tend to see it more as a way of understanding what we're going through now. Think of what's happening in Egypt. When Mubarak fell it was so inspiring. It broke so many stereotypes – democracy wasn't supposed to be something that people would fight for in the Muslim world. It vindicates revolution as a process, not as an event. So there was a revolution in Egypt, and a counter-revolution and a counter-counter revolution. What we learned from it was the importance of organisation."

This, surely is the key to understanding Marxism's renaissance in the west: for younger people, it is untainted by association with Stalinist gulags. For younger people too, Francis Fukuyama's triumphalism in his 1992 book The End of History – in which capitalism seemed incontrovertible, its overthrow impossible to imagine – exercises less of a choke-hold on their imaginations than it does on those of their elders.

Blackwell-Pal will be speaking Thursday on Che Guevara and the Cuban revolution at the Marxism festival. "It's going to be the first time I'll have spoken on Marxism," she says nervously. But what's the point thinking about Guevara and Castro in this day and age? Surely violent socialist revolution is irrelevant to workers' struggles today? "Not at all!" she replies. "What's happening in Britain is quite interesting. We have a very, very weak government mired in in-fighting. I think if we can really organise we can oust them." Could Britain have its Tahrir Square, its equivalent to Castro's 26th of July Movement? Let a young woman dream. After last year's riots and today with most of Britain alienated from the rich men in its government's cabinet, only a fool would rule it out. For a different perspective I catch up with Owen Jones, 27-year-old poster boy of the new left and author of the bestselling politics book of 2011, Chavs: the Demonisation of the Working Class. He's on the train to Brighton to address the Unite conference. "There isn't going to be a bloody revolution in Britain, but there is hope for a society by working people and for working people," he counsels.

Indeed, he says, in the 1860s the later Marx imagined such a post-capitalist society as being won by means other than violent revolution. "He did look at expanding the suffrage and other peaceful means of achieving socialist society. Today not even the Trotskyist left call for armed revolution. The radical left would say that the break with capitalism could only be achieved by democracy and organisation of working people to establish and hold on to that just society against forces that would destroy it."

Jones recalls that his father, a Militant supporter in the 1970s, held to the entryist idea of ensuring the election of a Labour government and then organising working people to make sure that government delivered. "I think that's the model," he says. How very un-New Labour. That said, after we talk, Jones texts me to make it clear he's not a Militant supporter or Trotskyist. Rather, he wants a Labour government in power that will pursue a radical political programme. He has in mind the words of Labour's February 1974 election manifesto which expressed the intention to "Bring about a fundamental and irreversible shift in the balance of power and wealth in favour of working people and their families". Let a young man dream. What's striking about Jones's literary success is that it's premised on the revival of interest in class politics, that foundation stone of Marx and Engels's analysis of industrial society. "If I had written it four years earlier it would have been dismissed as a 1960s concept of class," says Jones. "But class is back in our reality because the economic crisis affects people in different ways and because the Coalition mantra that 'We're all in this together' is offensive and ludicrous. It's impossible to argue now as was argued in the 1990s that we're all middle class. This government's reforms are class-based. VAT rises affect working people disproportionately, for instance.

"It's an open class war," he says. "Working-class people are going to be worse off in 2016 than they were at the start of the century. But you're accused of being a class warrior if you stand up for 30% of the population who suffers this way."

This chimes with something Rancière told me. The professor argued that "one thing about Marxist thought that remains solid is class struggle. The disappearance of our factories, that's to say de-industrialisation of our countries and the outsourcing of industrial work to the countries where labour is less expensive and more docile, what else is this other than an act in the class struggle by the ruling bourgeoisie?"

There's another reason why Marxism has something to teach us as we struggle through economic depression, other than its analysis of class struggle. It is in its analysis of economic crisis. In his formidable new tome Less Than Nothing: Hegel and the Shadow of Dialectical Materialism, Slavoj Žižek tries to apply Marxist thought on economic crises to what we're enduring right now. Žižek considers the fundamental class antagonism to be between "use value" and "exchange value".

What's the difference between the two? Each commodity has a use value, he explains, measured by its usefulness in satisfying needs and wants. The exchange value of a commodity, by contrast, is traditionally measured by the amount of labour that goes into making it. Under current capitalism, Žižek argues, exchange value becomes autonomous. "It is transformed into a spectre of self-propelling capital which uses the productive capacities and needs of actual people only as its temporary disposable embodiment. Marx derived his notion of economic crisis from this very gap: a crisis occurs when reality catches up with the illusory self-generating mirage of money begetting more money – this speculative madness cannot go on indefinitely, it has to explode in even more serious crises. The ultimate root of the crisis for Marx is the gap between use and exchange value: the logic of exchange-value follows its own path, its own made dance, irrespective of the real needs of real people."

In such uneasy times, who better to read than the greatest catastrophist theoriser of human history, Karl Marx? And yet the renaissance of interest in Marxism has been pigeonholed as an apologia for Stalinist totalitarianism. In a recent blog on "the new communism" for the journal World Affairs, Alan Johnson, professor of democratic theory and practice at Edge Hill University in Lancashire, wrote: "A worldview recently the source of immense suffering and misery, and responsible for more deaths than fascism and Nazism, is mounting a comeback; a new form of leftwing totalitarianism that enjoys intellectual celebrity but aspires to political power.

"The New Communism matters not because of its intellectual merits but because it may yet influence layers of young Europeans in the context of an exhausted social democracy, austerity and a self-loathing intellectual culture," wrote Johnson. "Tempting as it is, we can't afford to just shake our heads and pass on by."

That's the fear: that these nasty old left farts such as Žižek, Badiou, Rancière and Eagleton will corrupt the minds of innocent youth. But does reading Marx and Engels's critique of capitalism mean that you thereby take on a worldview responsible for more deaths than the Nazis? Surely there is no straight line from The Communist Manifesto to the gulags, and no reason why young lefties need uncritically to adopt Badiou at his most chilling. In his introduction to a new edition of The Communist Manifesto, Professor Eric Hobsbawm suggests that Marx was right to argue that the "contradictions of a market system based on no other nexus between man and man than naked self-interest, than callous 'cash payment', a system of exploitation and of 'endless accumulation' can never be overcome: that at some point in a series of transformations and restructurings the development of this essentially destabilising system will lead to a state of affairs that can no longer be described as capitalism".

That is post-capitalist society as dreamed of by Marxists. But what would it be like? "It is extremely unlikely that such a 'post-capitalist society' would respond to the traditional models of socialism and still less to the 'really existing' socialisms of the Soviet era," argues Hobsbawm, adding that it will, however, necessarily involve a shift from private appropriation to social management on a global scale. "What forms it might take and how far it would embody the humanist values of Marx's and Engels's communism, would depend on the political action through which this change came about."

This is surely Marxism at its most liberating, suggesting that our futures depend on us and our readiness for struggle. Or as Marx and Engels put it at the end of The Communist Manifesto: "Let the ruling classes tremble at a communist revolution. The proletarians have nothing to lose but their chains. They have a world to win."

Y. 46

The Communist Party of India (Maoist) as the Major Component Part of Communist Movement in India

Wang Jing[1]

Abstract: The rise of the Maoist movement in India since the mid-1980s has been the result of India's social ills accompanied by neoliberal poison and the sharpening of some old contradictions coupled with newborn contradictions. Compared to the armed struggle of Telangana Rebellion in the late 1940s and the Naxalbari Insurrection in the 1960s, this recent wave of Maoist communist movement performs a more resolute struggle and has a more mature strategy, which is a significant step forward in the history of the communist movement in India. The Communist Party of India (Maoist) established in 2004 with a strong army and a considerable number of militia, advocates emulating the Chinese revolution to launch a people's war, and ultimately achieve socialism in India. The Communist Party of India (Maoist) is the most powerful armed force in the current international communist movement. The Communist Party of India (Maoist) has become one of the most important threats for India's ruling classes. The final outcome of the struggle between the two parties, will directly affect the future of India and the world communist movement.

Key words: Communist Party of India (Maoist); communist movement of India; Maoist Movement; armed struggle

---

1 Wang Jing, specially invited researcher in the World Socialism Research Center, attached to CASS; research assistant in Marxism Research Institute.

The rise of the Maoist movement in India since the mid-1980s has been the result of India's social ills accompanied by neoliberal poison and the sharpening of some old contradictions coupled with newborn contradictions.

As compared to the previous communist movements, the leaders of this recent wave of communist movement, namely Communist Party of India (Maoist), have summarized the experiences and lessons of the decades-long peasant movement, drawn lessons and adapted their theories to national conditions similar to the historical experience of the Chinese revolution, and has firmly chosen Mao Zedong Thought as their guiding ideology. The recent Maoist movement communist movement performs a more resolute militant struggle and has a more mature strategy, which is a significant step forward in the history of the communist movement in India.

At present, the three most influential communist forces in India are the Communist Party of India, the Communist Party of India (Marxist) and the Communist Party of India (Maoist). The previous two parties advocate struggle via parliament although they combine parliamentary struggle with extra parliamentary struggles and they have won state power and governed for many years in the three states of India. Unfortunately, they failed to be elected in 2010 due to improper handling of the contradictions in the Kerala region between the interest of peasants and that of the monopoly enterprises.

The Communist Party of India (Maoist) has a strong army and a considerable number of militia. They follow the example of the Chinese revolution to launch a guerilla war as the part of people's war, thus ultimately achieve socialism in India. As a continuation of the Naxalbari Insurrection of the 1970s, the Maoist Movement led by the Communist Party of India (Maoist) has already surpassed the Naxalbari Insurrection of the 1970s and the massive Telangana Rebellion of the mid-1940s.

I. History of the Communist Movements of India: The Split of the Indian Communist Party

The Communist Party of India (CPI) witnessed several split-ups within its 90 years of history. Established in 1920, the CPI split into Communist Party of India and Communist Party of India (Marxist). In April 1969, the Communist Party of India (Marxist) split into Communist Party of India (Marxist) and Communist Party of India (Marxist-Leninist). In the early 1970s, the Naxalbari peasant movement failed and the Communist Party of India (Marxist-Leninist) split into more factions, and in 1990s when armed struggle of the peasants witnessed another upsurge, two factions of the Communist Party of India (Marxist-Leninist) joined hands to form the Communist Party of India (Maoist) in 2004. The phenomenon of constant splits within the Communist Party was pretty rare in the history of the international communist movement. It was due to the sectarian conflicts that the strength of the CPI was greatly undermined and the Party failed to achieve success in the communist movement.

Among the various major factors that caused the splits in the CPI, include the direct or indirect influence generated by the Communist Party of Great Britain, the Communist Party of Soviet Union, the Communist Party of Yugoslavia and the Communist Party of China. In addition, almost every big controversy and upheaval in the international communist movement has impacted the CPI directly. The several split-ups within the CPI are closely related to the internal splits or upheavals in the international communist movement, and this influence has been more obvious in India than in the other countries. The primary cause for this is that the CPI has failed to form a mature theoretical system to guide the communist movement in India and that it has failed to form a core of leadership collective to unite the communist forces in the whole country. The CPI has a long-lasting debate on the nature of Indian society and the regime led by the Congress Party, also the role and nature of this party, and on whether it should follow the revolutionary road of the Soviet Union or that of China. The disagreements in ideological issues have caused the CPI to split into several factions thus its power was significantly weakened.

The split of Communist Party of India in 1964

As early as 1946-1947, the CPI has gone through a long heated debate on whether they should support the Congress Nehru Government or not and on whether they should support the bourgeoisie or not. This debate, planted the seeds of the future divisions in the party.

In 1964, intense inner power struggle and a separatist movement began to take place in the CPI. The Sundarayya faction and the Dange faction held the Seventh Congress of the CPI under the name of CPI respectively in Calcutta and Bombay. The former faction believed that the Congress Party represented the big bourgeoisie and advocated the political line of anti-imperialist, anti-feudal and anti-big-bourgeoisie people's democratic revolution led by the proletariat. Dange faction, being supportive of the Congress Party's policies, believed that the Congress Party, which represented the interest of the national bourgeoisie, was the leading the ongoing national-democratic revolution.

In the mid-term election held in Kerala in February 1965, the Dange faction was recognized as the official CPI by the state election committee, and therefore, the Sundarayya faction was compelled to change its name into CPI (Marxist).

The split of the Communist Party of India (Marxist) in 1969

When the international communist movement went through big split and a re-grouping, the CIP (Marxist) faced another threat of split, though it has just separated from the CIP. Encouraged by the success of Kerala parliamentary elections, some party members proposed to follow the parliamentary road to realize people's democratic revolution. While another group believed that the situation was mature for the revolution in the view of increasing social contradictions in the Indian society, and the revolutionary situation worldwide, considering the rebellion of the "New Left" in Europe and the influence of changes in China, especially the "Cultural Revolution". On 22 April 1969, radical faction of the CPI (Marxist) founded the CPI (Marxist-Leninist) with Charu Majumdar as its general secretary. This radical party became the third communist power on the political stage of India.

The CPI, the CPI (Marxist) and the CPI (Marxist-Leninist) became the representatives of the right wing, the centre-left wing and the ultra-left wing respectively. The CPI and the CPI (Marxist) made certain achievements on the parliamentary struggle road, while the CPI (Marxist-Leninist) resolutely took path of armed struggle.

The split of the CPI (Marxist-Leninist) in the 1970s and the rise of the Maoist Movement in the 1980s

The vigorous Naxalbari peasant uprising erupted after Charu Majumdar, the leader of the CPI (Marxist-Leninist), was arrested and died in the prison and the movement turned to a low ebb. The armed struggle of the party in the countryside did not last very long and the CPI (Marxist-Leninist) split again. During the 1970s, communist movement in India was at a low ebb. The armed guerrillas of by the CPI (Marxist-Leninist) either cease their activities or went underground with a scope of narrowing the armed struggle. The whole Party organization was lax in discipline. "According to the statistics of the early 1980s, the Party has split into 27 small factions with no more than 10 thousand people. Most of the activities had stopped, or existed in name only. It was no longer a nation-wide party."[2]

Though the Naxalbari Insurrection failed, the armed struggle in the countryside did not stop. With the continuous armed struggle with a smaller scale, the fire of Naxalbari Insurrection was carried on in Bihar and Andhra Pradesh states. Since the mid-1980s, the armed struggle of the peasants saw a rising trend. The Maoist Communist Centre of India (MCCI) in Bihar, the CPI (Marxist-Leninist-Liberation) and the People's War Group (PWG) factions, which all belonged to the CPI (Marxist-Leninist), were the three most influential factions with armed forces.

---

2   Fan Yuchuan, "Past and Present of the Communist Party of India". Scientific Socialism, 1992/2.

On 21 September 2004, the MCCI and the CPI (Marxist-Leninist) (People's War Group) officially merged to form the CPI (Maoist) in the forest district of central India. After merger, the Maoist faction's strength greatly improved and rapidly impacted the other neighboring states from Bihar and Andhrapradesh. "According to official data, armed activities of the Maoist faction have occurred in the 53 counties of 9 Indian states till April 2003. After a year and a half, this number has increased to 125 counties of the 12 Indian states by September 2004. On 2 April 2006, Dugar, Secretary of the Interior Ministry of the India, told the press that 13 government officials were afflicted by Naxalites due to attacks. Among the 602 counties of India, 125 have witnessed armed Maoist attacks."[3]

II. Historical Comparison: Three Climaxes of the Armed Struggle throughout the History of Communist Movement in India

Three big armed peasant struggles have occurred throughout the history of communist movement in India, which pushed the communist movement in India to one climax after another. A close look at the three movements would show that the armed struggle of the CPI has gradually matured amid twists and turns.

Armed uprising of the peasants in Telangana, Andhra Pradesh state, during July 1946 to October 1951

The impressive spread of power and influence of this struggle was pretty rare in the modern history of India. "The armed struggle affected 3,000 villages of the district, and overthrew the reactionary Nizam regime within an area of 16.000 square mile and with the participation 3 million people. The struggle established a people's regime, confiscated 1 million acres of land from the landlords and distributed them among the peasants which possessed minimum land. During its zenith days, the struggle had expanded to the 7 counties of Telangana and Andhra Pradesh, influencing 12 million people."[4]

The armed struggle was initiated spontaneously by the peasants but gained an entirely new appearance due to the participation and leadership of the CPI Branch of Andhra Pradesh, but it suffered a violent defeat in the end, due to the intervention and cruel massacre of the army, ordered by the ruling Congress Party in its later period.

---

3 Sun Peijun, "Armed Struggle in the Countryside by the Naxalites: The Chief Domestic Threat for India". Journal of Sichuan University (Social Science Edition). 2006/5.
4 Pu Sundarayya, The Struggle of the Talangana People in India, Its Experiences and Lessons, Joint Publishing. 1997, p. 1.

After the violent crackdown, the Congress Party sent the leader of "Sarvodaya Movement (Common prosperity)", Vinoba Bhave, to carry out the so called "Land Gift Movement" and conducted an intense anti-communist propaganda and also tried to appease the peasants. The balance of class power went through great changes. Moreover, a divergence appeared within the Andhra Pradesh Communist Party and the CPI Central Committee with regard to the nature of the uprising. The rift was in fact a continuation of the debate on the nature of the Congress Party and regarding its role after winning the independence of India, and this disagreement has always affected the path of armed struggle to a large extent.

They could not decide whether they should take the advice of the Communist Party of the Great Britain and stop the armed struggle, or they should insist on this political line. Therefore, they sought advice from the Communist Party of the Soviet Union, the Party that enjoyed highest authority in the international communist movement, in those days.

The delegates sent to Moscow by the CPI has only received a vague answer from Stalin: "It seems it has been difficult to carry on the struggle (even in the first half of 1951). I feel sorry that the CPI has failed to defend the struggle. However, whether to continue the struggle or to stop it, the final decision should be made by the CPI."[5]

After three years of arduous struggle in defending their hard-won basis, the CPI declared a moratorium for the armed struggle on 21 October 1951.

This spontaneous struggle achieved great success due to the participation and leadership of the Andhrapradesh Branch of the Communist Party. But after the failure of the uprising, a large number of party members and citizens were killed. The fruits of the revolution were lost, and the Andhrapradesh Branch of the Communist Party as well as the entire CPI split into two camps, politically and ideologically. This ideological divergence continued till 1963 and finally caused the organizational split of the Party in 1964 with the aggravation of inner-party struggles.

Armed uprising of the peasants in Naxalbari region of Darjeeling, West Bengal during 1967 to 1971

After the independence of India, the Congress Party, which represented the interest of the bourgeoisies and the landlord class, has carried out an incomplete land reform. After the reform, the fundamental interest of the Zamindar landlord class in the countryside of India was preserved. Firstly, this class kept a good deal of their privately owned plot and some of their land was transferred to new landlords by the government.

---

5 Book by Sun Shihai, Politics, International Relationship and Security of South Asia, P 40.China Social Science Press, 1998.

Secondly, they received a huge sum of compensation from the government, while other powerful landlords and rich peasants became new landlords with land ownership as well. In essence, this reform was merely an adjustment and distribution of interests within the upper class in that it simply transferred part of the lands from the big landlord class to the hands of the middle and smaller landlords.

After this reform, it was the interests of the lower class, namely the interest of the farm laborers, employed peasants and land-lost farmers, which was damaged. Therefore, after the land reform, instead of decreasing, the number of landless farmers has rapidly increased. Therefore, statistically, the number of landless farm laborers was 2.752 million in 1951, and it had increased to 31.5 million, 45.6 million and 56.0 million respectively in during the years of 1961, 1971 and 1981.[6]

Compared to the land reform in China, land reform in India was an obvious failure, and that was why subsequent peasant uprisings have occurred in India.

In May 1967, another peasant uprising broke out in Naxalbari, Darjeeling, north of West Bengal. Naxalbari, extends in the long and narrow border area between Nepal and East Pakistan, and it is the only passage from the northeast states to the downstream flat area, which is strategic for India's security.[7]

This pro-China and pro-Maoist armed rebellion, when erupted out in such a strategic region, caused a panic in the central government of India, which was already in political and economic plight. Ajoy Mukherjee, the then Chief Minister and Minister of the Interior Ministry, immediately sent 1,500 police troops to assist the local security forces to suppress the insurrection. Within two month, the government has arrested 1,300 people, including most of the leaders of the uprising.[8]

The uprising was suppressed in a short period of time, and the remaining forces of the revolution resorted to underground struggle.

The uprising has not been put down completely and the influence of the Naxalbari Insurrection has continued. The CPI (Marxist) stopped its support for the uprising in the half-way and took a tacit attitude towards the suppression operation conducted by the government of India.

---

6   Class Relations and Technological Changes in Indian Agriculture. New Delhi, 1980, p. 41; Indian Reserve Bank. Indian Economy: Basic Statistics. Bombay, 1983, p. 5. Quote from Huang Sijun. Research on Indian Land System. China Social Science Press, 1998, p. 321.
7   Francine R. Frankel, India's Political Economy after Independence. China Social Science Press, p. 432, 1989.
8   Ibid., p. 432.

Thus, in September 1967, branches of the party in several states separated from the CPI (M). Large number of pro-Naxalit revolutionaries quitted the CPI (Marxist) in Andhrapradesh and West Bengal. The Naxalites established All-India Coordination Committee in Calcutta to prepare for the organization of a new party. Later, Naxalites appeared in more states such as Kerala, Karnataka, Punjab and Tamil Nadu.[9]

On 22 April 1969, the CPI (Marxist-Leninist) was established with Charu Majumdar as its Party Secretary. The Party declared its opposition against the absolute "fraud of the parliamentary system" and instead advocated immediate revolution through people's revolutionary war. The fundamental task of the Party was "liberating the rural area through armed agrarian revolution, winning and using the rural areas to encircle the cities, liberating the cities at the last stage and completing the revolution in the whole country". According to statistics, the CPI (Marxist-Leninist) had 20 to 30 thousand party members across the country and it had recruited its activists from university students and urban intermediate middle class.[10]

Although the vigor of Naxalbari Insurrection had deceased to low tide since 1972, its influence have continued during the consequent decades in India.

The scattered armed forces have continued to remain after the failure of Naxalbari Insurrection

The CPI (Maoist) was founded on 21sr September, 2004, through the merger of the Maoist Communist Centre of India in Bihar (MCCI) and the People's War Group of Andhrapradesh. The adoption of neoliberal policies by the Indian government after the collapse of the Soviet Union was one of the major reasons that triggered the rapid development of the armed forces of the CPI (Maoist). In essence, the socio-economic character of Indian society, since independence is capitalist embodying remarkable degree of remnants of feudalism. Due to the existence of a wide range of poor people in India and a strong left-wing forces , the Congress Party of India has proclaimed its political path as the third path of democratic socialism in the 1960s, although it cannot truly realize its many policies that contain socialist values.

But in its early period, Congress Party of India's left-leaning political line has to a degree, opposed and restricted the big bourgeoisie and the big landlord class in India.

However, the situation has changed since 1991.During 1989-1991, with the collapse of Soviet Union and Great upheaval in the Eastern Europe the world communist movement has encountered a setback and decline and the world saw the rise of neoliberal ideology.

---

9   Ibid., p. 439.
10   Ibid., p. 439.

In early July of 1991, the announcement of the New Economic Policy of the N. Rao[11] government led by the Congress Party has marked neoliberal concept, advocated by the right-wing capitalists gaining the dominant status in India. After neoliberal reforms in India, its GDP has recovered but the lives of the masses have deteriorated. The alliance between the government and big businessmen, which generated the Enclosure Movement, the Land Acquisition Law and the Special Economic Zones Act, has impoverished and many farmers have lost their small farms, caused a huge wave of urbanization of the poor. These conflicts have led to a new round of communist movement.

The CPI (Maoist) led the public to defend the interest of the masses, resisted the exploitation of Indian people by the foreign capital, and criticized other neoliberal policies. The CPI (Maoist) political organ wrote: "the policy of liberalization, privatization and globalization is an offensive against world's working class. They want to bind the hands and the feet of the workers despicably to facilitate the exploitation of the plutocrat". The Ninth Congress of the CPI (Maoist) in 2007, called on the people to "further strengthen the people's army, deepen the mass base of the party and wage a broad-based militant mass movement against the neoliberal policies of globalization, liberalization, privatization pursued by the reactionary ruling classes under the dictates of imperialism. People should, resolutely defend their land and houses, resolutely beat back the destructive and brutal and savage 'horde of capitalism".[12]

From 2004 till present, movement of the CPI (Maoist) has reached certain scale, formed a "red corridor" in India or even effecting the whole South Asia Region. The CPI (Maoist), characterized by having specific creed, strict party constitution, standardized solid organization system, is led by a systematic Marxist theory, and leads a guerrilla liberation army and armed militia, is able to maintain its power and able to develop itself although faced by comprehensive and ruthless suppression of the Indian ruling class.

---

11   Rao, also called the „Father of Indian Economic Reforms," is best remembered for launching India's free market reforms that rescued the almost bankrupt nation from economic collapse. He was also commonly referred to as the Chanakya of modern India for his ability to steer tough economic and political legislation through the parliament at a time when he headed a minority government.

Rao's term as Prime Minister was an eventful one in India's history. Besides marking a paradigm shift from the industrializing, mixed economic model of Jawaharlal Nehru to a market driven one, his years as Prime Minister also saw the emergence of the Bharatiya Janata Party (BJP), a major right-wing party, as an alternative to the Indian National Congress which had been governing India for most of its post-independence history. Rao's term also saw the destruction of the Babri Mosque in Ayodhya which triggered one of the worst Hindu-Muslim riots in the country since its independence.

12   Call of the Unity Congress – 9th Congress of the CPI (Maoist), http://www.satp.org/satporgtp/countries/india/maoist/documents/papers/callofunity.htm.

III. The status quo of the armed struggle since the establishment of the CPI (Maoist)

The CPI (Maoist), representing the united forces of Maoists after its foundation in 2004, has developed rapidly and expanded its range of activity to more than half of the Indian territories. The CPI (Maoist) has established two red corridors in India and the South Asia Region from Pashupati in Nepal to Tirupati in India.

According to statistics, among the 28 states in India, red corridor runs through 22 states, and the CPI (Maoist) has a control over one third of the Indian territories and population as of 2009. The CPI (Maoist) intended to establish revolutionary base areas in Dandakaranya forest, which runs across five states including Orissa, Madhya and Andhra including Dantewada, Bijapur and Sukma districts in Chhattigarh. As early as July 2001, the Maoists of Nepal, India, Bangladesh, Sri Lanka and Bhutan have formed "South Asia Maoist Coordination Committee" which hold regular meetings and coordinate their actions. They support each other and aim to expand the "red corridor" to the whole South Asia.

The 9th National Congress of the CPI held in 2007, has marked the completion of the merger between Maoist Communist Centre of India (MCCI) and the People's War Group, thus the unity of the Party has reached a new height.

The Congress is a continuation of the 8th Congress of the CPI (Marxist-Leninist) after 36 years, and it is a continuation of the CPI (Marxist-Leninist) struggle.

The Congress adopted the five basic documents of the unified Party— Hold High the Bright Red Banner of Marxism-Leninism-Maoism; the Programme of the Party; the Constitution; the Strategy and Tactics of the Indian Revolution and the Political Resolution on the current International and Domestic situation—after thoroughgoing and intense discussions in a free and frank manner. It also focused its attention on a review of the past practice of the two erstwhile Maoist parties since their formation in 1969, the three-year post-Congress review of the erstwhile PW from 2001 to 2004 and also the 2-year practice of the newly formed party. Besides, it passed resolutions on the important political issues of the day—both international and domestic—made the necessary organizational changes and elected a new central committee. The Congress was the culmination of the process that has been going on throughout the Party over the last two years where the documents were discussed in depth and Conferences were held at the area, district, regional and the State level and hundreds of amendments were sent to the Congress from below The Congress also passed a number of political resolutions on numerous current events like: world people's struggles, support to the nationality struggles, against Indian expansionism, on post-Khairlanji Dalit upsurge and against caste oppression, against Hindu fascism, against SEZs and displacement, etc. Resolutions were also passed on the strengthening of the three magic weapons of the Party, People's Army and the United Front. The two-year financial balance sheet of the unified Party was presented to the House. After that the outgoing CC presented its collective self-criticism, pin-pointing the main areas of its weakness and invited the Congress delegates to present their criticisms. After this process a new CC was elected, which then reelected Com Ganapathi as the General Secretary of the Party.

The Party Constitution of the CPI (Maoist) stipulates that the CPI (Maoist) is the vanguard party of the proletariat, guided by Marxism-Leninism and Mao Zedong Thought, and its activities would remain underground during the whole development process of the new democratic revolution. The short-term objective of the Party is to overthrow imperialism, feudalism and comprador bourgeoisie through protracted people's war, complete the new democratic revolution, establish people's democratic dictatorship under the leadership of the proletariat, and strive for the building of socialism.

The final objective is to realize communism and eliminate the exploitation system through "continuous revolution" led by the proletariat. The meeting has reaffirmed the general line of the new democratic revolution with agrarian revolution as its axis and protracted people's war as the path of the Indian revolution that had first come into the agenda with the Naxalbari upsurge.

The short-term mission of the Party is "to advance people's war, transform the people's liberation guerrilla army into people's liberation army, transform the guerrilla warfare into mobile warfare, and transform the guerrilla areas into base area". The 9th Congress of the CPI (Maoist) has been a milestone in the history of Indian communist movement.

The most impressive strength of the CPI (Maoist) is its military power. When we evaluate and compare its military power in history, the fourth generation of CPI(Maoist) has formed a full-prepared army with considerable scale, and its armed struggle has expanded throughout India. The people's war led by the army, is largely supported by the common people, although frequent brutal suppression operations by the Indian government, it does not show signs of losing power. The people's liberation guerrilla army of the CPI (Maoist) was originally established on 21 December 2000, the predecessor of which was "people's guerrilla army" led by the CPI (Marxist-Leninist) (People's War Group). In 2004, after the two parties merged, the armies were also merged into the "People's Liberation Guerrilla Army" The symbol of the army is sickle and hammer with a machine gun transversely lay in between. Nambala, the leader of this army, stated that the establishment of the guerilla army aims to "overthrow the control of imperialism,

Feudalism, and comprador bureaucratic capitalism", namely "realizing socialism through new democratic revolution"; the purpose of the army is "overturning the regime through armed struggle" and "the people's liberation guerrilla army has strongly united with the masses and has become part of their lives and hope".[13]

A senior leader of the Party, Rao once said that they intended to achieve the nationwide victory of the revolution by 2025.[14]

The people's liberation guerrilla army is gaining stronger support from the people, and its fighting members embrace people from all walks of life. The "People's Liberation Guerrilla Army" is formed of three types of forces: Main Force: This is the decisive force, built, trained and modeled more or less on the lines of any professional Army. It comprises military companies, platoons, and special action teams which have the ability to participate in operations anywhere, based on the needs of the movement, on the instructions of the military commissions/commands. It is the best equipped and trained force of the CPI (Maoist). This force will have to be further expanded and equipped if the PLGA is to turn into the PLA.

Secondary Force: It mainly comprises local/special guerrilla squads and district/ division level action teams. Selected personnel from these forces are taken into the main force and, thus, it acts as a feeder for the latter. A squad of 10 to 12 guerrillas may have one or two assault weapons. The remaining personnel are equipped with assorted weapons or even a .303 rifle. The squad leader need not be a local; however, the rest of the squad consists of locals from the area of its operational responsibility.

Base Force: This consists of the People's Militia or 'Jan Militia' equipped with assorted weapons. The self-defense squads, GRDs and ARDs at the RPC level, form part of the base force.

In 2007, a high police officer in the Basta district of Chhattisgarh, has commented: the militia has received professional knowledge in burying and detonating landmines by trained underground guerrilla forces. It is estimated that the number of militia has reached 30.000 in Basta alone, more than five times the size of the local police troops. At present, the

---

13 CPI India (Maoist) Central Military Commission: "Let us intensify People's War with the aim of defeating 'Operation Green Hunt' – War on People! Call of Central Military Commission, CPI (Maoist) on the occasion of PLGA 11th anniversary", People's March, vol. 4, 2011.
14 Indian Maoist Army Will Launch Large-scale Revenge. People.cn (New Delhi). 28 November 2011. http://world.people.com.cn/GB/16418395.html.

Maoist have discarded their olive colored uniform and mingled with the common people, which makes it very hard to identify them. "The Central Intelligence Department only have the names of 300 Maoists, the files do not contain photographs of two thirds of them." While it is impossible to obtain any information about their activities from the villagers.[15]

In recent years, the guerrilla army of the CPI (Maoist) have organized several large-scale battles. On 6 February 2004, they have attacked Koraput, Orissa, and emptied an arsenal, in which 528 weapons were hid. On 13 November 2005, the guerrilla army of the CPI (Maoist) and the underground workers operated a jailbreak in Janabad, Bihar, and released more than 900 prisoners, including numerous Maoist fighters and leaders. On 26 March 2006, in Orissa approximately 200 armed cadres of the CPI-Maoist shot dead three police personnel and took hostage at least two Government officials in attacks on a police station, a camp of the Orissa State Armed Police, the local jail and a bank at Udayagiri in the Gajapati district.

In West-Bengal, on September 21, 2011, two police personnel of the Bomb Disposal squad were killed and 29 others, including some senior police officers and journalists, were injured when a land mine planted by the CPI-Maoist exploded in the Lalgarh area of West Midnapore district.

On 6 April 2010, Central Reserve Police Forces of India (known as the largest paramilitary security force of the world) and the police of Chhattisgarh jointly encircled the Maoists in Dantewada region of Chhattisgarh, but their military operation failed and government forces have lost more than 80 officers and soldiers.[16]

In addition to the military combat in the remote neighboring areas adjacent to guerrilla base areas, the CPI (Maoist) also attaches great importance to the activities in bigger cities. The preparations for the underground work in cities include the following two aspects. Firstly, establish a vast and extensive underground network. Secondly, to establish a secret military organization network, the purpose of which is to preserve strength rather than participate in decisive battles. Through such well-planned goal oriented activities the Party is able to develop its political and military preparation, gather, reinforce and consolidate its power among the masses. Faced with the continuous expansion of the CPI (Maoist), Indian government carried out the "Operation Green Hunt" to suppress the Maoist Party forces, and gave a hard blow to it causing great losses of its troops. At the moment,

---

15 The Times of India report: "Operation Green Hunt: CoBRA Forces Being Flown In", The Times of India, 2009, p. 11.
16 CPI India (Maoist) Central Military Commission: "Let us intensify People's War with the aim of defeating 'Operation Green Hunt' – War on People! Call of Central Military Commission, CPI (Maoist) on the occasion of PLGA 11th anniversary", People's March, Vol. 4, 2011.

deeming the CPI (Maoist) as the biggest threat to domestic security, the Indian government mobilizes all its resources throughout the country in an unprecedented scale and applies the most advanced weapons and special forces to suppress them.

Future prospects of the CPI (Maoist)

The three possible future prospects of the CPI (Maoist) are the following:

Firstly, it may lose its effective strength, declines, consequently it will be forced to carry out its armed struggle in smaller remote districts with scattered forces.

Secondly, it may continue the status quo as a strategic stalemate against the enemy, which means it will greatly preserve its forces and will continue to engage a protracted a seesaw battle.

Thirdly, it may succeed to turns the crisis into opportunities, progresses rapidly, and achieves nationwide victory. Among the three, the second scenario is most likely to happen.

Throughout the history of the communist movement in India, from Telangana Rebellion of the 1950s to Naxalbari Insurrection of the 1970s, then to the Maoist Movement of the mid-1980s, this third wave of armed struggle shows a more strong momentum and grows steadily.

Though international communist movement has been at a low ebb in the 1990s, the CPI (Maoist) continued to expand without any external support from any major power, and has developed its support against the brutal suppression operations from the ruling class. The support by the exploited classes might be the only feasible explanation for such a unique phenomenon. Currently, the CPI (Maoist) has become the Party with the most powerful armed forces in the current international communist movement, and its armed forces poses the biggest threat to the ruling class in India. The final outcome of the struggle between the two sides will directly affect the future of India and even the world communist movement.

Y. 47

Review of the New Program of the Communist Party of Belarus

Kang Yanru[1]

Abstract: The Communist Party of Belarus adopted its new Program on 17th December 2011, at its 10th Congress, while the global financial crisis was continuing and Belarus has faced a serious currency crisis. Although the Communist Party of Belarus has kept its main goals, the Party was compelled to review its past practices and the current events scientifically in the new situation, review its stand and status in the political space of Belarus, and re-define the main ideology, ideas and values with a contemporary view. The new Program expounds on the characteristics of the current world, analyzes the crisis of contemporary capitalism, the inevitability of socialism in Belarus, defines the maximum and the minimum Program of the Communist Party of Belarus, the social basis and class foundation of the Party, political strategies in the current stage, and ideological and organization work of the Party.

Key words: the Communist Party of Belarus; Program; financial crisis

---

1 Kang Yanru, specially invited researcher in the World Socialism Research Center, attached to CASS, doctoral student of the Marxism Research Institute.

The Communist Party of Belarus adopted its new Program on 17th December 2011 at its 10th Congress, while the global financial crisis was continuing and Belarus was faced with a serious currency crisis. Previously, the Program utilized by the Communist Party of Belarus was the one passed at the 7th Congress in 2003. Valentin Reon, Secretary of the Communist Party of Belarus who is in charge of the Party's ideology work, believed that the necessity of the new Program was determined by the situation at home and abroad, especially due to the world financial crisis that erupted in 2008, which has effected the thoughts and attitudes of billions of people.

Although the Communist Party of Belarus has kept its main goals, the Party was compelled to review its past practices and the current events scientifically in the new situation, review its stand and status in the political space of Belarus, and re-define the main ideology, ideas and values with a contemporary view.[2]

The new Program[3] expounds on the characteristics of the current world, analyzes the crisis of contemporary capitalism, the inevitability of socialism in Belarus, defines the maximum and the minimum Program of the Communist Party of Belarus, the social basis and class foundation of the Party, political strategies in the current stage, and ideological and organization work of the Party.

I. Contemporary capitalism has fallen into a systematic crisis

The Communist Party of Belarus believes that the principle difference between capitalism and socialism has not been eliminated after a century, and the capitalism, which occupies a dominant position in the world, has not changed its nature. In capitalist society, the material production and spiritual development are subject to the law of profit pursuit and maintains its greedy nature. Therefore, capitalism seeks maximum profit by all possible means in production, and accumulates capital through full exploitation of the people and abuse of natural and material resources of mankind, and this accumulation fully neglects social or environmental consequences of this accumulation.

The globalization led by the capitalist society aggravates the antagonistic contradiction worldwide. The concentration of industrial capital and financial capital as well as the appearance of transnational corporations and multi-national banks facilitated by globalization accelerate the process of

---

2 Elena Shamina, A Review on the new edition of the PBC Program, It is the time of the Communist of Belarus, Journal of New Times, No. 38 (717) 18. 09. 2010.
3 The program of the Communist Party of Belarus [Adopted by the X (XLII) Congress of the CPB on December 17, 2011], http://www.solidnet.org/belarus-communist-party-of-belarus Direct or indirect references related to the new Program of the Communist Party of Belarus are translated from this article.

economic and political globalization. The oligarchs, who control most of the material resources of the world, determine the policies of the capitalist countries without exception. Under the influence of financial capital, the pursuit of speculative profit reduces the possibility of the industrial capital's increase. Consequently, problems such financial crisis, worsened exploitation and widespread unemployment will occur. Rather than bring the achievements of human civilization to benefit the world and the people, the transnational capitals intend to control the world, and their greed turns them into suppliers of cheap material resources and intellectual resources.

At the same time, through the control of political process, the world's oligarchs create a false appearance and advertise a scene of stable and powerful capitalism in the contemporary world so as to divide and weaken the labor movement, isolate the advanced group in the working class, try to ease the social contradictions in certain countries, and also oligarchs try every means to turn these internal contradictions into international conflicts.

The bourgeois propaganda that contemporary capitalism is humane, civilized, classless and that it provides high-quality life for people is groundless. Currently, economic crises of capitalism cannot be prevented, on the contrary they erupt more frequently. In addition, contemporary capitalism sharpens the issues of ecology, demographic and ethnic-national issues, widens the gap between the rich and the poor worldwide, and intensifies the exploitation of the working class and all laborers, and causes ever-more sharper contradiction between labor and capital. The laborers' struggles to protect their own rights are suppressed by the states, who have increasingly become the defenders of big capital's interests. In recent years, the existing contradictions hav aggravated, and other contradictions caused by the globalization of are more clearly manifested as follows: the contradiction between labor and capital, contradictions among imperialist groups, contradictions among transnational enterprises, contradictions among multinational banks, contradictions between rich countries and poor countries, contradictions between rich and poor in the society, contradictions between south and north and corresponding antagonistic contradictions worldwide, conflicts due to racial and ethnic issues, contradictions between local residents and immigrants with regard to subsistence and employment. The capitalist social structure form has reached its bearing limits. Capitalists openly use scientific and technological progress to produce weapons used to destroy life and destroy mankind.

For the development of the international society, the capitalist production and consumption pattern is a dead end. This has been proved sufficiently by the ongoing crisis in the world, such as new regional wars and world wars, repartition of the world, human-made disasters, cultural retrogress, spiritual degeneration, worldwide financial crisis and economic crisis, etc.

The Communist Party of Belarus believes that contemporary capitalism has fallen into institutional crisis and it is unable to solve the innate problems caused by unlicensed pursuit of financial increase. Thus, it is necessary for us to find a new people-oriented development road, which will generate fundamental changes in productivity, production pattern and consumption pattern, guide the development of science and technology in a direction that benefits all human beings, and protect the global ecological balance. Based on social equity, the socialist development road protects the interest of the laborers and respects their right and freedom. It is the road that will lead us out of the crisis, save the human civilization from the threats of wars, national conflicts, poverty and moral degeneration, eliminate the economic and political basis for terrorism, and get rid of other social problems generated by capitalist regime.

II. Socialist Development Path – The Struggle Goal of the Communist Party of Belarus

The Great October Revolution has epoch-making significance in the human history. The October Revolution paved the way for the path of socialism and national equality for the mankind, and promoted the creativity of the working class, the peasantry and the intellectuals. People of Russian Empire founded the Union of Soviet Socialist Republics, realized large-scale modernization within a short period of time, completed impressive cultural undertakings, brought its development to the forefront of the world in the fields of education, technology, industry and agriculture, and made a breakthrough in space. A new state system and social system with historical significance, namely Soviet Multinational Federal System represented by the working class, came into being. In the world history, the Soviet Union became the first country that guaranteed on a national scale individuals' right of labor, rest, free education, free medical service, residence and social pension insurance.

The basic values of the Soviet Union were collectivism, patriotism, harmonious interaction between, individuals, society and state, pursuit of truth has become the highest ideal, goodness and righteousness, and equality of citizens regardless of their ethnic-national origins, regions or other differences. These values and qualities were an important prerequisite for the masses to welcome the socialist ideals.

The Communist Party of Belarus believes that the collapse of the Soviet Union was caused by the two major factors. On the one hand, it failed to overcome the development gap between itself and that of the developed countries. On the other hand, its overlook of class struggle offered an opportunity for the political degenerates to restore capitalism. The Soviet

Union carried out its socialist construction against the background of arduous class struggle and constant imperialism aggression. Therefore, large amount of resources were devoted to the field of national defense to the neglect of people's welfare. That was why consumption level of the Soviet Union, though increased, still lagged behind that of the developed capitalist countries.

The Cold War, did not allow the Soviet Union leadership to make necessary reforms in the political system. During the socialist construction the Soviet leadership failed to attach sufficient importance to the lessons of class struggle, which has caused fatal consequences. Just for this reason, the perfection of the political and social economic systems has been slow. And the major principles of Leninism, namely the important principles inner-party life, the democratic centralism and collective leadership were weakened. Consequently, careerists and believers of capitalist ideology have penetrated into the Party and led to the degeneration of some leading cadres. The Soviet Union failed to take necessary actions to counter the subversive activities of the imperialist countries and their agents. Pseudo reformers, political degenerates and capitulationists got into the executive level of the Soviet Union. The hope of the Soviet people to live in a united state was trampled upon in the referendum held on 17th March, 1991. The socialist construction was suspended due to setbacks. The Communist Party of Belarus believes that the nationality of the Belarus suffered a heavy blow from the collapse of the Soviet Union, but the preserve of the economic policy and Soviet moral values saved Belarus from complete social breakdown and crisis.

As a part of the Communist Party of the Soviet Union, the Communist Party of Belarus inherits and carries forward the ideological and organizational line of the CPSU, and strongly defends the interests of the laborers under the existing political system and national development pattern, gives due consideration to the current contemporary social and economic development trends.. Guided by the scientific methodology of Marxism-Leninism, the Communist Party of Belarus upholds socialist values and ideals, the national interests, and the cultural and historical traditions of Belarus. The main goals of the party are: people's power, social justice, social equality and socialism. The Party supports all forms of solutions which will help the realization of the interest of the working people, given the diversity of solutions in the current era. While it fights for a socialist transformation, it also advocates and fights for feasible reform measures within the framework of the current system and laws, the party rejects violent social actions that undermine the domestic peace damages state peace, thus rejects the trends of bourgeoisie and the petty bourgeoisie extremism.

III. The maximum and the minimum program of the Party

The maximum Program of the Communist Party of Belarus is to build socialism. It believes that socialism can eliminate exploitation and can achieve a distribution of wealth based on quantity of labor given to society, and also considers the quality and results of labor. Based on scientific planning and management, socialist society can achieve higher labor productivity and economic productivity with the application of innovative and energy-saving industrial technologies. The socialist society is a society that will realize democratic politics and advanced spiritual culture in their true sense, and will promote the development of individuals and the autonomy of the laborers.

The class basis of the Communist Party of Belarus is the large working class. The Communist Party of Belarus aims at protecting the interest of the laborers who receive fair return on the basis of their labor contribution. The Party protects all laborers—laborers from state-owned business and private sector of economy, laborer employed by individual enterprise, laborers who receive low-level social welfare, including the retirees and the disabled, salary earners, manual workers and brain workers.

The Communist Party of Belarus has existing and potential alliances to realize its goal, including Socialist Party and Progressive Patriotic Party, which are composed by labor organization, peasant organization, women's organization, veterans organization, youth organization, creation organization and educational organization. On the basis of unified strategic objectives, the Communist Party of Belarus, together with other parties and organizations, commit themselves to protecting the national interest of Belarus and opposing the counterrevolutionary restoration of the capitalist.

The Communist Party of Belarus, after analyzing the major trend of reality and world development, the balance of political power home and abroad, and the interests of different classes of Belarus as well as their relationship, comes to the conclusion that the construction of socialist is an inevitable process in Belarus. To realize the proposed objective and ideal, the Communist Party of Belarus will apply the Constitution to control state power through legal political struggle.

The minimum Program proposed by the Communist Party of Belarus includes the following demands:

Fight for the consolidation of the Republic of Belarus, without neglecting the goal of strengthening the people's political power, fight for the consolidation of the current political system in the main, to ensure the stability of national economy, politics and national security, and defend to the basic laws and civil liberties of people. Fight to overcome bureaucratism, red tape, autocracy, protectionism and corruption thus improve the efficiency of state's management system by the optimization of its operational systems and mechanisms.

Strive for the goal that laborers are represented at all levels of power organs, and also at all levels of self-government bodies, in a qualified manner, strive for defending the collective rights of the working class,

Promote the conditions to strengthen local autonomy and local self-government, and help citizens to realize their demands.

Prevent that, proponents of state capitalism and capitalism enter and dominate the state organs, prevent the country from turning capitalist, propagate the advantages of socialist development path to the public, and explain the people the anti-historical nature as well as the evil results of capitalist restoration.

Advocate and promote the development, re-integration process within the former Soviet Union territories. Advocate the creation of a win-win relationship between Belarus and Russia within the framework of cooperative alliance.

Maintain and develop social-orientation of the national economy, so that it can guarantee a high-level of welfare for citizens and ensure social security of the lower classes and strata. Advocate and promote the state plays its regulatory function regarding the economic fields such as industry, agriculture and credit financing, advocate that the key economic fields which affect the national security is controlled by the state.

Fight against the plunder of the state and collective property. Prevent that the individual merchants and non-public sector of the economy, use state or collective property for profit-seeking activities. Advocate that the state maintains and consolidates, state ownership of land, natural resources, ecological system, transportation communication, cultural and historic heritage of the country.

Advocate resuming a more socially responsible and progressive tax system, advocate that the private sector of economy undertakes more social responsibilities, including the private enterprises that implement labor ownership and protect citizens' self-employment; continue to provide free secondary and higher education, guarantee the high quality of education through the positive experiences accumulated during the Soviet Union period.

Guarantee high-quality free medical service; maintain and develop Belarus's potential in science and technology, enlarge the scale of scientific and technological talents, improve the quality of the talents, increase financial and material support for scientific research, develop knowledge-intensive production, innovation and energy-saving technology; ensure the popularity of its culture, develop national-spirit-based Belarus culture, restrict the influence of pop culture on society and the commercialization of culture, create a good environment for citizens' mental and moral health; maintain the secularity of the state, protect people's spiritual freedom and their beliefs of atheism, respect the traditional religion which affects spiritual morality in a positive way; social divergence, contradiction, and protest within the framework of law are allowed.

Fight crime in all spheres of society, defend people's individual security, social security and freedom, ensure freedoms provided by the Constitution; defend and maintain the national independence and integrity of Belarus, thus enhance its international status and national defense capabilities, and improve its reputation across the world.

IV. The Organizational and Ideological Construction of the Communist Party of Belarus

Founded in December 1918, the Communist Party of Belarus went through the common pain of temporary failure in the process of socialist construction together with the Communist Party of the Soviet Union. The Communist Party of Belarus was one of the first parties, which could restore its organizational structures and actively fought against the anti-communist frenzy supported by the capitalists in the post-Soviet region. The Communist Party of Belarus can be evaluated as a true Party of the working class, which is able to answer all the urgent questions with regard to social development, because it has accumulated experiences and lessons of its own history and also experiences and lessons of the history of the international communist movement.

The Communist Party of Belarus carries out its activities, basing itself on the theories and practices of Marxism-Leninism, inherits and develops its experiences accumulated during socialist construction. The major purpose of its activities is to serve the people and the nation.

As an independent political organization, the Communist Party of Belarus recognizes the independence of all the other communist parties. Agreed on comradeship, mutual-aid and collective spirit, the Communist Party of Belarus and other communist parties develop their relationship with unified class interests and political & social objectives. The Communist Party of Belarus supports the unification of moral ideal and political basis accomplished by the communists of the international communist movement and the labor movement in the past centuries. As a formal member of the Communist Party of the Soviet Union, the consolidation of the Communist

Party of Belarus is important for the voluntary re-establishment of the alliances among the former Soviet states and the establishment of a united communist party. The Communist Party of Belarus develops cooperative relations with communist parties, anti-imperialist social movements and the world trade-union movement.

In order to enhance its political influence on social progress, the Communist Party of Belarus intends to work in the following fields: guarantee that the Party's representatives and members participate in important social political activities and organizations, which are of great importance for the interests of Belarusian people.

• participation in election campaigns and increasing their presence in the bodies of legislative and representative government at all levels, local self-government, as well as in the activities of executive authorities;

• combining various forms struggles and coordinating of the activities of leading party groups in representative bodies, maximizing their influence to protect the interests of working people;

• exposing the anti-people nature of bourgeois parties and movements, as well as bourgeois and nationalist ideology as the main ideological targets ;

• improving the forms of political work in labor collectives, in trade union, workers', peasants' and patriotic movements, in creative, women's, youth, veterans', environmental, charitable and other public associations;

• promoting interaction with trade unions in the economic and political spheres, intensification of workers' struggle for their rights and legitimate interests;

• holding political actions in support of the just demands of labor collectives, employees and the unemployed;

• defending civil rights and freedoms in Belarus, protecting the rights and dignity of compatriots abroad;

• scientific protection of national history and culture, moral support for the honor of a citizen, promote patriotism and internationalism thoughts among people.

According to the Communist Party of Belarus, top priorities that need to be solved with regard to inner-Party life include the following:

• Ideological and organizational strengthening of the party, primarily its foundations–primary organizations;

• Ensuring the ideological unity of party ranks and adherence to the principle of democratic-centralism in accordance with the Program of the PBC;

• renewal and consistent rejuvenation of the party's leadership, wide involvement of active representatives of youth and women in party ranks;

• democratization of the inner-party life, excluding the phenomena of bureaucracy and worship of leaders, systematic and regular updating of all elective bodies and leading cadres;

• The CPB in its fight against open and hidden opponents of socialism opposes manifestations of unacceptable tolerance, unjustified compromises and cooperation, a falsely understood party discipline to persons who do not fulfill the Party's organizational Charter and Program;

• systematic political enlightenment of the Communists, introduction of advanced socialist consciousness into the Belarusian society, promote scientific understanding of the Belarusian and world realities, promote the development of basic and applied sciences, including social sciences.

Analyzing the current situation of Belarus, the Communist Party of Belarus points out that Belarus has completed the transition to market economy in the first decade of the 21st century, established a relatively solid foundation for the legal supervision regarding economic stability, economic and social development, established a multi-sector economic structure including the non-public sector, and established a competitive market infrastructure for commodities, services, capital, labor force. Based on the strategic tasks for stable economic development, Belarus has successfully contained the speed of population decline. Poverty level has reduced to one third of the original level, the structure of production and consumption has been improved, and measures for educational development, health care, housing construction, environmental protection and reasonable utilization of natural resources have been implemented. However, the worldwide financial crisis broke out in 2008 impeded the completion of the social development target in Belarus.

The export-oriented small companies of in Belarus are vulnerable to fluctuations in the world economy, and suffers great problems from the decrease of demand by European and Russian markets. On 24th May 2011, the Government of Belarus announced that the exchange rate of the Belarus ruble against US dollar was dropped from 3155:1 to 4930:1. The sudden devaluation of currency triggered panic among the people, and people rushed to purchase products from chain stores and exchange currency in the banks. This devaluation has given a serious blow to the national economy.

To alleviate the crisis, the government of Belarus on the one hand continues to reform in the social field and increases pension with the aggravation of inflation, and on the other hand carries out the privatization policy in a considerable scale and sells part of the national asset which relates to national economic security, such as Belarus Gas Transportation Company, Belarus Iron and Steel Plant and Minsk Automobile Factory. People are worrisome whether this policies will cause Belarus, lose its economic independence, thus gradually lose its political independence, and whether Belarus will be able to continue its development miracle.[4]

In its new party congress The Communist Party of Belarus decided to continue supporting the social-oriented economic policy adopted by President Lukashenko, on the one hand, and emphasizes the harmonious interaction among the three: individuals, society and the state, highlighting the leadership of the state, on the other hand. The party emphasizes the importance of defending the basic economic and political system, and calls on the people to carry forward the spirit of collectivism and patriotism in times of crisis. However, the Communist Party of Belarus failed to propose concrete measures for solving the crisis in the Program or in the other Resolutions agreed in the 10th Party Congress, besides it did not provide detailed suggestions for improving the current economic structure. In order to make its propositions and values attractive and be accepted by more people, gain more votes, increase its influence in the future domestic political process, the Party should expand its social base and work out a realistic strategies and positions for transition to socialism.

---

[4] According to World Bank, the high rate of economic growth in Belarus – an average of about 8% annually from 2001 to 2011 – has helped it to reduce poverty almost seven-fold.

Y. 48

New Exploration of the Socialist Development Path of the South African Communist Party in the New Period

Nie Yunlin[1] & Cheng Guangde[2]

Abstract: The South African Communist Party (SACP) is an important force in the world socialist movement. After 90 years of its hard exploration on the socialist development road, it has formed a unique theory. The SACP believes that the future socialist society of the South African will have four basic characteristics: firstly, it should realize democracy, equality and freedom; secondly, it should practice the socialization of main economic sectors; thirdly, it should adhere to the organic combination of "efficient planning" and "beneficial market"; fourthly, it should persist in sustainable development. In addition, the SACP has also developed its own theory and strategy on the transition to socialism adapted to local characteristics. As for the development stages of social revolution, the SACP has developed a theory which combines democratic revolution with socialist revolution. As for the basic strategy for the transition to socialism, the SACP chose a strategy of revolutionary amelioration. As for the basic program for the transition to socialism, the SACP formulated a basic program known as the "four pillars" (political work, economic work, ideological work and grass-roots work). The SACP believes that strengthening the Party building is the fundamental guarantee for the transition to socialism, and it includes four aspects: innovating the targets, policies and contents of Party's activities; the strengthening of the ideological and theoretical construction; the strengthening of the building of Party organizations; and the improvement of the Party's administrative ability.

Key words: the South African Communist Party (SACP); socialism; development path

---
1 Nie Yunlin, Professor of the Research Institute of Politics, Central China Normal University.
2 Cheng Guangde, doctor of Wuhan University of Technology

With 130 thousand Party members, the South African Communist Party (SACP) is an important power in the world socialist movement and the most powerful, most influential party among the communist parties of Africa. The SACP was founded in 1921. Its 90 years of arduous struggle could be divided into three stages – from 1921 to 1952 was the period of "struggle and forced dissolution of the Party" the initial period"; from 1953 to 1994 was the period of "reconstruction of the Party and characterized by the anti-racist struggle"; from 1995 on was the period of "struggle for democracy and socialism".

The establishment of the democratic regime of South Africa in 1994 marked the end of the apartheid which has lasted for more than 300 years, and ushered in a new era in the South Africa. On its 9th Congress (1995), the SACP formulated the political line "Socialism is the future, build it now!" And through the modification and supplement of political line on the 10th Congress (1998), the 11th Congress (2002) and the 12th Congress (2007), the SACP worked out a more systematic theory and strategy to lead the South African people's struggle for democracy and socialism. The SACP's membership has gone through cycles over the years reflecting important political developments (1928 – 1.750 members; 1991 – 10.000; 1995 – 75.000; 2002 – 19.385; 2007 – 50.000; 2012 – 150.000; 2015 – 213.551).

I. The Four Basic Characteristics of the Future Socialism

Democracy, equality, freedom

Influenced by Marxism-Leninism and the political thoughts of the West due to its historical contacts with the Netherlands and the United Kingdom, besides drawing lessons from the drastic changes in the Soviet Union and Eastern Europe, the SACP intends to ensure "democracy, equality and freedom" in the construction of the socialist society in the South Africa.

The SACP believes that the socialist society should guarantee democracy in all aspects of social life. Socialism of the South Africa does not deny the main content of political democracy such as one man one vote, regular multi-party elections, constitutional government and judicial independence, etc. Socialist democracy should not deny such democratic forms but should seek to achieve more extensive democracy in all aspects of social life through indirect, direct or participatory democracy.

The SACP believes that equality is the intrinsic requirement of socialism. The SACP commits itself to eliminating the gaps existing in the capitalist society in terms of income, wealth, rights and opportunities. Unlike what is propagated by the capitalists, the equality advocated by the SACP is not mechanical or compulsory consistency among people, because under the socialist system, everyone should enjoy relative independence, since socialist citizens have different skills, attitudes, hobbies, culture and different status due to division of labor, and the SACP has no intention of eliminating such differences but will seek to achieve basic equality in terms of income, wealth, rights and opportunities.

The SACP believes that advanced democracy and equality should be based on freedom. Advocators of capitalism emphasize "free choice" and advertise "individualism", but the control by minority of capitalists over the majority of people deprives the majority from their rights and opportunities and from free choice. Socialism will increase, rather than reduce, the right of choice for individuals and groups of citizens. Socialism aims to eliminate poverty and hunger, fight against humiliation and ignorance, eliminating the fear of unemployment, class, sexual, racial discrimination or ethnic-national oppression.

Socialization of the major economic sectors

According to the SACP, "socialization of the major economic sectors" is another basic characteristic of the future socialist society. The SACP emphasizes that the socialization of the major economic sectors is the fundamental requirement for realizing "new representative democracy", substantive equality and extensive freedom, and at the same time, this is one of the major differences between the SACP and the Social Democratic Party. The SACP's ideas and propositions with regard to the socialization of the major economic sectors are as follows.

First of all, different from the concept of "nationalization plus state planning"[3], socialization of economy is an extensive concept with rich connotation. Nationalization is an important approach to establish state owned sector of economy by nationalizing the means of production previously owned by private enterprises. Socialist nationalization is the important foundation for the proletariat to control the lifelines of national economy, consolidate the established political power and carry out socialist construction. The state owned sector of economy is the objective requirement for the development of socialization in production. In a sense, nationalization (state-ownership) is the foundation of socialization and it will develop into socialization after it has developed to certain level. Thus, we could say that nationalization (state ownership) is the initial form of socialization (common ownership by the whole society). Nationalization phase is the low-level phase of socialization and socialization phase is the high-level phase of nationalization. That is to say, although state (nation) represents the members of the society, state is in essence a tool of class rule. It is the

---

[3] Programme of the South African Communist Party, SACP adopted by the 9th Congress, April. 1995, http://www.sacp.org.za.

interest of the ruling class rather than the interest of the whole society that a state represents.

Secondly, in essence, socialization of economy "grants economic power to the working class"[4]. Instead of simply emphasizing the legal form of ownership, socialization of economy shifts its emphasis to the control capability and control right of the laboring people over the property of means of production. It manifests itself as two aspects: firstly, improving the workers' ability to influence the workplace; second, enhance the workers' control over the social power generated by the ownership of means of production, which includes the enhancement of the workers' decision-making power on the investment policies of the state, on the level of social profit and choosing the project which should be prioritized.

Adhere to the organic combination of "efficient planning" and "beneficial market"

This theory of the SACP was proposed under the influence of three factors – firstly, the lessons of the Soviet Union and Eastern Europe's failures in socialist construction; secondly, the successful experience of combining "planning" and "market" seen in socialist construction of China and some other socialist countries; thirdly, it evaluates the experiences of the market economy adopted in the Western countries. The contents of this theory can be divided into the following three aspects:

Firstly, socialist society should implement an efficient planning. The SACP believes that the planned economy adopted by certain socialist countries through administrative orders have proved inefficient or unable to meet the demands of a contemporary economy which increasingly becomes complex. The economic planning in a socialist democracy should be different from the all-inclusive administrative orders. Socialist economy needs planning, but it should be efficient planning, because without effective planning and coordination by the government, even a contemporary capitalist economy cannot operate normally. In a socialist society, if the socialized sectors of the economy holds the dominant position, a more efficient and rational planning can be possible. The government of a socialist country should set targets for the development of the key economic sectors such as infrastructure and public services, and make a plan for other departments like training and education. As a democratic process, socialist planning process includes negotiation, regular evaluation of the results and post-plan adjustments. Secondly, socialist economy requires a "beneficial market". In a socialist economy, market will still play an important role in distribution and planning, but market will not have the final decision-making power.

---

4 Programme of South African Communist Party, SACP adopted by the 9th Congress, April. 1995, http://www.sacp.org.za.

The key fields of society, including health, education, housing, postal service, communication, urban transportation, water and electricity, should be de-commodification. Health-care, education, housing, the environment, culture and information should not primarily be commodities.

It does not mean that the products offered (supply) by these sectors should be free of charge, rather it indicates is that their prices and distribution among the population should not be decided by the market. The de-commodification of the above key fields of the society does not reject the existence of the market, but gives it only limited functional scope. SACP says:

For those fields that should be regulated by the market rules, SACP says: insofar as markets continue to be an important regulator of distribution, we must also engage with them. Markets are not some "neutral" reality, and there is no such thing as a "free market." The current markets reflect the accumulated power of capital. We need to intervene with collective social power on the market to challenge and transform the power relations at play within it.

Thirdly, efficient planning and beneficial market should be combined. Socialist economy requires both planning and market. Without market, efficient planning will lose its vitality; conversely, without planning, the flaws of market will inevitably impede the healthy and sustainable development of socialist economy. Closely related and mutually dependent, planning and market should work together to promote the advance of socialist economy.

Adhere to sustainable development

Based on ecological views of Marxism, the SACP emphasizes that socialist society should adhere to sustainable development mode. In the early 1920s, when the SACP started to visualize the construction of socialist society for the first time, they thought that like capitalist society, the construction of socialist society should be based on unlimited exploitation of natural resources and production. And in 1980s, when the SACP spoke of the experiences of the "established socialist society" in the Soviet Union and others, they favored the idea of "hasty catch up" in economy and supported the idea of accelerated process of modernization. After deeper exploration, the SACP finally came to realize that the concept of sustainable development is the only proper mode of socialist construction in the early 21st century.[5]

In socialist construction, both immediate interests and long-term interests, current interests of citizens and interests of future generations, economic and social interests, also interests of socio-economy and interests of

---

[5] South African Communist Party Constitution, SACP adopted by the 12th Congress, July. 2007, http://www.sacp.org.za.

environment and ecology should be taken into consideration. The SACP points out that future socialist society will realize sustainable life, sustainable family, sustainable society and benign and sustainable utilization of natural resources.

II. Theories and Strategies of Transition to Socialism

The SACP believes that the South Africa is a dependent and developing capitalist country. The major social contractions of the South Africa include the contradiction between the South African people and the imperialism, and the contradiction between monopoly capital of the minority white, squire and the majority of African people. After a scientific analysis of the South Africa's societal nature and social contradictions, the SACP has expounded on the development stage of the South African social revolution, puts forward the joint struggle theory of the two parties (SACP and ANC), consequently proposed its basic programme and basic strategies.

Development stage of the South African social revolution: combining of the two revolutions

The SACP believes that at the current stage, the ongoing revolution in the South Africa is national-democratic revolution in nature. The South Africa is in the process of transiting to socialism, and the major task at present stage is "defense, promote and deepen the achievements of the "1994 democratic breakthrough". For SACP the current government of South Africa is the new democratic government. The new democratic government has to play a leading role in ensuring effective coordination and coherence in the RDP. Without this the RDP (Re-construction and Development Program–the new government's main policy frame) work will not succeed. This implies an effective public sector, especially in areas that are critical to the major focus of the RDP: urban and rural infrastructural development.

Conforming to the immediate interests as well as the long-term interests of the working class and other social classes, this current task is the most direct demand of South Africa's transition to socialism. Now, the South Africa's national-democratic revolution is closely related to and it is inseparable with its struggle for socialism. Guided by the political line "the future belongs to socialism and build it now." the SACP defines its thought pn the development stage of revolution as stage "the combination of (national) democratic revolution with socialist revolution".[6]

The SACP's understanding of the relationship between national-democratic revolution and socialist revolution has seen a gradual development. On the 8th Congress of the Party held in 1991, the SACP had advocated

---

6 SACP Political Program adopted by the 10th Congress, July. 1998, http://www.sacp.org.za.

the theory of two-stage revolution, because the SACP thought that the target and the tasks of the (national) democratic revolution were completely different from those of the socialist revolution. On the 9th Congress of the Party held in 1995, the SACP put forward a new political line that "the future belongs to socialism and build it now", but this line could not receive unanimous approval in the Party. On the 10th Congress of the Party held in 1998, the traditional theory of "two-stage revolution" was still quite popular. Finally, on the 11th Congress of the Party held in 2002, the Party reached a consensus after debates and concluded: "at the present stage, we should on the one hand recognize that the socialist construction will go through the two stages, namely the (national) democratic revolution and the socialist revolution, and on the other hand, the two revolutions are closely related and interdependent. This is formulated as the theory of "the combination of the (national) democratic revolution and the socialist revolution". It was on this Congress that the SACP gave up the "two stage theory" put forward in the early 1990s. In 2007, this new theory "the future belongs to socialism and build it now", was further perfected during the 12th Congress of the Party.[7]

The SACP believes that the (national) democratic revolution is not a part of the capitalist revolution, instead, it is an essential stage for the South Africa's transition to socialism.[8] It is neither a roundabout path nor a delaying of the historical course, but the most direct route towards socialism. In addition, the socialist revolution of the South Africa is not a new stage after the (national) democratic revolution, but a new stage and higher of the (national) democratic revolution. This new stage provides advantageous situation, impetus, capacity and even nurtures and provides socialist factors for the transition to socialism, because defending, promoting and deepening of democratic achievements is the material prerequisite for the socialist revolution. The democratic revolution trains a powerful team of the working class and conducts large-scale education and propaganda among the working class and among the vast majority of working masses. At the same time, the value, analytical methods and organizational system of the socialist society are equally important for the success of the struggle at present and equally important for the future. Therefore, at present, the South Africa must adhere to the socialist concepts, values and sense of organization, and keep a positive attitude towards socialism. All in all, the (national) democratic revolution and the socialist revolution are not contradictory but complementary.[9]

---

7   Ibid.
8   Ibid.
9   Ibid.

Basic strategy of the South Africa's transition to socialism: revolutionary amelioration

Based on the situation home and abroad after the establishment of the South Africa's new government in 1994, the SACP made "revolutionary amelioration" (revolutionary advance, improvements and progress) the basic strategy of the South Africa's transition to socialism.

The SACP points out that Marx and Engels considered "non-peaceful means" and "peaceful means" as two different struggle forms of the working class and its party to achieve the victory of socialist revolution. As for which means should be the dominant struggle form, will be decided by the revolutionary situation and the balance of class forces.

The SACP believes that the form of transition from capitalism to socialism will depend on the characteristics of the times, international situation and national conditions, and the form of transition will be decided by the major force of the transition, namely the working class. As early as 1991, the SACP has proposed the idea of "revolutionary amelioration" in the 8th Congress, indicating that the SACP would carry out the socialist transition of the South Africa in a peaceful way. On the 10th Congress held in 1998, the SACP has pointed out that "the SACP will not conduct socialist attacks against the capitalists of the country"[10].

The SACP stresses that both the struggle for national liberation and the struggle for socialism are carried out when the country, the region and the world are controlled by capitalism, therefore, in order to achieve their objective, they should not simply adopt either amelioration (peaceful means) or revolution (non-peaceful means), but should combine them together and adopt "revolutionary amelioration". Rather than making some cosmetic changes, this kind of amelioration should touch the core of the capitalist power, and gradually change the balance of class forces to a full-fledged level. To win achievements in the strategy of "revolutionary amelioration", the SACP should consolidate and enlarge the united front and unite all the possible positive forces. With regard to the Inkatha Freedom Party[11], the

---

10 Ibid..
11 Inkatha Freedom Party (IFP), cultural movement and political party in South Africa that derives its main support from the Zulu people. Inkatha was founded in 1975 in the black homeland of KwaZulu by Mangosuthu Gatsha Buthelezi, chief of the Zulu people and the chief minister of the homeland. Its purpose was to work against apartheid (the official South African policy of racial segregation) and to encourage the political and cultural aspirations of South African blacks. Under Buthelezi's leadership, Inkatha advocated an evolutionary struggle against apartheid and declared its willingness to accept special power-sharing arrangements that would fall short of majority rule in a post-apartheid South Africa. In early 1994, IFP announced that the IFP would boycott the country's first free elections. The IFP over more than two decades has also liked to present its economic policies as „liberal", as „pro-free market". However, what essentially holds the IFP together is the dominant

SACP proposes to take a friendly stance and cooperate with them so as to win their support premised on prioritising the needs of the African rural and urban poor.

Basic program of the South Africa's transition to socialism: "four pillars"

Based on the political line "the future belongs to socialism and build it now", the SACP formulated the basic program for the South Africa's socialist transition – the "four pillars". This is the medium-term target of the SACP in the process of establishing the leadership of the working class, and it is the guide of action for the realization of socialism.

The "program of the political work" of the socialist transition is formulated as follows: "the strategic Medium Term Vision (MTV) of the South African Communist Party is to secure working class hegemony in the State in its diversity and in all other sites of power."[12] The SACP believes that the political performance of the current South African government (it is a coalition of three partners including SACP) is not satisfactory, therefore SACP emphasized: "we are working to establish a strong, activist, national democratic developmental state buttressed by our mass base.[13]

Only if supported by the working class mass basis and mass activism can ensure that the developmental state play its role." "A progressive and democratic developmental state has a duty to address the socio-economic dualities in our country,building strong SACP branches and districts is central to organize the primary motive force of the National Democratic Revolution, building a strong and dynamic Alliance will go a long way in transforming the harsh reality of CST (Colonialism of Special Type)."[14]

Regarding the status, function and future action guide the SACP states: "first of all we should understand that the SACP has played the role of "managerial party"[15] rather than ruling party since the "1994 democratic breakthrough."

Secondly, the SACP thinks the post-1994 state requires significant transformation and defines the task of the party as follows: This includes amongst other things:

---

personality of its long-standing leader, its institutional apparatus rooted in traditional and patriarchal domination of the KZN rural hinterland, and Zulu ethnic allegiances, especially amongst the rural poor, and amongst marginalized urban dwellers. The IFP is the only other political party (outside of the ANC-alliance) with a substantial mass-base among the African urban and especially rural poor.

12 Ibid.
13 Ibid.
14 Ibid.
15 Ibid.

a) Redressing the damaging impact of privatisation and restructuring policies that have weakened the capacity of the state and exposed key strategic areas to the dominance of private capital;

b) Addressing the lack of a clear cadre development policy in the state;

c) Building the strategic capacity of the state to drive developmental programmes;

d) Rebuilding critical sectors of the public service, including health care and education, that are still reeling from the effects of years of down-sizing and other restructuring measures;

e) Transforming the key area of local government, often the weakest sphere of governance.

Thirdly, the SACP puts forward three guiding principles for the electoral politics: firstly, electoral politics are an important but not an exclusive terrain for the contesting of state power.

Working class power in the state is related to working class power in all other sites, including the imperative of developing organs of popular power, active forms of participatory democracy and social mobilisation.

Secondly, throughout the struggle, the SACP's election strategy should be guided by the overall strategy; three, strategic Medium Term Vision of the South African Communist Party is to secure working class hegemony in the State in its diversity and in all other sites of power.

In the "program of the economic work", the SACP points out that to get rid of financial crisis, the South Africa should change the structure of the economy which retains the basic features of an export-oriented and import-dependent economy, with an under-developed domestic market–and "establish the economic leadership of the working class". For this aim, the following policies should be followed:

1. A national democratic, state-led industrial policy promoting a labour-intensive manufacturing sector is the basis to transform, diversify and build a vibrant economy. This industrial policy should link actively with and support our major infrastructure development, skills development, and equitable spatial development.

2. To campaign for and ensure the re-nationalization of companies in strategic sectors such SASOL and Mittal Steel with an ultimate aim of nationalizing and socializing the commanding heights of the economy in line with the vision of the Freedom Charter.

3. To call for improved beneficiation of minerals and measures to regulate and stimulate the fabrication of raw materials into finished and semi-finished products.

4. To call for increased investment in infrastructure and the ramping up of the public works programmes as a basis to provide economic and social infrastructure and employment.

5. Integration with the region should be on the basis of a strong industrial policy to provide basic goods in South Africa and the region.

6. Trade and macroeconomic policy should be subordinated to the logic of an industrialisation strategy to meet basic human needs.

7. Procurement policies should be reviewed to support local production and support broad based empowerment, employment, and small business development.

8. Any agricultural and industrial process in the production of bio-fuels should be legislatively regulated to guarantee food security and avoid possible food price hikes. Agricultural and Rural Development".[16]

In the "program of the ideological work" of the socialist transition, the SACP has pointed out: "with the democratic breakthrough in 1994, various social ideological trends have flourished. Under the influence of these diversified ideologies, communism, social democracy, active national liberation movement of the third world, and the neo-liberalism compete with each other and counter balance each other". Faced with the complex situations and serious challenges, the SACP believes that the neo-liberalism is the most important ideological trend posed against SACP's defending, promoting and deepening of the national democratic revolution. Therefore, major strategic target in the ideological field should be neo-liberalism.

The "program of the grass-roots work" of the socialist transition includes the rural part and the urban part. In terms of the "work places" in the cities, the SACP's target is: SACP Medium Term Vision identifies the workplace as one terrain within which working class hegemony must be built.

SACP also acknowledges the serious strides and victories brought about by the 1994 political breakthrough with regard to the transformation and democratisation of the workplace.[17]

Therefore, the following requirements should be fulfilled by the struggle of the "work place". First, all industrial strategies should center on the developmental manpower resource strategy, protect the least-advantaged workers, guarantee their economic interests and political rights, and train their professional skills. Second, support the development of the trade union movement, and promote the development of the informal labor organizations through the trade union movement. Third, supported by working class's struggle for leadership, the SACP aims to promote the development and transformation of the public and private workplace.

16　Ibid.
17　Ibid.

Fourth, SACP aims to intensify the campaign for the establishment of workplace SACP units in all industries. Furthermore, these workplace units must be continuously serviced and monitored for sustainability,

Every Province should have training sessions for both shop stewards and workers on Marxism-Leninism. This programme should be linked to the SACP Medium Term Vision, with specified targets, so that the working class could play their pioneer role and facilitate the transformation of the working places.

As for the communities of the countryside, the SACP puts forward the following basic requirements: "firstly, we should interfere in the land market, this requirement is essential because the land market itself is unable to complete the redistribution of land, that is to say, the land market will not automatically transfer the land from the low-efficient owners to high-efficient users. We should campaign for the expropriation and redistribution of land within the context of a reformulated agricultural development policy. In that context the "willing seller-willing buyer' principle should be effectively abolished to allow for a more effective and rapid land reform program.

And the state shall help the peasants with implements, seed, tractors and dams to save the soil and assist the tillers as part of a sustained agrarian reform.

We should call for the restructuring of the Land Bank to redirect its funding to small-scale farmers and cooperatives.

Secondly, launch a rural society movement including rural women, farmers that have lost their land and workers, and encourage the poor people to participate in the movement. Three, develop rural education and carry out a campaign to eliminate illiteracy.

III. Struggle Practices for Democracy and Socialism

After the victory of the "1994 democratic breakthrough", the SACP has carried out active and effective struggles in the fields of politics, economy, society and foreign relations – the SACP takes the advantage of its role as a coalition partner in the government and follows a policy of unity-struggle-unity towards its bigger partner ANC (party) led by Mandela; it opposes the remnants of the racist discrimination by whites, and strives for democracy and peace; it promotes the development of "socialist-oriented economic forms"; it actively copes with the burdens financial crisis upon the workers and people; it leads the "Red October Movement" to enhance the influence of the working class; it supports the Plan of New Partnership for Africa's Development promotes the foreign policy of promoting an African agenda and South-South cooperation and devotes its efforts to the revitalization of the Africa; it criticizes the imperialism-dominated globalization and endeavors to realize a "win-win common globalization".

When leading the struggle of the masses, the SACP attaches great importance to the Party building, believing that strengthening the Party building is the fundamental guarantee for the transition to socialism and will determine the destiny of the socialist revolution in the South Africa.

1. The innovation of the targets, policy and content of Party's activities

When it was established in 1921, the SACP has announced unequivocally that it is the vanguard of the working class. After it won its legal status in 1990, the SACP clearly stated that the Party should build itself into a "vanguard party of a mass character" to adjust itself to the new situations.

2. The strengthening of ideological and theoretical construction

Due to negative impacts of the collapse of the Soviet Union and the drastic changes in the Eastern Europe, the SACP has put great efforts to strengthen its ideological and political work and arranges orderly discussions within the Party to unite the Party ideologically and tries hard to increase the theoretical level of the party and strengthen the correct views among the members. Besides, the SACP constantly innovates the Party's theory so as to provide a correct theoretical and strategic leadership to the South African people's struggle for democracy and socialism.

3. The strengthening of the combat capacity of the Party organizations

The SACP adheres to the principle of democratic centralism in its organizational line, actively practices and enhances inner-Party democracy, and perfects the institutional structure of the Party and develops the institutions. The SACP constantly enlarges its party cadres with the organizational principle of "quality prior to quantity", and seeks to recruit qualified members from all walks of society.

4. The improvement of the Party's administrative ability

Before the "1994 Breakthrough" the SACP undertook a single role of being a revolutionary party, after the "1994 Breakthrough" it has assumed the dual roles of both revolutionary party and "ruling partner". As a party participating in the management of state affairs, the SACP has thousands of party members working in the leading state departments and institutions. Therefore, SACP undertakes the important task of training the cadres and members of the Party in terms of political education and administrative abilities.

Y. 49

Post-War History of the Japanese Communist Party's Movement as Narrated in the Autobiography Book by Mrs. Tetsuzo Fuwa

Zheng Ping[1]

Abstract: Mrs. Tetsuzo Fuwa published an autobiography in 2012, entitled A Road Never Regrettable – Living Together with Tetsuzo Fuwa. She has narrated some important aspects of the Japanese Communist Party which has successfully led the socialist movement in the era after the World War II, which includes, leading the trade union movement, constructing a broad democratic united front, participating in the National Diet and local elections, and struggles to achieve social transformation by winning majority in the parliament.

Key words: the Japanese Communist Party; Tetsuzo Fuwa; Nakako Ueda

---

1 Zheng Ping, specially invited researcher in World Socialism Research Center, attached to CASS, associate researcher in the Marxism Research Institute.

In April 2012, 83-year-old Nakako Ueda, wife of Tetsuzo Fuwa, published her autobiography "A Road Never Regrettable – Living Together with Tetsuzo Fuwa"2. The content of the book includes the 15 years long Sino-Japanese War and the 60 years history of post-war Japan, and more importantly reflects the author's acquaintance and belief in Marxism and her life as a communist since 19 years old. Nakako during all his past life, together with her husband Tetsuzo Fuwa, has strived for the realization of the revolutionary cause, as comrades-in-arms. In addition, the book depicts the history of the socialist movement in Japan after the World War II, from the perspective of the history of the socialist movement.

I. From a "Militant Girl" to a Japanese Communist

Nakako narrates the reason why she joined the Japanese Communist Party (JCP) in her autobiography. She has written that when the World War II was over, the Japanese society was flooded with all kinds of new social trend of thoughts, new literature and new feelings and a new cognition. The US occupation army, who led the administration of Japan, adopted the policy of criticizing and eliminating militarism and advocating democracy, which spread a strong and instantaneous wave of democracy all over Japan. Against such a background, the JCP started to rebuild the party and conduct activities as a legal party. Nakako, who had experienced the deep pain brought by the war, get acquainted about the JCP's anti-war movement during the WWII and was especially impressed by the propositions and slogans put forward by it, such as "sovereignty not belongs to the Mikado (Holy King) but to the people", "peace is the priority", "men and women are equal", "join the young and charming" "all citizens should enjoy the right to vote". Born in a "proletarian" family, the 19-year-old Nakako, who cherished the ideal of "building a better society", joined the JCP – an organization that unites and adds the power of an individuals, to the power of a collective organization of millions" in July 1948 when she was a student in the Tokyo Technical College.

After joining the JCP, Nakako Ueda actively participated in study and reading activities offered by the primary-level party organizations to improve her knowledge and consciousness, and at the same time, she delivered the Party brochures in electric cars, participated in the puppet show activities in factories, gave speeches in the streets and participated in the electoral activity to support Kyuichi Tokuda—first chairman of the Japanese Communist Party after World War II—who was candidate for the House of Representatives. Simply put, she "went wherever there was a red banner". In March 1949, Nakako became a professional revolutionary cadre after her school graduation and worked in a regional committee of the JCP in Tokyo.

---

2 Nakako Ueda. A Road Never Regrettable – Living Together with Tetsuzo Fuwa. Chuokoron-Shinsha, 2012.

Actually, Nakako's impressions about the JCP has been similar to that felt by many Japanese people in the post-War era. Tetsuzo Fuwa, (former leader of the JCP) who joined the JCP, a year earlier than Nakako, was also a young radical who turned to communism in the latter period of the WWII.

Established in July 1922, the JCP was forced to work illegally before the end of the WWII and was severely suppressed, its members and leaders were arrested and tortured by the police. Its legal status was recognized after Japan had surrendered in the war. Suffered from the aggressive war launched by the Japanese militarism, many people in Japan began to notice and evaluate the JCP in a new light and began to support the basic propositions of it. Many people, who shared similar experiences as Nakako and Tetsuzo Fuwa, joined the JCP, and the Party's ranks had greatly enlarged. When the 4th Congress of the JCP was held in December 1945, it had only 1,813 active members; three month later, when the 5th Congress was held in February 1946, the number had reached above 6,000; and when the elections for the House of Representatives was held in January 1949, the number of JCP members had surpassed 100,000. According to the speech given on the 90th anniversary of the Party's establishment by the JCP Chairman Kazuo Shii in July 2012, today the JCP has all together 318,000 members. Although its membership has seen some decrease in the last decade, it still enjoys great vitality and is supported by a considerable number of people outside the party in terms of its propositions. As of April 2017, it enjoys 21 seats out of 480 seats in the House of Representatives (in the 2014 general election, the JCP received 6.06 million votes, or 11.37%) and 14 seats out of 242 seats in the House of Councilors (in the 2016 election, the JCP received 6.02 million votes, or 10.74%).

II. Organize Trade Union Movement, Learn the Reality of the Grass Roots Worker's Lives

Nakako mentions that shortly after her graduation she experienced the contradiction between her "romantic ideals" and the reality, when she worked in the regional committee of the Party. Under the background of the cold war between the US and the Soviet Union and the establishment of the People's Republic of China, the US Occupation administration adjusted its policies in Japan. The "Red Purge" campaign was launched all across Japan and a large number of communists and sympathizers were kicked out of their jobs in the government offices and the major enterprises. The Soviet-centered "Communist Information Bureau" denounced the line of "peaceful revolution under the Allied Occupation" adopted by the JCP in the post-war era, a denunciation which triggered heated debate within the JCP and which led to the liquidation of the Party for a certain time. It never occurred to the young Nakako that the Party would split, and she had no idea, what was happening at the executive level. Young Nakako, could not believe that the Soviet Union, who has achieved revolutionary success, would make such a wrong judgment, but she could also not understand why the hard working JCP was criticized. The confused Nakako decided to return to the start and learn the realities of the trade union work and the labor movement in factories.

In April 1950, Nakako went to work in a casting factory to organize the union work of the JCP and was warmly welcomed by the workers with songs. During this period, Nakako devoted herself to develop the labor movement. She participated in the negotiations between the laborers and enterprise managers for the purpose of raising the workers' wages and bonuses; she initiated the establishment of Women Trade Union to improve the working conditions and to change attitudes towards the female workers; she organized the meeting of exchange for workers and farmers; she took part in the workers' parades regardless of the police's suppression, she reorganized the police hit trade union, and visited the arrested comrades.

Through these activities, Nakako got a better understanding of the stances of the laborers and the capitalists. In those days the labor union leaders and negotiators did not have the courage to represent the demand of the workers due to the fear of losing their jobs, during the tough negotiations led by Nakako, the factory owner attempted to bribe her and offered her a better job in a private talk, because the little brother of the factory owner was tortured and killed in prison because of his involvement in the left wing movement.

In addition, through these experiences, Nakako realized that it was very important to put herself in other's position with empathy when thinking and dealing with problems. When the workers strove to establish the trade union, they refused to seek help from the Labor Office in the factory, but would consult Nakako after work hours, not because she was good at working or reasoning, but because she was willing to share her lunch box with the workers.

Leading and organizing the trade union movement unswervingly has been one of the important activities of the JCP after the WWII. In July 1946, number of trade unions established had increased to 12,000 thousand, and the rate of the workers organized in the unions has exceeded 40%. The communist led "Japanese Congress of Industrial Organizations" had organized 1.63 million members, twice that of the trade union members led by the Socialist Party. When Nakako had participated in the movement of the grass roots workers' movement, Tetsuzo Fuwa also worked for 11 years in a primary level Steel Union. His major tasks included analyzing the economic situation, discussing the rationalization of workers' wages and labor time, and drawing up the policies of the trade union movement. In addition, he was also present at the hearth of the labor movement and led struggles against the dismissal of workers and for fair wages. However, with the improvement of the workers' living and working conditions, the workers' enthusiasm to organize in trade unions has weakened. Therefore, after evaluating the current status of capitalism in Japan, the JCP put forward a new demand to fight against the deregulation of the labor market: to fight against the increasing poverty in the working class. Chairman Shii claimed that "poverty comes from broken rules for decent work, we should be able to impose social regulations in order to curb large corporations' craze for profit. Consequently, the JCP advocated and demanded the "regulated economy versus capitalism without rules" thus led the labor movement towards a right direction. Shii commented: there are no rules governing in Japan, EU is worth studying as an economy governed by rules, JCP is aiming to make Japan a capitalist country with high level rules, like an European-style capitalist society. Of course, the solving of these problems will not touch the pillars of capitalism.

III. Lead and Participate in the Citizen Movements and Strive to Establish the Broadest Democratic United Front

Nakako narrates one of the political activities in which she has participated after she got married. In March 1953, Nakako married Tetsuzo Fuwa. In 1956, she resigned from her position in the regional party committee after she fell sick due to overwork, and in 1959, she gave birth to their first-born daughter. Under this new condition, Nakako, as a female communist, shifted her focus of activity to the citizen movement. She participated in and led the residents' community self-governance, negotiated with relevant governance departments, fought for the residents' rights stipulated in the Constitution, and sought to improve their living conditions. For example, she took part in the movement against the "Japan-US Security Treaty", supported the movement demanding the establishment of kindergartens and primary schools in the residential districts of the cities, fought for the right of free vaccine for all the children, opposed the public school's collecting regular fees from the families of the pupils, objected to the fare increases of the electric cars, and demanded strict examination of the city water. After her daughter went to primary school, Nakako returned to the front line of the women's movement led by the JCP and served as the party branch secretary and was elected as the member of the standing committee of the JCP led "New Japanese Women's Association", in which she organized the study club of scientific socialism and designed various cultural activities to attract the participation of the residents. In addition, she organized a special activity for the members of the middle-school parents working group.

After the war, the JCP advocated to work in the mass organizations in various fields to promote the democratic revolution through the establishment of a broad democratic united front. Leading people's struggle for rights and better life, and working hand-in-hand with various democratic organizations are the major activities promoted by the JCP. Nakako's efforts in leading and participating in the citizen movements have achieved satisfactory results. She and her comrades united the individual citizens and fought for democracy and rights to the uttermost and finally won great achievements in promoting governmental and social reforms, within the capitalist system. We could say that the JCP's strategies and efforts of combining the socialist movement with citizens' movement and establishing the broad democratic united front have paid off.

IV. From the District of the Commons to the World of Parliamentary Politics, Breaking the Old Concept of Money Politics

Nakako's revolutionary activities has changed with the change of Tetsuzo Fuwa's position and tasks he undertook. In her autobiography, Nakako mentioned that Tetsuzo Fuwa was elected to Japan's parliament (lower house called the House of Representatives,) in 1969 for the first time. And Tetsuzo Fuwa was elected as the general secretary of the JCP in 1970. Due to these changes, Nakako gave up her work in women's movement and began to assist her husband, which indicated that she has abandoned her proposition that men and women are equals. Nakako has admitted that the legislation work in the parliament consumed most of her time and energy. To better lead the legislation work in the parliament, they moved to the living quarter of the commons in Tokyo and spent great efforts to build good relationships with the neighbors so as to win their support. On behalf of her husband, Nakako propagated Fuwa's election propositions in the electoral area either by propaganda car or walking from door to door. She helped her husband's work in the election of district councilor, senator, governor and senate election, and she even assisted the wedding parties and funeral ceremonies in the electoral area. Nakako tried her best to adapt herself in different environments and tried to influence those people who have prejudice against communists. With empathy she placed herself in other's position, communicated with the ordinary people using their language, sharing their customs, and learnt how to wave to the public from the electoral car, and tried to figure her appearance and conduct suited to a public figure. She spared no effort to seek the residents' recognition. Taking "assisting a public leader" as a new job, Nakako constantly cultivated and improved herself. Through the unremitting efforts by the election campaign team, Tetsuzo Fuwa got 525.600 votes and won 14.4% of the votes in his first election. In his second candidate, he got 789.590 votes, 21% of the total, and his approval rate went up to fourth place from the top. After once he was elected, Fuwa was elected and has served for 11 successive terms in the parliament.

These episodes narrated by Nakako vividly and strikingly reveal the facts related to electoral politics in Japan. To cite an example, when Fuwa participated in the election for the first time, the citizens still perceived him as a rich person above the ordinary people. Therefore, a deputy from the town (municipal) parliament who supported the conservative was quite perplexed regarding Fuwa's election victory, he said: "Fuwa has no personal relations in the town parliament or the trade union, and there was no big corporate which recommended him. Besides, it seems that he is not rich. How did he get elected?" Yet since then, this man member has become Fuwa's loyal supporter.

The above comment by the deputy serving municipal parliament reveals that in the so-called democratic electoral politics of the capitalist system, professional politicians, bureaucrats and financial circles acted in collusion. While Fuwa, as a congressman came from the ordinary people, reflected people's voice, represented the masses in the political stage and elevated the public to a level of participating in political affairs. All these indicate the success of JCP's propositions, such as the idea of placing sovereignty in the people and empowering the people to utilize their right to vote, properly for their own interests.

V. The Parliamentary Road is Difficult within the Capitalist System

Soon after she joined the JCP, Nakako has participated in the activities to support the General Secretary of the JCP Central Committee Kyuichi Tokuda's election campaign for the Diet. Later, she further experienced 11 election campaigns for Tetsuzo Fuwa. Nakako wrote: "the election campaigns do not sail smoothly each time. At first, I naively believed that public support will remain consolidated as we participate more and more elections. However, it is far from the truth, because each election is deeply influenced by the current trend and political situation of the time. Once the JCP gained a victory and ascended to power, it always faced severe attacks and targeted by a certain power. Fuwa's percentage of votes kept rising steadily, but in the fifth election, he was elected only with 4,000 votes ahead of the second candidate."

Actually, the results of the various general elections after the WWII prove Nakako's observation, and also proves the difficulties of the parliamentary road to power chosen by the JCP. For example, the JCP won 5 seats in the House of Representatives in 1946 (only accounting for 1.078% of the total 464 seats); in 1949 after the promulgation of the new Constitution of

Japan, the JCP achieved an unprecedented success and won 35 seats (accounting for 7.511% of the total 466 seats); but in 1952, the JCP suffered a big defeat. Later, in 1969 when Tetsuzo Fuwa ran for the elections, the JCP won 14 seats (accounting for 2.881% of the total 486 seats); in 1972, the seats of JCP increased to 38 (accounting for 7.739% of the total 491 seats); but in the new century, especially after the emergence of the new trend of "favoring a two-party political system as in the USA" promoted by the financial capital circles in 2003, Japan sought exclude communists and other progressive parties from the political system, and weaken them in the election contests. This new tendency has aggravated the difficulties of the JCP, consequently the seats of the Party dropped to 9 (accounting for 1.875% of the total 480). This situation has continued up to 2010 and improved gradually since 2017.

After the WWII, the JCP was put in an awkward position due to changes in the international and domestic political strategic pattern. It was faced by critical questions which needed urgent answers which included: how to understand and apply the general principles of Marxism, how to understand the domestic conditions of Japan after the WWII, and how to integrate the general principles of Marxism with the new realities of Japan. Shortly after the war, in terms of the correct path of revolution, the JCP encountered the dispute between the "peaceful revolution under occupation" and the "violent revolution under occupation". Then in 1958, the JCP put forward the path advocating "struggles for peaceful revolution", and later on, the party was more and more inclined to take the path of winning the power by majority support including the parliament. When the JCP revised its Party Program in 2004, the party congress stipulated: "A change Japanese society needs at present is a democratic revolution instead of a socialist revolution. It is a revolution that puts an end to Japan's extraordinary subordination to the United States and the tyrannical rule of large corporations and business circles, a revolution that secures Japan's genuine independence and carries out democratic reforms in politics, the economy, and society. Although these are democratic reforms realizable within the framework of capitalism, their full-fledged achievement can be made possible through a transfer of state power to the forces that represent the fundamental interests of the Japanese people from those representing Japan's monopoly capitalism and subordinate to the United States. Success in achieving this democratic change will help solve problems that cause the people to suffer and pave the way for building an independent, democratic, and peaceful Japan that safeguards the fundamental interests of the majority of the people." And the congress admitted that socialism in Japan will maintain the market economy", and the next step would be to strive to build socialist & communist society: "in the next stage of Japan's social development, the task is to overcome capitalism and carry out socialist transformation and advance to a socialist/communist society. In the hitherto seen world, there has been no real socialist transformation taking place on the basis of the advanced economic and social achievements of the capitalist era. Working in a developed capitalist country to advance toward socialism/communism is a new historic task in the 21st century."

The political program of the JCP indicates that they would carry out socialism construction on the basis of the highly developed productive forces, which conforms to the basic principles of Marxism. Considering the political and social realities of Japan, the JCP attempts to advance the social construction and improve the current welfare system within capitalism so as to create conditions for the realization of socialism. From the autobiography of Nakako, we are able to learn that in actual practice, the JCP actively participates in the national and regional parliamentary elections in order to control more administrative resources and powers. However, the ups and downs in the historical course of election results achieved by the JCP reveal that the parliamentary approach of realizing social reforms within the framework of capitalism seems to be limited and shaky. The pro-capitalist parties never give up their efforts to suppress the communist party and will never tolerate the development of the communist party. They may even join hands to fight against the communist party leaving aside their different party interests.

VI. Struggle at the Forefront to Build a Better Society

In her autobiography, Nakako introduced several questions raised by Fuwa in the parliamentary struggles when representing the JCP. For example, in 1974, Fuwa demanded an investigation related to "nuclear leakage from an US nuclear submarine". After meticulous survey and analysis, Fuwa has found out how prime minister Tanaka Kakuei has manipulated unreliable survey data to prove the "safety" of the nuclear submarine and deceived the public. After Fuwa's efforts, U.S nuclear-powered ships stopped entering Japanese ports for 183 days, until the new investigation commission was established. In addition, Fuwa disclosed the secret nuclear treaty between Japan and the US, and expounded on the problems between the common earthquakes and nuclear energy plants in Japan. Nakako has written: currently there is nothing new in the media reports about the nuclear energy production in Japan, because all the points have been predicated by Fuwa long previously. Tetsuzo Fuwa also touched upon the issues of closing US military bases in Japan, constant rise of commodity prices, and deaths and illnesses from overwork, etc.

Nakako's introduction well demonstrates that JCP has always been struggling at the forefront to resolve the issues related to national sovereignty of Japan and the people's livelihood and has appealed to the public and developed active struggles against the capitalist regime in order to defend people's rights. Till Fuwa's last term in the Diet ended in 2003, Fuwa has confronted 18 prime ministers of Japan. The questions he raised and his speeches in the Diet received high attention from the society, but most of the questions have remained unsolved although they were directly or closely related with people's lives. All these facts prove that the JCP has always been sincere in defending the interests of the citizens and that the issues brought forward by the JCP are forward-looking and insightful.

Nakako and Fuwa – the revolutionary couple – have been sharing their lives for more than 60 years since they have met each other, and they have never changed their common life goal – making changes and transforming Japan so that each citizen can enjoy a dignified life. Just as they have expressed in their wedding vows: "We get married here, and we vow to stay together and unite in a concerted effort to strive for the peace and liberation of the world." This is probably the common wish of the 320.000 communists in Japan. Through a reading Nakako's autobiography and Tetsuzo Fuwa's autobiography "Testimony of the Age" which was published in 2011, we can get a better understanding of the JCP's activities in the post- war era from multi-perspectives including theories, practice, the foreground and the backstage of political developments.

Y. 50

On the Nature of the Current International Meetings of Communist and Workers' Parties

Nie Yunlin[1]

This article presents the initial fruits of the research project titled "Research on the Theories and Practices of Communist Parties in the Contemporary Capitalist Countries" sponsored by the Ministry of Education.

Abstract: The current annually held International Meeting of Communist and Workers' Parties has become a multilateral communication platform for the world's communist and workers' parties. The multilateral communication platform is based on the common ideological basis of Marxism-Leninism, it opposes imperialism and international monopoly capital, fights for peace, democracy, progress and socialism, which are set as its political basis for joint activity. The platform of Parties operates on the basic principles of equal rights, respect for differences of ideas and positions, and non-interference in internal affairs, and it is built on the common goal of strengthening communications, promoting friendship, exchanging work experiences and ideas, promoting the development of world socialist movement. If we say, the development of bilateral relations between the parties has been the main form of unity and cooperation of the world socialist movement, after since the drastic changes of the Soviet Union and Eastern Europe, then we can say the International Meeting of Communist and Workers' Parties is an important complement to the formation of unity and cooperation in the world socialist movement.

Key words: the nature of International Meeting of Communist and Workers' Parties, unity and cooperation

---

1 Nie Yunlin, specially invited researcher in World Socialism Research Center, attached to CASS, Director and researcher of the Foreign Marxist Parties Research Center, at the Central China Normal University in Wuhan.

After the drastic changes of the Soviet Union and Eastern Europe, international communications within the world socialist movement was severely damaged. Through concerted efforts of the communists all over the world, the international communications among the communist parties of different countries gradually resumed since mid-1990s. In 1999, the first session of the International Meeting of Communist and Workers' Parties was held in Athens, Greece. Since then, the annual International Meeting of Communist and Workers' Parties has become an important activity as one part in the development of the world socialist movement. Till 1999 to present, the meeting has been held annually and regularly for 13 times.

I. The Birth of the International Meeting of Communist and Workers' Parties

The world socialist movement is both a social movement rooted in national space and an international social movement, the development of which requires an extensive international contacts, especially in an era where economic globalization rapidly develops and the general monopoly capitalism has developed into international monopoly capitalism. The high degree of internationalization of capital determines that any movement targeting should be international, and all the more so, when it comes to socialist movement.

After suffering the severe setback brought by the drastic changes that occurred in the Soviet Union and Eastern Europe, the communist parties of the capitalist countries gradually gained a firm foothold and made serious efforts to further consolidate their positions and development, since mid-1990s. Therefore, by then, it became a common pursuit to resume the international contacts and exchanges among the communist parties of different countries. This development trend could be manifested in the following manifold activities by the communist parties.

Bilateral relations developed extensively between the communist parties and has become the main form of international contact and cooperation in the current world socialist movement

The communist parties, such as the Communist Party of China, the Japanese Communist Party, the French Communist Party, the Communist Party of the Russian Federation, the Communist Party of India (Marxist), the Communist Party of Brazil, the South African Communist Party and the Party of the Workers of Belgium, overcame difficulties, put their differences aside, and actively developed bilateral relations based on the principles of independence, equality, mutual respect and non-interference of their internal affairs.

Communist parties of certain countries voluntarily undertook the responsibility of holding small-scale or regional international meetings when the conditions were not mature enough for the worldwide meeting of communist and workers' parties

For example, in April 1992, the Workers' Party of Korea held an international meeting in Pyongyang; in 1993, the Communist Party of India (Marxist) and the Communist Party of Nepal (Marxist-Leninist) held the international meeting on "Contemporary World Situation and the Truth of Marxism". Communist parties of certain countries have organized regional meeting, for example, the Socialist Party of Mexico held two regional meetings successively in Latin America; together with political parties of other countries, the Communist Party of Greece organized party meetings of the Balkan region and the Eastern Mediterranean region. Since the mid-1990s, the preparation efforts for the resumption of the International Meeting of Communist and Workers' Parties have accelerated. In 1997, together with the commemoration of the 80th anniversary of the October Revolution, the Communist Workers Party of Russia held a commemorative international meeting in St. Petersburg, the Communist Party of Cuba held an international symposium on the effectiveness of socialism, and communist parties of the Mediterranean region held their second meeting.

Before resuming contact and association among the communist and workers' parties, many parties have provided suggestions for holding the worldwide meeting of the communist and workers' parties

In 1993, Guss Hall, the chairman of the Communist Party of the USA, proposed to hold the international meeting of the world communist parties. In March 1998, the Communist Party of Canada published an open letter to communist parties of other countries, suggesting holding international meetings so as to reach a common position based on negotiation. To map out the draft of the joint statement, the Communist Party of Canada, the Communist Party of the USA and the Communist Party of Australia established a working committee in advance.

During 22 to 24 May 1998, when it came to the 150th anniversary of The Communist Manifesto and 80th anniversary of the Communist Party of Greece, the Communist Party of Greece held an international meeting on the theme of "Communist Party at Present" in Athens, and published the announcement that a worldwide meeting of the communist and workers' parties would be held.

In 1999, the first session of the International Meeting of Communist and Workers' Parties was held in Athens with the theme of "Capitalist Economic Crisis, Globalization, and Reaction of the Labor Movement". Altogether, 56 representative communist parties and workers' parties from 46 countries have participated in the meeting. The participant parties have been isolated from each other for quite some time and some of the parties were newly established, their communications were not much. Therefore, this meeting mainly served for information exchange and the parties would express their stances and propositions regarding key issues. This international meeting, though attracted little attention by then, ushered in a new approach for the communist parties to develop multilateral relations and provided a platform for the parties to communicate with each other. The holding of the International Meeting of Communist and Workers' Parties provided important institutional reference for the meetings held subsequently.

It can be seen that the appearance of the annual International Meeting of Communist and Workers' Parties was no accident; instead, it was the result of series of initiatives and activities.

Firstly, after the drastic changes of the Soviet Union and Eastern Europe, communist parties of different countries scientifically analyzed the nature and lessons of these changes and reiterated their commitment to Marxism and the ideal of communism in their bilateral exchanges, and thus they reached consensus ideologically and theoretically.

Secondly, certain countries voluntarily undertook the responsibility of holding small-scale international meetings and regional meetings, which provided the platform for bilateral communications among the communist and workers' parties. All these activities have enabled the communist and workers' parties to resume their contact network, after drastic changes in the Soviet Union and Eastern Europe and after severe offensive by the international monopoly capital. This was the organizational preparation.

Thirdly, the initiatives and active efforts by the communist parties of countries like Greece, India, Brazil, USA, and Canada facilitated the eventual beginning of the International Meeting of Communist and Workers' Parties, among which the Communist Party of the Greece has made outstanding contributions.

II. Development of the International Meeting of Communist and Workers' Parties and the Formation of the Meeting System

From 1999 to 2011, the International Meeting of Communist and Workers' Parties has been held for 13 times regularly and annually. The first seven meetings (1999-2005) were held in Athens. From 2006 on, the meeting went out of Greece and was held in relevant countries of the five continents in turns: 2006 in Lisbon, Portugal, 2007 in Minsk, Belarus, 2008 in Sao Paulo, Brazil, 2009 in New Delhi, India, 2010 in Tshwane, South Africa, and 2011, in Athens, Greece. The International Meeting of Communist and Workers' Parties going global represents that the world socialist movement recovers and develops after the setback caused by drastic changes of the Soviet Union and Eastern Europe, and indicates that the meeting has gained an international nature.

The number of parties participating in the International Meeting of Communist and Workers' Parties is unstable, the maximum being 73 parties from 62 countries in 2005 and the minimum 54 parties from 41 countries in 2001. The International Meeting of Communist and Workers' Parties discusses a wide range of social political problems, such as economic globalization, capitalist economic crisis, world situation after "9.11", anti-imperialism war, environmental protection, trade union movement, labor movement, the establishment of anti-imperialism and anti-monopoly untied front, and the fight for peace, democracy, sovereignty, progress and socialism. All the important issues concerning capitalism and socialism would become the central topics for discussion in the meeting.

After more than a decade of development, the International Meeting of Communist and Workers' Parties has not only reached a considerable scale, but also established a set of operation mechanisms to ensure the normal operation of the meeting.

Publishing of a meeting announcement

As early as 1999, when the International Meeting of Communist and Workers' Parties was held for the first time, the working procedure of publishing information bulletin was established. Publishing an announcement regarding the coming meeting, via internet became an important procedure of the meetings, and this notice has been one of the most significant means for the people to be informed about the meeting.

Publish a joint political statement

The adoption of a joint statement by the International Meeting of the Communist and the Workers' Parties is not a simple matter. The first two meetings were not able to issue any joint statement. There was only a unilateral statement issued by the Communist Party of Greece, which indicated that the first two meetings failed to reach consensus among the participants.

In 2002, the third session of the International Meeting of Communist and Workers' Parties discussed the "9.11" issue and the world situation afterwards. Representatives presented at the meeting unanimously opposed to the misleading slogan "without war – without terrorism" raised by some people. The real intention of the slogan was legalizing the strategies of imperialism and confusing revolutionary violence with terrorism so as to deprive people of their rights of revolutionary struggle. Therefore, the meeting published the first joint statement through consultation, denouncing that "imperialism is the terrorism of resistance movement" and reiterating their commitment to "providing strong support for people's struggle for social rights and national independence". Thereafter, the International Meeting of Communist and Workers' Parties established the working procedure for publishing joint statement. The joint statement of the meeting seeks common ground while reserving differences. It only records the agreed political thoughts and the joint action demands, not the disputes.

Publishing a declaration of resolutions agreed and signed by a number of the Parties

The resolutions adopted in the international meetings are generally approved by all the communist and workers' parties. But, we look into the history of the international communist movement, there occurred such cases as heated controversies, and which finally led to the division of the movement. Therefore, the International Meeting of Communist and Workers' Parties has changed the traditional mode of meeting operation and the way resolutions are issued. To be more specific, any motion proposed by a group of Parties does not need to be approved unanimously. Those who agree with a motion can just sign their Party names on it. In other words, if the party disagrees with the motion, he does not need to sign. In this way, the number of undersigned parties on each resolution is different. Some of them might be signed by all participants, while some others might be signed by some parties. Sometimes, certain resolutions only received about 10 signatures. Obviously, the parties not signing on the resolution will not be bound by it. The operation mode of unanimous approval in the past has changed into joint signature of certain like-minded parties. This kind of special resolution fulfills the parties' need to express their interests and wishes, and avoids disputes among parties with different opinions. Such practice will not damage the unity and cooperation of the parties and will promote the stable development of the world socialist movement. In a sense, this is a new type of cooperation which seeks common ground on major issues while leaving aside minor differences.

Principles of operation of the international meeting

The International Meeting of Communist and Workers' Parties, which is usually participated by 60 to 70 countries each year, has set certain rules to maintain its smooth operation. Different from the "Three Internationals" in the history of the communist movement, the current International Meeting of Communist and Workers' Parties does not have a common political program and constitution, but has some principles formed in its practices, such as equal rights, respect for differences and non-interference of other parties' internal affairs.

The introduction "working group" mechanism

As an international meeting, the preparation work of the International Meeting of Communist and Workers' Parties has been conducted by the International Department of the Communist Party of Greece for long years. To change such situation, the sixth session of the meeting held in 2004 made the decision of choosing a working team to prepare the next meetings. The responsibilities of the working groups include: first, organize the time, location and theme of the meeting; two, prepare documents for the meeting; three, invite new communist and workers' parties to participate in the meeting and carry out the works of joint action. To be a member in certain working group is open to all the participant parties. The first working group included the Communist Party of Greece, the Communist Party of Bohemia and Moravia, the Communist Party of Spain, the Communist Party of the Russian Federation, the Communist Party of Lebanon, the South African Communist Party, the Communist Party of Cuba and the Communist Party of Brazil. Later, the Portuguese Communist Party, the Communist Party of India and the Communist Party of India (Marxist) also joined the working group. Since then, the preparation work for the international meeting was no longer the sole responsibility of the Communist Party of Greece, but became a shared responsibility undertaken by all parties. The parties can issue press statement about the working group meetings. See The Press Statement by the Portuguese Communist Party, Meeting of the Working Group: http://www.lcparty.org/index.php?option=com_content&id=2177:meeting-of-the-working-group-of-the-international-meetings-of-communist-and-workers-parties.

Establishment of the informative website: www.solid.net

As early as 1999, when the first session of the International Meeting of Communist and Workers' Parties was held, the Communist Party of Greece has established the information website www.solidnet.org for the participant parties, and published meeting statements, resolutions and announcements through the website. Later, the website has become an important bridge between the international meeting and the parties, the working class and the people of the world.

III. Functions and the Nature of the International Meeting of Communist and Workers' Parties

As a meeting with worldwide influence, the functions and nature of the International Meeting of Communist and Workers' Parties receive much attention. First question, what is its nature? The parties participating in the meeting have had different expectations regarding the nature of the meeting in the past.

Knicks Eritak, member of the International Department of the Communist Party of Greece, described in the article "On the International Meeting of Communist and Workers' Parties" that as far as back in the year 2000, when the second session of the meeting was held, participant parties have expressed several different opinions regarding the nature of the meeting. Their opinions could be summarized into three groups. The first group thought that the meeting should be transformed into a general meeting of the "left wing parties". They have put some pressure during the debates to change its composition regarding participants, thus eventually, the meeting would lose its communist nature during its development. The second group believed that the meeting should maintain its communist nature and shoulder to implement an anti-imperialist strategy, and organize coordinating secretariat to coordinate the relations among the participant parties and facilitate common actions. For example, in the second session of the meeting, some parties proposed this secretariat to coordinate actions, but the proposition was not approved. The third group has also argued that the meeting should maintain its communist nature, but the cooperation and unity should not be operated as it had in the first seven decades of the 20th century. It should not be empowered with strong leading organs, instead it should be a platform for the parties to develop multilateral relations and a means express their solidarity. In the subsequent meetings made in the later years, there were many other parties expressing their opinions on the nature and the development direction of the "Meeting". The following three aspects can be deduced, regarding the nature of the "International Meeting" from the previous 13 meetings:

Firstly, the International Meeting of Communist and Workers' Parties has maintained its communist nature and there is no possibility that it may develop towards an "International Meeting" "left wing parties".

Secondly, the "International Meeting" does not develop in accordance with the second expectation, either. Although the "International Meetings" have made some common action plans regarding anti-imperialist and attempted coordination among the parties, it did not commit itself to facilitating "unanimous joint actions". Thirdly, generally direction of the "Meetings" developed according to the third expectation or opinion, it has developed into a "platform for the parties to develop multilateral relations among themselves and express their wills for solidarity".

Functions of the "International Meeting"

The International Meeting of Communist and Workers' Parties, during its existence for more than a decade, has mainly undertaken the following functions:

(1) The communist and workers' parties exchange their thoughts and opinions, publish their understandings and views of the important political, economic and social problems of common concern.

The important issues of the world include the nature and basic reasons of the drastic changes of the Soviet Union and Eastern Europe, the 9/11 terrorism attack, the new development and changes of capitalism, the new changes of the working class, the economic crisis broke out in 2008 and its development trend, etc.

(2) The communist and workers' parties report their respective working conditions, demonstrate their new progress in the struggle for peace, democracy, sovereignty, progress and socialism, and exchange their working experiences with each other. To be more specific, the communist parties of capitalist countries mainly introduce the development situation of the labor movement and other social movements in their countries, and inform about the roles played by the communist party. While the communist parties of socialist countries mainly introduce their achievements in socialist construction and their innovations in the aspects theories and practices.

(3) The communist and workers' parties propose strategies and tasks to face the new situations. For example, due to recent global economic crisis, "the Meeting" called on all the communists to stand in the forefront of the fight against the capitalist governments' attempt of shifting the burden of economic crisis over the shoulders of peoples; and defend the economic and social rights of the working class and the toiler masses. "The Meeting" called on all the communists to struggle against the transnational monopoly capital and its neoliberal policies and establish an international anti-imperialist and anti-monopoly united front for the victory against monopoly capitalism.

(4) The international "Meeting" initiates limited joint actions regarding certain struggles

For example, the "Meeting" appealed to the communist parties and the masses all over the world to support Cuban people's anti-imperialist struggle and oppose US imperialism's economic blockade on Cuba's economy. The "Meeting" also called communist parties and people of all countries to support Cyprus people's struggle against the occupation of Turkey and for united Cyprus. The meeting appealed to the communist parties of all countries to support Indian people's protection of the environment and to oppose the America-led transnational monopoly companies' action of environmental damage; the meeting appealed to communist parties all over the world to launch activities in honor of the October Revolution and to commemorate the centenary anniversary of the Pravda newspaper.

From the examples mentioned above we may come to the conclusion that the contemporary International Meeting of Communist and Workers' Parties has become the multilateral communication platform for the world communist and workers' parties.

This multilateral communication platform is based on Marxism-Leninism, as the common ideological basis, and fights against imperialism and international monopoly capital, for peace, democracy, progress and socialism, which are set as its political basis for joint activity. The platform operates on the basic principles of equality, respect for differences, and non-interference in others' internal affairs. If we say, the development of bilateral relations between the parties has been the main form of unity and cooperation of the world socialist movement, after since the drastic changes of the Soviet Union and Eastern Europe, then we can say the International Meeting of Communist and Workers' Parties is an important complement to the formation of unity and cooperation in the world socialist movement.

The contemporary International Meeting of Communist and Workers' Parties is different from the Moscow Meetings hosted by the Soviet Union in the 1950-60s. The Moscow Meetings followed the principles of following one central leader (the Communist Party of the Soviet Union), accepted and followed one revolutionary road (the road of October Revolution), and implicitly adopted a unique pattern of socialist construction and development (the Soviet pattern) as the only model. The purpose of the Moscow Meetings was to ensure that the world socialist movement does not deviate from the above three "uniform" modes. However, the contemporary world socialist movement has encountered tremendous changes, in the last 40 years. Currently, the communist parties tend to follow a revolutionary path suitable for their own conditions under the independent leadership of the communist party and construct socialism with their respective features. Diversity is an important feature of the contemporary world socialist movement. Against such background, the International Meeting of Communist and Workers' Parties will not and could not carry on the practices of the Moscow Meeting.

Since the International Meeting of Communist and Workers' Parties is held against the background and historical conditions of the current quite diversified nature, which we can clearly observe in the world socialist movement, consequently, it will impossible to build an artificial "unity" in the world socialist movement. Just as Manuera San Bernardino, the General Secretary of the Central Committee of Portuguese Communist Party, has commented on this point during the 13th session of the "International Meeting": "Although the conditions and experiences of many communist parties are diversified, and although we have different approaches and opinions, we should still continue to strengthen the International Meeting of Communist and Workers' Parties and should be united as one to oppose capitalism, promote social progress, maintain peace and develop socialism. However, currently the unity and cooperation within the socialist movement are different from previous times, today for us, unity and joint action and their necessity does not mean following identical policies or does not mean deliberately building communist movement. Instead, our current situation suggests that we should exchange our different and diversified social reform experiences and unite to develop concerted efforts among us for our specific goals."

Y. 51

An Analysis of the "International Meetings of the Communist and Workers' Parties" from 1999 to 2011[1]

Wang Ximan[2] & Wang Zifeng[3]

Abstract: "International Meeting of the Communist and Workers' Parties" has emerged with requirement of the times require since 1991, near to the end of the 20th Century. After ten years of its development, it has gradually grown into an international meeting with socialist properties, which promotes unity and cooperation Marxist Workers' parties leading anti-imperialist and anti-monopoly struggles within the capitalist countries. In the new period of world socialist movement, studying its emergence, development process, composition and operation mechanisms, characteristics, its theory and practice, constitutes great when we explore ways and methods to strengthen unity and cooperation within the world socialist movement.

Key words: International Meeting of the Communist and Workers' Parties; anti-imperialist and anti-monopoly struggle; world socialist movement

---

1 This article is the research fruit of the project titled as "Research on the International Meeting of Communist and Workers' Party in the Contemporary World" sponsored by .the national social sciences fund for the young scholars.
2 Wang Ximan, Specially invited researcher in World Socialism Research Center, attached to CASS, Associate Prof. in the Research office of Marxism with Chinese Characteristics, in the College of Marxism, Liaoning University.
3 Wang Zifeng, Specially invited researcher in World Socialism Research Center, attached to CASS, postgraduate student in the College of Marxism, Liaoning University.

After the drastic changes that occurred in the Soviet Union and Eastern Europe, especially after 1999, the international communist movement has established a new cooperation form, namely the annual "International Meeting of the Communist and Workers' Parties". The "Meeting" was first initiated by the Communist Party of Greece, and later on it has been hosted in turn by communist parties of the capitalist countries and the "Meeting" is participated by representatives of the communist parties and workers' parties from all over the world. Generally, focusing on the themes of "peace, democracy, sovereignty, progress and socialism", the member parties exchange opinions, work out resolutions and carry out joint actions to promote the unity and revitalization of the international communist movement. At present, the Communist Party of China is an observer member of the "Meeting".

I. The Birth and Development of the "International Meeting of the Communist and Workers' Parties"

Historical circumstances for the birth and development of the meetings

After the drastic changes that occurred in the Soviet Union and Eastern Europe, the International Meeting of the Communist and Workers' Parties did not come into being right away, but has gone went through a long process of exploration. To be more specific, the birth and development of the "Meeting" has gone through three stages.

The first stage: brewing and preparation period (1991-1998)

Soon after the drastic changes that occurred in the Soviet Union and Eastern Europe, the Marxist workers' parties, who have survived the anti-communist persecution and the restraints of big party, resumed bilateral ties and sought to develop multilateral relations. During this period, Marxist workers' parties such as the Workers Party of Korea (North), the Communist Party of Nepal (Marxist-Leninist), the Communist Party of India (Marxist), the Communist Party of Greece, the Russian Communist Workers Party–Communist Revolutionary Party of Russia and the Communist Party of Cuba, successively hosted several regional meetings attended by the communist and workers' parties. For example, in 1992, the Workers Party of Korea held an international meeting in Pyongyang; in 1993, the Communist Party of India (Marxist) and the Communist Party of Nepal (Marxist-Leninist) jointly hosted an international meeting with the theme of "Contemporary World Situation and the Validity and Relevance of Marxism", which was participated by 30 parties. In the mid-1990s, the Socialist Party of Mexico has hosted two international meetings which were mostly attended by the parties in Latin America.

Together with political parties of other countries, the Communist Party of Greece and European and North African parties hosted meetings attended by the communist parties of the Balkan region, the Eastern Mediterranean region.

In 1997, when commemorating the 80th anniversary of the October Revolution, the Communist Workers Party of Russia held a commemorative international meeting in St. Petersburg, and in the same year the Communist Party of Cuba held an international seminar on the "validity and relevance" of socialism. These regional meetings laid the foundation for the formation of the International Meeting of the Communist and Workers' Parties.

The year 1998 was a crucial year for the development of the International Meeting of the Communist and Workers' Party. In 1993, Gus Hall, the Chairman of the Communist Party of the USA, proposed to hold an international meeting of the world communist parties. Five years later, in March 1998, the Communist Party of Canada, the Communist Party of the USA and the Communist Party of Australia drafted a joint statement on "Hold a World International Meeting of the Communist Parties themed with 'Multilateral Agreement on Cooperation and Unity." Later this joint declaration was sent to communist parties of other countries by the Communist Party of Canada by a written letter. In the year of the 150th anniversary of The Communist Manifesto and in the 80th anniversary of the establishment of the Communist Party of Greece, the Communist Party of Greece held an international meeting on the theme of "Communist Party at Present", and in this meeting other participant parties agreed to hold the annual joint "Meetings" beginning with the year 1999 as the first session.

The second stage: birth and initial period (1999 to 2005)

From 1999 to 2005, the seven annual sessions of the International Meeting of Communist and Workers' Parties were hosted by the Communist Party of Greece in Athens, which played an important role in the development of the "Meeting". In 1999, the website of the Meeting, the www.solidnet.org was established, and also an "Information Bulletin" began to be published, and a joint declaration against NATO attacks and expansion of NATO was agreed. In 2000, the second session of the meeting suggested to establish the Secretariat to coordinate actions, but could not be realized. During the annual meetings between 2001 to 2003 no agreement could be reached on the following issues due to differences: "the nature and future of the Meeting", "joint struggle against imperialism", "attitude towards fight against terrorism" and "opposing to opportunist parties". But since 2002 the participant parties have been able to make unanimous joint statement to fight against imperialism and to support the righteous struggle of people around the world, and joint declaration called on taking active joint actions.

In 2004, the "Meeting" decided to establish a working group, the major responsibilities of which included deciding the time, place and theme of the meeting, preparing documents for the meeting, inviting new parties and facilitating the realization of joint actions. Meetings of the working group are open for all the participant parties.

In the course of time we can observe that the "Meeting" has attracted a high participation rate. Since its establishment, the minimum number of the participant parties was 54 in 2001 and the maximum being 73 in 2005. The participation rate is stable and maintains a high level.

The third stage: development and improvement period (2006 till present)

The development of the International Meeting of Communist and Workers' Parties is first reflected in its various meeting locations. Till now, it has been held on all the continents of the world except the Oceania. After it convened for the first 7 sessions in Athens, the meeting moved to other countries – 2006 in Lisbon, Portuguese, 2007 in Minsk, Belarus, 2008 in Sao Paulo, Brazil, and 2009 in New Delhi, India. Besides, a special international meeting was held in Damascus, Syria. Then in 2010, the meeting was held in Tshwane, South Africa, and it returned to Athens in 2011. In 2012, the meeting was held in Beirut, Lebanon, and this was followed by Lisbon, Guayaquil, Ecuador, Istanbul, Turkey, Hanoi, Vietnam.

In addition to diversified gathering locations, the content of the meeting has gone through various changes. After years of struggle against non-Marxist, non-socialist opinions, the theme of the meetings has transformed from "anti-imperialist struggle" to "the future of socialism" after 2005. The number of parties participating in the meeting has increased as well, the maximum has reached 78, accounting for the 60% of the world communist and workers' parties.

Historical circumstances for the birth and development of the "Meeting"

The gradual emergence and the development of the International Meeting of Communist and Workers' Parties was no accident, but was the result of a series of historical factors that have developed after the drastic changes in the Soviet Union and Eastern Europe.

Firstly, the new changes of capitalism driven by the scientific and technological revolution and the revolutionary development of capitalist productive forces have constituted an important factor, as its international environment. During 1990s, with the rapid development of new high-technologies, science and technology and the productive forces, and new changes such as economic globalization, technology informatization (IT technology), political democratization, cultural diversity, social welfare, middle class phenomena and de-ideologization, continue to impact the social structure of capitalist society. Meanwhile, capitalism further transformed from state monopoly capitalism to international finance monopoly capitalism. The imperialism attempts to establish reactionary international system globally, which causes the aggravation of local conflicts, consequently causes regional conflicts and wars. As for how to deal with the new changes within capitalism, how to survive and develop in the new circumstances of and how to cope with the imperialist offensive have become serious external challenges faced by all the communist parties all over the world. Consultation on these issues through bilateral and multi-lateral meetings can be the most effective methods.

Secondly, the world socialist movement has suffered a major setback and the need to enhance internal contacts and communications have been the main driver of the "Meeting". The world socialist movement has lived a serious trouble after the drastic changes in the Soviet Union and Eastern Europe. Except bilateral ties between certain number of parties, the internal contacts and communications within the world socialist movement ceased. Encountered by the anti-communist attacks by the capitalist class, most of the communist parties and workers parties have fallen into a difficult position. Therefore, resumption of contacts and and communications among the communist and workers' parties have become an inevitable choice. The parties needed to discuss the significant issues of the movement, such as the nature of the era we are passing through, the future of socialism, and the proper reforms and transformations regarding communist parties, to be more clear over these issues has become crucial for the communist parties, that they can find a proper socialist development path suitable to their national conditions.

Thirdly, the gradual recovery and reorganization of the communist and workers' parties have provided the internal force that pushed, the international "Meetings." During the first decade after the collapse of the Soviet Union and socialist states in the Eastern Europe, the communist and workers' parties went through the toughest time regarding their activities. By the end of the 20th century, they have gained a firm foothold after insistent struggles. For example, the Communist Party of Greece has strengthened its position in the national parliament and the South African Communist Party has become one of the coalition partners of the ANC led government. That is to say, these parties were able to participate in the International Meeting of Communist and Workers' Parties held either in their own country or abroad. These developments have laid a solid organization foundation for the development of the meeting.

Fourthly, the experiences and lessons of the international communist movement provided the historical basis for the emergence and development of the "Meeting". Since its birth in 1847, the Marxist working class party subsequently established the International Workingmen's Association, the Second International, the Third International, and the Communist Information Bureau under the ideological guidance of the proletariat internationalism to enhance the unity and cooperation within the international communist movement.

And the Marxist working class parties have held International Meeting of Communist and Workers' Parties respectively in the year 1957, 1960 and 1969. We could say that the experiences and lessons of the Marxist working class parties in establishing international organizations and holding international meetings were important in the international communist movement, thus this past experience has provided the historical basis for the new round of cooperation via the International Meeting of Communist and Workers' Parties.[4]

Fifthly, the Marxist theory is the theoretical basis for the emergence and development of the "Meeting". Marxism has a comprehensive theoretical system which includes, Marxist theories of strategy and tactics, proletariat internationalism, proletarian party building, capitalism, imperialism and socialism which provide the main basis for the theoretical innovation pursued by the communist and workers' parties, and this comprehensive theoretical system also provides powerful weapons to cope with various challenges and in solving all kinds of problems.

Sixthly, the concerted efforts by certain Marxist working class parties, represented by the Communist Party of Greece, have been the direct cause for the emergence and development of the meeting. The Communist Party of Greece adheres to the basic principles of Marxism and socialist development road, it has expanded its influence in the process of manifold struggles. From 1999 to 2005, it has hosted 7 sessions of the "Meeting" successively, which has made outstanding contributions to the emergence and development, of the International Meeting of Communist and Workers' Parties.

---

4 See, Statement of 81 Communist and Workers Parties Meeting in Moscow, USSR, 1960. New York: New Century Publishers, 1961. https://www.marxists.org/history/international/comintern/sino-soviet-split/other/1960statement.htm.

II. The Current Situation of the International Meeting of Communist and Workers' Parties

Till 2011, the world International Meeting of Communist and Workers' Parties has been held for 13 times. The meeting was first held in Athens, Greece on 21 June 1999, and since then it was held annually. Specific number of the parties and countries participating in the meeting is as follows: in 1999, 56 communist and workers' parties from 46countries participated in the meeting; in 2000, 60 parties from 47 countries; in 2001, 54 parties from 41 countries; in 2002, 62 parties from 50 countries; in 2003, 59 parties from 47 countries; in 2004, 64 parties from 51 countries; in 2005, 73 parties from 62 countries; in 2006, 63 parties from 50 countries; in 2007, 72 parties from 59 countries; in 2008, 66 parties from 55 countries; in 2009, 57 parties from 47 countries; in 2010, 51 parties from 43 countries; and in 2011, 78 parties from 59 countries. In terms of the meeting dates, the first five sessions of the meeting were held in mid-to-end of June; later on, in order to summarize the experiences of the past year and make plans for the new year, the meetings were held in the fourth quarter of the year since 2004, often in December.

Though the participant parties are varied, they could be generally divided into two groups—the parties guided by Marxist ideology and the parties guided by Marxism-Leninist ideology. Most of the parties are communist parties with legal status in capitalist countries—namely, political parties performing within the established political system, and some have been the ruling parties of socialist countries. The number of parties which participated in the meeting is large. Till now, 101 parties have participated in the "Meeting", accounting for 78% of the total communist parties in the world.

To be more specific, the following parties have taken part in the meeting: the Communist Party of Cuba, the Communist Party of Vietnam, the Workers Party of Korea, the Lao People's Revolutionary Party, the Communist Party of China, the Communist Party of Albania, the Algeria Party for Democracy and Socialism, the Communist Party of Azerbaijan, the Communist Party of Australia, the Communist Party of Argentina, the Communist Party of Armenia, the Communist Party of Austria, the Communist Party of Belgium, the Workers' Party of Belgium, the Communist Party of Bangladesh, the Workers' Party of Bangladesh, the Brazilian Communist Party, the Communist Party of Brazil, the Communist Party of Great Britain, the New Communist Party of Great Britain, the Communist Workers Party of Bosnia and Herzegovina, the Communist Party of Bolivia, the Communist Party of Bulgaria, the Party of Bulgaria Communists, the Communist Party of Canada, the Socialist Workers Party of Croatia, AKEL, the Cyprus's Progressive Party of Working People, the Communist Party of Bohemia and Moravia, the Communist Party of Denmark, the Danish Communist Party, the Communist Party of Egypt, the Communist Party of Finland, the Communist Party of France, the Communist Party of Macedonia, the United Communist Party of Georgia, the Communist Party of Germany, the Communist Party of Greece, the Guyana's People's Progressive Party, the Communist Party of Columbia, the FARC-EP of Colombia, the Communist Worker Party of Hungary, the Communist Party of India, the Communist Party of Estonia, the Communist Party of Ireland, the Workers Party of Ireland, the Communist Party of Iraq, the Communist Party of Kurdistan-Iraq, the Party of Italian Communists, the Communist Refoundation Party of Italy, the Communist Party of Jordan, the Communist Party of Kyrgyzstan, the Madagascar's Congress Party for the Independence, the Socialist Party of Latvia, the Communist Party of Lebanon, the Socialist Party of Lithuania, the Communist Party of Luxembourg, the Communist Party of Malta, the Communist Party of Mexico, the New Communist Party of Netherland, the Communist Party of Norway, the Communist Party of Kazakhstan, the Communist Party of Pakistan, the People's Party of Palestine, the Communist Party of Palestine, the Communist Party of Paraguay, the Peruvian Communist Party, the Communist Party of Peru (Patria Roja), the Communist Party of Poland, the Communist Party of Philippines–1930, the Communist Party of Portugal, the Communist Party of Romania, the Communist Party of Belarus, the Communist Party of the Russian Federation, the Russian Communist Workers' Party – Communist Revolutionary Party, the Communist Party of the Soviet Union, the Communist Party Alliance–the Communist Party of the Soviet Union, the Party of Communists of Serbia, the New Communist Party of Yugoslavia, the Communist Party of Spain, the Communist Party of the Peoples of Spain, the Left Wing Alliance of Spain, the Party of Communists of Catalonian, the South African Communist Party, the Communist Party of Sri Lanka, the Communist Party of Slovakia, the Communist Party of Sudan, the Communist Party of Syria (Bakdash faction), the Communist Party of Syria (Faisel faction), the Communist Party of Syria (United), the Communist Party of Sweden, the Communist Party of Turkey, the Turkey's Party of Labor, the Communist Party of Ukraine, the Union of Communists of Ukraine, the Communist Party of Venezuela, the Communist Party of United States of America, the Communist Party of Tajikistan, the Communist Party of Uruguay, and the Communist Party of Chile, etc. Some other communist parties and workers parties unable to participate in the meeting have also sent their congratulations messages.

The themes of the International Meeting of Communist and Workers' Parties have been different each year. They cover a wide range of significant topics, including important current events or significant theories and historical problems, such as anti-imperialism, capitalist economy, globalization, socialism, the status and role of the communist parties, trade union movement. To be more specific, the theme of the 1999 meeting was "Capitalist Economic Crisis, Globalization and Reaction of the Labor Movement"; in 2000, "Experiences of Strengthening Alliance and Unity of the Contemporary Communist Parties"; in 2001, "Communist Movement and Trade Union Movement"; in 2002, "New Situations of the World after the "9/11" terror attacks; in 2003, "Anti-war, Anti-Capitalist Global Movement and Communists"; in 2004, "Anti-imperialist Struggle and Communism".

In 2005, "Development Trend of the Current Capitalism: Economic, Political, Social Influence and Choice of the Communist Party"; in 2006, "Crisis and Opportunities Offered by the International Situation, Strategies of y Imperialism and the Energy Problem, People's War, Socialist Experiences of Latin America and Prospect of Socialism"; in 2007, "90th Anniversary of the October Revolution: Pertinence and Validity of Ideal, Communists' Anti-Capitalist Struggle for Socialism"; in 2008, "New Phenomena in the International Situation, Aggravated Contradictions between Democracy, Society, Environment and Imperialism, Struggle for Peace, Democracy, Sovereignty, Progress and Socialism, and Joint Action of Communist and Workers Parties"; in 2009, "International Capitalist Crisis, Struggle of Laborers and People, Alternative Solutions, Function of the Communist Party and the Working Class Movement"; in 2010, "Aggravating Crisis of the Capitalist System, the World Communists' Anti-imperialism Struggle for Sovereignty, Cooperation, Peace, Progress and Socialism"; in 2011, "Socialism is the Future."

III. Theoretical propositions and Practical Activities of the International Meeting of Communist and Workers' Parties

Theoretical propositions of the "International Meeting"

Though topics of each meeting are different, they have mainly covered the themes and issues, such as capitalism, socialism and changes regarding communist parties. Looking at the speeches and resolutions of the previous meetings, we might summarize its main theoretical perspectives as follows:

Firstly, its views on the age we are passing through.

Most parties of the "Meeting" believe that the world is now in the process of transiting from capitalism to socialism, which is determined by the dialectical motion between productive forces and productive relations. The basic contradiction of capitalism determines that capitalism will inevitably be replaced by socialism eventually. The parties of the "Meeting" have also pointed out that the drastic changes that occurred in the Soviet Union and

Eastern Europe cannot change the historical course and trend of social development, because "the final victory of the socialism-communism society conforms to the law historical development, and the social course will not be affected by a singular event in history".

Secondly, its opinions on the new changes that have occurred within capitalism.

The parties of the "Meeting" generally believe that with the rapid development of the third technological revolution and revolution of productive forces, the capitalist economy, politics, culture and society have encountered profound changes. Developed capitalist countries are still in their highest and latest stage of capitalism—stage of imperialism. They are still transiting from state monopoly capitalism to international monopoly capitalism, and attempt to establish a barbaric, reactionary international imperialist system. The globalization, which is the globalization of capitalism in essence, is a process to establish an imperialist "new world order". In the last hundred years capitalism has enhanced its self-regulating and self-renewal ability, and tries to entrap the labor movement into the framework of capitalist order. It is the basic contradiction of capitalism that has caused current international financial crisis and debt crisis. The offensive that was started by imperialists and their so-called "bailout plans" and "austerity measures" by the capitalist governments all aim to shift the burdens of crisis over the shoulder of peoples of other countries. The decline of the western "welfare state" policies also indicates the plight of the capitalist governance. And the only way out is to overthrow the existing power system through joint action. The so called "human rights" "anti-terrorism" "disappearance of the working class" propagandas are only excuses for defending the rationality of capitalism and the imperialist aggression.

Thirdly, evaluation of the contemporary world socialist movement.

The parties of the "Meeting" believe that the world socialist movement is marching forward positively by accumulating experiences and lessons, and that socialism has made indelible contributions to people's struggles for peace, liberation, unity and progress. The reasons for the drastic changes in the Soviet Union and Eastern Europe have occurred due to are manifold complicated factors—internal, external, theoretical or practical, and also including the counterrevolutionary reform process of Gorbachev since 1985. But the collapse of the Soviet Union is not the failure of socialism, instead it has been a failure of a specific historical pattern of socialist construction. This historical pattern has lacked certain essential features of socialism, this pattern has even contradicted certain features of socialism. The existing socialist countries, like Vietnam, North Korea, Cuba, Laos and China, are carrying out reforms consistent with their national conditions. Thus the superiority and vitality of socialism are gradually manifested in these countries, which will be manifested more clearly as the history moves forward. The paths for developing socialism can be diversified, this diversity is inevitable, and different countries should independently explore a socialist development path suitable for their own national conditions. In labor movement and people's struggles, communist parties and workers parties should play their roles, enhance ideological propaganda, adjust strategies and tactics based on realities, employ all possible struggle forms and should fight for democracy and socialism. In the international communist movement, the struggles for national and social liberation and the socialist movement are unified. We should establish the broadest international social alliances, and alliances of workers which belong to different parties so as to fight against imperialism and monopoly capitalists, establish the international political alliance of world's all communist parties, and adopt joint action to oppose capitalism, imperialism, all kind of opportunisms and reformism.

Fourthly, ideas on the establishment of new kind of Marxist workers parties.

The parties of the "Meeting" believe that under the new circumstances, the establishment of a new type of Marxist workers party will determine the future of the socialist revolution and construction. At present, the objective of party building is to improve the fighting capacity and leadership skills of the communist and workers parties. In practice, innovative methods should be adopted to carry out the party building, in the current new circumstances. Firstly, the guidance of Marxism must be insisted on so as to enhance the ideological education of the party members. Secondly, the social and class basis of the party should be broadened and strengthened, and the proportion of young party members and female party members should be increased. Thirdly, the cultivation and training of the party leaders should be emphasized, so that the new leaders working at the grass-roots level will be improved through the practices at grassroots level. Fourthly, the links between the party and the people should be enhanced; the party should increase its contact with the labor unions, youth organization, women's and students' organization. Fifthly, bilateral and multilateral communications between parties of different countries should be strengthened.

Practical activities under the leadership of the "International Meeting"

(1) Activities to defend socialist movement and labor movement. For example, activity to commemorate the 60th anniversary of the world anti-fascist war was held on 9 May 2005, joint activity to commemorate the 90th anniversary of the October Movement was held on 7 November 2007.

(2) Activities to support righteous struggle of people around the world. For example, 29 November has been fixed as the day to support the struggle of the Palestinians. The parties of the "Meeting" have demanded for several times to release the five Cuban patriots and demanded that they should returned back to Cuba.

(3) Launching assemblies and demonstration activities to oppose capitalism and its machine. For example, when NATO held the summit in Lisbon in 2010, communist parties of many countries, such as Greece and Portugal, held large-scale demonstrations. The 13th session of the "Meeting", which was held in 2011, agreed to organize large-scale assemblies and demonstrations during the NATO Summit in Chicago in 2012. The parties of the "Meeting" has made numerous statements to denounce the Iraq War and the Libya War started by imperialism.

(4) Launch different kinds activities to support the labor movements in order to oppose the rule of the bourgeoisie and oppose the exploitation of monopoly capital.

Such activities became more frequent after the capitalist economic crisis in 2008. The annual meetings held after the year 2008 all reviewed the situation of the labor movement led by the communist and workers parties and issued resolutions to enhance international cooperation. It is worth mentioning that under the influence of the meeting, the Greek labor movement led by the Communist Party of Greece has become the vanguard of the European labor movement. The 13th session of the International Meeting of Communist and Workers' Parties passed the resolution to support the class struggle of the Greek working class and expressed tributes to the Communist Party of Greece and the Greek working class. In the evening when the 13th session of the "Meeting" came to an end, member parties participating the "Meeting" took part in the 43rd day of the strike organized by the iron workers of Greece. Each state sent a representative of the communist and workers parties to deliver a speech to the workers on strike, expressing their support for the strike of the Greek iron workers.

(5) Launch all kinds of environmental protection activities. The Delhi Declaration, which was published on the 11th session of the "Meeting" in 2009, pointed out the major responsibilities of the capitalist system with regard to the present environmental crisis problems; the South African Communist Party suggested to hold a "Meeting" on the issue of "Climate Justice" in 2012.

IV. Principles, Characteristics and Nature of the International Meeting of Communist and Workers' Parties

Principles of the meeting

(1) Independence. The parties have the right to participate or not participate in the meeting, and they have the right to sign or not sign a resolution. More importantly, they have the right to choose different socialist development paths.

(2) Complete equality. The participant parties, be it from socialist countries or capitalist countries, enjoy equal status regardless of their size. No party has the privilege over the rest. The "Meeting" is held in an equal, democratic and free atmosphere.

(3) Mutual respect. Due to certain historical factors and different development situations, the parties have disputes and disagreements. But all the parties have their respective advantages and disadvantages, strength and shortcomings, experiences and lessons, successes and failures; therefore, they will respect each other in the "Meeting" and seek common basis while reserving differences.

(4) Mutual non-interference into others affairs. The "Meeting" insists that the domestic affairs of each party should be dealt with by itself. No resolutions and statements of the "Meeting" should interfere with the internal affair of any party or any country.

Characteristics of the "International Meeting"

(1) Flexibility. The "Meetings" are organized in a flexible way. It is not an international organization having a centralized leadership, and it has no standing leading organ, nor a fixed Program and constitution. It only sets up a working group so as to maintain the continuity of the "Meeting" and make preparations for the meeting.

(2) The principle of realistic attitude. The themes and topics of all previous meetings are related to the urgent issues of the times. Participant parties have proposed suggestions and expressed opinions with regard to the issue based on their own realities.

(3) Class character. The parties participating in the "Meeting" all belong to the category of Marxist working class parties. They adhere to the socialist ideal and seek interests for the working masses.

(4) Controversial ideas and positions. Due to certain historical factors and different development situations, the parties have different opinions on some issues. They do not have agreement regarding the guidance of Leninist ideology, or how to establish anti-imperialist international front,

or how to evaluate the imperialist organizations, or how to deal with social democratic parties and opportunist trends and parties, especially on the Left party of Europe.

(5) Non-alliance principle is still prevalent. Though some parties have suggested to establish an anti-imperialist international alliance and a stronger political alliance in the international arena, no such suggestions were approved till today.

Nature of the "Meeting"

First of all, the "Meeting" is an international meeting organized by the communist parties of the capitalist countries to struggle for peace, democracy, sovereignty, progress and socialism, and to oppose capitalism, imperialism and monopoly capitalism. This nature is not only manifested by the Marxist nature of the participating parties, but also manifested in the themes and propositions brought forward in the previous sessions. The previous meetings have demonstrated positions on the issues such as international situation, war, capitalist economic crisis, cooperation of the communist parties and socialism, and the meetings have reached the consensus that "socialism is the future" and that "international cooperation and unity of the communist and workers parties should be strengthened" which all demonstrate their theoretical stock.

Secondly, the "Meeting" has been a significant form to promote the development of the world socialist movement by providing an important platform for the world communist and workers parties to enhance communication, and exchange opinions and exchange their working experiences. After the drastic changes in the Soviet Union and Eastern Europe, developing bilateral party-to-party relations had became the major form of communication among the communist and workers parties of different countries. Later the annual "Meeting" has provided a platform for the communist and workers parties all over the world to communicate and contact with each other. Besides, the "Meeting" makes new attempts to enhance the cooperation within the international proletariat and to establish extensive united front. Gradually, the "Meeting" has developed into a new form of unity and cooperation within the world socialist movement.

V. The Communist Party of China and the "Meeting": Harmony in Diversity

The relationship between the Communist Party of China and the International Meeting of Communist and Workers' Parties could be described as "harmony in diversity". Namely, regarding adhering to basic principles, the CPC does not seek agreement and consistency on every issue, but recognize, tolerate and respect the differences so as to achieve common strength. As the observer of the "Meeting", the CPC has participated in the "Meeting" for eight times and has sent low-profile representatives to deliver speeches. We give our full support to the holding of the "Meeting". At the same time, generally the International Meeting of Communist and Workers' Parties recognizes the achievements made by socialism with Chinese characteristics. But, as the ruling party of the world's biggest socialist country, we should make more efforts in promoting the progress of the meeting. Given the current situation, we should first of all become a full member of the "Meeting". Secondly, we should send our important leaders to participate in the "Meeting" and clarify our stance and views. Thirdly, we should apply to host the International Meeting of Communist and Workers' Parties in our country and enhance our communication with the Marxist parties of other countries. Fourthly, we should advocate the establishment of a regular contact and communication mechanism to facilitate the cooperation and unity among the parties.

Y. 52

The Brussels Meetings: The Analysis of the 21st Meeting of the International Communist Seminar[1]

Wang Ximan[2]

Abstract: The recent crisis of the capitalist system is ongoing since four years, imperialism stirs up trouble in every corner of the world, while workers' movement and the struggles by broad masses demonstrate ups and downs with a general upward trend. Under such a complex situation, the 21st International Communist Seminar was held in Brussels as scheduled, with the theme of sharing "experiences on the relation between the immediate tasks of communists and their struggle for socialism" The meeting adopted a series of statements on current issues of the world, and stressed that the communists should use the opportune situation offered by the capitalist economic crisis. The participants exchanged views and experiences on the relation between the immediate tasks of communists and their struggle for socialism. Participants came from Africa, Asia, the Middle East, the Americas and Europe. At sessions devoted to each of the continents, every delegate presented his party's analysis of the capitalist crisis and its consequences in his country, the anti-worker and anti-people austerity measures put in place, the popular protest movement against them, and the party's work and demands in such conditions. Also explained and discussed was each party's understanding of the struggle for an alternative to capitalist society, for socialism. At the very moment the NATO Summit was meeting in Chicago, USA, the Brussels Seminar adopted a resolution saying "no" to NATO and calling for its abolition. There were also Seminar resolutions on solidarity with Cuba, on the situation in the Arab world and particularly in Palestine, and in support of the "no" vote in the referendum in Ireland on the European fiscal treaty, on May 31. Before concluding the three-day Seminar, the participants agreed to meet again from 24 to 26 May 2013, to discuss a related topic: the front and alliance work of communist and workers' parties, both for immediate demands and for longer-term goals.

Key words: International Communist Seminar; urgent task; socialism

---

1   This article is the research fruit of the project titled as "Research on the International Meeting of Communist and Workers' Party in the Contemporary World" sponsored by .the national social sciences fund for the young scholars.
2   Wang Ximan, specially invited researcher in World Socialism Research Center, attached to CASS, Associate Prof. in the Research office of Marxism with Chinese Characteristics, in the College of Marxism, Liaoning University.

The 21st Meeting of the International Communist Seminar was held in Brussels as scheduled between May 18-20, 2012. The seminar has stressed that the urgent task of communists should be to analyze the current crisis of the capitalist system, from a Marxist standpoint and called for active participation in the workers' and people's struggles and stand in the forefront of the fight for socialism.

The International Communist Seminar has become an important event in the development of the world socialist movement. Since 1992, the International Communist Seminar hosted by Workers' Party of Belgium is held in Brussels each year in May with its aim being defending Marxism-Leninism and proletarian internationalism while opposing revisionism. Up to now, about 150 Marxist parties and organizations from the regions of Africa, Latin America, North America, Asia and Europe have participated in this seminar, including the Communist Party of China. Besides, the seminar also established its conference website www.icsbrussels.org and proceedings are published in the quarterly journal titled Studies on Marxism, in French and Dutch since 2000.

I. Background of the 21st International Communist Seminar

The 21st International Communist Seminar has gathered against an extremely complicated, severe backdrop of events and developments.

1. With the constant spread of the current profound and lasting capitalist economic crisis in the world, it is an urgent premise for Marxist working class parties throughout the world to deeply analyze reasons, the essence and development of this crisis when adjusting their strategies.

The subprime crisis in the US burst out in the summer of 2008 and rapidly turned into a worldwide capitalist economic crisis which constantly deteriorated at the end of 2009, causing sovereign debt crises in many developed capitalist countries, among which Portugal, Italy, Ireland, Greece and Spain were hit the most. Besides, the numerous developing countries also had serious problems of economic crisis and sovereign debt crisis. With the capitalist world trapped in economic crisis, we can't help asking these questions like how did this capitalist financial crisis break out and evolve, and how to evaluate the bailout and the austerity policies by the capitalist governments of European Union in particular. We should analyze the future trend of these developments, their influences on the global socialist movement and the ways they can use to play their due roles. Correct answers to these questions have become a significant task faced by the Marxist working class parties throughout the world.

2. With the gradual escalation of the imperialist offensive and aggression, constant local wars and conflicts triggered by them, thus the fight against the imperialist forces has become an important content of the current global socialist movement.

Besides ongoing wars in Afghanistan, Iraq and Libya, imperialist powers have began to stir up troubles in every corner of the world and intervene in the sovereignty of other countries by the way of in "color revolutions and instigate the "Arab Spring".

For example, nowadays Syria and Iran are faced with the threat of violence coached by several western forces and national wars and civil wars are likely to occur. In Latin America, imperialism implements all-around intervention policies, uses threat of force and target the peoples' movement and progressive political forces of the region. At the end of 2010, the Lisbon NATO summit even passed the so-called new the NATO strategy which is titled as "Actively Participate in the Modern Defense". The summit statement said: NATO should remain ready to play an active role in crisis management operations, whenever it is called to act. The new Strategic Concept urges Allies to invest in key capabilities to meet emerging threats and agree to develop within NATO the capabilities necessary to defend against ballistic missile attacks and cyber attacks. "This is an action plan … which sets out clearly the concrete steps NATO will take." "It will put in place an Alliance that is more effective, more engaged and more efficient than ever before."This move in Lisbon has more openly revealed the aggressive character of NATO.

The Chicago NATO summit held in 20-21, May of 2012 has been most prominent summit the largest one in the history of NATO with leaders and representatives from about 60 countries and which also included several international organizations. The Chicago summit has aimed to establish a concrete practical action plan according to the ideas and consensus reached in the Lisbon summit. Meanwhile, inner conflicts and struggles within the Western alliance especially between the EU and US imperialist powers have also become increasingly fierce.

Consequently, current workers' movement and people's struggle both include fights for social, anti-imperialist national, and class liberation on the one hand, and struggles for socialism on the other hand. The struggles for socialism and national and anti-imperialist liberation struggles are inseparable and should be properly combined. To explore proper methods to combine these struggles organically have become a key strategic task and realistic option for the Marxist working class parties of each country.

3. While the struggles by workers' movements and just struggles of the peoples of Europe and the world is surging, it has become an urgent imperative task to provide them a correct leadership In Europe, workers and the masses in the above mentioned five countries—Portugal, Italy, Ireland, Greece and Spain—who were hit the most by sovereign debt crisis have launched huge demonstrations against "austerity" and "bailout" policies of the monopoly capitalist governments. In the USA, the demonstrators of the "Occupy Wall Street" movement who claimed to represent the 99% of the population have s received worldwide attention.

In Middle East and North Africa, there are surging workers' movements and people's struggles against hegemonism and neocolonialism of western developed countries. In Latin America, peoples seeking for justice have launched all kinds of demonstrations and meetings to protest and combat the aggression by the US-imperialism. In Asia, people in countries like Afghanistan, Nepal and Korea have set good examples in fighting against imperialism and hegemonism. However, current workers' movements and peoples' struggles are characterized by loose organization, their class consciousness are, lack clear orientation and mature strategies, besides lack powerful prestigious leaderships and scientific theories suited to their struggle paths.

Therefore, it is an urgent task of current workers' movements and peoples struggles a) to unify thoughts, b) adjust their strategies to suit the current situation, c) reinforce ideological struggles and ideological clarity.

4. It has been 20 years since the occurrence of drastic changes in the Soviet Union and Eastern Europe, while the global crisis of the capitalist system is there for four years. It is of vital importance for Marxist working class parties throughout the world to further summarize and theorize the experiences and lessons of world socialist movement, especially we should summarize and theorize the experiences and lessons of the fights against the recent crisis, especially the parties of the countries hit severely by the crisis and which have fought hard, have more chances to do this.

Before the drastic changes in the Soviet Union and Eastern Europe, the forces of socialism showed strength and used to be one of the two major rival forces in the world, with both precious struggle experiences and bitter lessons of failure.

In 1990s the world socialist movement had descended to a lowest level. Nevertheless, after 20 years' of development, the global socialism has achieved a partial revival in certain regions of Asia, Africa and Latin America: the Nepal-Unified Communist Party (Maoist) has ascended to power, Moldova Communist Party and the AKEL-Cyprus Labor People's Progressive Party have gained parliamentary victories.

And in Europe's developed capitalist countries which are hit severely by the crisis, workers' movements and peoples' struggles have seen surging, all these show that world's socialist forces are fighting bravely, although the low tide still prevails.

Therefore, it has become an important task for the Marxist workers' parties throughout the world to learn from the experiences and lessons, and adjust their strategies to the current situation.

II. A Brief Overview on the 21st International Communist Seminar

The 21st International Communist Seminar was attended by 59 communist and workers' parties coming from 49 countries. During the three-day conference, the delegates were frank, open, fraternal and comradely and conducted a series of discussion and exchanged opinions and experiences on the conference topic: "sharing experiences on the relation between the immediate tasks of communists and their struggle for socialism".

In order to help communists living in different countries to better understand the reality of other countries, information and experience exchange sessions were arranged. Delegates communicated with each other and introduced their opinions concerning the current capitalist crisis, its consequences, austerity measures taken by the governments against workers and people, people's movements against those austerity measures and the way Marxist parties conducted their activities under such circumstances. Moreover, each party has also elaborated its understanding of transforming the capitalist society towards socialism and its understanding of fighting for socialism. Finally, the conference passed a statement called "Final Conclusion" signed by the delegates of 40 parties.

After negotiations and discussions, the 21st seminar has passed the following four resolutions:

1. Since the NATO summit was being held in Chicago US, the seminar passed a decision called 'stop NATO, abolish NATO' signed by 43 parties.

The resolution said: On the occasion of the NATO summit of Chicago, we declare our principled opposition to this imperialist alliance, whose continued existence is a threat to world peace and to the rights and the well-being of the workers and the peoples of the world. Over the past years, the US and NATO have waged wars of aggression against Yugoslavia, Iraq, Afghanistan and Libya. Today, they are threatening and planning more militarization, interventions, aggressions and outright wars on all continents, in a context of ever-deepening crisis of the world capitalist system, in an effort to further advance and impose the dominance of monopoly capital.

We, Communist and Workers' Parties present at International Communist Seminar in Brussels, will continue our opposition and mobilization against any and all imperialist interventions and wars. We express our solidarity with all forces that resist imperialist occupation and aggression and defend the sovereignty and independence of their countries. We will continue our struggle to oppose and abolish NATO. By struggling to bring an end to this imperialist alliance, we are contributing to the cause of world peace.

2. With regard to the referendum to be held in Ireland on May 31st 2012 about whether to accept the new financial pact with the EU, the seminar passed a decision titled "vote NO in the Irish referendum" signed by 48 parties.

As is shown in the Ireland resolution, the communist and workers' parties that attended the 21st International Communist Seminar regarded the new financial pact between Ireland and EU as a threat to working people of all countries. The resolution said: "Therefore, we support the act of voting "no" in the May 31st Ireland referendum, which if passed means that people of Ireland and people of other European countries would continue suffering from economic difficulties, which is a new round of savage capitalist offensive against the working classes and the poor of Ireland."

3. The conference passed a resolution concerning problems of the Arab world and Palestine which was signed by 48 parties. The resolution pointed out: "the 21st International Communist Seminar supports the just demands and struggles of the Arab people for freedom, democracy and social justice. The Arab people of relevant countries are concerned to achieve—more than ever—an economy which is able to distribute the produced wealth among all residents rather than, an economy dominated by the monarch, business class and bourgeoisie."

Participants have also opposed to the US-Israel strategy aiming to divide and oppress the Middle East countries and strongly condemned the neo-interventionism pursued by the US imperialism and its NATO allies which targets the Arab countries and stirs up trouble in their domestic affairs.

Meanwhile, they also denounced the land occupation policy of Israel squeezing Palestinians and demanded that it immediately stops its settlement constructions in Palestine lands.

Finally, participants demanded that a fair solution of the Palestine issue, could only be based on establishing a true Palestine state and respecting the right of Palestine refugees, which demand returning back to their motherland.

4. The conference passed the resolution as "Solidarity with Cuba" which was signed by 52 parties. According to the resolution, participants reiterated solidarity unity with Cuba and the Cuban Communist Party. The resolution read: "we call for an immediate end to US's financial, economic and business embargo and blockade targeting the island, the so-called "flexible blockade" policy led by the Obama administration has become unbearable and be immediately stopped. The US should not continue to ignore the demands of the international community which forbids such kind of genocidal policies. The United Nations has already passed 19 resolutions which stipulate that that such sanctions violate the international law. The US president should take fair actions and release those five Cuban patriots imprisoned in America, including Rene Gonzalez who is forced to stay in America for 3 years by the US government, who has actually extended his term of penalty in America. Only solidarity can help our five comrades returning back to their motherland." When it comes to EU, the resolution demanded the following: the EU should abandon its common position with the US and acknowledge the self-determination right of the Cuban people, their right to decide about their future freely without intervention and that of their Socialist Revolution. The current unilateral intervention policy led by the EU towards the island won't hold water. By virtue of their tenacity, courage, unity with most of the exploited and their efforts made to defend their benefit and ideal, Cuba, Communist Party of Cuba and Cuban people have set a good example for the revolutionists throughout the world."

At the end of the seminar, participants unanimously agreed that the 22nd seminar would be held in May 24-26, 2013 with a related topic being 'the front and alliance work of communist and workers' parties—for current demands and long-term goals". Later the topic was changed as: "The attacks on democratic rights and freedom in the world capitalist crisis. Strategies and actions in response"

III. Main ideas of the 21st International Communist Seminar

This seminar held discussions centering on the topic "sharing experiences on the relation between the immediate tasks of communists and their struggle for socialism" and arrived at the following ideas in a general consensus.

The overall crisis of capitalism opens the path to socialism

The primary task of current communists throughout the world is to grasp the nature of the crisis obsessing the entire global capitalist system for the past 4 years. At present, the most important ideological task is to conduct Marxist analysis on the essence of the capitalist crisis. The significance of Marxist criticism lies in helping workers and people of all countries to figure out the root causes of global economic disasters and reveal the relationship between all sorts of capitalist offensive and the savage capitalist system, thus make them clearly grasp the root source leading to numerous problems like the food crisis, ecological and environmental problems, aggressive wars, gap between the rich and the poor, crisis of the bourgeois ideology and bourgeois parliamentary system.

To have a Marxist analysis on the capitalist crisis, we should insist that the current crisis is a systemic crisis of the capitalist system, and admit that we are going through a crisis of relative over-production and excessive accumulation of capital. The so-called financial bubble is just a reflection of this crisis in the field of circulation, and once these financial bubbles blow up, then the contradiction between the actual purchasing power of the poor and the over-production will become even sharper. The Marxist analysis apparently differs from the analysis which evaluates the current crisis as "financial defect" or a "debt crisis". Instead, just as Marx put it, the root cause behind every capitalist crisis, lies in the contradiction between socialized nature of production and private ownership of the means of production.

We must fight against the so-called exit strategy which judges the capitalist system as intact and fleckless. The various measures implemented by the bourgeoisie to tackle the crisis, in fact aim to restore the profit margins of the capital and aims to rescue themselves, by victimizing and harming their competitors and workers.

In the crisis conditions social democratic governments once again proved their role as a faithful manager of capitalism and a major attacker against the people. Failure of all those policies adopted by the bourgeoisie governments have caused public turn to extreme nationalism, xenophobia, religious fundamentalism and neo-fascism. The bourgeoisie made use of these reactionary political tendencies, racial and religious conflicts to conceal antagonistic class contradictions, while imperialists have taken advantage of them to expand their sphere of influences, history of the 1930s has proved this fact. Therefore, the communist party and the workers' party should unite and rally around common beliefs, that is, by learning from the past lessons, they should rebuild socialist faith so as to liberate workers and people from exploitation and suffering. The left-wing reformism advocates that Keynesianism can alleviate the problems of the market economy and prevent crises and exploitation, which all means fooling the public.

The planned economy based on public ownership of the means of production is the only inevitable way to create an economy which can satisfy needs of people and maintain sustainable development of nature (ecology) and economy. Doom of imperialism and the victory of socialism are the premise of establishing sustainable peace among the peoples of the world but also the prerequisite of building an international order without domination and exploitation. The current crisis of capitalism has sparked a new hope for socialism, but winning new battles in the socialism struggle depends on the vanguard role of communist party and the workers' parties, i.e. their persuasion and organizational successes.

Participate in and lead workers' and peoples' struggles

The crisis of the capitalist system creates new opportunities for communist and workers' parties to lead the people in their struggles for socialism, but the socialist ideology cannot spontaneously become subjective belief of people. The mission of communist and workers' parties, is to take their realistic position and circumstances into account in their countries, and correctly judge the level of organization and consciousness of the working class and people, the balance of contrasting class and political forces, in order to figure out the proper means to improve and strengthen their subjective consciousness, accordingly mobilize and organize them.

Besides, the counter-revolutionary subversion of socialism in the Soviet Union and Eastern Europe has caused confusion in the general public and is utilized by the world bourgeoisie to defame the image of socialism. The current overall crisis of capitalism has crisis has broken the above anti-communist propaganda.

It will greatly conductive to the development of class consciousness, to evoke the masses through their struggle practices and raise their sense of struggle.

The goals of struggles should reflect the actual demands of workers and their families such as employment, wage increase, social rights, public services, education, medical care, retirement, housing and higher living standards etc., which can prevent them from excessive exploitation by employers, but these reforms will not change the status of the working class as wage slaves.

However, only throughout daily struggles can the communists win the trust of the working people, prove them that they are the most loyal advocates of their general or long-term interests, they are the ones who fight to establish a more favorable balance of power relationship in the struggle against the monopoly capitalist class, thus can prepare and lead the masses for a greater victory, in the ultimate confrontation. Communists should assume vanguard roles in struggles. They, while struggling with right opportunism, should remain vigilant about the disturbances of left opportunism. It is certainly a mistake to disdain the daily struggles for actual demands, there is no insurmountable barrier between economic and political struggles.

Currently, urgent political issues include the launching of anti-imperialist class struggles and opposing violent offensives of imperialism and imperialist interventions, fight against human rights violations arising, therein.

On the other side, problems like unemployment, price hikes, increasingly deteriorating public services, homelessness, etc, initially emerged as economic and social problems. However, if communists and the people treat them as issues of class struggle against imperialism, these economic and social problems can easily become political issues.

Throughout all these struggles, communists should proactively explore the prospect of overturning capitalism through socialist revolution, since only the socialist revolution can rapidly and ever improve the living conditions of the working masses.

Thus, communist and workers' parties should vigorously publicize the solution of seizing power and the strategy of establishing people's power, so as to promote the socialist alternative. This is the true response to the crisis of capitalism and to the capitalism system of exploitation.

Strengthen the influence of communist and workers' parties in the current struggles

We, communist and workers' parties, commit ourselves, to the struggle for socialism, social progress, democratic rights, proletarian internationalism, world peace and environmental protection. When working in labor unions, democratic movements, environmental movement and peace movements, communist and workers' parties should emphasize that, socialism is the only way to achieve social progress, people's democracy, environmental protection and world peace, so as to expanding their influence. Because, as long as the monopoly capitalists control the state, it will be impossible to achieve sustainable reforms in any social sphere of life.

In order to carry out daily struggles and guide them towards socialism, communists should give top priority to working hard in all sorts of organizations of the exploited and labor unions. Labor unions should become the mass organization of the working class in their struggle against capitalists. It is our important strategic task, to establish and strengthen labor unions which uphold the class struggle route, and promote them to expand their influence among the masses of workers.

The current situation is mature enough for establishing an anti-imperialist and anti-monopoly alliance. The goal of this alliance is to defeat all sorts of imperialist intervention and aggression and fight for establishing people's power and the realization of profound, radical and revolutionary changes.

"The 21st International Communist Seminar" has been an important event in the second decade of the 21st century for communist and workers' parties of the world in strengthening their contacts, exchanging opinions and work experiences and has promotes the development of world socialism. This seminar was not only supported by the Marxist working class parties, from all continents, but also responded to the current complex and severe international situation, as well as provided timely guidance for the urgent tasks and struggles faced by the communist and workers' parties all around the world. We believe that as long as the communist and workers' parties of the world adhere to the guidance of Marxism and the socialist ideals, constantly adjust their strategies based on international situations and domestic conditions and continuously strengthen communication and cooperation on the basis of proletarian internationalism spirit, the world socialist movement will gradually elevate to a new situation of unity and cooperation.

Y. 53

For Equality, Democracy, Peace and Socialism[1]
On the 26th Congress of the Communist Party of Israel

Wang Ximan[2] *& Wang Zifeng*[3]

Abstract: The Communist Party of Israel with its 93 year-history, adheres to Marxism-Leninism as its guideline, and socialism as its lofty goal. It is one of the important left-wing forces in Israel and Middle East, and also an important component part of the world socialist movement. Focusing on the theme of "equality, democracy, peace and socialism", the 26th congress of the Communist Party of Israel has analyzed the political and economic situation of the current world, especially the Arab regions. The congress has put forward the major measures and strategies in response to the complex situation, set the major tasks of the Party for the next years, expounded on the direction of development of peace, democracy and socialist movement in Israel.

Key words: the Communist Party of Israel; equality; democracy; peace; socialism

---

1　This article is the research fruit of the project titled as "Research on the International Meeting of Communist and Workers' Party in the Contemporary World" sponsored by the national social sciences fund for the young scholars.
2　Wang Ximan, specially invited researcher in World Socialism Research Center, attached to CASS, Associate Prof. in the Research office of Marxism with Chinese Characteristics, in the College of Marxism, Liaoning University.
3　Wang Zifeng, Specially invited researcher in World Socialism Research Center, attached to CASS, postgraduate student in the College of Marxism, Liaoning University.

The Communist Party of Israel held the opening ceremony of the 26th Congress in Haifa and also held a three-day discussion in Nazareth for during March 15-17, 2012. Apart from several hundred delegates from the Communist Party of Israel, the congress was attended by the representatives from the Palestine liberation organization, Palestine People's Party, Left Party from Germany, the Communist Party of Germany, the Communist Party of Spain, Workers' Party of Belgium, the Communist Party of Italy, the Communist Party of Britain, the Red-Green Alliance from Denmark, the Communist Party of Greece, the Communist Party of Portugal and AKEL, Progressive Party of Working People from Cyprus. The central committee of the Communist Party of Israel submitted to the congress a report titled as "fighting for equality, democracy, peace and socialism". The congress held discussions focusing on various themes, including the current global capitalist economic crisis, changes within Israel capitalism, the situation in the Arab world and relevant struggles of people, the situation of the Israel working class and the activities of the Party among the working class, the Party's struggles to realize justice and lasting peace, to defend democracy and curb fascism, struggles for the equality of Arab minorities in Israel, struggle against Jewish Zionism and its goal of "21st century socialism".

I. The global capitalist economic crisis and changes within Israel capitalism

According to the 26th Congress of the Communist Party of Israel, the global crisis which originated in the USA has quickly spread to all core capitalist countries and even to their peripheries. Given the fact that capitalist class always strives to reduce the labor cost, especially in this era of globalization. In such circumstances, the contradiction between overproduction and workers' impoverishment is increasingly sharpening, including in these core capitalist countries. The current economic crisis of capitalism erodes democracy, the historical achievements of the working class and the achievements of world peace.

With the constant increasing of wealth and power in the hands of a handful of capitalist groups called the "tycoons" of Israel, capitalist economy and politics of Israel are further militarized.

Military expenditures of Israel has risen to about 1/2 of its national budget. And in addition to the yearly military expenditures, government realizes huge amount of extra military expenditures The wars launched, almost regularly, in every several years by consume huge sums of funds. For example, cost of Gaza war and financial losses it has caused during December 2008 to January 2009 has reached up to 5.5 billion Israel shekel (about 1.432 billion dollar). And the cost of the second Lebanon war, in the summer of 2006 has reached 30 billion Israel shekel (about 7.811 billion dollar).

Since 1985, the Israel government has formulated many economic policies to support the big capitalist groups. The government also implemented privileged tax policies to favor these capitalist groups, and has tried every mean to marginalize labor unions to serve their interests, reducing unemployment pays, reducing public subsistence allowances of the front-line workers and especially women workers, and also promoted flexible labor and temporary workers, lowered the wages and reversed the labor laws. The current economic plan aiming to "promote the free market reforms" actually serves the capitalists, thus won the support of all parties in the governing coalition. The natural result of the increasingly concentrated capital is no other than social inequality and constant expansion of poverty. In 2000, the inequality of the Israel economy ranked second among the OECD countries only next to USA. In 2010, one quarter of Israel population was living below the poverty line. During those eight years ranging from 2002 to 2010, the number of poverty-stricken children increased have from 20% to 36% while the poverty rate among of Arab families has increased from 18% to 20% and from 49.5% to 57% respectively.

In recent years, Israel labor unions have sprung up and strikes broke out one after another such as the 2010 lawyer strike in the public sector, the 2011 workers' strike and doctors' strike in the field of public health for the purpose of improving the employment environment.

During these labor struggles, the Communist Party of Israel provided workers with the creeds of social class struggle, and demanded higher wager and better work environment for them. The Party emphasized: "currently, we should also offer the working class a more profound understanding of the capitalist exploitation system and essence of the bourgeois state. Over the past ten years, the Communist Party of Israel played an even more important role in some political problems and in the struggles for democracy. However, the Party is not satisfied with the level of party and labor union activities among workers.

II. Political situation of the world and Middle East

The Communist Party of Israel believes that the political situation in the past several years has been quite turbulent.

As for the entire world situation, social and political protests have occurred everywhere in 2011

After the "Arab Spring" since December 2010, a wave of social anger swept the region including Israel. Protestors and demonstrators took the streets and squares in countries all around the world, workers, women and the youth showed their anger against capitalism and the austerity policies by governments, which meant shifting the burden of economic crisis over the shoulders of peoples. In the beginning giant corporations and governments, especially those in the US, were quite hesitant about those protests, but they soon dispatched armed policemen to violently suppress the protests, on the other side western governments have strengthened their military activities and interventions in Middle East and North Africa, concurrently. At present, in the Arab world, the imperialist forces have started coaching and manipulating some local forces even reactionary forces including fundamentalists, to utilize struggles of people for democracy and social justice into a direction favorable to their interests.

In terms of political situation in Middle East, the Communist Party of Israel has especially pinpointed to the destructive activities of imperialism led by the US in Middle East.

The Communist Party of Israel has declared: In Israel, we support human rights and seek to overthrow the tyrannical regime that abuses human rights and civil rights, and replaced by an advanced democratic government. Since December 2010, social and democratic movements of peoples have began to shake the Arab world which have been the most unique and significant event in the recent decades." The party report added: the so-called democracy and freedom, human rights advertised by the US and its allies including Israel are quite hypocritical, in fact their presence in the region damages the democracy and freedom. Actually, historically they are the obstacles of democratic revolutions in the Middle East and hindered the realization of democracy and human rights in the Arab world, which is demonstrated in their attitudes regarding Palestine, Iraq, Lebanon, Afghanistan, Yemen and Libya. The same applies to their current attitude towards Syria."

The Communist Party of Israel believes that the surging protests Arab people, have profound social class and political sources, neoliberal policies followed by the governments is the true cause behind the worsening poverty, high unemployment rates and oppression and increasing corruption within Arab countries. With the help of multinational corporations, capitalist powers have already transformed the countries like Egypt and Tunisia into a heaven of capital and foreign capitalist investors, thus these countries have become a hell for workers and vast social classes including the middle class. The US aims to strengthen its control over the reactionary regimes in the region, whose class basis are local big capitalists and the landlord class who rely on global capital.

The phenomenon that the parties supported by Islamic movements has surged and gained majority in the general elections of Sudan, Tunisia and Egypt indicates that the Arab countries are undergoing a religious wave of Islamic revivalism which is nurtured by people's indignation.

With regard to the current Syria crisis, the Communist Party of Israel, has warned the people towards the humanitarian disasters caused by upgrading violent civil wars in Syria and the Party rejects direct or indirect military interventions by imperialist forces.

The Communist Party of Israel has criticized the attitudes and efforts by certain members of the Arab League Union, Turkey, the US, NATO and the Israel government, to surrender Syria to the hegemony of the US led western countries. Imperialism supports and will continue to support the hated tyrant governments in the Middle East, and imperialists' aim of overthrowing the tyrant Syrian government will not liberate Syrian people from oppression, transform it to another foothold of imperialism in the Middle East. The Communist Party of Israel favors the just demands of the Syrian people, opposes to tyranny and supports the fights for democracy, freedom and social progress, but rejects any act of intervention into Syria's domestic affairs.

The Communist Party of Israel has often stressed that its fundamental standpoint is to fight against imperialism, hand in hand with the Arab peoples. To respond to Arab people's opposition and anger, the Communist Party of Israel has even revised its slogan as: fighting against imperialism and affiliated regime implementing tyranny together with the Arab people, it salutes people on their continuous struggle against imperialist and Zionist intervention, and for free and just Lebanon and Syria.

The situation in Israel proper as well as in the Palestinian Occupied Territories is grave. As far as the occupation is concerned, Israel colonization of the territories is not only going on under the auspices of USA and its financial and political support, but actually only getting deeper and crueler. Natural resources like water and land are regularly robbed by Israeli Zionist authorities for the sake of Jewish settlers; Palestinians' freedom of movement, worship and assembly are strictly limited; peaceful demonstrators and non-violent protesters are often arrested, beaten, and occasionally even shot; and trees, fields and other assets owned by Palestinians are burnt and damaged on a daily basis by Jewish settlers, while Israeli soldiers and other officials ignore that fascist vandalism, as if we were talking about KKK in Alabama under George Wallace.

III. Political situation in Israel

When evaluating the political situation in Israel, the Communist Party of Israel emphasizes the importance of striving for the equality of Arab minorities in Israel.

According to the report presented to the Congress: Arab population keeps growing in Israel, but their situation is deteriorating, racist-ethnic discrimination is obvious, therefore, fights for the equal rights of the Arab minority has become particularly important, by the mid-2011, the Arab minority in Israel—except the Palestinians of East Jerusalem and Syrian Arabs living around the Golan Heights Syrian Arabs, has reached 1.33 million people, accounting for the 17.7% of the Israel the population."

In comparison, in 2001 the Arab population in Israel was only 957.000. In 2000, the unemployment rate among the Arab population was two times more than that among the Jews. In the third quarter of 2011, Israel's unemployment rate was 5.7% while the same rate among the Arabs was between 13-15%. Actually, since Israel state was founded, the bourgeois democracy has kept declining, which finds its main expression in the lack of a democratic constitution and constant promotion of the fundamentalist Zionist ideology and promotion of all sorts of discriminatory ideologies targeting Arab minorities. Recently, the Zionist fundamentalism under the cloak of so-called New Zionism is promoted whose core opinion defends the Israeli occupation of Palestine lands and supports new Israeli settlements in over these lands, denies the rights of Arab citizens of Israel, propagates xenophobia and justifies use of violence against Arabs. Therefore, actually the Israel's political regime is one with limited democracy, which often uses armed police forces, infringes the current laws of the constitution when implementing an all-around discrimination against Arabs. In particular, since the Netanyahu government established in 2009, the government passed a series of discriminatory and anti-democratic laws and decrees and a number of Arab celebrities and intellectuals including Mohammad Barakeh an Arab, serving in the Political Bureau of the Communist Party of Israel, were arrested.

The party organ wrote on the discriminative legislation: "the racist bill, supported by most Likud ministers as well as all Israel Beitenu, Shas and Ha Bayit Ha Yehudi ministers, and opposed by Labor ministers as well as Likud members Dan Meridor, Michael Eitan and Benny Begin, has drawn sharp criticism amongst civil rights organizations and in the Arab public. "[Demanding] an oath of allegiance from non-Jewish naturalizing citizens is opposed to democratic principles", said the Association for Civil Rights in its response. "The formula of the oath presented by the government in itself undermines the bases of democracy in Israel", said ACRI in its letter to Netanyahu. ACRI called upon the government to oppose the bill, to stop its de-legitimization of the Arab minority in Israel and to act immediately upon its obligation to ensure equality for all citizens of the state." "The solution proposed by our party remains the most practical and applicable solution, despite the settlements, the killings, the Apartheid Wall, the political, social and economic persecution of the Palestinian people, and the theft of Palestinian resources such as water and land. This solution is the "Two State" solution, based on the borders on June 4, 1967, with East Jerusalem as the Palestinian capital, and a just solution for the refugees according to the resolutions of International Law."[4]

Disappointment with the peace process, existential anxieties, and a sense of uncertainty about the future have wrought major changes in Israel's political life. After the failure of Camp David and the outbreak of the second intifada, the left-of-center political parties began a sharp decline. The presence of the once powerful Labor Party was reduced to only 13 of the Knesset's 120 seats in the 2009 elections, and that of the Meretz Party, to Labor's left, to just three. Liberal and left-wing non-parliamentary movements such as Peace Now are virtually silent, and civil and human rights activists commonly face accusations of treason.

The solution proposed by our party remains the most practical and applicable solution, despite the settlements, the killings, the Apartheid Wall, the political, social and economic persecution of the Palestinian people, and the theft of Palestinian resources such as water and land. This solution is the "Two State" solution, based on the borders on June 4th, 1967, with East Jerusalem as the Palestinian capital, and a just solution for the refugees according to the resolutions of International Law.

The Communist Party of Israel has been the first party to put forward the policy of equal rights for the Palestinians after the founding of the Israel state, defended that their national minority rights should be stipulated in the constitution, as one part of Arab minorities. Currently, the Communist Party of Israel advocates the 2-State solution for the Palestinian issue, it has launched many campaigns against oppression and discrimination towards minorities and advocated that Jews should ally with Arabs in democratic struggles.

---

4   The majority of Palestinians (51%) and Israelis (58.5%) support a two-state solution to the Israeli-Palestinian conflict. So reports the new Palestinian-Israeli Pulse: A Joint Poll published on Monday, August 22, by the Israel Democracy Institute and the Palestinian Center for Policy and Survey Research in Ramallah. The poll, which surveyed 1,270 Palestinians and 1,184 Israelis, focused on the public's views on a permanent peace agreement, the ability to trust and compromise with the other side, and mistrust and fear of the other. See the web of the Communist Party of Israel http://maki.org.il/en/?p=98

The Communist Party of Israel believes that only by evaluating the current problems of Arabs as a part of Israel's democratic development, expanding human rights and strengthening struggles for equality will be the correct strategy to solve their ethnic-democratic issues. Therefore, the interest of Arab minority is at large common with Jews in eliminating the threat of fascism and developing the democracy.

A unique experience of the Communist Party of Israel in the past several decades: "Mass popular actions" strategy

The Party has successfully carried out the "mass popular actions" strategy among Arabs and Jews in the past several decades, which is unique for the Communist Party of Israel.

Strictly speaking, the "mass popular actions" strategy refers to putting forward common slogans and promoting joint struggles of the working class and other progressive forces, namely the Communist Party of Israel has worked in conjunction with all patriotic political and popular movements to broaden the struggle.

An example has been the historical victory of Nazareth front in 1975. And also, during the 2008 Tel Aviv municipals election, the party proposed the campaign slogan of the "common city for everyone and all Israeli people including Arabs", the call won tens of thousands of votes, got the support of many sot young people, thus defeating McCarthyism and anti-communist propaganda of the right wing forces.

In the summer of 2011, a huge wave of social protest once again swept Israel with its participants consisting of the middle class, low waged employees, the general public, mothers, students and almost all workers. At the very beginning, the protests mainly targeted the rising housing costs and rents, but it gradually developed into a social protest in just one week. On September 3, 2011, the protests reached a climax with the massive assembly of masses with 500.000 participants which had not only put forward many specific economic demands but also shouted slogans against neo-liberalism and social gaps, privatization and social and public level inequalities caused by neo-liberalism.

The Communist Party of Israel and Hadash[5] also came up with the slogan "people demand social justice" and distributed thousands of leaflets which said: "if the government continues to oppose its people, then people will oppose and rebel against the government." Besides, the leaflets said: "Netanyahu government is serving corporate giants and tycoons rather than serving people's interests, we called for a genuine political change."

The militants of the Communist Party of Israel also organized protests in the Arab neighborhoods and in the districts where Arabs and Jews lived together, in order to promote joint struggles of Arabs and Jews. The Communist Party of Israel believes that Arabs participating in the joint struggles has a double meaning: firstly, it is a strong blow against the discriminatory policies of the Israel government, because Arabs suffer from poor housing or lack houses and from social welfare cuts, the poverty rate among them being twice higher than the national average, thus participation by Arabs demonstrates their extreme discontent and resistance against discriminatory policies of the Israel government. Secondly, Arabs' participation in social struggles is a strong blow against the right-wing political forces which try hard to exclude Arabs from the social and political stage of Israel. Besides, their participation also manifest that they are an indispensable part of Israel's democratization process. Although, struggles against capitalism have weakened in the first decade, the social protests that occurred in the summer of 2011 has indicated that, those progressive forces which participated the protests have not only opposed the rule of neoliberal capitalism, but also opposed the fascist tendencies of the Israel government. Although the entire Israel society feels suffocated by the circumstances of the geopolitical deadlock and erosion of democracy, the 2011 protests have strongly proved that there are social forces in the society advocating progressive changes revolution in Israel and the protests have also paved the way for breaking such suffocation.

---

5 Hadash – (the Democratic Front for Peace and Equality) was established in 1977. The aim of its founders was simple: to unite most of the supporters for peace, equality, democracy and workers' rights, Jews and Arabs, in order to create a political alternative to the government's policy of occupation and exploitation. Activists from the main protest movements of the time—the Land Day Protest against expropriation, and the Black Panthers Protest against discrimination; as well as adherents of different peace movements and academics, joined in the establishment of Hadash. The basic principles of Hadash as a broad leftist movement included the unique demand for the evacuation of all the territories which were occupied in June 1967 and the establishment of a Palestinian state alongside Israel—a claim that other movements began supporting only in later years. The principles stressed subjects such as workers' rights, social justice, opposition to privatization, democratic liberties and human rights, equality for the Arab minority, ethnic groups, women, the protection of the environment and the disarmament of mass destruction weapons.

The Communist Party of Israel has also analyzed the recent situation Palestine-Israel conflict

According to the Communist Party of Israel, Netanyahu's party Likud and its partners in the governing coalition regarded the domination or hegemony of the US in Middle East as the guarantee for Israel to permanently occupy territories of Palestine, increase new Jewish settlements and prevent the formation of a Palestinian state, alongside Israel—based on the territories and border lines set on June 4, 1967. During the past few years, the US and Israel colluded to prevent Palestine from entering the United Nations as a formal state and abandon the possibility of peaceful solution of the Palestine-Israel conflict. 2011 was the peak year of Jewish settlements in the West Bank and East Jerusalem. The policies of the Netanyahu government chose to undermine all the potential opportunities for peace, between Palestine and Israel and rejected the war-like situation in the Middle East, which also meant an attack on the Israeli democracy. Since the 1967 war, the occupation of Palestinian territories has eroded Israeli democracy just like cancer cell. This right-wing government of the Jewish settlers has tried all means to strengthen domestic oppression, trampled on the principle of equality and freedom of speech and even set up large-scale concentration camps for Arabs. Besides, numerous right-wing forces and the right-wing government also tried to brainwash the citizens with the massive propaganda of "Israel is faced with a survival threat".

Therefore, the Communist Party of Israel has stressed that on the one hand it should take a path of lasting peace so as to oppose to the permanent occupation policy of the Israel government which it believes to be the barrier of peace between Israel and Palestine and peace between Israel and Arabs in the Middle East, which is also the major reason for the erosion of democracy and pervasive racism. The Israel government made use of permanent occupation and wars it entailed to constantly erodes the rights of Arabs through reverse legislation, expropriating land and demolishing houses.

On the other hand, it infringes Palestinian people's right to self-determination. The Communist Party of Israel defines people's right to self-determination as both the Palestinian people's right to self-determination, and their founding a sovereign state, and the recognition of Jewish people's right to self-determination.

The Communist Party of Israel has always emphasized that Israel is not a sole and exclusive state of the Jews, but a secular state where both the majority Jews and a great number of Arab minorities should be equally represented. As a result, the Communist Party of Israel demands the elimination of all forms of discrimination against Arabs, acknowledges civil rights of Arab minorities in Israel.

Thereafter, the Communist Party of Israel put forward the following plans of peace between Palestine and Israel. Firstly, peace is built on the basis of Israel ending its occupation over all Arab territories it plundered through aggressive wars since 1967 and respecting the sovereignty of Israel, Palestinians and Arabs under peaceful and secure circumstances. Secondly, Arabs in Palestine will achieve the self-determination right and establish a sovereign state, alongside Israel on the West Bank of River Jordan, the Gaza Strip and the East Jerusalem. Thirdly, the problem of refugees in Palestine should be solved in accordance with the United Nations resolution under the framework of peaceful negotiation between Israel and Palestine. Fourthly, Israel should withdraw from the East Jerusalem it occupied and the independent Palestine will own its sovereignty. Based on willingness of people of two countries, the West Jerusalem will serve as the capital of Israel while the East Jerusalem will become the capital of the independent Palestine. The peace agreement will cover the entire Jerusalem and ensure cooperation of the West and the East in the field of municipal administration and a free access to this religious holy land. Fifthly, all Jewish settlements in the occupied area will be demolished. Sixthly, the Golan Heights will be returned back to Syria. Seventhly, Israel should withdraw from Lebanon. Eighthly, the peace agreement will be produced on the basis of peaceful coexistence and not interfering in internal affairs of other countries. Each side will declare cease of war and respect sovereignty and territorial integrity of all nations, including Israel and the independent Palestine. Besides, each side has the right to live within an organized and secure national border without threat of violence. Ninthly, the Middle East should be de-nuclearized and then clear away weapons of mass destruction including chemical and biological weapons. Israel will sign the international nuclear non-proliferation treaty.

The Communist Party of Israel stressed that in order to realize the peace plan, it is necessary for Jews and Arabs to launch protests against occupation and wars doing damage to Palestinian people and Israel people and to strive for international solidarity. Under the guidance of these principles, the Communist Party of Israel will try all possible means to consolidate the peaceful camp of Israel. Israel and Palestine are the same in that fate of people of two countries is based on getting rid of occupation and establishing everlasting peace which is conducive to mobilizing the general public to resist against discrimination and racism and fight for equality and social justice.

IV. Current tasks of the Communist Party of Israel

The Communist Party of Israel identifies itself as a revolutionary and international party of both Jews and Arabs under the guidance of Marxism-Leninism, and a party striving for justice and peace, a party fighting for democracy, equality and social justice and as a party that adheres to the goal of socialism. This identification indicates the essence of the party and its standpoint is demonstrated in its unique standpoint towards the Israeli politics. Against the backdrop of people's increasing distrust towards the capitalism system, mobilization of hundreds of thousands of people led by the banner of social justice, worsening international isolation, violence and occupation policies, Israel communists, Jews and Arabs are undertaking great responsibilities.

In the following several years, urgent tasks of the Communist Party of Israel were set as follows. Firstly, make great efforts to strengthen the Communist Party of Israel and expand its activities among workers, youngsters in particular so as to promote development of the Israel communist youth league. Secondly, make stronger efforts to boost cooperation among all democratic forces in the struggles against the Israeli fascist tendency and set up a more extensive anti-fascist front so as to stop the extreme right-wing forces. Thirdly, the left-wing parties and forces of Israel, should gather and rally around a clear, definite political agenda, go beyond ideological divergences, and consolidate solidarity and friendly relations.

Main content of the political program put forward by the Communist Party of Israel is as follows: the 2-state solution should abide by the borders set up on June 4, 1967; we should oppose to occupation, Jewish settlements and wars; advocate complete equality for the Israeli Arabs; promote partnership between Jews and Arabs; oppose to all sorts of racial segregation; fight for environmental and social progress and genuine equality of women. Fourthly, continue efforts to unite Arabs in Israel and launch the democratic struggle against discrimination, racism, demolishing of houses and expropriation of Arab lands so as to ultimately, realize equality of all citizens and minorities. Fifthly, promote the friendship between Jews and Arabs in state institutions and institutions involving parties and promote such friendly relations in the Israel society as a whole. Sixthly, deepen ideological and political education of party members and spread Marxism-Leninism among the youth, women and the general public. Seventhly, expand the number of Israeli Communist Party members. Eighthly, overcome the organizational shortcomings in the Party work, inspire party members' sense of responsibility and strengthen the unity among the party organizations, especially the unity and coordination, between grass-root organizations, local organizations and the central organizations. Ninthly, enhance the influence of the Communist Party of Israel in public consciousness. Tenthly, make full preparation for the coming congress of the Labor Unions Confederation, the 19th Parliamentary and Municipality elections.

V. Socialism for the 21st century

The Communist Party of Israel believes that neither the ideal of socialism nor socialism itself hasn't come to an end. This truth is determined by the social realities of the 21st century.

Ever since disintegration of the Soviet Union and the upheaval in Eastern Europe, the bourgeois parties have tried to convince people that revolutionary changes in the world have become impossible.

But, even today the world-shaking Russian revolution still continues to inspire the people who have a firm belief in Marxism. Obviously, the disastrous social realities of the 21st century like the widening social and economic inequalities, sufferings, poverty, wars, commercialization of interpersonal relationship, commercialization social safety services and destruction of ecological climate conditions determine that the world is in need of revolutionary changes. As we can see from the historical experience of the 20th century, genuine revolutionary changes aim to achieve that the entire world operates in a better and more democratic way. Even in the current Israel, the socialist ideals haven't disappeared in the public opinion. With the deteriorating economic inequality caused by the rapid capitalist globalization and frequent occurrence of social and ecological disasters, more and more people seek an alternative social system which could replace capitalism.

Moreover, the Communist Party of Israel also pointed out that socialism can be realized in diversified ways and any country shouldn't just blindly copy the pattern of other countries, but should constantly innovate and develop socialism according to changes in the situation.

Even though some changes have taken place in capitalism and even though there occurred changes in the historical conditions, yet communists and other people equipped with the ideals of democracy and socialism have successfully found ways for progress and reform.

The experiences since the mid-19th century, tells us that there is more than one way forward to promote profound changes in democracy and society, and that there can't be any socialist development mode that can be applied to the progress of all countries.

Every communist and each national democratic movement must base itself on the national conditions and international situation of his country into account before determining the way to unite victims of capitalism so as to achieve the regime change, and they should seek the truth on the following problems:

To what extend can the bourgeois democracy, such as the universal suffrage can be used in uniting forces, build strength and promote political changes? What should be the central goal of the current political struggles? What will be the content of the next level of struggle, to achieve the just society of workers?

The Communist Party of Israel thinks that the revolution under its leadership should be carried out under the conditions of the twenty-first century, within which new social movements have emerged, the Party should utilize the new struggle means by the new century.

Therefore, the essence of problem is how to combine the socialist ideology with the realities of Israel so as to create the forces for the socialist transformation. The party congress declared: our urgent task now is to organically combine all social movements, such as the movement against Jewish occupation and for peace, movement fighting for social and national equality of Arab minorities, the movement striving for democracy and freedom, movement fighting for women's equality and the movement against imperialism, thus lead the oppressed people onto the development path of socialism.

Y. 54

The 17th and 18th Meetings of the Sao Paulo Forum and the Development and Consolidation of the Latin American Left Forces

Xu Shicheng[1]

Abstract: The Sao Paulo Forum (FSP) has experienced the course of 22-year development since its establishment. The foundation and growth of FSP have played an important positive role in its rise, development and consolidation of the Latin American Left wings. The Sao Paulo Forum is the most important forum of the Left wing parties and organizations of Latin America and world. The annual meeting of the Sao Paulo Forum is a significant gathering of the Left wing parties of Latin America and world. In 2011 and 2012 the 17th meeting and the 18th meeting of the Sao Paulo Forum took place in Nicaragua and Venezuela respectively.

Key words: Sao Paulo Forum; the 17th and the 18th meetings; Brazilian Workers' Party; Latin American Left wings

---

1 Xu Shihao, executive director at the World Socialism Research Centre, attached to CASS, researcher at the Institute of Latin America.

The Sao Paulo Forum (FSP) which is a coordinating organization of the left- wing parties and organizations of Latin America has experienced the course of 22-year development since its establishment. The foundation and growth of FSP have played an important positive role, and has affected the rise, development and consolidation of the left-wing forces in Latin America and has led to great changes in the political pattern of Latin America. The Sao Paulo Forum is the most important forum of the left-wing parties and organizations of Latin America and world. The annual meetings of the Sao Paulo Forum are a significant gathering of the left-wing parties of Latin America and world. In 2011 and 2012 the 17th meeting and the 18th meeting of the Sao Paulo Forum took place in Nicaragua and Venezuela respectively. This paper will mainly introduce the recent conditions of these two conferences and development and consolidation of left-wing parties in Latin America.

I. Development course of the Sao Paulo Forum (FSP)

As the most representative and influential coordination and consultation and negotiation organization of Latin America, which includes the overwhelming majority of the left-wing parties and organizations of Latin America. FSP was founded in early June of 1990 by Brazil Labor Party with great support from left-wing parties and organizations of Latin America including the Cuba Communist Party. In the period, from the late 1980s to the early 1990s, the world socialist movement was at a low ebb as a result of the collapse of Soviet Union and Eastern European socialist countries, numerous left-wing parties and organizations in Latin America were at a loss both ideologically and theoretically, thus there occurred an urgent need of a platform for discussion so as to pinpoint and grasp the new political direction.

Meanwhile, with the rapid development of capitalist globalization especially the development of neoliberal globalization has exerted negative influences on developing countries including those Latin American countries.

These negative developments, have triggered the critique of capitalism by the left-wing parties and organizations of Latin America, re-consider the socialist alternative and seek alternative solutions against neo-liberalism. Under such circumstances, the left-wing parties and organizations of Latin America have begun to seek new forms of solidarity and cooperation. In early June 1990, the left-wing parties and organizations of Latin America held the first assembly in St. Paulo, Brazil and have discussed on the significant economic, social and political problems of the world and Latin America and about how to deal with the offensive of neo-liberalism., and this conference has reached consensus on the issues of the situation and prospects of Latin America.

The purposes of the Sao Paulo Forum include opposing the capitalist globalization and neo-liberalism, advocating legal and proper struggles to replace the existing irrational and unreasonable international order and support struggles for democratic future and a benign global governance. Sao Paulo Forum is characterized by a wide-range of participant forces and parties, advocates democratic and free forms of organization and also generates radical and open propositions. In the second meeting held in Mexico in 1991, the left-wing parties and organizations of Latin America, formally named their annual meeting as the Sao Paulo Forum. Since the third meeting held in the capital city of Nicaragua-Managua in1992, in addition to the left-wing parties and organizations of Latin America, the FSP also invited communists and representatives of the left-wing parties and organizations of other regions to attend the meeting as observers.

II.The 17th meeting of the Forum held in Managua

Between 17-21 May, 2011, the 17th meeting of the FSP convened in the capital city of Nicaragua-Managua, and 640 representatives coming from 48 parties and organizations of 21 Latin America and Caribbean and 33 specially invited delegates of 29 parties from 15 Asian, African and European countries participated the FSP meeting. The Nicaraguan president Ortega attended the opening ceremony and delivered a speech. Besides, people present at the meeting also included chairman of the Cuban National People's Congress Alarcon, the former Brazil president Lula and Maduro, the foreign affairs minister of Venezuela. The meeting passed a basic document and a final statement.[2]

The basic document consists of four chapters whose content are as follows: According to the first chapter, development of the Sao Paulo Forum can be divided into three stages. Stage one (1990-1997), oppose to neo-liberalism and seek alternative solutions. Stage two (1998-2009), numerous Latin American left-wing parties as members of the Sao Paulo Forum have won victories in general elections and ascended to power. The third stage (2010-) is not over yet, during which capitalism is faced by a global crisis and the world hegemony of the USA was shaken. Besides, in this period, imperialism and the right-wing forces of Latin America began to conduct counterattack.

---

2 For full text of the basic document and the final statement, please refer to http://foro-desaopaulo.org/?p =531.

At this last stage, the member parties of the Sao Paulo Forum are faced with the following challenges:

1) to maintain the conquered spaces, especially our status as governments,

2) keep fighting to defeat the right-wing forces they rule,

3) to deepen the changes and reforms where we govern,

4) accelerate the process of unity, solidarity and regional integration,

5) defeat the counterattack of imperialism and the right-wing forces,

6) support social struggles

7) to advance in finding a political and peaceful solution for the situations of Honduras and Colombia

8) expand the debate aiming to find alternatives to neo-liberalism and capitalism,

9) to make a qualitative leap in the organic functioning of the São Paulo Forum

10) to expand dialogue, integration, cooperation and unity of action among Latin American and Caribbean left-wing forces;

11) to expand the capacity of the Latin American and Caribbean left-wing forces to elaborate (theoretical analysis, program, strategy, tactics, specific themes), in particular by adopting a propositional attitude in relation to the central and most outstanding issues.

The document highlighted that the FSP should follow the two basic principles, namely the spirit of solidarity and the significance of respecting different opinions and views of various parties.

The second chapter of this document has analyzed the current situation in the world and especially that of Latin America and Caribbean region.

The third chapter has analyzed the challenge spheres faced by the left-wing forces of the Latin America as follows:

A) the cultural, ideological, theoretical, educational and communication fields;

B) the field of social struggles;

C) the field of electoral struggles;

D) the field of parliamentary action;

E) the field of governments;

F) the fields where we oppose to right-wing and neo-liberal governments;

G) the field of integration process;

H) the field of strategy debates.

The fourth chapter has mainly discussed about the necessary organizational changes in the organs of the FSP.

The fourth chapter has pointed out that the operation of the FSP must be improved qualitatively. Only in this way can it consolidate the dialogue, integration, cooperation and unity of action between the left-wing forces of Latin America and the Caribbean region and enhance the ability of conducting theoretical analysis on the issues of the left-wing forces of Latin America and the Caribbean region, thus formulating strategies and solutions to specific problems.

III. The 18th meeting of the Forum held in Caracas

Between 4-6 July, 2012, the 18th meeting of the forum took place in the capital city of Venezuela-Caracas for the first time. More than 800 representatives coming from over 50 countries and 100 parties and members throughout five continents attended the meeting. In attendance were representatives of practically all of the FSP's member organizations, including El Salvador's FMLN, Nicaragua's Sandinistas, Guatemala's URNG (all three of them former guerrilla groups), the Cuban Communist Party, Ecuador's Alianza PAIS, Uruguay's Frente Amplio, Bolivia's Movement Toward Socialism and the Puerto Rico Socialist Front, as well as leftist and socialist political parties from countries like Mexico, Costa Rica, Panama, Dominican Republic, Haiti, Barbados and Argentina. The Venezuelan president Chavez hosted the closing ceremony and delivered a speech.

The theme of this meeting was "the challenges faced by left-wing forces of the Latin America in terms of political and economic integration" and its slogan has been is uniting people throughout the world to fight against neo-liberalism and for peace.

The meeting was divided into 14 special discussion groups on the following topics: defense and security, descendants of black Africans, democratization of information, environmental protection, climate changes, immigration, social movement, aborigines, food safety and drugs raid.

Before and during the formal meeting, it held a series of activities, including the 3rd youth meeting, the 1st women meeting and a seminar on peace, national sovereignty and the issue of decolonization.

On the opening ceremony of June 4th, Valter Pomar, executive secretary of the forum and a leader of the Brazil Labor Party, has pointed out: "this meeting has gathered together the great majority of the pro-people's democracy, anti-neoliberal, socialist, communist and patriotic, left-wing parties in Latin America and the Caribbean region. Therefore, it is not just an assembly of the left-wing forces of Latin America, but of the global left-wing forces".

Ramon Balaguer, secretary at the secretariat of the central committee of the Cuban Communist Party and the head of the international relations department of the Party, and Falcon the Chairman of Brazil's Labor Party also gave a speech in the opening ceremony. Roman Balaguer stressed: "socialism is the only alternative to substitute neo-liberalism, today Venezuela under the guidance of Chavez is a pioneer in global patriotism, revolutions and international struggles".

The meeting screened a video greeting by Lula who was former president of Brazil and the founder of FSP. He said: "Mr Chavez, thanks for what you've done for Latin America. Your triumph is our triumph. Only under your guidance can the Venezuela people make significant achievement.' He also stressed: "at the time when our Labor Party (PT) proposed to establish the SPF in 1990, Cuba was the only country in Latin America which was led by a left-wing party, and people could hardly imagine that, in just 20 years the left-wing parties would come to power in so many countries like Venezuela, Ecuador, Bolivia, Nicaragua and Brazil and so many new reforms taking place in Latin America."

The Venezuela president Chavez who had just had a medical operation 9 days ago has attended the closing ceremony on June 6th and delivered a speech.[3]

Chavez, called on the world's left-wing parties, organizations and social movements to carry on changing the world with the perspective of democratic left-wing and also emphasized: "the victory of the Venezuela revolution was closely related to support of revolutionary governments in Latin American and the support of Bolivarian Alliance for the Americas and the South American Union of Nations. In Venezuela we will win the general elections of October 7th which will be a historical struggle helping Venezuela's transition to a new world." He also emphasized that his re-election on October 7th, would allow the continuation of the revolution in Venezuela, and put forward the 2013-2019 national plan for Venezuela (election program) whose goal was to ensure Venezuela's transition to socialism. Chavez stressed: "Latin America should unite together to fight against imperialism, consolidate the new system which will replace capitalism and march on the path of socialism".

The meeting passed the document of "Caracas Declaration" (Statement for short) and the appeal to the peoples all around world uniting together to support Venezuela.[4]

---

3 For the abstract of Chavez's speech, please see http://www.avn.info.ve/contenido/ch%C3%A1vez-se-est%C3%A1-ganando-batalla-hist%C3%B3rica-transici%C3%B3n-al-mundo-nuevo.
4 For full text of the declaration published in the 18th meeting of FSP, please see http://alainet.org/active/56298.

The statement was made up of 41 points. It stressed that this meeting was held against the backdrop of severe structural crisis of capitalism and the current global economic crisis was far from being over. Latin America and Caribbean region is no exception. Thanks to efforts made by Latin American progressive and left-wing forces, "endless long night of neo-liberalism" has been reversed to a certain extent. The statement also pointed out that imperialism and right-wing forces of Latin America have tried all possible means to fight against the growth of progressive and left-wing forces of Latin America, such as the recent two "coup d'état" attempts and the mutiny of policemen in Bolivia; "coup d'état" attempts of Venezuela in 2002; and the "coup d'état" of Honduras in 2009 to overthrow the legal government led by Celaya; "coup d'état" attempt of Ecuador in 2010; "coup d'état" of Paraguay in 2012 to overthrow the legal government led by Fernando Lugo.

And in some Latin American countries, the right-wing forces have made use of media and media companies under their control to fight against the ruling left-wing governments, produce instability and challenge democracy and its democratic mechanisms. Besides, the declaration stated that in recent years Latin American progressive forces had won general elections in Brazil, Nicaragua, Argentina and Dominica. The declaration said: Presidents Dilma Rousseff and Cristina Fernández de Kirchner together with President José Mujica, a few days ago decided to suspend the coup government of Paraguay from MERCOSUR until democracy was restored in this country and at the same time approved the incorporation of Venezuela—as a full member—into the most important political and economic bloc in this part of the world". The declaration praised the progress made by the integration organization of ALBA, Andean Community and South American League and the foundation of a joint community between Latin American and Caribbean countries; pointed out that imperialism attempted to promote the Pacific League so as to weaken the integration of Latin American and South America. The statement supported Puerto Rico's struggle for independence, fight against American's blockade of Cuba, supported Paraguay people's struggle, and opposed to recognize the governments which came to power through coups; supported the Haiti people and supported Columbia's peace process with FARC guerilla army; supported the broad front of Guatemala's left-wing forces and struggles of the Honduras people, called on the progressive and the left-wing forces to support the democratic elections in Venezuela and fight against attempts by right-wing forces which aimed to create chaos and instability; called for Latin American people, progressive and left-wing forces to fight against neo-liberalism and struggle to build a peaceful, democratic and just world. At last, the statement suggested that it is possible to have another world, since we are building a socialist world.

IV. Evaluation of the FSP and consolidation and development of left-wing forces in Latin America

With a history of 22 years, the FSP has become such influential as to be the most important forum of left-wing parties and organizations in Latin America and world. The annual meetings of the FSP has already become an important meeting of Latin America's and world's left-wing parties. When FSP was founded in 1990, Cuba was the only Latin American country which was ruled by a left-wing party, namely the Communist Party of Cuba.

Nowadays, Left wing parties have come to power in more than ten countries such as Venezuela, Brazil, Argentina, Bolivia, Ecuador, Uruguay, Nicaragua, Salvador and Peru etc. FSP has already become a platform of Latin American left-wing parties and organizations to unite, support, communicate and cooperate with each other and a new political platform in Latin America. Development of FSP plays an important center which promotes the growth of Latin American left-wing forces and has brought great changes to the political pattern in Latin America.

Membership of FSP keeps increasing ever since its establishment 22 years ago from only 48 parties and organizations in 1990 to 84 parties at present. Among those parties and organizations, there are communist parties, who adhere to Marxism, like the Communist Party of Cuba, Argentina, Bolivia and Brazil, many Latin American left-wing nationalist parties such as the Brazil's Labor Party, Mexico Democratic Revolutionary Party, the Sandinista National Liberation Front in Nicaragua and the Uruguay broad front, some new left-wing parties that have just been found like the Venezuela Unified Socialist Party, the Ecuador Sovereign State Party and the MAS (Movement towards Socialism) in Bolivia, as well as some legal parties evolving from former guerilla movements such as the Guatemala National Revolution Union and the Farabundo Marti National Liberation Front in San Salvador Those parties joining the FSP like Mexico Democratic Revolutionary Party, the Sandinista National Liberation Front of Nicaragua and the Uruguay Broad Front are also members of the Socialist International. Other parties such as the Brazil Labor Party, the Communist Party of Cuba, Mexico Democratic Revolution Party and the Uruguay Broad Front are also members of Permanent Conference of Political Parties of Latin America and the Caribbean.

To seek fundamental political consensus, the FSP used to merely touch upon socialism in all previous basic documents without taking the realization of socialism to be its fundamental slogan or guideline. Nevertheless, there were still many representatives of member parties who kept discussing and exploring socialism and deepened their understanding of socialism through fighting against neo-liberalism.

For example, just as Ernesto Cardenal, the former minister of culture of the Sandinista National Liberation Front of Nicaragua, an advocator of liberation theology trend, put it: "as to the third world and the majority of the poor, capitalism is disastrous and the failure of capitalism is prior to that of socialism. The failure of socialism is only the failure of false socialism rather than the genuine socialism. On the contrary, capitalism that failed is a real one rather than a false one. Socialism failed because it was not realized, while capitalism failed because of its realization"

In spite of different opinions advocated by various Latin American left-wing parties, they are generally constantly exploring socialism in the process of seeking an alternative patterns to neoliberal capitalism.

In addition to the Communist Party of Cuba's adherence and practice of scientific socialism, the Brazil's Labor Party which is the core of the FSP, advocates labor socialism trend, the Unified Socialist party led by Venezuela president Chavez and President Correa who is also the leader of the Ecuador Sovereign Alliance, have together put forward the proposition of 21st century socialism trend, Morales, the leader and president of MAS (Movement towards Socialism) in Bolivia, came up with the idea of "community socialism". All of these ideas can be seen as explorations for an alternative program against neo-liberalism, thus add new contents to the connotation of socialism.

The FSP put forward a series of strategies and suggestions for Latin America's left-wing progressive forces, including how to develop left-wing political forces in Latin America, formulated strategies and plans, accumulating forces to ascend to state power. The fact that the FSP could manage to develop on the basis of extremely diversified politics and ideology and produced some basic political consensus manifests its great vitality. The FSP mainly focuses on parliamentary struggles, i.e. elections and other legal struggles, promoting alternative policies against neo-liberalism and aims to improve the social distribution structure. It has already become a principal political way for member parties of the forum to take part in legal politics and elections.

Latin American left-wing parties and organizations attending the FSP have different views, on certain issues, and it seems to be difficult to unify all those standpoints and opinions. Some radical left-wing parties and organizations hope that the forum would become an organization like the Third International (Communist) or the Socialist International with relatively rigorous organizations and definite political guidelines while some other parties and organizations propose to maintain the current relatively loose mechanism of coordination. The FSP laid emphasis on diversity, debates concerning the common issues without harming each other, coexistence between divergence and unity as well as exchange of experience, coordinate actions and mutual support among parties.

In recent years, among those member parties of the Forum, some parties have ascended to power while some parties became coalition partners in governments. However, there are still some opposition parties. There are significant differences between those left-wing parties which have ascended to power or not. Besides, even among the ruling parties, the Communist Party of Cuba is different from the Brazil's Labor Party in terms of policies. There are also differences in the policies of the Latin American left-wing governments. For example, Cuba and Venezuela explicitly oppose to establish a Free Trade Zone in America, but Nicaragua as a member of the free trade agreement between Central America and the US didn't withdraw from this institute, after the Sandinista National Liberation Front came to power again in early 2007.

Even within the same left-wing parties such as the Brazil's Labor party, there are also differences before and after they ascend to power. Some, Latin American left-wing parties and organizations, members of the FSP, before they ascend to power oppose to economic reforms of neo-liberalism, the establishment of an American Free Trade Area and the recommendations of the International Monetary Fund and the World Bank.

However, after they ascended to power, Latin America's left-wing governments like the Brazil Labor Party Lula and the Rousseff's government in Brazil, often followed some economic policies of neo-liberalism for the sake of stability, but on the other side they have attached great importance to alleviate poverty and resolve social injustice problems. Even, though there are some conflicts between some governments ruled by left-wing parties and the World Bank, they still have to fulfill those commitments made by former right-wing governments. Therefore, hereafter only the course of time will tell whether the FSP could better coordinate standpoints, opinions and actions of Latin American left-wing parties and organizations so as to give full play to its positive role. Since the communist parties of Latin American countries play an important role in the FSP, in addition to those Latin American Nationalist left-wing parties, left-wing political forces that attend the Forum also consist of numerous Marxist parties and organizations. Apart from the Communist Party of Cuba, a lot of Communist Parties in Latin America are members of the FSP.

It is a strategic goal of the FSP and a basic political consensus of member parties to seek an alternative program against neo-liberalism. In its previous meetings, the FSP conducted analysis on the formulation and implementation of strategic plans. Afterwards, it went on to put forward concepts like alternative solutions, alternative model, pattern, alternative strategies, alternative society and alternative order in the proceeding documents, aiming to replace neo-liberalism. Generally speaking, the FSP members believe that the neo-liberalism has failed in Latin America and they seek a more solid unity of Latin American social progressive forces and boycotted the establishment of a Free Trade Zone of America through carrying out parliamentary and extra-parliamentary mass movements.

However, the FSP is just a coordination and consultative organization of the Latin American left-wing parties and organizations, so its influence and function are limited. Development and reform in Latin American countries will mainly depend on proper policies formulated by domestic left-wing parties and organizations based on national specific conditions. Without any central official leading organ, the FSP has an executive secretariat and a working group responsible for organizing meetings, including determining the topic of each meeting, drafting documents and holding meetings twice or three times a year. Its working group is made up of 17 parties and organizations.

Y. 55

Review of the Eleventh Congress of the Communist Party of Turkey:
Forging Socialist Alternative against Reactionary Power and Push Forward Socialism

Yu Weihai[1]

Abstract: In June 2012, the Communist Party of Turkey (TKP) held its 11th National Congress, which analyzed in detail the Turkish ruling class plus the ruling Justice and Development Party (AKP), and the domestic class situation in Turkey. The TKP's 11th National Congress has stated that although the AKP has been ruling Turkey for 10 years and has won substantial support and reputation, the AKP is primarily and more than anything, a bourgeois party, whose position represents the interests of the reactionary capitalist class. On the other side, behind the cover of prosperous AKP rule, various contradictions and crisis are hidden behind. And, the TKP states that the people's social dissatisfaction and discontent has been steadily on the increase, which provides the Party with the best historic opportunities to propagate the socialist revolution, because only socialism can resolve the problems in the capitalist system.

Key words: 11th National Congress of the Communist Party of Turkey; class situation; socialist revolution

---

1 Prof. Yu Weihai, Research Center for Foreign Marxist and Communist Parties, Central China Normal University, Wuhan, China.

The author Prof. Yu Wehai is a guest researcher in the Chinese Academy of Social Sciences Research Center of World Socialism. He is also researcher of the postdoctoral research center of Central China Normal University which is called research center of Marxist Political Parties Abroad.

In 2012 Years, at the 9-10 of June, the convening of the 11 National Congress of the Communist Party in Ankara of Turkey, was attended by more than 600 representatives of the Party General Assembly.[2]

The General Assembly of the TKP made an analysis on the Turkey's Justice and Development Party (AK Party) which rules Turkey since November 2002 after taking office. Justice and Development Party (AK Party) has won victory in three consecutive elections and earned a stable rule without sharing this rule with other political parties.

But on the other side Erdogan's government rule with controversial policies, have triggered widespread concern and certain opposition among the public on the issues of: religion, the Kurds, the international and regional issues and democratization. In the General Assembly of the TKP (Communist Party of Turkey) many contradictions and crises in government policies were analyzed,

From the perspective of the fighting tasks, the General Assembly of TKP in its political resolution has set the task of "overthrowing the reactionary forces and forging the socialist alternative"…"The level of situation in Turkey points to the direction of the socialist power or socialist revolution."

The conference delegates have completed two days of intensive work by electing executive bodies of the Party. Below you will find an outline of the main contents of the General Assembly resolution promulgated in TKP's party congress in June 2012.

I. On the political regime of the ruling class

Any political party or government is the representative of the interests of a particular class or stratum, which is also the case with AKP (Justice and Development Party). The Communist Party of Turkey believes that the AKP is in essence a bourgeois political party, and main ring of the support for AKP is the big and medium-sized capitalist classes of the Turkey. The Communist Party of Turkey has pointed out that although the AKP represents of course rather one part of the capitalist class, namely the (Islamist) green capitalists or the Islamic bourgeoisie) to some extent, AKP never

---

[2] The party encountered 2 splits, in July 2014 and August 2015, consequently there are currently 3 parties, coming from the same communist tradition which was founded in 1978. Decided by a protocol neither can use the name TKP anymore. (The current names are KP, HTKP and TKH)

stands in conflict with the rest of the bourgeois class which have also increased their profits immensely under the AKP rule. The interests of this party and the bourgeois class are essentially coincident. It is precisely because the AKP government implements the neoliberal laisser-faire policy and the policy of unlimited freedom for capital that AKP government is basically welcomed by the whole bourgeois class, which also manifests the reactionary nature of the bourgeoisie. The AKP government of the past ten years has fully reflected the reactionary nature of the bourgeoisie. The cabinet formed by the reactionary AKP government are compatible with the plunder of public resources in the form of financial fund transfers to capitalist class, diminishing labor rights in favor of capital and coincides with the aim of opening up new spaces for bourgeoisie and international monopoly capitalists, support these aims with legal regulations.

The ruling party AKP shows a clearly pro-American line, plus a religious character and implements pro liberal-market policy. The pro-American and religious character of the Second Republic of the AKP is perfectly compatible with its pro-market policy. As a counter-revolutionary formation, AKP's religionization of political and social life is largely embraced and supported by the imperialist power centers as well as by the Turkish bourgeoisie due to the militant bourgeois attitude in question.

İts "reform" efforts such as the introduction of 4+4+4 system in the education system as a comprehensive site of struggle in the coming period is a striking example of how AKP's religious policies overlap with its pro-market policies which coincides with the imperialist policies of the United States in the international and regional scale. Consistent support of the US is not only a result of the passionate backing of AKP to regional projects of imperialism. It is, at the same time, a result of the desire – as a militant bourgeois party – of the AKP for complete removal of barriers to capital and its venture to carry the same militancy to the neighbor regions that are geographically close to Turkey.

The party resolution further stated: the current government takes its power from oppressors and the social support for the government, this power which did not show any sign of diminishing in the last decade, in fact has been increasing as revealed and can be observed in many occasions, and this support continues to feature a broad laborer profile, too.

The resolution said: Thus, our determination in the 10th Congress of our Party, which evaluated that all basic institutions and parties of capital headed towards being adapted to the Second Republic have been completely corroborated, and that all actors within the system, including the subjects like Turkish Armed Forces (TSK) and Republican People's Party (the CHP), which are accredited with a certain extent of resistance, have also taken their places in the new regime (of the Second Republic). Therefore, of course it is extremely important to melt and weaken the supporter base of this party, to rescue those social groups whose interests do not in fact overlap with AKP, particularly the working class, and to win them over to socialism. However, only those who obey AKP and only those who accept (compromise) the Second Republic can approve the idea that supporters of AKP are more convenient and should be prioritized (in order to win to our side) in terms of strengthening the socialist alternative.

After the referendum of September 9th 2010, Communist Party of Turkey has issued a statement, pointing out: "it is still an urgent task to increase the resistance of social groups opposing to AKP and to rescue them from the other options inside the system by attracting them to the organized political struggle." The resolution analyzed: there is a quite broad group, the majority of which consists of laboring classes, which increasingly reacts to AKP, and which is also ready to support a strong and credible socialist alternative. It is almost impossible to redirect the social basis of AKP's support to the left without winning over some parts of this group. The Communist Party of Turkey believes that it is necessary to actively fight to win this part of the population. Any understanding which does not put broad social groups opposing AKP at the center will not serve anything but will help to legitimize the Second Republic

II. The revolutionary forces of Turkey: The Strategy of the Communist Party

The working class

The working class of Turkey is not only the primary force of the socialist revolution in Turkey, but also the most important social assurance (base) to downgrade the current political power.

As a matter of fact, one of the most substantial tasks of the Communist Party of Turkey is to create the conditions and instruments for the working class of Turkey to undertake these historical and current tasks within certain wholeness.

The success of the efforts in this direction primarily depends on making correct realistic evaluations regarding the objectivity (objective status) of the working class of Turkey. In the current situation. Communist Party of Turkey believes that due to the constant weakening of trade union organizations of Turkey, and the decreased efficiency of socialist ideology and politics in the aftermath of the coup d'état of 12 September 1980,all these have undermined the unity of the working class and caused an erosion in the class unity. And the new designs of the capitalist class relating to the organization of production had such a negative impact which has greatly damaged the unity of the working class. Thus the party thinks that the situation of the Turkey's working class is not optimistic. Although being homogenous in terms of their historical interests, the working class of Turkey has structurally become highly heterogeneous. Under these circumstances, the unity of the class can solely (only) be assured on the "political level".

Besides privatization, flexible production, flexible labor, subcontracted work, which are important elements of neoliberal attacks; practices like the liquidation of some industrial sectors, deindustrialization and rapid expansion of service industry, all these have changed the composition, ideological options and cultural habits of the working class. It is impossible to organize the working class by ignoring these realities. "Therefore, in view of these new factors and differences related to the situation of the working class, the party cannot follow the old-fashioned way, we must correctly evaluate the positive aspects of the differentiation among the working class. The Party is in need of developing struggle instruments that each sector of the working class requires, the Party should expand and deepen the political perspective that will carry the working class to unity and avoid the idea that ignores the intra-class richness and thus the Party should fight hard to overcome the problems which are and were created by using the old methods.

Under these conditions, the Congress of the Communist Party of Turkey has decided to develop a model in the organization of workers, which considers the specificity of each sector and especially aims at deepening its work in certain prioritized sectors, and will predicate the leading capacity of the organization upon the workers coming from the field and will plan a complete agenda related with the work among the laboring class. And this work should be attached not to a bureau but directly to the Central Committee.

The resolution said: The (positive) role and limitations of trade unions precisely become evident at this very point of time. The trade union organizations will have crucial roles (only) in a practice that will deeply address the various divisions and differentiation among the working class. Undoubtedly, many trade unions do not bear the characteristics of being struggle organizations with their current positions. Nevertheless, we have to put more effort into the work of increasing the number of party members in the trade unions of all branches if possible, and fight for the conversion of trade unions into class-oriented organizations. During that time, we should avoid those common (vulgar) methods that would level and ignore differences among the class, but aim to find the most appropriate form for each sector with a creative perspective and be brave to develop different instruments in the fields where trade union organizations do not exist or where they are insufficient.

Hence, the fundamental aim for the Communist Party of Turkey in this period is not seeking for the "unity of trade unions" or focusing on setting general principles related to the whole trade union formations, but instead Communist Party of Turkey should vigorously develop the organization of the working class at all branches and should strive to add a political content into this organization.

Since 2011, the Communist Party of Turkey has re-activated its Workers' School. And the resolution says that this school should be converted into one of the most essential organizational instruments of the Party by further summarizing and institutionalizing this Workers' School experience from the point of view of the party's ideology. According to the party's ideology Workers' School offers major opportunities that provide workers to be acquainted with the party and promotes them to be increasingly organized. The Workers' School should also play an educational role so that the proletarian culture can dominate the inner-party life and should enable that those laborers working in heavy conditions will not be distant from the Party works.

The resolution adopted in 11th National Congress of the Communist Party of Turkey added that the Party should approve one each working plan that involves the political and organizational goals of the Party related to the prioritized sectors with regards to the Party work.

Youth

The situation of the youth has become even worse compared to the past years. To make a living or even get married, most of the young workers are forced to shoulder a heavy debt burden, they try hard deal with the risk of unemployment. Besides, the political power (rule), which cuts off the dynamism of the youth and imposes a lifestyle that restricts their freedoms, but political power also faces difficulties in obtaining the intended result. Thus, the youth straddles or vacillates between this above reality and the ideological-cultural values imposed upon them and easily becomes open to new ideas or quests.

The Communist Party of Turkey believes that a considerable part of the youth which will turn into laborers, and a great number of young people that have to work beginning from their early ages should be won towards socialism so that they will reject liberal, religious and nationalist ideologies. More efforts should be mobilized in this regard. Specific instruments have to be developed and particular importance should be given to vocational schools (those related with practical postsecondary education and job training) when trying to organize the young workers, and the party should focus on "youth" activities in the trade unions and vocational education schools.

The TKP believes that "one of the ways of reaching young workers and reducing their concerns of being fired from their jobs is to contact with them in living spaces and localities (communities). Therefore the Party works in the communities will gain more and more importance within the forthcoming period of the Party. Party works should strengthen the youth with cultural and ideological elements against the inputs of the system that are corrupting, individualist, and which alienate them from the life and realities.

The Communist Party of Turkey has decided to increase the amount of party work targeting young university students which would reinforce their reference and pioneering positions of communist students at universities. That needs a further detailed planning in the forthcoming period. Accordingly the party emphasizes to consider the new transformations started in the university organizations of the party this year is the only option to increase the ideological and political impact of socialism.

The courses of socialism in the universities (Socialism Schools) started by the Party in 2012 should be led towards institutionalization. The Communist Party of Turkey hopes that these Socialism Schools should be institutionalized in the way that they would meet the different requirements and should be responsible all the year around—permanently—and these Socialism Schools should become one of the central instruments of the university organization.

The further and direct contribution of the Party members from university students to the theoretical, political and cultural production of the Party should be paid attention and planned carefully because it can accelerate the individual development of students, diminish the risk of formation of castes (closed groups) within the Party and lead up and promote the dynamics of efficient cadre policy.

Women

Despite of the fact that the women occupy a place that cannot be undermined in the society, which led the AKP to power and supported this party in the direction of its (AKP's) intended social and other (reactionary) transformations, it is obvious that a major part of worker and student origin women do not accept the lifestyle imposed on them by the current political regime of AKP. The women as a significant force are coming to the forefront to settle the account with the Second Republic (of the AKP).

Although this refusal by women is still distant from wholeness and remains uncertain in respect of class characteristic, these do not trivialize the importance of their resistance. Besides almost all reactions in different ways to the patriarchal discourse and practices of the reactionary AKP, it is also possible to imbue these reactions of women with a revolutionary political content. The important point here is that the AKP which leads the political power, cannot conceal its intensions to downgrade the position of women in the production process and the scientific-cultural life. The women in Turkey are being forced to change their roles or relinquish some of them. This process can be felt in middle class women who seek for individual ways out and who attempt to create some free living spaces for themselves. However, a considerable part of the women who are under pressure are women with working class and student origin and they are not in such a position as the middle class women, that means they cannot produce individual solutions. The Communist Party of Turkey appreciates, encourages and supports all kinds of opposition against the oppression of women, and regards that the political struggle sphere is the primary field to liberate the women at most. Additionally the party members should not consider this idea of the party as a class reductionist or exceedingly simplified approach. The political struggle in Turkey today will not only radically strengthen the women in their struggle for equality but also will make them more resistant to the hypocritical and reactionary ethical blockade that the women face. Just at this point the Party should abandon such an understanding which deepens the social gender differences, which cuts the links of the women question and attempts to drag the women to a practice of struggle that has a different agenda. Instead, the Party should adopt and develop another approach, that confronts the women with current exploitation system and the ruling political power, thus push them forward in the struggle for socialism. The realization of localization goal of the party and the realization of the needs of the Communist Party of Turkey will largely be the result of politicization of the broad masses of women by the Communist Party of Turkey. The Party should prepare and provide those conditions in which women can undertake much more duty and responsibility in the Party life; and the women organizations of the Party, instead of seeking for an abstract equality, should be made immanent in all works of the Party, the women should be linked to all other resistance pivots (forces in the society). Only in this way can the Party reach its target of localization or socialization. (Mass base)

The women works of the Party must be integrated with the ongoing organizational works among workers, the women works of the Party must also be integrated with other sectors, the university and high school organizations, the organization of Alawite laborers and the organization of culture-art workers.

The Kurdish people

The Communist Party of Turkey thinks that today in Turkey the political channel, to which the equality and freedom demands of the "Kurdish people will flow, remains obscure." The party thinks: the Kurdish political movement, which has a great responsibility in helping AKP's ruling power to become settled and established, also manages to be one of the political forces that raise most grave difficulties for the AK Party (AKP). The causes of this fact is—undoubtedly—not only related with the political culture of the Kurdish political movement but also related with the impossibility of the solution of the Kurdish question under the capitalist conditions. TKP writes: "The political zigzags of the Kurdish political movement towards the American and European imperialism is a phenomenon that should be discussed in an all round manner as well."

The Turkish Communist Party points out that the attitude of Kurdish political movement in the fight against the religionization of the Turkish society also includes a complication or uncertainties namely its policy makes zigzags and vacillates. On the one hand, the Kurdish political movement wants to conserve and defend the results—namely the secular gains—of the Kurdish awakening (enlightenment) on the other hand Kurdish political movement acts with an illusion, thinking that certain "reactionary maneuvers (attempts)"[3] could be a "liberator" for Kurds.

The Communist Party of Turkey refuses being a part of this above unpleasant negative general picture, "in the pretext of defending" the claims of the Kurdish people. It will be an improper political tactic for Turkey's communists (TKP) which tries to impact the Kurdish politics and Kurdish people by being part of this unpleasant picture. It will be an improper political tactic, because of the fact that the Kurdish political movement is not a passive (ineffective) movement which is open to all kinds of outside intervention and secondly that the "the socialist ideology" of the TKP cannot tolerate such a "flexible" (concessionist) attitude. All these means that the political channel, to which the equality and freedom demands of the "Kurdish people will flow, remains obscure."

But, Communist Party of Turkey on the other side, does not believe that the Kurdish political movement has already entered—or will ultimately enter— into an irreversible evil road, that would compromise the Second (reactionary) Republic (the new regime of Turkey). And the Communist Party of Turkey on the other side, does not believe that that the Kurdish political movement is discharging the revolutionary elements within its body. Such an idea would be a very simple one and will lead to political errors. Instead of following such erred ideas and instead of evaluating the Kurdish political movement (Kurdish dynamic) with this or that criterion, the TKP should—in this period—"concentrate on those efforts" that can change the political balances of Turkey, defend the just claims of the Kurdish people from a socialist perspective, develop an explicit attitude towards the oppression

---

3 Ed note: Here with the wording of "reactionary maneuvers (attempts)" the Party resolution means reactionary maneuvers by imperialist powers such as USA and EU plus, those attempts by the political forces in power in Turkey.

against the Kurdish people and Kurdish political movement. But on the other side, the Communist Party of Turkey —should in no way depart from or betray the "independent line of the socialist movement regarding the themes of reaction, liberalism, and imperialism." In any case this independent line should continue to be the principled attitude of the Communist Party of Turkey.

Remaining in this framework and context, TKP targets to establish an explicit, honest and constructive communication and solidarity with the representatives of the Kurdish politics and aims that the organization of the Party among the Kurdish people, particularly in Western regions of Turkey, should be reinforced and channels and instruments to address the Kurdish people's demands should be developed.

The Alawites[4]

The Communist Party of Turkey attaches great importance to the progressive Alevitan movement and the problems of Alawites.

The reactionary AK Party (AKP) has been carrying out an aggressive negative policy towards the Alawites from the very beginning, especially since the imperialist interventions in Arab geography that has gained a new content. In the final analysis, the Alawites have always been seen as a problematical section by the capitalist order forces (regime/ the order front) because of the fact that the Alawites are prone (open) to a culture of resistance and they are open to progressive thoughts in this Arabic geography.

At the same time, the Alawites, who act as an important resisting force against inequality and reaction, will add an immensely significant pro-people value to the revolution in Turkey by reproducing themselves within the axis of labor. TKP, in order to guarantee this positive possibility of winning them to the axis of labor, should aim to add "nonreligious" inputs (nonreligious discourse) to those divisions of ideology and divisions of class that are present among the Alawiten people. The party resolution says: "this very policy constitutes the difference between TKP and others when approaching the Alawiten people".

The Communist Party of Turkey, believes that the Alawismis such a complicated and rich cultural phenomenon that cannot be reduced to an issue of religious sect. That would be a great mistake. On the other side, evaluating Alawism with a supra-class approach, or setting aside inner conflicts or variances and (ideological and political) differences among Alawites,

---

4   Alawites are a certain distinct group living in all regions of Turkey with different beliefs and cultural orientation. There goes on a academic and political discussion whether they are part of Islam or not (Ed. Note). They have some similarities and differences from those similar believers in the Middle East (Arabic and Iran nations) which are called the Shiite community. A part of Alawites belong to Kurdish nationality.

and furthermore supporting those efforts that attempt to institutionalize or organize the Alawiten people as a religious sect and to transform them so that these people become a part obeying the Turkish capitalist system are impossible and unacceptable for the TKP.

TKP, which defends that the religious issues must be separated from politics, cannot be an advocate for any religious belief. However, while TKP defends the freedom of belief and worships the freedom of atheism, it also supports the claims of equality demanded by the Alawiten people.

In this context, a courageous and principled attitude should be developed both on the policies regarding the organization of the Alawites and also related to the policies directly linked with the works of the Party. The efficiency and organization of the Party within the Alawiten laborers should be reinforced in conjunction with the expansion and localization (socialization) targets of the Party.

The Intellectuals

The Communist Party of Turkey believes that it is necessary to correctly view the relation between intellectuals and the working class. TKP points out that the intellectuals are important supporters of the struggle of the working class, and working class must also cultivate their own intellectuals. Therefore, on the one hand, the Communist Party of Turkey must enhance its advanced nature and enhance its creative thinking and there is an urgent need to pay great efforts to improve the socialist struggle of the political research and analysis capability. On the other hand, the party tries to organize the sphere of science, the sphere of culture and art with different instruments.

The Assembly of Socialist Intellectuals, initiated and established by the TKP in the previous years, has attracted great attention and has provided opportunity for respectful scientists, intellectuals, artists and politicians of Turkey to cooperate on a free and productive socialist platform. This unique instrument of the Party should be strengthened. The Association of University Councils, Nazım Hikmet Cultural Center, Nazım Hikmet Academy, and Marxist-Leninist Research Center are the other institutional instruments operating in this field of intellectuals and each of them nurtures the opportunities and issues together that require to be dealt by the Party. The prioritized task of the Communist Party of Turkey in this period is to correlate the advanced thought, promote the theoretical productivity, creative and free art imbued with partisanship. While the intellectual members of the party, themselves have great responsibility in adhering to the partisan intellectual attitude, central organs of the party should also give some leadership to them (intellectuals) so that the mistaken idea of the anti-partisanship is avoided. This anti-partisanship (not taking political sides) attitude (or idea) which regards that those intellectuals who take political sides means that these individuals have quality problems, and this mistaken idea sometimes appears in the communist movement as well. In this context, a radical transformation should be carried out on the goals and organization of theoretical, cultural and artistic works of the Party in the upcoming period. A more clear and revolutionary perspective related to each field should become apparent in the next phases of the Congress process.

Overseas Turkish citizens

The Communist Party of Turkey should reconstruct its work multi-dimensionally related to the citizens of the Republic of Turkey living abroad. This section has not been paid attention centrally in the struggle against capitalism so far. This work among overseas Turkish citizens should simultaneously take into consideration, on the one hand that immigrants living in European countries, partially in Germany should be linked with the struggle in Turkey, on the other hand the party should help them in their struggles against the problems they face in the countries where they live and the party should help them to participate in the class struggles of the host countries Although these two goals are inter-correlated, it is clear that different goals and tools should be developed at each level. The Communist Party of Turkey, for which the opportunities are increasing day by day, will take fast and effective steps in this direction in the forthcoming period and will institute Party representations and sub-organizations in some foreign countries where there are Turkish immigrants. The Party will also take certain measures for the members living in such countries to promote their political development, but TKP thinks that—for its members—carrying out an extensive political work is impossible in these host countries. In any case—for its members—to contribute to the class struggles in those countries and to contribute to the struggle of TKP in Turkey, both of the two are not an easy task for the members.

III. The Conditions and the Strategy of the Socialist Revolution in Turkey

The Communist Party of Turkey, on the basis of the analysis of the major social class relations, has proposed that the rule of the reactionary AKP regime is losing the social foundation of its rule. Although the people still surrender to the ruling class, there are all kinds of other indications that the Turkish society is undergoing a positive change quietly which provides an excellent opportunity for the socialist struggle of Turkey. Therefore, the Communist Party of Turkey decided to take the initiative to organize all kinds of resisting forces in the struggle for socialism.

1. In Turkey, the increasing social discontent, is creating the conditions of the struggle for socialism. Under the AKP government the Turkish economy seems to enjoy great success. AKP, has controlled the effects of the global crisis of capitalism to (Turkey) by depending to the external resources on one hand, on the other hand, the AKP, has developed effective demagogic methods to maintain the credibility of its "economic success" story. But, this "economic success" story has gradually turned into a monstrous lie. Continuation of "external financial support" (hot money), which has so far protected the Turkish economy from a heavy blow (under the world economic crisis conditions) not only depends on Turkish-US relationship, but will also depend on the situation that is created and that will be created by the complex dynamics (developments) of the middle east region.

For a period of time, the growth in Turkey has been created by the plundering of public resources and transferring them to capitalist class. But the debt burden of the poor people of Turkey, who have only benefited a small share of this economic growth is no longer sustainable. Since the unemployment has become a widespread and permanent phenomenon, and since the price inflation has increased to a rate that it is no longer possible to hide it by tricking the statistical figures, all these show that the economy of Turkey has become excessively fragile and show that it is ceasing to be a trump card of the AKP. That means the "economic success" story of the AKP can no more be a trump card for this party.

In fact, it will be impossible to keep and maintain the structural problems of Turkish economy under control. These structural problems are gradually becoming more serious, and after a certain point the incoming hot money (cash follow) "support" will not be able to "cure" these structural problems. There are some people who have been negative against the AKP for ideological and political reasons, but which were previously affected by its discourse of "economic success"; but now these people have started to feel anger against this party. And among those (former voters) supporters of the AKP, the concern and worries for future economic prospects becoming apparent. The new steps and attempts taken by AKP to religionize both the political life and the social life do not receive vast public support at all. On the contrary, these policies lead to frustration and resistance. It is nonsense to think that the cheap success won by the AKP when it transformed the army leadership and the judiciary power (leaders of high judicial organs), which were strategically crucial political issues, will be repeated in other or in every department of the society. Although oppositional sectors have given an unorganized and non-integrated (split) impression till today, the reactions by the people against the interventions to their lifestyle, and Islamic intervention to the cultural and educational policies (spheres) imposed by the AKP are increasing. The fact that these reactions by the public are non-continuous, local and have a weak class characteristic, do not reduce their importance and efficiency. But fighting against the political rule cannot depend on waiting for an economic crisis. The solution is attached to the politicization of the working class, and the leading the reactions in the society to organized status. "More important is that there is no need for a deepening economic crisis, for the toiling masses to situate themselves against the political rule and the exploiter order the political rule represents. Although the AKP government has a powerful voter support, it is extremely weak, and every day it gives such inputs, that politicizes and polarizes various sectors of the society.

Correct handling of the internal contradictions of the bourgeoisie

The internal conflicts of the coalition of reactionism plus liberalism, which has provided the power to AKP to stay in power for ten years, and which has provided the power to AKP to lead the historical transformation, will be one of the most important issues of politics in the upcoming period. These internal conflicts sometimes arise due to different interests among religious sects supporting the AKP, and sometimes due to the problems of sharing the political and economic power, between the leadership cadres of the AKP and a particular religious sect supporting them. And in some cases internal conflicts arise due to frustration by the liberals (on some subjects) due to some political practices of the AKP. Generally the liberals are in the ruling coalition but they sometimes have partial and limited opposition.

The Communist Party of Turkey believes that such conflicts are never unimportant, they cannot be evaluated as being outside the interests of the practice of revolutionary politics as well. Relaxations (weakening) within the internal structure of bourgeois politics and the disintegration signs observable within the block of ruling coalition are not only the signs of weakening of the ruling power. The resolution says: "such developments and the disintegration signs means that we should define new themes in our ideological and political struggle." And such developments and the disintegration signs also means that the working masses are more open to political awareness and political propaganda.

However, from the point of revolutionary politics, putting these internal contradictions of the ruling coalition in the center of our political struggle and siding with one side during these conflicts as the main axis of our political struggle, will be mistaken and will cause fatal results. Today, there is no benefit for the working people, in siding with any party in the division between the AKP and the Turkish Military Forces (The army) as well as siding with any party in the division between the AKP and the CHP (Republican Peoples Party). This applies to the case when there are frictions and divisions between the AKP and those religious sects supporting it or to the case when there are frictions and the divisions between the liberals and religionists (cadres of religious circles or religious communities). The latter case alone has no capacity to change the existing balance of political powers in Turkey.

On the contrary, taking these divisions and frictions as the basis of political struggle should be evaluated as giving help to the deeper establishment of the Second Republic regime. If the left forces ever try to make some discourse inputs to "deepen" these "conflicts", or ever try to take a position in these "imagined" and pseudo political polarizations" , and if the left forces support one of the "conflicting" sides, it will be an unforgivable strategic mistake. Choosing the one side against the other one is a stance that should never be taken, because it will mean helping the capitalist domination to cover its temporary shortcomings, and this mistaken stance will divert the new oppositional quests occurring in the society into the "classical old channels" once again.

"What makes these inner contradictions valuable from the point of revolutionary politics are the new opportunities that they give us for the publicity of the socialist alternative, the new opportunities they give us for the exposition of the system and that the working class can win new progresses in terms of organizational and political aspects. Any problem and frustration occurring within the ruling coalition block undermine the ability of persuasion and the legitimacy of this block. Any problem and frustration occurring within the ruling coalition block cause the system, lose its fighting concentration – albeit temporarily – against the left forces and laborers."

The Communist Party of Turkey must pursue an effective struggle in the society against those trends which invest hope to the cracks occurring in the coalition of liberals and religious reactionaries, this effective struggle is even necessary related to the section of people which is called as those leaning towards the left. But this struggle has to be implemented as the part of whole (integrated) strategy, in which "the socialist alternative" of the TKP vigorously, effects all the weakening points of bourgeois politics. It should not be implemented in a manner which is indifferent to the developments in the bourgeois politics, not be implemented in a sectarian (closed-door) manner or in an expressionist (exaggeratedly) manner.

The Turkish Communist Party proposed to take the initiative and actively organize various resistance forces

The Communist Party of Turkey has pointed out that it cannot spend its time by idly waiting the days when the policies of the AKP become completely bankrupt. AKP is a special party that has undertaken certain historical missions to fulfill and it has been implementing a challenging transformation plan. There is no possibility of this transformation plan to become an established reality of Turkey, there is no possibility that Turkey will accept this outdated old jacket that is planned for it. A struggle strategy must be developed in order to raise and organize the hope among the people, the hope to move forward with patient but quick steps, the hope which seizes every moment and every day as an opportunity to grow. In this context, instead of basing our work and our struggle on "an expected economic deterioration that will awaken the people", we "should develop new propaganda techniques" to win them, we should be aware that already "the facts of the country" are persuasive and convincing enough, if the vanguard party processes these facts in a correct and effective way.

The people will not surrender

The Turkish Communist Party has pointed out that the struggle to win the political power cannot be based on the expectations for the occurrence of an economic crisis. More importantly, there is no need for a deepening economic crisis so that the laborers will be ready to take positions against the political power and so that they will fight against the system of exploitation, this political power represents. Finally, TKP evaluates that the AKP and its government has an extremely weak foundations despite its strong electoral support, therefore every day this party creates some new political inputs (so-called debates) which results in the politicization of different sectors of the society and which results in the polarization of some sectors of the society against this party.

The thesis which suggests that more people have fallen into despair and that they surrender to the ruling political power can convince only those who observe the social life through the aspect of the institutions of the system and from the prism of monopolistic capitalistic media. The number of people who think "something has to be done" against the gloomy practices of the AKP government is not less at all than the number of those people who think "nobody can stop the AKP government."

On the revanchist attacks of the Second Republic regime against the previous historical reality

The problems which have historical sources will never be solved by the Second Republic regime, on the contrary will deteriorate. Our party defends the achievements of Republic established in 1923, we will not allow the revanchist Second Republic regime accuse the former regime's realities freely, and criticize the so-called left supporting its this accusation policy. The common aspect of the 2 regimes is the "so-called bourgeoisie dictatorship", we have an answer against the policy of beautifying itself with the crimes of the past regime: "Only the working class has the capacity of judging bourgeoisie rule."

Considering this fact, Communist Party of Turkey will strengthen the discourse which is political and the discourse which leads to the confrontation of the fighting parties, related to the problems brought about by capital domination; besides put the Party's core perspective of socialist power in every theme of discourse to the central position[5]. This will be the attitude of the party to socialist opportunities, but also the immediate task of the Communist Party of Turkey.

---

5 TKP advocates a Lukàcsian "totalism" discourse and opposes partialist discourse in the political struggle.

PART FIVE

Lessons Drawn from the Collapse of the Soviet Union

Y. 56

Ideological Realm and the Role of Intelligentsia during the Reverse Evolution of the Soviet Union

Zhou Xincheng[1]

Abstract: The ideological realm has been the sally port in the process the "Soviet Evolution". The hostile forces have promoted and manufactured counter-revolutionary public opinions, promoted the negation of the history of the Communist Party of Soviet Union and the Soviet socialist practices as their central agenda, launching an attack against the leaders of the Communist Party of the Soviet Union as the grabbing point, and used the gradual de-ideologization as the method. Meanwhile, the policies of democratization, openness and pluralism (the Glasnost and Perestroika) put forward by Gorbachev has given a green light to hostile forces to further nurture counter-revolutionary public opinions. During the reverse evolution of the Soviet Union, some intellectuals have played notorious roles. The reason they became the grave-diggers of Soviet socialism is closely related with the political atmosphere, the ideological work of CPSU and the international environment of the Soviet Union at that time.

Key words: reverse evolution of Soviet Union; ideology; intelligentsia

---

[1] Zhou Xincheng, a guest researcher in the World Socialism Research Center, attached to CASS, and tutor of doctorate students at the Institute of Marxism of Renmin University of China.

It has been more than 20 years since the disintegration of the Soviet Union and collapse of the Communist Party of Soviet Union, which is the most tragic event in the history of the international communist movement that left us bitter lessons. It is noteworthy that ideological changes centering on the negation of the history of the Communist Party of Soviet Union and the socialist practices of the SU are the precursor of the reverse "evolution" of Soviet Union, during which some intellectuals have played notorious roles.

I. Ideological confusion and changes have been the precursor of reverse "evolution" of Soviet Union with negation of the history of the Communist Party of Soviet Union and the socialist practices of the SU as the core agenda

In socialist countries, hostile forces can only restore capitalism through grabbing state power and paralyzing the ruling communist party, only if the communist party itself is in an ideological disorder and poorly organized, if its combat effectiveness is wakened. Therefore, hostile forces must start from the ideological field. Just as Comrade Mao put it, we must shape public opinions and do ideological work before overthrowing a regime. This rule applies to both for the revolutionary class and the counter-revolutionary class. This objective law has been proved by the disintegration of the Soviet Union and great upheaval Eastern Europe.

Let's look at the ideological situation of Soviet Union in late 1980s. Ligachev, serving as a member and the secretary of the Secretariat Department of the Political Bureaus of the Central Committee of the CPSU at that time, described in its memoirs titled The Mystery of Gorbachev: "since the fall of 1987, many newspapers in the Soviet Union began to distort and slander its history. Articles exposed were just like storms sweeping all tools of public opinions. What ultra-right newspapers tried to describe was not a multidimensional history narration, nor a history with paradoxes—achievements versus failures—but instead just dark stains. According to those articles, the brilliant past of the SU was completely meaningless, and our ancestors had only suffered from torture in this land, thus cutting off the continuity of history. Such kind of unjust, malicious slanderous and false narratives alarmed and irritated the social atmosphere. As a result, people began to target at the Communist Party of Soviet Union, its history which in my opinion is a bitter yet glorious history and finally the people and their memory of history".

How could those anti-communist and anti-socialist fallacies apparently distorting historical facts become the mainstream ideology and control public opinions as a whole in those days? Behind these were the humane and democratic socialist ideological line put forward and implemented by the leading group led by Gorbachev in the Central Committee of the Communist Party of Soviet Union. Shortly after Gorbachev ascended to power, he put forward the so-called slogans of "pluralism in ideology" and "transparence" (the Glasnost and Perestroika) and democratization. The democratization he advocated was democracy without class, without dictatorship over hostile elements and centralized leadership, thus giving a green light for the furious attack by the anti-communist forces. Transparence, meant permitting anti-communist forces to enormously exaggerate those wrong and negative phenomena in the history and reality of Soviet Union. As for pluralization or diversificiation, it was mainly about legalizing the discourse and deeds negating the leadership of communist party and the guiding role of Marxism, which caused and unrestrained ideological freedom for the bourgeois liberalism.

All these guidelines of "democratization", "transparence" and "diversificiation" were like a one-way street in that people were only allowed to propagate anti-communist and anti-socialist discourses rather than being tit for tat. Anti-communist forces were free to launch parades, gatherings and strikes while the CPSU was not allowed to fight back.

Freed by these guidelines, hostile forces could unscrupulously carry out anti-communist and anti-socialist activities while the feet of the CPSU were tied up and could do nothing but suffer from attacks by hostile forces. In his memoirs, Ligachev, in details described an event which bewildering him. "When numerous articles by hostile forces which negated and attacked the history of the Communist Party, the Political Bureau of the Central Committee of the Communist Party of Soviet Union, turned a blind eye to it, without raising any objection. As a response, a prominent intellectual Nina Andreyeva published an article which advocated a practical and realistic analysis on the history of the party. This time, the Political Bureau of the Central Committee, reacted to Nina Andreyeva's article, held meetings which attacked her, initiated "critical articles" to fight back and started an investigation to find out the backstage supporter of her act".

According to Ligachev this was an obvious double standard. On the one hand, the leadership allowed ideological pluralism towards those anti-communist and anti-socialist articles; on the other hand, it initiated investigation and suppressed those rebuttal articles defending socialism. This case obviously reveals the nature of the democratization, transparence and diversification promoted by Gorbachev.

During the collapse of Soviet Union, public opinions manufactured by anti-communist and anti-socialist forces have focused their propaganda to completely negate or even attacked the history of the Communist Party of

Soviet Union and the socialist practices of the Soviet Union. In their opinion, the CPSU was an organization which not just committed mistakes, but it was a criminal organization which led a fascist regime.

The victory of the Great Patriotic War was nothing but a big fascist defeating a tiny fascist aggressor. They regarded the socialist system as a socialism characterized by totalitarian lines, military socialism and bureaucratic despotism, and socialism had brought people nothing but disasters. They even belittled the October Revolution to be a coup initiated by a few gangsters which deviated Russia from its natural path of human civilization, and considered 70-plus years of socialist course, as a historical mistake.

Publicity, advertised farewell to the past and demonization of the past which were the main content of the hostile publicity. Socialist course was blemished as a piece of infamous history that people should reject. Hostile forces completely denied and attacked the history of the Communist Party of Soviet Union and socialist practices of the SU, which aimed to shoot two birds with one bullet.

On the one hand, they openly advocated to end the governance by the Communist Party and chase it from the political arena with such kind of historical nihilism propaganda, and even demanded trialing and suppression of the CPSU. They also explicitly demanded to abandon the socialist system and restoration of the capitalist system. On the other hand, they made use of such publicity to pacify those forces resisting the hostile forces, which made communists believe they belong to a wrong organization and even feel guilty.

They also used such publicity to reduce socialism to a derogatory term, thus depriving people of their trust in socialism. Once this public opinion becomes the mainstream, attack launched by hostile forces on the party and socialism would turn into just actions taken for granted, thus making it hard for people of integrity to defend the party and socialism. When Gorbachev announced his resignation, and the end of the Soviet Union and when Yeltsin banned the CPSU, there were hardly any organized protests within the entire Soviet Union, let alone forceful struggles, which are quite incredible for the Communist Party of the Soviet Union with a 90 years glorious revolutionary tradition and Soviet Union, a world power with a history of 70 years. However, this fact can be easily grasped after getting to know the violent anti-communist and anti-socialist publicity spread in those days, which helps us to better grasp why the western hostile forces regarded ideological work as the primary task to realize the strategy of "peaceful evolution".

Anti-communist and anti-socialist forces initially started from completely negating proletarian revolutionary leaders and as the second step focused on denying the history of the party and socialist history. Evolution of the Soviet Union was not accidental and neither did Gorbachev's foreign policy of "new thinking" was accidental. If we evaluate the origin of political thoughts propagated in the Gorbachev era, they could be traced back to the period of Khrushchev when the evolution of Soviet Union actually began to take root.

Khrushchev set an extremely bad example by completely negating Stalin in his secret report to the 20th Congress of the Communist Party of the Soviet Union in 1956 which had caused severe consequences and triggered anti-communist and anti-socialist waves across the world. In the preceding 30 years, the ideological trend of complete negation of Stalin had always been generally dominant in the party and Soviet Union, which prepared the ideological foundation for Gorbachev to initiate the path of humane and democratic socialism. Upheavals of Soviet Union in 1980s used the sally port of publicity which advocated destroying all related to "Stalinist ideology", completely demonizing the Stalinist pattern and demanded drawing a line with all forms of Stalinism, including "new Stalinism". At that time, Stalin had already been dead for over 30 years, so why was Stalin mercilessly assaulted like this? Apparently, those people did not really aim to target Stalin, but demonize the Communist Party of Soviet Union and the socialist system. Compared with Khrushchev's attacks against Stalin in mid 1950s, the anti-Stalinist wave during the Gorbachev era was so weird as to include slandering means coming from nothing, attack and slander against Lenin and negation of Marx and Engels. They demonized the proletarian revolutionary leaders and labeled Marxism-Leninism as an evil ideology. This publicity, pinpointed that the socialist system and Communist Party led by the thoughts of these revolutionary leaders were not tenable.

It is of great value to notice that the hostile forces, negated and attacked the Communist Party and socialist practices by starting from denying Stalin and Lenin. The lesson we can draw from this fact it is that we must evaluate the history of the communist parties and the history of the socialist countries with a realistic, practical and scientific methodology and be alert against the speeches, articles and works distorting and vilifying proletarian revolutionary leaders and the socialist system, let alone allowing them to spread wantonly.

Those anti-communist and anti-socialist forces have gradually induced the Soviet people to accept their proposition of restoring capitalism system. In addition to complete negation of the CPSU and the socialist practices, hostile forces also strived to publicize the features of their aspirations regarding their model society, and depicted a "wonderful society" in terms of economy, politics and culture after the complete abandonment of the Soviet society.

They seldom directly expressed their intentions and aspirations, instead utilized a strategy of de-politicization and de-ideologization, i.e. they put forward some ambiguous so-called new slogans and concepts, to depreciate the original, scientific and clear-cut concept. With such a strategy of blemishing, they tried to coach the masses towards the evil path, in the absence of vigilance.

Gorbachev's attitude is typical: after he ascended to power in 1983, he was determined to "reform" the country according to his "new principles" and advocated that "both the face and nature of the society" should be completely changed. However, he followed a gradual approach when delivering his ideas and polices, he always tested the reaction of the public, and if the reaction was weak, he marched forward.

For example, regarding politics, he initially insisted on the leadership of the Communist Party and rejected the multi-party system. But later, he held that the multi-party system was not an issue of principle and declared that any provision of the constitution could be amended, including the Article Six which stipulated the leadership of the Communist Party in building socialism. Afterwards, he declared: "we should not indulge in the fair of the devil when discussing the reform of the multi-party system" and finally, he advocated the abolishment of the Article Six and introduction of the Western multi-party system.

Regarding the economic sphere, when talking about the ownership system, in the initial stage he advocated adhering to the public ownership system.

Later, he advocated a mixed economy with diverse components without mentioning the leadership and dominance of the public sector, a step further he advocated de-nationalization of major enterprises.

And finally announced the implementation of privatization, and the eradication of public ownership. As for the economic operating mechanism, initially he only talked about making full use of the commodity-money relationship , then went on to advocate an abstract market economy regardless of the ownership system, and finally declared that the public ownership system was "incompatible with the market economy, thus a market economy based on private ownership is necessary".

Regarding the Ideological sphere, initially, he claimed to remain loyal to the intellectual heritage Marx-Engels-Lenin, and free people from the dogmatic understanding of them", in the second step, he began to criticize : "Marx did not predict the vitality of capitalism" and "Lenin didn't have a complete socialist construction program." And, in the final stage, he announced that "Marxism-Leninism's theory of socialism is out of date and has to be abandoned, and so on."

Some people have argued that Gorbachev's ideas saw a gradual change in the course of time, I will not agree this view, his gradual style regarding ideological issues was a kind of trick and image building and preparation of the public, in fact he has always been consistent in his final goal.

In November 1991, he admitted: "I aimed to change the old system, I came to this conclusion, the moment I ascended to power. Nevertheless, the society was not yet fully prepared, so I might end up accomplishing nothing, if the question of transformation was debated just like this."

This better explains the truth regarding him, after the disintegration of the Soviet Union and collapse of the party, he wrote: "My life's work has been accomplished. I did all that I could, I feel in peace"

To be clear that the reverse evolution of the Soviet Union has started in the ideological field, is a thought-provoking lesson obtained at a painful price.

II. A part of the intelligentsia has played notorious roles, and a specific analysis of their acts is necessary

Guiding ideology of the leading group of the CPSU headed by Gorbachev, namely the humanitarian democratic socialism played a decisive role in the occurrence of the historical event of Soviet Union's collapse and its evolution to capitalism. However, no one can deny that some part of the intellectual group has played notorious roles in the entire evolution process, after all, those books, articles and public opinions were all created by them.

In the Soviet Union, there appeared some intellectuals, their numbers were relatively small, but their effect grew geometrically, who worshipped "freedom, equality, fraternity" of liberalism, who vigorously opposed to the leadership of the Communist Party and viciously attacked the socialist system. They served as the vanguards in attacking the party and socialism and preaching restoration of capitalism. The US scholar David Kotz, an expert on the "reverse evolution" of the Soviet Union drew the conclusion that the intellectual group was one of those three main groups, which fought for the capitalist restoration in the Soviet society. Generally speaking, it is right to say that Soviet intellectual group has played a big role, in the "evolution", but it would not be scientific to say that they were the social class foundation of the capitalist restoration in the Soviet Union.

Because, the intellectual group is never an independent group or class and it is always subordinate to, serves or cheers for a certain class. In a word, intellectuals are just like the hair's relation to the skin. Since it is impossible for the hair to exist and survive separated from the skin, the so-called independent public intellectuals haves never existed in the world.

In essence, the great majority of Soviet Union's intellectuals tended to support the socialist path, and advocated the standpoint of the working class, but we should also admit that there were indeed some intellectuals, in the Soviet Union who were on the side of capitalism, and took part in the fierce struggle between capitalism and socialism, thus became the "pioneer" and advocate of the overthrow of the socialist system.

Then how come that those intellectuals which were educated in the socialist system turn into grave-diggers of Soviet socialism?

In spite of the fact that Soviet Union had already fulfilled the socialist transformation regarding the ownership of production means as early as the mid-1930s and eliminated the economic base of the exploiting class, the historical materialism tell us that, although social being determines the social consciousness, ideology enjoys a relative autonomy. Therefore, bourgeois ideology will not disappear immediately, along with disappearance of its economic base but stubbornly resist and emerge in various fields. There is still a long way to go before completely solving conflicts between two types of ideologies—wrong and right—and the two paths which may become more intense under certain circumstances. More importantly, there were numerous serious failures in the practical work of Soviet Union, which have pushed some intellectuals to the oppose socialism. This is a lesson that we should learn from.

Most of those intellectuals that playing the most notorious role in the collapse of Soviet Union were nurtured since the mid-1950s, some of them were even promoted to leading positions in party and government and in the ideology related departments

The fact that those people who belonged to the intellectuals group actively opposed to communism and socialism and preached capitalism was certainly related to their growing environment and conditions. After the 20thCongress of the Communist Party of the Soviet Union in 1956, Khrushchev put forward a series of revisionist opinions which were not criticized or boycotted within the Communist Party of the Soviet Union but instead kept spreading until they became the dominant ideology. Those opinions completely negated Stalin, which actually paved the way for the attack targeting the history of the party and socialism. The supra-class humanitarian thoughts that were advertised as "for the sake of all people and their happiness" even became the programmatic goal of the party.

The doctrine of "the party for all the people" and "the state for all the people" aimed to negate the doctrine of class struggle and proletarian dictatorship, thus was directly targeted against Marxism. The "nuclear deterrence doctrine" became the theoretical foundation of the idea advocating "interests of all humanity are above all."

These revisionist opinions of Khrushchev were not only the ideological source of Gorbachev's "New Thinking" doctrine but also the pioneer of formal anti-communist and anti-socialism ideology. Khrushchev's secret report delivered at the 20th Congress of the Communist Party of the Soviet Union stirred up chaos and confusion among the party and people, so Marxist ideological education began to exist in name only. It's no exaggeration to say that the Khrushchev period laid an ideological foundation for Soviet Union's later reverse evolution. No wonder there were quite a number of people who rejected Marxism from the bottom of their hearts, since they grew up in an environment dominated by a series of revisionist opinions. It better explains the later phenomenon that, when Gorbachev put forward the "humanitarian and democratic socialism" line, many people just accepted it without any resistance and even actively demanded that it should become the guiding ideology of the party. This was why, they quickly turned to the opposite side of the party and socialism, when Gorbachev advocated "the democratization, transparency and ideological pluralism".

Ever since the mid-1950s, Soviet Union has ignored the education of Marxist outlook on life and Marxist values, and the "official" ideological and political work was trapped in formalism and dogmatism, thus unable to solve practical problems

In Soviet Union, the group of intellectuals was a part of the working class and received much care in the Stalin era. As an important strata in building the socialist society, if they united with workers and farmers and serve the latter whole-heartedly, then they would no doubt become the backbone of socialist construction cause.

However, if they stuck to individualist outlook on life and individualist values, separated themselves from workers and farmers and devoted themselves to private gains, then they might spontaneously tend to liberalism and capitalism, which could make aspire to place them superior to workers and peasants, because capitalism—by virtue of their technological and scientific knowledge—offer them some minor advantages compared to working classes.

Unfortunately, since the mid-1950s, the Communist Party of Soviet Union, began to completely neglect the political and ideological work, which led the intellectuals to the pursuit of individual material interests at the expense of the interests of the great majority, thus many of them have lost their ideals and beliefs. Consequently, these people were prone to be involved in the swirl of capitalism. David Kotz has analyzed the attitude of intellectuals during the upheaval in the SU: "there were real material interests, behind the behavior of some intellectuals, when the opening-up was pushed by Gorbachev, in comparison they found that their colleagues were enjoying much higher living standards in almost all aspects of life in the Western capitalist countries." More importantly, it appeared to them that western scholars and intellectual enjoyed more privileges than the working classes, which is generally true, although often this fact is exaggerated. Intellectuals in Moscow tended to complain that the material life of their western colleagues was slightly better than or basically the same as blue-collar workers, which they thought as an evidence of social injustice. "Intellectuals was effected by such kind of mindset have easily assumed a negative attitude towards socialism, and were fascinated by capitalism".

As for the external international environment, the Western countries implemented the strategy of peaceful evolution towards socialism countries while intelligentsia is the class affected by capitalist ideology the most.

Soviet Union began to build socialism against the backdrop of backward economy and culture surrounded by imperialism. Capitalism still plays a dominant role in the global economy, technological and military spheres while the bourgeois ideology also holds a leading role in the global ideological field. Since mid-1950s, imperialism has initiated the strategy of "peaceful evolution" towards the socialist countries, the most important component of which was the ideological infiltration. Besides, intellectuals group is the strata which has the most frequent contacts with the capitalist world. Under such an international background, it was inevitable that some intellectuals would exist in socialist countries, which worshipped capitalism. However, the problem lies in the fact that after the 20th Congress of the Communist Party of Soviet Union, Soviet Union implemented the doctrine of "three harmonies" with the Western world, and undermined the class struggles in the international sphere, accompanied by the advocate of the so-called "common values of all humankind" and to consider the so-called "common interests of all humankind" which ignored the threat posed by the strategy of "peaceful evolution" of the West, which intensified influence of Western bourgeoisie ideology and western values among the Soviet intellectuals, promoted pro-Western sentiments among them, thus the capitalist path became an alternative ideology in the Soviet Union.

Of course, this doesn't mean that the intellectuals of the socialist countries are bound to oppose socialism. Actually, the majority of the intellectuals in the Soviet Union tended to advocate socialism and only a minority of them served as the pioneers of anti-communism and anti-socialism. But, once this minority was allowed to capture the control of public media outlets and when some of them occupied key positions in the party and government, their negative role in the ideological and political sphere has made evil effects. As we have discussed above, it is very important for us give more care and trust the intellectuals group, at the same time strengthen their ideological and political education, so that they can truly master the Marxist stand, point of view, and Marxist methodology, so that they can develop their proletarian world view, correct outlook on life, and values, foster their bonds with the broad masses of workers and peasants and cultivate affection for the working people among them, which is crucial for them in adhering to the socialist path and doing a good job in building socialism.

Y. 57

Twenty Years Since the Fall of the USSR: Whose Fault? And What to Do?

Yuri Prokofyev[1]

translated by Zhang Shuhua[2]

Abstract: This article represents an eye-witness reflection on the causes of the demise of the USSR and some thoughts about the future course of Russia. The author argues that three groups of people have contributed to the demise of the USSR. The first group is the Soviet Party (CPSU) and political elites who were unable to face the challenges of the times. Some of them have even betrayed. The second group includes the external forces led and manipulated by the United States, who, out of their own political and economic interests, attempted to overthrow the USSR. And the third group refers to those including the intelligentsia, who had little idea about what the transformation of the socio-political systems of Soviet Union mean, consequently the third group did not rise up to defend their motherland from disintegration. Currently, it is crucial for Russia to unite with some of the former constituent republics of the Soviet Union and take the opportunity of the Customs Union and Unified Economic Zone including Russia, Kazakhstan and Belarus, with a view to establish an Eurasian Union.

Key words: demise of the USSR; causes; Russia; future

---

1 Born in February 20th 1939. Before the banning of the Communist Party of Soviet Union, Yuri Prokofiev used to serve as the first secretary of Moscow Municipal Party Committee from 1989 to 1991 and member of the Political Bureau of the Central Committee of the Party from 1990 to 1991. Even though he didn't officially join in the State Emergency Committee which led the 8/19 event in 1991, he was actively involved.

Afterwards, he was investigated and trialed by the Yeltsin regime. He had published two books titled as "Before and After the Banning of the Communist Party of Soviet Union—Memory of the First secretary of Moscow Municipal Party Committee of the CPSU (2005) and Kill the Communist Party of Soviet Union—testimony of first secretary of Moscow Municipal Party Committee of the CPSU (2011) which has exerted great influence in Russian public. After the collapse of the Soviet Union, he had successively led several large-scale high-tech defense industry enterprises and engaged in social and political activities, served as the Chairman of the 'Motherland—All-Russia Socialist People's Movement' and also Presidium member and Chairman of the Strategic Culture Foundation.

2 Zhang Shuhua, deputy director of the World Socialism Research Center, attached to CASS and he is the Dean of the Information Intelligence Research Institute.

20 years ago, the vast Eurasian continent suffered geopolitical catastrophe which almost completely changed the global course of history, thus creating a new world configuration, in which millions of people belonging to newly established emerging countries have been separated by national borders.

Soon later, on December 25th 1991, the flag of the Soviet Union was replaced by a tricolour flag of Russian at the top of the Kremlin. From then on, the Russian empire had been disintegrated and lost millions of square kilometres of land and nearly half of its population.

Upon the 20th anniversary of the demise of USSR, two major Russian TV Channels successively played various documentaries such as "The Demise of the USSR and The Collapse of an Empire" among which I believe the latter much better conforms to the historical realities.

What is the Soviet Union? In terms of its geographical features, it is a Russian empire and a powerful country built by its people after centuries of hard work, covering an area ranging from the Baltics to the Pacific Ocean and from the Arctic to the Pamirs. As an empire which used to include the 1/6 of the world's land area, its spiritual blood consists not only the Russian national characteristics accumulated for centuries but also includes the spiritual culture of many other races living in this land.

Was it impossible to avoid the demise of USSR? If we believe the arguments of people like N. Svanidze or Mrekin[3], the demise of the USSR would be fatal and its planned economy was doomed to collapse, they have blindly argued that national conflicts are not man-made, "only caused by natural reasons."

Nevertheless, facts are facts. Based on objective facts, some renown economists, historians and politicians have came to those conclusions which are completely opposite to that of Svanidze and Mrekin. In fact, it was an inevitable trend for the Soviet Union to renovate its economic and political system, but the lack of the ability to timely cope with the challenges posed by the change of times didn't mean that it was necessary to break up its complete social and political system. In other words, it is unworthy to destruct the Soviet Union, a Russian empire that had come into being after a thousand years, a geopolitical entity which had stood the tests of the 20th century.

---

3 Born in April 2nd 1955, Nica Svanidze is the professor of history in the Russian Cultural University and a host in some historical TV programs, but a part of viewers and public have criticized his historical opinions and saw him as a person joking with history and advocating selective historical memory. And, Mrekin, born in June 12th 1957 is a TV program producer related to modern Russian history and political interviews and commentary. Besides, he has also published multiple historical books.–note of the translator.

The author of "A Hundred Years' Development of Russian Economy", Vasily Simchera, the vice director of Russian Economic Research Institute has revealed the following facts in his book. Before the reforms of Gorbachev, the average annual growth rate of the Soviet Union economy was 4%-5%, but it had sharply decreased to 2.4% during the period from 1986 to 1990 (Gorbachev Era). Even so, given the same low growth rate, Russia's current GDP cannot be 1600 billion US Dollars in 20 years, but normally it should have been 4300 billion US Dollars, which could ensure an average monthly wage of 2000 US Dollars for the workers. In 1980s, the industrial production of our country was characterized by ample investment and advanced technological level. Then after 20 years, even if calculated at an annual growth rate of 2%, the per capita GDP of Russia should have reached to circa. 20-22 thousand Dollars just like Japan rather than the mere fancy of catching Portugal at present.

I have to reiterate that at that time, it was definitely necessary for the Soviet Union to carry out certain structural adjustments, introduce a market mechanism for its agricultural sector, light industry and trade as well as facilitate the application of new scientific and technological discoveries. It was obvious that Soviet Union shouldn't destroy the entire economic and political system, rather implement modernization reforms by using its resources and potentials. If these reforms would achieve, it would be quite possible for the SU to reach an annual economic growth of 8-10%. However, the party and government accomplished nothing, remained passive. According to a calculation by a CIA analysts, by the mid 1980s, the economy of the Soviet Union had accounted for 15-16% of the global GDP, but currently Russia's share is less than 3%.

With the subversion of the socialist system, people's moral codes were also destroyed, the ideals of communism which inherited people's pursuit of justice, mutual help, solidarity for thousands of years, were all paralyzed. Unfortunately, all these ideals have sunk together with the Soviet Union. Currently, people just have one road left, that is, a money-oriented, selfish life.

Of course, the demise of Soviet Union has been a fact and what's done cannot be undone, which entails two eternal and classic questions of Russia, namely whose fault was that and what to do?

I. About whose fault?

There are various judgements concerning the reasons behind the sudden demise of the superpower Soviet Union and the Communist Party of Soviet Union which had 19 million members. Different people have different opinions.

First of all, its demise was not just an overnight thing, rather an accumulated product of a period including several decades. If we have to find out whose fault, then I guess there were three groups who destroyed the SU.

The first group is elites in the party and government of the Soviet Union or at least the great majority of them. Among them, some were just foolish and hasty while others served as traitors, purposely since they were quite clear about what they were doing and conscious about their relevant advantages and disadvantages. Soviet Union was not well prepared for the severe tests, because its party and state leadership had failed to timely renew its social and political system, all of which has laid the foundation for the so-called reforms of Gorbachev. It was just because of a series of policies introduced during the reform period of Gorbachev (1985-1991) that have caused the destruction of the Communist Party of Soviet Union and Soviet Union. The details of Gorbachev's misdeeds were the following:

(1) Cancellation of the 6th article of constitution and depriving of the Communist Party of Soviet Union from the task of leadership to the state and social life. As a result, there occurred a vacuum of authority and leadership, governance. Later, the Communist Party of the Russian Federation was founded in the summer of 1990, which once again destructed the unity of the Communist Party of Soviet Union. From then on, this new founded party (KPRF) became a union of communist parties of various league republics rather than the core of cohesion of Soviet Union.

(2) The Soviet Union government and the Central Committee of the CPSU passed a series of resolutions in the economic field which brought extremely severe damages to Soviet economy that were unable to repair.

Among them, the most influential ones were the Soviet Union State Enterprises (Joint) Law which caused to unauthorized price rise of enterprises, the Law of Soviet Union Cooperatives which led to flooding cash flow of Rouble and serious inflation and thirdly the Economic Calculation Law which gave rise to the beggar-thy-neighbour phenomenon and paralyzed the cooperation among republics.

(3) The first step and also the most severe step leading to the demise of USSR was the Declaration of National Sovereignty of Russian Federation passed in the Russian Federation People's Congress.

This declaration (the Treaty of the Union[4]) explicitly put forward that the law of the socialist Soviet Union in Russia should be based on laws of Soviet Union. The introduction of this document was actually a direct consequence of power struggles between Yeltsin and Gorbachev.

(4) Some officials who held power directly got involved in destructive activities at that time.

Otherwise, under the conditions of the planned economy, it was impossible for the government to shut down all tobacco companies or household cleaners producing enterprises at the same time. But it did happen, and shelves in stores of Moscow and other cities were all empty while roads heading to the capital were crowded with hundreds of trucks loading meat, edible oil and cheese.

By August 1991, similar destructive activities had almost achieved to weaken the CPSU, put state management into chaos and aroused dissatisfaction among the general public through sharply lowering the level of daily material life. Of course, this might not be directly caused by external forces but they have imposed pressures in different ways. In the last three or four years the leaders of the party and the state had succumbed to these pressures, which led to the final disaster.

The 19/8 coup became the ultimate turning point, resulting in the ban on CPSU and led to drastic changes in the social and political system.

As for traitor behaviour of the highest leadership in the party and state, we should mention Gorbachev, Yakovlev, Shevardnadze as well as those people signing the Belovezhskaya-Pushcha Agreement[5], including Yeltsin, Kravchuk (Ukraine), Shushkevich (Belarus) and their accomplices Burbulis, Gaidar, Schach and Kozyrev [then-Russian Foreign Minister].

Of course, we cannot forget and ignore the role of Gorbachev who was the gravedigger of the CPSU and Soviet Union. He was the one who initiated and implemented those acts paralyzing the national unity and social and political system. Besides in Reykjavik and Malta, Gorbachev also gave promises to the US president that he would dissolve the Warsaw Pact and the Council of Mutual Economic Assistance (COMECON), allow the separation of three Baltic republics from the Soviet Union and promised that SU would never interfere with domestic affairs of Moldova. He was supposed to stop the signing of the Belovezhskaya Pushcha (Belavezha Accords) because at that time the Belarus KGB organization had already notified him of this secret meeting and prepared to kill him at any time.

---

4   Treaty of the Union is the critical element in reordering both the political and economic relations between the republics and the center.

5   The Minsk agreement was drafted by the three presidents, at Viskuli residence in the Belovezhskaya Pushcha (Belovezh Forest) on 8 December. Also known as the Belavezha Accords is the agreement that declared the Soviet Union effectively dissolved.

The former Belarus leader Kobich later confessed that he was actually confused at that time because they violated the constitution and committed the crime of treason. Then he went on to say that if he was Gorbachev, he would dispatch a troop of Alpha Special Forces, arrest and send them to the Moscow prison. The fact that Gorbachev adopted a wait-and-see policy and allowed the signing of the Belovezhskaia-Pushcha Agreement was the last blow for the demise of the Soviet Union.

The second powerful group which was involved in dissolving Soviet Union was the external forces

On the one side, western countries always feared from the giant Russian empire, while on the other side coveting its natural treasure at the same time. During the opposition with the Tsarist Russia at first phase and Soviet Union later, the western powers, the US and the UK in particular, always stuck to the purpose which ranged from eliminating Russia as their rival in the past to prevent Russia from becoming their rival again. To achieve these purposes, western countries have adopted various strategies and plans.

(1) Allen Dulles Minutes and Colby Plan by the CIA[6]

The latter was implemented by Reagan and President George Bush Senior. The US well knew that the Soviet Union economy suffered from intense pressure as a result of the cold war armament race, so they seized the opportunity to make up the myth of star wars, aiming to push the Soviet Union into a new round of arms race and completely paralyze its economy. At last, they have achieved their aim.

(2) The US kept exerting pressure on oil producing countries.

Soviet Union used to purchase consumer goods with its oil exports income to compensate its shortcomings in terms of domestic light industry production. At first, in 1976 due to sharply increasing global oil production, Saudi Arabia chose to lower the price of oil which is a strategic raw material for Soviet Union's export income and foreign exchange reserves. Due to a sharp increase of oil production by Saudi Arabia , price of oil each barrel sharply reduced from 35-40 to10-11 dollars per barrel, almost close to the cost of oil production in the Soviet Union. Consequently, the economy

---

6 The Dulles Minutes refers to the document called "The Task of America towards Russia" put forward by the United States National Security Council on August 18th 1948. Russia used to hold that the plan of dissolving Soviet Union through ideological and cultural infiltration was secretly carried out by director of the CIA, Allen Dulles. The CIA Cathy plan refers to a series of secret action plans conducted by the CIA against the Soviet Union. Russia believed that those six years when William Colby served as the director of CIA in early 1980s were a period characterized by the most rampant anti-Soviet activities all over the world during the Cold War. In addition to the US president Reagan, CIA led by Colby were the direct external reasons leading to the rapid demise of Soviet Union. -note by the translator.

of the Soviet Union suffered greatly. It could no more import normally due to lack of foreign exchange reserves, store shelves were empty and leading to extreme dissatisfaction among Soviet people.

(3) CIA and other Information organizations belonging to western countries cooperated with each other to establish an active fifth column in the Soviet Union by making use of all sorts of activist groups and non-governmental (NGO) organizations.

The people who worked for the fifth column came from the representative figures of the intelligentsia. There has been an accurate comment by the writer Sergei Zaregin to the effect that intelligentsia was aware of what they were doing and what the consequence would be.

Under the support of the Central Propaganda department led by Yakovlev, almost all the media organs of the Soviet Union at that time were controlled by those people who advertised "the necessity for change". They tried all possible means to advertise that people should spare no efforts to comprehensively change the Soviet economic and socio-political system. At that time, about 50 figures who used to express their views in newspapers or TV shows and instigated the general public with "radical and revolutionary" opinions, including Popov, Shmelev, Leisy Zikin and Abromovich. Soon after, the anti-Soviet ideological trend Union finally became the mainstream trend in the media.

The third group who buried the Soviet Union was just the Soviet Union itself.

Most of people in Soviet Union especially residents in the big cities tended to just blindly follow the changes without having any idea of their essence and consequences. Even, some of them cheered the propaganda and added fuel to the fire. However, in some small and medium-sized cities, the great majority of people didn't care much and acted indifferently.

This was because people were poverty-stricken that they had no time to follow the power struggle between Gorbachev and Yeltsin and its danger. Just as the Hungarian economist Janos Kornai put it, people didn't care much about the future of the social system, for them buying sausages was more important. People tended to welcome the new changes believing that capitalism meant the access to all sorts of products in the stores while people can still enjoy the welfare provided by a socialist system today. But they were completely mistaken, the socialist system of the Soviet Union provided people with the best social security and an optimistic social spirit. This is just what most of the Russian citizens lack and long today.

To sum up, gravediggers of the demise of Soviet Union were the party and state elites who were unable to deal and face with challenges of times and even chose a path of betrayal, secondly the external western forces led by the US who sought their own political and economic interest with the purpose of destroying the Soviet Union, and thirdly those figures among the intelligentsia who had no idea of those consequences that would arise by the change of the social and political system and didn't defend against the disintegration and split of the nation.

II. On "what to do?"

At present, we definitely cannot return back to Soviet Union for no man can swim twice in the same river. Nevertheless, Russia can't just struggle with the target of survival, as it has been striving for in the two decades. This target is far from enough to defend the vast territories of Russia that stretches over 9 time zones with only 140 million population. Russia, should have a population of at least 0.2 to 0.25 billion. Besides, in view of its current population situation, even though the situation may see some improvements in the future, yet this rate of improvement will not be sufficient for the new century. Therefore, today we have only one way left, that is, to unite with a part of former republics of the Soviet Union, namely those new independent countries in an Eurasian Union.

Just like at the end of an endless tunnel, there appears the first light of morning, namely a customs union and unified economic zone including Russia, Kazakhstan and Belarus. I am convinced that there will be other countries that would benefit from joining this union to form an Eurasian Union which will be located in the region covering a part of the Russia-Soviet Union's historical territories.

Y. 58

A Round Table Discussion: The Disintegration of the Soviet Union and the International Financial Crisis — The Yin-Yang Imbalance

Li Shenming, hosts guests from the Austrian Academy of Sciences led by Helmut Denk

Wang Xiaoju[1]

Abstract: In December 2011, Prof. Helmut Denk, President of the Austrian Academy of Sciences, accompanied by other five guests visited the CASS. CASS scholars in the fields of philosophy and social sciences and Austrian natural scientists had a thorough discussion on the collapse of the Soviet Union and the current global financial crisis, from the unique perspective of pathology. Arnold Suppan, the vice-President of the Austrian Academy of Sciences, pointed out that the root cause of the collapse of the Soviet Union was within the Soviet Union itself. Li Shenming, vice-President of the CASS has argued, that— in a certain sense—social movement could find rules from the macroscopic physics. Essentially, the collapse of the Soviet Union twenty years ago and the global financial crisis since 2008 can also be seen as a kind of "Yin-Yang imbalance".

Key words: disintegration of the Soviet Union; global international financial crisis; Yin-Yang imbalance

---

[1] Wang Xiaoju, guest researcher at the World Socialism Research Center, attached to CASS, also researcher at the Institute of World History, CASS.

Li Shenming (vice-President of the CASS and the director of the World Socialism Research Center): It's our great honor to host Prof. Helmut Denk, President of the Austrian Academy of Sciences, and his companions in our CASS, and we are happy that you have suggested the theme of discussion as the collapse of the Soviet Union 20 years ago and the current global financial crisis. I am also glad to know that, Prof. Helmut Denk is a scholar of pathology. The collapse of the Soviet Union, to a certain sense, can be evaluated as a social malady and we can employ some principles of pathology, when reflecting on the reasons of the disintegration of the SU and the current global international financial crisis which I believe may be a unique perspective. Natural and social sciences are interlinked, and both the nature and the human society are essentially material in different forms. Besides, physical forms are constantly in motion which all have regularities or laws of motion that can be discovered and recognized. Men can recognize and master their laws and utilize them to guide their social practices. According to Chinese traditional philosophy, men are actually an integral part of nature, so it can be said that there are consistencies in the development laws of the nature and human society. Our today's exchange between scholars of natural sciences and scholars of philosophy and social sciences may generate some new sparks of thought, which could be very beneficial. In my opinion, there are three things worthy of evaluation in the 20th century. The first thing is the October Revolution. For the first time, a new type of country—the Union of Soviet Socialist Republics came into being. The second was is the founding of the socialist People's Republic of China in 1949. The third was the collapse of Soviet Union 20 years ago which has marked that the world socialist movement was suffering a great setback, and that it entered the era of low ebb development. The global international financial crisis in 2008 was essentially the crisis of the capitalist system, especially the crisis of neo-liberalism. Politicians, scholars and people across the world are all pondering about where the humankind is heading towards. The topic of today's discussion will focus on the collapse of the Soviet Union, 20 years ago and the deepening of the global international financial crisis. I hope that each of you can freely air your opinions.

Arnold Suppan (vice-President of the Austrian Academy of Sciences and renowned expert of Eastern European history): Lately, I met an old Russian man who lived the October Revolution as a senior aristocrat, and I talked with him about reasons of the October Revolution. He said that the reason was quite simple, namely the extreme discrepancy between the rich and the poor in Russia at that time. I myself have conducted research on the history of Eastern Europe, so I think the influences of the October Revolution is so far-reaching that not only the Russian empire had been overthrown but also the Austro-Hungary empire had collapsed. It may need another century to clarify the significance of the October Revolution, more comprehensively. After the Second World War, Soviet Union as one of those victorious nations had achieved consolidation in various mechanisms. Other Eastern European socialist countries like Poland, East Germany and Czechoslovakia all had made revolutionary strides. Even though, people could observe some signs of the collapse of the Soviet Union in Stalin's era, it was turning point, when Gorbachev decided to reduce the burden of the Soviet Union, that the Soviet Union began to disintegrate, at that turning point, he "asked" the Soviet allies in the Eastern Europe to work out their own ways for salvation.

Although, the Warsaw Treaty Organization, at that time, could sustain and maintain itself for a longer period of time, militarily, the alliance in the spheres of economy and culture, was greatly weakened.

In the 1980s, it was the socialist Soviet Union that suffered from the structural crisis, but today it's the entire western world, which faces the crisis. At present, the world still has no correct answer towards the current ongoing global financial crisis. There are also different solutions and opinions, which vary greatly, in Brussels, the headquarter of the European Union. Besides, I should say, the historians have been too late to give their opinions.

Li Shenming: In terms of major significant historical events, there have hardly been any unified understanding for quite a long period of time, but Marx had already seen clearly and predicted the essence and laws of human society and the laws of historical development. As for the root cause of the current international financial crisis, Marx had already given a definite answer more than 140 years ago. He said in his book Das Kapital that the most fundamental reason underlying all real crises was nothing but poverty of the masses and their limited consumption. However, the capitalist production still has the energy to develop productive forces regardless of this situation, as if only absolute consumption of the masses was the limit of developing production.

After the drastic changes in Eastern Europe, and the Soviet Union, due to disappearance of the universal and comprehensive socialist social welfare in the socialist countries, West was freed from a social welfare competitor, the Western capital began to rampantly embezzle labor, thus caused polarization between the rich and the poor all over the world. Besides, with the rapid development of high technology driven by the information technology, the labor productivity has greatly improved while the amount of workers hired has sharply reduced and there were even factories without workers. As a result, there occurred a significant increase in unemployment rate and drastic decrease in effective social demand throughout the world.

Relative surplus of production has appeared not because of the lack of production capacity, but the lack of consumption capacity in the society. This current international financial crisis is essentially a crisis of relative surplus of production. L. Blanqui, the leader of early labor movement in France, advocated eliminating capitalism with violent terroristic means, which Marx disapproved and found it impossible for a minority of people to fulfill such a great event. He held that the great majority of people could only liberate themselves through relying on those oppressed and exploited people. Marx was right, because he was a complete materialist who upheld only masses could push history forward, while Blanqui advocated the viewpoint of heroes making the history. The reason for demise of the Soviet Union is different from the eruption of the 2008 global financial crisis, but both of them were essentially caused by the movements of contradictions, related to the imbalance in the entire society due to increasing gap between the rich and the poor.

Arnold Suppan: After the World War II, there were not only a few rich aristocrats but also some people in the middle class in some Western European countries while the amount of the poor who lived in relatively poor conditions was just a minority. The same applies to Austria. However, the problem lies in the sharp contrast between a wealthy society and high level of debt by the state. Bankruptcy of the Lehman Brothers has also exerted great influence on us. In response, Austria adopted two measures, namely exercised strict control over the state debt in order to reduce the state debt and began to pour money into the society to stimulate consumption which were indeed contradictory. In Europe, countries like Germany, Netherlands, Sweden and Czech Republic adopted the first method while countries such as Greece and Spain employed the second method, namely loose monetary policies.

Li Shenming: This financial crisis is just at its early stage. American society can maintain long-term social stability, because it enjoys the advantage of its currency being the world currency. To a certain sense, the US is different from Europe in terms of its social security system and the ordinary American people usually spend less in their daily life. For example, the same shirt produced in China is sold at 700 RMB but just 9 dollars in the US. In other words, a shirt is nearly ten times higher in China compared to America. Besides, since the financial crisis, real estate (home) prices in the US also fell by more than a half and the oil price in the US is also cheaper than China.

Through it exhausts the resources of other countries, pollutes the ecological environment of other countries and although it imports people's daily necessities with cheap dollar, the US has managed to receive a huge amount of state debt up to 1.5 trillion dollars. Later, the US manipulated its exchange rate and depreciated dollar and forced other countries to appreciate their currencies so as to depreciate the value of dollar bonds held by them, which is completely a parasitic attitude. The US just made use of this method, which is different from social welfare attitude of Europeans, in order to maintain its so-called advocacy of domestic people, but there are still more than 40 million people living below the poverty line and over 50 million people without health insurance in the US.

In contrast, some European countries adopted another type of social security system, including endowment insurance, health insurance and unemployment insurance—which has caused heavy financial over the state budgets. The Stalin's era laid a foundation for universal and comprehensive social welfare in the Soviet Union, which included free supply of daily necessities like baby diapers and milk to people from cradle to grave, which greatly disappointed the capitalist world. During the competitive game with the Soviet Union, western countries have learned some social welfare policies form the Soviet Union so as to ensure the long-term social stability. One important content of Roosevelt's New Deal was to narrow down the income gap through fiscal expansion and increasing jobs, thus alleviated social conflicts in the US. However, this reference (the socialist system) collapsed together with the demise of Soviet Union, consequently the capitalist world was rewarded by a new opportunity, began to increase labor exploitation, this has been the basis Mr. Giddens' "third road". The professed "third road" was in fact the road one between a social democratic capitalism within the frame of capitalism and a savage capitalism, not a third road, compared to capitalism and socialism. This policy proposition completely caters to the interests of the international monopoly capital and results in widening gap between the rich and the poor all around the world, thus maintaining the turmoil in current world. The world has to head towards a better destination, but it must experience quite a long historical period and an uneven or a roundabout path. We should be convinced that we will definitely reach that destination.

Anton Zeilinger (Director of the Institute of Quantum Optics and Quantum Information at the Austrian Academy of Sciences): Some basic laws of physics can play a role in human society. For example, all concepts within a theoretical system should be consistent instead of conflicting. Besides, metaphysical things are always less important than abstract super organic things such as the relationship between individual information and basic principles. Quantum physics is based on the uncertainty principle of materials, so it is of vital importance to look at things from a certain perspective. A social and political system will not exist for long if its basic philosophy and practice are not consistent. Nevertheless, there were indeed discrepancies between Soviet Union's later practices and basic philosophy of the October Revolution, so it is in this sense that Soviet Union was bound to collapse. The philosophy pledged by the US president was also inconsistent with some of their practical actions. There is a saying in Europe that basic philosophies of human beings come from Christianity which however is not put into practice. These problems are quite thorny, but we are obliged to solve them at last. In physics, all things have invariants. There are also some invariants in a theoretical system and in a society within which some basic concepts and principles can't be changed. If they do change, the whole theoretical system and the society will also change. I believe human society will have a better future and our ultimate goal is to constantly improve the living quality of people.

Li Shenming: Those super-organic things are regular things abstracted from numerous metaphysical things, which is just the cognitive process of practice, cognition, practice and further cognition emphasized by Chairman Mao Zedong in his "On Practice". The fundamental guiding philosophy or ideology of a state or a party must follow a consistent practice, otherwise a state or a party will not last for a long time, which reveals the root cause which has led to the collapse of the Soviet Union. After the October Revolution, Russia was a socialist country whose power was genuinely held by the communist party. During the Stalin era, Soviet Union was still a socialist country guided by the communist party, despite severe mistakes of Stalin, in his era the nature of the party and society continued to remain, its nature began to change with the Khrushchev era.

Helmut Denk (President of the Austrian Academy of Sciences): In the medical field, wisdom of traditional Chinese medicine is very commendable. According to the traditional Chinese medicine, health of human being or even the entire society requires harmony which embodies an all-round balance in all aspects.

Balance of both biology and society as a whole should not be disturbed, otherwise changes will take place in the society, be it forwards or backwards, longing for a new harmonious and balanced state within its system.

Li Shenming: I really appreciate president Denk's praise of traditional Chinese medicine. As a NPC delegate, each year I submit numerous proposals aiming to rejuvenate China's cause of traditional Chinese medicine. The concept of balance and harmony you just mentioned is quite important for understanding the entire human society. The collapse of the Soviet Union 20 years ago and the global financial crisis since 2008 can be seen as a kind of "Yin-Yang imbalance" at root.

Law of motion of the society, in a certain sense, can be better discovered from the macroscopic physics. There is the theory of "Yin-Yang imbalance" in Chinese philosophy, Chinese medicine theory in particular. Given the severe gap between wealth possession and income distribution, any country would suffer from imbalance, which also reflects the so-called principle of conservation of energy in physics. The outburst of the October Revolution was just because of a great gap between the upper class and the lower class, and the root cause leading to the collapse of Soviet Union lies in the degeneration of the USSR, and its leadership did not serve and represent the fundamental interests of the ordinary people.

Here we can compare the party and the state and their power organs to be Yang and the ordinary people to be Yin.

If Yang can represent and serve the fundamental interests of the Yin, then the latter will support and advocate leadership of the former and the society will enjoy and achieve development thanks to the Yin-Yang balance. In the reverse situation, Yin and Yang will gradually become imbalanced, and the party and authority which lose the support of people will not last long.

Accompanied by the external factor that western powers wanted to topple the Soviet Union, the collapse of Soviet Union was just a matter of time. Looking at its form, the collapse of Soviet Union seems to be peaceful, but it was essentially a drastic upheaval and big imbalance. This global financial crisis is also a kind of "Yin-Yang imbalance". In this crisis, the productive forces within the framework of capitalist production relations can be compared to Yang while the limited consumption capacity of the masses can be compared to Yin. If Yang outweighs Yin, then the imbalance will cause the financial crisis.

Chen Zhiye (Honorary member and researcher at the Chinese Academy of Social Sciences):

In the past 20 years, the collapse of Soviet Union has always been an important problem studied by historians and scholars from other disciplines.

In the Chinese academy, there are two different types of opinions concerning the root cause of the collapse of Soviet Union. One believes that it was caused by the Stalin system while the other holds theories and policies implemented by Gorbachev should be blamed. The Soviet Union system during the late 1920s and the early 1930s was a historical phenomenon which was consistent with fundamental theories and reality at that time. Back then, Soviet Union was under the siege of imperialist countries and lagging behind would leave it vulnerable to external attacks. Stalin achieved success because he has turned Soviet Union into the first level industrial power in Europe and the second largest in the world, rapidly just in two short two five-year plans and then defeated the strong German fascists in the World War II.

After the World War II, especially during the recovery stage, it was necessary for the Soviet Union to reform its mechanisms. However, both Khrushchev and Gorbachev didn't carry out correct and serious deep reforms. Particularly, Gorbachev attempted to replace the system of Soviet Union with the Western political system which caused the inconsistence between theoretical concepts and reality. Besides, during Gorbachev's era, Western countries began to exert increasing influence and infiltration targeting the Soviet Union. Gorbachev didn't pay enough attention, but trusted western countries and facilitated their efforts. Therefore, his so-called reform would definitely cause the collapse of the Soviet Union and the CPSU.

Arnold Suppan: It is undeniable that Stalin did enhance the strength of Soviet Union and played an important role in defeating Hitler through mobilizing marshals, generals and people of the whole country to join the cruel fight. However, he also exerted severe control over his people. Before the World War II, as a result of government policy problems, Stalin had caused death of millions of people, the great famine in regions like Ukraine and also launched purges against his previous colleagues and marshals. For me, it is hard to determine the influence of western politicians on Gorbachev, I think the collapse of Soviet Union to a great extent was an internal explosion.

Li Shenming: To evaluate right and wrong of events and historical figures, we should put them in the historical long river rather than confining to a short period of several decades. There is no doubt that Stalin had made mistakes or even serious ones in the elimination of counterrevolutionaries, but how should we look at his contributions and mistakes?

We should place him under a specific historical environment of the Soviet Union at that time as the only socialist country which was under the siege of the capitalist world. In fact, western countries had constructed numerous fifth column troops in the CPSU and the state, so if the fifth column troops was not eliminated, then it would be impossible for the Soviet Union to win the Great Patriotic War or even the World anti-Fascist war during the Second World War.

When it comes to the serious mistakes during the elimination of counterrevolutionaries, both Stalin and other people like Khrushchev were responsible. While serving as secretary of Krai province located in the Russian Far East, Khrushchev had once ordered to kill more than 60,000 people, and after he became the CPSU head he destroyed all relevant documents and materials.

Therefore, sometimes there may be inconsistencies between documents and the real history and archives may also be faked. Besides, Western countries also exaggerated Stalin's mistakes geometrically. For example, during his rule of 29 years, Stalin executed more than 780.000 people, however Western writers said it was only 20 million just during the "1936-38"—the period of elimination.

Since, Stalin attempted to establish a brand new socialist system for the benefit of the great majority, he would definitely run against more slander and attacks. The US had killed more than 20 million Indians, but it didn't mention it at all. In 1965, the CIA had once supported the Indonesian military forces to kill 500.000 to 1 million Indonesian communists whose blood turned the rivers into red, but no one knows about this, till today. No one can imagine the amount of people killed and tortured during the McCarthy era in 1950s. The western powers use of their huge financial sources to launch all sorts of media which could transmit a lot of false news to people all over the world, thus cause illusions. Actually, this process is promoted with invisible ideology. People want to defend ethics, but actually they get false information. The practice has proved that the mass graves in Kosovo and Iraq's mass destruction weapons were all false news transmitted by the US as the pretext for its invasion. There are information wars in the world, and in a certain sense the collapse of the Soviet Union was a result of numerous lies by capitalist forces. Unfortunately, such kind of situation still continues to happen, and the same rule applies to the present China's socialism with Chinese characteristics. I can't agree more with the opinion of vice-president Suppan that the fundamental reason underlying the collapse of Soviet Union lies within the Communist Party of Soviet Union. To be specific, inconsistency between its words and action, betrayal of its people plus external intervention of the western countries together has caused the collapse of the Communist Party of Soviet Union and USSR.

Bernard Plunger (Director of Scientific Research Office and International Relations Department of Austrian Academy of Sciences): As a younger historian, I was born in 1968, namely in the period of Vietnam War. While studying in my hometown in 1989, I was quite astonished by the great event of the fall of the Berlin wall. Ten years later, East European countries began to join the European Union. Recalling the history, I believe the present situation is in a better balance and I am full of confidence in the future of globalization. Those well-educated young generations of the 1990s will be the driving force to unite Europe.

Li Shenming: Joining of some Eastern European countries to the European Union or NATO has not only created a new balance but also led to a new imbalance and problems. In a certain sense, European Union now implements a foreign expansionist policy similar to that of Brezhnev. Like Soviet Union, it is also impossible for the EU to shoulder an increasingly heavy burden, if it continues, this will cause a new imbalance. The severe situation of sovereign debt crisis in Europe just reflects this new imbalance.

Robert Ussing (Deputy Director of the Institute of Quantum Optics and Quantum Information at Austrian Academy of Sciences): I was born in a town quite near to the iron curtain wall about which I knew little for I was just a child and knew nothing about the world. However, the collapse of Soviet Union turned our attention to Europe. Retrospecting the history since 1989, politicians have been quite successful in carrying out reforms, but now Europe encounters a new crisis, namely the financial crisis. Nowadays, many leaders and politicians of major countries tend to follow the media commentators, so they are just short-sighted politicians. China is also undergoing rapid transformations, and it also leaves a deep impression on the world with its fast economic development and changes in its governance system. Besides, the powerful leadership demonstrated by the Chinese leaders is not carefully noticed the western leaders and countries.

Li Shenming: I would like to hear director Anton Zeilinger's opinion towards the collapse of the Soviet Union.

Anton Zeilinger: At the end of 20th century, I went to Poland and met an old fisherman who had a good but time-honored boat. But, the boat could still be used to catch fish, so I was quite amazed and asked him why. He told me he inherited the boat from his father who told him that it was a good boat left behind by ancestors and each year, he just needed to paint it several times without randomly repairing or refining. In this way he could still make better use of it today. This is a true story. If I could be able to tell Gorbachev this truth, then Soviet Union may avoid the fate of demise.

Li Shenming: Director Anton Zeilinger's example is very persuasive. Thank you. Today, scholars of China and Austria have conducted beneficial exchanges and harvested a lot, scholars of natural science and philosophy and social science in particular. Let's express our heart-felt thanks to the visit of president Denk once again.

Y. 59

Soviet Scholars' Debates on the 20th Congress of the CPSU and "the Sixties Generation"

Ma Xiaoming[1]

Abstract: At the 20th Congress of the Communist Party of the Soviet Union (CPSU) in 1956, Khrushchev delivered a secret report which defamed and totally negated Stalin, which dealt a heavy blow to people's belief in communism and the Soviet socialist system. This Congress started the process of bourgeois liberalization and caused a deep split in the social ideology of the Soviet society. The young generation of "the sixties" represented by Gorbachev and Yakovlev who were influenced by the idea of liberalization of the 20th Congress of the CPSU, inherited Khrushchev's practice of negating Stalin and Khrushchev's initial bourgeois humanitarian thought, which was advocated at the 20th Congress of the CPSU. These two figures put forward the theories of "humane democratic socialism" and carried out the so-called "democratization" and "glasnost" movement that completely denied the Soviet socialist system in the second half of the 1980s under the cloak of reform, which ultimately became cause of the dissolution of the CPSU, and the disintegration of the Soviet Union.

Key words: 20th Congress of the Communist Party of the Soviet Union; "the Sixties"; Gorbachev; Yakovlev

---

[1] Ma Xiaoming, a guest researcher of the World Socialist Research Center, Chinese Academy of Social Science, a doctoral candidate at the graduate school of Chinese Academy of Social Science.

At the 20th Congress of the Communist Party of the Soviet Union (CPSU) Khrushchev delivered a secret report which defamed and totally negated Stalin, destroyed the core and backbone of the CPSU ideology and Soviet Union's highly unified values dominated by communist ideals. This Congress started the process of bourgeois liberalization which caused deep split in the social ideology of the Soviet society. The young generation of "the Sixties (1960s)" who were influenced by the idea of liberalization of the 20th Congress of the CPSU later turned into deleterious forces hidden in the Party, leading to the CPSU's losing its leadership position and the collapse of the Soviet Union.

The 20th Congress of the CPSU started the process of "social democratization" and bourgeois liberalization.

Democratic intellectuals of the Soviet Union evaluated the Khrushchev's reform era as "Khrushchev Thaw" period or spiritual emancipation of the society, and have spoken highly of Khrushchev's criticism towards Stalin's personality cult and the preceding process of "social democratization" and bourgeois liberalization. Around 1988, liberal democrats began to pay attention to research on the ten years' history of Khrushchev era especially the relationship between the 20th Congress of the CPSU and the reforms. Historian Aksyutin compiled the relevant articles of liberal democrats like V. Borotsky and published a book titled Khrushchev: Memories of Contemporaries.

In their opinion, the 20th Congress of the CPSU had not only started the process of democratization but also regarded Khrushchev's criticism of Stalin's personality cult in the period between the 20th Congress of the CPSU to the 22nd Congress of the CPSU as an integrated process whose objective historical significance lied in democratization, which has led to replacement of the Stalin's "barracks communism" based on completely new and different socialist principles.[2]

They held that the "democratization" process initiated by Khrushchev was consistent with the later reform direction of Gorbachev.[3]

They have argued that Khrushchev "did not negate the fundamental principles of the Soviet socialist system, and his measures of modernization and reform has started the process of liberalization.[4]

In fact, this so-called "democratization" was a bourgeois liberalization which both abandoned Marxism-Leninism and proletarian dictatorship. Later, Gorbachev inherited this completely different principles of

---

2 Aksyutin, Khrushchev: Memories of Contemporaries, translated by Li Shubo etc., the Oriental Press, 1990, p. 105.
3 Ibid., p. 106.
4 Aksyutin, Khrushchev's "Thaw" and the Public Sentiment in the USSR, 1953-1964, Rosspeng 2010 , 2nd edition, p. 5.

socialism" and followed the path of socialism led by democratic socialism ideology, which radically negated Marxism-Leninism. Democratic intellectuals of the Soviet Union have appreciated Khrushchev's courage in negating Stalin at the 20th Congress of the CPSU and believed such kind of "fearless move" of him which took "personal risk and fame" has brought ideological emancipation for people. Poet A. Voznsersky even generously forgave the humiliation brought by Khrushchev's move due to this great merit, because he believed Khrushchev had achieved most important step which "liberated the people since after 1956."[5]

Gorbachev's analysis of the 20th Congress of the CPSU and opinions of liberal democrat intellectuals are similar, Gorbachev wrote in his memoirs: "this was the first attack against the totalitarian system and also the first attempt for Soviet Union to head towards democratization."[6]

Such kind of "democratization" experience has exerted tremendous ideological effect on the generation of the "sixties."

II. Direct influence of the 20th Congress of the CPSU on the "reform" thoughts of the generation of the "sixties."

The "sixties" were also called the "boys of the 20th Congress". Andre Graciov, the advisor and the press secretary of Gorbachev, published the first Russian biography of Gorbachev in 2001 titled "The Mystery of Gorbachev" in which he explained the concept of the "sixties". To be specific, the "sixties" refer to those liberal intellectuals whose world view was formed in the late 1950s and early 1960s, namely the "Khrushchev Thaw" period, and they worshipped respect for human rights, individual freedom and openness.[7]

By delivering a secret report at the 20th Congress of the CPSU which negated Stalin, Khrushchev exerted great and chaotic influence on the political environment, social ideology and international communist movement, thus greatly effecting the young generation that had just stepped in society, that is, the "sixties".

With the political influence of the 20th Congress of the CPSU, the sixties prepared for and carried out reforms without doubting the necessary connection between the 20th Congress and reforms. Russian historian Aksyutin pointed out that Khrushchev's secret report helped the "sixties" to get rid

---

5 Aksyutin, Khrushchev: Memories of Contemporaries, translated by Li Shubo etc., the Oriental Press, 1990, pp. 134-137.
6 M. Gorbachev: Memoirs, translated by Shu Tao etc., Social Sciences Academic Press, 2003, pp 99-103.
7 Andre Graciov: The Mystery of Gorbachev, translated by Shu Tao, Et.al, Central Compilation & Translation Press, 2005, p. 19.

of the fear, they felt, get access to new thoughts and opinions concerning the society and politics and step in society as a generation who could transform the society. It was definitely not accidental that for children born in 1956 to lead the reform but conformed to the logical development during Khrushchev's era: "thanks to such phenomenon during the 1950s and the 20th Congress that today's reforms gave become possible."[8]

Apparently, through recalling the 20th Congress and Khrushchev's secret report together with his contemporaries, Aksyutin, attempted to find theoretical origin and basis for the later "reforms".

Khrushchev's secret report accelerated the relaxation process which had secretly started after the death of Stalin in 1953, so people tended to connect the relaxation with the 20th Congress or Khrushchev.[9]

A group of Soviet Union intellectuals deeply influenced by the "Khrushchev Thaw" (social democratization) later became open dissidents who vigorously promoted the humanistic "human rights" thoughts and the social democratization" and ultimately won recognition of Gorbachev.

Soviet historian L. Medvedev held that Khrushchev's secret report has "polished" people's eyes and made more people especially the youth believe that the party had marched on the road of ethical purification, namely the party had embarked the path of building a "democratic society". "There even appeared a generation called the generation of the 20th Congress, which stood in the forefront of reform."[10]

Nevertheless, this path of "purification" was actually a dangerous road of bourgeois restoration.

According to analysis of Andre Graciov it was because of the phenomenon of the "sixties" that resulted in changes in political ideology of Gorbachev who had always attempted to realize the ideal of the "sixties".[11]

However, the ideal of the "sixties" was to carry out reforms and complete the half-way "social democratization" started by Khrushchev. In his memoirs, Gorbachev analyzed reasons accounting for the failure of "social democratization" after the 20th Congress, he said: "Khrushchev didn't and couldn't conduct further and deeper analysis on the causes of totalitarianism, because such an analysis would require him to break his old framework of beliefs. Therefore, Khrushchev's criticism on personality cult seemed to

---

8 Aksyutin: Khrushchev: Memories of Contemporaries, translated by Li Shubo etc., The Oriental Press, 1990, pp. 27, 181, 216.
9 William Taubman, Khrushchev, Moscow „Young Guard", 2008, p. 337.
10 Malkovich, Taco, et. al., Theories on the Stalin Model by Foreign Scholars' Theory on the Stalin Model, edited by Li Zongyu, Central Compilation & Translation Press, 1995, p. 476.
11 Andre Graciov: The Mystery of Gorbachev, translated by Shu Tao etc., Central Compilation & Translation Press, 2005, pp. 28-29.

be sharp but in fact incomplete, because he had set a certain limit in advance, therefore Khrushchev's democratization was stalled just from the very beginning."[12]

It was because of such kind of subconscious critical approach about "Khrushchev's incomplete democratization" that Gorbachev has made great efforts to compensate the "disappointment" of the "sixties" after becoming the new generation of Soviet Union leaders, thus Gorbachev started a new round of "social democratization" reforms in Soviet Union.

During the reform period, in 1980s, influenced by spirit of the 20th Congress, the "sixties" began to sing the "sagas" of half-way reform attempt by Khrushchev, and they carried forward practice of Khrushchev's negating Stalin and upholding bourgeoisie humanism of the 20th Congress. They vigorously advocated "democratization" and "openness", completely negated the Soviet, put forward the theory of "humanitarian democratic socialism" and finally led the CPSU into a path within which the Party lost its leadership position and the disintegration of the Soviet Union. Among the "sixties" namely the "generation of the 20th Congress", the most representative ones were Gorbachev, who was "the father of reform", and Yakovlev, was "the designer of the reform", whose opinions had changed dramatically after the 20th Congress in 1956.

III. Changes in the thoughts of Gorbachev and Yakovlev after the 20th Congress

When Gorbachev, saw Khrushchev's secret report submitted to the 20th Congress, he had already graduated from Moscow University and had worked in the youth league of Stavropol Krai for one year. According to Andre Graciov, it was from then on that Gorbachev could be classified into the "sixties" group.[13]

Like other democrats, Gorbachev appreciated the criticism of Stalin by Khrushchev in the secret report at the very beginning. The probable reason for Gorbachev's easy and natural appreciation of Khrushchev's criticism on Stalin's personality cult was related to his being born in a victim family of "the great purge". To be specific, his grandfather—a farmer—was sent to the labor camp in 1934 since he failed to fulfill his sowing plan and was treated as a "saboteur" and was punished as being a member or follower of the "right-wing Trotskyist counter-revolutionary organization". Besides, grandfather of Gorbachev's wife was executed by the decision of a group of three people. Therefore, Gorbachev spoke sincerely and bluntly to Ikeda

---

12 Gorbachev: Gorbachev's memoirs: truth and confession, translated by Shu Tao etc., Social Sciences Academic Press, 2002, p. 57.
13 Andre Graciov: The Mystery of Gorbachev, translated by Shu Tao etc., Central Compilation & Translation Press, 2005, p. 19.

Daisaku, a Japanese scholar, that he felt grateful for the 20th Congress of Soviet Union and had actively took part in exposing "Stalin's personality cult and dictatorship"[14].

After the 20th Congress, as a cadre of the Communist Youth League, Gorbachev offered a plan of publicizing the ideas of the 20th Congress to the youth to his superiors, and got approval.

Following the 20th Congress, the 22nd Congress more deeply affected Gorbachev's anti-Stalin thoughts. Historian Medvedev wrote that the 22nd Congress had a decisive effect on Gorbachev's world view, because the 22nd Congress was the first time for Gorbachev to attend the party congress as a delegate.

Besides, the 22nd Congress bluntly talked about crimes of Stalin and passed the resolution of removing Stalin's remains from the Lenin Mausoleum, renaming of several cities named after Stalin and other Stalin era politicians. The 20th Congress and the 22nd Congress contributed to the "great renewal" of Soviet society and the Soviet Party and made deep imprints on the life Soviet country life, which couldn't be erased even during the later period of stagnation."[15]

It was the 20th Congress and the 22nd Congress of the Party that paved the way for the leading Soviet officials like Gorbachev and democrat intellectuals Medvedev to lay an ideological foundation for advocating "anti-Stalinism" and "democratic socialism".

Andre Graciov explicitly pointed out that there were multiple sources for Gorbachev's "democratization" thought. "While Gorbachev served as the party secretary of Stavropol Krai (province), he had already become quite interested in the Euro-communism trend by Italian communist leaders which advocated to establish socialism with legal means and he also read numerous works of "critical Marxists" like Gramsci, Turati and works of contemporary non-Marxists and new philosophers like Sartre and Marcuse and representatives of the Frankfurt School. Consequently, "pagan" communist or the socialist romantic school of the Prague Spring or Italian communists and other Euro- communists all became aspirators of Gorbachev."[16]

The socialist Romanticist Czech Z. Mlynar, who was a classmate of Gorbachev during his college days, later became one of the leaders of "the Prague Spring". In 1967, Z. Mlynar had once traveled to Stavropol to visit

---

14 M. Gorbachev, Ikeda Daisaku: Spiritual Lessons of the 20th Century, Translated by Sun Lichuan, Social Sciences Academic Press, 2005, p. 44.
15 Markovich, Taco etc., Foreign Scholars' Theories on the Stalin Model, edited by Li Zongyu, Central Compilation & Translation Press, 1995, p. 476.
16 Andre Graciov: The Mystery of Gorbachev, translated by Shu Tao etc., Central Compilation & Translation Press, 2005, pp. 41, 95.

Gorbachev after Gorbachev was elected as the Party general secretary he was invited to visit Moscow even though he was expelled from Czech Communist Party due to "the Prague Spring" and was exile in Austria. While serving as the general secretary of Soviet Union, Gorbachev carefully read private publications, book published in foreign countries reading materials, and some foreign publications which were only for internal reading or "non-public written materials" distributed within a small range, besides he was interested to read "Marxist History" series written by independent writers. With these readings he acquired "the factual basis" which has allowed him to abandon "all those deep-rooted, superficial and untrue" views of the party concerning the history of the Soviet Union.[17]

Historian A. Chernyaev, born in 1921, was a decade older than Gorbachev, old enough to have served in the Soviet military during World War II. In February 1986 the nearly sixty-five year old Chernyaev was called upon to join Gorbachev's team as a senior foreign policy aide, and later in 1993 he published the autobiographic book titled as 'My Six Years with Gorbachev', in which described changes in revolution opinions of Gorbachev in details. He pointed out that foreign reading materials Gorbachev read had exerted an important influence on decisions of Gorbachev.

Much of his book consists of Chernyaev's journal entries, linked together by remarks and reflections added later for context and narrative continuity. While this technique allows Chernyaev to portray himself, with some justification, as a prescient observer of the unfolding realities of the 1980s (such as when he writes that in 1986 he advised Gorbachev to begin thinking about the matter of German unification).

According to Chernyaev, Gorbachev read widely, was familiar with samizdat and tamizdat critical of the Stalinist system, and in particular was heavily influenced by Stephen Cohen's book on Nikolai Bukharin. By 1987-88, the Soviet leader spoke of returning to the "true" Lenin (i.e., the Lenin of NEP), whom he constantly "consulted" in seeking answers to contemporary problems. By the suggestions recommendation of the author and people around him, Gorbachev decided to lift the ban on Bukharin. On November 7th 1987, in his speech in the commemoration meeting of the 70th anniversary of October Revolution, Gorbachev praised Bukharin and his personal role, thus paved the way for the revision of the entire Soviet ideology based on the book "A Concise History of the Communist Party of the Soviet Union" which was revised by Stalin, thus prompted the first wave of completely re-evaluating all sorts of values."[18]

---

17 Anotoly C. Chernyaev, Six years with Gorbachev On Diary Entries, Moscow Publishing group „Progress"–„Culture" 1993, pp. 183-184.
18 Ibid., pp. 183-184.

Even though Gorbachev could never bring himself to let go of Lenin, eventually, partly under the influence of Aleksandr Solzhenytsin's Lenin in Zurich, he was able to see the first Bolshevik as an ordinary person capable of making mistakes. (p. 213)

. While the general secretary made overtures to the reform-minded intellectuals for their support, Chernyaev remarks that Gorbachev was really "more concerned with keeping the leaders of the traditional intelligentsia close by and making sure that none of them were offended" (p. 211). In his desire to bring both camps together, he kept one foot squarely planted in each and thereby succeeded in alienating both the liberal intellectuals—many of whom eventually defected to Yeltsin—and their conservative counterparts. Meanwhile, Chernyaev and Yakovlev consistently urged Gorbachev to purge those apparatchiks who did not support perestroika. Instead of making a firm alliance with the democratic-minded reformers, Gorbachev felt betrayed when they criticized him—yet, to the consternation of his liberal advisers, he abided the attacks of Soviet hardliners.

Chernyaev writes that by the summer of 1990, "conditions were ripe for a break with the Party, with socialist ideology, and with the old way of governance." It was time, in other words, "to admit that perestroika is a revolution that means transformation of the existing order." But, Chernyaev sadly admits, "this didn't happen" (p. 293). The result was that Gorbachev remained beholden to a Central Committee that was full of Ligachev's and Polozkov's people—the conservatives—and therefore the Soviet leader was rendered powerless before the Party (p. 294).

Yakovlev, "the designer of reform", in his memoirs, also attached great importance to the impact of the 20th Congress on his generation. In 1956, Yakovlev attended the 20th Congress, when he was an instructor of the CPSU party school. Khrushchev's secret report played a decisive role in his departure from the Marxist world view. In his biography, he said that people always "kept asking him when and why he began to deviate from Marxism". My first step was, to deviate from the actual embodiment of Marxism, deviated from the so-called 'socialism'. This is because, I had once very carefully studied the classic works of Marxist-Leninist writers in details, that I could be able to see that "the eternal truth of this doctrine" appeared increasingly dim to me with more questions and gaps, and my previous rich imagination and enthusiasm also weakened. This evolution of mine is not paradoxical, it has its own logic. Of course, Khrushchev's report at the 20th Congress in 1956, and his new evaluations played a decisive role in correcting my views.[19]

---

19 A.N .Yakovlev: A Cup of Bitter-Bolshevism in Russia and Reform Movement, p 14.

He highly praised Khrushchev's negation of Stalin at the 20th Congress and referred to it as a breakthrough from barbarism to civilization, from nature of animals to restoration of reason as well as from non-rationality to responsibility, thus shocking the social spiritual world and being the only soil of freedom.[20]

After the 20th Congress, Yakovlev appealed to leave his position in the Central Committee of the CPSU, to pursue his studies. He studied in the Graduate School of the Academy of Social Sciences attached to the Central Committee of the CPSU, from 1956 to 1960, in this period he was sent to the Columbia University as one of those first four students sent to USA, after the World War II.

Thanks to his study in the USA, he became even firmer in doubting Marx's and other classical Marxist writers, negated the socialist system of Soviet Union and engaged himself to restore liberal capitalism in the country. He said: "the 20th Congress has caused a stir and variety of contradictory reactions in my mind, my re-evaluation of the past and present was formed, in such a context......after the 20th Congress, I went to USA when I was relatively young and although I had quite contradictory ideas then, the idea of human freedom had already taken root in my mind.[21]

After the 20th Congress, Yakovlev's world outlook has gradually changed, and finally became completely opposed to the leading ideology of CPSU, opposed to political system of Soviet Union and the Marxist ideology.

He worked abroad for 11 years (1972-1983, as the Soviet ambassador to Canada) "he had not only accumulated a "certain amount of theoretical and practical knowledge in this period, but also became more confident that the dominant ideology of Soviet Union became increasingly corrupted and that the Soviet political system was on the verge of perishment.[22]

In 1983, Gorbachev visited Canada, and shortly after this visit Yakovlev, returned back to Russia, Gorbachev appointed him as the director of the Institute of World Economy and International Relations attached to the Soviet Academy of Sciences and soon allowed him to enter into his private writing group.

Soon later, Yakovlev was appointed as the minister of the Central Propaganda Department of the CPSU in 1985, and in 1986 he was appointed as a director in the General Secretariat Department of the Central Committee of the CPSU in charge of ideological problems, finally in 1987 he was elected as a and member of the Political Bureau. Promoting the

---

20 Ibid., p. 19-21.
21 Ibid., p. 20-22.
22 Ibid., p. 27.

reforms together with Gorbachev, he became famous as the "designer of reform". In the very beginning, while he was preparing speech drafts for Gorbachev, Yakovlev used to boast his loyalty to the party, talked about firm belief in the socialist cause and advertised ardent love for the SU, but he always sought the opportunity to deliver his real opposite views which were gradually demonstrated in his reform policies. Many politicians of the former Soviet Union have noted that Yakovlev was duplicitous and Machiavellian. For example, Andropov referred to him as "an evil liar" while Kryuchkov, the former chairman of the KGB, said Yakovlev would always wear a fake mask.[23]

At the 28th Congress of CPSU held on July 2nd 1990, Yakovlev has praised the three major events in the "reforms": formulation and implementation of the new political ideology, guiding the work of rehabilitation committee for victims of political repressions in the past, thirdly the implementation of "democratization" and "openness" (glasnost).[24]

All these three major policies were centered around the same theme, that is, pushing the Soviet Union from the socialist system to capitalism, since Yakovlev he believed "the bourgeois slogans of freedom, equality and fraternity demonstrated a lofty idealism based on sober and practical concern."[25]

In the beginning phase of reforms, Yakovlev vigorously promoted "democratization" and "openness" which were the main means employed to overthrow the leadership of CPSU and the restoration of capitalism. In the 28th Congress Yakovlev openly declared that the aim of reforms is to break the so so-called backbone of the "totalitarian system".[26]

The two groups in the transformation of the Soviet Union

Under the guidance of such reform ideology, it's no wonder that Soviet Union would perish and get disintegrated at last. Khrushchev's move at the 20th Congress was first step in emancipating the mind of people (Khrushchev Thaw) with the advocate of bourgeois liberalization and "democratization" which gave some people a hope for system changes, while at the same time made the younger generation who used to believe in the socialist system of Soviet Union become suspicious of the Soviet system,

---

23 W. Kryuchkov: Personal file 1941-1994, Oriental Press, 2000, p. 255.
24 Yakovlev: Yakovlev's theory of new thinking of reform and the fate of the Soviet Union, translated by Gao Hongshan and Feng Yousong, Jilin People's Publishing House, 1992, pp. 204-207.
25 Yakovlev: A Cup of Bitter-Bolshevism in Russia and the Reform Movement, translated by Xu Kui, Zhang Danan, Xinhua Publishing House, 1999, p. 339.
26 Yakovlev: Yakovlev's theory of new thinking of reform and the fate of the Soviet Union, translated by Gao Hongshan and Feng Yousong, Jilin People's Publishing House, 1992, pp. 203.

which caused changes in their ideology and political standpoint. One these two types of groups later became the "intellectual elite of the sixties" while the second group became the political elite which led the "reforms". For the communist regime, the most important influence of the 20th Congress lies in the liberalization of its ideology, and its fatal consequence was to foster the opposition forces which led to the disintegration of the Soviet Union and collapse of the CPSU.

Y. 60

The Social Situation in the Former U.S.S.R. Territories, 20 Years after Its Disintegration

Xu Hua[1]

Abstract: The collapse of the Soviet Union has its 20 year's history. Now peoples living in the territories of the former Soviet Union are facing more and more political, economic and social problems. Through Western eyes, no country which belonged to the former Soviet republics including Ukraine where the "Orange Revolution" took place has really become a democratic country. The majority of the countries including Russia not only couldn't realize economic growth and structural optimization in their transition process to market economy, but also encountered economic decline. The situation has turned for the better only in recent years, and economic development of only Azerbaijan, Belarus, Kazakhstan, Russia, Turkmenistan and Baltic countries have surpassed the levels achieved in 1990 and 1991. In addition, in Russia, Kazakhstan and other countries, the social polarization between the rich and the poor has become serious. 10% of the richest people holding 80% of countries' income. In this situation, if the income gap further widens, and the injustice in the distribution of natural resources and social wealth continues, still more severe social conflicts or disturbances may break out in the territories of the former Soviet Union.

Key words: dissolution of the Soviet Union; politics; society; economy

---

1 Xu Hua, associate researcher at the Research Institute of Russia, Eastern Europe and Central Asia, of the CASS.

2011 was the 20th anniversary of the collapse of Soviet Union, but during this important period Russia appeared to be silent as a whole. Except the anniversary meeting held by the Communist Party of Russia (CPRF), the Russian government didn't hold any official events or meetings and ceremonies, while the academic circles of the former Soviet republics also didn't come up with any significant and thought-provoking research achievements.

Twenty years have passed, now both Soviet Union and its socialism are just by-gone. The kind of western affluent and democratic life promised by Russian liberals hasn't appeared in the territories of the former Soviet Union.

I. The social sphere

In early September 2005, after a terrorist incident in the Beslan school of North Ossetia, Caucasus of the CIS, Putin, as the Russian president at that time, announced in a televised speech that the collapse of Soviet Union was a serious geopolitical disaster and the great majority of people ended in vain. During the past 20 years after the collapse of Soviet Union, Russia has suffered from population decline, deterioration of health care, shortened life span as well as widening gap between the rich and the poor.

According to the latest results of Russian nationwide census on December 15th 2011, in just eight years between 2002-2010, the population of Russia was reduced by 23 million to 142.857 million with a rate of 1.6%.[2]

In the following over 20 years since 1989, Russia has conducted three nationwide population census successively in 1989, 2002 and 2010. The results showed that in the first ten years after 1989, the annual decrease rate was 0.09% while that of 8 between 2002-2010 was 0.09%. Before the collapse of Soviet Union, the total population of Russia was 147.022 million in 1989 which reduced to 145.164 million in 2002. The average life span of Russians over the recent 20 years was much lower than the average level of European countries, ranking 100th in the world. In the last two years, the average life expectancy of Russians has reached 70 among of which men is around 69.[3]

The number was only 58.6 in 2005, ranking the last among the European countries.[4]

---

2 See report of RIA on December 15th, 2011, http://ria.ru/society/20111215/517756244.html.
3 Putin declared at the government meeting on January 20th, 2012 that after years of great efforts life expectancy has increased to 70.5. See, http://demoscope.ru/ weekly/2012/0495/rossia01.php.
4 Medvedev encouraged Russian men to catch up with women. See http:// ria.ru/society/20111015/460147314.html.

With the disintegration of the Soviet Union, more than 24 million residents speaking Russian were forced to stay at the border towns of Russia, thus becoming aliens being forgotten. After the disintegration of Soviet Union, the living condition of the Russian speaking residents of former Soviet republics has deteriorated. In the newly independent countries led by national leaders, Russian minorities living in these countries have a lot of sufferings, even a part of them became are homeless today. By 2010, there were still about 10 million Russians scattered in the CIS (Commonwealth of the Independent States) and Baltic region states.

In a report called Comparison between Russia and European Union countries delivered on December 14th 2011, Surinov, the director of Russian State Bureau of Statistics, stated that the present Russia is the poorest and most unfair country in Europe.[5]

As is shown in the above statistics, compared with 27 European countries, former eastern European countries like Russia, Bulgaria and Romania were in the lowest rank in both consumption and gross domestic product per capita. Despite its vast territories, abundant resources and high economic aggregate, Russia still lagged behind in most social development indicators. For example, before the global financial crisis, the gross domestic product per capita of Russia in 2008 if calculated with the purchasing power parity was 15,900 Euro, but Russia still fell behind European countries in terms of social development. Human development index of Russia in 2010 was 0.72 while that of Romania and Bulgaria, the two least developed European countries, were 0.74 and 0.76 respectively. The health care budget expenditure of Russia only accounted for 4% of the GDP while that of European countries between 6% to 8%. Due to factors like insufficient health care expenditures, Russia's death rate from cardiovascular diseases and traffic accidents has been the highest in Europe. In 2011, the proportion of people dying from coronary artery diseases in Russia was 352 cases per 100,000 people, which was 6 times higher than Belgium, four times higher than Austria and even twice higher than the poorest Bulgaria. The indicator of death rate resulting from blood disease and infectious diseases have also remained at a high level and even ranked the highest in Europe. The death rate of traffic accidents in Russia was 20 per 100,000 people while that of Romania and Bulgaria was 12 to 13 and the average number of European Union countries was 10.

According to the report, compared with other European countries, Russian society is characterized by the highest income gap with a Gini coefficient of 0.42 while that of Germany, Austria and Spain were less than

---

5 Article by Sergeev M. The first in Europe—on mortality and inequality—However, Russia is far from being the poorest country. Nezavisimaya newspaper, December 14, 2011, http://www.ng.ru/economics/ 2011-12-14/1_smertnost.html.

0.35. The former Soviet Union upheld the goal of eliminating class differences and had once established an advanced social security system, free education, free medical care and offered economical homes for its citizens which was envied. Up to now, as a result of factors like difficult living conditions and high living expenses, Russians can't afford to raise children, which is also an important cause for the low birth rate of Russian people.

In the past 20 years, corruption has prevailed in the Russian society. To be specific, the phenomenon of corruption and gangland crimes had been quite rampant during Yeltsin's era that lasted 9 years, and it became even worse during the era of Putin. During the period of President Medvedev, corruption became more hidden and universal. During the anti-government demonstrations that erupted in the late December 2011, Russian netizens labeled the United Russia Party led by Putin as a party of burglars and liars. Over the past 20 years, corruption has already become the cancer of Russian society which is difficult to cure. In 2010, as is reflected by corruption perceptions index ranking released by an independent international organization, among those 178 countries and regions throughout the world, Russia ranked 154th in corruption together with Cambodia, Kenya and Laos.

II. The political sphere

On December 27th 2011, the Japanese newspaper, Asahi Shimbun published an editorial to the effect that 20 years ago the last Soviet leader Gorbachev said on his resignation that he hoped each republic would be prosperous and people would live in a democratic society after the Soviet disintegration. Nevertheless, twenty years later, neither independent republic has realized that wishful prediction.

In the political field, the CIS states, for example Russia used to imitate or copy the western political system, but neither of them managed to step in the threshold set by western countries in the past 20 years. Even today, Russia is still the target of critiques by the western media, and like most of the CIS states Russia is listed as an autocratic and authoritarian country by the western countries. According to the western media, Yeltsin's era was a period characterized by domination of super-rich oligarchs and prevalent corruption while Russian governed by Putin almost returns back to the former autocratic and authoritarian Soviet system. Political systems of newborn Central Asian countries also have too centralized power systems. For example, in Kazakhstan and Uzbekistan, the leaders which were inherited from the former Soviet Union have led these countries for over 20 years, and used the methods of persecuting political opponents and election frauds. In the Republic of Belarus, president Lukashenko still maintains his long-term autocratic rule. In Ukraine democratization was expected to make progress after the Orange Revolution, but the ruling party still suppresses the opposition parties and groups.

On December 2nd 2011, in the US's "New York Times" website an article was published titled "Walking Through 20 Years of Russia" written by Ariel Cohen, a senior researcher of the American Heritage Foundation.[6]

According to the above article, upon the 20th anniversary of Soviet Union collapse, the western public feel disappointed when they are evaluating the success and failure of reforms in Soviet Union. "The disintegration of the Soviet Union failed to bring people a promising prospect as anticipated by many people in western and eastern countries, because most of the power positions are still in the hands of former state officers. Due to a lack of belief, moral depravity and growth of crime rate, Russia still fails to become a government serving the people dutifully and has not still set up a transparent and participatory governance system based on rule of law." Just as a western joke puts it, to establish an autocratic system in a democratic state is just like cooking fish soup in a fish tank while setting up democratic system on the basis of autocracy is like breeding fish in fish soup.

In his article Ariel Cohen has argued that apart from three Baltic states (or perhaps Georgia), no former Soviet republic is genuinely qualified as a democratic country, including Ukraine which underwent through the Orange Revolution.

Finally, Ariel Cohen has written: "the Russian people are not happy, today Russia has the highest rate of drug addiction, corruption and suicide. Meanwhile, it is Europe rather than Russia where the senior officials and billionaires of this country make their holidays, deposit their cash money and educate their children. Russia is not a democratic country but an authoritarian country characterized by numerous crimes and paternalism." According to Robert Gates, the former US secretary of defense and the current director of the CIA, "Russia is an oligarchic country with its power in the hand of secret service."

III. The Economic sphere

20 years ago, the CIS (The Commonwealth of Independent States) state Russia abandoned the planned economy of the former Soviet Union which used mechanism state regulation, this country adopt a shock therapy economic reforms in the hope of developing a western type of free market economy. However, the process of market transformation in most of the

---

6 Cohen A., „Walking Through 20 Years of Russia", The New York Times, 2 Dec. 2011, http://www.nytimes.com/2011/12/03/opinion/russia-20-years-along. html?_ r =2.

countries including Russia not only failed to achieve economic growth and optimized structure but encountered with a dramatic economic decline and faced two serious economic crises in 1998 and 2008. On November 26th 2011, RIA-TV broadcasted an analysis by the economic commentator Vlad. Grinkevich titled "The Russian Economic Reform: 20 Years in Circles".[7]

According to the analysis: "Russia has already conducted economic reforms for 20 years and now it's time to sum up. Unfortunately, the results are not satisfactory. Even though Russia got rid of its old planned economy, yet it has cost Russia a declining industrialization, it lags behind the developed countries, it is reduced to a supplier of raw materials for the global economy and gradually marginalized economically".

Grinkevich has commented: "In the Soviet era during the period from the mid-1980s to 1991, the Soviet Academy of Economics had suggested some radical economic reform plans, but due to hesitation and resistance by and quarrels among the Soviet leaders, these plans were never implemented. What's worse, at the end of 1980s, decline of oil prices in the international markets and due to political crisis in the Soviet Union political its economy was pushed to the verge of collapse, and from then on, the economic crisis has further deepened and the disintegration of Soviet Union became inevitable.

The policy of economic privatization has exerted severe negative influences, which was manifested by a high inflation rate of 2500% in 1992. Besides, the consequence of economic privatization was so brutal and unlawful that even liberals have criticized the privatization of Russia's state property as being a dirty and unfair business. Some Russian economists have argued that it was a great mistake to implement the decision of privatizing state-owned assets, under the conditions of hyperinflation, because the privatization accounts or privatization checks or vouchers received by the ordinary citizens rapidly lost their values.[8]

Such kind of privatization was doomed to be full of all sorts of unfair and dirty businesses. The second stage of privatization, has caused more severe problems.

---

[7] V. Grinkevich, Reform of Russia: 20 Years in Circles, http://ria.com/analytics/20111125/497973465.html (in Russian language).

[8] The approach advocated the free distribution of state-owned enterprises to the whole of the Russian population. That idea was based on the proposition that the Russian people had participated in the creation of national wealth, including all productive assets, during previous decades and therefore were entitled to share in the nation's material assets. To achieve citizen ownership, advocates proposed the creation of privatization accounts or privatization checks or vouchers. After extensive discussions, this approach became the basis for Russia's first privatization program in 1992.

It was extremely absurd to do the privatization of the assets of the large scale state-owned companies through the notorious mortgage auction method. It should be the privatization, based on an honest, open sale of state property at the fair, the real price. Since then Russian economy turned into a barbaric, sturdy and maleficent capitalist economy just as described by Dickens. Such kind of privatization will continue to harass Russia.

Currently, the superpower Soviet Union which once challenged the US no longer exists. 20 years later, the average living standards of Russians will only level off with that of the late 1980s. Over the past 20 years, the industrial power of Russia has sharply declined with its average labor productivity equaling to 6% to 10% of the US. Despite, continuous growth of oil prices in the international markets in the recent years, financial budget of Russia is still hovering on the verge of deficit. Social security expenditures of the state is stretched and can only be met with tinkering. Besides, government's expenditures on education, health care and other public services also continues to decline, year after year without recovery.

IV. Economic situation of the counties in the former USSR regions

20 years ago, Ukrainian leaders had announced that after independence Ukraine would soon become the richest country in Europe. However, this period of 20 years has been just like a nightmare for this country and life seems to return back to the origin. On November 11th 2011, Russia's newspaper "The Independent" published an article by V. Vashanov, the director of the Center for Economic Research at the OECD, a division of the Russian Ministry of Economic Development and the Russian Academy of Sciences.

In this article titled "Pros and Cons of Post-Soviet Independent States: Striking the Balance, Vashanov wrote: Over the past 20 years the economies of the most post-Soviet independent countries have failed to reach the level of Soviet Union in 1991. Now 20 years have passed, and by 2010, in addition to those three Baltic countries, quite few countries like Azerbaijan, Kazakhstan and Russia have managed to surpass the level of 1991 in terms of their GDPs. In contrast, other former Soviet republics are all struggling. What's worse, the global financial crisis that erupted in 2008 has slowed the pace of economic development and has exposed them to predicament once again."[9]

---

9 Vashanov V., Twelve Years After the Decay, Nezavisimaya Gazeta, November 11, 2011, http://www.ng.com/ideas/2011-11-11 5_20years.html.

Over the past 20 years, except the Republic of Belarus, the trade volume of Russia and the CIS states generally were reduced by 1/3. From 1991 to 1995, the GDPs of former Soviet countries have dramatically declined. Over the first ten years after the disintegration of the Soviet Union, only Estonia managed to surpass the level of the year 1991 regarding its GDP. In the last 20 years, the economies of many countries which had separated from the Soviet Union in 1990 have mainly relied on their energy industries like oil and natural gas production and exports. For example, Azerbaijan can exploit 4 billion tons of oil, and Kazakhstan's oil and gas production is also increasing.

Compared with 1991, the growth rate of Kazakhstan's gas and natural gas production per capita in 2009 were 210% and 50% respectively. When it comes to Turkmenistan, its natural gas production ranked top 5 in the world and its oil production is the fourth among post-Soviet countries. Nevertheless, the foreign currency revenues of these former Soviet countries gained through oil and natural gas exports have failed to fundamentally improve social life of people. For example, the average nominal monthly salaries of workers in Uzbekistan is less than 200 dollars with a high level of invisible unemployment rate. Labor force of some Central Asian countries have no choice but to earn money through working in Russia.

After the disintegration of the Soviet Union, the population of Russia has decreased greatly, but compared with the period of Soviet Union, per capita output of many important industrial products are still in a decreasing trend, that is, in electricity the decrease rate is 4.3%, oil 7.2%, coal 23.7%, cement 35%, ferrous metal rolls 20% and meat (industrially processed) 40%. The only exception is the grain yield which has increased by 14% in 2010.

The global financial crisis has exerted the most negative effect against the Republic of Belarus. By the mid-2011, the currency of the Republic of Belarus suffered a severe devaluation and people's average income decreased by 25% to 30% while its foreign debt has constantly increased.

As the second largest country after Russia, Ukraine's manufacturing industry possesses leading position among the Former Soviet countries. By virtue of its multiple and abundant mineral resources, Ukraine is regarded as a great mining country in Europe. In history, the extraction of coal, iron ore and manganese ore in Ukraine used to take the lead in Europe, but in the past 20 years after the disintegration of the Soviet Union, its economy kept deteriorating. In the recent 10 years, Ukraine's oil and natural gas reserve keep decreasing. Currently, Ukraine itself can only supply 10% to 12% of its domestic oil needs and 22% of its domestic natural gas needs, thus has become heavily dependent on Russia with its energy relying heavily on Russia. The situation of Ukraine in the past 20 years is strikingly similar to Russia, despite a 12% decrease in Ukraine's population, nearly all of its economic indicators have declined sharply: the electric energy production per capita was reduced by 44%, oil by 18%, coal by 54%, cement by 51%, ferrous metal rolls by 57% and processed meat by 74%. The only exception is the grain yield which has increased by 34%.

In those CIS states like Armenia, Georgia and Moldova, their domestic social and economic situations since independence have all encountered deterioration to a certain extent.

Armenia used to be an industrialized country with a strong potential of science and technology, but since after the 1988 earthquake plus its military conflicts with Azerbaijan, its economy has failed to recover. Ever since 1990, Armenia's economic development has encountered a great frustration. The highway and railway transportation between Armenia and Azerbaijan was halted due to conflicts while its railway connection to Russia via Georgia was also halted as a result of conflicts between Georgia and Abkhazia. Over the past 20 years, the electric energy output per capita of Armenia has reduced by 53% with its production reduced by 70%. In 2010, the average nominal monthly wages of workers were less than 280 dollars.

The situation in Georgia has also been terrible with an all-round decline in per capita output of its major industrial products, that is, electric energy production saw reduction of 42%, coal 31%, cement 51%, grain yield 14% and processed meat 93%. The average nominal monthly wages of Georgian workers were only about 250 dollars.

The social and economic development of Moldova since its independence 20 years ago has been unsatisfactory. In 1992, there occurred military conflicts in the Dnieper river region, which caused the actual separation of the Transnistria region10 which has been the richest industrial region of the former Moldova Republic under the USSR.

In the other regions of Moldova, their output of electric energy, cement, grain and processed meat saw reductions by 90%, 45%, 20% and 93% respectively with the average nominal monthly wages for workers being about 240 dollars. Agriculture as the leading sector could only manage to survive as a result of severe aging of technical equipment, deficient investment and rising price of fuel based fertilizers.

---

10 Transnistria is a small breakaway state located between the Dniester River and Moldova's eastern border with Ukraine. In November 1990, limited fighting broke out between Russian-backed pro-Transnistrian forces and the Moldovan police and military. The fighting intensified in March 1992, and lasted until an uneasy yet lasting ceasefire was established on July 22, 1992.Transnistria's Russian-speaking population believes that its identity would be overwhelmed by the ethnic Moldovan majority and thus sees the Russian military presence as protection.

By 2010, the living standard of the citizens of Kyrgyzstan and Tajikistan have been far lower than that of Soviet Union era levels. With the successive outburst of putsches and domestic revolutions, Kyrgyzstan has suffered political unrest, regime changes and constant ethnic conflicts, thus its national economy has been beset with crises. The electric energy output per capita of Kyrgyzstan saw a reduction by 42% while the production of mining, engineering and food industry all has reduced. When it comes to its foreign debt, even though the Paris club had exempted the majority of its foreign debts, its remaining foreign debt still around 2.7 billion dollars (accounting for about 60% of Kyrgyzstan's GDP). The per capita income of Kyrgyzstan has been almost the lowest among the CIS states after Tajikistan. The per capita income of Kyrgyzstan was only 151 dollars in 2010, and its GDP per capita being just 840 dollars.

The social and economic situation of Tajikistan has been even worse. The civil war between 1992-1994 has caused to an all-round collapse of its national economy and 100,000 people were wounded or lost their lives (far higher than the number of casualties during the Great Patriotic war). As a result, a huge amount of labor force became disabled. The war has devastated the country, which required more than 7 billion Dollars to restore its economy. Factors leading to decline of production also include the damaged former economic connection and failure in market economy reforms. All sorts of enterprises, be it small or large, in industries of machine manufacturing, light industry and food processing industry have suffered severe losses and encountered bankruptcies one after another. The monthly wages in Tajikistan ranked the least among all the former Soviet republics with only 70 dollars, and its per capita GDP was also the least with just 745 dollars.

Generally speaking, currently the economic situation of those countries like Armenia, Georgia, Kyrgyzstan, Moldova, Tajikistan, Uzbekistan and Ukraine are worse than the Soviet Union era with a low per capita GDPs ranging from 880 to 2,500 dollars and an average wages around 300 dollars.

While analyzing the economic situation of former Soviet countries over the past 20 years, Vashanov pointed out: "only Azerbaijan, the Republic of Belarus, Kazakhstan, Turkmenistan and Baltic countries have managed to surpass their 1990-1991 levels with their per capita GDP ranging from 6,000 to 9,000 dollars while that of Baltic countries were around 10,000 dollars. The average monthly per capita incomes of the CIS states were about 400 to 600 dollars and that of Baltic countries were between 800-1.100 dollars. Of course, these data are quite limited and cannot truly reflect the great gaps and polarization of income among the people. For example, the gap between rich and poor in Russia and Kazakhstan has been quite serious: the 10% richest people in the society possess 80% of the total national income.

Under such circumstances, if the income gap among the Russian population continues to widen, unfair distribution of natural resources and social wealth continues, if these are coupled with badly managed ethnic policies, Russia may face severe social conflicts, which could lead social divisions and chaos, meaning the repetition of the old mistakes by the Soviet Union.

Y. 61

The Russian Scholars Are Beginning to Explore the Contemporary Value of the "Soviet Civilization"

Li Ruiqin[1]

Abstract: When commemorating the 95th anniversary of the October Revolution in 2012, Russian scholars put forward that they should explore Soviet civilization's contemporary value in combination with the comprehensive degradation of Russian social sciences. They think that the fundamental character of Soviet civilization was to eliminate exploitation and embodied the principle of all-round social equality in society. Soviet civilization has made significant contribution to Russia and the whole world. At present, in order to find a way to come out of the current global crisis, the world will inevitably divert attention to studying the experiences of the Soviet civilization.

Key words: Soviet civilization; contemporary value

---

1 Li Ruiqin, a guest researcher of the World Socialism Research Center, attached to CASS, also an associate researcher in the Institute of Marxism.

Ever since the collapse of Soviet Union 20 years ago especially after the heavy attack of the 2008 global financial crisis, reflection on the national development path, has become a top priority by Russian people from all walks of life. They try to sum up, theorize and reflect on the 70-year historical experience of socialist construction in Soviet Union from different perspectives and standpoints, which is the key focus point. Echoing, the social emotions of the society, Russian scholars began to reflect on reevaluating Stalin, reevaluating the history of Soviet Union and its achievements..

When commemorating the 95th anniversary of the October Revolution in 2012, Russian scholars put forward that they should explore the contemporary value of the Soviet civilization, together with the comprehensive degradation of Russian social sciences.

For example, on October 16th 2012, Russian Pravda held a round-table conference titled experience and lessons of the Soviet civilization; and recently Zyuganov, general secretary of the central committee of the Communist Party of Russian Federation, published a long article called The Memory of the Future-Soviet Civilization on October 25th 2012. And, SG Kara-Murza, the famous contemporary Russian political commentator has published a book of two volumes titled The Soviet Civilization.

The famous Russian website called Opposing the TV Screen" also especially allocated a column for debates on the Soviet civilization etc.

Even though at present there are only quite few Russian scholars studying the Soviet civilization independent from the current ruling authority in Russia, yet they are still convinced that in the history of Russia, indeed there has been a remarkable Soviet civilization led by the guidance of Marxism-Leninism. This point is particularly worth further thinking for those people living in socialist countries. The following are the current focus of Russian academics:

I. The fundamental nature of the Soviet civilization was eliminating exploitation.

According to Zyuganov, the general secretary of the Communist Party of Russian Federation: " it is a complex and arduous cause to study the Soviet civilization and what we can do today is just determining and proposing the outline of this scientific and political study issue. Ever since 1917, a new type of civilization has taken shape in the world, thanks to which the working class became the master of the society. As a result, it fundamentally established a kind of civilization different from the one examined by Oswalt Spengler and Toynbee."

Zyuganov added: "Marx and Engels established the theory of scientific communism, was developed in the works of V.I. Lenin, and then I.V. Stalin. The correctness of the scientific findings of Marxism-Leninism and the errors in the utopian schemes of the bourgeois revolutionaries were proved in the course of formation of the socialist system. In this case, the Soviet social order was organic and stage of development of our original native Russian–Russian civilization. For the first time in world history classes, living on the operation, have lost their privileges. Authorities parasites and speculators, and the continued pursuit of profit by robbing other people has to stop. Soviet civilization was the first in which the principles of triumph: "He who does not work shall not eat" and "lord of the world will work." From the first days of Soviet power were taken to ensure that the most pressing social and political rights of the working man. Labor, exalted in society awards and a variety of measures to promote, in a matter of honor, valor and heroism.[2]

Scholars attending the round-table conference of Russian Pravda mentioned that as the first civilization in the world, which genuinely embodied and led by the Marxism-Leninism, the Soviet civilization was different from the civilization proposed by the bourgeois revolutionaries or communists like Trotsky. During the October revolution, people like Trotsky just mechanically affirmed the role of the French bourgeois revolution and attempted to stop Soviet Russia from attempting the practice of socialist construction, before the triumph of western proletarian revolution.

Starting from the fact that socialist revolution was an inevitable outcome of Russian social development, Lenin and Stalin led Russian people to establish this new type of civilization. Therefore, the Soviet civilization is the outcome generated by extensively absorbing the experience of people in Russia and other countries.

The scholars have argued that: "the most important and fundamental distinctive feature of the Soviet civilization lied in that it has established a society dominated by public ownership and created splendid material and spiritual wealth. All former civilizations of human history were founded on the basis of private ownership. Western civilization has made significant contribution to development of humankind, but now it is heading towards self-destruction, because the private ownership will inevitably lead to perishment." "Another important feature of the Soviet civilization was that it conforms to the historical development and national conditions of Russia. Since April 1917, Lenin had began to think about possible prospect of Russia and attempted to practice the theories emphasized by Marx and Engels: "a revolution should fit to historical features of each country, then it will be feasible for different countries, realizing their revolutions with various properties."

---

2 Gennady Zyuganov, Soviet Civilization–A Memory of the Future, Soviet Russia, 25/10/2012.

According to classical Marxist writers, the revolution was first started by French workers followed by Germany, but the Russian revolution came fore as the caprice of world history.

It was not only because of the fact that Russia was the weakest link of the imperialist chain due to the most authoritarian Tsarist rule and the heaviest exploitation of the laboring people but also the fact that the Russian working class was characterized by village farmer's state of mind and possessed the capability of unifying most social classes.[3]

Another scholar wrote in his book titled as "The Key to the Future" that the Soviet civilization, that appeared in Russia in the first half of 20th century, can be classified as a humanitarian civilization, among various civilizations in the contemporary world. It has demonstrated many "firsts" in the long history of human civilization.[4]

To be more specific, it was the first time to establish the notion of prohibiting exploitation in terms of social ideology.

The conquest of nature requires the help of science and technology, in the Soviet society, science was for the first time declared as a social productive force.[5]

Soviet civilization, for the first time announced the death of the religious doctrine and advocated atheism.

It was the first country which explicitly declared, social creativity, as one of those basic human rights, in the society. This human right aimed to guarantee that all-round and comprehensive development of human beings can replace, that "dull" kind of labor, and this kind of human right aimed to gradually eliminate differences between manual labor and mental labor.[6]

As mentioned above, scholars were basically in agreement regarding the evaluation the Soviet civilization.

It is a new type of civilization which developed on the basis of public ownership characterized by the guidance of the scientific theory of Marxism-Leninism, elimination of exploitation and oppression, working people becoming masters of their country and the emergence of the most glorious new value of labor.[7]

---

3 Round table in the editorial board of Pravda, What are the experience and lessons of the Soviet civilization, http://za.zubr, in: Ua 2012/10/16/18249.
4 Alexander Lazarevich, The Key to the Future: The Soviet Civilization, http://technocosm.narod.com/k2f /soviet_ civilization.htm.
5 Ibid.
6 Ibid.
7 Round table in the editorial board of Pravda, What are the experience and lessons of the Soviet civilization, http://za.zubr, in: Ua 2012/10/16/18249.

This new civilization of the Soviet Union conforms to objective laws of Russia and historical development which was an inevitable outcome of social development of Russia in early 20th century.[8]

The Soviet civilization has been a new form of civilization in the history of human society, representing the general trend human development in the future.

II. The Soviet civilization has comprehensively embodied the principle of social equality

According to general secretary Zyuganov: "since the Russian working class accounted for the great majority in the society, the Soviet civilization has been the best realization of civilization in Russia. It has indeed adopted the practice of social equality principle, which didn't remain only as a promise.

In the world history, it was the first time, that all the members of the society could have a free access to free learning opportunities and various medical, health care services. Soviet people's expenditure on housing, public utility service and transportation was quite negligible, which didn't change in throughout the Soviet Union history, and the food expenditures were affordable."

For the first time, "Soviet civilization" put an end to patriarchal system, and put an end to the unequal status of women who had suffered from oppression and discrimination. In the first year after the establishment of the Soviet regime, it implemented the principle ensuring women's political equality and women were granted the right to get the same pay for the same job, which was neglected in many countries all around the world.

Besides, the "Soviet civilization" also devoted huge efforts to protect women and children in that women could enjoy paid leave before and after delivery, nation-wide free clinics and free maternity hospital network were set up throughout the country and almost all nurseries and kindergartens were free. Mothers were esteemed by honor and respect. At the height of the Great Patriotic War, Soviet Union had set up many awards for mothers with more than one child: medal for mother, glorious mother and heroic mother. The International Women's Day on March 8th has been one of the most favorite festivals of Soviet people."

"Soviet civilization has attached greater importance to the education of teenagers and youth, it formed a new type of targeted pattern of adult public education and family education. During their growth, children received all-round protection so as to protect them from being seduced by immoral and

---

8   Ibid.

bad habits. Soviet Union was the first country to found a pioneer organization of children while most of the young people have joined youth mass organizations, Communist Youth League (Komsomol).

Such kind of new pattern combining collective education with family education as family, kindergarten, school, vanguard of adolescents and youth league provided the best learning and practical situation for the younger generation to cultivate a healthy moral spirit."

"In order to protect the children's physical and mental health, the state established a nation-wide network covering all medical and health organizations. With these policies, infant mortality rate was significantly reduced, healthy growth of the younger generations was enhanced, and the life expectancy in the Soviet Union saw an increase of %112."

Moreover, healthy growth of the younger generations promoted sports, and the Soviet state paid great attention to support sports activities, and Soviet athletes always ranked among the best in Olympic games and in other international contests."

Soviet civilization established the principle of ethnic-national equality for the first time. For centuries, there had always been national oppression, conflicts and violence in Russia. In the first year after the establishment of the Soviet regime, all nations were able to enjoy a new relationship based on equality and fraternity or brotherhood. Soviet civilization created favorable conditions for development of national culture and established education facilities responding to the demands of different ethnic-nations and promoted ethnic languages. To be specific, Soviet civilization, supported the research of new words for those ethnic groups, that had weaker languages. and it also built art and theater groups having national characteristics including all nations living in the SU, thus promoted the traditional and national culture of various nations,

Soviet civilization promoted ethnic-national literatures, which in turn contributed to the civilization in the whole Soviet Union. In the Soviet Union era, a large number of excellent works in the fields of music, literature, painting, architecture, drama and cinema films were created. Many excellent works created by Soviet writers like Sholokhov, Shostakovich, Prokofiev, Mayakovsky, Sviridov, Mukhina, Eisenstein and Khachaturian were listed among the world cultural treasure house. Bright reflection of the depth of feeling of the Soviet people was the Soviet song that created the country's best composers and performed her best singers. The whole world applauded the musicians, vocal and ballet ensembles, which exhibited all over the world creations of Soviet culture.[9]

---

9 Gennady Zyuganov, Soviet Civilization–A Memory of the Future, Soviet Russia, 25/10/2012.

Fourier, a great French utopian socialist thinker, once made a famous comment: "the degree of emancipation of woman is the natural measure of general emancipation," which indicated that the female's social status is significantly important for human development.

Besides, the ideas and slogans of equality among nations and equality, freedom and fraternity were declared by the bourgeoisie through since the French Revolution, but they were never realized. In history, it was only the "Soviet civilization" that used practical measures to initiate remarkable achievements, which has proved the scientific and practical features of Marxism, the great science which aims human liberation.

The world's first civilization was built on a scientific basis. Soviet civilization brought to life the judgment of Marxism-Leninism on the continuous development of society from capitalism, divided into antagonistic classes, to a new society with friendly classes, to socialism, and then to walk towards a classless communist society.

III. "Soviet civilization" has made great contributions to Russia and the world.

In his long article titled 'The Memory of the Future- Soviet Civilization', Zyuganov concentrated on the contributions of the Soviet civilization.

Contribution to the freedom of the Soviet Land

First of all, Soviet civilization has proven its ability to defend against enemy attacks. During the Second World War, our country has demonstrated unsurpassed in the world to achieve the creation of the perfect weapon: the legendary "Katyusha", T-34, IL-2. Nazi soldiers informed the German minister of armaments A. Speer, they prefer Soviet submachine German. These achievements were based on unsurpassed in the world of technical level of the Soviet defense industry. Attempts to create a copy of the German gunsmiths of the T-34 have failed because they were not able to smelt the same stainless steel and produce the same motor of aluminum. War show a higher level of military art, shown by Soviet generals Zhukov, Rokossovsky, Konev, Wasilewski and others, led by Supreme Commander Stalin. The war has proven and unmatched ability of the Soviet state to implement the evacuation of thousands of industry and millions of people and organize the defense industry in the rear. Evidence of perfection of Soviet civilization began a rapid recovery of the country and devastated the beginning of peaceful development. At the same time Soviet civilization was able to mobilize industrial production, science and technology, in order to take a few years to catch up to the U.S. nuclear weapons and to protect the country from the U.S. imperialists was preparing destruction of hundreds of millions of our cities and the Soviet people. The steady performance of five-year plans or other economic development became a guarantee of stable development of Soviet society. The belief that "tomorrow will be better than yesterday," was typical of Soviet civilization, reflected in the relationship between people and the works of Soviet culture.

In addition, the country also gave top priority to development of science and technology, thus leading the world in terms of research on aerospace. To be specific, it launched the first man-made satellite in the world, conducted the first flight to space and set up the first nuclear power plant in the world. The country took active measures to develop its industrial production and science and technology, and caught up U.S in a short time by developing nuclear weapons, thus freeing the country from destruction and threat of American imperialism. In the minds of people, those heroes achieving feats in the great patriotic war would never fade.

Secondly, Soviet Union was the planned economy that knows no crisis, business failures and unemployment. Soviet planning system provided steady movement to an ever higher level of production in terms of quantity and quality. For several decades, the Soviet industry, the share of which in the beginning had no more than 4% of world production, was to produce about 20% of the industrial output of the planet. During the years of Soviet civilization, there were thousands of modern enterprises, and hundreds of new cities, reflected the aspirations of the Soviet people to create a "city of gardens". Built on a scientific basis, the Company shall ensure priority development of research in all fields of human knowledge. The first artificial satellite, the first human flight into space, creating the world's first nuclear power plant and other achievements are prime examples of successes of Soviet science and technology.

The new man of the Soviet Civilization

One of the major achievements of Soviet civilization–unprecedented in the history of the formation of the Soviet man. Rejection of bourgeois morality as a relic of the past accompanied by the development of such qualities as integrity, and sometimes selfless performance of his public duty, patriotism, and willingness to help not only our neighbor, but also people from distant lands and countries. Embodied in the provisions of the Moral Code of the Builder of Communism: "Man to man–a friend, comrade and brother."

Soviet people became more educated and well-rounded. Our country has become the most popular in the world. Rapidly growing interest in the literature, to the scientific and popular journals and books on science and technology. Soviet man was not limited philistine, withdrawn into the sphere of their private interests and personal life. In Soviet civilization lived and worked great people work, education and culture, which became an example for the younger generation, such as Stakhanov and Gaganova, Korolev and Kurchatov, the researchers of the Arctic Ocean and Antarctica, Chkalov and Gagarin, the famous production organizers, engineers and technicians. Heroism is not fading in people's memory exploits of the Soviet people in the Great Patriotic War: Zoe Kosmodemyanskaya, Alexander Matrosov, the Young. The examples of his duty million Red Army soldiers and selfless heroes home front during World War II grew generations of Soviet people.[10]

Soviet civilization's contribution to the world

According to Zyuganov: the successful development of the Soviet civilization was an example for the world. Under the influence of the Soviet Union's ruling classes in the capitalist countries have been forced to install an 8-hour day and go for a variety of social and political concessions to the working people. Under the influence of the Soviet example in the capitalist countries to take measures to eliminate the inequality of women. An example of the Soviet Union made the racists in the U.S. to take their positions and refuse from the blatant practice of racial or ethnic discrimination. After the launch of the Soviet satellite in the Soviet Union rushed a delegation of American educators who have studied the experience of the Soviet education. The American education system is divided into a period of "up to the satellite" and "after the satellite." In capitalist countries, they began to try to resort to plan its economic development. Soviet example stimulated the development of space research and development in other areas of science and technology.

However, the impact of Soviet civilization of the world was not limited to a focus on its positive examples. The Soviet Union fought for the preservation of world peace by pulling back in the 1920s, a program of general and complete disarmament, speaking for the collective security, and to curb the aggressors. Soviet civilization has become a major force to crush the march of Hitler's Germany, militarist Japan and their allies against humanity. The threat of enslavement of the peoples of the world and the infinite genocide was eliminated primarily by the Soviet civilization. Achieving balance in having weapons of mass destruction, Soviet civilization managed to prevent the outbreak of a global nuclear catastrophe and the transformation of the world into a desert. Thanks to the continuous efforts of the Soviet Union a new world war was averted.

Like any true civilization, the Soviet Union had a powerful impact on the surrounding—near and far—the world. USSR contributed to the formation of the Soviet type of social systems everywhere—in Europe, where the situation socialist commonwealth countries such as East Germany,

---

10 Ibid.

Bulgaria, Poland, Yugoslavia, Czechoslovakia, in Asia (China, Vietnam), the Americas (Cuba), Africa (Angola and Mozambique). And the pockets and the germs of Soviet civilization preserved in some of these countries after the collapse of the USSR. And some, such as China, even strengthened, largely adopting the "red" civilizational initiative of the Soviet Union, and the tree of instilling her own millennial culture.[11]

IV. Consequences of Soviet civilization after its destruction

Zyuganov wrote: the overthrow of the socialist system and the collapse of the Soviet Union followed by the destruction of the Soviet civilization. Ceased the work of hundreds of industrial enterprises established in the Soviet era. Went into decline agriculture. Scientific, educational and cultural institutions were closed. City, built in the years of Soviet five-year plans are falling into disrepair and become breeding grounds for crime and social conditions. Millions of people are out of work and confidence in the future. Suicide rates increased dramatically. The birth rate has fallen sharply, and the population began to decline. Soviet civilization was replaced by the era of bourgeois barbarism. The decline of knowledge, cultural degradation, furious growth of alcoholism and drug addiction accompanied triumph immoral principle: "Man to man–the wolf." In a country where the triumph of militant morality of selfishness, ideal for the younger generation has become a speculator, nazhivshiysya to fraudulent manipulation, looting of public property, and steal millions. As people remember the lost Soviet life, and the memory is hard to destroy, the Russian criminal bourgeoisie seeks to prove the viciousness of the Soviet civilization. Improvised media every day convince the population of Russia is that 74 years of Soviet civilization was only a historical failure. They are trying to discredit the great stories every day, every significant event of Soviet life, slander communist doctrine. However, this cannot be achieved.[12]

People say that the USSR, Soviet civilization became a legend of our time, a kind of Kitezh-hail the twentieth century. This is not entirely true. They were not so much a legend as a dream, turned to the future. Indeed, history suggests that the existence of the great civilizations is, as a rule, a kind of pulsating character. They know the times of the rise and fall times, sometimes so deep that the impression of their deaths. But time passes, and such a revival of civilization again, rushing to the heights of development. The death of the Soviet Union was scrapped in the development of the great Russian civilization, which, raising the Soviet system, said the world main way of further human progress. And suffered a setback back on many years ago.

---

11   Ibid.
12   Ibid.

Therefore, the current Russian bourgeoisie aims demonize the Soviet civilization, and every day the media controlled by the bourgeoisie tries to convince the Russians that the 74-year Soviet civilization was a historical failure. According to scholars attending the round-table conference of Pravda on October 26th 2012, ever since the collapse of Soviet Union 20 years ago, Russia could not surpass the level of primitive capitalism without any breakthroughs in the field of economy or in the fields of culture, philosophy, theory and thinking.

Current, Russia fails to optimize social relations in Russia and cannot achieve ethnic unity among nationalities.

Retrogression in all fields can be seen as the reward of anti-civilization movement of Russian neo-liberalism, they cannot offer any constructive vision or program for the world, instead Russian neo-liberalism has only the ability of absorbing residual of western spirituality.

The current Russian society is full of worsening corruption and polarization, which reproduced morbid social phenomena such as lack of belief, violence, drug abuse, alcoholism, demoralization, rampant and narrow pragmatism and the deepest pessimism. All these have triggered a tide of suicide, global terrorism threat and increasing war like relations among people, all these are marks of barbarism. A scholars commented: as a rule, the history has shown that the existence and development of a great civilization, needs to cope with the characteristics of the times. During the development process of a civilization, it might face and suffer severe hardships. However, with the passage of time, the "Soviet civilization," which represents the direction of human progress will revive and rejuvenate again and achieve a higher degree of development."[13]

V. The contemporary value of Soviet civilization against the background of the current global economic crisis

A scholar attending the round-table conference of Pravda said: "the world today is faced with a fundamental transformation. Both the NATO, implementing aggressive offensive policies, and the US by its global expansion attempts to impose their will to the entire world. Under such new circumstances, the world's interest towards Soviet civilization has greatly increased, which is closely related with the global crisis, which involves almost 200 countries and many regions of the world. Seeking the way out and seeking solutions for this crisis, inevitably, many researchers have shifted their attention to the experience of Soviet civilization.

---

13 Round table in the editorial board of Pravda, What are the experience and lessons of the Soviet civilization, http://za.zubr, in: Ua 2012/10/16/18249.

Even Obama, had to talk about the necessity of strengthening social life and the importance of strengthening the role of state and need to restrict some aspects of capital operations, during his 2012 election campaign platform. The seemingly prosperous Europe has also encountered with severe challenges.[14]

Party general secretary, Zyuganov said: that Asian countries have suffered the deepest disaster in the crisis, but socialist countries like China and Vietnam could overcome the crisis, since they had one thing in common, namely a rational government regulation characterized by effective management and planning and the implementation of a social oriented fiscal policies. These were just the solutions which were adopted by the Soviet state in the past."

"In the current decayed and corrupt era, the choice of civilization is more acute than any other time. Russia must seriously study the experience of the 'Soviet civilization', and strive to maintain the memory of this unique and independent civilization so as to put an end to the current corrupt bourgeois regime. Therefore, we must apply achievements of the Soviet civilization, into the new historical stage of Russian social development, in order to effectively build the socialism of 21st century.[15]

---

14 Ibid.
15 Gennady Zyuganov, Soviet Civilization–A Memory of the Future, Soviet Russia, 25/10/2012.

Y. 62

A Proposal to Translate and Publish the Revised Editions of Stalin's Collected Works Volumes 14-18

Ouyang Xiangying[1]

Abstract: The Chinese edition of "The Collected Works of Stalin" includes 13 volumes, which conforms and corresponds with the first 13 volumes of the Russian edition. Originally, the Russian edition was planned as 16 volumes, but actually total 18 volumes were published. The 17th and 18th volumes include Stalin's poems, letters, telegrams, speeches and instructions. The new revised content of 14th to 16th, i.e. the three volumes are different compared the old edition and the new edition contains a large number of new supplements and its publication was completed recently in 2011. The 16th volume is divided into two parts, the first part of it is a collection of articles from September 1945 to December 1948, the second part of the 16th volume includes articles from December 1948 to 1952, which are written in the period of the post-war reconstruction and the post-war economic development of the Soviet Union. The time from the end of World War II to Stalin's death is the main historical stage is covered in the 16th volume of the revised new edition, it is also an important period during which Stalin led the construction of the Soviet Union and effected important changes in the international political and economic setup. The revised Russian version of the "Stalin Complete Works" especially, the volumes 14-18, which are recently published, can offer us new historical references for us to sum up the experiences and lessons of history, regarding the politics, economy, military and diplomacy of the Soviet Union. They also provide more materials for to studies on Stalin thought and practice, and also about the history of the development of the international communist movement, we can especially read the communications between Mao Zedong and Stalin and examine the early relationship between the Soviet Union and China. This article focuses on the main content of the Russian version of the "Stalin Complete Works", 16th Volume.

Key words: Complete Works of Stalin; history of International Communist Movement; socialist camp; Stalinism; Soviet archive

---
1 Ouyang Xiangying, associate researcher in the World Socialism Research Center of the CASS, and the Deputy director of the Institute of World Economic and Political Research.

I. About the publishing of the "Works"

In 1946, Marx, Engels-Lenin Institute, attached to the Communist Party of the Soviet Union (Bolshevik) started to compile The Complete Works of Stalin, which should include 16 volumes as planned, and they were published by National Political Literature Press. The first 13 volumes were released smoothly. But, after Stalin's death, Khrushchev ordered to terminate the publishing of the rest volumes and ordered the destruction of the works regarding several volumes which were already prepared for publication.

According to the "Acknowledgment" notice in the 1st Volume: "it says the 14th volume will include the works of Stalin from 1934-1940, the 15th volume will include the History of the Communist Party of the Soviet Union (Bolsheviks), Short Course, and the 16 volume covers Stalin's works during Patriotic War".

In 1960s, The Hoover Institution on War, Revolution, and Peace (USA) published the last three volumes of The Complete Works of Stalin, but this publication has made major adjustments to these three volumes.

In the 15th volume, of History of the Communist Party of the Soviet Union (Bolsheviks) Short Course was not completely included as planned in Russia, and the 14th volume included a short summary of Stalin's famous article Dialectical Materialism and Historical Materialism. The 15th volume was changed to include Stalin's works during the Patriotic War and the 16th volume was changed to include Stalin's works after the Great Patriotic War. Though the Hoover edition is was largely approved by Russian left-wing scholars, they have never stopped their interest to study and publish a more accurate version of Stalin's works. In 1997, in the 80th anniversary of October Revolution, the last three volumes (13-15-16) were published by Moscow Writers Publishing House with Richard Kosolapov as the leader and Herrebonikov Workers University as the chief editor, this Russian publication has adjusted the content of the 14th, 15th, and 16th volumes according to Hoover edition. In 1997, the print run was only 2000, which were sold out within one or two months. Later, in 2004 and 2006, the Russian publisher has edited and published the 17th and 18th volumes.

The 17th volume includes Stalin's poems, letters, telegrams during 1895-1932, compiled by Central Scientific Method Committee of the Communist Party of the Soviet Union, and published by Tver Northern Crown Science Press.

The 18th volume included numerous supplementary speeches, reports, letters, telegrams, conversation transcripts, Stalin's directives and commands, etc. he made between 1917-1953 which were not published before.

Some of the material in this 18th volume can be seen in the previous volumes, but in this 18th volume a different version of the same material is included, which were endorsed by the Ideological Department of the Central Committee of the Communist Party of the Soviet Union, jointly compiled by Herrebonikov Workers University, and these 2 volumes were published by "Union" Information Publishing Center.

At the same time, in 2007, the materials endorsed by the Ideological Department of the Central Committee of the Communist Party of the Soviet Union, and Herrebonikov Workers University were revised by Richard Kosolapov and included in the revised edition publication of the 14th, 15th, and 16th volumes. The 2007 edition was a revised edition of the 1997 edition, which was published by Tver Northern Crown Science Press.

Richard Kosolapov was the chief editor of the revised edition of 2007, and the revised 14th volume included prewar articles from March 1934 to June 1941, with a 1.6 times increase in the included materials. The 2007 edition was published by the "Union" Information Publishing Center in 2007.

The 2007 edition of the 15th volume is divided into three parts, the first part of it is a collection of articles from June 1941 to February 1943, the second part includes works from February 1943 to November 1944 and the third part contains works and literature from the November 1944 to September 1945, 10 times increase compared to the 1997 edition, The 2007 edition is reprinted in 2009 and in 2010.

The 2007 edition of the 16th volume is divided into two parts, the first part of is a collection of articles from September 1945 to December 1948, the second part includes articles from December 1948 to 1952, the period of the postwar reconstruction and the post-War economic development of the Soviet Union, with 3 times increase of content material compared with the old edition.

This 2007 edition is also recently published by the ITRK Press, Moscow, in 2011.

II. Main content of the16th volume (1945-52)

Over a half of the 16th volume of The Complete Works of Stalin involves diplomacy and only a small part includes works regarding the domestic issues of the Soviet Union, which is inseparable from the complex international situation of Soviet Union at that time.

The articles in this volume reflect the domestic and international situation and issues of the Soviet Union during 1945-1952, as well as Stalin's evaluations and answers to these issues. The main content of the 16th volume can be divided into three categories.

I. The relationship between socialist camp and capitalist camp

Under the banner of "European Recovery", the Marshall Plan has established a division in the continent: thus anti-Sovietism and pro-Americanism which divided Europe into two camps, and the relationship of the two camps was finally evolved into a hostility.

The socialist Soviet Union was faced with a question whether, among the two systems (socialism and capitalism) socialism is better than capitalism and if socialism was equal to totalitarianism or tyranny.

In a variety of interviews, Stalin discussed the Soviet Union's relationship with USA, Germany, Japan, British, and Italy etc. For instance, in April 4th 1946 Conversations with Schmidt, the American Ambassador,[2] and April 15th 1947 Conversations with George Marshall, US Secretary of State.[3]

refers to the disputes of relations between the US and the Soviet Union and Stalin's critiques to US regarding the world order, in the post- World War II era,

Here, Stalin has manifested an uncompromising stance, from which the US side became to think over the necessity of cooperation with Soviet Union in order to solve the problems of Europe.

However, in 1946, when answering the questions of reporters from Pravda regarding Churchill's famous speech, Stalin has emphasized the growth of the communist parties in the European region after World War II, refuted Churchill's provocative comments regarding Soviet Union-Poland relationships, and expounded on the accusations against the Soviet Union, regarding the so-called "totalitarianism, tyranny and police system" issues.[4]

In addition, the 16th volume includes some private correspondence, such as Premier Stalin's Private Letter to Prime Minister Attlee (September 24th 1945), and Premier Stalin's Private Letter to Truman, President of the United States (October 26th 1945), which provides historical references for us to learn more about the then international situation, as well as the course of struggle and the sharpness and complexity of the contradictions between the two camps.

---

2 The Complete Works of Stalin Russian edition, part 1, 16th volume, pp. 258-273
3 The Complete Works of Stalin Russian edition, Part 1, of the 16th volume, pp. 500-510.
4 The Complete Works of Stalin Russian edition, part 1, 16th volume, pp. 221-227.

II. The internal relations within the socialist camp

As for Soviet Union's relationship with Eastern European countries, although Molotov Plan was proposed to control any alienation tendency from the Soviet Union, Soviet Union still had some disagreements with the new born Poland, Czechoslovakia, Yugoslavia, Romania, Bulgaria and Hungary etc. on some detail problems such as development stage, socialism construction mode and who will lead the construction or several other historical and practical issues, which can be seen in Stalin's telegram to Tito, president of Yugoslavia.

His letter to Wilhelm Pieck, president of East Germany; and conversation with Zoltan Tildy, president of Hungary etc. With the growth of socialist camp, the Soviet Union had to strengthen the communication with China, North Korea, and Vietnam, and tried to coordinate its international position together with them.

From the 16th volume, it can be seen clearly that around 1947, Stalin had vacillating attitude between the Kuomintang and the Communist Party of China, which can be seen from his friendly relation with Chiang Kai Shek at the beginning of 1947. In his telegram to Chiang Kai Shek on January 3rd 1947, Stalin thanked him and responded New Year greetings to Chiang Kai Shek, and also extended his New Year greetings to Chinese people.[5]

Another telegram for inviting Mao to Moscow: Stalin was the real sender and recipient of this telegram: To Comrade Terebin [trans. note: Terebin (real name Andrei Iakovlevich Orlov] was a Soviet medical doctor and Soviet operative in Mao's base in Yan'an]. Convey to Mao Zedong that the VKP(b) CC [trans. note: sesoiuznaia Kommunisticheskaia Partiia (bolshevikov), the All-Union Communist Party (of the Bolsheviks)—the Soviet Communist] considers it desirable to have him come to Moscow without any kind of disclosure about it. If Mao Zedong also considers this necessary, then, it appears to us, it is better to do this through Harbin. If needed, [we] will send a plane. Telegraph the results of the talk with Mao Zedong and his wishes. F[yodor Fedotovich] Kuznetsov [trans. note: Chief of the GRU (Soviet military intelligence)]. Though Kuznetsov's signature appeared on several cables to and from Orlov, Stalin was the real sender and recipient of this telegram.[6]

Due to a variety of reasons such as civil war and international situation, Mao Zedong could not make his journey to Moscow until the end of 1949, in this volume there are many telegrams about Mao Zedong's visit to Soviet Union.

---

5 Complete Works of Stalin, Part 1, the 16th volume, p. 454.
6 The Complete Works of Stalin, part 1 of the the 16th volume, Moscow, ITRK Press, Moscow, 2011, p. 562.

Stalin's telegram to Mao Zedong on April 20th 1948 is a very controversial document.

Mao Zedong, sent two telegrams to Stalin on November 30th 1947 and March 15th 1948 respectively.

For the first telegram, Stalin replied that we agree with the assessment of the situation given by Comrade Mao Zedong. We have doubts only about one point in the letter, where it is said that "In the period of the final victory of the Chinese Revolution, following the example of the USSR and Yugoslavia, all political parties except the CCP should leave the political scene, which will significantly strengthen the Chinese Revolution." We do not agree with this. We think that the various opposition parties in China which are representing the middle strata of the Chinese population and are opposing the Guomindang clique will exist for a long time. And the CCP will have to involve them in cooperation against the Chinese reactionary forces and imperialist powers, while keeping hegemony, i.e., the leading position, in its hands. It is possible that some representatives of these parties will have to be included into the Chinese people's democratic government and the government itself has to be proclaimed a coalition government in order to widen the basis of this government among the population and to isolate imperialists and their Guomindang agents."

But, in the second telegram, Stalin wrote that he agreed on all conclusions in Mao's telegram, and the plans about setting up a central government and enrolling liberal bourgeois representatives into the government were all right.[7]

Before being compiled in this book, this telegram was published in Russian Language, in the book titled, "The Documents of the 20th Century Sino-Russia Relations, the 5th volume, Soviet-China Relations during 1946-February 1950, p. 411-412".

Accordingly, Mikoyan, the former Soviet Union leader, wrote that it was due to Stalin's suggestion that Chinese Communist Party changed its policy on bourgeois parties. As for the authenticity of these two telegrams and Mikoyan's views, Chinese scholars have different opinions. Some believe that this is an important file about the future and destiny of democratic parties in China and some think that it was just Mao Zedong's idea to implement this policy, and some scholars doubt the authenticity of this telegram.

As a matter of fact, the Soviet Communist Party and Stalin have made many "suggestions" or "instructions" to the Chinese side before and after the founding of the People's Republic of China, but not all of these were proper, which is also one of the reasons why China pursued an independent development policy later.

---

7 Complete Works of Stalin, the 16th volume, part 1, pp. 629-630.

On January 6th, 1949, Stalin advised Mao Zedong to call a meeting of the Political Consultative Conference immediately before summer and establish the Democratic Coalition Government with the nationalist party:

Similarly, we think that your reply, if you are asked, should be tentatively like this:

The Communist Party (China) is always in favour of peace in China because the civil war in China was started not by the Communist Party, but by the Nanjing Government, which should be held responsible for the consequences of the war. The Chinese Communist Party is prepared for talks with the Kuomintang however, without the participation of those war criminals who unleashed the civil war in China. The Chinese Communist Party stands for direct talks with the Kuomintang without any foreign mediators. The Chinese Communist Party specifically considers the mediation of such foreign powers that are themselves participating in the civil war by using their air force and navy against the Chinese People's Liberation Army, as such a power cannot be acknowledged to be neutral and objective in the task of stopping the war in China. We think this is what, tentatively, your reply should be…[8]

On January 22nd, 1950, Stalin's conversation with Mao Zedong covers two aspects.[9]

One issue was the Soviet-China relations, and the other issues were the China's Northeast and Xinjiang affairs, involving the conditions of the Soviet-Sino New Treaty, China Changchun Railway, Lushun Port Agreement, the status of Dalian, Soviet-Sino Loan Agreement, Trade Agreement with Xinjiang and Manchuria, and pilots that Soviet Union would send to China, etc.

But according to researches by the Chinese Scholars, the date should be corrected as January 22nd 1950, and it was Mao Zedong's third conversation with Stalin during his first visit to Soviet Union. After the outbreak of Korean War, Stalin sent many telegrams to Mao Zedong and Zhou Enlai, talking about many affairs such as North Korean War and military aid (see also Telegrams To Mao Zedong, (May 26th, 1951).[10]

Stalin sent telegrams even related to specific battle plans (see the Telegrams To Mao Zedong (May 29th 1951), published in The Complete Works of Stalin, the 16th volume, part2, p 339), and also about the conditions of the North Korea peace negotiation (see also Telegrams To Mao Zedong (July 3rd 1951).[11]

---

8 Complete Works of Stalin, the 16th volume, ITRK Press, Moscow, 2011, part 2, p. 1.
9 About the time of this conversation with Stalin, according to The Complete Works of Stalin, the 16th volume, part 2, p. 10, the date was January 22nd, 1949.
10 Complete Works of Stalin, the 16th volume, part 2, p. 338.
11 Complete Works of Stalin, the 16th volume, part 2, p. 59.

Meanwhile, it includes many telegrams to Kim Il-sung. From August to September 1952, Zhou Enlai visited Moscow secretly, and talked with Stalin about North Korean Situation, domestic situation of China and five-year economic development plan of the People's Republic of China, and Lushun Port Agreement according to Mao Zedong's directives. The talk also included a plan of constructing a Sino-Soviet railroad through territory of Mongolian People's Republic or Xinjiang.

Zhou Enlai's talk was the second time and also the last time that Stalin met with a top leader of Chinese Communist Party and the People's Republic of China in Moscow after Mao Zedong's visit and before Stalin's death. Since the Soviet Union archives were declassified recently, the content of these telegrams have attracted close attention from both governments and academic circles.

III. Domestic Affairs of the Soviet Union and "Stalinism"

There were also domestic problems in Soviet Union such as economic development, unity among ethnic-national minorities and regarding the consolidation of the Soviet regime etc., and Stalin's opinions on these issues can be seen from a large amount of commands, decisions, talks, and telegrams. One of the along work of Stalin was the Economic Issues of Socialism Economy in the USSR which is of great theoretical value, and provides us a great reference value for us to understand the economic policies, realities, and system evolution of Soviet Union.[12]

However, the book Joseph Vissarionovich Stalin: A Brief Biography– The 2nd Revised Edition talks about Stalin's strict and truthful revision of this biography by Stalin. This biography writes that that Comrade Stalin was indeed modest, and Stalin always insisted that he was Lenin's student, and never exaggerated his own merits. But, at the same "he had to establish authority to consolidate the proletarian regime with him as the core." Brief Biography wrote: Khrushchev's false charges on Stalin are irrelevant and untenable.

Compilation status and our suggestions

Central Compilation and Translation Bureau hasn't translated the Russian edition of the 14th,, 15th16th . Volumes of The Complete Works of Stalin,, and have no translation plan yet, so there is no Chinese version. However, some articles, usually the published articles and telegrams, have been embodied in The Collected Works of Stalin 1934-1952, translated by Central Compilation and Translation Bureau in 1984 and published by People's Publishing House in 1985, and some others have been embodied in the

---

12 Complete Works of Stalin, the 16th volume, part2, pp, 221-227.

limited-readership publication Marx, Engels, Lenin and Stalin Research archives. We have no complete Chinese version of the planned old edition by Russian editors, or the supplemented and completed volumes of 14th,15th, 16th which is the new edition, we also don't have the highly informative 17th,18h volumes. Along with the deepening of the research on Stalin in China and the world, and the constantly emerging controversies, the incompleteness of the Complete Works of Stalin, will be a problem for our systematic research.

The supplemented and completed version of the 14th, 15, 16th volumes of The Complete Works of Stalin is of great value. Different from the original plan they mostly include published articles and speeches, this new revised edition also includes some files marked with "confidential" "secret", mostly gathered from the declassified Soviet archives, including archives from Russian State History of Social Politics Archives, Russia Federal Ministry of Foreign Affairs Archives, and Russian Presidential Archives, which are all with great historical reference with authentic and specific volume numbers and page numbers.

In these volumes, the meetings of Communist Party of the Soviet Union (Bolshevik) Central Committee Political Bureau and Council of Ministers of the Soviet Union were all recorded with numbers, the minutes of the talk, time, place, and recorders' signatures. The diaries of the Soviet and China top leaders and foreign leaders are all marked with years and page numbers, for instance, Stalin's letter to Dimitrov on August 12th 1947 is collected from Dimitrov's diary. Upon learning of a treaty between Yugoslavia and Bulgaria, Stalin ominously wrote to Comrade Dimitrov on August 12, 1947: "The opinion of the Soviet government is that [Yugoslavia and Bulgaria] have made a mistake...despite the warnings of the Soviet government."[13]

And some files are collected from foreign archives, such as The Welcome Luncheon Speech to Bulgaria Government Delegation Visiting Kremlin Excerpts from the talk on March 19th 1948, which is received from Belarus Central National Archives.[14]

Stalin's talk with British Foreign Minister Ernest Bevin on October 24th, 1945 was translated from English to Russian from the book called "Ministry of Foreign Affairs and Kremlin: British Reference Documents on about Anglo-Soviet Relations in 1941-1945".[15]

The richness of this new edition regarding reference sources and its accurate extensive cover is worthy of our attention.

---

13 Complete Works of Stalin, the 16th volume, part 1, p. 526.
14 Complete Works of Stalin, the 16th volume, part 1, p. 600.
15 Complete Works of Stalin, the 16th volume, part 1, p. 141.

I think the compilation of a complete ""Complete Works of Stalin" as a Chinese edition is necessary for the following reasons.

Firstly, from the aspect of socialist construction, the researches on Stalin and Soviet Union model is of great reference value so as to understand the path of Chinese revolution and construction , its reference value of Stalin's works should not be negated due to its some historical limitations.

Secondly, from the aspect of academic research, at present there are many controversies over Stalin at home and abroad, and we lack systemic and authoritative primary sources to analyze and refute or debate various opinions.

Thirdly, from the aspect of translation, already we have abundant translation basis of articles and works about October Revolution and the socialist construction in the Soviet Union, but these articles are not complete, especially because some important documents are only recently declassified, which means we lack unified edition. In a word, we should properly understand the reference and the historical value of "The Complete Works of Stalin".

Y. 63

The Analysis of Social Structure and Classes of Russia by the Russian Communists
"Theory and Practice of Foreign Communists" Research Report II

Liu Shuchun[1]

Abstract: Since the early 21st century, communists in the Russian Federation have surveyed the changes in the present-day Russian economy and social classes by means of class analysis. They believe that the restoration of capitalism in Russia was a top-down, unnatural and retrogressive process, and resulted in the polarization of the society. The conflict between labor and capital became the main contradiction of the society. The Russian ruling classes today are composed of oligarchies, neo-bourgeoisie, and upper-class bureaucratic groups, who possess the basic means of production and have the real power. On the contrary, the working class and suppressed small entrepreneurs who account for the great majority of the population are under oppression. Only one thirds of the national income is at their disposal. What is more, they are constantly threatened by unemployment and uncertainty. The so-called "middle class" is nothing but the "myth" fabricated by the ruling class to maintain stability. The "modern proletariat" is composed of manual and mental laborers. They are, as a whole, weak in class consciousness. Therefore, uniting all groups of working people and fostering class consciousness among the modern proletariat are the most urgent tasks to be accomplished by communists.

Key words: Russian communists; class structure; analysis of classes

---

1 Liu Shuchun, executive director of World Socialism Research Center, Chinese Academy of Social Sciences (CASS), researcher of Marxism Research Institute.

It has been 20 year since the collapse of the Soviet Union. During these 20 years, through the transformation of politics, economy, and society, the economic base and the superstructure of Russia has changed dramatically. How to understand the present-day structural changes in the Russian economy and the resultant changes in social class and strata is the premise for communists to design their strategic goals and action program.

I. The restoration of capitalism has led to the polarization of society and confrontation between labor and capital

In regard to the social system established in Russia after the collapse of the Soviet Union, CPRF led by Zyuganov has defined it as "comprador and criminal capitalism" "barbarous primitive capitalism" "oligarchic and bureaucratic' capitalism" etc. The Party has argued that capitalism is restored in Russia and argued that with this capitalist restoration, the changes in economic structure and political system has resulted in the polarization of the society, and triggered the profound confrontation between the working class and capitalists and also caused frequent systemic crises. The party proposes socialism as an alternative system.

The program of 2008 made by CPRF led by Zyuganov has made representative analysis on the polarization of society and main social contradictions after the collapse of the Soviet Union.

According to this 2008 program: the restoration of capitalism has inevitably led to the exploitation of man by man, the deep cleavages in the society, and the polarization of social classes. On one pole is the so-called class of "strategic proprietors" whose core was initially made up of bank speculators and exporters of raw materials. It is closely linked with the West economically and has a pronounced comprador character. National capital, in spite of seeking to develop the domestic economy, has not lost his class character. The number of dollar millionaires and billionaires in the country is growing. On the other pole is the huge mass of impoverished people of wage-earners crushed by the threat of unemployment and a sense of insecurity. The antagonistic contradiction between hired labour and capitalist is back in Russia. The state machine which underpins this order of things fully expresses the interests and the will of the bourgeoisie and its elite as represented by the oligarchs."

At the same time, the political report presented by the Central Committee, of the CPRF to the 13rd National Congress, which was held in 2008, has pointed out: "the change of system brought crisis to the nation, which was manifested in the following: the country is in the grip of a systemic crisis. The restoration of capital entailed a shrinking of industrial and agricultural production, the degradation of science, education and culture. In spite of the flood of petrodollars, not a single sector of the economy has made any substantial progress. The population is shrinking. The citizens are debarred from participating in running the affairs of society. Even the norms of bourgeois democracy are flouted. Elections to government bodies are increasingly turning into a farce. The gulf between the rich and the poor, between the new tightwads and the majority of the people is widening. Working people have been deprived of most of their social, economic and civil rights. Proletarization of the majority of our fellow countrymen is accompanied by social stratification. The absolute impoverishment of much of the population, veterans and pensioners continues. Millions of children are tramps who do not attend school. Contradictions between regions, between town and countryside are becoming sharper.

The flames of interethnic conflicts are blazing. The Russian question acquired a particular relevance during the years of capitalist restoration. The Russians today are the biggest divided people on the planet. An open genocide of a great nation is taking place. The Russian population is decreasing. The historical culture and language are being eroded. The solution of the Russian question and the challenges of building socialism are essentially the same thing."

Therefore, CPRF firmly believes that "The CPRF is convinced that the salvation of the Motherland can only come through a revival of the Soviet system and through following the path of socialism. History has again put the peoples of our country before the same choice as in 1917 and 1941: either a great power and socialism or further destruction of the country and its conversion into a colony. We are not talking about turning back, but about moving forward towards a renewed socialism cleansed of the mistakes and delusions of the past, a socialism that meets the realities of today." In the CPRF's opinion: "the current evolution of economic structure in Russia is an unnatural process, and the current Russian capitalism is different from western capitalism and even different from the initial capitalism in Russia. It is abnormal, and its result is retrogression but not progress.

A.V. Koubitsky, the chief editor of monthly theoretical journal "Kommunist" published by the ruling CPSU in the former Soviet Union, and professor in the Philosophy Department of Moscow State University, has described the features of Russian capitalism as follows:

1. The present-day Russian capitalism is not a result of natural development, but a top-down, retrogressive process caused by combined external and internal factors.

This retrogression is brought about by the common efforts of anti-communist and anti-party elites among the Russian Communists and hand-in-hand with the forces of international imperialism. This capitalism cannot fit the Russian culture and tradition.

2. The restoration of capitalism in Russia is not what Lenin had analyzed in 1899 "The Process of the Formation of a Home Market for Large-Scale Industry."

In many aspects, "new" Russian capitalism has deviated and departed from production and does not possess a corresponding industrial and agricultural basis. It is supported % 75 by foreign trade and finance, and relies directly foreign support which is vital for its existence.

3. During recent 20 years, Russia has formed various economic structures, including four kinds of social economic compositions: state capitalism (those original enterprises which are owned by the whole people), private capitalism (privatization of production), small commodity economy and cooperatives.

Among these compositions, only the cooperatives have the potential for future socialism, and other three are extremely unstable as long as the political power is not transferred to the working people. These first three sectors are suffering the pain of the current capitalist evolution and experiencing the grinding by the market. Under these circumstances, the current idea of re-implementing "Lenin's new economic policy of 1921" which is proposed by some "left-wing" scholars and politicians" is unrealistic and couldn't be realized. Unless, the socio-political system in Russia encounters a fundamental change in class relations, its entering into a path of socialism via state capitalism, seems impossible.

II. The polarization in the class structure, the working class accounts for the great majority of the population

In the CPRF's opinion, the 20-year of social differentiation in Russia has formed new class composition, which is different from former Soviet Union where the middle-income class accounted for the overwhelming majority in the society, also different from the olive-shape society we see in the developed western countries where middle class accounts for the big majority. Consequently, Russia has become a polarized society with a minority of super-rich people, and a majority of poor people.

The political report of the Central Committee of the Communist Party of Russian Federation, presented to the 13rd National Congress has analyzed the recent class composition in Russia. According to the report, the ruling classes of Russia include, the oligarchy, new bourgeoisie and top-level bureaucracy, who hold the essential means of production and also hold real state- power in the country.

These stratums were formed after the "coup d'etat" by Yeltsin and Co. after which the illegal plunder of social wealth and state assets had begun, consequently the rich and super-rich people in Russia account less than 3% of the population.

In addition, since 1991, a new type of stratum the official-entrepreneur has grown up rapidly, objectively speaking they are a part of the ruling classes. Consequently, generally speaking, the ruling class plus the middle class which serve them altogether account for 12%-15% of the population. However, the upper parts of ruling classes is not monolithic, among them there is the comprador oligarchs which closely collude with western capital and there is the elite-bureaucrats group—these two groups are the most powerful sections, within the ruling classes—which are not well accepted by the western countries, the elite-bureaucrats group, advocate a kind of reactionary patriotism, they are trying hard to protect themselves and their capital from the threats posed by their greedy "partners" in the West.

The big majority, 85%-88% of the population includes two main groups, the wage earner working class and the suppressed small entrepreneurs. Based on the above analysis, the report has pointed out that the main contradiction of Russia is between oligarchic capitalists who illegally plunder most of the social wealth and the workers who have lost their political and economic power.

"Consequently, the main task of the CPRF is to combine social class struggle with the national liberation struggle and create conditions for the transition to socialism."

In 2008, the party leader Zyuganov has also made a quantitative analysis, regarding the "working class" and "small entrepreneurs" in Russia, during the discussions when the Party was amending its program. He said: "currently, in Russia there were 60 million wage earners, which include mental laborers, manual workers, farmers, and intellectual laborers such as the teachers, doctors, engineers, scholars, and job seeking people. There are 5 million small private entrepreneurs and altogether 38 million retirees. These 103 million people make up the great majority who have created and are creating the social wealth of Russia, but their share only account for the 1/3 of the GDP. Such extremely unfair distribution of wealth will lead Russia to disastrous situation."

This party made another analysis in 2014 as following: There is yet another contradiction which has grown sharper within "new bourgeoisie" which has seized the command heights in the economy. We see a conflict between two parts of comprador capital. One part of is formed by "state" capitalists who are one with the authorities and hope to grab the juiciest pieces of state property through privatization. The other part are "Liberal capitalists". They were on top of things in the 1990s but have lost ground when property was redivided.

While these two branches of the bourgeois class are engaged in the tug-of-war and worshipping different "gods", citizens are supposed to look at their struggle as the essence of the main contradictions in the country. But that is not so: no one has yet managed to deceive the laws of social development.

The CPRF considers the preservation of the working class as an economic as well as a political minimum task.

If high-skilled workers join its ranks the working class will be able to become aware of its basic interests more quickly and precisely and to understand their direct link with Russia's return to the path of socialist development.

The number of workers in Russia is considerable. There are more workers today than there were in 1917. There are more of them than at the time of the 1959 national census. Two important facts have been established. First, the working class has a vital stake in socialism. Second, it is the most numerous social group in Russia. This means that it can play the leading role in the struggle for a sweeping transformation of society. Wherever we Communists manage to arouse this force it is reckoned with by the owners of enterprises and bureaucrats. But if it is to perform the vanguard role the CPRF must expand its influence in the workers' milieu. A party organization acquires authority and influence at the grassroots level precisely when workers themselves are actively involved in its activity, when there is no gap between the declarations on the proletarian character of the Communist Party and its daily work. It is also important to seek out leaders from amongst workers, to help them to come into their own as leaders, to teach and educate them.

Another party and another class analysis

The Union of Communist Parties-Communist Party of the Soviet Union, led by Oleg Shenin, which separated their struggle path with the CPRF led by Zyuganov, in 2001, has also made a more detailed analysis on the class composition of the current Russia, in the party program approved in the 5th Party Congress in February, 29th, 2004. The party defined the task of supporting the working class struagle, relying on this class and unite them. This party analyzes the current capitalism as bank capitalism: the "new" capitalism in Russia is %75 as bank capitalism, therefore it is moribund capitalism."

1. The composition and demands of the contemporary proletariat in the Russian Federation

The contemporary proletariat of Russia is reproduced again during the process of the restoration of capitalism, and it is composed of two basic parts.

One is industrial workers, with a population of 10 million, accounting for about 12% of the working-age population. These workers' main interests and demands are: participating in the production management of enterprises and the solution of social affairs, active labor unions, stable production, and a fair wage. The other group is the large number of intellectuals, with a population of 14 million, including engineers, professionals, scientific researchers, teachers, doctors, and other "mental laborers". The Party has defined the fundamental interests of intellectuals as follows: human right, individual freedom and political freedom, and they demand to reach the wage level of industrial workers, since their wages were very low in those days.

2. Agricultural proletariat and semi-proletariat accounting for 7 million
The Party aims to promote the revival of cooperative movement and cooperatives and will urge the government to provide support for the cooperative movement, and give support to the agricultural economy that should be established on the basis of state-owned land and collectively owned means of production. 3. Large number of urban semi-proletariat which account for half of the working-age population (circa over 40 million)

These people mainly work as staff in the non-productive sectors, also employees in trade and service industry, clerks, various practitioners, apprentices, low earning part of the proletariat. Also there are the marginalized stratums which include noneconomic employees, the workers with minimum skills and the unemployed.

The party should fight to guarantee the realization of these groups' following demands: ensure full employment, wages should not be under the minimum living standards. Defend them from mobbing and bully of the bosses, demand free training and opportunities so that they can improve their skills and so that they can acquire normal jobs.

4. Petty bourgeoisie stratums which includes nearly 10 million individuals

This group includes: low-end of the middle-sized entrepreneurs and secondly, all kind of petty proprietors, such as the farmers, labor aristocracy, middle-managers etc. The members of the petty bourgeoisie stratums are the mobile (upwards or downwards) but also the unstable part of the society.

Their status and incomes can change every day even every hour. Some may ascend to an upper status and join the ranks of capitalists, but more often, they descend to a lower status and join the ranks of the proletariat. This kind of dual characteristics of these stratums, leads to the their unstable political stances, consequently they vacillate between "far-left" and right positions. The party thinks that these stratums are still the main social and political pillar of the current bourgeoisie Russian society. The task of the party is to neutralize the petty bourgeoisie stratums, and try to prevent that their majority do not side with the current order, prevent that they do not support, ultra-right and nationalist political forces.

In a word, the Party, defined its strategic task as all kinds of laborer groups (the first 3 groups above which account for 71 circa million, particularly the first two groups of industrial workers and intellectuals, and strive , to overcome the distrust between them. The is Party believes: once these two groups united together and realize that they are part of the same class, their power as the contemporary proletariat would be much stronger than the combined forces of the bourgeoisie. Such united proletariat will be able to lead the middle class stratums (the fourth group above) and can guarantee the social and political re-transformation in Russia. In addition to the Party's official documents, recently the topic as "how to understand the contemporary proletariat?" is popular and often appears in the communist media.

On 5th July,2011, a nameless article Who Belongs To the Contemporary Working Class in Russia? has been published in the website of Communist Party of Russian Federation (CPRF). This article has analyzed the two major opposing classes in the current Russia based on the latest statistics in Active Population in the Russian Economy issued by Statistics Bureau of the Russian Federation. The article concludes that currently proletariat still accounts for the majority of Russian population, among which the industrial workers are the major part of it.

Firstly, the article provides the relevant data regarding the two class structure in Russia: the entrepreneurs and wage laborers

The author has pointed out: "according to the Russian official data, in 2010, 84% of employed population worked in legally established enterprises and business corporates, their employers account for 1.4% of the population, who belong to the big and middle bourgeoisie.

64.560.000 workers are employed by 947.000 employers, which is the most essential class reality of the Russia: 65 proletarians work for one master.

Secondly, in 2010, the 4.1% of the working-age population are engaged in those enterprises without corporate organization (small businesses), and 0.6% of the population work and manage their own businesses, who are the fundamental part of the petty bourgeoisie stratums. In this second sector, total workers account for 9.2% of the total population.

Thirdly, 2.2% of working-age people are engaged in agricultural and forestry or forest protection as part of the private household enterprises.

Shortly to say, in whichever economic sector, the current population is engaged with, it can be seen that the society is composed of two main groups: the entrepreneurs and wage laborers. Therefore, the principle contradiction of the Russian society is still the confrontation between capitalists and laborers.

The article analyzes the similarities and differences between contemporary proletariat and and the proletariat in history . The author has written: "today the working class is still exploited. However, there are some differences between traditional working class and the current working class. Firstly, modern working class has a higher educational background. Before the October Revolution, only 2.8% of the population in Russia were literate, but today only 4.3% of the workers have no complete secondary education background, and even among the 8.7 million unskilled workers, over 7 million have received complete secondary education. Secondly, contemporary working class accounts for the largest population in Russia. During October Revolution, workers accounted for less than 10% of the working-age population, while the currently workers account for as high as 50% of the working-age population. Thirdly, the skills enjoyed by the current working class is quite different from the past. A century ago, most of the industrial laborers did not have advanced skills, while today among the 35.1 million workers, nearly 24 million of them work in industrial—even post-industrial—sectors, including highly skilled workers, computer programmers, operators, drivers, etc. and some of them work in transportation, communication, and energy sectors. All these worker groups account for more than 2/3 of Russian working population. The high proportion of workers with advanced skills constitute the objective premise for the acceleration of social development. The past experiences of revolutions prove that, the workers with advanced skills form the part who can most actively defend the interests of proletariat."

The article did not ignore the analysis of the unemployed groups: "according to official statistics, of 2010, there are 7 million unemployed population in Russia, while according to estimations by experts, there are 9-9.5 million jobless in Russia. And 75% of them can be evaluated as the labor reserve army. And 23% of the jobless, are the mental laborers and office workers. For capitalists, the best option is the existence of unemployment, which ensures that the minimum wage level can be maintained. The logic is simple: the unemployed people are an integral part of the working class. During the first decade of the 21st century, although the number of jobless people is so huge, the number of working class in Russia has remained stable, i.e. its number has reached over 35 million. This is the main social foundation of the socialist movement in the contemporary epoch".

III. The myth of "middle class"

Since the 21st century, the concept of "middle class" has been prevalent in Russia, which is not only widely used in sociology academy, but also popular among ruling elite groups. However, Russian communists find this concept improper when analyzing the essence of social class changes. They believe that the formation of the so-called "middle class" in Russia is just a myth.

The article titled as the "Middle Class": The Myth and Reality

The "Political Education" the theoretical journal of the Russian Communist Party, has published an important article titled as the "Middle Class" The Myth and Reality, in its issue 2011/3 co-authored by R. Trofimov and V. Truchkov.

The article points out: the concept "middle class" has first become popular with the emergence of the "consumer society" in the latter part of the 20th century in the Anglo-American academy, and gradually became an important part of the bourgeoisie ideology."

With the restoration of capitalism in Russia, the social economic structure has changed rapidly, which compelled the ruling class of Russia to use the concept of "middle class". The reasons are as follows:

Firstly, as the contradiction between labor and capital would intensify objectively in Russia, the victors of the 1991-1993 struggles—the ruling class—were bound to wishfully seek a reliable social class, as the basis of their rule.

Secondly, the ruling class needed that the traditional Soviet values in the spiritual life of the Russian youth should be weakened and substituted by consumerism.

Besides, there are also some common properties of the pre-Soviet Russia and the former Soviet Union, which have pushed the ruling class to instill the concept of "middle class" in the minds of the society.

Firstly, the capitalist mode of production in the pre-Soviet Russia was indeed not a natural phenomenon, its social basis was limited, in other words, it was weak and unstable.

Secondly, in the former Soviet Union the "middle class" was eliminated, destroyed. Also, currently, the wages of most doctors, primary and secondary school teachers and mental workers engaged in culture, science, and higher education, is far lower than that in Soviet Union era.

Thirdly, in the current Russia, social gaps and the distribution of wealth has been polarized. In short, specifically, it is the restoration of capitalism in Russia that has caused the ruling class to enthusiastically construct the ideological concept of "middle class".

The two authors have also analyzed the rise of the "middle class" concept in Russia: in the 1990s, in Russia, "middle class" was a possibility, rather than a reality. Till the end of 1990s, politically speaking, various domestic powers were still in a precarious balance, economically, almost half of the commodity or service output came from state-owned companies, and the workers of the state-owned companies accounted for nearly a half of the total working people. The concept of "middle class" became really popular in 2000s, while in these days economic situation created an illusion that Russia had stepped in a mass consumption society, and ruling elites did their best to implement the concept of "middle class". In November 2008, in the "2020 Strategy" forum initiated by Unified Russia party led by Putin, the chief deputy director of the presidential office B. Surkov asserted: "during the economic depression period, protecting the middle class should be the main task in Russia." President Medvedev, also affirmed:" by 2020, the population of "middle class" in Russia can reach 60-70% of the population." However, the two authors have argued that, the strong emphasis made by the leading authorities, on the formation of the "middle class" is due to the need by them (ruling class) to such a "middle class" to guarantee their long-term stable rule.

The academic circles in Russia cannot reach a consensus if there is such a "middle class" or is it a just a virtual phenomenon. For instance, E. Guttmacher, the dean of the Social Policy Center attached to Institute of Economics in the Russia Academy of Science, commented. common people regard middle class as a class between the rich and the poor, which however is dangerous and deceptive, because, the members of the so-called 'middle class' are more likely to be the poor, and the 8-year economic growth in Russia hasn't guaranteed the formation of such 'middle class'. Even worse, the channels for an upward of social mobility promotion don't work at the moment."

Therefore, the two authors have argued: "not only in public common sense but also in academic circle, the problem of ambiguity around this concept has emerged, i.e., ambiguously a social group in Russia is regarded as the "middle class", which is imagined to be fond of acting with the criteria of "mass consumption society" in the one hand, and has the opportunity of obtaining wealth, wholly or partially, on the other hand."

Thus, the concept of "middle class" is not only an ideological myth, but also an economic myth. In the view of these two authors: "this group should be seen as a part of petty bourgeoisie, whether from the aspect of its social composition, interests, tastes or from the aspect of their political ideology and life style, this group has its own specific objective premise and can be defined with the social classification criteria, thus it is a social reality. But the concept of the so-called "middle class", is a virtual phenomenon and mainly exploited as a bourgeoisie ideological paradigm."

IV. Enhancing the class consciousness of the proletariat is the urgent task of the communists

As the advanced vanguard part of the proletariat, communists should undoubtedly depend on and represent the interests of proletariat.

At present, all the communist parties of the world take "modern proletariat" as their social foundation. While regarding the composition of "contemporary proletariat", just as mentioned above, they advocate that it includes both the manual and mental workers. They generally agree that the class consciousness of "contemporary proletariat" in Russia is rather weak.

The political report presented to the CPRF's 13rd National Congress has pointed out: "at present although the oppressed class is discontent with current situation, they are still in the state of political apathy and fear, due to control of the existing system, laborers largely lose class consciousness. The report said: We take some of the blame for the fact that the working class has undeveloped socialist consciousness. Only the Communist Party can introduce it into the proletarian struggle. Otherwise a very different kind of ideas will dominate their minds. We are duty-bound to bring to the masses scientific knowledge of socialism and proletarian dictatorship. What is needed is not a short-lived propaganda campaign but long-term systematic work."

Even those workers belonging to different ethnic-nationalities are alienated to each other, which means that it is not easy to unite and educate the working class and seize the political power, thus enhancing of their class consciousness is indeed is a matter of urgency.

The Union of Communist Parties—Communist Party of the Soviet Union, led by Oleg Shenin also thinks that contemporary proletariat in Russia is still spiritually in a "lax and passive" state and need to improve their class consciousness. The party program points out: "the social foundation of the communist movement is proletariat, both in the past, today and in the future, i.e., it is the class which has lost the ownership of production means. They are the only social force that can eliminate bourgeoisie system, but now they are still the 'lax and passive' class. Thus, the task of instilling socialist consciousness to contemporary proletariat is urgent. The Union of Communist Parties-Communist Party of the Soviet Union holds that in order to achieve this task, communists' programmatic goal should not only include helping them to seize the ownership of production means, but also guarantee the realization of their rights, which were announced and promised but in fact not implemented during the first stage of socialism which refers to the Soviet period. —underlined by the author."

Some theorists of the communist parties have made an in-depth analysis on the economic and social reasons why the class consciousness of Russian working class is weak. They think that, this is related with the industrialization of marginalized periphery countries, but the weakening of class consciousness of the working class caused by the transformation of labor process in the post-industrialized developed countries is a totally different issue.

W. Trushkov wrote in the article titled, "By Grasping Marxism, Human Being Will Have A Better Future": "in Russia, even though the working class is limited with the scope of manual workers, working class is still the largest social group, accounting for more than a half of the whole working-age population. This fact refutes the claim that there is "no proletariat" in current Russia, but the current problem is that, among the group of heavy industry workers, the unskilled part overweighs the skilled part. During 1999-2006, in Russia's working class structure, unskilled workers group has seen most rapid growth. Of course this kind of strange phenomenon is related with the nature of capitalism in Russia, and the primary economic law of capitalism is the profit pursuit. For capitalists, the cost of unskilled workers is low, and they do not undertake the cost for professional training, so capitalists have chosen to hire unskilled worker, rather than adopting the advanced and sophisticated technologies. Therefore, the path of Russian capitalism, has promoted such kind of industry, which has led to the growth of unskilled workers, and the increase of proletariat and the decrease of class consciousness are the two traits of the current Russia."

Sergei Stelloyev wrote, in his the article titled: "In Commemoration of the Anniversary of Karl Marx's 190th Birthday" which was published in Marxism Today: "this phenomenon we see in Russia has also occurred in other countries. In some marginalized countries (Russia also belongs to these countries after the collapse of Soviet Union), the de-industrialization has become obvious, which caused loss of social status by the broad masses in the society. Social being determines social consciousness. The "1991 reform", has paved the way for the backward and raw-material producing industries which means, de-industrialization process, and this process in Russia is also the objective process which has abandoned the class-consciousness of broad masses. In such circumstances, the task of the communists is the same as 100 years ago, i.e., enhancing the class consciousness of working class, providing the spiritual means for millions of workers to defend their own interests, and instilling the socialist ideology into people's minds.

Since the global economic crisis in 2008, there occur frequent large-scale strikes and protests in the Western countries, but seldom in Russia. Why? The above article analyze this question as follows: "the workers are afraid of losing their jobs, passively follow their leaders who are inert at the moment, and admire the rich". The Russian communists believe: only when the workers have consciously realized the possibility of a victory, they will display their struggle strength. However, this consciousness won't drop down out of the sky, but will be instilled by the political party of working class. The consciousness of the possibility of winning the battles against exploiters directly depends on the people's trust in the Communist Party. Of course, this trust does not originate from the lofty, grand title of the "Communist Party" itself, but depends on its constant efforts to instill consciousness to working class in its daily struggles.

Y. 64

The Collapse of the Soviet Union and East Europe: Reflection and Criticism by the Communist Party of Australia

Yang Chengguo[1]

This paper is the initial research result of Young Researchers- Humanities and Social Sciences Program sponsored by the Ministry of Education. Research subject: Communist Party of Australia and the International Meeting of Communist & Workers' Parties' and the 'International Communists Seminar in Brussels" and Research on communist parties of the capitalist countries.

Abstract: The disintegration of the former Soviet Union and great upheaval in the East European socialist countries has been a major setback in the world socialist movement, and has greatly hit the communist parties in Australia. However, in Australia many of the staunch Marxists have shown great courage to overcome the difficulties. In 1990 the Socialist Party of Australia—renamed the Communist Party of Australia in 1996—conducted and in-depth analysis of the collapse of the former Soviet Union and East Europe. The analysis not only admitted the great achievements of the socialist countries in the 20thcentury, but also pinpointed to the mistakes of some socialist countries and their causes, it also analyzed the factors behind such a change and the impacts of the disintegration of the former Soviet Union and the great upheaval in the East European socialist countries. The analysis has pointed out that this reverse change does not mean the failure of socialism, and the fundamental trend of socialism finally replacing capitalism has not been changed. 2011 is the 20th anniversary of the disintegration of the Soviet Union and the collapse of socialist countries in East Europe. The analysis of the Australian Communist Party provides us with new perspectives with important reference value.

Key words: the Communist Party of Australia; collapse of the former Soviet Union and East European socialist countries; socialism; capitalism; achievements and lessons

---

1 Yang Chengguo, special researcher of World Socialism Research Center, Chinese Academy of Social Sciences (CASS), Dean of Research Center for Contemporary Marxist Political Parties, Nanyang Normal University.

The disintegration of the former Soviet Union and East European socialist countries has been a major setback in the world socialist movement, and effected the dissolution of former Communist Party of Australia in 1990, but in the Socialist Party of Australia which was split from the Communist Party of Australia in 1971 has survived. Aiming at the difficult situation caused by the collapse of the former Soviet Union and East European socialist countries, the Socialist Party of Australia has made a special meeting and issued a statement which conducted an in-depth analysis of how to evaluate the collapse of the former Soviet Union and East European socialist countries and the historic achievements and lessons of the practice of these countries.[2]

From October the 4th- 7th 1996, in its 8th National Congress, the Socialist Party of Australia was renamed as "the Communist Party of Australia". The congress declared that the party would carry on the tradition of former Communist Party of Australia. The re-constructed Communist Party of Australia adopted the new party program in its 10th National Congress held between September 30th to October 3rd 2005, and summarized and re-evaluated the historical process of the 20th century world socialist development.

The Communist Party of Australia advocated: we should analyze the collapse of the former Soviet Union and East European socialist countries in a frank and open attitude, and should not cover up the mistakes or ignore the great achievements made by socialist countries. We should fully examine the facts and avoid simple explanation and conclusions, and aim to draw lessons and reveal the nature of the collapse of the former Soviet Union and East European socialist countries, in order to fully carry out the socialist work in Australia.

The crisis in the socialist world in the late 1980s and early 90s underlines the danger of underestimating the capacity of imperialism to undermine socialism through its huge system of anti-communist agencies and its powerful use of ideological subversion. It also underlines the role of right-wing revisionism in opening the way for counter-revolution by whittling down and finally destroying communist ideology and Party organization.

The mistakes of the past and the pressures and blandishments of imperialism opened the way for widespread acceptance of a return to the capitalist system in some of the socialist countries."

---

2 Socialist Party of Australia, "Political Statement," http://www.agitprop.org.au/ lefthistory/199009_special_congress_statement.htm.

I. Historical achievements of the socialist countries in the 20th century

The Communist Party of Australia has argued: "the evaluation of the collapse of the former Soviet Union and East European socialist countries is inseparable from the development history of socialism movement" , and the Party spoke highly of the historical achievements of socialist movement in the 20th century. It pointed out that: "in the 20th century the socialist revolutions and the national independence movements of many nations have won a global victory. The great Russian October Revolution of 1917 has been the first victory of socialism revolution, and from then on the oppressed people for the first time conquered the political power and started to establish a new society without private ownership, exploitation or greed for profit. Meanwhile, the world's political pattern also changed dramatically. The historical social transition from capitalism to socialism has thus started. After World War II, some countries in Europe, Asia and Caribbean Sea regions have joined the family of socialist countries. The industrial and agricultural foundations of these newborn socialist countries were weak and also were war-torn countries, but they were not afraid of difficulties, and overcame all difficulties, achieving a great successes in socialist construction, which have made significant positive influences on the development of the whole mankind. These historical achievements of socialism will never be erased from the history of humanity. The party said. The crisis in many socialist countries was not a consequence of public ownership of the economy and working class power. It was rather a result of an inadequate understanding and application of socialist principles, a failure both to see what was wrong and how to correct it. Socialism itself did not fail."

Concrete achievements:

1. The establishment of the economic system of public ownership of the means of production and working people's political power led by the working class. They have terminated the rule of capitalist class, eliminated the phenomenon of exploitation of workers for private profits, and made working class and other progressive democratic forces have mastered the state power and truly became the real masters of the country. Socialism is a humane form of society, that aims to satisfy people's ever increasing, cultural and material needs and promotes people's all-round abilities as the impetus of social development, thus substitutes the pursuit of profit as the driving force of social development of society.

2. Improvement of people's life standards

Socialist countries have developed strong public owned industry and collectively owned agriculture, reduced or even eliminated unemployment; vigorously developed the cultures of ethnic-national minorities, eradicated illiteracy and provided education opportunities for all. They have widely established public health service agencies and promoted social security services. Cuba has exceeded all other Latin American countries in the aspects of medical service, education quality, housing and working conditions etc. China, after accomplishing the new-democratic revolution and socialist transformation smoothly, has made great progress in industrial and agricultural development and gradually became one of the powerful countries in the world. If it were not the socialist revolution and the leadership of the Communist Party, China would remain a backward country under the imperialist aggression.

3. Prposed a new concept of democracy: Socialist participatory democracy

People's right to work and right to rest has been guaranteed, and women's rights equal economic and social rights were given priority.

4. They promoted scientific and technological progress

Socialist counties stepped to the forefront in the field of space technology and other scientific fields. With the growth of their economies and industries, socialist counties became to possess a large proportion in the total production and trade in the world.

5. Equality among all nationalities

A new principle of equality among all nationalities and peoples has been established, the formerly exploited and oppressed minority nationalities have started a new life in the socialism societies. The minority nationalities were carefully protected, their national languages were promoted and supported, their economic development and economic interests were maintained.

6. Promoted the struggles of the peoples for socialism, in the capitalist countries

The improvement of the economic and social status of people in the socialist countries encourages the people in capitalist countries to strive for socialism. As a result, capitalist countries have achieved great progress in many aspects, such as democratic rights, social welfare, and economic rights etc.

7. Socialist countries have fought for safeguarding world peace.

During World War II, the Soviet Union played a key role in defeating fascism. Socialist countries in Europe, Asia and Caribbean region, have declared the fight for peace as their own responsibility for the first time in world history, and claimed that "world war can be avoided". After World War II, since the socialist camp countries have reached a balance in military strength with imperialist countries, the aggressive policies of imperialists were restrained, which avoided the possibility of the outbreak of the world war.

8. Proposed a new form of international economic relations – based on mutual aid, cooperation, specialization and integration, aimed at improving the level of economic development of each participating country and aiming eliminating economic inequality between them. With the collapse of the world colonial system, The people of vast colonies have won national independence.

However, this independence is still somewhat controlled generous economic assistance and other forms of support to the Third World countries, they supported their economic development through mutually beneficial trade deals.

All of these achievements constitute a historic leap, which have the prospect of creating a classless society without exploitation and oppression. The achievements of socialist countries have inspired millions of people in the world, and showed that it is possible to establish a new social system, and paved way for the working people and progressive people to master the political power.

II. Causes and impacts of the disintegration of the Soviet Union and the upheaval in the East European socialist countries

The Communist Party of Australia thinks that although socialist countries have made great achievements in the 20th century, at the same time some serious mistakes were committed during the construction of socialism. Since these mistakes were not corrected for a long time they have caused fatal effects.. These mistakes were caused by departing from Marxism, and impossible to say that these mistakes were inherent to socialism, all of which have hindered the development of the cause of socialism.

The mistake of overstepping the stage of social development

The Communist Party of Australia has analyzed that the Soviet Union has made the mistake of overstepping the stage of social development. In 1930s, the Soviet Union leaders headed by Stalin had also realized the construction of socialism should be carried out in stages, but they had eliminated all forms of private ownership when the conditions were not ripe, only state ownership and collective ownership were left. This has led the Soviet leadership prematurely declare that the socialism has won the final victory, and they have ignored the roles of other forms of ownership during the transition period. Moreover, this mistake of overstepping the stage of social development didn't disappear after the death of Stalin. In 1960s, Khrushchev has declared that the Soviet Union had started to "lay material and technological foundations for communism", and his successors also declared that the Soviet Union had entered the stage of "advanced socialism". This was the continuation of overestimating the achievements of socialism and "overstepping the stage of social development." This kind of mistake has brought negative impacts in the economic, political and social spheres, and this was the deep reasons why Andropov called for realistic reforms after he became the General Secretary of the CPSU.

Lenin has mentioned many times when implementing the NEP (new economic policy) that the idea of direct transition from capitalism to communism would be wrong. When he talked about the transformation of individual economy and scattered small commodity economy to large-scale social production, in order to re-build the whole new social economic system, he pointed out: "this transformation process will a very long process." Lenin had warned: "never proceed too fast, or attempt to shorten this process".

However, Lenin's successors didn't realize or didn't accept that during the long-period of transition from capitalism to socialism, "although the principle of public ownership and socialist economy will play a key role, the currency- commodity relations as well as some economic laws of the capitalist economy" will continue to be in effect. During the socialist transition period, private enterprises, cooperative enterprises, leasing companies, joint ventures and other forms of ownership will continue to survive in some fields of the economy. However, socialism requires that public ownership should be the leading ownership in the fields: such as industry (especially key industries), land ownership and national resources, minerals and energy sources, power generation, transportation, communication, banking sector etc. Meanwhile, socialism requires that a central plan of orientation should be maintained, in order to make sure the main direction and key point of economic and social development, the planning aims to allow workers' democratic participation in the production process, such plan can facilitate the implementation of effective and efficient management, and the utilization of advanced technology, thus it can guarantee the dynamic development of socialist economy.

Socialist countries have formed highly centralized economic system

In the Soviet Union, during its period of transition to socialism, some flawed phenomena have emerged: a kind of rigid, over-centralized and bureaucratic economic system was formed. This kind of system couldn't properly handle the relations between the central and local enterprises, between managers and worker masses, and egalitarianism became prevalent which violated the distribution principle of socialism, the distribution according to work—all of which contradicted the development laws of socialism. Socialist plan doesn't require that each detail of the economic development should be approved by a central planning agency, but must point to overall goals and define the economic guidelines. The rigid and over-centralized system of the Soviet Union had developed further during the period of World War II, and then became a fixed pattern of economic development for other socialist countries after the World War II. Historical experience shows that this kind of over-centralized system had many disadvantages, and led to the growth of bureaucratic style in the socialist countries. These bureaucratic elements often issued unrealistic orders, frequently abused their powers, restrained the initiative and enthusiasm of workers and their grass-root level participation in production affairs, which all led to the inefficiency of production, and restricted product variety in the markets of and decline in product quality, etc.

What was more serious: this system has led to the alienation of workers from the production process, and due to such alienation working people who served the society could neither control the social products which they have produced, nor could they control the socially owned public property.

To avoid such flaws as mentioned above, the economic system of the socialist countries should be constantly adjusted and innovated, but the rigid economic system was inapt to reforms and innovations. Consequently, the Soviet Union and East European socialist countries fell behind the developed capitalist countries, economically and technologically, lagged behind in the application of technology, and couldn't meet domestic demand of people in the aspects of quantity, quality, and variety, regarding the consumption goods. Thus people's living standard has stagnated, the capacity of investment and accumulation capacity of their economies has weakened, economic growth rate declined, which all caused to the defeat of socialist countries in the economic competition with capitalist countries.

The stagnation in the construction of socialist democracy

In the initial period of its development, Soviet Union were faced serious situation of armed intervention by 14 imperialist countries and domestic counterrevolutionary insurgency, for this reason the young proletarian state had to establish a strong state apparatus, in order to defeat the armed intervention of imperialists, meanwhile applied strict domestic controls, adopted severe repressive measures against the counterrevolutionary destructions and sabotage. In such case, the state could not but impose certain restrictions on the realization of democratic rights, thus the state power was centralized power and the state apparatus was strengthened. Consequently, a highly centralized political system was formed in the USSR.

With the victory of revolution against the imperialist armed intervention and with the end of civil war, the Soviet national economy was gradually restored, the domestic situation was gradually normalized, then began the socialist construction period, was coming, which meant that the conditions have undergone a fundamental change.

However, in new period, the class struggle method that was used during the struggles against the foreign armed intervention and during suppression of the domestic counterrevolutionary insurgency, was not changes, instead the class struggle method was utilized mechanically, in the peaceful socialist construction period.

Although the socialist construction has accomplished successive victories, a bigoted, hostile and skeptical atmosphere still continued in the state governance of the Soviet Union, and the erroneous doctrine of "socialist society includes constantly sharpening class struggles" has guided the socialist practice of the Soviet Union. This doctrine has led to the further development of the highly centralized political system, neither the Soviet state system nor the Communist Party of the Soviet Union has established a sound form and structures of socialist democracy or developed the inner-party democracy.

This kind of situation badly undermined the development of socialist democracy, people's democratic rights, the right to vote , respect for individual freedoms, and restricted the participation of individuals and restricted the expression of different opinions, and the violations of socialist legal system by the leading state organs and politicians have occurred repeatedly. As a result of all these people lacked real opportunities to influence or control the government's decision making, gradually people's creativity and initiative were weakened, leading to the serious decline of people's participation degree. Consequently, working class and the vast majority of laboring masses became alienated from the political life day by day, and the political regime was also alienated from the people.

The mistakes of the Communist Party in the process of leadership

The leadership status and the vanguard advanced character and leadership role of the Communist Party originates from Marxism, and adherence to it – the most advanced and the most scientific social theory.

This principle originates from Marx and Engels' scientific class analysis of the society and analysis of various social forces and different class interests, and their judgment on how to maintain the interests of the working class and all working people. This principle originates from Marx and Engels' deep understanding on the law and direction of social development. However, in the social practice of the Soviet Union and East European socialist countries, this correct concept of "the leadership role of the Communist Party" was distorted. Firstly, in the Soviet Union and East European socialist countries, although working class was declared as the ruling class, in real life, the working class didn't play the leading role in the field of economy and politics at all. Secondly, the different functions of the Communist Party and state were not differentiated clearly and often overlapped which resulted in the intertwining of between the Party and the government, which greatly restricted socialist democracy. Last, the labor unions, women's organizations, and youth organizations etc. often became official organizational structures, rather than being social organizations of the masses.

The Communist Party of Australia has evaluated that the phenomenon of severe violation of democratic-centralism principle existed in the Soviet Union and East European socialist countries, such as lack of criticism and correction systems, lack of an accountability system, even existed the practices of suppressing critiques from inside and outside the party, and so on.

All these practices have led to the persistence of mistakes in the leadership system of the Party. Thus, the communist parties of these countries, could not focus their efforts on the political work and political education of the people, also could not focus their efforts on the key task of winning people's support for the Party policies.

As a result, the Party's blood-and-flesh bonds with the people were undermined, and people's sense of trust in the Communist Party was weakened. Although "the leading role of the Communist Party" was stipulated in the constitution of socialist countries, this was not supported by the people.

The work in the ideological sphere did not receive due attention

The Communist Party of Australia has evaluated: dialectical materialism is not as widely spread and deeply rooted as idealism. Idealism is the philosophical basis of bourgeois and feudal ideologies. Some erroneous thoughts that have arisen during the socialist construction period were the expressions of idealist world outlook. In the Soviet Union and East European socialist countries, although there existed Marxism education, however it was usually formalistic and dogmatic. Consequently, understanding and application of Marxism, in the studies, by many people was one-sided and fragmented, which meant that the complete system and essence of Marxism was not grasped comprehensively.

In the late 1980s, though many mistakes of the past were recognized, but many others were not recognized, such as the pursuit of rapid changes. The dogmatism was criticized, but the liberal supra-class and non-class theories prevailed.

Bourgeois ideology based on idealism and metaphysics, besides the old ideas and habits from the old society which have been dominant for centuries are deeply rooted in people's minds. On the contrary, the dialectical materialism world-view of the working class, socialist ethics and advance socialist culture was not widely spread and disseminated among the people.

Marxism-Leninism is a creative and ever developing science, and it must be utilized as the fundamental guideline to solve problems, and the solutions should be sought on the basis of real world changes. If the thoughts fall, behind the objective changes, it is inevitable to occur a gap for the intrusion of bourgeois ideology, thus we can become unable to respond effectively to the newly emerging problems.

The Communist Party of Australia has argued: "ignorance of the timely reform of the overly concentrated and centralized economic and political system was one of the reasons of the drastic changes in the Soviet Union. Meanwhile, the "humanistic, democratic socialism" advocated by Gorbachev under the banners of "openness" "democratization" "multi-party system" "pluralism" and "free choice", has copied the political systems and economic forms of the Western Europe, which caused the complete change in the direction of socialist development, and the attempt to achieve rapid "change" and rapid "results" has caused enormous social and political instability and chaos, have eventually destroyed socialism.

For example, the "draft outline" of the CPSU mentioned the need for an appropriate relationship between planning and market forces, but in Gorbachev's report to the Party Congress, only mentioned the "market economy" and planning wasn't mentioned at all. Gorbachev's report appealed that "equal economic and political rights" should be provided to different ownership forms in the economy including privately owned businesses, but he didn't say anything about the leading role of public ownership sector of the economy. The Communist Party of Australia believes that socialism means "maintaining the dominate role of working class, and leading role of public ownership, and besides a proper form of central planning, currency control and financial controls in the macro-economic level.

In addition, Gorbachev's another theory was "the value of all mankind is superior than class value", but in fact, Gorbachev thought that the class does not have any value and in practice he ignored the interests and class stand of the working class. And, in his conception, there has been a tendency of underestimating the threat of imperialism, refused to admit the necessity of ideological struggle between two ideologies, and denied the contradiction between the two systems. Gorbachev's concept erased class content of Lenin's "peaceful coexistence" concept, and he was inclined to advocate policies that would appease imperialism. Whit this conception, Gorbachev has argued to give up struggles for national liberation, socialism, and social progress, with the pretext that these struggles would threat the maintenance of the world peace, and provoke wars.

The disintegration of the Soviet Union and the upheaval in East European socialist countries has led to the capitalist offensive against working class, across the world and also in existing socialist countries, and an offensive against the liberation movements in the former colonies. Depending on its current advantageous status in the world's power balance, imperialism claims to establish a "new world order", which just means utilizing political, economic and military means to re-construct a hegemonic capitalist world, besides the tendency of international easing, disarmament and international cooperation was reversed. This new situation led to imperialist countries' invasion of Iraq and other countries, and led to threats targeting various independent countries. When socialist countries were striving for peaceful coexistence and disarmament, imperialist countries were armed to the teeth, were trying their best to use ideological and economic means to promote "peaceful evolution" of socialist countries.

The Communist Party of Australia has pointed that one of mankind's greatest tragedy is that, the Soviet Union and East European's return to capitalism didn't solve their problems. Their each step further along this capitalist road, will bring about inevitable evil consequences of the capitalist system. The evils and fundamental features of capitalism had once impelled 1/3 of the world population to move towards socialism, and today its nature hasn't changed. The system under which, livelihood of millions of people are faced with poverty, where workers are exploited and social polarization widens and where a handful number of people rule the majority, cannot meet the needs of the people, which just means that it will not last long.

The final conclusion of the Communist Party of Australia reads as follows: "the crisis of the Soviet Union and East European socialist countries is not caused by public ownership and workers' being the masters of the state, but the misunderstanding and improper application of the principles of socialism. The disintegration of the Soviet Union and the great upheaval in East European socialist countries was caused by the complex internal and external factors. These problems are not inherent in socialism, they can be avoided and overcome. Therefore, the disintegration of the Soviet Union and the great upheaval in East European socialist countries is not the failure of socialism, itself. The currently existing socialist countries have avoided these problems and future socialist countries can also avoid such problems.

Y. 65

Scientifically Revealing the Reasons Behind the Collapse of the Soviet Union — A Summary of the Academic Seminar: *"Scientifically Revealing the Reasons Behind the Collapse of the Soviet Union and Upholding Socialism with Chinese Characteristics"*

Gao Yong[1]

Abstract: The disintegration of the Soviet Union is a huge historical tragedy for the people in the Soviet Union and even in the world. The collapse of the Soviet Union enlightens us that the pivotal factor for persevering in socialism is to persist in correct guiding ideology and a correct basic line. When studying the problems and flaws of the Soviet Union, we must be clear about its main trend and its essence. The Soviet Union model of socialism has persisted in the basic systems of socialism, such as the system of distribution according to work and adhered to the Marxist and Leninist guidelines. But its problem lay in the flaws of concrete political and economic systems, and flaws in the operating mechanisms. Starting with the Khrushchev era, the Soviet Union gradually gave up the Marxist guidelines, denied the leaders: Stalin and Lenin, and purposely blurred the distinctions between two regimes purposely, which later finally led to the overthrow of the socialist political regime. Stalin represented the class, the basic line, and the basic social system, denying Stalin meant denying everything related to him, the inevitable result must be national subjugation.

Key words: collapse of Soviet Union; socialism; Marxism; class analysis; standpoint

---

1   Gao Yong, Special Research Fellow at the World Socialism Research Center, attached to CASS, Researcher in the Marxism College of Tsinghua University.

On May 19th 2012, Academic Seminar of Scientifically Revealing the Reasons of Collapse of Soviet Union and Upholding Socialism with Chinese Characteristics was held in Tsinghua University. Zhu Jiamu, the former vice-president of Chinese Academy of Social Sciences (CASS); Liang Zhu, the former vice-president of Peking University; Deng Wei, Deputy Secretary of Party Committee Tsinghua University; Ai Silin, Deputy Dean of Marxism Department Tsinghua University, attended the meeting. The specialists and scholars from Chinese Academy of Social Sciences, Tsinghua University, Peking University, Renmin University of China, University of Science and Technology Beijing, China University of Geosciences, Henan University and Expand Association, such as Zhou Xincheng, Cao Changsheng, Liu Shulin, Li Wei, Xin Xiangyang, Dongfang Yi etc., and over 30 representatives from newspapers and press institutions, such as Studies on Marxism, Leading Journal of Ideological & Theoretical Education, Red Flag Semimonthly, China Education Daily and China Social Sciences Press, were also present in the meeting. Attendees discussed seriously the reasons and lessons of the collapse of the Soviet Union, and believed that at present scientifically revealing the reasons of collapse of Soviet Union from Marxism standpoint, views and methods and drawing lessons is the inescapable responsibility for scholars engaged in Marxism study especially those engaged in the ideological and political theoretical studies, so that we adhere to the direction of socialism with Chinese characteristics and promote the cause of China's revitalization.

I. Different opinions on the collapse of the Soviet Union reflect the differences in political standpoints and lines

Scholars all agreed that the wording "upheaval or collapse of the Soviet Union" is more accurate than "disintegration of the Soviet Union", because "disintegration" only refers to the change in the state form but does not include the change of the party, while "collapse/upheaval" includes both the changes in the party and the state. Since these two decades, the academic circle has various and even opposite opinions on the collapse of the Soviet Union. Attendees have argued that for both communists and anti-communists, the collapse of the Soviet Union is a serious political issue. By the collapse of the Soviet Union, the anti-communists aim to prove the failure of communism, and they attribute this collapse to the aptness of socialism to the survival and development of mankind and to its nature, so they advertise the democratic socialism. For communists, to reveal the real reasons behind the collapse of Soviet Union is related with the current struggles of the existing socialist countries, specifically that they will avoid to have such tragedy in the future, which is also related to the future of the whole human being.

The collapse of the Soviet Union enlightens us that apart from reforming and improving the economic structures, the key factor for adhering to the socialist path is to persist in correct guiding ideology and correct basic line. To persevere in socialism, we must be certainly clear that imperialism will not give up its goal of eliminating socialism. Starting with Khrushchev, the Communist Party of Soviet Union gradually began to abandon the communist guidelines. In 1959 after the U.S-Soviet Camp David talks, Khrushchev widely advocated the so-called U.S.-Soviet reconciliation, giving up the struggle and confrontation with capitalist camp, and "the Spirit of Camp David" mentioned by Khrushchev meant the U.S-Soviet dominating the world together. The ultimate goal of socialism is to eliminate imperialism, so if the cognition of imperialism becomes blurred, will the socialism still survive?

Different circles hold different opinions on whether the collapse of the Soviet Union was a good thing or not. Some argue that the collapse of the Soviet Union has been a historical progress, the collapse conforms with the right direction of the human civilization. And some argue that, the collapse of Communist Party of the Soviet Union has been a loss in the status of world socialism movement, and it was a great retrogression of history. The opposite opinions on this issue show that this is a question of class standpoint, and only class analysis method can explain it. If looking from the standpoint of capitalist class, the collapse of the Soviet Union will be regarded as a historical progress; if looking from the standpoint of proletariat and working people, the collapse of the Soviet Union will be regarded as historical tragedy. Some people argue that the failure of the Soviet "reform" lies in the imperfection of its reform method, and if it could adjust the reform method positively, it would well succeed. This seems impossible. The key problem of Gorbachev's reform was the wrong guiding ideology and the wrong basic line, not the specific reform measures he applied .

There are two opposite world outlooks and cognitive, methodical approaches regarding the studies on the collapse of the Soviet Union: one is persisting in the Marxist standpoint, views and approach in studying the collapse of the Soviet Union; the other is taking non-Marxism as the guideline, evaluating the collapse of the Soviet Union one-sidedly and statically, and which even distorts the facts and makes quotes out of the real context, just to provide basis for their arguments, by any means.

These two attitudes struggle with each other regarding evaluation of the every major aspect of the collapse of the Soviet Union. Western monopoly capitalist class believes that only capitalism is the most perfect social system for humankind and Russia, was from the beginning made a mistake to choose the socialist system, thus the collapse of the Soviet Union has enabled Russian people return to the capitalist civilization path. Consequently, they attribute the collapse of the Soviet Union to October Revolution.

While from the standpoint of proletariat and working people, we recognize that the collapse of the Soviet Union has been a historical retrogression, has been a great historical tragedy for the people of the world. The real purpose of those people who deny Stalin and Lenin, is to negate Marxism and pave the obstacles in the history of socialism thus open the avenues for democratic socialism.

We should realize that as long as there are conflicts and struggles between these two ideologies and systems of socialism and capitalism in the world, the conflicts and struggle between these two cognitive lines will exist. Therefore, we should keep clear mind, firmly persist in and apply the standpoint, views and methodology of Marxism when analyzing and evaluating the collapse of the Soviet Union, and be courageous to fight against all non-Marxist erroneous views.

II. When studying the problems and flaws of the Soviet Union, we must be clear about its main trend and its essence

Attendees of the meeting have argued that, the Soviet Union model of socialism has persisted in the basic systems of socialism, such as the system of distribution according to work and adhered to the Marxist and Leninist guidelines. But its problem lay in the flaws of concrete political and economic systems, and flaws in the operating mechanisms. When studying the flaws of the Soviet Union, we must grasp the main rend and its essence.

Attendees of the meeting have argued: "besides the differences in standpoints, the opposing academic viewpoints also follow different research methodologies."

When looking from the viewpoint which focuses on the historical facts, we shouldn't only examine the surface phenomena one-sidedly and statically, but should observe all the historical facts in the historical process of human history, and grasp the main trend and the essence of historical facts. We should be clear about if it is—in the final analysis—progressive or retrogressive in the course of human history, and if the Soviet system had the viability, if it represented a rise, if it represented continuous improvement and development of things in the course of history or it represented decline, decay and if it had a hopeless future. We should be firstly very clear regarding these major fundamental criteria.

In the history of the development of the cause of socialism, there have been mistakes. If we only focus on some phenomena, and do not look into the main trend and the main nature, randomly deny the historical course, the true reality of the socialist system will be distorted.

Mao Zedong has been the first one who has discovered this problem. He thought that there were severe mistakes in Khrushchev's secret anti-Stalin report, both from the aspects of content and methodology, and he said if the sword of Stalin was lost, the true reality of the socialist system would be distorted.

Therefore, we must catch the holistic essence and nature of historical events comprehensively. Phenomena are not equal to truth, only the essence can reveal the truth. Some people write or compiled voluminous books, attempting to prove their opinions with numerous archival materials and considering these archival material as the "truth". As a matter of fact, archival material can only reflect some phenomena, which might not be the "truth". The truth must include the main trend and the essence, in order to possess the scientific research value. Depending on a piece of archival material to make judgments or conclusions and ignoring the analysis of the essence cannot reveal the truth of the main trend. Nowadays, some people tend to study history with rich archival materials archives, and propose sensational "truths" reveal "inside stories" regarding historical figures and events, based on some bits of archival materials. It is true that, valuable archives are important materials for historical research, and archives can reflect historical facts, but historical truth is not directly reflected in them. Apart from archives, we can mention some more important historical facts. Some studies ignore the facts that millions of people are familiar with, and adopt an ostrich policy, instead of to explore new things to reveal the dark side of them, they try to find things in the "archives" what they wish to find as "the truth". Such study will never find the truth of history, instead seriously distort the development direction of history. When Stalin took over Russia, it was an underdeveloped country, when Stalin passed away, Russia had become a developed country. Russia defeated Hitler depending on the socialist system. These two facts reflect the essence of the socialism of the Soviet Union. Some scholars have pointed out that in the face of divergent opinions, we should study the methodology used in the article "More on the Historical Experience of the Dictatorship of the Proletariat" that was published in 1956, and accordingly differentiate basic systems of the Soviet Union from its specific systems and differentiate basic systems from the flaws in the operating mechanisms.

The model of socialism in the Soviet Union persisted in the basic system of socialism, the system of distribution according to work and persisted in the Marxist and Leninist guidelines. These are true, its flaws lay in the imperfection of its concrete political and economic systems, and in the operating mechanisms.

III. The leadership groups of the Soviet Union were seriously divorced from the masses, which has led to the degeneration of the CPSU and the collapse of the Soviet Union

While tracing the reasons of the collapse of the Soviet Union, the attending scholars have all agreed that: from the time of Khrushchev to Gorbachev the ideological and political degeneration of the CPSU has been the main reason.

When discussing if there appeared a privileged class in Russia, attendees discussed it carefully. Some scholars have argued that before the collapse of the Soviet Union, "there had been privileged stratum phenomena to a certain degree, but there did not yet emerge a privileged stratum, that was in an antagonism with the fundamental interests of the people. Some have argued that there had emerged a privileged stratum in Russia, otherwise it would be hard to explain how the people belonging to the same class, could partly advocate the capitalist road, and some part demanding the improvement of socialism.

As for the question if there emerged a privileged stratum in Russia, we should draw a clear line with such theories as the "alienation in the socialist society" and the theory advocated by Djilas's book "The New Class" and similar theories. The collapse of the Soviet Union is that "the political regime or power is overthrown" as the result of a minority group that betrayed the socialist system, which were not prevented or restricted.

As for the question if there emerged a privileged stratum in Russia, scholars have suggested that this issue needs to be further explored. However, there did emerge a special interest group in Russia, which played as the foundation of imperialist meddling, and a group of traitors who have betrayed the socialist system. Mao Zedong once analyzed that "after the problem of ownership is solved, governance issues and correct handling of the relations among people would become the key problem."

When Mao Zedong read the "political economy textbook" of the Soviet Union, he emphasized the significance of people's participation in state governance. The collapse of the Soviet Union warns us that only solving the problem of ownership of production means will not be enough, still the socialist regime may change. Another problem is the people who hold the leadership may divorce from the masses and indulge in bureaucratism.

Attendees have argued that there were several problems which the socialism of the Soviet Union didn't solve properly or handle well.

Firstly, the problem of the relation between the policy of promoting material interests and the principles of Paris Commune was not properly solved. The core principle of the Paris Commune was that officials' wages should not be higher than workers' average wages. The leadership cadres stratum should give up the mentality of fame and wealth, otherwise it will be very dangerous. Whether you call it "the bureaucracy stratum" or not, a special interest group has emerged in Russia.

Secondly, the issue of the relation between ideal and history was not properly solved. The strength of our ideals, greatly originates from history, and how to look into history is a major issue. The reverse evolution of the Soviet Union started by denying Stalin, denying the history of socialism. In a socialist country where the true history of socialism is distorted, such socialist regime will inevitably collapse.

Thirdly, the issue of the relation between the quality and quantity of party members was not properly solved.

Lenin paid great attention to the quality of party members: "Our party is the ruling party, and naturally an open party, and the one who joins it may gain a position to enjoy some powers. Therefore during this period—when the party is enjoying great prestige, we have to fight against bad elements, and prevent old socialist dregs sneaking into our ruling party……. Only those who participate the party when the Party and our communist movement are in trouble…… may be truly loyal to the cause of workers' liberation."[2]

Attendees have argued that that the primary and key issue about any research on the Soviet Communist Party should figure out, who were the people that facilitated collapse of the Party, which will explain the root cause of the destruction of the Soviet Communist Party. Therefore, we should thoroughly study and reveal the social forces which have destroyed the Soviet Communist Party, otherwise our relevant research over the recent 20 years' will go nowhere. Making a clear distinction between the people and the enemy is not only the primary issue of a revolution, but also the key in researching history and summing up historical experience. In order to analyze which forces and who destroyed the Soviet Union, we should use Marxist theory of class struggle and class analysis method to see the problems clearer. It is obvious that it was Gorbachev who declared the dissolution of the Soviet Communist Party, and it was Yeltsin who decided the disintegration of the Soviet Union. Their main means used in destroying the Soviet Union was to deny Stalin, because Stalin represented the class, the line, the basic socialist system, and denying Stalin meant denying everything related to him, which would definitely lead to ideological subjugation. Those people like Gorbachev who talked about the Party building should not be taken seriously.

---

2   Lenin, "Collected Works, Volume 38, People's Publishing House, 1986, p. 311.

IV. Abandonment of the guiding status of Marxism in the realm of ideology and other superstructures was the primary ideological reason behind of the collapse of the Soviet Union

One of the outstanding manifestations of the evolution of the Soviet Union was that, with Khrushchev, the guiding status of Marxism was gradually weakened, the leadership deviated from it, and the guiding status of Marxism was finally abandoned. This is an important lesson from the death of the Soviet Union.

Some scholars have argued that the CPSU was the pillar of the Soviet Union, without the Communist Party, the Soviet Union could not exist.

If there you do not have a strong political support, the reform you will implement is bound to failure. The former chairman of the USSR Council of Ministers Nikolai Ryzhkov has reminded us that we should draw a lesson from the Soviet Union and persist in the leadership of the Communist Party in our reforms.

To maintain the Party's unity, we should never practice factionalism, and never abandon the guiding status of Marxism. Some attendees have argued that currently, the discourse system of academia in China looks quite problematic, for instance, the term "citizen" has replaced "people"; "tolerate" has replaced critique; "voluntary participation" has replaced "communist dedication" ; "universalism" has replaced proletarian internationalism; and "top level" has replaced "grass root level", which is seriously unfavorable for the guiding status of Marxism.

Some scholars have argued that the deep reason behind the collapse of the Soviet Union was the abandonment of Marxism in the realm of ideology: "if you give up the guidance of Marxism in the field of ideology, the change of the nature of the party will become a matter of course. The collapse of the Soviet Union was not accidental, but an inevitable result of a series of degenerations, before the collapse of the CPSU, its transformation was already realized. Gorbachev et.al have discarded Marxism from the all spheres of ideology, and implemented a comprehensive attack against the history socialism, in all aspects including the social ideology, literature and art, so that people would not have a basic belief in socialism.

Other attendees have argued that: "it was the ignorance and even departure the centralized guiding status of Marxism in the realm of ideology regarding major issues and indulging in liberal pluralism in the realm of ideology, has led to unchecked spread of non-Marxist and anti-Marxist thoughts, which is a key factor leading to the collapse of the Soviet Union.

For example, in the field of philosophy, Marxism was replaced by abstract humanism, which has led to the change of the nature and departure from the guiding ideology the CPSU accordingly leading position of the Party was shaken. In the field of economic construction, the new liberal view of economics has shaken the economic foundation of the socialist system, and caused that the economic reform deviate from the self-improvement of the socialist system.

In the field of politics, "humanistic democratic socialism" was advocated which meant that the guiding position of Marxism-Leninism and the leading role of the CPSU was given up. In the field of historiography studies, the history of the Soviet Union was totally denied, which has caused the "legitimacy crisis" of the leadership of the CPSU and the socialist system. In the field of literature, the wave of critical liberalism played a leading role in creating anti-communist, and anti-socialist paving the way to the disintegration of the Soviet Union. The collapse of the Soviet Union reveals that we must always uphold the guiding status of Marxism in the realm of ideology, correctly understand and deal with the contradictions in the realm of ideology, we should control and guide all kinds of new and conventional mass media outlets, be vigilant against the western ideological infiltration and give effective response to it; strengthen the education of party and government cadres at all levels and the masses, strengthen the belief and grasp of Marxist beliefs and faith, establish the ideals of communism and strengthen socialist beliefs, improve the ability to resist the adverse effects of foreign thought trends.

V. Several generations of the Soviet Union leaders have lost their faith in communist ideals, which caused Soviet reform go astray

The selection of successors for the Party and state is always the key issue of Marxist party and state building. After resigning, the former US president Nixon has made a deep investigation on the Soviet Union and East European countries, and finally has concluded that the vast majority of the state leaders in these countries had lost their enthusiasm in socialist ideals, and become bureaucrats seeking for fame and fortune. Such a state will be vulnerable. Unfortunately, later facts have proved his judgments. This warns us of the supreme importance of socialist and communist ideals for the cadres of Party, from a negative side.

Some scholars have argued that the problems regarding the central leadership level of the CPSU has been one key reason in the collapse of the Soviet Union. After the chaos of 1989, Deng Xiaoping especially emphasized the importance of selecting the proper the central leadership and its core. He said: "If the socialism should progress well, if the government should maintain long-term stability, the key is that we must do a good job in managing the Party affairs." This judgment of comrade Deng Xiaoping came from the lessons of the collapse of Soviet Union and the two CPC General Secretaries' which could not resist bourgeois liberalization, properly. Since the death Deng Xiaoping and other revolutionaries of the older generation, our party can still lead the people to prudently deal with risks emerging in the political and economic fields, one after another, the key lies in that the leadership of our Party Central Committee has always been in the hands Marxists. Among all our works, the selection of successors especially for the central successors is always the crucial issue, which is also of the utmost importance for our Party to withstand the test of being a party in the ruling position for long decades, the tests of the market economy, and the opening-up, and to ensure that our country does not change its color, which is of supreme significance.

Some scholars have suggested that the main reason for the disintegration of the Soviet Union lies in the problem in leadership. "From Khrushchev to Gorbachev, has been a process of consciously deviating from socialism, changes from quantitative to qualitative, which have accumulated the ideological and social foundation for the collapse of Soviet Union, consequently such person as Gorbachev emerging was not accidental. Some scholars have commented that the degeneration of the CPSU has encountered a long process from Khrushchev to Gorbachev. During this long process, through local and partial changes occurred, which was a quantitative accumulation. The obvious indication of the degeneration of the CPSU was the open abandonment of the communism banner and raising the banner of "humanistic democratic socialism". Abandonment of the communism banner of communism marked that CPSU was completely degenerated, and had embarked the evil path of capitalist restoration. Those who destroyed the Soviet socialist system were the "boys" of the Khrushchev era. This shows that the education of the youth with socialist and communist ideals and beliefs is extremely important.

VI. Privatization reforms have led to the collapse of the economic basis of the Soviet Union

Some scholars have introduced Pichurin, a renowned scholar from the Russian Academy of Engineering who has analyzed the reason of the collapse of the Soviet Union from the aspect of national economy management. Pichurin, has evaluated that the collapse was not a natural process, but facilitated by internal and external enemies. The late reforms in the Soviet Union had caused a serious economic crisis. With the pretext of overcoming the crisis, "caused by transition to marketization" the central ministries and agencies together with the governments of the independent republics have designed a joint action plan which said: "the socialist economic system has already been invalid" thus the direction of transiting to capitalism was established."

Gorbachev's radical economic reform had paralyzed the essential elements of the socialist economy, which meant that and the socialist economy has ceased to exist in the Soviet Union during 1989-1991. The "Soviet Union Ownership Law", promulgated in 1990 which violated the constitution, reversed the laws regarding "land ownership, use and distribution rights, ownership of resources," thus dissolved the whole economic system. Introduction of the measure of regional economic accounting (for independent republics) in the late reform period has promoted the surging of the nationalist forces. Nationalist forces vigorously began to propagate that, living in an independent country would be much better, which mislead the people.

The deterioration of people's lives was precisely due to abandonment of the socialist economic management system, but in those days, all the media has made unfair comparison between socialist economy and capitalism, favoring capitalist countries.

Some scholars have pointed out that the maintenance of the public ownership is the fundamental basis of the socialist countries, the fundamental basis of the Communist Party in power, which should not be shaken. Socialist reform can only be further improved, by consolidating and developing the leading position of public ownership, thus prevent embarking the path of privatization.

The collapse of the Soviet Union is one the greatest political event in the history of mankind in 20th century. It has rendered the greatest lesson, was the greatest setback, in the development of the international communist movement and scientific socialism, and has been a great historical retrogression.

Since the Khrushchev era, the Soviet Union has gradually abandoned the guiding status of Marxism, denied and blemished its party leaders Stalin and Lenin, deliberately blurred the distinction between the two social systems, and finally led to the collapse of the socialist regime.

Y. 66

Unveiling the Truth and Thought-provoking "8/19" Event — The Archives of the Beijing Television (BTV)
The documentary film "The Disintegration of the Soviet Union: Exposal of the "8/19" Event" received massive echoes

Li Yan[1]

Abstract: In the past narrations on the Soviet Union history, especially in 1990s, the "8/19" event was often evaluated as a resistance made by "die-hards" against the reform, or it was seen as an unsuccessful "state coup" launched by the senior leaders of the CPSU. Not only it was unable to save the Soviet Union, but also it accelerated the collapse of the CPSU and the disintegration of the Soviet Union. According to the latest classified historical materials of Russia, Gorbachev was not unwitting of the plans and actions of the "emergency committee". After the coup was initiated, despite disagreements among the putschists and below par execution of the coup, etc, the secret support given by some Western countries actually played a key role in Boris Yeltsin's "reversing the situation" and gaining "victory". To reveal the truth of the event is important to clarify some historical facts during the process of the disintegration of the Soviet Union, and will help people to have a better understanding and get a correct judgment.

Key words: Soviet Union; "8/19" event; Gorbachev, The column of Archives Beijing TV

---

1 Li Yan, guest researcher at the World Socialism Research Center, attached to CASS, and associate researcher at the Institute of World Economics and Politics.

The documentary film "The Disintegration of the Soviet Union: Exposal of the "8/19" Event" (I, II, III-Three Episodes) was broadcasted after review, in 3 days, between March the 14th-16th 2012.

Li Shenming, the Deputy Dean of Chinese Academy of Social Sciences (CASS), Dean of Institute of World Economics and Politics was the general counselor of the documentary film, and Chen Zhihua, Wu Enyuan, Zhang Shuhua, Liu Shuren were the counselors for the documentary.

Yu Zhenqi, the former ambassador to Belarus, commented that "this documentary film is worth watching and provides many little-known materials. When the '8/19' event happened in 1991, I was the Deputy Director of the Soviet Union Eastern Europe Division of Ministry of Foreign Affairs, and learnt a lot about the course of the event. Today, I know it much better. For example, many people think that when '8/19' event happened, Gorbachev was under house arrest, while now it seems not, which clearly shows that Gorbachev was a double-dealer." He added impressively that "it's not easy to find so many precious archive material to make this documentary film."

Cui Qimin, the Chief of Central Foreign Affairs Office Propaganda Bureau, who was the Director of Policy Research Office the Chinese Embassy in Russia. He said: this documentary has an educational significance and I will advise other comrades to watch it."

Prof. Yu Sinian, from the Central China Normal University, one of the chief experts of International Communist Movement History, the editor of the key textbook of the Central Marxist Theoretical Construction and Research Project, commented: "this documentary is a classic, not only informative, but also convincing proof that Gorbachev and Yeltsin were the key characters leading to the disintegration of the Soviet Union. The production of this film is also excellent, and it's not easy to make such a political commentary film. I hope this film would be re-broadcasted in CCTV and provincial TVs, and students should be promoted to watch it." He also hoped to see the continuation of such themed documentary works.

Hu Yuequn, historian and Secretary of Chengdu Sports Bureau, Party Committee, had a lot of feelings after watching the film. She commented that the lessons of the disintegration of the Soviet Union was worth thinking deeply: firstly, in a certain sense, it was such leader as Gorbachev that ruined the Soviet Union, so the selection of worthy leaders is closely related to the destiny of a country and is very important. Secondly, as the ruling party, the Communist Party must maintain close ties with the masses and eliminate corruption, especially corruption among the party officials. Meanwhile, we must develop productive forces, improve people's livelihood, and avoid social polarization between the rich and the poor."

Li Yan, associate researcher of the Institute of World Economics and Politics attached to CASS commented that this film series revealed the "8/19" event happened in Russia in 1991 comprehensively and specifically, some the characters and scenes are very specific, vivid and impressive. Objectively, speaking the people don't know well about Russian history and condition, when thinking on the history of the disintegration of the Soviet Union, will feel difficult to figure out why the "State Emergency Committee" which had held almost all supreme authorities and powers of the state, who decision-making ability, and who should normally act with strong determination beforehand, didn't take timely measures in time and declared a state of emergency."

After watching this film, it is clear that apart from missing the best time because of weak faith and hesitation, another important reason is the collusion of hostile forces both inside and outside. Here Gorbachev's "double-dealer" face had been clearly exposed. The latest book "Memories and Reflections: the 20 Years after Breakup of Soviet Union, the memoirs of Lukjanov and Yazov etc. fully proves this point.

A Russian friend who lives in China said in interview that this documentary film is a breakthrough in the exploration of materials and the reveal of historical facts, because in the time of Gorbachev's reform, Gorbachev and Yeltsin etc. were influenced by the US and other western countries, on which there is no complete analysis and evaluation both in the former Soviet Union or present Russia.

This film tells the people that the Soviet Reforms and the disintegration of the Soviet Union cannot be only attributed to internal factors within the Soviet Union, but external factors also played important roles. To a certain extent, the disintegration of the Soviet Union is the result of years of foreign anti-Soviet and anti-communist activities. Of course, when watching this film, people may have mixed and contradictory feelings. On the one hand, this film describes the process of the disintegration of the Soviet Union with many unpublished internal data and even confidential data, and reveals some little-known details, which is very convincing. On the other hand, as a Russian, in the face of these real historical materials, he couldn't help recalling the "reform" period he experienced at that time, and recollected the collapse of country, the stagnation in the social development, and difficulties he and all people have suffered, which was deeply engraved on his mind.

The "8/19" event in the Soviet Union shows that the starting point of reform should aim defend the interests of the country and the people, especially the stability of the country and the people's peaceful livelihood. Reforms should adhere to the Party's leadership and take the socialist path.

We should be vigilant at all times and never take it lightly that, the western countries headed by the US, implement all kinds of subversive activities against the socialist countries,

A comrade from General Office of the State Council, after watching this film has commented: "having watched the Beijing TV program for three consecutive days, I salute the persons who have contributed! Its dialectic is so vigorous. Just as what Du Mu said in his poem "Lamenting the Epang Palace" that 'The man of Ch'in, having no opportunity of lamenting himself, was left to be lamented by later generations; and the later generations who lament Ch'in, but refuse to learn a lesson from him make later generations lament the later generations."

Andreyev, a Russian agency representative in China, after watching the film said that: "firstly, congratulations to BTV and China's Soviet Union history researchers for making such wonderful and authentic documentary." He expressed full agreement that the film was a historical breakthrough with its representation, analysis and meanings, "I have never watched such a documentary with in-depth analysis on the historical events of the Soviet Union, which demonstrates that China's research on the Soviet Union has achieved great success in the aspects of mastery of historical materials and restoring authenticity. Secondly, from this documentary, it can be seen that Gorbachev reforms and the disintegration of the Soviet Union was not only caused by internal problems of the Soviet Union, but also external factors have played great roles, indeed.

Before this documentary, there was no complete and factual analysis and introduction about the influence of western countries on Gorbachev and Yeltsin during the Gorbachev's reform period either in the former Soviet Union or present Russia. Their role in the disintegration was not known.

Therefore, this is a "breakthrough". Andreyev agreed on the analysis of the causes of the collapse of the Soviet Union, which in a certain sense was the result of years of anti-Soviet and anti-communist actions from outside the country.

Thirdly, the process of the Soviet reform and the collapse and the way of present Russian society development should be deeply summarized and lessons should be drawn. We can be sure that United States and some other Western countries have never stopped sabotaging and restraining the socialist countries, especially their effect in internal subversive and sabotage activities. We should be vigilant and guard against them resolutely.

Fourthly, Gorbachev's behavior before and after the "8/19" event is not accidental or temporary "maneuver". In fact, after the disintegration of the Soviet Union, people had known that Gorbachev was "opposing" the system, and his "opposition" had just started with his meeting with Mrs. Thatcher in 1984. Many Russian officials began to think that Mrs. Thatcher was very brilliant with her ideas. After their first meeting, Gorbachev changed a lot in his ideological concepts and understanding of the socialist system, and Mrs. Thatcher didn't only influence Gorbachev, but many others in the Soviet Union.

Several months after Gorbachev was back from London, the Soviet Union's national TV station sent three journalists to make an exclusive interview for Mrs. Thatcher.

They asked some questions about Soviet Union sending its troops to East Europe in the World War II and the results achieved after the World War II.

Also asked her opinions on the socialist system and communism, and questions about oil exploration in each country and international oil price etc. Their questions were simple and direct in a sense just like "pediatrics", while Mrs. Thatcher was like a skillful teacher, who was answering the questions of "lazy students", and took this opportunity to criticize the reforms of the Soviet Union, rather than making constructive comments.

At that time, this interview was broadcasted in the national TV stations, which were actually propaganda for Mrs. Thatcher. Now from the documentary film "The Disintegration of the Soviet Union: Exposal of the "8/19" Event", it could be seen clearly that the interview program was just prepared for Mrs. Thatcher, who could destructively criticize the Soviet socialist reform, without proposing constructive suggestion. After watching this brilliant documentary, we can understand that it was not accidental to arrange such a program to popularize Margaret Thatcher.

Fifthly, in the final part of the documentary, the analysis on Russia's social situation in the Putin era is correct. During the 20 years from the later stage of the Soviet Union to the collapse of the Soviet Union, Russia basically relied on selling energy resources in order to survive. This kind of development lacks creativity and innovation, which cannot be regarded as successful from the long-term aspect.

Y. 67

The Party Committees of Various Regions and Departments Have Organized A Campaign of Group Watching of the TV Documentary: "20 Years' Reflections on the Soviet Union's and CPSU's Perishment: The Russians Narrating"
The Broadcast Has Received Intensive Echoes and Responses

A News Report by China Fangzheng Press

Abstract: A lot of precious historical data in the documentary panoramically reveal the profound lessons of the Soviet Union's collapse, which allow us more deeply think about some major theoretical and practical problems such as: what is essentially important for the Marxist political parties in power, what should be the Party's soul and how should be political life of such party guided, and how should the purity of the Party maintained. Watching this TV documentary is of great practical significance, so as to deeply understand our Party which is faced by "four threats" as analyzed by the General Secretary Hu Jintao: the Party should exercise control over itself, and should make a scientific summary on running the Party strictly, need to educate the Party members to be vigilant against danger; need to further strengthen ideals and faith in socialism with Chinese characteristics; the need to keep the Party's advanced character and purity; and need to unswervingly follow the path of socialism with Chinese characteristics.

Key words: TV documentary 20 years' reflections on Soviet Union's collapse; lessons; warm response

"20 Years' Reflections on the Soviet Union's and CPSU's Perishment: The Russians Narrating" the TV series produced by World Socialism Research Center, attached to CASS, and was co-published by the Central Commission for Discipline Inspection (CCDI) and China Fangzheng Press.

It was designed as an educational documentary. This TV Documentary film series contained 4 episodes, published in parts with the title of "Be Vigilant Against Threats, III). The series was published with a large circulation and generally well accepted by the masses and received warm response from the vast number of party members and cadres.

I. Localities and departments attached great importance, and made timely arrangements

In order to spread the spirit of the symposium and work conference titled as the "National Anti-corruption Publicity and Education" the Central Commission for Discipline Inspection, together with some various localities and other various government departments have mobilized the masses to watch the above mentioned TV documentary series.

Over 30 provinces (including municipalities and autonomous regions) evaluated this documentary as a lively textbook for the education for party members and cadres, which would help to improve their vigilance.

Chen Lun, the standing member of the Jilin Province's Provincial Commission for Discipline Inspection, has suggested: "this documentary should be seriously watched under our scrupulous organization, so as to further enhance the public awareness among the leading cadres, to sharpen their communist ideals and faith, and promote their determination in our practice, i.e, the path of socialism with Chinese characteristics."

Shandong Province's Provincial Commission for Discipline Inspection also suggested to watch the documentary as an important part of strengthening the education of party members for purifying the party, it suggested that this activity should be combined with the ongoing education activity of the party themed as "Adhere to Political Ethics, Maintain the Purity of the Party". The leader of the commission called: "do a good job of organized education."

Liaoning Province's Provincial Commission for Discipline Inspection issued special circular: "combine this activity with our province's anti-corruption propaganda and educational work" , "we should watch the documentary "20 Years' Reflections on the Soviet Union's and CPSU's Perishment: The Russians Narrating" and "strengthen the work of education regarding maintaining the Party's purity education, and further develop cadres' political, ethical and integrity education." The Provincial Commission suggested combining watching with learning.

Jiangxi Province's Provincial Commission for Discipline Inspection included an evaluation of the results of watching and learning activity combined with the said TV documentary in the principal content of annual comprehensive evaluation of its propaganda and education work.

Guangxi Autonomous Region's Commission for Discipline Inspection, issued a circular themed as "Circular on Developing Educational Activities, for Clean Government and Maintaining Purity Forever", and suggested watching "the documentary" as an important part of educational activities, for the Party members and the leading cadres, the circular said: "consciously resist all kinds degeneration, corruption and erroneous thoughts."

Yunnan Province carried out a "reflection and learning activity" and suggested the documentary as an important teaching material.

The Organization Department of the Shanxi Province's, Provincial Party Committee evaluated the documentary as an educational reference which should be watched by the Party cadres.

The relevant departments attached to the Central Propaganda Ministry purchased the video publication of "the documentary" and donated them to provincial and ministerial level study groups and to some experts and scholars, as the study reference.

Central Political and Law Commission, work committee, attached to Central Committee of the CPC, Working Committee of the Central State Organ, the Ministry of Public Security, State-owned Assets Supervision and Administration Commission (SASAC), the State Tobacco Monopoly Administration etc. suggested their subordinate units to watch the documentary. Chinese Academy of Social Sciences (CASS) presented the documentary to its experts and scholars and organized a discussion conference. The Central Party School and the National School of Administration included the documentary into class teaching curriculum, it was watched and discussed in the classes, and two forums were organized.

II. Well organized watching campaigns: masses have responded enthusiastically and warmly

From the central authorities to grassroots level units such as neighborhoods, factories, working places, including mines and army units, school campuses, various such units have carefully and enthusiastically watched the documentary and discussed it in forms of study groups, party classes, reading classes etc. In the units where the documentary was watched in an organized manner, party members and cadres have enthusiastically discussed it.

Both the Offices, departments and bureaus attached to the Central Commission for Discipline Inspection, and Chinese Academy of Social Sciences (CASS) bureau-level leading cadres organized reading classes to watch the documentary.

Shanghai's Commission for Discipline Inspection has attached great importance to and specially appointed a cadre in charge of organizing "watching and studying" the documentary.

In Shanghai, more than 2000 county-level party members and leading cadres have watched the documentary, and over 30 forums were held, and over 100 pieces of written feedbacks received.

In the Jilin Province the documentary was broadcasted for over 400 times, more than 50 thousand people have watched it, 85 forums were held, and more than 1300 written feedbacks were received.

Guangxi Autonomous Region's Commission for Discipline Inspection has utilized the documentary as an education material for new department-level cadre training, organized discussions. In 2011, Guangxi Autonomous Region, utilized the documentary for the education of 214 district-level cadres, to maintain Party's purity and political education.

Shandong's Shandong Provincial Commission for Discipline Inspection, used the documentary as an opportunity to organize training classes for provincial (city and district) secretary of Committee for Disciplinary Inspection, organized 140 county-leveled secretaries to watch this documentary and discussed in groups, which received warm response from the trainees.

Liaoning Province combined the watching of the documentary with the activity "Uncorrupted Party Activities" which was held for main leading cadres from cities, counties and towns in the province, on the theme "Maintain Party Discipline, Keep Party's Purity", the trainings took the content of this documentary as an important part education.

The Party committees and leading cadres at all levels, and combined it with incorrupt legislation test for new leading cadres held in each regions of the province; took the content of this documentary as an important study materials of the incorrupt legislation test for new leading cadres held in each regions of the province, and included it into the question bank of incorrupt legislation test for new leading cadres.

Besides, the documentary was used as the basic learning material for fighting against corrupt politics and education for a clean government in the training of leading cadres, adopted it as important content of training organizations for leading cadres. On the other side the documentary was used in the various central theoretical study groups.

Forums and thematic conferences were held and writing articles on theme was promoted, party members and leading cadres were organized to study and exchange views extensively and carried out in-depth discussions.

In the Tibet Autonomous Region, over 40 units directly under Tibet Autonomous Region carried out discussion after watching this documentary. Guiyang City in the Guizhou Province, organized leading committees, especially the heads of the committees to watch this documentary, and promoted studies and forums, combined learning with practical work in various ways.

Xinjiang Uygur Autonomous Region's Farming and Animal Husbandry Bureau, Jiangsu Nantong's Prefecture-level City Party School, Wulan County in Qinghai Province Public Security Bureau, Xi'an's Public Bus Transportation Factory, the 7th Division of the Xinjiang Production and Construction Corps, Guxi township government in Anhui Province, tens of thousands grassroots units all over the country saw watching this documentary as an opportunity, and organized Party members and cadres to hold forums, exchanges, composed reviews and comments, and deepened the effects of the learning.

III. Audience gave high recognition and generally commented favorably

After watching "the documentary", majority of the audiences have described the documentary as "vivid, thought-provoking and impressive." They all positively commented: "through a lot of precious historical data and materials and true witnesses of the events, this documentary panoramically reveals the profound lessons of the sudden collapse of Soviet Union, which has been the first socialist country in the world, which was led by a communist party for over 70 years. Thanks for such a rare ideological and political learning material."

Comrade Zhou Benshun, General Secretary of the Central Political and Law Commission has watched the film, and suggested that all political and legal organs across the country should organize watching and studying this documentary.

Wang Qijiang, the Deputy Secretary-General Comrade Wang Qijiang made special comment: "I have watched this documentary, and I think it's good. I advised our organs to organize the party units to watch it." Liu Guchang, the former Vice-Minister of Foreign Affairs, and China's ambassador to Russia, has pointed out: "this documentary is good, with many first-hand informative materials, and it is convincing, we should let more people to watch this film." Chen Jin, the deputy director of Central Literature

Research Office, after watching it, commented: "It is great!" used three letters to describe the documentary.

Li Yongqing, the vice-president of the Shandong Provincial Party Committee, commented after watching this documentary: "in this documentary, a lot of precious historical data panoramically reveals the profound lessons of the Soviet Union's collapse, and its leading party the CPSU, which urge us to think more deeply about some major theoretical and practical problems, what is essentially important for the Marxist political parties in power, what should be the Party's soul and how should be political life of such party guided, and how should the purity of the Party maintained. Watching this TV documentary is of great practical significance, so as to deeply understand our Party which is faced by "four threats" as analyzed by the General Secretary Hu Jintao: the Party should exercise control over itself, and should make a scientific summary on running the Party strictly, need to educate the Party members to be vigilant against danger; need to further strengthen ideals and faith in socialism with Chinese characteristics; the need to keep the Party's advanced character and purity; and need to unswervingly follow the path of socialism with Chinese characteristics.

Many audiences also called and spoke highly of this documentary, which has combined political, ideological and artistic qualities. An audience from Yunmeng town of Hubei said: "in the recent years few works have touch me so deeply, indeed this documentary was touching. After watching it, I lived mixed feelings and thousands of new thoughts."

CITIC Group watched this documentary and evaluated it a satisfactory. After watching, the CITIC invited the film's creative artistic staff to give a lecture on what they thought and encountered during the course of its production. Many units which have watched this documentary expressed: while our entire Party and our people of all nationalities are confident to welcome the successful convocation of the 18th National Congress of the Party, this documentary is of great practical significance, for educating the Party members to be vigilant against threats and strengthen the ideals and faith in socialism with Chinese characteristics; to maintain the advanced character and the purity of the Party, and unswervingly follow the path of socialism with Chinese characteristics.

IV. Warning effect is remarkable, and the educational aspect is of great significance

Through watching and studying the documentary, the audiences were deeply inspired and educated, and generally commented: people have compared the glorious parties the Chinese Communist Party and the CPSU, honor and disgrace, rise and fall, it is thought-provoking. Vast number of party members and cadres have expressed these feelings: we should earnestly draw lessons from the Soviet Union's collapse and the CPSU's demise, keep vigilant against threats, cherish the hard-won brilliant situation in our country, maintain a high degree of unity around the Central Committee of the CPC, live up to the expectations of the party and the people, and fulfill the tasks given by the Party and the people.

On the eve of "July 1st" Day, the Party Committee which is organized in Beijing's Commission for Discipline Inspection, organized over 200 party members and cadres to watch the film. After watching it, many of them commented: "we must draw lessons from history, profoundly learn from the lessons of the Soviet Union's collapse and Soviet Communist Party's decline, further strengthen communist ideals and beliefs, always maintain the purity of the Party, unswervingly follow the path of socialism with Chinese characteristics.

County-level secretaries who have attended the Shandong's Provincial (city, region) Commission of Disciplinary Inspection training class, the leader of the class said: "20 Years' Reflections on the Soviet Union's and CPSU's Perishment: The Russians Narrating" is vivid education material, it impressively demonstrates causes, external and internal causes of the Soviet Union's collapse and Soviet Communist Party's decline by the means of real person's experiences and people concerned at that time, it deeply analyzes the reasons, and renders profound warning and reflection opportunity for Party members and cadres. We should draw lessons from it, improve ourselves, be pure Party members all the time, and strive to be loyal guards of the Party and closely unite with the people."

Trainees who have participated the training class of the Jiangxi provincial department of technology, Disciplinary Inspection and Supervision Department, after watching the film commented as follows: This documentary offers a true political education, also education for our aim of clean government, and offers Party discipline education. We should carefully combine the lessons and problems in the film with the actual situations of China, which will be of great educational meaning.

In the a prefecture-level city of Xinyu in the Province, the party members and cadres were moved after watching the film and a leader commented: "ignoring the interests of the people and masses has been the fundamental reason of Soviet Union's collapse and CPSU's demise".

Party members and cadres elected to the People's Congress of the Guiyang City, after studying and discussing the film have made such a brief summary: "Soviet Union's collapse and Soviet Communist Party's demise is caused by the "diversified" guiding ideology adopted by this party and adopting of western multi-party political system, and the economic privatization policy. Painful lessons of this big event are heavy and alarming. When we are building socialism, at the same time we should strengthen our ideals and faith in socialism with Chinese characteristics, adhere to the Party's leadership, take economic construction as the central work, adhere to the view of people-oriented development, promote social harmony, and strive for revitalizing the Chinese nation."

V. Further deepen the warning value, and highlight the long-term effects

As far as we know, in many provinces of the country and many departments and units are continuing to promote the watching and studying of the documentary film "20 Years' Reflections on the Soviet Union's and CPSU's Perishment: The Russians Narrating" there are many essays written, forums and other kind of activities being held, all of them aim to further deepen its long-term warning value of this documentary.

On the basis of watching and studying Twenty Years' Reflections on Soviet Union's Collapse and Soviet Communist Party's Decline, Liaoning Province planned to develop keynote speech on political ethics and a composition writing competition among the Party members and leading cadres in the whole province in the second half the 2012, in order to constantly strengthen the systemic, targeted and effective features of anti-corruption educational work.

Guiyang city of the Guizhou Province planned to further develop "watching and discussing" the documentary together with Municipal Committee Organization Department and Propaganda Department, focusing on solving Party members and cadres' problems of ideals and faiths, team building, honesty and self-discipline.

Many Party Members, Cadres and even Senior Party Cadres, suggested that the Central Commission for Discipline Inspection, together with other relevant Departments of the Central Government, should either separately or jointly issue a written statement, that calls upon all Party Membership and related masses, together with all university teachers and students, to study the spirit and implement the required action, contained within the important speech made by Hu Jintao at the Provincial Level Main Leadership and Cadre Seminar, delivered on July 23rd, 2012. This action will assist in the building of good public opinion and creating a conducive atmosphere, that will welcome the convening of the forthcoming 18th National Congress of the Communist Party of China (CPC).

Y. 68

A Review of A Spectacular Event : The Educational TV Film "20 Years' Reflections on the Soviet Union's Collapse and the CPSU's Perishment: The Russians Are Narrating" —The Heart-Shaking, Vivid, Educational TV Film Penetratively Reveals the Lessons of the Soviet Union's Disintegration and CPSU's Perishment

Liu Ruisheng[1] & Li Yan[2]

Abstract: "20 Years' Reflections on the Soviet Union's Collapse and the CPSU's Perishment: The Russians Are Narrating" is an educational TV film. It was produced by the film creators led by a team appointed by the World Socialism Research Center, attached to CASS. Since its broadcast in 2012, the Propaganda and Education Office under the Central Commission for Discipline Inspection, has issued an official circular to all of its branches and its organizations at all levels, and also required the Party members and leading cadres above the county level to watch this film. At present, over 50 ministries and commissions such as departments under the CCP, central government organs etc. and over 30 municipalities and autonomous regions, over 2000 cities and counties, thousands of basic units have watched this film in forms of central study group, Party classes, reading classes etc. Twenty Years' Reflections on Soviet Union's Collapse and CPSU's Perishment: the Russian Are Narrating has received close attention from national leading officials and academic circles, and aroused strong repercussions in China.

Key words: educational TV film; collapse of the Soviet Union; Russian telling; strong response

---

[1] Liu Ruisheng, Executive Director of the World Socialism Research Center attached to CASS, Associate researcher in the Institute of News and Communication by CASS.
[2] Li Yan, guest researcher at the World Socialism Research Center, attached to CASS, Associate researcher in the Institute of World Economic and Political Studies.

Editor's note: The film crew of World Socialism Research Center of Chinese Academy of Social Sciences has been to Russia for three times for extensive interviews, and it took over two years to make this educational TV film: "20 Years' Reflections on the Soviet Union's Collapse and the CPSU's Perishment : The Russians Are Narrating" (Be Vigilant Against Threats, Part III and IV). The consultants of this film were: Chen Kuiyuan, Li Li'an, Zhang Quanjing, Teng Wensheng, Wang Weiguang, Zheng Keyang, Jiang Chengkang, (Russian) G. Osipov, (Russian) M. Titarenko, (Russian) O. Zhukov, (Russian) F. Dobrincov etc. Li Shenming has been the Chief-editor.

On March 7th 2012, the Propaganda and Education Office under the Central Commission for Discipline Inspection, has issued an official circular to all of its branches and its organizations at all levels, and also required the Party members and leading cadres above the county level to watch this film.

At present, over 50 ministries and commissions such as departments under the CCP, central government organs etc. and over 30 municipalities and autonomous regions, over 2000 cities and counties, thousands of basic units have watched this film in forms of central study group, Party classes, reading classes etc. "20 Years' Reflections on Soviet Union's Collapse and CPSU's Perishment: the Russian Are Narrating" has received close attention from national leading officials and academic circles, and aroused strong repercussions in China.

Since its broadcast, the film has received close attention from the leading officials of the Party, state and academic circles, and aroused strong repercussions in China. Also a six-part academic version of the documentary is being produced. Already, the 4 Episodes version was watched by the Party members and leading cadres above the county level, across the country. Below a part of the feedbacks will summarized:

I. Reveal the painstaking lessons of Soviet Union's collapse and Soviet Communist Party's decline vividly and impressively

A number of central leaders, leaders of the Central Military Commission and leaders of the ministries and commissions have made instructions or sent messages praising and suggesting the film or captioned it. Some central leaders have proposed fair amendments in advance, some central leaders have commented that the film was quite good and has great educational value, some former central leaders even wrote comments and notes which were over ten-page, some leading comrades from ministries gave clear instructions advising their subordinate units to organize watching events, and some provincial leaders purchased this film at their own expenses and gave them as presents to others.

Li Lian, the former member of the Standing Committee, and general-secretary of the organ, has pointed out: "It has a clear guiding ideology, and the film is has been carefully divided into several sub-topics for discussion, offers vivid pictorial information, plus includes Russian's personal narration and comments I appreciate. Currently, the overall situation of our country is quite good, however some facts are also very worth of attention. The economical, political, and ideological situations before the Soviet Union's collapse reflected in this film is shocking, and currently we need such works to further strengthen our sense of crisis, so that we should never encounter a situation as faced by the Soviet Union. We have acquired great achievements during the reform and opening up, but must be still vigilant, and unwaveringly adhere to the path of socialism with Chinese characteristics.

General Secretary Hu Jintao stressed the importance of upholding the Four Cardinal Principles in his "July 1st" speech. One of the Four Cardinal Principles is dictatorship of proletariat, i.e., people's democratic dictatorship. One of the primary reasons of Soviet Union's demise was the abandonment of the dictatorship of proletariat, which has been clearly explained in this TV film. In socialist countries if there is no pure leadership by a proletarian party, it's difficult to keep the maintain the color of the country. In our country, currently we are paying great efforts to oppose economic corruption, at the same time we are opposing political, ideological, theoretical phenomena which deviates from the basic theory of the party, from its basic program, its basic principle, and basic standpoint. This film sends a warning signal against ideological laxity. We should find ways, so that more people can watch this film, draw lessons from, and raise consciousness. This film is in complete accord with the spirit of Hu Jintao's speech in the 90th anniversary of the foundation of the Party. It embodies quite practical educational significance."

Zhang Quanjing, the former minister of the Central Organization Department, has pointed out: the "Be Vigilant" educational series are getting better and better, deeper and deeper, more and more concrete specific, in comparison from the first, to second, and to the present third part. The third part is vivid with its images, clear and includes shocking facts, and better than the first two parts.

The film expounds and underlines Gorbachev, makes a thorough introduction to the essence of his "new thinking" in foreign policy, "openness", and "democratization", and more profoundly elaborates his anti-Marxism-Leninist, anti-Stalinist, and anti-socialist stand. In the past, we didn't know who constituted the fifth column in Soviet Union, and after watching the film, we can clearly understand that, Gorbachev and his group gang were the fifth column. One of the most fundamental reasons for the collapse of the Soviet Union was the betrayal of Marxism-Leninism. Gorbachev's usurping the power, was also a very important reason, because no matter what numerous lessons we can draw, this latter one is the most important. Chairman Mao Zedong said that the threat of "peaceful evolution" is in the party, from its top leaders, which has been fully proved by the betrayal of Gorbachev group. Hu Jintao, the General Secretary of the Party Central Committee has repeatedly stressed the need to strengthen the ideals of and faith in communism and socialism with Chinese characteristics. Currently, some people don't talk about ideals and faiths, which is wrong. Just precisely because communism is distant and ideal, we must promote faith in it. Our Party has ideals and faiths in communism since its foundation days. I have joined the revolution during War of Liberation period, in those days we all talked about ideals and faiths, and so many martyrs devoted their lives to realize ideals and faiths. Why cannot we talk about them today? Generally speaking, this film is wonderful and of great practical and educational significance, and the next step is to do a good work in spreading it. We are thankful that, the World Socialism Research Center has produced such a brilliant work."

Liu Guchang, the former Vice Minister of Foreign Affairs, Chinese ambassador to Russia, pointed out: "this documentary is quite good, informative, and includes a lot of first-hand information and is convincing, we should let more people watch it."

Zhao Xidi, the former Chinese ambassador to Belarus, said that "this film reveals the reasons CPSU's perishment, includes the historical lessons that we should draw from it, and some views on the Soviet Union's collapse, which are all tenable theories and views. The material is very informative."

Yu Hongjun, Vice Minister of the International Department, attached to CPC Central Committee, said that "When I have watched this film. I have understood that a great effort is in it, the creative producing team has done a good job. It is skillfully designed to include the Russian's narrations, this has been a wise idea, it has is a brilliant design. The whole film is very positive from the aspect of educational significance, I have suggested it to many Party members, especially when the CPC as the ruling party is faced with many challenges in the coming decade, it will play an important role. Summarizing the lessons of the Soviet Union's collapse and the CPSU's demise, and seeing the corrupt practice of the late Soviet system and mechanisms have a warning value for us. We should persist in our own way, never follow the late Soviet example. To maintain socialist system, we should adhere "three-favourables"[3] idea of comrade Deng Xiaoping, advantage measures and continue to implement the scientific concept of development."

Cheng Baoshan, Deputy Political Commissar of Second Artillery Unit, after watching, has praised it and, has recommended the compact disk to more units and comrades.

Wang Huaichen, secretary of Sichuan Provincial Committee, Provincial Discipline Inspection Commission, said that "at present many leading officials of the Party are studying the lessons of Soviet Union's collapse, and this film is a very good teaching material."

Li Qiqing, former deputy director of Compilation and Translation Bureau, mentioned that "exploring the historical lessons of Soviet Union's collapse and CPSU's perishment is a major topic, and this film answers this question scientifically, and has reached a high cognitive level. This film concentrates and reveals the truth of Soviet Union's collapse by means of Russian's narrations, and it is very convincing and theoretical. This film is shocking and enlightening."

II. Remember lessons of the Soviet Union's disintegration: during reforms we should always bear the masses' interests in mind and stick to the socialist orientation

Pang Xianzhi, the former director of Literature Research Center of the CPC Central Committee, said that "thanks for the comrades in the World Socialism Research Center of the CASS, you have produced a very good film, and did n very important work."

Zheng Keyang, the former director of Policy Research Office of the CPC Central Committee, pointed out: "this film is very good. Compared with the previous "Be Vigilant" it has common points and also differences. This new one focuses on the evil role of late political leaders in the Soviet Union, and gives the observations of Russians from all walks of life, regarding the major event that occurred 20 years ago.

The film includes a large amount of precious data and information, and further explains the causes of Soviet Union's collapse in a very persuasive way. It has collected interesting interviews and materials which are very difficult to reach. This film is both creative and also it has a remarkable depth. Soviet Union's demise is a mirror for us, a reference; obviously the conditions and situations in China and the SU are different, but the laws of

---

3   Deng Xiaoping's three favorable in reform practice are favourable to developing the productivity in the socialist society, favourable to consolidating China's comprehensive national strength and favourable to raising the people's living standards.

development of political parties are similar. We should pay attention to the lessons of Soviet Union's collapse and the CPSU's perishment, which is life and death importance regarding the destiny of the Party, so we must warn all Party members to carefully draw lessons. As the companion to the previous volume of the "Be Vigilant", the recent one approaches from another aspect, and deepens our understanding regarding Soviet Union's collapse that occurred 20 years ago. It is good and great."

Jin Chongji, the former vice-director of Party Literature Research Center of CPC Central Committee, commented: "after watching, I have been greatly inspired, it is wise that the film has adopted the way of Russian's narrations, which has made it more convincing."

Li Qiufang, the head of the Discipline Inspection Unit in CASS attached to Central Commission for Discipline Inspection, pointed out: "the lessons of the CPSU falling from power, have offered us a great warning, consequently we have focused on how to ensure that the power of our ruling party does not detach from the people, and our party cares for boldness, innovation, opposes rigidity, stagnation, so as to lead socialism with Chinese characteristics, to new victory, our CPC should be vigilant against threats, continue to emancipate our minds, always keep nurture the Party's blood-and-flesh ties with the people, maintain the advanced nature of the Party, progressiveness, persistently fight for the cause of the people, and constantly improve the Party's governing capacity."

Liang Zhu, the former vice-president of the Peking University, commented: "the film is meaningful, after watching it, I have summarized two points which are very convincing: firstly, to sum up the historical lessons of Soviet Union's collapse from Marxist viewpoint. We should understand the exact causes for the demise of the Soviet Union. In our Party, some people attribute it to Stalin model and the Soviet Union system, which is completely wrong. We shouldn't deny there were some mistakes in the Stalin era, but it will not be appropriate attribute the collapse to these mistakes, this approach will not help us to correctly summarize lessons of the history. Secondly, the film embodies a strong sense of reality and practical meaning, it offers a good reference value for our Party in adhering to socialism, how to promote reform and opening up, and how to prevent against corruption and degeneration. If we can correctly sum up the historical lessons of the demise of the Soviet Union, we will benefit greatly. This film should be popularized in universities and colleges, and will be helpful for us to properly understand the lessons of Soviet Union."

Zheng Dexing, the secretary-general of the Central Literature Research Office has pointed out: "the film, which has coincided with the 90th anniversary of the foundation of our Party, the lessons of Soviet Union's demise and CPSU's perishment are impressive, and it is necessary for us to carry out Party education. This impact of this educational film gives a shocking effect and remarkably inspiring. Although, previously I knew the events generally, but after listening the narrations of the persons involved, 20 years after the events, I have felt them more deeply and objectively. This film reveals that some leaders of the CPSU have used "reform" as means for seeking personal gains, which finally led to the demise of the party. This is too horrible. We should prevent against such tragedies occurring in other socialist countries, especially in China."

Han Jiugong, director of the Institute of the Party Building Research attached to Central Organization Department, has commented: "this film contains vivid scenes and visually very impressive, and it embodies narrations by former leading cadres of the Soviet Union, as well as narrations by experts and scholars, common Russian soldiers and a number of Moscow residents; letting them narrate the events in the process of Soviet Union's collapse, is indeed convincing. The commentary is also good, gives clear information and messages, also thought-provoking. It's meaningful to launch this film on the occasion of the 90th anniversary of the foundation of the Party."

Chai Shangjin, from the General Administration Department the State Council, has pointed out: "through this film, we can directly watch and examine the demise of the Soviet Union, and hear the narrations by the former members of the CPSU, Political Bureau such as Ryzhkov, Ligachev, who have evaluated how Gorbachev used "reform" to coach Soviet Union to its collapse and the CPSU to demise—step by step—in the fields of politics, economy, and diplomacy. After Gorbachev ascended to power, he paid great efforts to promote the "new thinking", "openness" and "democratization" reforms, his aim was to end the so-called "one-party dictatorship" of the CPSU and establish the western type of multi-party parliamentary system. With these initiatives, in practical politics he eliminated the leadership of the CPSU in the political sphere, recognized the legality of dissidents like Sakharov and others, and promoted anti-Soviet Yakovlev, to a key position in the Party, these steps by Gorbachev have inevitably led to unchecked surge of various anti-communist associations and anti-socialist activities in the society. The narrations by witnesses of the events allow us to see clearly that Gorbachev's so-called "new thinking" and "reform" were in fact "getting rid of a capable lieutenant". All prove that, he was the culprit of Soviet Union's demise and CPSU's perishment."

Prof. Mei Rongzheng, from the School of Marxism attached to Wuhan University, commented: "this film analyzes the background, reasons, process, nature, and consequences of the Soviet Union's collapse and CPSU's perishment realistically with narrations Russians, with most vivid and persuasive facts and analysis. After watching I was so touched that, I stayed awake at night to think over it. All the Party members who are loyal to the cause of communism will feel shocked and upset when watching it. No one should forget the greatest historical tragedy of the 20th century."

Sun Weiping, the deputy director of the Institute of Philosophy, attached to CASS, and Prof. Yu Sinian, from the Institute Political Sciences, attached to Huazhong Normal University, have commented: the documentary film "20 Years' Reflections on Soviet Union's Collapse and CPSU's Perishment: the Russian Are Narrating" gives a shocking effect, full of warning, and embodies a strong sense of urgency, and has an outstanding educational quality. It is a kind oral history work with interviews, narrations, site visits which revisits a major event. Through many witnesses, and authoritative figures who have direct experienced the disintegration of the Soviet Union, this film displays the emergence of the serious problems in the CPSU and how these problems have developed in the later phases, which are critical for correctly understanding the reasons behind the disintegration of the Soviet Union, consequently it is very convincing.

The historical lessons of the upheaval in the Soviet Union will be reflected for a long time in the future, and this documentary will promote these reflections, with its informative character and it directly reflects the events with clear and accurate materials, which has a great inspirational meaning for Chinese Communist Party's political practice. The Russian narrators have shown their real feeling and gave first hand information which help the audience to understand the issue more profoundly. Such a convincing TV film has been very attractive for the audience, and also an outstanding research result."

Fan Jianxin, vice-president of the Institute of Marxism, attached to CASS, pointed out that "the lesson we learn from the CPSU's can be summarized as follows: any successful socialist reform can only be the self-improvement and development of the socialist system. Reform must adhere to socialist direction, and we should allow no pretext for eroding the basic system of socialism, and no pretext for promoting capitalist liberalization. A noteworthy feature of the Soviet Union's collapse is the deviation from socialist reform direction, such as capitalist privatization was advocated to replace socialist public ownership in the economic sphere, which destroyed socialist economic foundation. In the political sphere, western systems were copied in an all-round manner, such as the multi-party system, presidential system, parliamentary system, which denied the leadership of the communist party and the dictatorship of proletariat. In ideological sphere, "ideological diversification or pluralism" was promoted while the guiding status of Marxism-Leninism was abandoned, and this resulted un-checked spread of anti-communist and anti-socialist bourgeois ideologies.

In the sphere of ruling party construction, the leadership of the Party was abandoned according to the requirements internal and external reactionary forces. On the other hand ethnic-national relations deteriorated, national separatism of Union Republics was accommodated, which led to a national crisis. All these facts advise us that show that reforms in socialist countries should adhere to socialist orientation and if the orientation is wrong, the reform will be bound to failure. Although this TV film narrates a Russian event, in fact it is closely related with the future and destiny of socialism. Debates and disagreements over the Soviet Union's collapse and CPSU's perishment is never a pure theoretical issue, instead a practical question about how to correctly understand the theory and practice of socialism, and how to treat the socialism with Chinese characteristics, its path, its theoretical system, which involves the contest between two roads and two systems, as well as the fundamental interests of the people and the development of human society. As long as we earnestly draw lessons from this major event, firmly adhere to the principles of scientific socialism and so that our reform always keeps the right direction, we won't repeat the same mistakes which has led to the collapse of the Soviet Union."

III. Reconsidering the causes of the Demise of the Soviet Union and its Political System: we should always pay attention to the struggles in the ideological field, be vigilant against attempts of "Westernize" and "divide"

Jiang Shuxian, former deputy director of Research Office of International Department, attached to the Central Committee of the CPC, has commented: "the research on the drastic changes in the Soviet Union, i.e, the research on such a great historical event, need to be based on facts, while Russian people's personal experiences and feelings are worthy of attention, which is also important. The footage team of the World Socialism Research Center has collected a large number of information and documents, interviewed with the witnesses of the event, and convincingly reflect how Gorbachev has ruined the leadership status of the CPSU, and the tragic consequences that effected the Russian people. This educational TV film profoundly reveals the whole process of the "peaceful evolution" led by the Western forces. The struggle between the "peaceful evolution" and restricting the peaceful evolution is one of the real struggles faced by the socialist countries, and we must never take this struggle lightly."

Chuai Zhenyu, the secretary of the Party committee, of the Institute of Finance and Trade Economics, attached to CASS has commented: "after watching the film, I got a much deeper understanding of the disintegration of the Soviet Union. Particularly, in this Party with 74 years of history, over

1.9 million members was expelled, great number of its members and Soviet people have remained 'oddly silent", which is dramatic, and reveals that the Party was in fact abandoned by the people.

The CPC must draw lessons from this fact, adhere to the guidance of Marxist theoretical system, strongly resist all kind of non-Marxism thoughts, and never allow the repetition of history regarding the perishment of the CPSU."

Li Fuchuan, researcher in the Institute of Russian, Eastern European, Central Asian Studies, attached to CASS, has evaluated: "Soviet Union's dramatic change and demise 20 years ago, in fact it was the first most successful Color Revolution by the western powers. However, in the past 20 years, it seems that other countries haven't drawn lessons from it, and the threat of "Color Revolutions" are spreading to other countries. For the political parties, which have seized power in violent or other uncommon ways, and the Parties which have been holding power for decades, how to prevent corruption within the Party, prevent the Party that it divorces from the masses, and prevent degeneration of its top leaders, is an issue of life and death for the political party, as well as the survival of the nation. In the past 20 years, with the economic integration surging across the world, western values have spread to other countries, together with western scientific and technological goods and consumption commodities, It is almost impossible to stop this. The popularization and development of the "Internet thing" has also become an effective tool for the western powers to instigate turmoil in other countries. The profound lessons of the demise of the Soviet Union and its Political System revealed in this educational TV film is of great practical meaning for the Chinese Communist Party that holds the power for 62 years and also for each of its ordinary party members and for every patriotic Chinese people.

Vigilantly guarding against the Western "color revolution" is an issue of life and death for the ruling political party. Soviet Union's collapse tells us and our party that we must adhere to the study of the Marxist theory, prevent embarking the "westernization road", prevent blind worshipping of it, prevent the penetration and induction of the Western values; profoundly clarify the theoretical content and aim of our political system reform, and keep a clear and sober minds and unify thoughts on 'what must be uphold' 'what and which path should explored' in political system reform."

IV. Some brief remarks and suggestions

Further expand the watching range, and advise to broadcast this film to all Party members

Party and government cadres should advise to expand the broadcasting range of this film after watching it. Sha Jiansun, the former deputy director of Party History Research Center of the Central Committee of the CPC, said: "this film has been modified over 30 times during its production, its creative work and shooting has not been easy, after these efforts now, it is very appealing and persuasive. We should expand its influence and let more people be educated."

Wu Yin, vice-president of the CASS, believed that "this film is extremely fascinating, we should expand its circulation range and let more comrades watch it."

Develop new ways of ideological and political education

Emeritus Prof. Zhou Xincheng, and former vice-president of Graduate School of the Renmin University, commented: "this film is of great educational meaning, and especially important for young college students. In the past, young college students simply believed in some comments and arguments made by Westernized and liberal elements, which propagated that Soviet Union's collapse was completely caused by the Stalin mode, and even said the Soviet Union's collapse was a kind of historical progress. They lacked the cognition about the responsibility of leaders such as Gorbachev, in the collapse, they weren't clear about the painful lessons of the Soviet Union's collapse and its disastrous influence on the Soviet people, as well as the responsibility of leaders such as Gorbachev. I believe that their opinions will change dramatically after they watch it and hypocritical views will be surpassed."

Prof. Cao Deben, from the School of Marxism at the Tsinghua University, commented: "this film represents some big events during the Soviet Union's collapse through interviewing Russian people from all walks of life. It sums up the historical lessons of the demise of the Soviet Union and its political system with a profound theoretical insight on the basis of latest research results in China. It is a great achievement in delving into the depths of history, great breakthrough in revealing the essence of events. I advise to take watching this educational TV film as a new way of ideological and political education."

It is a good teaching material for the education of college students with Marxist theories

This TV film contains rich historical data, as well as popular theoretical analysis and vivid explanation. Zhang Leisheng, secretary of the Party Committee, in the College of Marxism, attached to Renmin University of China, pointed out: "the field interviews included in this TV film is scientific and practical, and the interviewees are broadly representative. The materials and historical data are repeatedly verified and screened, and some important historical figures who played roles in those days have been are deeply analyzed. It is an achievement in the TV broadcasting which embodies historical events and scenes and has opened up a new way for ideological and political education work. I advise to list this film should be listed among the teaching materials for ideological and political education, and I recommend college teachers to show this film in teaching, and lead students to revisit and discuss the film and events. The education should discuss the demise of the Soviet Union and political system, combining education with thought-provoking questions: 'Why did Soviet socialism came to the end? Whether the Soviet Union's collapse means the end of socialism ? How to strengthen the construction of ruling party?' etc., so as to deepen their understanding of the difficulties and long-term character of building socialism in the economically-backward countries, and strengthen their consciousness on the importance of building the ruling party."

Prof. Liu Shulin, dean of the Tsinghua University, and leader of the Research Center for College Moral Education, a key research base of the Ministry of Education, has made the following evaluation: "Be Vigilant I, II" both films have received warm response from the students, and most of them is convinced, I have seen no opposition or resentment against basic ideological education. The third documentary film is more comprehensive than the first two, and we can see the improvement compared to the first two, its effect is much persuasive. The third is film is more penetrative because, it has adopted Russian people arguments and narrations in the documentary. It should be seen as a gift for the 18th National Congress of the CPC. As for the circulation, I suggest it should not only be taken as educational film within the Party, but should be promoted more widely. We should also let undergraduates, graduates, master students, majority of the young people should watch it. They are the forefront edge of our education. If we can spread this film among broader masses, its educational significance will be displayed more vigorously."

Recommendations to broadcast this film in the mainstream media outlets such as the CCTV

Huang Hong, the major general from the National Defense University, has watched the film and commented: "I often watch TV movies and series, I'm seldom moved with them, because I usually notice too much unrealistic additions in them. However, I was indeed moved by the ""20 Years' Reflections on the Soviet Union's Collapse and the CPSU's Perishment : The Russians Are Narrating" Regarding the demise of the Soviet Union and its political system, no one can feel what Russian people felt, who have experienced and lived in the events directly. What they saw and lived makes all kind of "defensive" arguments for the major disaster brought by Gorbachev and Yeltsin in the 20th century look pale and hypocritical. This is not a theoretical problem, in fact it is torturing every conscience of the soul. Needless to say, the facts and data displayed in the film are enough to make people alarm and reflect on them. Gratitude to the World Socialism Research Centre for raising the following relevant centennial subject for the Russian people to consider: Was there anything inherently wrong with the choice of Socialism?'

I think the "Be Vigilant" series should not only serve as a brilliant teaching material within the Party, but also included among the teaching materials which the college students should use as reference. Such valuable TV documentary should be broadcasted in the prime time range of the mainstream media such as the CCTV and others, I think it will surely score a high rating. I would like to extend my warm congratulations both to the artistic creative team and the shooting team!"

www.ingramcontent.com/pod-product-compliance
Lightning Source LLC
LaVergne TN
LVHW090034080526
838202LV00043B/3322